AUTODESK® REVIT®
ARCHITECTURE 2011

NO EXPERIENCE REQUIRED

AUTODESK® REVIT®
ARCHITECTURE 2011

NO EXPERIENCE REQUIRED

Autodesk®
Official Training Guide

Eric Wing

Wiley Publishing, Inc.

Senior Acquisitions Editor: Willem Knibbe
Development Editor: Stephanie Barton
Technical Editor: Jon McFarland
Production Editor: Dassi Zeidel
Copy Editor: Liz Welch
Editorial Manager: Pete Gaughan
Production Manager: Tim Tate
Vice President and Executive Group Publisher: Richard Swadley
Vice President and Publisher: Neil Edde
Book Designer: Franz Baumhackl
Compositor: James D. Kramer, Happenstance Type-O-Rama
Proofreader: Publication Services, Inc.
Indexer: Robert Swanson
Project Coordinator, Cover: Lynsey Stanford
Cover Designer: Ryan Sneed
Cover Image: Eric Wing

Library of Congress Cataloging-in-Publication Data

Wing, Eric, 1970
 Autodesk Revit architecture 2011 : no experience required / Eric Wing. — 1st ed.
  p. cm.
 Summary: "Learn Revit Architecture step by step with this project-based tutorial. Revit Architecture is the leading Building Information Modeling (BIM) software for architects and others in related fields. Written by renowned Revit trainer Eric Wing, this simple, yet engaging tutorial teaches you the program's basics.   You'll find concise explanations, focused examples, step-by-step instructions, and an engaging hands-on tutorial project that will take you from an introduction to the interface and Revit conventions right in to modeling a four-story office building. Explains views, grids, and the program's editing capabilities, and then progresses as the building's design would in the real world. Encourages you to work with structural grids, beams, and foundations and shows you how to add text and dimensions, as well as understand how to use dimensions as a design tool. Walks you through building floors layer by layer and joining them to exterior and interior walls, and creating and editing roofs and ceilings as well as stairs, ramps, and railings. Even with no experience, Revit Architecture and its accompanying Web site will support you as you learn Revit at your own pace."— Provided by publisher.

ISBN 978-0-470-61011-4 (pbk)
ISBN 978-0-470-90465-7 (ebk)
ISBN 978-0-470-90467-1 (ebk)
ISBN 978-0-470-90466-4 (ebk)

 1. Architectural drawing—Computer-aided design. 2. Architectural design—Data processing. I. Title.
 NA2728.W482 2010
 720.28'40285536—dc22
          2010016218

Dear Reader,

Thank you for choosing *Autodesk Revit Architecture 2011: No Experience Required*. This book is part of a family of premium-quality Sybex books, all of which are written by outstanding authors who combine practical experience with a gift for teaching.

Sybex was founded in 1976. More than 30 years later, we're still committed to producing consistently exceptional books. With each of our titles, we're working hard to set a new standard for the industry. From the paper we print on, to the authors we work with, our goal is to bring you the best books available.

I hope you see all that reflected in these pages. I'd be very interested to hear your comments and get your feedback on how we're doing. Feel free to let me know what you think about this or any other Sybex book by sending me an email at nedde@wiley.com. If you think you've found a technical error in this book, please visit **http://sybex.custhelp.com**. Customer feedback is critical to our efforts at Sybex.

Best regards,

NEIL EDDE
Vice President and Publisher
Sybex, an Imprint of Wiley

To my dad.
You would have pretended to understand
what you were reading in this book
just to make me feel good.
I miss that.

Acknowledgments

Before I ever even pondered writing a technical book such as this one, I was the guy who bought them and studied them from front to back. This specific page, however, I always thought was somewhat superfluous… bordering on self-indulgent. As I sit here now, after finishing 23 chapters, I can categorically say that this section only scratches the surface of the list of people close to me who have been tremendously inconvenienced by my unavailability and, conversely, by my temperament during the rare occasions when I was available. Of course topping this list is my wife, Jennifer, and the kids, Cassidy and Jacob. You guys always come through for me, and there is no way I could have written one single chapter without your support, and yes, you get to go to Disney again, like last year.

Also, I'd like to thank Grandma and Baci for constantly watching and being with the kids.

On the technical side, thanks to Willem Knibbe for acquiring the book and working with me on my manuscript and for his constant patience as I lumbered through each chapter. To Jon McFarland for his complete thoroughness in the technical editing of the book. I'd also like to thank Stephanie Barton for her great developmental editing, Dassi Zeidel for helping get the book to the printer, and copy editor Liz Welch for making sure I made sense. I'd also like to thank Nick Cerro at C&S Companies for setting the stage for me and for getting me high-profile speaking engagements in support of my previous books. One more thanks goes to Franco Zavaglia for providing me with a great cover rendering for the book.

ABOUT THE AUTHOR

Eric Wing lives in Syracuse, New York, with his family. He is the BIM Services Manager for C&S Companies, which is a full-service engineering/architectural firm headquartered in Syracuse. Eric obtained his degree in architectural engineering from Delhi University. In addition to writing this book, Eric has written *Revit Architecture No Experienced Required 2010* and *Revit Structure Fundamentals*, and he co-authored *Mastering Revit Structure*. Also, Eric is the manager of the Autodesk Usergroup training program (ATP), and is a columnist for the *AUGIWorld* magazine publication. He also writes a monthly Revit column for AUGI's *HotNews*. In addition to writing, Eric is a nationally recognized speaker, consultant, and trainer. He is also a bass player in a Syracuse band called Jemba when time allows.

Contents at a Glance

CONTENTS

CHAPTER 3   Creating Views   97

CHAPTER 4   Working with the Revit Tools   155

CHAPTER 5 Dimensioning and Annotating 199

CHAPTER 6 Floors 241

CHAPTER 7 Roofs 285

CHAPTER 11　　Schedules and Tags　　505

CHAPTER 22   Project Collaboration   895

CHAPTER 23   BIM Management   913

INTRODUCTION

Ah! Why does one need a big, thick technical book? Well, it is true that the best way to learn is to just do it! But do you ever just *do* it and not fully *get* it? Books can serve either as the basis for learning or as a supplement for your learning. No one book will teach you everything you need to know about a specific application, but you may never learn everything you need to know about an application without a book. When written appropriately, the book you purchase starts you off using good practices. If you have already started, the book serves as a desktop reference. And lastly, a book can merely serve as confirmation that you are approaching an application in the correct manner.

Revit Architecture is no exception. Although this application has proven to be easy to learn and easy to get the feel of, it is still a deep, sometimes complicated application with many procedures that require step-by-step instruction to fully understand. And to be honest, some of these features just don't work in the real world.

Also, this book has been written by an author who is "in the trenches" using Revit Architecture, Revit Structure, and Revit MEP simultaneously every day. So, yes, you could figure out all this information on your own, but sometimes it is nice to let someone else figure it out for you and pass that knowledge along to you in the form of a book.

Instead of lengthy paragraphs of text that ultimately lead to nontangible information, this book addresses each subject in a step-by-step approach with literally over a thousand pictures and screenshots to make sure you are on track.

Also, this book uses an actual project and will relate to real-world scenarios. As you follow the step-by-step procedures in the book, you will be encouraged to try many procedures on your own, and also to embellish the procedure to fit your own needs. If you would rather stick to the instructions, this book allows you to clearly do so as well. The book's project uses a five-story office building with a link (corridor) to a three-story multiuse building. The book's website provides the model (plus additional families) you will need for each chapter so that you can just open the book, jump to your chapter of interest, and actually learn something! Also, this book is flexible enough that you can substitute your own project if you do not want to follow the book's examples.

Although there are more than 900 pages, this book does not waste time and space with examples of other people's triumphs, but is designed for you to open it to any random page and learn something.

Who Should Read This Book

Autodesk® Revit® Architecture 2011: No Experience Required. Does that mean if you have used Revit you won't find this book advanced enough? No. This book is designed for anyone who wishes to learn more about Revit Architecture. Also, this book is intended for architects, architectural designers, and anyone who is using a CAD-based platform to produce architectural-based drawings.

What You Need

Building information modeling (BIM) can be tough on hardware. This book recommends that you have 4GB of RAM with a 4GB processor. Also, you should be running at least 512MB for your graphics. If you are under these specifications (within reason), in some cases you will be fine. Just realize, however, that when your model gets loaded, you could start slowing down and crashing. All Revit applications are intended to run on a PC-based system. Windows XP or higher is recommended. If you are running on a 64-bit operating system such as Windows Vista or Windows 7, be sure to load Revit as 64-bit to take full advantage of the allocated RAM.

What Is Covered in This Book

Autodesk® Revit® Architecture 2011: No Experience Required covers the full gamut of using the software; the book is organized as follows:

Chapter 1: The Revit World   Chapter 1 introduces you to the Revit Architecture 2011 interface and jumps right into modeling your first building.

Chapter 2: Creating a Model   Chapter 2 starts right off with placing walls, doors, and windows. Also, this chapter is designed to point you in the right direction in terms of using reference planes and all-around best practices.

Chapter 3: Creating Views   Chapter 3 shows you how to navigate the Revit Project Browser and how to create new views of the model. Also, you will learn how to create specific views such as elevations, sections, callouts, plans, and of course our favorite, 3D perspectives.

Chapter 4: Working with the Revit Tools   In Chapter 4, you will learn how to use the everyday drafting tools needed in any modeling application. You will become familiar with such actions as trim, array, move, and copy. Although it seems remedial, this is one of the most important chapters of the book. It gets you on your way to the "Revit Feel."

Chapter 5: Dimensioning and Annotating   In Chapter 5 you will learn how to annotate your model. This includes adding and setting up dimensions, adding and setting up text, and using dimensions to physically adjust objects in your model.

Chapter 6: Floors   Yes! Just floors. In Chapter 6, you will learn how to place a floor. You will also learn how to add materials to a floor and how to pitch a floor to a drain.

Chapter 7: Roofs   In Chapter 7 we discuss the ins and outs of placing roofs. You will learn how to model flat roofs, sloping roofs, pitched roofs, and roof dormers. In addition, you will learn how to pitch roof insulation to roof drains.

Chapter 8: Structural Items   In Chapter 8 you delve into the structural module of Revit Architecture. The topics we cover include placing structural framing, placing structural foundations, and creating structural views.

Chapter 9: Ceilings and Interiors   Chapter 9 focuses predominately on interior design. We cover placing and modifying ceilings as well as adding specific materials to portions of walls and floors. You will also learn how to create soffits.

Chapter 10: Stairs, Ramps, and Railings   Chapter 10 focuses on the creation of circulation items. You will learn how to create a simple U-shaped multistory staircase to start; then we move on to creating a custom winding staircase. From there you will learn how to create a custom wood railing. You will be adding ramps to the model in this chapter as well.

Chapter 11: Schedules and Tags   In Chapter 11 you will start bringing the BIM into your model. This chapter focuses on adding schedules and adding annotation tags to specific objects and materials in your model. Most importantly, in this chapter you will learn how your model is parameter driven and how these parameters influence the annotations.

Chapter 12: Detailing   In Chapter 12 you will learn how to simply draft in Revit. The procedures allow you to draft over the top of a Revit-generated section, or create your own drafting view independent of the model. You will also learn how to import CAD to use as a detail.

Chapter 13: Creating Specific Views and Match Lines   In Chapter 13 you will learn how to take advantage of the multitude of views you can create, and how to control the visibility graphics of those views to create plans such as furniture and dimensional plans.

Chapter 14: Creating Sheets and Printing   Chapter 14 explores how to produce construction documents using Revit. The procedures include creating a new drawing sheet, adding views to a sheet, creating a title block and a cover sheet, and plotting these documents.

Chapter 15: Creating Rooms and Area Plans The focus of Chapter 15 is to create rooms and areas. The procedures lead you through the placement of rooms, and you will learn how to set the properties of those rooms. We also discuss how to create room separators and how to create gross area plans. This chapter also guides you through the creation of a color fill floor plan.

Chapter 16: Advanced Wall Topics In Chapter 16 you will focus specifically on the creation of compound walls. By using the Edit Assembly dialog, you will learn how to add materials, split walls, and add sweeps and reveals such as parapet caps, brick ledges, and brick reveals. Creating stacked walls is also addressed.

Chapter 17: Creating Families Chapter 17 focuses on the topic of creating families. The procedures start with a simple wall sweep family, and then move on to creating a door family with an arched header. You will also learn how to create an in-place family.

Chapter 18: Site and Topography In Chapter 18 you will learn how to place a topographical surface into your model. We also discuss how to control point-by-point elevations in your site. Splitting and then creating subregions to create swales and berms will be covered. You will also learn how to utilize an imported CAD site plan and place a toposurface over the top of the CAD lines. We also explore rotating your project to true north.

Chapter 19: Rendering and Presentation In Chapter 19 you will learn how to use the Revit rendering tools using the mental ray rendering engine built into the Revit GUI. This chapter also shows you how to create walkthroughs as well as solar studies.

Chapter 20: Importing and Coordinating Revit Models Chapter 20 focuses on the ins and outs (pun intended) of importing and exporting CAD formats as well as linking Revit Structure models. The procedures include configuring CAD layering settings as well as linking and importing AutoCAD for plans and sections. You will also learn how to link Revit Structure and perform a copy/monitor operation as well as use the Revit collision detection.

Chapter 21: Phasing and Design Options Chapter 21 explains how to create an existing floor plan, then moves through demolition into new construction. You will also learn how to create alternates using design options.

Chapter 22: Project Collaboration In Chapter 22 you will learn how to use Revit in a multiuser environment. The procedures in the book will lead you through activating worksharing, and then creating a central model. You will then move on to creating local user files as well as saving to central and placing *requests to relinquish*.

Chapter 23: BIM Management   Our final chapter, Chapter 23, shows you how to create a Revit template you can use at the start of each Revit project. You will also learn how to configure settings such as line weights, dimensions, text, and custom tags, such as levels structural grids and view titles.

Included with the book are Revit Architecture project files that follow along with the instruction. Each chapter will have one or more actual Revit models completed up to the point of the instruction of that specific chapter—or even that specific section of the chapter—to allow the reader to jump in at any moment. Also included with the book are custom families that accompany the lessons, and additional families and projects that can be downloaded as a bonus. You can download the accompanying files at **www.sybex.com/go/revit2011ner**.

Contacting the Author

As you are reading along, please feel free to contact me at ewing@cscos.com, and I will be glad to answer any question you have. In addition, if you would like me to come speak or train at your firm, feel free to give me a shout. You can also visit my company's website at **www.cscos.com** and click the BIM link. You can also go directly to **www.bimnation.com**.

Sybex strives to keep you supplied with the latest tools and information you need for your work. Please check the website at **www.sybex.com**, where we'll post additional content and updates that supplement this book if the need arises. Enter **Revit Architecture** in the Search box (or type the book's ISBN—**9780470610114**), and click Go to get to the book's update page.

The Revit World

Before we get started, I think we should set the record straight. I'm sure you have seen plenty of presentations on how wonderful and versatile this 3D Revit revolution thing is. And I'm sure you may be thinking, "This all seems way too complicated for what I do. Why do I need 3D anyway?"

The answer to that question is: you don't. What do you do to get a job out — that is, after the presentation has run its course and you are awarded the project? Your first step is to redraw the plans. Next comes the detail round-up game we have all come to love: we pull the specs together, and then we plot. This is quite a simple process, and guess what? It works.

Well, it has worked up until this 3D thing showed up. Now the process seems to be this convoluted approach in which we have no real clue where things come from, drawings don't look very good, and getting a drawing out the door takes three times as long.

▶ **The Revit Architecture interface**

▶ **The Project Browser**

▶ **File types and families**

The Revit Architecture Interface

Toto, we are not in CAD anymore!

If you just bought this book, then welcome to the Revit world. In Revit, you will find that the vast majority of the processes you encounter are in a flat 2D platform. Instead of drafting, you are placing components into the model. Yes, these components have a so-called third dimension to them, but a logical methodology drives the process. If you need to see the model in 3D, it is simply a click away. That being said, remember this: there is a big difference between 3D drafting and modeling.

N O T E   The preceding paragraph will be the longest one of the book. This book is designed to cut to the chase and show you how to use Revit Architecture in a step-by-step fashion without having to read through paragraph after paragraph just to find the answer you are looking for. Datasets are provided at the book's accompanying website (www.sybex.com/go/revit2011ner), but you can also use your own model as you go through the book. If you do not wish to read this book cover to cover, don't! Although I recommend going from front to back, you can use the book as a desk reference by jumping to a desired topic. The datasets will be added in phases to accommodate this type of usage. Either way, get ready to learn Revit Architecture!

With that preamble behind us, let's get on with it.

First of all, Revit has no command prompt and no crosshairs. Stop! Don't go away just yet. You will get used to it, I promise. Unlike most CAD applications, Revit Architecture is heavily pared down, so to speak. It's this way for a reason. Revit was designed for architects and architectural designers. You do not need every command that a mechanical engineer would need. An electrical engineer would not need the functionality that an architect would require.

What you will find as you start getting comfortable with Revit is that there are many, many choices and options behind each command.

Let's start at the beginning:

1. To open Revit Architecture, click the icon on your desktop (see Figure 1.1), or choose Start ➢ All Programs ➢ Autodesk ➢ Autodesk Revit Architecture 2011 ➢ Autodesk Revit Architecture 2011 (see Figure 1.2).

2. After you start Revit, you see the Recent Files window shown in Figure 1.3. The top row lists any projects you have been working on; the bottom row lists any families you have been working on.

FIGURE 1.1 You can launch Revit Architecture from the desktop icon.

FIGURE 1.2 You can also launch Revit Architecture using the Windows Start menu (this shows the Windows Vista operating system).

3. If you are firing up Revit for the first time, both of these rows will be blank. At the bottom of each row, you can choose to create a new model or open an existing one (see Figure 1.4).

4. In the upper-left corner of the Revit window, you will see a big purple R. Click the purple R and choose New ➢ Project.

5. The New Project dialog shown in Figure 1.5 opens. You can use the default template or no template, or you can create a new template by clicking the Project Template radio button. (We will cover template creation later in the book.) For now, just click OK to create a new project using the default template. You do not need to alter anything in this dialog.

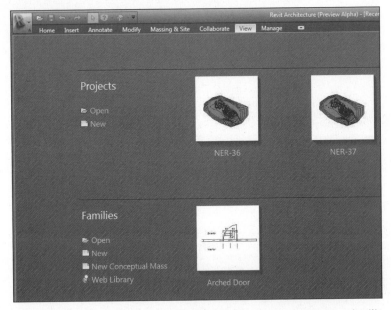

FIGURE 1.3 The Recent Files window lists any recent projects or families you have worked on.

FIGURE 1.4 You can create a new model or browse for an existing one.

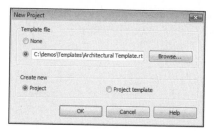

FIGURE 1.5 The New Project dialog allows you to start a new project using a preexisting template file, or you can create a new template file.

Now that the task of physically opening the application is out of the way, we can delve into Revit. At first, you will notice many differences between Revit and CAD. Some of these differences may be off-putting, while others will make you say "I wish AutoCAD did that." Either way, you will have to adjust to a new workflow.

The Revit Workflow

Revit has a certain feel that you AutoCAD converts will need to get a grasp on. This new workflow may be easy for some to adapt to, whereas others will find it excruciatingly foreign. (To be honest, I found the latter to be the case at first.) Either way, it is a simple concept. You just need to slow down a bit from your AutoCAD habits.

Executing a command in Revit is a three-step process:

1. At the top of the Revit window is the Ribbon, and built into the Ribbon is a series of tabs. Each tab contains a panel. This Ribbon will be your Revit launch pad! Speaking of launch pad, click the Wall button on the Home tab, as shown in Figure 1.6.

2. After you click the Wall button, notice that Revit adds an additional tab to the Ribbon, with options specific to the command you are running, as shown in Figure 1.7. This tab allows you to make different choices based on the placement of a wall. You may also notice that Revit places an additional Options bar below the Ribbon for more choices.

FIGURE 1.6 The Ribbon is the backbone of Revit Architecture.

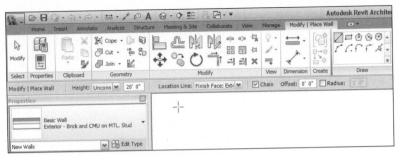

FIGURE 1.7 The Options bar replaces the command prompt from AutoCAD. Microstation users will be more familiar with this method.

3. After you make your choices from the Ribbon and the Options bar, you can place the object into the view window. This is the large drawing area that takes up two thirds of the Revit interface. To place the wall, simply pick a point in the window and move your pointer. The wall starts to form. You can press the Esc key to exit the command.

Using Revit is not generally as easy as this, but keep in mind this basic three-step process:

1. Start a command.

2. Choose an option from the temporary tab that appears.

3. Place the item in the view window.

Revit appears to offer a fraction of the choices and functionality that AutoCAD or any drafting program offers. This is true in a way. Revit does offer fewer choices to start a command, but how many choices does an architect or architectural designer need? Revit keeps its functionality focused on architecture and construction. Revit gets its robust performance from the dynamic capabilities of the application during the placement of the items and the functionality of the objects after you place them in the model. Never judge a book by its cover — unless, of course, it is the book you are reading right now.

Let's keep going with the main focus of the Revit interface: the Ribbon. You will be using the Ribbon exclusively within Revit.

Using the Ribbon

You will use the Ribbon for the majority of the commands you execute in Revit. As you can see, you don't have much choice to do otherwise. However, this is good because it narrows your attention to what is right in front of you. When you click

> You will hear this throughout the book: always remember to look at your options. With no command prompt, the Options bar will be one of your few guides.

an icon on the Ribbon, Revit will react to that icon with a new tab, giving you the specific additional commands and options you need. Revit also keeps the existing tabs that can help you in the current command, as shown in Figure 1.8. Again, the focus here is to keep your eyes in one place.

In this book, I will throw a few new terms at you, but you will get familiar with them quickly. We just discussed the Ribbon, but mostly you will be directed to choose a tab, and to find a panel on that tab.

To keep the example familiar, when you selected the Wall button, your instructions will read: "On the Build panel of the Home tab, click the Wall button."

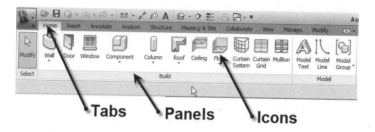

FIGURE 1.8 The Ribbon breakdown

WHAT'S THAT TOOLBAR ABOVE THE RIBBON?

This toolbar is called the Quick Access toolbar. It is filled with some popular commands. One special function of this toolbar is the cursor icon. You use this icon when you wish to terminate a command. If you want to add to this toolbar, simply right-click any icon and select Add To Quick Access Toolbar. To the left of this toolbar is the Revit Home button. Clicking this button gives you access to more Revit functions that will be covered later in the book.

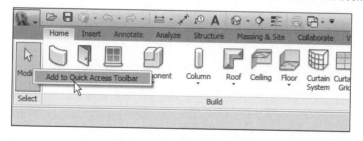

Now that you can see how the ribbons and the tabs flow together, let's take a look at another feature within the Ribbon panels that allows you to reach beyond the immediate Revit interface.

The Properties Interface

When you click the Wall button, an entirely new set of commands appears. This new set of commands combines your basic Modify commands with an additional tab specific to your immediate process. In this case that process is adding a wall. You will also notice that a Properties dialog appears to the left of the screen. If you do not see the Properties dialog, click the Properties icon that is displayed in Figure 1.9. In the Properties dialog is a picture of the wall you are about to place. If you click on this picture, Revit will display all the walls that are available within the model. This display is called the Change Element Type menu (see Figure 1.10).

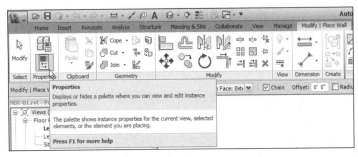

FIGURE 1.9 Click the Properties button to display the Properties dialog. Typically the dialog is shown by default.

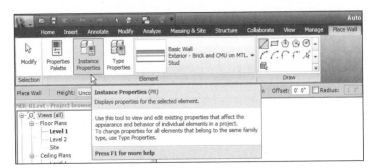

FIGURE 1.10 The Properties button gives you access to many variables associated with the item you are adding to the model.

The objective of the next exercise is to start placing walls into the model:

1. Open Revit Architecture using the default template.

2. On the Home tab, click the Wall button.

3. In the Properties dialog, select Exterior - Brick and CMU on MTL.Stud.

Element Properties

Hidden within the Options bar is a single button. There are two different sets of properties you will deal with in Revit: Instance Properties and Type Properties. Instance Properties will be available immediately in the Properties dialog when you place, or select, an item. If you make a change to an element property, the only items that are affected in the model are the items you have selected.

The Properties Dialog

The Properties dialog is new to Revit Architecture 2011. As just mentioned, the Properties dialog will display the Instance Properties of the item you have selected. If no item is selected, this dialog will display the View Properties.

In addition to accessing the Instance Properties, you can click the Edit Type button to open a dialog displaying the Type Properties of the selected item (see Figure 1.11). By making a modification here, you will change every occurrence of that item in the entire model.

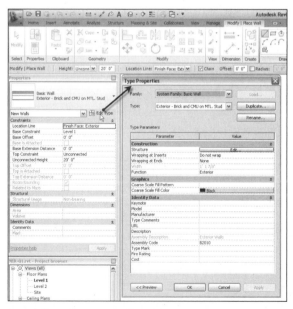

FIGURE 1.11 The Type Properties dialog gives you access to the parameters associated with the element you have selected.

Let's take a closer look at the two categories of Element Properties in Revit.

Instance Properties

The items that you can edit immediately are called parameters, or Instance Properties. These parameters will change only the object being added to the model at this time. Also, if you select an item that has already been placed in the model, the parameters you see immediately in the Instance Properties dialog will change only that item you have selected. This makes sense — not all items are built equally in the real world. Figure 1.12 illustrates the Instance Properties of a typical wall.

Type Properties

The Type Properties (see Figure 1.13), when edited, will alter every item of that type in the entire model. To access the Type Properties, click the Edit Type button in the Properties dialog, as Figure 1.14 shows.

FIGURE 1.12 The Instance Properties will change only the currently placed item or the currently selected item.

At this point, you have two choices. You can either make a new wall type (leaving this specific wall unmodified) by clicking the Duplicate button, or you can start editing the wall's Type Properties, as shown in Figure 1.15.

WARNING   I cannot stress enough that if you start modifying Type Properties without duplicating the type, you need to do so in a very deliberate manner. You can easily affect the model in unintended ways. We will discuss the specifics of all the wall's Type Properties in Chapter 16, "Advanced Wall Topics."

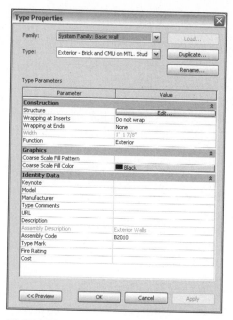

FIGURE 1.13 The Type Properties, when modified, will alter every occurrence of this specific wall in the entire model.

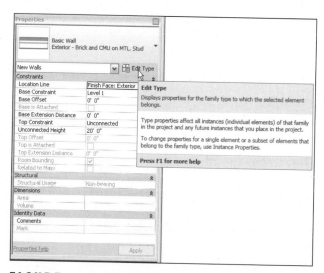

FIGURE 1.14 The Edit Type button allows you to access the Type Properties.

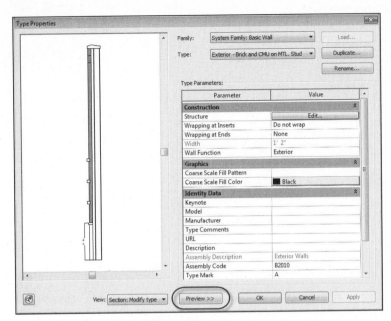

FIGURE 1.15 The Type Properties are used to modify the wall system's global settings. Click the Preview button at the bottom of the dialog to see the image that is displayed.

Now that you have gained experience with the Type Properties dialog, it is time to go back and study the Options bar as it pertains to placing a wall:

1. Since we are only exploring the Element Properties, click the Cancel button to return to the model.

2. Back in the Options bar, find the Location Line menu. Through this menu you can set the wall justification. Select Finish Face: Exterior (see Figure 1.16).

3. On the Options bar, be sure the Chain checkbox is selected, as Figure 1.16 shows. This will allow you to draw the walls continuously.

4. In the Draw panel, there is a series of sketch options. Because this specific wall is straight, make sure the Line button is selected, as shown in Figure 1.17.

Get used to studying the Ribbon and the Options bars — they will be your crutch as you start using Revit Architecture! Of course, at some point you need to physically start placing items in the model. This is where the view window comes into play.

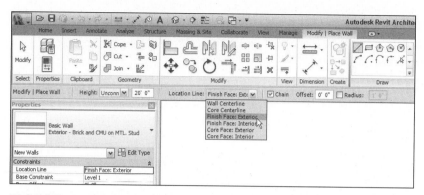

FIGURE 1.16 By selecting Finish Face: Exterior, you know the wall will be dimensioned from the outside finish.

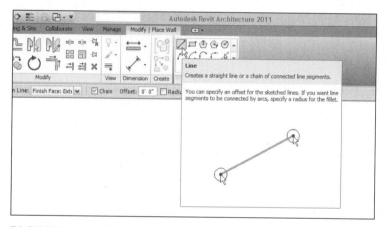

FIGURE 1.17 You can draw any shape you need.

The View Window

To put it simply, "the big white area where the objects go" is the view window. As a result of your actions, this area will become populated with your model. Notice the background is white — this is because the sheets you plot on are white. In Revit, what you see is what you get … literally. In Revit, you aren't counting on color #5, which is blue, for example, to be a specific line width when you plot. You can immediately see the thickness that all your "lines" will be before you plot (see Figure 1.18). What a novel idea.

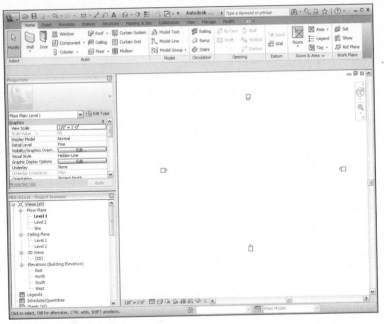

FIGURE 1.18 The view window collects the results of your actions.

To continue placing some walls in the model, keep going with the exercise. (If you have not been following along, you can start by clicking the Wall button on the Home tab. In the Properties dialog box, select Exterior - Brick and CMU on MTL.Stud. Make sure that the wall is justified to the finish face exterior.) You may now proceed:

1. With the Wall command still running and the correct wall type selected, position your cursor in a similar location to the illustration in Figure 1.19. Now, pick a point in the view window.

2. With the first point picked, move your cursor to the left. Notice that a two things happen: the wall seems to snap in a horizontal plane, and a blue dashed line apparently locks the horizontal position. In Revit, there is no "Ortho." Revit will align the typical compass increments to 0, 90, 180, 270, and 45 degrees.

3. Also notice the blue dimension extending from the first point to the last point. Although dimensions cannot be typed over, this type of dimension is a temporary dimension for you to use as you place items. Type 100, and press the Enter key. (Notice you did not need to type the foot mark ('). Revit thinks in terms of feet. The wall is now 100' long (see Figure 1.19).

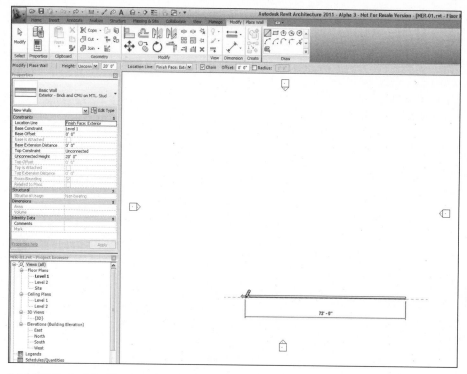

FIGURE 1.19 The procedure for drawing a wall in Revit Architecture

4. With the Wall command still running, move your cursor straight up from the endpoint of your 100′-long wall. Look at Figure 1.20.

5. Type 80 and hit Enter. You now have two walls.

6. Move your cursor to the right until you "run into" another blue alignment line. Notice that your temporary dimension says 100′–0″. Revit understands symmetry. After you see this alignment line, and the temporary dimension says 100′–0″, pick this point.

7. Move your cursor straight down and type 16, and hit Enter.

8. Move your cursor to the right and type 16, and hit Enter.

9. Press the Esc key.

Do your walls look like Figure 1.21? If not, try it again. You need to be comfortable with this procedure (as much as possible).

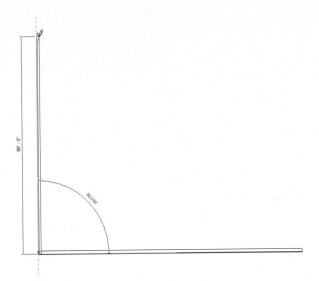

FIGURE 1.20 How Revit Architecture works is evident in this procedure.

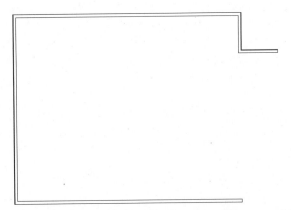

FIGURE 1.21 Working with Revit starts with the ability to work with the view window, and learning the quirks and feel of the interface.

To get used to the Revit flow, always remember these three steps:

1. Start a command.

2. Focus on your options.

3. Move to the view window, and add the elements to the model.

If you start a command, then focus immediately on the view, you will be sitting there wondering what to do next. Do not forget to check your Options bar and the appropriate ribbon tab.

Let's keep going and close this building by using a few familiar commands. If you have never drafted on a computer before, don't worry. These commands are simple. The easiest but most important topic is simply how to select an object.

Object Selection

Revit has a few similarities to AutoCAD and MicroStation. One of those similarities is the ability to perform simple object selection and to execute common modify commands. For this example, we will mirror the two 16′–0″ L-shaped walls to the bottom of the building:

1. Type **ZA** (zoom all).

2. Near the two 16′–0″ L-shaped walls, pick (left-click) and hold down the left mouse button when the cursor is at a point to the left of the walls but above the long, 100′–0″ horizontal wall.

3. You will see a window start to form. Run that selection window past the two walls. After you highlight the walls, as illustrated in Figure 1.22, let go of the mouse button, and you have selected the walls.

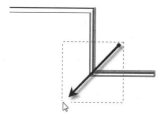

FIGURE 1.22 Using a crossing window to select two walls

There are two ways to select an object: by using a crossing window or by using a box. Each approach plays an important role in how you select items in a model.

Crossing Windows

A crossing window describes an object selection method in which the window being placed only needs to cross through the objects in order to select them. A crossing window will always start from the right and end to the left. The crossing window, when being placed, is represented by a dashed-line composition (see Figure 1.22).

Boxes

A box is an object selection method that will only select the items that are 100 percent inside the window being placed. This method is useful when you want to select only specific items while passing through larger objects that you may not want in the selection set. A box always starts from the left and works to the right. The line type for a selection window is a continuous line (see Figure 1.23).

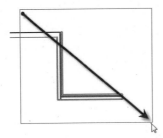

FIGURE 1.23 To select only objects that are surrounded by the window, select a box. This will leave out any item that may only be partially within the box.

Now that you have experience selecting items, you can execute some basic modify commands. Let's begin with mirroring, one of the most popular modify commands.

Modifying and Mirroring

You will find that Revit Architecture requires that you select items first and then execute a command. This is true for most action items, and is certainly true for every command on the Modify toolbar.

1. Make sure only the two 16′–0″ walls are selected.

2. Once the walls are selected, you will see the Modify Walls tab appear. On the Modify panel, click the Mirror Draw Axis button, as shown in Figure 1.24.

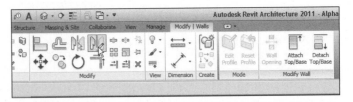

FIGURE 1.24 The Ribbon adds the appropriate commands.

3. Your cursor will change to a crosshair with the mirror icon illustrating that you are ready to draw a mirror plane, as shown in Figure 1.25.

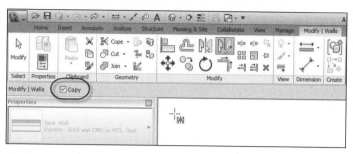

FIGURE 1.25 There are options you must choose for every command in Revit.

4. Make sure the Copy checkbox is selected (see Figure 1.25).

5. Hover your cursor over the inside face of the 80′–0″-long vertical wall until you get reach the midpoint. Revit will display a triangular icon, indicating that you have found the midpoint of the wall (see Figure 1.26).

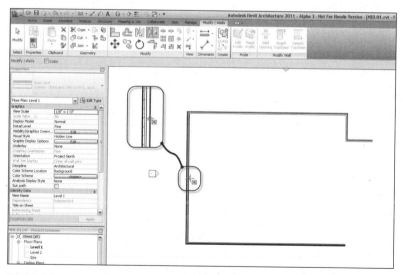

FIGURE 1.26 Revit has snaps similar to most CAD applications. In Revit, you will only get snaps if you choose the draw icon from the Options bar during a command.

6. When the triangular midpoint snap appears, pick this point. After you pick the point where the triangle appears, you can move your cursor directly to the right of the wall. You will see an alignment line appear,

as illustrated in Figure 1.27. When the alignment line appears, you can pick another point along the path. When you pick the second point, the walls are mirrored and joined with the south wall (see Figure 1.27).

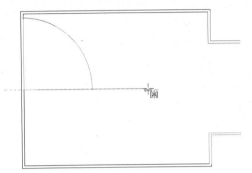

FIGURE 1.27 Mirroring these walls will involve first, picking the midpoint of the vertical wall, then second, picking a horizontal point along the plane.

Now that you have some experience mirroring items, it is time to start adding components to your model by utilizing the items that you placed earlier. If you having trouble following the process, retry these first few procedures. Rome was not built in a day. (Well, perhaps if they had Revit, it would have sped things up!) You want your first few walls to look like Figure 1.28.

FIGURE 1.28 Your building should look like this illustration.

Building on Existing Geometry

Now that you have some geometry to work with and you have some objects placed in your model, Revit starts to come alive. The benefits of using building information modeling (BIM) will become apparent quickly, as explained later in this chapter. For example, because Revit knows that walls are walls, you can add identical geometry to the model by simply selecting an item and telling Revit to create a similar item.

Suppose you want a radial wall of the same exact type as the other walls in the model. Perform the following steps:

1. Type **ZA** to zoom the entire screen.

2. Press the Esc key.

3. Select one of the walls in the model — it does not matter which one.

4. Right-click on the wall.

5. Select Create Similar, as shown in Figure 1.29.

 N O T E   New to Revit 2011, when you right-click on an item, you can choose to repeat the last command. You can now also select all items that are only in the current view.

6. On the Modify | Place Wall tab, click the Start-End-Radius Arc button, as shown in Figure 1.30.

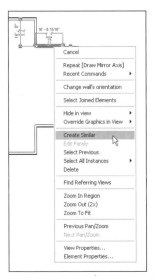

FIGURE 1.29 You can select any item in Revit and create a similar object by right-clicking and selecting Create Similar.

7. Again with the Options? Yes. Make sure your Location Line is set to Finish Face: Exterior.

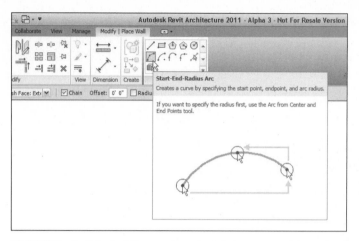

FIGURE 1.30 Just because you started the command from the view window does not mean you do not have to look at your options.

8. With the wheel button on your mouse, zoom into the upper corner of the building and select the top endpoint of the wall, as shown in Figure 1.31. The point you are picking is the corner of the heavy lines. The topmost, thinner line represents a concrete belt course below. If you are having trouble picking the correct point, don't be afraid to zoom into the area by scrolling the mouse wheel.

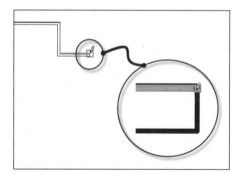

FIGURE 1.31 Select the top corner of the wall to start your new radial wall.

9. Select the opposite, outside corner of the bottom wall. Again, to be more accurate, you will probably have to zoom into each point as you are making your picks.

10. Move your cursor to the right until you see the curved wall pause. You will also see an alignment line and a tangent snap icon appear as

well. Revit understands that perhaps you want an arc tangent upon the two lines you have already placed in your model.

11. When you see the tangent snap icon, choose the third point. Your walls should look like Figure 1.32.

12. Press Esc to terminate the command.

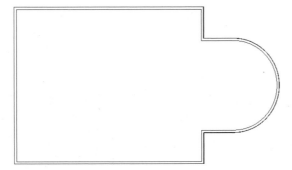

FIGURE 1.32 The completed exterior walls should look like this illustration.

Just because you have placed a wall in the model does not mean the wall looks the way you would like. In Revit Architecture, you can do a lot with view control and how objects are displayed.

View Control and Object Display

Although the earlier procedures are a nice way to add walls to a drawing, they do not reflect the detail you will need to produce construction documents. Well, the great thing about Revit is that you have already done everything you need to do. You can now tell Revit to display the graphics the way you want to see them.

The View Control Bar

At the bottom of the view window, you will see a skinny toolbar (as illustrated in Figure 1.33). This is the View Control bar. It contains the functions outlined in the following list:

FIGURE 1.33 The View Control bar controls the graphical view of your model.

Scale   The first item on the View Control bar is the scale function. It gets small mention here, but it is a huge deal. In Revit, you change the scale of a view by selecting this menu. Change the scale here, and Revit will scale annotations and symbols accordingly (see Figure 1.34).

FIGURE 1.34 The scale menu allows you to change the scale of your view.

Detail Level   The detail level allows you to view your model at different qualities. You have three levels to choose from: Coarse, Medium, and Fine (see Figure 1.35).

FIGURE 1.35 The detail level control allows you to set different view levels for the current view.

If you want more graphical information with this view, select Fine. To see how the view is adjusted using this control, follow these steps:

1. Click the detail level icon and choose Fine.

2. Zoom in on a wall corner. Notice the wall components are now showing in the view.

T I P   When you change the view control in a view, it is not a temporary display. You are telling Revit how you want to plot this view. The view you see on the screen is the view you will see when it comes out of the plotter.

There are other items on the View Control bar, but we'll discuss them when they become applicable to the exercises.

The View Tab

Since Revit is one big happy model, you will quickly find that simply viewing the model is quite important. Within Revit, you can take advantage of some function-ality in the Navigation bar. To activate the Navigation bar, first go to the View tab, then click the User Interface button. Make sure the Navigation bar is activated, as shown in Figure 1.36.

One item we need to look at on the Navigation bar is the steering wheel.

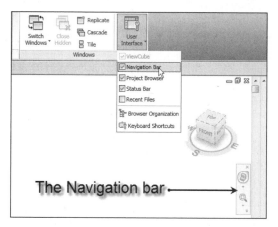

FIGURE 1.36 The View tab allows you to turn on and off the Navigation bar.

The Steering Wheel

The steering wheel allows you to zoom, rewind, and pan. When you click the steer-ing wheel icon, a larger control panel will appear in the view window. To choose one of the options, you simply pick (left-click) one of the options, and hold the mouse button as you execute the maneuver.

To use the steering wheel, follow along:

1. Pick the steering wheel icon from the Navigation bar, as shown in Figure 1.37.

2. Once the steering wheel is in the view window (as illustrated in Figure 1.37), left-click and hold Zoom. You can now zoom in and out.

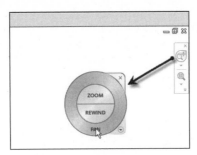

FIGURE 1.37 You can use the steering wheel to navigate through a view.

3. Now click and hold Rewind in the steering wheel. You can now find an older view, as shown in Figure 1.38.

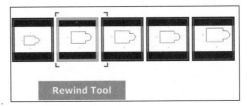

FIGURE 1.38 Because Revit does not include zoom commands in the Undo function, you can rewind to find previous views.

4. Do the same for Pan, which is also found on the outer ring of the steering wheel. After you press and hold Pan, you can navigate to other parts of the model.

Although you can do all of this with your wheel button, some users still prefer the icon method of panning and zooming. For those of you who prefer the icons, you will also want to use the icons for the traditional zooms as well.

Traditional Zooms

The next items on the Navigation bar are the good old zoom controls. The abilities to zoom in, zoom out, and pan are all included in this function, as shown in Figure 1.39.

Of course, if you have a mouse with a wheel, you can zoom and pan by either holding down the wheel to pan or by wheeling the button to scroll in and out.

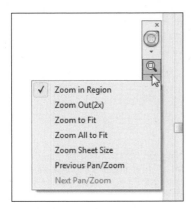

FIGURE 1.39 The standard zoom commands

Thin Lines

Back on the View tab, you will see an icon called Thin Lines, as shown in Figure 1.40. Let's talk about what this icon does.

In Revit Architecture, there is no such thing as layers. Line weights are controlled by the actual objects they represent. In the view window, you see these line weights. As mentioned before, what you see is what you get. Sometimes, however, these line weights may be too thick for smaller-scale views. By clicking the Thin Lines icon, as shown in Figure 1.40, you can force the view to display only the thinnest lines possible to still see the objects.

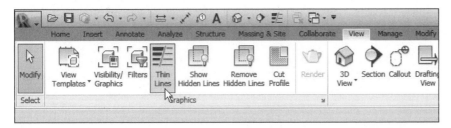

FIGURE 1.40 Clicking the Thin Lines icon will allow you to "operate" on the finer items in a model.

To practice using the Thin Lines function, follow along:

1. Pick the Thin Lines icon.

2. Zoom in on the upper-right corner of the building.

3. Pick the Thin Lines icon again. This toggles the mode back and forth.

4. Notice the lines are very heavy.

The line weight should concern you. As mentioned earlier, there is no such thing as layers in Revit Architecture. This topic is addressed in Chapter 13.

3D View

The 3D View icon brings us to a new conversation. Complete the following steps that will move us into the discussion on how a Revit model comes together!

1. Click the 3D View icon, as illustrated in Figure 1.41.

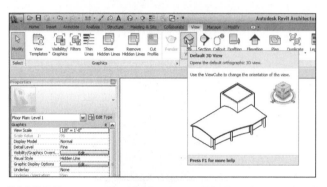

FIGURE 1.41 The 3D View icon will be heavily used.

2. On the View Control bar, click the Visual Style button and choose Shaded with Edges, as illustrated in Figure 1.42.

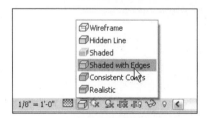

FIGURE 1.42 The Visual Style button enables you to view your model in color. This is typical for a 3D view.

A word of caution: if you do turn your shadows on, do so with care. This could be the single worst item in Revit in terms of performance degradation. Your model *will* slow down with shadows on.

3. Again on the View Control bar, select Shadows Off and turn the shadows on, as illustrated in Figure 1.43, and again in Figure 1.45.

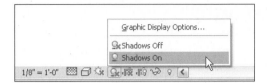

FIGURE 1.43 Shadows create a nice effect, but at the expense of RAM.

Within the 3D view is the ViewCube. It is the cube in the upper-right corner of the view window. You can switch to different perspectives of the model by clicking on the quadrants of the cube (see Figure 1.44).

FIGURE 1.44 The ViewCube lets you freely look at different sides of the building.

 TIP The best way to navigate a 3D view is to press and hold the Shift key on the keyboard. As you holding the Shift key, press and hold the wheel on your mouse. Now move the mouse around. You will be able to dynamically view the model (see Figure 1.45).

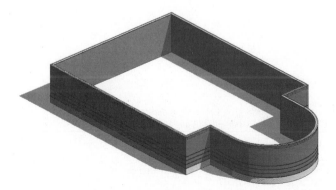

FIGURE 1.45 The 3D model with shading and shadows

Go back to the floor plan. Wait! How? This brings us to quite an important topic in Revit: the Project Browser.

The Project Browser

Revit is the frontrunner of BIM. BIM is sweeping our industry for a reason. One of the biggest reasons is the fact that you have a fully integrated model right in front of you. What this means is that when you need to open a different floor plan, elevation, detail, drawing sheet, or 3D view, you can find it all right here in the model.

Also, this means our workflow is going to change. In most cases, it is going to change drastically. When you think about all the external references and convoluted folder structures that comprise a typical job, you can start to relate it to the way Revit uses the Project Browser. Within Revit, you are using the Project Browser instead of the folder structure previously used in CAD.

This approach changes the playing field. The process of closing the file you are in and opening the files you need to work on is restructured in Revit to enable you to stay in the model. You never have to leave one file to open another. You also never need to rely on external referencing to complete a set of drawings. Revit and the Project Browser will put it all right in front of you.

To start using the Project Browser, follow along:

1. To the far left of the Revit dialog is the Project Browser (see Figure 1.46).

FIGURE 1.46 The Project Browser is your new Windows Explorer.

2. The Project Browser is broken down into categories. One category is Floor Plans. In the Floor Plans category, double-click on Level 1.

3. Next, double-click on Level 2. Notice that your display level is set to Coarse. This is because any change you make on the View Control bar is for that view only. When you went to Level 2 for the first time, the change to the display level had not been made yet.

4. In the view window, you will see little icons that look like houses (see Figure 1.47). These are elevation markers. The elevation marker to the right might be in your building. If this is the case, you need to move it out of the way.

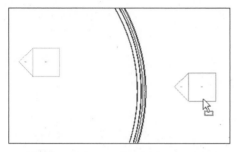

FIGURE 1.47 Symbols for elevation markers in the plan. If you need to move them, you must do so by picking a window. There are two actual items in an elevation marker.

5. Pick a box around the elevation marker. When both the small triangle and the small box are selected, move your mouse over the selected objects.

6. Your cursor will turn into a move icon. Pick a point on the screen and move the elevation marker out of the way.

7. In the Project Browser, find the Elevations (Building Elevation) category. Double-click on South.

8. Also in the Project Browser, notice there is a 3D Views category. Expand the 3D Views category, and double-click on the {3D} choice. This will bring you back to the 3D view you were looking at before this exercise.

WARNING Hey! What happened to my elevation? You are in Revit now. Items such as elevation markers, section markers, and callouts are no longer just "dumb" blocks. They are linked to the actual view they are calling out. If you delete one of these markers, you will delete the view associated with it. If you and your design team have been working on that view, then you lost that view. Also, you must move any item deliberately and with caution. This elevation marker you moved has two parts. The little triangle is actually the elevation. The little box is the part of the marker that records the sheet number the elevation will wind up on. If you do not move both items by placing a window around them, the elevation's origin will remain in its original position. When this happens, your elevation will look like a section, and it will be hard to determine how the section occurred.

Now that you can navigate through the Project Browser, adding other components to the model will be much easier. We can now begin to add some windows.

Windows

By clicking on all of these views, you are simply opening a view of the building, not another file that is stored somewhere. For some users this can be confusing. (It was for me.)

When you click around and open all these views, they stay open. You can quickly open many views. There is a way to manage these views before they get out of hand.

In the upper-right corner of the Revit dialog, you will see the traditional close and minimize/maximize buttons for the application. Just below them are the traditional buttons for the files that are open, as shown in Figure 1.48. Click the X for the current view.

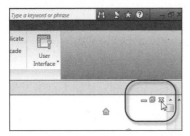

FIGURE 1.48 You can close a view by clicking the X for the view. This does not close Revit, or an actual file for that matter — it simply closes that view.

In this case, you have multiple views open. This situation (which is quite common) is best managed on the View tab. To utilize the Window menu, perform the following steps:

1. On the Window panel of the View tab, click the Switch Windows button, as shown in Figure 1.49.

2. After the menu is expanded, look at the open views.

FIGURE 1.49 The Switch Windows menu lists all the current views that are open.

3. Go to the {3D} view by selecting it from the Window menu by clicking the 3D icon at the top of the screen or by going to the {3D} view in the Project Browser.

4. On the Windows panel, click Close Hidden Windows.

5. In the Project Browser, open Level 1.

6. Go to the Windows panel and select Tile Windows.

7. With the windows tiled, you can see the Level 1 floor plan along with the 3D view to the side. Select one of the walls in the Level 1 floor plan. Notice it is now selected in the 3D view to the side. These views you have open are mere representations of the model from that perspective. Each view of the model can have its own independent view settings.

BUT I USED TO TYPE MY COMMANDS!

You can still type your commands. In the Revit menus, you may have noticed that many items have a two- or three-letter abbreviation to the right. This is the keyboard shortcut associated with the command. You can make your own shortcuts or you can modify existing keyboard shortcuts — if you navigate to the View tab. On the Windows panel, click the User Interface button. In the drop-down menu, click the Keyboard Shortcuts button. Here you can add or modify your keyboard shortcuts.

You are at a good point now to save the file. And this brings the book to a good point to discuss the different file types, and their associations with the BIM model.

File Types and Families

Revit Architecture has a unique way in which it saves files and utilizes different file types to build a BIM model. To learn how and why Revit has chosen these methods, follow along with these steps:

1. Click the save icon (see Figure 1.50).

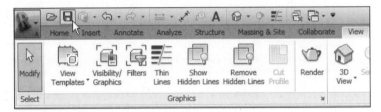

FIGURE 1.50 The traditional save icon will bring up the Save As dialog if the file has never been saved.

2. In the Save As dialog, click the Options button in the lower-right corner (see Figure 1.51).

FIGURE 1.51 The Options button in the Save As dialog lets you choose how the file is saved.

3. In the File Save Options dialog, you will see at the top a place where you can specify the number of backups, as shown in Figure 1.52. Set this value to 1.

   Revit provides this option because, when you click the save icon, Revit duplicates the file. It will simply add a suffix of "001" to the end of the filename. Each time you click the save icon, Revit will record this save and add another file called "002," leaving the "001" intact. The default is to do this three times before it starts replacing the 001, 002, and 003 with the three most current files.

4. Under the Preview section, you can specify which view this file will be previewed in. I like to keep it as the active view. That way, I can get an idea if the file is up-to-date based on the state of the view. Click OK.

5. Create a folder somewhere, and save this file into the folder. The name of the file used as an example in the book is called NER.rvt. (NER stands for "No Experience Required.") Of course, you can name the file anything you wish, or you can even just do your own project using the steps and examples from the book as a guideline.

FIGURE 1.52 The options in the File Save Options dialog box let you specify the number of backups and the view for the preview.

Now that you have experience adding components to the model, it is time to investigate exactly what we are adding here. Each component is a member of what Revit calls a *family*.

UNDERSTANDING THE REVIT ARCHITECTURE FILE (.rvt)

The extension for a Revit Architecture file is .rvt. There are three separate Revit applications: Revit Architecture, Revit Structure, and Revit MEP. All three Revits share the same .rvt file extension. You can open a Revit file produced in any of these three applications directly. You do not need object enablers to read items that do not pertain to that discipline.

System and Hosted Families (.rfa)

As mentioned earlier, a Revit model is based on a compilation of items called families. There are two types of families: system families and hosted families. A system family can be found only within a Revit model and cannot be stored in a separate location. A hosted family is inserted similar to a block (or cell) and is stored in an external directory. The file extension for a hosted family is .rfa.

System Families

System families are inherent to the current model and are not inserted in the traditional sense. You can only modify a system family through its Element Properties within the model. The walls you've put in up to this point are system families, for example. You did not have to insert a separate file in order to find the wall type. The system families in a Revit Architecture model are as follows:

> Walls
>
> Floors
>
> Roofs
>
> Ceilings
>
> Stairs
>
> Ramps
>
> Shafts
>
> Rooms
>
> Schedules/quantity takeoffs
>
> Annotation items
>
> Views

System families define your model. As you can see, the list pretty much covers most building elements. There are, however, plenty more components not included within this list. These items, which can be loaded into your model, are called hosted families.

Hosted Families

All other families in Revit Architecture are hosted in some way by a system family, a level, or a reference plane. For example, a wall sconce is a hosted family in that, when you insert it, it will be appended to a wall. Hosted families carry a file extension of .rfa. To insert a hosted family into a model, follow these steps:

1. Open the NER-01.rvt file or your own file.

2. Go to Level 1.

3. On the Home tab, select the Door button.

4. On the Modify | Place Door tab, click the Load Family button, as shown in Figure 1.53. This will open the Load Family dialog.

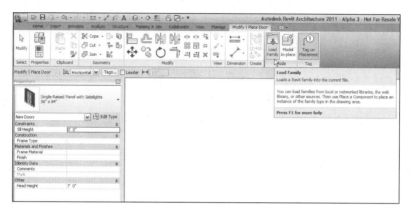

FIGURE 1.53 You can load an .rfa file during the placement of a hosted family.

5. Browse to the Doors directory.

   Note that if you are on a network, your directories may not be the same as in this book. Contact your CAD/BIM manager (or whoever loaded Revit on your computer) to find exactly where they may have mapped Revit.

6. Notice there is a list of doors. Select Single-Raised Panel with Sidelights.rfa, and click Open.

7. In the Properties dialog, click the change element type menu, as shown in Figure 1.54. Notice that not only did you bring in the raised panel door family, but you also have seven different types of the same door. These types are simply variations of the same door. You no longer have to explode a "block" and modify it to fit in your wall.

8. Select Single-Flush 36" x 84", as shown in Figure 1.54.

9. Zoom in on the upper-left corner of the building, as illustrated in Figure 1.55.

10. To insert the door into the model, you must place it in the wall. (Notice that before you hover your cursor over the actual wall, Revit will not allow you to add it to the model, as shown in Figure 1.55.) Once your pointer is directly on top of the wall, you will see the outline of the door. Once you see this, pick a point in the wall. The door is inserted. (We will cover this in depth in the next chapter.)

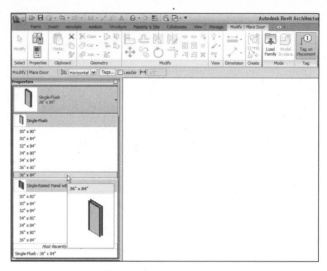

FIGURE 1.54 Each family .rfa file will contain multiple types associated with that family.

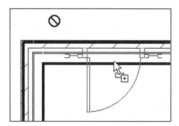

FIGURE 1.55 Inserting a hosted family (.rfa)

You will be using this method of inserting a hosted family into a model quite a bit in this book and on a daily basis when you use Revit. Note that when a family is loaded into Revit Architecture, there is no live path back to the file that was loaded. Once it is added to the Revit model, it becomes part of that model. To view a list of the families within the Revit model, go to the Project Browser and look for the Families category. In the Families category, you will see a list of the families and their types, as Figure 1.56 shows.

The two main Revit files have been addressed. Two others are still crucial to the development of a Revit model.

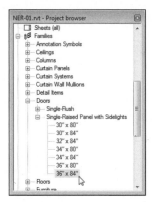

FIGURE 1.56 All of the families are listed in the Project Browser.

Using Revit Template File (.rte)

The .rte extension pertains to a Revit template file. Your company surely has developed a template for your own standards or will soon. An .rte file is simply the default template that has all of your companies standards built into it. When you start a project, you will use this file. To see how an .rte file is used, follow these steps:

1. Click the Application menu button and select New ➢ Project.

2. In the resulting dialog, shown in Figure 1.57, click the Browse button.

3. Browsing will throw you into a category with several other templates. You can now choose a different template.

4. Click Cancel twice.

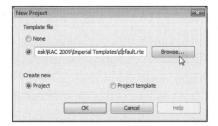

FIGURE 1.57 A new Revit model is based on an .rte template file.

Whenever you start a project, you will use the .rte template. When you start a new family, however, you will want to use an .rft file.

Using Revit Family Files (.rft)

The .rft extension is another type of template, only this one pertains to a family template. It would be nice if Revit had every family fully developed to suit your needs. Alas, it does not. You will have to develop your own families. You will start with a family template. To see how to access a family template, perform these steps:

1. Click the Application menu button, and select New ➤ Family to open the browse dialog shown in Figure 1.58.

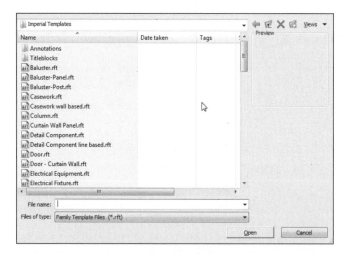

FIGURE 1.58 The creation of a family starts with templates.

2. Browse through these templates. You will most certainly use many of them.

3. Click the Cancel button.

Tempting? I know! We will thoroughly cover creating families in Chapter 17, "Families." As mentioned earlier, you will get to a certain point when you run out of Revit-provided content. If you are feeling brave, go ahead and play around in one of the templates. You have nothing to lose (except time).

Are You Experienced?

Now you can...

☑ navigate the Revit Architecture interface and actually start a model

☑ find commands on the Design bar and understand how this controls your options

☑ find where to change a keyboard shortcut to make it similar to CAD

☑ navigate through the Project Browser

☑ understand how the Revit interface is broken down into views

☑ tell the difference between the two different types of families, and understand how to build a model using them

Creating a Model

Now that you have a solid working knowledge of the Revit Architecture interface and you understand how it differs from most other drafting applications, it's time to move on to creating the Revit model.

The first chapter had you add some exterior walls to the model, and this chapter will expand on that same concept. You will also be placing some of the components, such as doors, that were introduced in Chapter 1, "The Revit World." Revit is only as good as the families that support the model.

To kick off the chapter, we will focus on the accurate placement of interior and exterior walls. We also have a lot to learn about the properties of walls and how to tackle tricky areas where the walls just won't join together for us.

▶ **Placing walls**

▶ **Using reference planes**

▶ **Adding interior walls**

▶ **Editing wall joins**

▶ **Placing doors and windows**

Placing Walls

In Chapter 1 we placed some walls and then added some exterior walls to the model. In this section you will be adding more walls to the model. While adding walls to the model is not difficult, we need to explore how to control these walls when adjacent items start moving around and corners get "fussy." Also, we will examine proven methods to ensure accuracy, so we can keep you from starting down the wrong path.

Adding Exterior Walls

To continue with the perimeter of the building, let's add some more exterior walls. The first few walls we added to our model were pretty basic in terms of layout. It would be nice to have only square geometry! The reality is you are going to encounter walls at different angles and dimensions to which you cannot just line up other walls. To get around this, let's add what are called reference planes to help us lay out our building. At the end of this section, our building's perimeter will look like Figure 2.1.

The objective of the next set of procedures is to establish some strong working points, and then add walls along those guidelines. We will also use these rules to make the necessary adjustments later in the section.

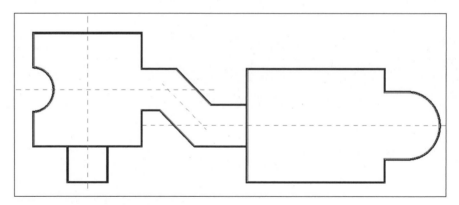

FIGURE 2.1 The footprint of our completed building

Using Reference Planes

Reference planes are construction lines that you can place in your model to establish center lines and to use as an aid for symmetrical geometry. If you add a reference plane in one view, it will show up in another. If you add one in a plan view, you can see that same plane in an elevation. This approach is a great way to build using a common reference. Also, reference planes, by default, will not plot.

The only drawback to reference planes is that they suffer from overuse. Try to use them only as what they are: a reference. To practice using reference planes, follow these steps:

1. Open the file you created in Chapter 1. If you did not complete that chapter, open the file called NER-01.rvt, which you can download from the book's website at **www.sybex.com/go/revit2011ner**. (You can also use your own building, but the dimensions specified here will not be consistent with your model.)

2. On the Work Plane panel of the Home tab, click the Ref Plane button, as shown in Figure 2.2.

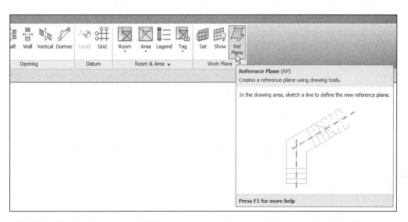

FIGURE 2.2: The Ref Plane command is on the Home tab's Ref Plane panel of the Ribbon.

3. Draw the reference plane through the center of the building, extending each end past the exterior walls. (Remember, this is a construction line. You can go long if you need to). See Figure 2.3 for an idea of where the line should go.

4. If the line is not the length you would like it, you can stretch it. First select the line; at each end, you will see blue grips. Simply pick (left-click) the grip and stretch the reference plane to the desired length, as in Figure 2.3.

5. Start the Ref Plane command again.

As you move through the exercises in this book, you will discover that the Ref Plane command is found elsewhere in the program.

6. Press Esc, and then click the Ref Plane button again. Now, on the Draw panel, click the Pick Lines icon, as shown in Figure 2.4.

7. Set the Offset to 15′–0″ (remember, you can just type 15), as in Figure 2.4.

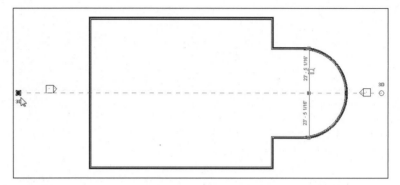

FIGURE 2.3 You can grip-edit reference planes to the required length.

FIGURE 2.4 Offsetting a reference plane

8. Hover your pointer above the mid-reference plane. Notice a blue alignment line will appear either above or below.

9. Move your pointer up and down. See the alignment line flip? When it flips to the top, pick the middle line. It will add the line to the top.

10. With the Ref Plane command still running, hover over the middle line again. This time, offset the alignment line down. Your plan should now look like Figure 2.5.

TIP   Notice you did not actually use the Offset command. Revit Architecture has the offset function built into most of the commands you will be running. You just need to remember to look at your temporary tab and your Options bar and you will be fine.

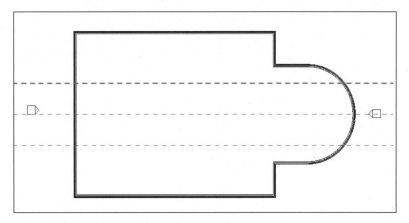

FIGURE 2.5 Reference planes are used here to aid in the placement of walls.

Adding More Walls

Let's add some walls. To do so, follow along with the next set of steps. (Before we start, here's a tip. In this procedure we're going to add walls in a counter-clockwise direction, so follow along in that manner. But keep in mind that Revit assumes you will add walls in a clockwise manner. In the future, try adding the walls clockwise; it "forces" the exterior of the wall to the outside.) OK, now back to adding walls!

1. Press the Esc key.

2. Select one of the exterior walls in the model and right-click.

3. Select Create Similar. (You can still start the Wall command from the Home tab. If you do, make sure you select Basic Wall: Exterior - Brick and CMU on MTL. Stud.)

4. On the Options bar, make sure Location Line is set to Finish Face: Exterior.

5. Start drawing your new wall from the intersection of the west wall (the one on the left) and the upper reference plane, as shown in Figure 2.6. Make sure you are using the face of the wall and not the ledge below. The blowup in Figure 2.6 can help you.

6. If the wall is starting on the wrong side of the reference plane, tap your spacebar. This will flip the wall to the correct side.

7. Making sure you have a horizontal line started, type **25** and press Enter

8. Press Esc.

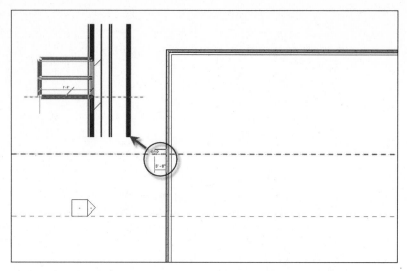

FIGURE 2.6 Drawing a single wall from a defined starting point

9. Do the same for the other side. Your plan should now look like Figure 2.7.

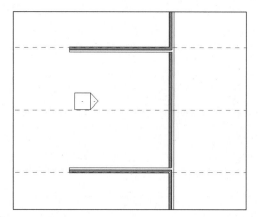

FIGURE 2.7 The two walls drawn here are 30′–0″ from finish face to finish face.

10. Start the Wall command again.

11. From the top 25′–0″ wall, pick (left-click) the corner of the finish face (again, the brick face and not the ledge below). The wall may be in the wrong orientation, so tap the spacebar to flip it if it is.

12. Move your cursor up and to the left at a 135° angle (Revit will snap at 45° intervals).

13. After you move your cursor far enough in this direction, Revit will pick up the north finish face of the building drawn in the previous procedure. After these two alignment lines appear, pick the point on the screen, as shown in Figure 2.8.

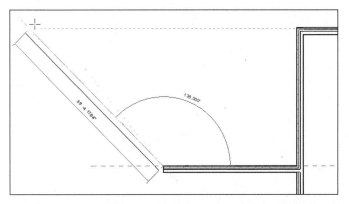

FIGURE 2.8 Allow Revit to guide you in the placement of walls.

14. After you pick this point, draw a horizontal wall to the left 25′.

15. From the left point of that wall, draw a wall up 25′.

16. From the top of that wall, draw another wall to the left 80′.

17. Draw a wall down 25′.

18. On the Modify | Place Wall panel, click the Start-End-Radius Arc button, as shown in Figure 2.9.

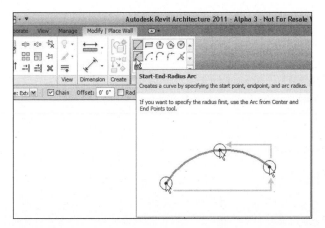

FIGURE 2.9 Draw a radial wall using the Start-End-Radius Arc method.

19. Because the Wall command is still running, the next point to pick is the endpoint of the arc. Pick a point straight down at a distance of 30'–0".

20. After you pick the second point, move your pointer to the right until Revit snaps it to the tangent radius. (You may not get a tangent snap, but Revit will hesitate when you have reached the tangency.) Once this happens, pick a point.

21. On the Draw panel, check the line button in the upper-left corner as shown in Figure 2.10. This will allow you to draw a straight wall again.

22. Draw a wall straight down from the end of the arc 25'.

23. Draw a wall to the right 80'.

24. Draw a wall straight up 25'–0".

25. Press Esc. Your building should look like Figure 2.10.

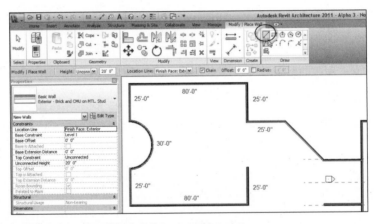

FIGURE 2.10 The building up to this point

The next few walls will be a little tougher. You will have to place them using the embedded offset function within the Wall command. Remember, you need to keep watching the Options bar for this one.

1. Start the Wall command.

2. On the Draw panel, click the Pick Lines icon, as shown in Figure 2.11.

3. On the Options bar, you will see an Offset input. Type 30 and press Enter.

4. Move your cursor over the outside face of the wall, as shown in Figure 2.12. When you see the alignment line appear below the wall, pick the outside face, as shown in Figure 2.12.

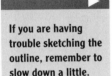

If you are having trouble sketching the outline, remember to slow down a little.

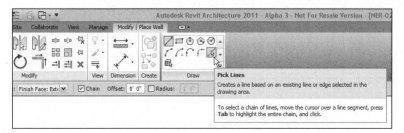

FIGURE 2.11 The Pick Lines icon from the Options bar lets you add a wall by using an offset from another object.

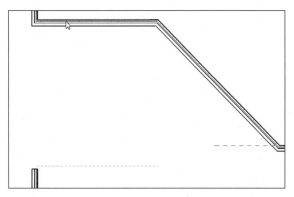

FIGURE 2.12 Adding a wall using the built-in offset function may take a few tries to get the method down.

5. Repeat the procedure for the angled wall. Make sure you offset the wall to the left (see Figure 2.13).

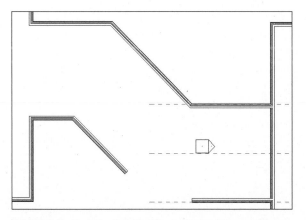

FIGURE 2.13 Creating the bottom of the corridor

Wall Adjustments

You've probably noticed that the walls are joining themselves together. This behavior is inherent to Revit. For the previous procedure, however, you will be left with a gap between the bottom two walls. It was too far for Revit to realize these walls need to be joined. You can fix this by following these steps:

1. Pick (left-click) the bottom diagonal wall. You will see a number of blue icons and dimensions appear, as shown in Figure 2.14. Each of these icons plays a role in the adjustment of the wall.

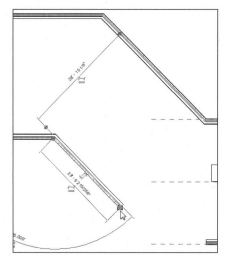

F I G U R E   2 . 1 4   By selecting a wall, you can make adjustments, such as stretching the ends, by picking the blue grips.

2. On each end, you will see a solid blue grip. Pick the right solid blue grip and drag the wall down to meet the reference plane, as shown in Figure 2.15.

3. Select the horizontal wall to the right.

4. Pick the left blue grip, and drag this wall's end to the left until you hit the bottom corner of the diagonal wall. The two walls will join together (see Figure 2.16).

5. We need to add another part of the building. Select and then right-click on one of the exterior walls and select Create Similar.

6. On the View toolbar, set the detail level to Coarse, as shown in Figure 2.17.

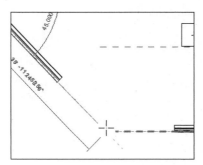

FIGURE 2.15 Stretching the wall using the blue grip

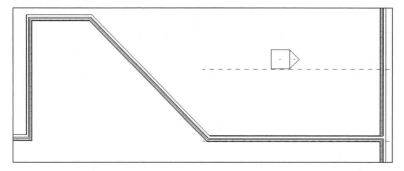

FIGURE 2.16 The walls are automatically joined when you "pull" the end of one into another.

FIGURE 2.17 Sometimes setting the graphic display to Coarse can make the placement of other walls easier.

7. On the Options bar, change the offset to 15′–0″.

8. Pick the midpoint of the wall, as shown in Figure 2.18.

9. Draw the wall 25′–0″ down from the wall by typing **25** and pressing Enter.

10. After you pick the 25′–0″ distance, move your cursor up, back toward the wall, as shown in Figure 2.19, resulting in a 25′ long wall.

11. Draw a wall across the front of the two walls, as shown in Figure 2.20. Make sure it is flipped in the right direction.

12. Set the detail level back to Fine. Your walls should look like Figure 2.20.

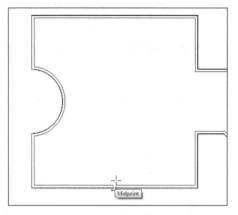

FIGURE 2.18 Adding the new walls requires picking the midpoint of this wall. Make sure your offset is set to 15′–0″ on the Options bar.

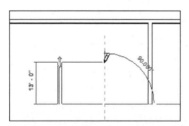

FIGURE 2.19 By using the Offset command as you draw walls, you can use one common centerline.

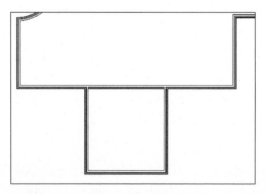

FIGURE 2.20 The completed walls for the south side of the building

DOES IT MEASURE UP?

In Revit, you can access the Measure function, which is the same as the Distance command in AutoCAD. To verify whether your walls are at your chosen distances, click the Measure icon as shown here. After you measure the distance, the Options bar will show you the result. The Measure icon is available on the Inquiry panel of the Modify tab.

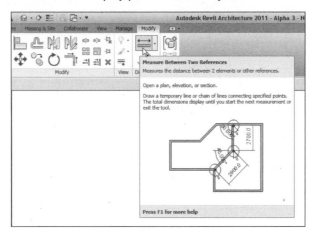

Adding Interior Walls

Interior walls are basically the same as exterior walls in terms of how they are placed in the model. This is a good thing. Luckily you can be slightly more relaxed with the justification. Now that the building has a footprint, you can see more easily whether or not the walls need to be adjusted.

We'll start with laying out an elevator shaft and a stairwell, using an 8″ CMU wall system. To follow along, either keep going with the model you are developing or open the file NER-02.rvt.

1. Zoom into the northeast corner of the building, as shown in Figure 2.21.

2. On the Home tab, click the Wall button.

3. In the Properties dialog, select Generic - 8″ Masonry, as shown in Figure 2.21.

4. For the starting point, pick the corner as shown in Figure 2.21. The wall will probably be in the wrong orientation, so if necessary, tap the spacebar to flip the wall's orientation.

5. Move your cursor downward and type **12**. The wall will be 12′–0″ long.

6. Move your cursor to the right and type **10**.

7. Move your cursor back up the view and pick the exterior wall.

8. Hit the Esc key. You should have three walls that look like Figure 2.22.

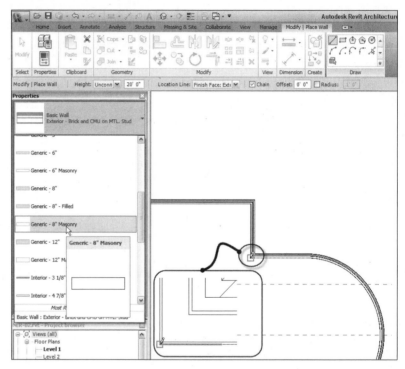

FIGURE 2.21 Start drawing the 8″ CMU elevator shaft in the corner indicated here.

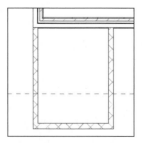

FIGURE 2.22 The elevator shaft begins to take shape.

At this point, you have some walls in the model. It is time to look at ensuring that these walls are accurately placed, so you need to check the dimensions.

Using Temporary Dimensions to Gain Control of Your Model

After you place items in a model, you usually need to make some adjustments. Revit does a good job with this; however, there are some rules that need to be adhered to. The goal here is to have a clear 10′–0″ dimension on the inside faces of the shaft. At this point, you should assume that you do not. This is where temporary dimensions come into play. To start working with temporary dimensions, follow these steps:

1. Select the right, vertical CMU wall. You will see a blue temporary dimension appear along the bottom wall. (If the dimension does not go to the point indicated, click the blue grip. This will move it to the correct location as shown in Figure 2.23.) This dimension indicates the centerline increments, as shown in Figure 2.23.

2. On the temporary dimension, you will see some blue grips. If you hover your cursor over one of them, a tooltip will appear indicating that this grip represents the witness line.

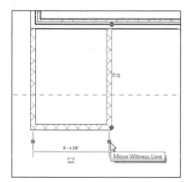

FIGURE 2.23 Temporary dimensions can be adjusted to measure from different wall faces by picking the witness line grip.

3. Pick the grip to the right side of the dimension. Notice it moves to the outside face of the wall. Pick it again, and notice it moves to the inside face. This is exactly where we want it.

4. Pick the grip to the left of the dimension twice to get it to read from the inside face of the CMU wall.

5. Notice the actual increment in the dimension is blue. Select the blue dimension, type **10**, and press Enter. The wall that was selected will move to accommodate the new increment, as shown in Figure 2.24.

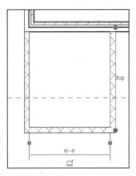

FIGURE 2.24 The selected wall is the wall that will move when you type the new dimension.

Temporary Dimension Settings

Revit measures the default dimension for the temporary dimensions from the center of the walls—which is typically the last place you want to take the dimension from. You can change some settings to fix this action:

1. On the Manage tab, click Additional Settings ➤ Temporary Dimensions, as shown in Figure 2.25.

2. In the Temporary Dimension Properties box, select Faces in the Walls group.

3. In the Doors and Windows group, select Openings, as shown in Figure 2.26.

4. Click OK.

5. Select the wall to the left. You may not see any dimensions at all. Always remember to look up at the Ribbon area. Click the Activate Dimensions button, and you will now see a 10′–0″ dimension.

6. Underneath the dimension, you will see a small blue icon that also looks like a dimension. If you hover your mouse over it, a tooltip will appear indicating that you can make the temporary dimension permanent, as shown in Figure 2.27. When you see this tooltip, click the icon.

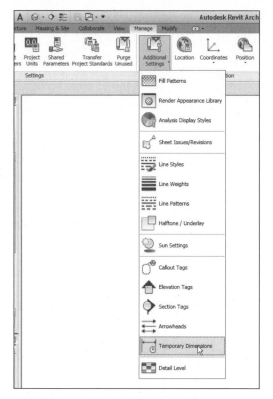

FIGURE 2.25 The Temporary Dimensions function lets you control where Revit measures the temporary dimensions.

FIGURE 2.26 The most popular configuration for Temporary Dimensions

7. Press Esc.

8. Select the right wall. Notice the permanent dimension turns blue. We know that anything that turns blue in Revit can be edited. You can change this increment anytime you wish.

9. Press Esc again without changing the dimension.

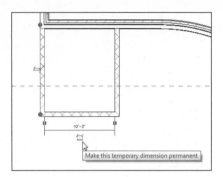

FIGURE 2.27 You can make temporary dimensions permanent.

We need one more shaft wall to create a separation between the exterior walls and the shaft, as shown in Figure 2.28. Perform these steps:

1. Select and then right-click on any CMU wall and select Create Similar.

2. On the Draw panel, click the Pick Lines icon.

3. On the Options bar, type **10** in the Offset field.

4. On the Options bar, be sure Location Line is set to Finish Face: Interior.

5. Offset the south CMU shaft wall (from the inner line). This will separate the shaft from the exterior and create a little chase.

6. Press Esc twice. Figure 2.28 shows the shaft wall. Make sure you check your dimensions before proceeding.

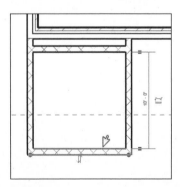

FIGURE 2.28 The shaft wall

The next task is to mirror these walls to the other side:

1. Pick a window around all of the masonry walls (a window with your cursor, not an actual window).

2. On the Modify | Walls tab, click the Mirror ➤ Pick Axis button, as shown in Figure 2.29.

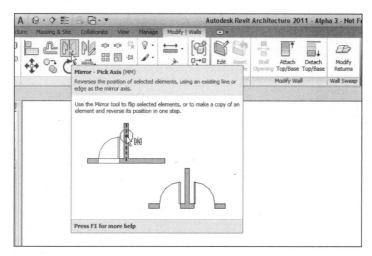

FIGURE 2.29 The Mirror - Pick Axis command is activated only when you have objects selected.

3. Pick the horizontal reference plane in the center of the building. Your walls are now mirrored, as shown in Figure 2.30.

4. Save the model.

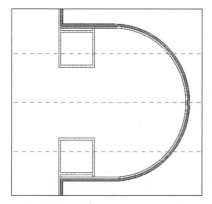

FIGURE 2.30 The elevator shaft is now mirrored.

We are starting to get the hang of adding different wall types—but we aren't done yet. We still need to add quite a few interior partitions.

DID YOU SELECT TOO MUCH?

If you picked a window around all of your walls and have more items selected than you wish, you can simply press the Shift key on your keyboard and pick the item(s) you want unselected. This will remove the item from the selection set. If the opposite happens and you want to add an item, press the Ctrl key and pick the item(s) you want added. Your cursor will always appear with a plus or a minus sign, as shown in the following image.

Placing Interior Partitions

The majority of your tasks in Revit involve placing interior partitions. Given the dimensional nature of placing these types of walls in Revit, you don't need to bother with reference planes as often as when you place the exterior walls.

Knowing that, creating interior partitions is somewhat easier than the exterior variety. With the exterior, careful placement and constant double-checking is crucial. With interior partitions, you can typically get the wall where you think you need it. You can then go back and make adjustments without disturbing too many adjacent items.

To start adding interior partitions, we will begin with the necessary lavatory and egress first, and then fill the spaces with some offices. When completed, this stage will look like Figure 2.31.

The objective of the next procedure is to start adding our interior partitions:

1. Open the building you have been working on. If you did not complete the last procedure, open the file called NER-03.rvt found on the book's website. Or, of course, you can keep going on your own project.

2. Make sure you are on Level 1.

3. On the Home tab, click the Wall button.

4. In the Properties dialog, select Interior - 6 1/8″ Partition (2-hr).

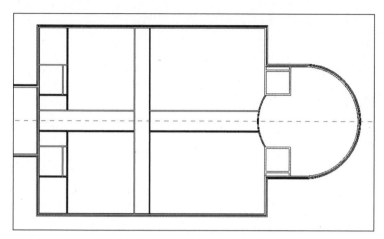

FIGURE 2.31 The east side of the building with egress and lavatories up to this point

5. On the Draw panel, click the Pick Lines icon.

6. For the Height, choose Level 2 from the menu (if it is not already the current selection).

7. For Location Line, choose Finish Face: Exterior.

8. On the Draw panel, click the Start-End-Radius Arc button (see the top right of Figure 2.32).

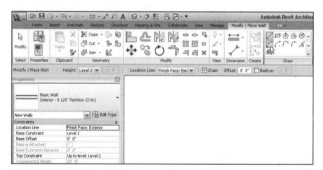

FIGURE 2.32 Choosing options should be old hat by now! The Start-End-Radius Arc button is at the top right.

9. Pick the left corner of the upper CMU walls.

10. Pick the left corner of the bottom CMU walls.

11. Move your cursor to the left, and specify a radius of 20′–0″, as shown in Figure 2.33.

12. Press Esc twice.

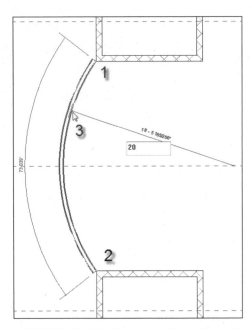

F I G U R E 2 . 3 3 Drawing arched radial wall requires a three-point method. It is similar to the Start-End-Direction command in AutoCAD.

We now need to add some corridor walls. You can do this using the center reference plane you established earlier:

1. Select and then right-click on the radial wall and select Create Similar.

2. On the Draw panel, click the Line button.

3. For Location Line, choose Finish Face: Interior.

4. For Offset (on the Options bar), add a 4′–0″ offset.

5. To start placing the wall, pick the intersection of the center reference plane and the radial wall, as shown in Figure 2.34.

6. Move your cursor to the left. Notice the wall is being drawn but at an offset of 4′–0″ from the "line" you are drawing up the middle of the building.

7. For the second point of the wall, pick the intersection of the vertical wall to the left.

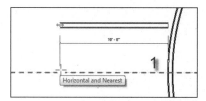

FIGURE 2.34 Drawing corridor walls using an offset can be a great timesaver.

8. Now move your cursor back to the right. Notice the other side of the wall is being drawn at a 4′–0″ offset. This time, it is on the opposite side of the reference line.

9. Pick the intersection of the reference plane and the radial wall as the second point, as shown in Figure 2.35.

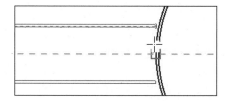

FIGURE 2.35 Completing the main corridor. You will still have to drag the walls together to join up.

Let's now clean up the gaps between the radial wall and the two corridor walls:

1. Make sure you are not still in the Wall command by pressing Esc or by clicking the Modify button to the left of the Ribbon.

2. Select the top corridor wall. On the right end of the wall is a blue grip. Pick it and drag the top corridor wall into the radial wall.

3. Repeat the step for the bottom wall (see Figure 2.36).

WARNING   Picking a grip on the end of a wall also means you are going to get a temporary dimension. Look at it! If it does not say 8′–0″ to the inside face of the corridor, you have a problem. It is much better to discover these discrepancies early in the design stage than to find out you have a dimensional issue when the drawings are going out the door. If the increment is not 8′–0″, first verify that the temporary dimension is going to the inside face. If not, pick the blue grip and move the witness line to the inside face of the walls. If the dimension is still off, move the witness line to the center reference plane. Now just type 4 and press Enter. Repeat the process for the other wall. Always check dimensions like this. The time you save could be your own!

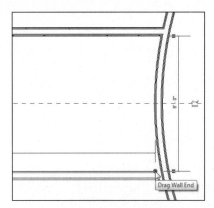

FIGURE 2.36 Getting a grip on the grips!

The next step is to get the lavatories in. These will show up at the west end (left side) of the building. Refer to Figure 2.37 for the dimensions and follow along:

1. Select and then right-click on one of the corridor walls and select Create Similar from the menu.

2. Look at your options, and create the lavatories shown in Figure 2.37. All of the dimensions are taken from finish inside face.

3. After you draw in the lavatory walls, mirror the walls to the other side of the building, as shown in Figure 2.38.

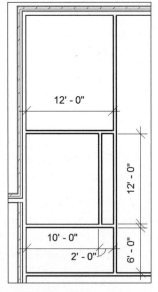

FIGURE 2.37 The lavatory at the west side of the building

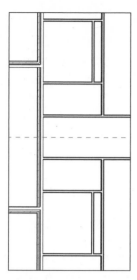

FIGURE 2.38 Both the Men's and Women's lavatories. The actual rooms will be added in Chapter 15, "Creating Room and Area Plans"

We now need another corridor running north and south, as shown in Figure 2.39. The best way to approach this task is to add another reference plane, and then add the walls in a similar fashion to the method applied to the east/west corridor. To open up the central area, some 45° walls will be added at 4'–0". Follow these steps to add the new walls:

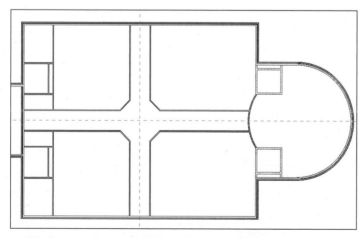

FIGURE 2.39 This is the finished corridor layout.

1. On the Work Plane panel of the Home tab, click Ref Plane.

2. Draw a reference plane from the midpoint of the top exterior wall to the midpoint of the bottom exterior wall.

3. Click the Measure Between Two References button. Make 100 percent sure this is the center of the building. You are going to rely heavily on this line.

4. Start the Wall command.

5. On the Options bar, be sure Location Line is set to Finish Face: Interior and that the offset is 4′–0″.

6. Pick the top intersection of the reference plane and the exterior wall.

7. Draw the wall down to the bottom of the building.

8. Keeping the Wall command running, draw the other side of the corridor by picking the same two points along the reference plane. When you are finished, hit Esc.

T I P   Are the reference lines really necessary? No, they are not. But it is a good, sound approach to laying out your building. These lines will be used heavily throughout the life of your project.

You now have an area in the middle of the building where four walls intersect each other. You can now add some 45° walls there to open the corridor at this area, as shown in Figure 2.40:

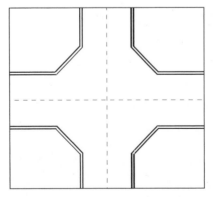

FIGURE 2.40 The corridor with the 45° walls added

---

1. Zoom into the intersections of the corridors.

2. On the Work Plane panel of the Home tab, click Ref Plane.

3. On the Draw panel, select the Pick Lines button and change the offset to 4′–0″.

4. From the finish inside face of the top, horizontal corridor wall, offset the reference plane up (see Figure 2.41).

T I P　It can be tricky to get the reference plane going in the correct direction. If it is being stubborn, and is still trying to offset the line down, just move your cursor up a little. The reference plane will change direction.

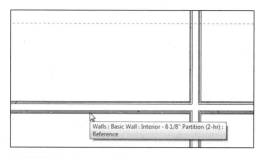

FIGURE 2.41　Adding yet another reference plane to the model. You will delete this one.

After you establish the reference plane, you can add the new wall. It can be as simple as just drawing the wall in, but there are still a few little procedures you should be aware of:

1. Start the Wall command by selecting and then right-clicking on one of the corridor walls and choosing Create Similar.

2. On the Options bar, be sure the wall's Location Line is justified from Finish Face: Interior.

3. Pick the intersection of the reference plane and the inside finished face of the left, vertical corridor wall (see Figure 2.42).

4. After you pick the start point, move your cursor to the left and down at a 45° angle (you can approximate the angle; Revit will "snap" you to the correct angle).

5. At a 45° angle, pick the endpoint at a location within the horizontal, top corridor wall. Once you are done, press the Esc key on your keyboard (see Figure 2.42).

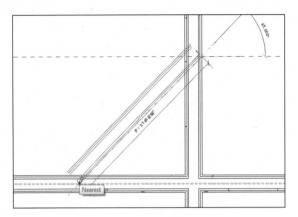

FIGURE 2.42 Adding the 45° wall

EYEBALLING WITH ACCURACY

You may notice when you are using temporary dimensions that the increment always seems to "snap" to even increments. This is no accident. If you choose Settings ➢ Snaps on the Manage tab, you will see values for Length Dimension Snap Increments and Angular Dimension Snap Increments. These values change based on the zoom percentage. The closer you zoom in, the smaller the increments get. You can also add to these values by typing in a semicolon and adding a new increment to the end of the list, as shown in this image:

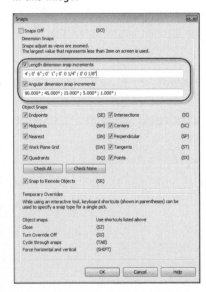

W A R N I N G   If you proceed with just assuming that these walls are 4′–0″ from the inside face, you may be making a big mistake. Take distances after you add walls—especially if the walls are not 90°.

The next task is to mirror the walls. This part is going to be easy since you put those reference planes in there!

1. Select the 45° wall.

2. Pick Mirror Pick Axis from the Modify | Walls tab.

3. Pick the vertical reference plane. And voilà! The wall is mirrored (see Figure 2.43).

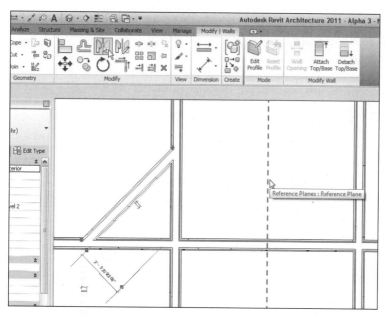

F I G U R E   2 . 4 3 Using the Mirror command in conjunction with a reference plane is a good example of thinking ahead.

4. Select the two 45° walls, and mirror them around the horizontal reference plane. You should now have four 45° walls, as shown in Figure 2.44.

5. You can now delete the vertical reference plane by simply selecting it and clicking the Delete button.

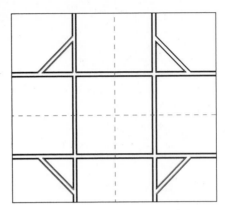

FIGURE 2.44 Stuck inside these four walls

Now it's time for some further cleanup. Although all of the modify commands will be featured in Chapter 4, "Working with the Revit Tools," we can still use some here. Already, we have borrowed the Mirror command from that chapter. We might as well borrow the Split command as well!

1. On the Modify panel of the Modify tab, click the Split Element button, as shown in Figure 2.45.

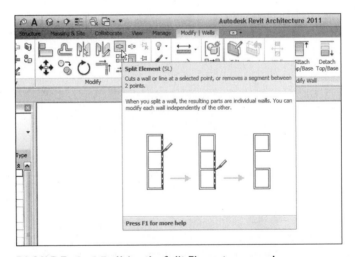

FIGURE 2.45 Using the Split Element command

2. Always look at the Options bar! Select the Delete Inner Segment option.

3. Pick a point along the top horizontal corridor wall near the intersecting 45° wall.

4. Pick the second point along the same wall, only on the opposite side (see Figure 2.46).

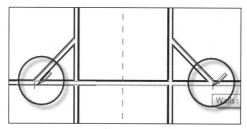

FIGURE 2.46 Split the wall at two points. If you've selected Delete Inner Segment, the result is to eliminate the wall between the two points.

5. Repeat the process for the other three walls. You should now have an open central area for your corridor, as shown in Figure 2.47.

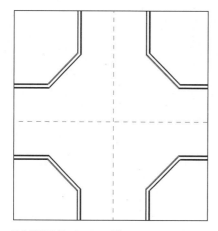

FIGURE 2.47 The open corridor

N O T E   If the Split Element command is giving you a splitting headache rather than splitting the walls, keep trying. We will also cover this in Chapter 4. Commands such as Split Element do require a different "touch" than with the AutoCAD Break command.

Looking back, we have accomplished quite a bit. Laying out walls and then modifying them to conform to your needs is a huge part of being successful in Revit, but we are not done yet. The next few processes will involve dealing with different types of walls that merge together. Historically, merging walls has been an issue in modeling software. Although Revit tends to clean these areas up a little better than other modeling applications, you must still cope with some "sticky" areas. Let's create a sticky situation!

Editing Wall Joins

There is a separate function in Revit that deals with editing wall joins specifically: the Edit Wall Joins command. It can come in quite handy. To get started, let's add some more walls to an already busy corner of the building:

1. Zoom into the northeast corner of the building, as shown in Figure 2.48.

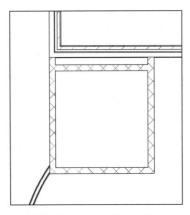

FIGURE 2.48 The northeast corner

2. Start the Wall command. Make sure it is the same 6 1/8″ two-hour partition you have been using.

3. To start the wall, pick the intersection where the CMU wall abuts the finish inside face of the exterior wall (see Figure 2.49).

4. The wall may be flipped in the wrong direction. If it is, remember to hit the spacebar. This will flip it up to the proper orientation. Look ahead to Figure 2.50 for the orientation.

5. Pick the second point of the wall at the corridor in the middle of the building. Press Esc twice. The intersection should look like Figure 2.50.

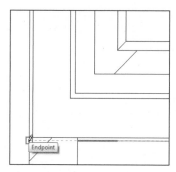

FIGURE 2.49 Adding to the mess in the corner

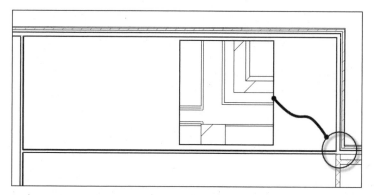

FIGURE 2.50 The wall and the resulting intersection

6. Zoom back in on the intersection. If the view does not resemble Figure 2.50 in terms of line weight, click the Thin Lines icon, as shown in Figure 2.51.

FIGURE 2.51 Click the Thin Lines icon to see how the walls are joining together.

7. On the Geometry panel of the Modify tab, click the Wall Joins button, as shown in Figure 2.52.

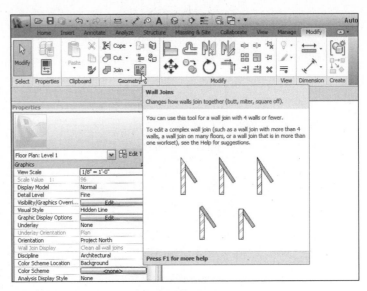

FIGURE 2.52 You'll find the Wall Joins button on the Modify tab.

8. Hover your pointer over the intersection. Revit will display a big box, as shown in Figure 2.53.

9. When you see the big box, pick anywhere within the area. This will establish that this is the intersection you wish to edit.

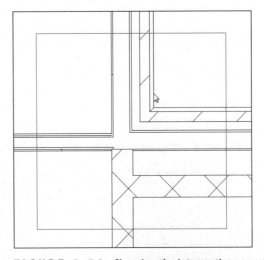

FIGURE 2.53 Choosing the intersection you wish to edit

After you pick the intersection, you will see some additional lines show up. These additional lines expose how Revit is actually looking at the corner.

10. On the Options bar, you will now see some choices for configuring this intersection. Select the Miter option, as shown in Figure 2.54. This option is the most popular.

Although a wall of this type would never have a 45° miter in real life, mitering the corner in Revit allows for a more uniform join between adjacent walls.

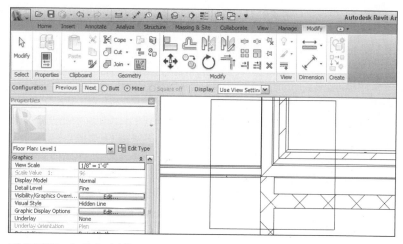

FIGURE 2.54 Adding a mitered join

Displaying Wall Joins

Usually, in a plan view such as this, there will be no wall joins shown at all. Typically only the outside lines join and an enlarged detail would show the specific construction methods. But in some cases, you would want Revit to reveal this information. In Revit, you have three choices for the display:

Clean Join   Clean Join will join together the same materials in each wall.

Don't Clean Join   Don't Clean Join will take one wall and indiscriminately run it straight through to the end.

Use View Setting   Use View Setting will take you to the View Properties, where you can specify the default for how to display the wall intersections (see Figure 2.55).

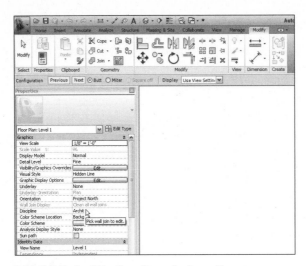

FIGURE 2.55 Choosing a display option

The objective of the next procedure is to investigate where the wall join settings are located:

1. Choose Use View Setting.

2. Press Esc a few times and click on the drawing.

3. Type VP to open the View Properties dialog.

4. In the Properties dialog, you will see a category for Wall Join Display. It is set to Clean All Wall Joins; it is also unavailable for editing. If your view's detail level is set to Fine, the default is to clean all joins. If it is set to Coarse, as shown in Figure 2.56, you have a choice between joining the same wall types or cleaning all joins.

5. Do not change anything here.

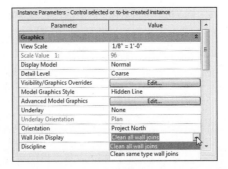

FIGURE 2.56 Choosing a Wall Join Display option in the view's properties

Disallowing Wall Join

You must deal with another important item when walls join together. In some cases, you may not want walls to automatically join even if they are the same exact wall type. To learn how to prevent this behavior, follow along:

1. Select the long, horizontal 6 1/8″ wall that comes into the corner, as shown in Figure 2.57. You will see a blue grip to the right of the intersection. This represents where the wall's extents are.

2. Hover directly over the blue grip.

3. After the blue grip highlights, right-click.

4. Select Disallow Join (see Figure 2.57).

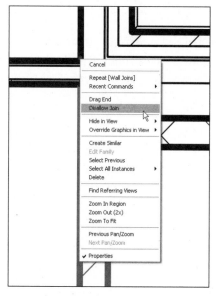

FIGURE 2.57 By right-clicking on the wall's end grip, you can tell Revit to disallow that wall's join function.

5. After the wall is un-joined, you can pick the same blue grip and slide the wall back to where you would want it to terminate. Of course, you will have to do this manually (see Figure 2.58).

6. After the wall slides into place, select it.

7. Notice there is an additional blue T-shaped icon. Hover your cursor over this icon; you will see that you can pick this icon to allow the walls to join back up again, as shown in Figure 2.58.

8. Click this icon to allow the join.

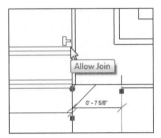

FIGURE 2.58 Allowing the walls to join back again

As mentioned earlier, your ability to edit wall joins can determine how quickly you start either liking, or disliking, Revit. This book took a few extra steps in the effort of joining walls, but the experience will carry through, project after project.

There is one more area we need to investigate before we leave this corner: the area within the chase. Suppose you do not want to run the gypsum into this area. This is a common situation that can cause people to have fits with Revit. Let's try to avoid those fits right now!

Editing the Cut Profile

A plan view is simply a section taken 4′–0″ up the wall from the finish floor. In Revit, you can manually edit the profile of any wall cut in plan. This is extremely useful if you need to take sections of drywall out of specific areas without creating or adding an entirely new wall. To do this, perform the following steps:

1. Zoom in on the right side of the elevator shaft at the intersection of the exterior wall, as shown in Figure 2.59.

2. Select the east CMU wall, and drag it out of the exterior wall by picking and dragging the blue grip at the end of the wall (see Figure 2.59).

3. Right-click on the blue grip on the endpoint of the wall.

4. Select Disallow Join.

5. Pick the blue grip and drag the wall end back to the face of the wall behind the gypsum (see Figure 2.60).

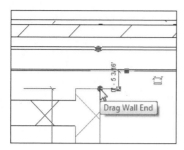

FIGURE 2.59 Pick the blue grip and drag the CMU wall out of the exterior wall.

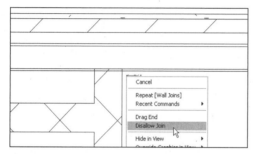

FIGURE 2.60 Pull the CMU out of the wall, disallow the join, and then drag it back into the face of the stud.

6. On the Graphics panel of the View tab, click the Cut Profile button, as shown at the top right of Figure 2.61.

7. Pick the finish face of the exterior wall. You are selecting the gypsum layer to be cut out of the shaft (see Figure 2.61).

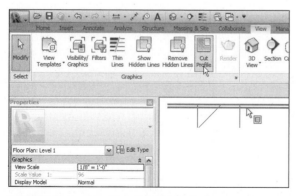

FIGURE 2.61 Click the Cut Profile button and select the gypsum.

8. You now need to draw a very short, vertical line from the inside face of the wallboard to the outside face, as shown in Figure 2.62. Press Esc.

9. Once the short line is drawn in, you will see a blue arrow. This arrow indicates the side of the material you wish to keep. If you pick (left-click) the arrow, it will flip direction. Make sure it is flipped to the right.

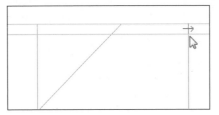

FIGURE 2.62 This line indicates where the wallboard will be cut. The blue arrow indicates the side of the material that will remain.

10. What you see here is called the Sketch Mode. Since you are done "sketching" the cut profile, click Finish Edit Mode, as you can see in Figure 2.63. Figure 2.64 shows the final result.

FIGURE 2.63 Clicking Finish Edit Mode will finalize the session and complete the command.

N O T E   If you receive an error that says "Ends of the sketched loop do not lie on the boundary of the face being modified" when you are trying to finish the sketch, it is because you have not drawn the line exactly from point to point. This line cannot cross over, or be shy of, the material you are trying to split. If you are getting this error, select the magenta line. You will see two familiar blue grips. Pick the grip that does not touch the face of the material and drag it back.

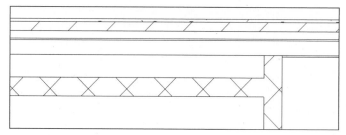

FIGURE 2.64 The finished wall with the drywall deducted from the core of the chase

Go through and do the same thing to the south side of the building, starting at the edit Wall Joins section.

There are plenty more walls left to add, but we need to save something for Chapter 4. At this point, it sure would be nice to start adding some doors and windows to the model!

Placing Doors and Windows

Adding doors and windows is one of the easiest things you will do in Revit Architecture. Finding the correct door or window becomes a bit harder. Creating a custom door or window takes time and patience. In this section, we will focus on adding these items to the model. Chapter 17, "Creating Families," will drill down into the specifics of creating these custom families.

Adding Doors

Placing a door in Revit Architecture can seem annoying and unnecessarily tedious at first. But like anything else in Revit, once you get the method down, you will find your groove.

1. Either continue working in your current model, or go to **www.sybex .com/go/revit2011ner** and navigate to the file called NER-04.rvt. The model is completed up to this point. Of course, you can translate these lessons to your own project as well.

2. On the Home tab, click the Door button (see Figure 2.65).

3. In the Properties dialog, choose Single-Flush: 36″ x 84″.

FIGURE 2.65 Adding a door

4. Move your cursor over to the south wall near the elevator shaft, as shown in Figure 2.66. Notice that if your cursor is not within a wall, you get the "NO" sign. Revit will not allow you to just place a door into space. A door is considered a hosted family.

5. After you get your cursor positioned approximately where Figure 2.66 shows, move your pointer up and down. Notice the door's direction will change. This is typical behavior for a door.

6. Press the spacebar. Notice the door swing will flip direction.

7. Make the door face outward and to the left, as shown in Figure 2.66. Then pick (left-click) a point on the wall. If you accidentally put it in wrong, don't worry—we can fix it. Press Esc.

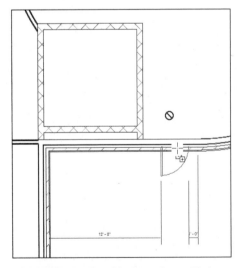

FIGURE 2.66 Placing a door will always require a host. Remember, you can press the spacebar to change the orientation, and move your cursor up and down to flip the direction.

Notice that when the door is placed, a tag shows up with an automatic number. In Revit, after you place a door you should go right back and select it. This will highlight the door and activate a few different options. Follow these steps:

1. Click the Modify button on the left of the Ribbon. This will disengage you from the Door command.

2. Pick the door you just added to the model. Notice there are blue temporary dimensions. Let's make sure these dimensions are going where we want them.

   a. On the Settings panel of the Manage tab, click Additional Settings ➤ Temporary Dimensions, as shown in Figure 2.67.

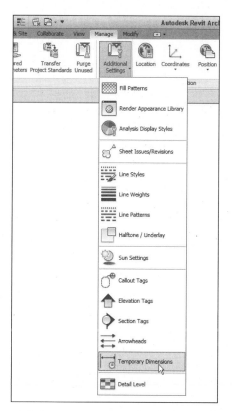

FIGURE 2.67 Select Additional Settings ➤ Temporary Dimensions.

   b. Make sure that Wall Dimensions are going to Faces and that Door Dimensions are going to Openings.

   c. Click OK.

YIKES, LOOK AT MY WALLS!

When you place a door or any opening into a compound wall, you need to tell Revit specifically how to wrap the materials. By default, Revit will stop the brick and any other finish right at the opening. Obviously this is usually not the case. The following steps will guide you through wrapping materials at an insert:

1. Select the exterior wall.

2. In the Properties dialog, click the Edit Type button, as shown here:

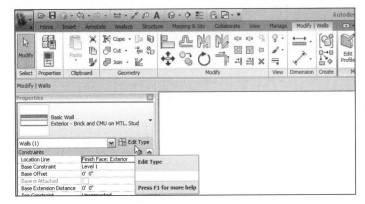

3. In the drop-down menu that specifies wrapping at inserts, select Both.

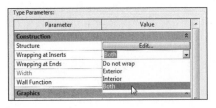

4. Click OK.

Now that we have configured the temporary dimensions the way we need them, we can start using them to manipulate the placement of our doors:

1. Select the door again.

2. Move the left witness line to the outside face of the CMU wall, as shown in Figure 2.68.

3. As you know, in Revit Architecture anything that turns blue can be edited. Click on the blue dimension that extends from the CMU wall, drag it to the right of the elevator shaft, and change it to 1'–0" (see Figure 2.69).

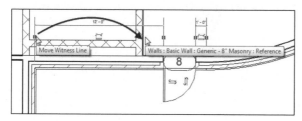

FIGURE 2.68 Moving the witness line to a more appropriate location

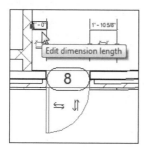

FIGURE 2.69 Changing the temporary dimension

Placing Wall Tags

Notice the tag that shows up? This is an automatic feature of Revit, as is the tag's number. Under normal circumstances, Revit will number it incorrectly. Luckily you can renumber it:

1. Select the door.

2. Pick (left-click) the number in the door tag.

3. Change the number to 101.

4. With the door still selected, notice you have flip arrows as well. If the door is not in the orientation you see in the previous figures, click these arrows to flip the door.

5. Mirror this door and its tag about the building's centerline.

> Most items that are added to the Revit model can be selected and flipped in the same method. Also, if you select the items to be flipped and press the spacebar, it will have the same effect.
>
>

Loading Families

It would be nice if the seven doors available in the Revit model were all you needed. They, of course, are not. Revit, like most other CAD and applications that use building information modeling, does not load every single component into the drawing or model. File size is just as much of a concern in Revit as it is in AutoCAD. If you need a different door, you have to go get it:

1. On the Home tab, click the Door button.

2. On the Modify | Place Door tab, click the Load Family button, as shown in Figure 2.70.

FIGURE 2.70 Click Load Family on the Mode Panel.

3. Find the Doors directory; navigate to Double-Flush.rfa and click Open.

4. Select Double-Flush: 72″ × 84″ from the Properties panel.

5. Place the double doors in the wall, as shown in Figure 2.71.

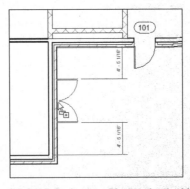

FIGURE 2.71 Placing the double doors

Normally the doors will automatically "find" the center of the wall. But to make sure, you can type SM. This will tell Revit that you want to snap to the middle.

6. Mirror the door and tag using the center reference plane.

7. Add bathroom doors, as shown in Figure 2.72. Use Single-Flush: 36″ × 84″?

8. Label them accordingly.

9. In the exterior wall that divides the east building from the corridor, add a Single Raised Panel with Side Lights: 36″ × 84″ door centered upon the opening.

10. Change the tag to read 100B, as shown in Figure 2.73.

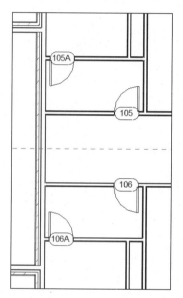

FIGURE 2.72 Adding lavatory doors. You will have to renumber the tags.

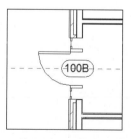

FIGURE 2.73 Adding a new corridor door. If this door is not loaded into your model, you have to click the **Load Family** button on the **Mode** panel of the **Modify | Place Door** tab.

We need to add more doors and interior partitions, but they will be best suited for Chapter 4 where we can be more accurate. In the meantime, however, let's add some simple openings.

Placing Openings in Your Walls

Openings are categorized with doors but need to be added to the model using the Component command. No, really. It's true. Follow along:

1. On the Home tab, click Component, as shown in Figure 2.74.

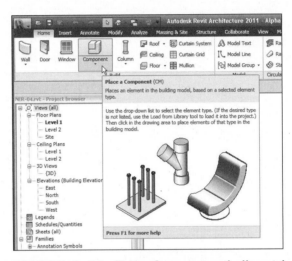

FIGURE 2.74 Clicking Component on the Home tab

2. On the Modify | Place Component tab, click the Load Family button.

3. Browse to the Doors directory.

4. Find the file called Opening-Cased.rfa and click Open.

5. Click the Edit Type button in the Properties panel.

6. Click Duplicate in the Type Properties dialog.

7. In the Name dialog, name the opening 84"×84" then click OK.

8. Under Dimensions, change Width to 7'–0".

9. Click OK. Then hit Esc to clear the command.

10. Zoom into the area shown in Figure 2.75, and place an Interior - 6 1/8" Partition (2-hr) wall as shown. This is the wall you will place the opening into.

11. Click Component, and place the opening into the wall as shown in Figure 2.75.

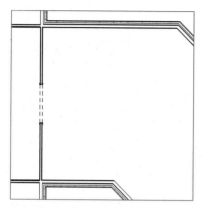

FIGURE 2.75 The new opening

Add two more doors, and we are finished with this section:

1. On the Home tab, click Door.

2. In the Properties dialog, pick Double-Flush: 72″ × 84″.

3. Add the double doors to the ends of the vertical corridor, as shown in Figure 2.76.

4. Label them as 100C and 100D.

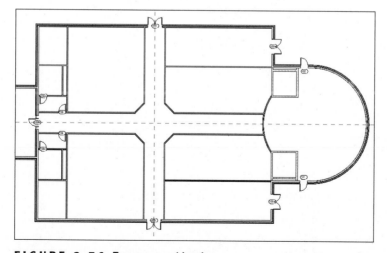

FIGURE 2.76 Two new corridor doors

Again, there are plenty more doors and partitions that we can add to the model, but they will be added in Chapter 4. Let's move on to adding some windows!

Adding Windows

Doors, windows, openings… it's all the same really. Once you have experience adding one, the other is just as easy!

The objective of the next procedure is to add some windows to the model.

1. On the Home tab, click the Window button, as shown in Figure 2.77.

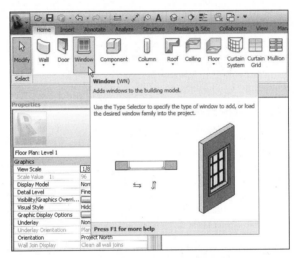

FIGURE 2.77 Adding a window is the same as adding a door.

2. Select the Fixed: 36″ × 72″ window from the Properties panel.

3. Add the window to the corner of the building, as shown in Figure 2.78. Be careful with the placement. If your cursor is toward the exterior of the wall, the window will be orientated correctly.

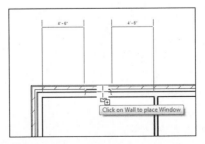

FIGURE 2.78 Depending on the side of the wall your cursor is on, you can add a window to the correct orientation.

4. Add two more windows to the west wall adjacent to the wall you just put the first window in. Use your temporary dimensions to ensure you are placing the windows 1'–0" from the opening to the wall.

5. Mirror the windows and tags (see Figure 2.79).

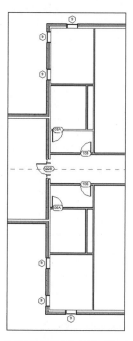

FIGURE 2.79 Placing the windows to the corner of the building and mirroring them

6. Select one of the placed windows. Notice the temporary dimensions and the flip arrows.

7. Change the tag to read A. (All of the windows are type A.)

8. You will get a warning stating that you are changing a type parameter. Click OK.

Now that the windows are in place, it is time to investigate how they are built by taking a look at their properties.

Window Properties

Again, just as with doors and openings, you can check the Element Properties to tweak the unit even further:

1. Select one of the windows.

2. In the Properties dialog, click the Edit Type button, as shown in Figure 2.80.

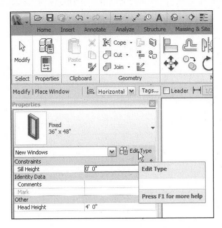

FIGURE 2.80 The Edit Type button in the Properties dialog

3. The contents of the Properties dialog that appears first contain the instance parameters. Anything you change here applies to only the one window you have selected. Click the Edit Type button.

 T I P   **If you know that you want to change an instance parameter (such as sill height) for every window in the model, you can. Knowing that an instance parameter only applies to one item, instead of picking just one window, you can pick a window, right-click, and choose Select All Instances. From there you can change every window's parameters in the Properties panel because you had every window selected.**

4. Scroll down until you see Type Mark. Notice this value is set to A. This is the property you changed by typing the value into the tag in the model. Revit works both ways. If you change a symbol in the model, it will change the parameter value within the family (see Figure 2.81).

Windows are among the most difficult items in Revit to use out of the box without any real customization. In Chapter 17, we will dive into creating some custom Revit windows. For now, however, remember the lessons learned in this chapter. They will go a long way.

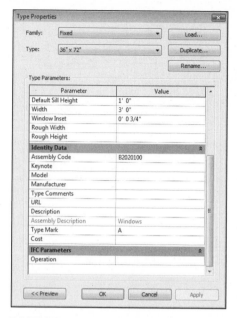

FIGURE 2.81 Changing a type parameter changes every window of that type.

Are You Experienced?

Now you can...

☑ **place exterior walls**

☑ **place interior walls**

☑ **add reference planes**

☑ **join walls**

☑ **use the Split command**

☑ **edit a cut profile**

☑ **add doors**

☑ **add openings**

☑ **add windows**

Creating Views

One of Revit Architecture's strongest points is the fact that it is one single model. This single model, however, has to be broken down into a tangible format that allows the user to navigate through a project. Chapters 1 and 2 featured the Project Browser (and it will be featured in this chapter as well), but what is the Project Browser managing? Well, it's simply managing views of the model. Here's an example: in the Project Browser, under Floor Plans you usually see Level 1. This is a view of the model that just so happens to be a floor plan. Under Elevations (Building Elevations), you see East Elevation, North Elevation, South Elevation, and West Elevation. These are exactly the same as the floor plans in the sense that they are simply views of the model.

▶ **Creating and managing levels**

▶ **Adding sectional and elevation views**

▶ **Controlling your views for aesthetic values**

Creating Levels

This chapter focuses on the creation of views and their relationship to the model. We will start with possibly the most important function in Revit: creating levels. The power of Revit comes with the single-model concept. By being able to add levels to a model, you are also adding floor plans. This two-way interaction is what makes Revit the BIM choice for many users.

As you wander through the floor plans in the Project Browser, you will see Level 1 and Level 2. Not every job you will work on will have only a Level 1 and a Level 2. Our task in this section is to create new levels that are appended to floor plans.

To follow along, open the model you have been working on, or go to **www.sybex .com/go/revit2011ner**, and browse to the Chapter 3 folder. Open the file called NER-05.rvt. If you wish, you can use an actual project you are working on. You will just have to replace any names and specific dimensions with ones that are applicable to your project. Perform these steps:

1. In the Project Browser, double-click on the South elevation. It is located under Elevations (Building Elevations), as shown in Figure 3.1.

    Notice at the right side of the building there are two symbols with a datum at the end. These are elevation markers. Unfortunately, right now they are somewhat obscured by the exterior wall. Zoom in to this area, as shown in Figure 3.2.

FIGURE 3.1 Finding an elevation in the Project Browser

TIP   If, as you progress through the next few steps, you don't see what is shown in the next two figures, try zooming in more and repeating the instructions.

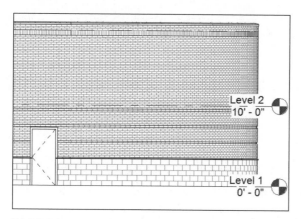

FIGURE 3.2 When dealing with levels, it is a good idea to zoom in close so you can manipulate them.

2. Select (left-click) Level 1. Notice you will get several blue icons, dimensions, and a lock.

   Where the actual level line intersects the datum bubble, there is a hollow blue circle (grip), as shown in Figure 3.3, except that your view will be slightly obscured by the wall. Move the bubble so that you can see the grip clearly.

3. Left-click (pick) and hold the pick button on the mouse. You can now drag the bubble to the right.

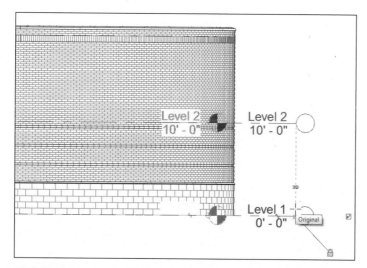

FIGURE 3.3 Picking the grip to drag the level out of the way

If you hover over any item in Revit Architecture and pause for a second, you will see what is called a tooltip. This will help you verify you are selecting the correct item.

4. When you get to a point where the Level marker is outside the building, pick a spot to place the bubble and the annotation.

5. Press Esc.

Now that the levels are physically in a position where you can work on them, you can start building on them.

Adding Levels

Adding an entirely new level in Revit Architecture is quite simple. But you need to adhere to certain procedures in order to ensure you add the levels correctly.

When you use the Level feature in Revit, two procedural aspects stand out. The first is to look at your Options bar after you start the command. The second is to click the Modify button when you have finished. It is easy to get confused as to how Revit wants you to proceed with adding a level, and it is also easy to inadvertently create multiple levels. Remember, in Revit you are always in a command.

To add a level, follow along:

1. On the Datum panel of the Home tab, click the Level button, as shown in Figure 3.4.

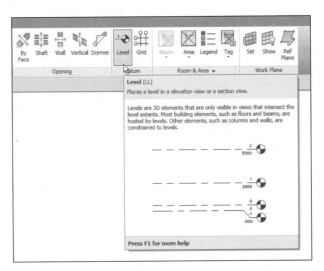

FIGURE 3.4 Adding a level from the Datum panel on the Home tab

2. On the Draw panel on the Modify | Place Level tab, you will see that you can either draw a line or pick a line, as shown in Figure 3.5. Make sure Pick Lines is selected.

3. Also, on the Options bar, you will see the Make Plan View option. Make sure it's checked.

4. At the end of the Options bar, you will see a field for an offset. Type 10 and press Enter. Basically the approach here is to pick Level 2 and create a new level that is offset 10′–0″ above (see Figure 3.5).

FIGURE 3.5 Choosing the options for the Level command

5. With the options set, hover your cursor over Level 2.

Notice that when you come into contact with Level 2, a blue dotted line appears. If you move your cursor slightly above the Level 2 line, the blue alignment line appears above Level 2. If you inch your cursor slightly below Level 2, the blue alignment line appears below Level 2.

6. When you see the blue line appear above Level 2, pick the Level 2 line, as shown in Figure 3.6.

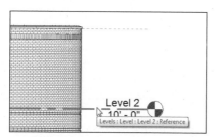

FIGURE 3.6 Waiting for the alignment to appear

T I P   You may notice that speeding through the commands as you may have done in AutoCAD is not helping you any in Revit. In Revit you may need to slow down a bit, and let Revit "do its thing." After you get the hang of Revit's behavior, you can speed up again.

7. You should now have a Level 3 at 20′–0″ (see Figure 3.7).

 W A R N I N G   Just because you have created a new level, this does not tell Revit to shut down the command. Notice the Options bar is still active and the Pick Lines icon still has the focus. If you start clicking around in the view area, you will start creating levels. Every time you pick a point on the screen, a new level will show up. Also, Revit does not care if you have a level on top of another level. This situation can get ugly fast.

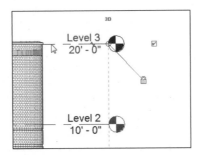

F I G U R E   3 . 7   The completed Level 3. Remember, you are still in the Level command until you tell Revit to stop.

8. With the Level command still running, create Levels 4, 5, 6, and 7. Your elevation should now look like Figure 3.8. Also, look at your Project Browser. It should not have any additional levels. You may also notice that you have new levels under the Ceiling plans category as well.

9. On the Select tab of the Ribbon, click the Modify button. You have now safely terminated the Level command. (You can also press the Esc key on your keyboard.)

Now that you have some experience adding levels, it is time to investigate the physical level to see how it can be manipulated and modified.

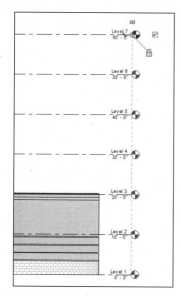

FIGURE 3.8 Levels 1 through 7 are now complete.

The Composition of a Level

Levels have controls that allow the user to adjust their appearance. As stated throughout the book, when you select a family you will see that multiple items turn blue. The blue color indicates that these items can be modified. When you select a level, a few additional items will appear.

To investigate further, follow along:

1. Zoom in on Level 7.

2. Select Level 7 by picking (left-clicking) on either the text or the actual level line itself. This will put the focus on the level line. Notice the text that turns blue. We know that any blue item can be modified (see Figure 3.9).

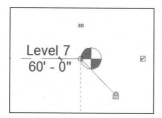

FIGURE 3.9 The selected level

3. Click on the blue Level 7 text. This will allow you to edit the name of the level.

4. Type **Parapet**, as shown in Figure 3.10, and press Enter.

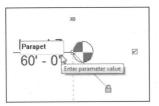

FIGURE 3.10 Renaming the level

5. Revit will ask you if you want to rename any corresponding views. Choose Yes (see Figure 3.11). Level 7 is now the Parapet level, as shown in Figure 3.12.

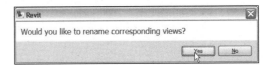

FIGURE 3.11 Click Yes to rename corresponding views.

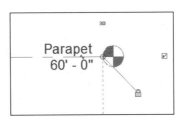

FIGURE 3.12: The renamed level

By renaming corresponding views, you are telling Revit to keep the level and its corresponding view named accordingly.

6. With the Parapet level still selected, click on the 60'–0" field.

7. Type **52** and press Enter. This will physically drop the level to the true elevation.

You will now have two slightly overlapping levels. This can be fixed by manipulating some of the controls that show up when you select the level.

Press the Esc key a few times to clear any command that may be active and follow along:

1. Select the Parapet level (if it is not still selected from the previous exercise).

2. The blue items will "light up." One of them is the choice to add an elbow, as shown in Figure 3.13. Click it, and Revit will bend the level.

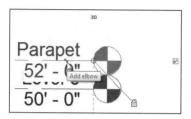

FIGURE 3.13 You can add an elbow to the elevation marker.

3. Now that you added the elbow, you need to move it. Notice the blue grip at each bend point. Pick the blue grip, as shown in Figure 3.14, and drag the Parapet level out of the level below.

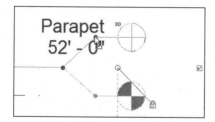

FIGURE 3.14 Dragging the level to a new position using the grips provided

4. The line of the level will still be in the way. Notice the two blue grips are still available. Pick and drag the horizontal line out of the way of the Parapet text, as shown in Figure 3.15.

◄

Can't you just type over the dimension? In Revit, you cannot have an inaccurate increment. If you type a new value to any increment, the model will change to reflect this new dimension.

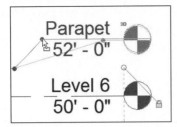

FIGURE 3.15 Making the final adjustments to the level

Now that you've established the Parapet level, it is time to make modifications to Level 6. Luckily the procedures will be the same as when you made the modifications to the Parapet level:

1. Press Esc to clear any commands.

2. Select Level 6.

3. Pick the blue text that says Level 6.

4. Rename it to **Roof**.

5. Press Enter.

6. Click Yes to rename the corresponding views.

7. Press Esc. Your levels should look like Figure 3.16.

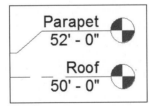

FIGURE 3.16 The Roof and Parapet levels

Other Level Adjustments

There are three more adjustments we still need to review before we can move on. If you notice, the level lines are projected all the way to the other end of the building. Only level heads and level data are displayed on the right side of the level line. You can control the other end of the level as well.

To follow along, pan over to the left side of the building where the level lines seem to just stop, as shown in Figure 3.17, and perform these steps:

1. Select the Parapet level.

2. Notice the small blue box to the left of the level? Pick it. It will turn the level information on at that end of the building (see Figure 3.17).

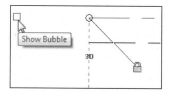

FIGURE 3.17 You can click the box that appears to turn the level information on at the other end of the building.

3. Turn the Roof level on as well. Use the blue adjustment icons (elbow icons) to move it out of the way (see Figure 3.18).

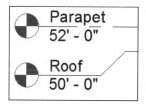

FIGURE 3.18 Controlling the visibility of the levels at the other end

With the two upper levels established, we can now constrain some walls up to these levels. Sometimes the best way to do this is to look at the model from a 3D view:

1. Click the Default 3D view icon on the Quick Access toolbar at the top of your screen, as shown in Figure 3.19.

2. The next step is to select all the walls you want to be extended to the Parapet level. In this case, only the east building will go all the way up to this level. Select the walls as shown in Figure 3.20. (Be sure to select all of the elevator shaft walls as well.) You must hold the Ctrl key to add to the selection.

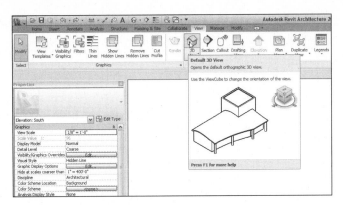

FIGURE 3.19 Clicking the Default 3D view icon

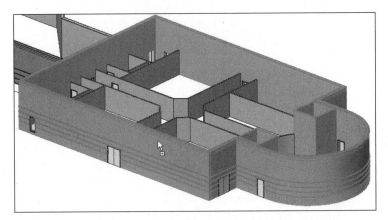

FIGURE 3.20 Selecting the walls that extend to the Parapet level

3. In the Properties dialog, under the Constraints category, change Top Constraint to Up To Level: Parapet, as shown in Figure 3.21. Your walls should now extend to the Parapet level, as shown in Figure 3.22.

4. In the Project Browser, double-click the South elevation under Elevations (Building Elevations).

5. Start the Level command again.

6. Offset Level 4 up 4′– 0″. Remember, you are in the Level command. You must choose Pick Lines on the Draw panel. Also, you must specify an offset of 4′–0″ on the Options bar.

FIGURE 3.21 Setting the top constraint to Up to Level: Parapet

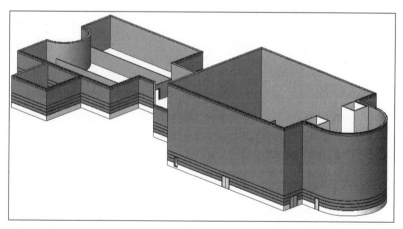

FIGURE 3.22 The walls on the east side of the building are now constrained to the Parapet level.

7. Offset another level up from the 4th level, 2′–0″, and then press Esc to terminate the command.

8. Rename the 4′– 0″ offset level to **West Parapet**. Click Yes to rename corresponding views.

9. Rename the 2′–0″ offset to **West Roof** (see Figure 3.23), and click Yes to rename corresponding views. You will have to add elbows to the levels to see the names and elevations.

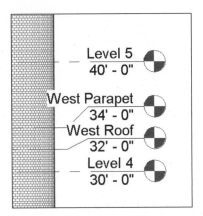

FIGURE 3.23 Adding two new levels for the west side of the building

See? Adding levels isn't all that hard. You just need to know how Revit wants you to do it. Now that we have some levels added, we can go back and configure how they are displayed:

1. Deselect the Display Bubble checkbox to the *right* of the level lines by clicking the Hide Bubble checkbox.

2. Display the bubbles to the *left* side of the level line by checking the Show Bubble box, as shown in Figure 3.24.

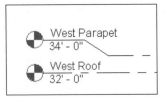

FIGURE 3.24 Using the display bubble toggles to switch the display to the appropriate side of the building

3. Pan back to the right side of the building. There should now be two blank level lines above Level 4.

4. Select the West Parapet level. Notice some blue icons still appear. One of those icons says 3D.

5. Pick (left-click) the 3D icon. It now says 2D. The larger hollow blue grip now turns to a smaller, solid grip. You can now drag the level end without dragging the rest along with it. It also ensures this modification does not affect other views (see Figure 3.25).

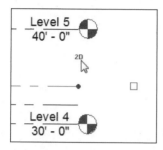

FIGURE 3.25 Turn off the 3D extents so you can drag the level end freely and without disturbing any other view.

6. Repeat the procedure for the West Roof level. Now both of the blank ends are set for 2D extents.

7. Select the west Parapet level, activating the grips.

8. Pick the blue grip and drag the end to the left side of the building approximately to the location shown in Figure 3.26. Notice that the two 2D lines are locked to one another.

9. Add another level 2′–0″ above Level 3 and call it **Corridor Parapet**. Click Yes to rename corresponding views.

10. Turn on the level information on the left side.

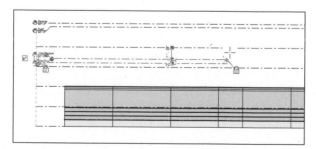

FIGURE 3.26 You can drag the 2D level ends wherever you want them.

11. Turn off the level information on the right side.

WARNING   On almost every project you will have to adjust a level's display in different views. Keep in mind that, if the 3D button is left on, moving the level in the current view will also move it in other views—sometimes for the better, and sometimes for the worse. Switching to 2D can eliminate some aggravation.

12. On the right side, turn on the 2D extents.

13. Drag the right side of the line to an area approximately as shown in Figure 3.27.

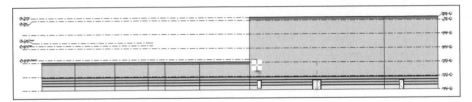

FIGURE 3.27 All of the levels are in place for now.

Now it's time to move these walls to their proper levels. Again, in this case it may be a little easier to go to a 3D view so we can get a good perspective on the results of constraining the tops of the walls. Perform the following steps:

1. Click the Default 3D icon.

2. In the 3D view, select the west side of the building, excluding the corridor and the three walls to the south, as shown in Figure 3.28. (You will need to press and hold the Ctrl key for multiple selections.)

3. In the Properties dialog, set the Top Constraint to Up To Level: West Parapet.

4. In the 3D view, your walls should grow to meet the new constraints.

5. Press Esc.

6. Select the corridor walls as well as the three south walls whose tops remain unconstrained. (You may need to rotate the view to see everything.)

7. In the Properties dialog, set the Top Constraint to Up To Level: Corridor Parapet (see Figure 3.29).

8. Go back to the South elevation. Adjust your levels to appear as shown in Figure 3.30.

9. Save the model.

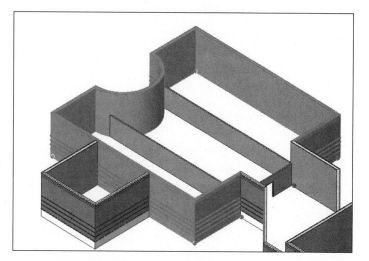

FIGURE 3.28 Selecting the west part of the building

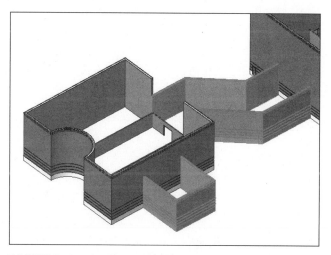

FIGURE 3.29 The final walls are constrained to the corridor parapet level.

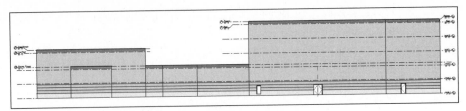

FIGURE 3.30 The final look of the building

Creating Building Sections

As your model starts to develop, you will begin to see areas that need further attention. (Certainly the area where the corridor hits the west building needs to be fixed.) This brings us to a good point. Sections in Revit Architecture, when placed into the model, not only help us build a set of construction documents, but also help us to physically work on the model. For example, we need to fix the east wall of the west wing. We don't have any good views established that focus directly on this area. This is the perfect place to add a section!

To begin, open your model, or go to **www.sybex.com/go/revit2011ner** and browse to Chapter 3. Open the file called NER-06.rvt. If you wish, you can use a project you are working on. You will just need to replace any names and specific dimensions with ones that are applicable to your project. To add a section and some cool wall modify commands, follow along:

1. Go to Level 1 and zoom in on the area where the corridor meets the west wing of the building.

2. On the Create panel of the View tab, select Section, as shown in Figure 3.31.

3. A section takes two picks to place into the model. You must first pick the point for the head; then you must pick a point for the tail. To place the section as shown in Figure 3.32, first pick a point above the corridor and to the right of the vertical wall.

4. After you pick the first point, move your cursor straight down the view. When you are positioned directly below the bottom corridor wall, pick the second point (see Figure 3.32). If the section is facing the wrong way, that's fine. We will fix that in a moment.

5. Now that you placed the section, it looks like we need to flip it to face the wall we intended to modify. Pick the section. You will see a few blue icons appear. We are interested in the icon that looks like two

arrows. This is a flip grip. It is the same thing we saw in the doors and windows (see Figure 3.33).

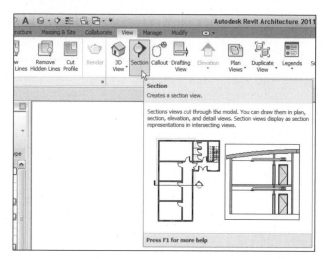

FIGURE 3.31 The Section command is found on the Create panel of the View tab.

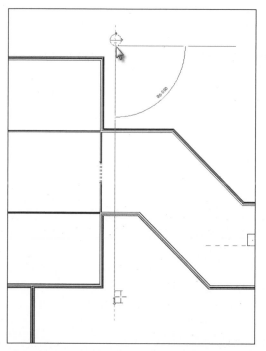

FIGURE 3.32 Placing the section into the model

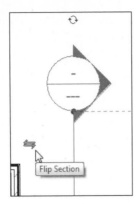

FIGURE 3.33 After you select the section, you will see the flip grip.

6. When you see the flip grip, pick it. It will flip the section into the correct direction.

WARNING   We may be jumping ahead here, but here's a word of caution: if you cut a section in Revit Architecture, then place detail components and draft over the top of that section, you are stuck. Do not flip or move the section after you have drafted over the top of a section. The results will be bad. The walls will move, not your linework, leaving you with a mess.

With the section flipped in the correct direction, you will see a dashed line that forms a box around part of the model, as shown in Figure 3.34. This forms the view extents of the section. Anything outside of this box will not be shown.

7. The vertical dashed line (to the left) will have a move arrow. Pick the move arrow and drag the crop region into an area as shown in Figure 3.34.

NOTE   If you don't have the section selected, you need to select it. You must pick the line of the section, not the bubble. When you pick the line, the section is selected.

8. With the section still selected, notice you have a small, blue break icon in the middle of the section (see Figure 3.35). Pick the break line (it is called the Gaps In Segments icon). The section is now broken, and you will have grips controlling the ends of the break lines (see Figure 3.35).

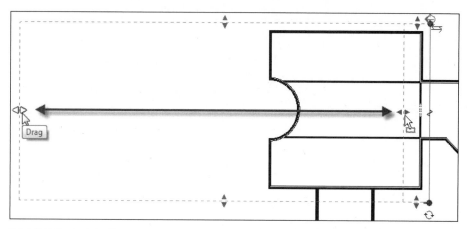

FIGURE 3.34 You can control how deep into the building you want the section to look.

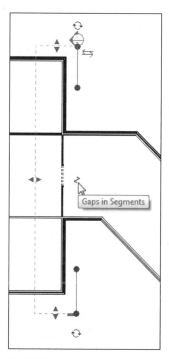

FIGURE 3.35 Adding a gap in the section. You can move your grips to be the same as the figure.

9. At each end of the section you will see a blue icon that resembles a recycle figure. This controls what the section head will display. By selecting this "recycle" icon, you can choose to have a section head, a tail, or nothing. At the tail of the section, cycle through until you get a section head (see Figure 3.36).

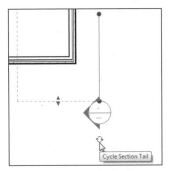

FIGURE 3.36 Cycling through the display choices

With the section cut, it is time to open the view we have created. In the Project Browser, you will now see a new category called Sections (Building Section). In this Sections category, you will have a view called Section 1. When you cut the section, you added a view to the project. This view will carry its own properties and can be drafted over (see Figure 3.37).

FIGURE 3.37 The Project Browser with the new section

TIP   Be organized. Just because you are using BIM, that does not negate the need for basic organization. The first thing you should do when creating a section (or any new view for that matter) is give it a name. If you don't, and leave it Section 1, Section 2, Section 3..., you find yourself wasting a lot of time looking for the right view.

At this point, you need to name the section and open the view. We can also fix the gap in the wall while we are at it. Just perform the following steps:

1. In the Project Browser, right-click on Section 1.

2. Choose Rename from the context menu (see Figure 3.38).

3. Change the name of Section 1 to **West Corridor Section**.

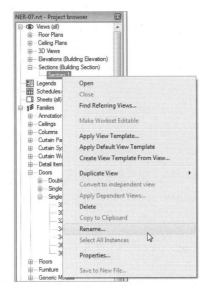

F I G U R E   3 . 3 8   You can rename the view by right-clicking in the Project Browser.

4. Click OK.

5. Double-click on the West Corridor Section in the Project Browser. This will open the section. You can see the two corridor walls and the west wing beyond.

6. You will notice immediately that the level information is running into the walls. To fix this, simply select the West Parapet level. (Remember: select the actual line, not the datum head.)

7. Slide the elevation markers to the right, out of the way of the walls (see Figure 3.39).

8. Repeat the process for Level 1 and Level 2 if necessary. Notice that when you slide these levels to the right, they will snap into place and align themselves to the rest of the levels.

9. Pick the left end of the level lines, and move them to the right as well. This will get all of the lines out of the way so that you can work on the section (see Figure 3.40).

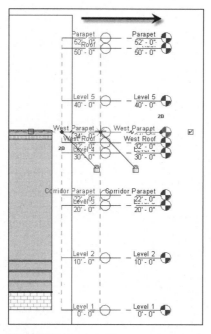

FIGURE 3.39 You can adjust the levels by picking and dragging the blue grip at the intersection of the level line and the datum bubble.

 N O T E   Notice that when you are adjusting the levels in the section the 2D icon appears. This means that any adjustments made here will not affect any other views. In a sectional view, Revit will automatically make the levels 2D. In an elevation view, however, Revit will make the levels 3D. If you want to make adjustments in an elevation, it is a good idea to turn these to 2D extents.

10. Also, add some elbows to the elevation markers. There are so many that the text elements collide with one another.

11. On the View Control bar, select Fine for the detail level, as shown in Figure 3.40. (Making adjustments like this to a view will become second nature to you very soon.)

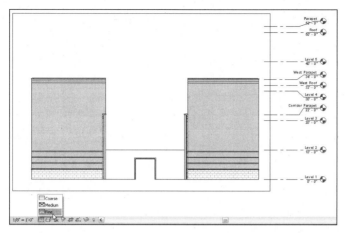

FIGURE 3.40 On the View Control bar, set Fine as the detail level.

Cutting a section is immensely helpful in terms of viewing the model from any perspective you want. To go even further, when you cut a section you can also work on your model by modifying any item the section.

Making Building Modifications in a Section

Now that you have a good look at this side of the west wing, it is obvious that this wall needs to be repaired. In Revit Architecture, you can make a modification to a building in any view. This is good and bad. Just remember that everything you do has a downstream effect on the entire model.

To follow along, open your model, or go to **www.sybex.com/go/revit2011ner** and browse to Chapter 3. Open the file called NER-06.rvt if it is not open already. If you wish, you can use a project you are working on and replace any names and specific dimensions with ones that are applicable to your project.

The following procedure will guide you through making a modification to a wall's profile while in a section view:

1. In the Project Browser, find the West Corridor Section and open it by double-clicking on the name West Corridor Section (if it is not open already).

2. In this section, select the east wall of the west wing, as shown in Figure 3.41.

3. After you select the wall, look to your Modify | Walls tab. There you will see a button that says Edit Profile, as shown in Figure 3.41. Click that button.

In Revit Architecture, you can also double-click on the actual annotation that refers to the view you wish to open. For example, if you want to open the West Corridor Section, and you are in a plan, all you have to do is double-click on the section bubble, and it will open the view. If you are in the section and you want to go back to a floor plan, you can double-click on a datum bubble, and Revit will open that view.

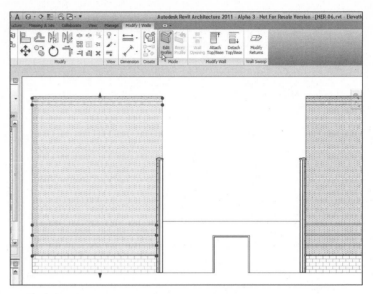

FIGURE 3.41 Clicking Edit Profile on the Modify | Walls tab

When you select a
wall, you will get
options to modify
that wall. Edit
Profile is one of
those options.

You will now be presented with a magenta outline of the wall. This magenta outline can be modified to alter the wall's profile. If you look at your Ribbon, you will notice that Edit Profile has been added to the Modify | Walls tab. This allows you to focus on the modification at hand (see Figure 3.42).

4. On the Draw panel of the Modify | Walls ➤ Edit Profile tab, select the Line button, as shown in Figure 3.42.

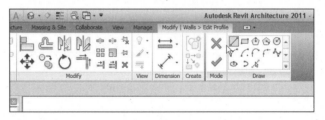

FIGURE 3.42 Adding additional lines to alter the wall's profile

5. With the Line command running, move your pointer to the right vertical magenta line.

6. Move your pointer up or down until you are aligned with Level 3, as shown in Figure 3.43.

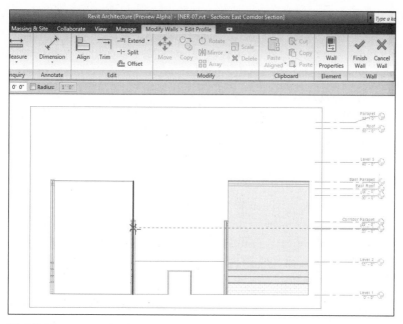

FIGURE 3.43 Revit will align your cursor to levels, allowing you to accurately sketch a new profile.

7. When you see that you are snapped and aligned with the magenta line and Level 3, pick this point. Your line will start.

8. Draw the line to the right until you intersect with the side of the wall to the right, as shown in Figure 3.44.

9. When you see the intersection snap show up, pick this point (see Figure 3.44).

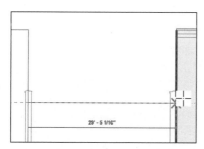

FIGURE 3.44 Drawing the line from the left wall to the right

10. Now, draw the line straight up the wall to the top. Make sure you do not snap to the top of the parapet. The point you want is to the top of the brick, as shown in Figure 3.45. (All you are doing here is sketching the profile of the wall.)

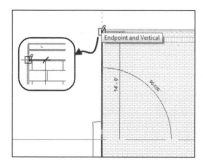

FIGURE 3.45 Drawing another line from Level 3 to the bottom of the parapet

11. Continue drawing the line from the right to the left across the top of the wall. Snap to the endpoint of the wall to the left, as shown in Figure 3.46.

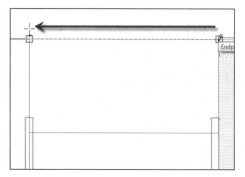

FIGURE 3.46 Drawing the line across the top

12. Press the Esc key, or click the Modify button on the Select panel.

13. Pick the vertical line to the left that goes from the bottom of the wall to the top.

14. Pick the top blue grip, and stretch the line down to Level 3.

15. You now have a closed loop, as shown in Figure 3.47.

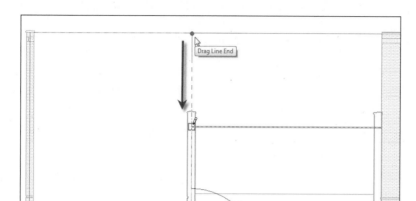

FIGURE 3.47 Closing the wall by stretching the line using grips

 WARNING If you do not have a perfectly closed, continuous loop with your magenta lines, Revit will not allow you to proceed with finishing altering the profile of this wall. Make sure you have no gaps, overlaps, or extra line segments aside from the six lines you need to form the wall's outline.

16. On the Wall panel of the Modify | Walls ➤ Edit Profile tab, click Finish Edit Mode, as shown in Figure 3.48. Your finished wall profile should look like Figure 3.49.

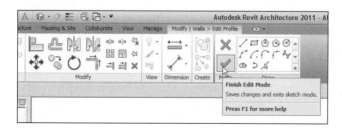

FIGURE 3.48 Clicking Finish Edit Mode

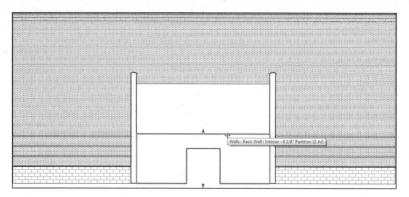

FIGURE 3.49 The finished wall profile

There is one thing left to do before we leave this section: select the 2 hr fire rated partition wall that is only constrained to Level 2. Now that we have opened up this area, the wall can now go up to Level 3. To constrain the top of this wall to Level 3, follow along:

1. Select the wall, as shown earlier in Figure 3.49.

2. In the Properties dialog, change Top Constraint to Up To Level: Level 3, as shown in Figure 3.50.

FIGURE 3.50 Choosing the properties to change a wall's constraints is becoming old hat!

3. The wall now meets the brick exterior.

4. In the Project Browser, double-click on Level 3.

5. Change the detail level to Fine (remember this is in the View Control bar at the bottom of the screen).

6. On the View tab, select the Section button.

7. Place a section as shown in Figure 3.51. Make sure the extents are similar to the figure.

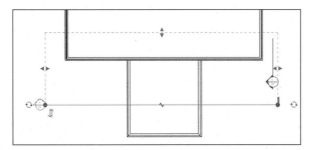

FIGURE 3.51 Adding another section to modify another wall

8. In the Project Browser, right-click on the new section and rename it to **West Wing South Wall Section**. We will use this section in Chapter 4.

Adding entire building sections is a great way to quickly break down the model into large segments so you can work. Another type of section, a wall section, however, allows you to view smaller portions of the item being detailed.

Adding Wall Sections

A wall section is basically the same as a building section. The only difference is that, when you place a wall section, Revit will hold the extents to a much smaller area. When you add a building section, Revit will want to extend to the farthest geometry. That being said, a wall section is usually placed to show only the item being cut, not allowing the geometry beyond to be seen.

Start by opening your model, or go to **www.sybex.com/go/revit2011ner** and browse to Chapter 3. Open the file called NER-07.rvt. If you wish, you can use a project you are working on and replace any names and specific dimensions with ones that are applicable to your project. To place a wall section, follow this procedure:

1. Double-click Level 1 in the Project Browser.

2. On the View tab, pick the Section button (the same one you picked for the building section).

3. In the Properties dialog box, select Wall Section, as shown in Figure 3.52.

WARNING   If you are directed to go to a specific floor plan and your view looks nothing like the one shown in the book, you need to make sure you are not in a ceiling plan. Notice in the Project Browser that you have floor plans and ceiling plans. The two are quite different. Make sure you are in a floor plan.

4. Also on the Options bar, change the scale to 1/2"=1'–0".

5. Add the section through the corridor wall that was modified in the previous section of this chapter, as shown in Figure 3.53.

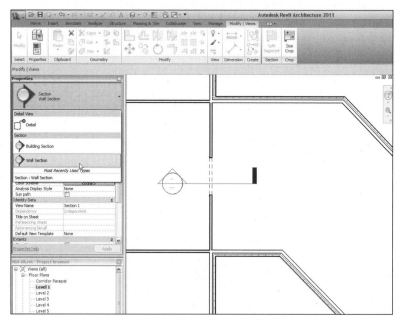

FIGURE 3.52 Changing the type of section from Building Section to Wall Section and adding it to the model

6. Right-click on the new section in the Project Browser. It will be in a category called Sections (Wall Section).

7. Select Rename.

8. Call the new section **Corridor Entry Section**. Click OK.

9. Open the Corridor Entry Section.

10. Change the detail level to Fine. Your section should look like Figure 3.53.

11. Save the model.

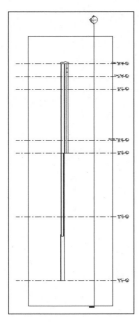

FIGURE 3.53 The wall section at 1/2″ = 1′- 0″

Now that we are narrowing down the types of sections we can use, it's time to venture into a specific type of section that can allow you to do a plan section detail.

Creating Detail Sections

There is a third type of section we need to discuss: the detail section. Revit refers to this type of section as a detail view, so that's how we will start addressing it.

To create a detail view, open your model, or go to **www.sybex.com/go/revit 2011ner** and browse to Chapter 3. Open the file called NER-08.rvt. If you wish, you can use a project you are working on and replace any names and specific dimensions with ones that are applicable to your project. Perform the following steps:

1. Open the view called Corridor Entry Section (if you do not have it opened already).

2. On the View tab, select Section (yes, the same section we have been using all along).

3. In the Properties dialog box, select Detail View: Detail.

4. On the Options bar, change the scale to 1 1/2" = 1'–0".

5. Place a section horizontally, as shown in Figure 3.54. Make sure the section is flipped so it is looking downward.

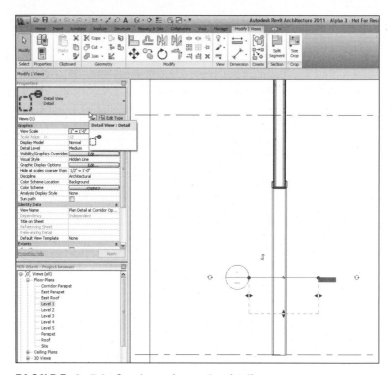

FIGURE 3.54 Creating a plan section detail

6. In the Project Browser, you will see a new category called Detail Views (Detail). Expand the tree, and you will see your new detail. It is usually called Detail 0, depending on how many details have been added to the model previously.

7. Right-click Detail 0 and select Rename.

8. Rename the detail to **Plan Detail at Corridor Opening** and click OK.

9. Open the Plan Detail at Corridor Opening view.

With the detail open, you may only be able to see two dashed lines. This is because the crop region needs to be expanded, as explained in the next section.

Crop Regions

The border that surrounds the detail is called a crop region. It dictates the extents of the specific view you are in. We can adjust this crop region and use it to our advantage. To learn how to make adjustments to the crop region, follow these steps:

1. Select the window surrounding the detail, as shown in Figure 3.55.

2. You will now see four blue stretch arrows at the midpoint of each line. Pick the top stretch arrows, and stretch the top region up until you can see the opening jamb, as shown in Figure 3.55.

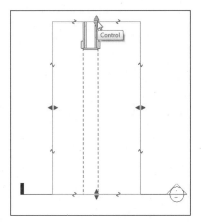

FIGURE 3.55 Stretching the crop region to view the detail

3. Repeat the process for the bottom so you can see the entire opening.

4. With the crop region still selected, notice there are break icons similar to the make elbow icons in the level markers. Pick the break icon, as shown in Figure 3.56. You can now slice part of the section away, resulting in two separate cropped regions.

5. Within the cropped regions, you will see blue move icons. If you do not see blue icons as shown in Figure 3.57, you need to select the crop region again.

6. Slide the sections closer together by clicking the top icon and moving the section down.

7. Save the model.

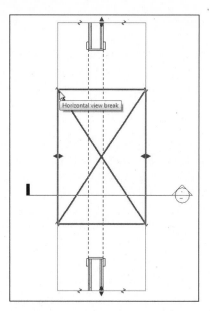

FIGURE 3.56 Splitting the section

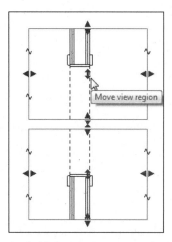

FIGURE 3.57 Sliding the view regions tighter together

Now that we have some nice control over how the details are being shown, we can go back and learn how to make the actual section marker more aesthetically pleasing.

Splitting a Section Segment

One more section item, and then we are done! Sometimes, it is necessary to split (or jog) a section. You do this when you need to show items that are not necessarily in line with one another. You can accomplish this in Revit Architecture as follows:

1. Open the Level 1 floor plan.

2. On the View tab, select the Section button.

3. In the Properties dialog box, select Building Section.

4. This time, pick a point above the corridor that connects to the east wing of the building for the section head, and then pick a point well below the bottom of the corridor, as shown in Figure 3.58.

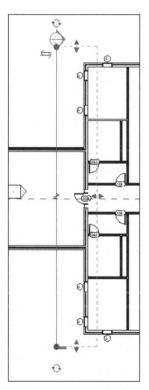

FIGURE 3.58 Adding another section to the model

5. In the Project Browser, find the section you just made and rename it to **East Corridor Section**.

6. Select the new section marker.

7. On the Modify | Views tab, click the button called Split Segment.

8. Pick a point along the section line just below the corridor, as shown in Figure 3.59.

9. Move your cursor to the right. Notice a jog appears in the section. Place the jog into the building. The section is now jogged into the building. Hit Esc twice to clear the command.

Finally! We are done with sections. Just remember that by adding a section to the model, not only are you preparing to build your construction documents, but you are also enabling access to specific elements, thus allowing you to make modifications you otherwise could not have.

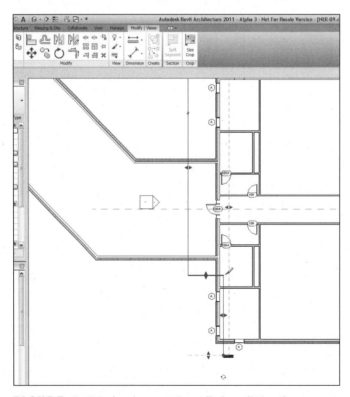

FIGURE 3.59 Jogging a section calls for splitting the segment.

Creating Callouts

Creating an enlarged area of your model is going to be an item on every project you do. Luckily in Revit Architecture, callouts are not only easy to add to your model but they directly link to the view they refer to as well. This is crucial for project coordination. Another nice thing about callouts is that you can make modifications to the callout view independently from the host view you pull the information from. The biggest change you will make is the scale. Yes, your callout can be at a different scale.

To follow along, open your model, or go to **www.sybex.com/go/revit2011ner** and browse to Chapter 3. Open the file called NER-09.rvt. If you wish, you can use a project you are working on and replace any names and specific dimensions with ones that are applicable to your project. Here's the procedure for adding callouts:

1. In the Project Browser, under Sections (Wall Section), open the Corridor Entry Section.

2. Find the View tab on the Ribbon.

3. On the View tab, click the Callout button, as shown in Figure 3.60.

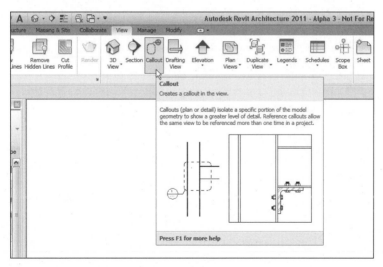

F I G U R E 3 . 6 0 The Callout button is located on the View tab.

4. On the Options bar, set the scale to **1 1/2" = 1'– 0"**.

5. Pick a window around the area where the corridor fire wall meets the exterior wall with the brick façade, as shown in Figure 3.61.

6. In the Project Browser, notice there is a new Sections (Building Section) item. Its name is Callout of Corridor Entry Section—which is fine just the way it is. Press Esc.

7. Select the callout you just added by picking any point along the line. Notice a bunch of blue grips appear. These grips enable you to stretch the shape of the callout.

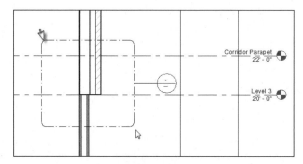

FIGURE 3.61 The callout area is directly related to the view it is calling out.

8. Pick the grip that connects the callout bubble to the leader coming from the callout window.

9. Drag the bubble to the location shown in Figure 3.62.

10. Pick the blue midpoint grip on the leader and create an elbow, as shown in Figure 3.62.

11. In the Project Browser, find Callout of Corridor Entry Section under the Sections (Building Section) category and open the view. (You can also double-click on the callout bubble to open the view.)

12. With the section open, select the crop region, as shown in Figure 3.63. After you select the crop region, you will see an additional region that consists of a dotted line. This is called an annotation region, and it gives you a "gutter" to place text outside the area that is physically being cropped.

13. Type **WT**. This will tile the windows you have open.

Notice that the callout window is selected along with the crop region in your callout. That is because the two objects are one and the same (see Figure 3.64).

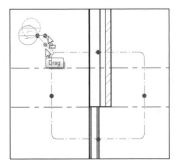

FIGURE 3.62 Adjusting the callout will be a common task.

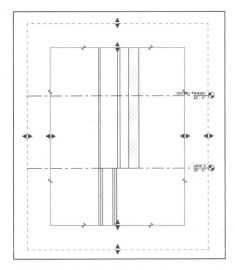

FIGURE 3.63 Selecting the crop region

14. Stretch the crop region closer to the actual wall, as shown in Figure 3.64.

15. Save the model. We will use this detail for future chapters to get it ready for construction documents.

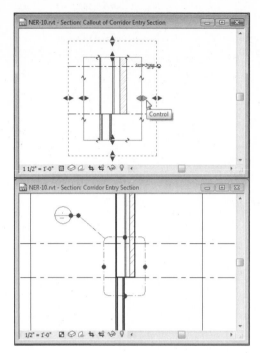

FIGURE 3.64 Modify the crop region by selecting it and stretching the grip.

Now that we have a callout created for a detail, it is time to go to the plan and create some callouts there. It would be nice to have some typical lavatory callouts as well as a typical elevator callout:

1. In the Project Browser, go to Level 1. (Make sure it is a floor plan, not a ceiling plan.)

2. Zoom in on the area shown in Figure 3.65.

3. On the View tab, select Callout.

4. Pick a window around the lavatory, as shown in Figure 3.65.

5. In the Project Browser under the Floor Plans category, you will see Callout of Level 1. Right-click on Callout of Level 1 and select Rename.

6. Rename it to **Typical Men's Lavatory.**

> The crop region and the callout outline are the same. If you modify one, the other changes accordingly.

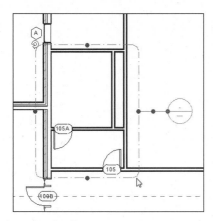

F I G U R E 3 . 6 5 Creating a plan callout

7. Open the Typical Men's Lavatory view.

8. Notice the detail level is set to Coarse. Change it to Fine.

T I P   You may have noticed that we have been opening up quite a few views. It is a good idea to close the views you don't need to have open because they could slow you down a tad. To close views, choose Window ➤ Close Hidden Windows.

9. Save the model.

10. Open the Level 1 floor plan if it is not open already.

11. Create a callout for the Women's room below the corridor (directly below the Men's room).

12. Call the new callout **Typical Women's Lavatory**.

13. Create one more callout around the elevator shaft in the east wing, as shown in Figure 3.66.

14. Call the new callout **Typical Elevator Shaft**.

Now that the "boring" views are out of the way, it is time create some perspective views of the model. Creating these views is just as easy but requires a specific procedure in which you'll take advantage of the Camera function.

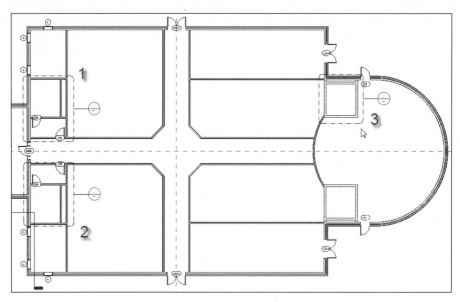

FIGURE 3.66 The plan showing the three typical callouts

Creating a Camera View

The camera view is by far the view you will have the most fun with. Revit Architecture seems to lend itself naturally to this type of view.

Taking a camera view is essentially telling Revit to look at a certain area from a perspective vantage point. Like a section or a callout, this view may never see the "light of day" in terms of going on a drawing sheet, but camera views are perfect to see how a model is coming along from a realistic point of view.

To follow along, open your model, or go to **www.sybex.com/go/revit2011ner** and browse to Chapter 3. Open the file called NER-10.rvt. If you wish, you can use a project you are working on and replace any names and specific dimensions with ones that are applicable to your project.

To create a camera view, follow along:

1. Go to the Level 1 floor plan.

2. On the View tab, click the drop-down arrow in the 3D View button and select Camera, as shown in Figure 3.67.

3. Pick a point in the main corridor of the east wing, and move your cursor to the left down the hallway. We want to take a perspective view as if we

were standing in the intersection of the two main corridors, as shown in Figure 3.68.

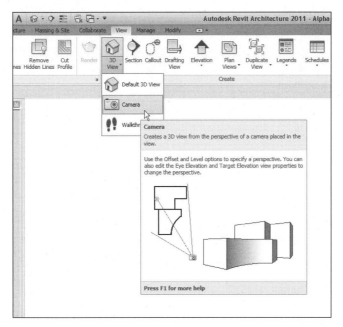

FIGURE 3.67 Adding a camera view

4. The second point you pick will be how far the camera "reaches" into the building. Pick a point past the corridor doors, as shown in Figure 3.69.

5. Unlike when you're placing a section or a callout, Revit will automatically open the new 3D view. This does not mean that it automatically has a name. In the Project Browser, you will see a new view within the 3D Views category. It is called 3D View 1. Right-click on 3D View 1 and name it **East Wing Corridor Perspective.**

6. On the View Control bar located at the bottom of the view, change the Visual Style to Shaded With Edges.

7. The next button to the right is the Shadows button. For a perspective view, turning the shadows on is okay for a relatively small view. In this example, go ahead and turn them on (see Figure 3.69).

When the camera is in place, you may find it difficult to modify it at first. You can do quite a bit to the view, but the following section will focus on modifying the actual camera in the plan.

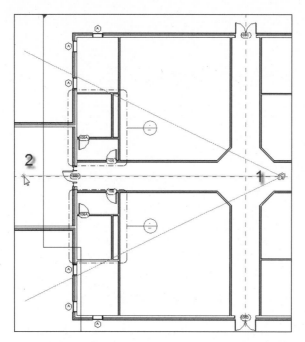

FIGURE 3.68 Placing the camera view in the main corridor

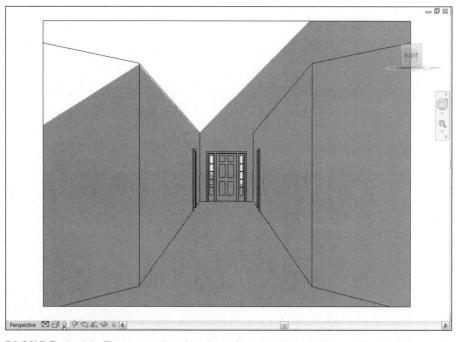

FIGURE 3.69 The perspective view down the east wing corridor

Modifying the Camera

After you place the camera into the model, Revit does not leave behind any evidence that the camera is there. If you need to make adjustments, or just see where the view is being taken from, perform the following steps:

1. Open the Level 1 floor plan.

2. In the Project Browser, find the East Wing Corridor Perspective view in the 3D Views category. Right-click on it and select Show Camera, as shown in Figure 3.70.

FIGURE 3.70 By finding the view in the Project Browser, you can tell Revit to show the camera in the plan.

The camera will now show up in the plan temporarily so you can see it.

In the view, you will see the camera icon itself, a triangle, and a straight line. You can physically move the camera, and you can also adjust the grip on the midpoint of the triangle to swivel and to look further into the model. Figure 3.71 shows the perspective view.

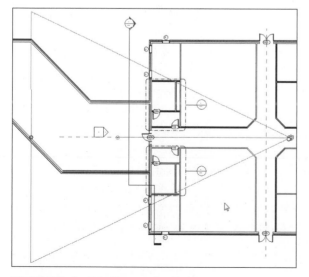

FIGURE 3.71 The perspective view

Creating an Elevation

I saved the best view for last... or at least the most popular. Elevations are essential for any project—so essential, in fact, that Revit provides four of them before you place a single wall into the model. The four shapes that represent houses that were in the model at the beginning of the book are elevation markers, as shown in Figure 3.72. These markers are typically handy but are most certainly in the way now. The first thing we need to do is to move one of them out of the way. The second thing we need to do is to create a few new ones!

To start manipulating elevations, follow along:

1. Go to the Level 1 floor plan. In the eastern part of the corridor, there is an elevation. Yours may be in a slightly different location than the book's example, but it needs to be moved nonetheless (see Figure 3.72).

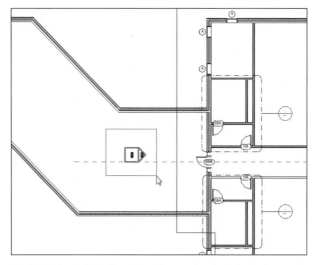

FIGURE 3.72 The elevation marker is right in the way!

The action we are about to perform is moving the elevation marker. To move an elevation marker, however, we need to break down what an elevation marker is composed of. It is actually two separate items. The square box is the elevation. The triangle is the part of the marker that activates the view, as shown in Figure 3.73. To move this elevation marker, you must pick a window around both items and move them together. If you do not, the actual view will stay in its original location, leaving you wondering what is wrong with your elevation.

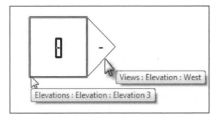

FIGURE 3.73 The elevation marker is broken down into two pieces. Both need to be moved together by picking a window around the entire symbol.

2. Pick a window around the elevation marker. Make sure you are not picking any other items along with it.

3. Move your mouse over the selection. Your cursor will turn into a move icon with four move arrows, as shown in Figure 3.74.

4. Drag the elevation marker to the west side of the building, as shown in Figure 3.74.

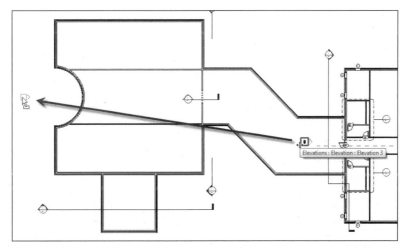

FIGURE 3.74 You can drag the elevation marker after the entire item is selected.

Now that the elevation marker is out of the corridor, it is time to make a new one. To do so, make sure you are in the Level 1 floor plan and follow along:

1. On the View tab, click the Elevation button, as shown in Figure 3.75.

2. After you click the Elevation button, move your cursor around the perimeter of the building. Notice that the elevation marker will follow the profile of the exterior walls. This is a great thing!

W A R N I N G   When you are choosing to create an elevation of a radial wall, or nonlinear item, be sure you know exactly at which angle you are placing the elevation marker. When you are in the elevation view, you may get a false sense of the true dimensions based on the view's perspective. Draw a reference plane if you need to, and then place the elevation on that plane.

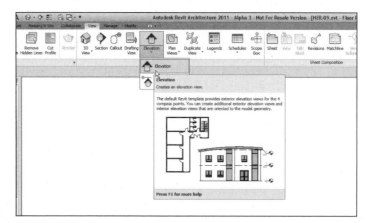

FIGURE 3.75 The Elevation button on the View tab

3. Pick a place for the elevation, as shown in Figure 3.76, and press Esc to terminate the command.

4. When the elevation is placed, select the triangle. You will see the same extents window as you saw in the previous section (see Figure 3.76). This controls how deep into the model you are viewing, and it also shows you the length of the section. Because you placed this elevation up against a wall, Revit will stop the elevation at that wall.

5. Pick the top grip and stretch the elevation past the wall, as shown in Figure 3.76.

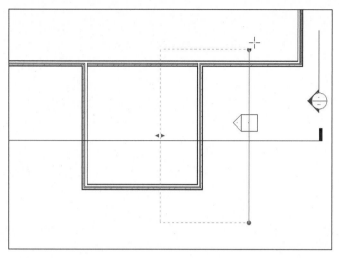

FIGURE 3.76 The elevation is placed. You can select the view arrow and move the extents of the elevation into the building.

6. In the Project Browser under Elevations (Building Elevation), you will see a new elevation. Right-click on it and rename it to **West Wing Southeast Elevation**.

7. Open the elevation.

8. On the View Control bar, change the scale to 1/4" = 1'–0".

9. On the View Control bar, set the detail level to Fine.

10. Save the model.

You have added a new exterior elevation. You can add an interior elevation as well. It is just as easy and much more fun!

Interior Elevations

The difference between an exterior elevation and an interior elevation is the same as the difference between a building section and a wall section. Both interior and exterior elevations are executed the same way: by selecting the View tab on the Design bar. The only difference is that you can make a choice between the two in the Type Selector in the Options bar. To add an interior elevation, perform these steps:

1. Go to the Level 1 floor plan.

2. On the View tab, select the Elevation button.

3. In the Properties dialog box, choose Elevation : Interior Elevation, as shown at the top of Figure 3.77.

4. Hover your cursor in the corridor near a point shown in the middle of Figure 3.77. Notice that when you move your cursor up, the arrow flips up. When you move your pointer down, the arrow flips down.

5. Make sure the arrow in the elevation target is pointing up and pick a point along the horizontal corridor, as shown at the right of Figure 3.77, to place the elevation. Once it's placed, press Esc to terminate the command.

6. After you place the elevation, you will notice that the extents will be outside the building (in most cases this occurs; if it does not, you are good to go). Select the elevation again, and on the right side, pick the blue grip and drag the right extent to the point shown at the right in Figure 3.77.

7. In the Project Browser, you will see that you have a new elevation under the Elevations (Interior Elevation) category. Right-click the new elevation (Revit will call it Elevation 1 - a, or something similar) and call it **East Wing Corridor Elevation**.

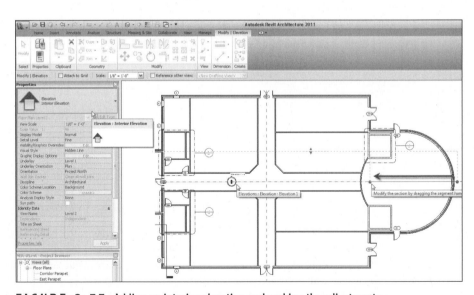

FIGURE 3.77 Adding an interior elevation and making the adjustments

8. Open the new view called East Wing Corridor Elevation.

9. Notice the crop region extends all the way up to the parapet. Select the crop region and drag the top down to Level 2, as shown in Figure 3.78.

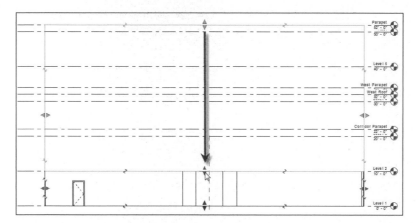

FIGURE 3.78 Stretching the grip down to crop the view

 N O T E   If you had floors already placed in the model, Revit would create the interior elevation to only extend to this geometry. Since we do not have floors, Revit does not know where to stop. If you happen to place an elevation without floors, and then you put them in later, Revit will not make the adjustment. You still have to create the interior elevation manually for the new floors.

Let's create some more elevations, shall we?

1. Go to Floor Level 1. Zoom into the east wing entry area, as shown in Figure 3.79.

2. On the View tab, select the Elevation button.

3. Place an elevation marker in an area similar to the one shown in Figure 3.79, and then move it to the center of the lobby.

In the elevation's view, you can drag the crop region down to show only that floor. If you would rather see all of the floors, perhaps you should use a section rather than an elevation.

 T I P   Notice that when you are trying to place the elevation in the entry area, it seems to be wandering all over the place. This is because the elevation is trying to locate the radial geometry. The safest bet in this situation is to find a straight wall and "aim" the elevation at that wall. In this case, you should aim the elevation at the bottom of the elevator shaft. When the elevation marker is in place, you can then move it to where you need it to be.

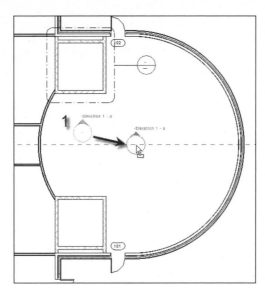

FIGURE 3.79 Add the elevation marker as shown here, and then move it to a new location.

4. With the elevation marker centered in the lobby, select the round bubble. Notice that four blue boxes appear, as shown in Figure 3.80. These boxes let you turn on multiple views. Turn on all four views, as shown in Figure 3.80.

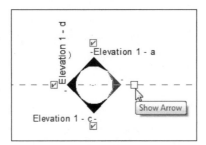

FIGURE 3.80 Turn on all four views in the lobby.

With the four elevations turned on, you have some naming to do! Up to this point, you have been going to the Project Browser to rename the elevations. Let's explore another way to rename an elevation and to view its properties as well.

Elevation Properties

With each view comes a new set of properties. For example, when you made the perspective view of the corridor you set Visual Style to Shaded With Edges, and you turned the shadows on. Normally, in an interior elevation you do not want to do this. Revit allows you to have separate view properties on a view-by-view basis.

To access the View Properties dialog, follow these steps:

1. On the interior elevation with the four arrows, select only the arrow facing up (north).

2. In the Properties dialog, notice you have a wealth of information about that view. You also have a multitude of options as well. The option we are going to change is View Name, as shown in Figure 3.81. Find View Name under the Identity Data heading, and change it to **East Wing Entry North Elevation**, as shown in Figure 3.81.

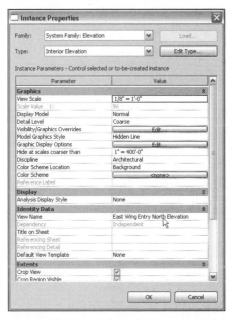

> By changing the value in the Properties dialog, you are, in effect, changing the name in the Project Browser. Again, change something in one place, and it will change in another.

FIGURE 3.81: Changing the View Name setting to East Wing Entry North Elevation

3. Select the East Wing Entry North Elevation again. Notice the view's extents are stretching past the entry atrium. Pick the blue grips at the end of the elevations and bring them into the atrium area, as shown in Figure 3.82. Also, drag the view limit up to show the radial exterior wall (see Figure 3.82).

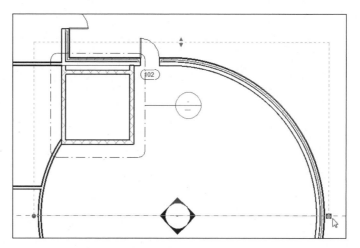

FIGURE 3.82 Making the adjustments to bring the view back into a reasonable range

4. Right-click on the elevation arrow facing left (west).

5. Change View Name to **East Wing Entry West Elevation**.

6. Right-click on the arrow facing down (south).

7. Change View Name to **East Wing Entry South Elevation**.

8. Right-click on the arrow facing right (east).

9. Change View Name to **East Wing Entry East Elevation**.

10. Select each elevation, and adjust the view's extents as you did for the north elevation.

11. Save the model.

Notice that the actual view names are showing up in the plan. This is nice, but unfortunately it leaves no room for anything else other than the actual view. Plus, no construction documents have these names right in the plan (at least none that I have ever seen). We can turn this feature off.

Now that we can place and modify annotations, let's delve into the physical properties of these annotations.

Annotation Properties

Annotations all have properties we can modify. To change the elevation symbol properties, follow along:

1. On the Manage tab, click Settings ➢ Additional Settings ➢ Elevation Tags.

2. At the top of the Type Properties dialog, you will see Family: System Family : Elevation Tag. Below that you will see Type. Change Type from 1/2" square to 1/2" circle (see Figure 3.83).

3. In the Type Parameters, under Graphics, change the Elevation Mark to Elevation Mark Circle - Upgrade : 1/2".

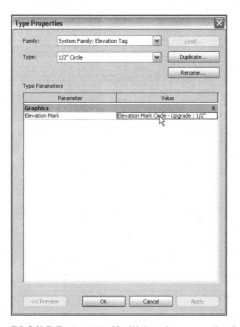

FIGURE 3.83 Modifying the properties for the elevation markers

4. Click OK.

5. Zoom back in on the elevation markers. They should look like Figure 3.84.

FIGURE 3.84 The revised, less obtrusive elevation markers

N O T E   It's Revit time! No longer will you see "dumb" placeholder information in a tag. When we create our construction documents and put these views on sheets, Revit will automatically fill out tags with the correct information. To take it one step further, you can tell Revit not to print these annotations if the views they represent are not on a sheet.

The ability to add elevations is a must. As you can see, physically adding an elevation is simple. It does, however, take practice to manipulate elevations to look the way you want.

Are You Experienced?

Now you can...

- ☑ create levels and constrain walls to stretch or shrink if the level's elevation information changes in any way

- ☑ cut wall sections and building sections through the model

- ☑ create detail views, allowing you to add plan sections through a wall or a building section

- ☑ create a callout view and control the crop region

- ☑ add a camera to the model, giving the user a nice perspective of a certain area

- ☑ create interior and exterior elevations within the model

CHAPTER 4

Working with the Revit Tools

You can get only so far with allowing a computer application to place architectural components into a model. At some point, the application needs to be flexible enough to enable users to employ their own set of drafting and modifying tools, thus allowing the architect or designer the freedom to create their own architecture and construction procedures. Revit Architecture does provide the basic modify and edit commands—which are quite common if you have experience with other drafting applications such as AutoCAD or MicroStation—but with a little more flair and some differences in procedure from that of a 2D drafting application.

▶ **The basic edit commands**

▶ **The Array command**

▶ **The Mirror command**

▶ **The Align tool**

▶ **The Split Element command**

▶ **The Trim command**

▶ **The Offset command**

▶ **Copy/Paste**

▶ **Creating the plans**

The Basic Edit Commands

In this chapter you will learn how to utilize the geometry you have already placed in the model to build an actual working plan. As you manipulate the plan, all of the other views you made in the previous chapter will reflect those changes. We'll start with the edit commands.

 N O T E   Like the previous chapters, it is important that you are comfortable with this chapter. If you are not comfortable with the first few chapters, I recommend skimming back through them. Sometimes you can pick up something you missed and have a "light bulb" moment.

You aren't going to get very far in Revit without knowing the edit commands. Up to this point, we have been avoiding the modify commands with a few exceptions. There will be some overlap in these chapters as many aspects of Revit span multiple topics.

The basic commands that we'll cover are Move, Copy, and Rotate. Then we will move on to Array, Mirror, Align, Split, and Trim. Each command is as important as the next at this stage of the game. Some are obvious, whereas others can take some practice to master.

The first command, Move, is one you'll recognize from previous chapters. Move is probably the most heavily used command in Revit.

The Move Command

The Move command is generally used to create a copy of an item while deleting the original item.

Begin by finding the model you are using to follow along. If you have not completed the previous chapter procedures, open the file caller NER-11.rvt found at the book's website, **www.sybex.com/go/revit2011ner**. Go to the Chapter 4 folder to find the file.

To use the Move command, perform the following steps:

1. With the file open, go to Level 1 under the Floor Plans category in the Project Browser.

2. Zoom in on the west wing.

3. Select the south wall of the bump-out at the south side of the west wing, as shown in Figure 4.1.

4. On the Modify | Walls tab, you will see the Move button, as shown in Figure 4.1; click it.

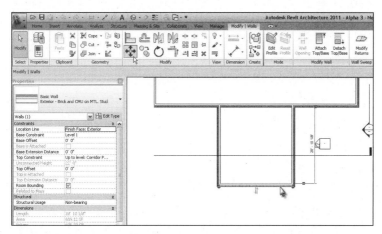

FIGURE 4.1 Select the wall to be moved. The Move button now appears on the Ribbon.

5. Now that the Move command is running, you see some choices on the Options bar:

Constrain If you check Constrain, you can only move at 0, 90, 180, or 270 degrees.

Disjoin If you check Disjoin, when you move the wall, any walls that are joined to it will not be affected by the move. The wall will lose its join.

Copy The Copy option turns the Move command into the Copy command. Conversely, you can uncheck the Copy command to return to the Move command.

6. To start moving the item, you must first pick a base point for the command. Pick a point somewhere toward the middle of the wall, as shown in Figure 4.2.

7. After you pick this point, move your cursor straight up. You will see a blue dimension. At this point you have two choices: you can either "eyeball" the increment, or you can type the increment you want (see Figure 4.2).

8. Type in the value 2'–6" and press Enter. The wall has moved 2'–6". Notice the adjacent walls move with it. In Revit, there is no stretch command (see Figure 4.3).

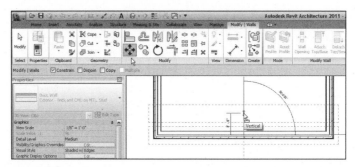

F I G U R E   4 . 2 Choices on the Options bar. The first point has been picked and the wall is being moved up.

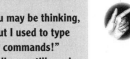

T I P   Revit Architecture will accept a few different values for feet and fractional inches. For example, instead of typing 2'–6" (which Revit will accept), you can type 2 6. Just make sure you have a space between the 2 and the 6. Revit will accept that value. If there are fractional increments, you can type 2 6 1/2", and Revit will accept the value. Or you can type 2'-6 1/2".

You may be thinking, "But I used to type my commands!" Well, you still can in Revit. If you type MV, Revit Architecture will launch the Move command. Remember, though, you need to select the item first!

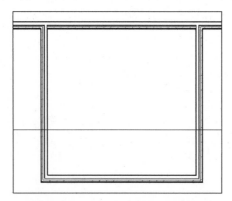

F I G U R E   4 . 3 Moving the wall 2'–6" also means that any adjoining walls will be adjusted along with it.

Now that Move is officially in the history books, it's time to move on to Move's close cousin: the Copy command.

The Copy Command

When you need to make duplicates of an item, Copy is your go-to player. The Copy command works like the Move command, except it leaves the initial item intact. You can also create multiple copies if necessary.

To start using the Copy command, follow along:

1. Make sure you are still in the Level 1 floor plan.

2. Zoom in so you are focused on the east wing in its entirety, as shown in Figure 4.4.

3. Pick the corridor wall, as shown in Figure 4.4.

4. Click the Copy command on the Modify | Walls tab.

5. Zoom in on the wall close to the midpoint of the selected wall and the intersection of the horizontal wall that divides this portion of the building (see Figure 4.4).

6. If you hover your cursor in the center of the wall (not near the actual finish faces, but the core of the wall), you will see a blue dotted center-line indicating that you have found the center of the wall.

   Also, if you move your cursor to the right a little, you can position your cursor so that it picks up the horizontal wall's centerline. After you pick up the horizontal wall's centerline, the centerline for the vertical wall will disappear. This is fine.

   You will now see that you are snapped to the endpoint of the horizontal wall. After you see this, pick the point (see Figure 4.4).

7. Move to the right until you pick up the midpoint of the horizontal wall. When you do, pick that point. If the midpoint doesn't appear, just type 22'3".

8. Repeat the procedure for the south side of the corridor, as shown in Figure 4.5. You will see that the ends of the walls do not meet. This is fine—we will modify these walls with the Trim command in a moment.

9. Save the model.

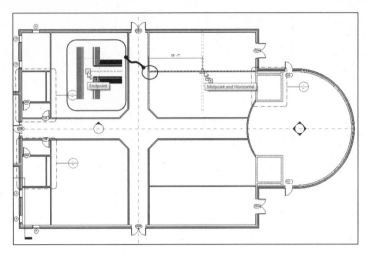

FIGURE 4.4 Creating a copy of the corridor wall

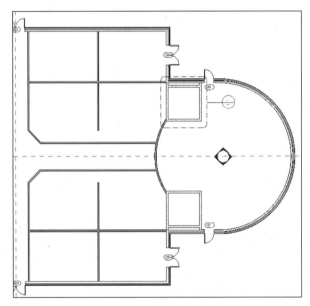

FIGURE 4.5 The two walls copied, segmenting the spaces north and south of the corridor

The next step is to rotate an item. Although the Rotate command is a simple concept, Revit does have unique processes involved in this command.

The Rotate Command

The Rotate command allows you to change the polar orientation of an item or a set of items. This command may take a little practice to understand. The good thing, however, is that when you have experience with the Rotate command, you will be better at other commands that share a similar process.

To use the Rotate command, follow along:

1. Open the Level 1 floor plan.

2. Zoom in on the radial portion of the west wing, as shown in Figure 4.6.

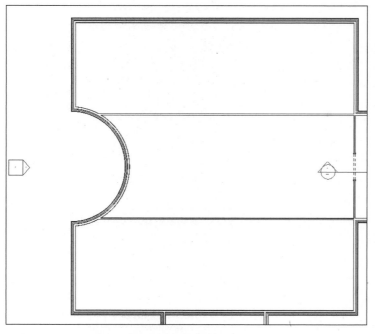

FIGURE 4.6 The radial portion of the west wing

3. We are going to add a new reference plane and rotate it by 45 degrees. To do this, in the Home tab click Ref Plane in the Work Plane panel. (See Figure 4.7).

4. In the Draw panel, click the Line button.

5. For the first point, pick the center point of the radial wall, as shown in Figure 4.7.

Notice that the Copy command is one click away from being the Move command. Remember to always look at the Options bar for choices.

6. For the second point, pick a point outside the radial wall (again, see Figure 4.7).

7. Press Esc.

 T I P   In Revit, sometimes finding the correct snap can be difficult. To overcome this, you can type the letter **S**, then the first letter of the snap you wish to use. For example, if you wanted to snap to the center of the arc, you would start the Ref Plane command (any command works here, but we are using a reference plane as an example) and type **SC**, place the cursor over the arc until the snap marker appears, and then click. This will snap to the center.

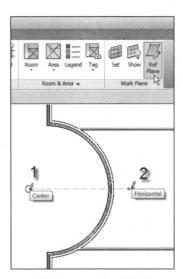

F I G U R E 4 . 7 Establishing a reference plane

 W A R N I N G   Be careful when you rotate items in this fashion. Figure 4.7 shows the second point extended past the radial wall, and that is where you generally want it; however, watch out for your snaps. When you pick the second point, be sure to zoom in on the area, ensuring you are not inadvertently snapping to the wrong point.

Now that you have added the reference plane, you can rotate it into place. (Yes, you could have just drawn it at a 45° angle, but we are practicing the Rotate command here.)

1. Select the reference plane you just drew.

2. On the Modify tab, select the Rotate button, as shown in Figure 4.8.

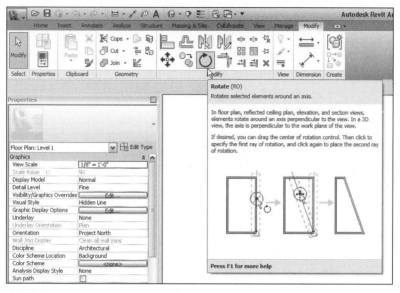

FIGURE 4.8 The Rotate command is active for the specific item you have selected.

3. After you start the Rotate command, look back at the reference plane. Notice the icon that resembles a recycle arrow in the middle of your line. Revit will always calculate the center of an object (or group of objects) for the rotate point (see Figure 4.9).

4. Zoom in on the rotate icon.

5. We must move this icon to the left endpoint of the reference plane. To do so, click and drag the rotate icon to the endpoint of the reference plane, as shown in Figure 4.9.

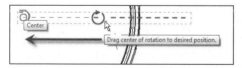

FIGURE 4.9 Click and drag the rotate icon to the endpoint of the reference plane.

6. With the rotate origin in the correct location, it is rotate time! Notice that if you swivel your cursor around the reference plane, a line forms from the rotate origin to your cursor. This indicates that the origin is established. You need to now pick two points. The first point you pick

You can start the **Rotate command** by typing **RO**; just be sure you have something selected first.

must be in line with the object you are rotating. In this case, pick a point at the right endpoint of the reference plane, as shown in Figure 4.10.

7. Now, when you move your cursor up, you will see an angular dimension. Once that angular dimension gets to 45°, pick the second point (see Figure 4.10).

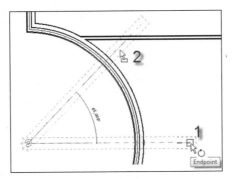

FIGURE 4.10 To rotate an item, you must specify two points.

8. Press Esc.

ROTATE OPTIONS

While you are in the Rotate command, don't forget that you have options. The most popular option is to create a copy of the item you are rotating, as shown in the following graphic.

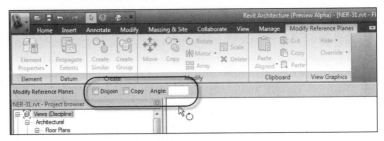

Another popular option is to simply specify an angle. This can be difficult, however, because the correct angle may be the opposite of what you think, resulting in you having to undo the command and then redoing the rotation with a negative (−) value.

As you are well aware, you'll use the Rotate command quite frequently. Now that you have some experience with the Rotate command and know how Revit wants you to move the pivot point, the next command, the Array command, will be easy for you to grasp.

The Array Command

When you need to create multiple duplicates of an item, or a group of items, the Array command will be the logical choice. The Array command in Revit functions in a similar fashion to the Rotate command. The similarities of the Array command also extend to the Array command in AutoCAD. You have two basic choices:

▶ Radial, which allows you to array an item around a circle or an arc

▶ Linear, which allows you to array an item in a straight line, or at an angle

Let's look at the Radial array first.

Radial Array

The Radial array is based on a radius. If you need items to be arrayed in a circular manner, then the Radial array is your choice. Again, after you start the Array command, do not ignore the Options bar. It will guide you through most of the command.

To start using the Radial array, follow these steps:

1. Select the 45° reference plane, as shown in Figure 4.11.

2. On the Modify | Reference Planes tab, select the Array button, as shown in Figure 4.11.

3. With the Array command active, you will see some choices available on the Options bar, as shown in Figure 4.12. For this procedure, click the Radial button.

4. Check Group And Associate.

5. Set Number to 4.

6. Click the Move To: Last button (see Figure 4.12).

7. With the options set, focus your attention on the object being arrayed. Notice the familiar rotate icon. Pick and drag the blue icon from the

midpoint of the line to the endpoint. The array will pivot around this axis (see Figure 4.13).

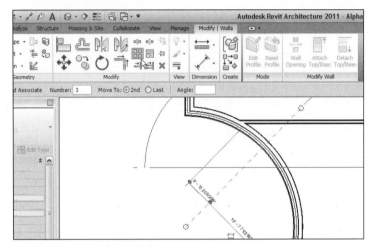

FIGURE 4.11 Select the item to be arrayed first, and then click the Array button on the Modify | Reference Planes tab.

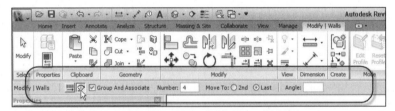

FIGURE 4.12 Setting the options for the Radial array

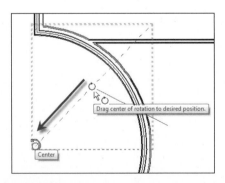

FIGURE 4.13 Drag the pivot icon to the endpoint of the item being arrayed.

8. With the pivot point in place, specify two points for the array. The first point will be a point along the angle of the item being arrayed. The second point will be a point along the angle you wish to end with.

9. Pick the endpoint of the reference plane you are arraying.

10. Move your cursor down until you see 90°. Then, pick the second point (see Figure 4.14).

11. Click (left-click) off into another part of the view. This will establish the array. You should have four reference planes at this point, similar to Figure 4.15.

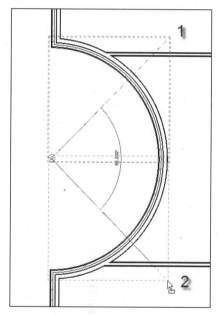

FIGURE 4.14 Specifying the two angles for the Radial array

12. Select (left-click) one of the reference planes. You will see a large dashed box surrounding the reference plane. You will also see a temporary arc dimension with a blue number 4 at the quadrant. It may be obscured by the arc, but it is there nonetheless (see Figure 4.15).

13. Click the number 4.

14. Change the count to 5.

15. You now have five reference planes, as shown in Figure 4.16.

Getting the hang of the radial array may take a few projects. The next array type, the Linear array, follows the same concept as the Radial array, but it is more straightforward. Yes, pun intended.

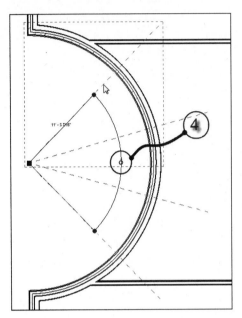

FIGURE 4.15 After the array is created, select one of the arrayed members. Notice you can change the count.

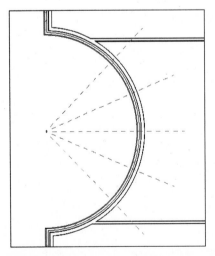

FIGURE 4.16 You can control the number of items in an array group after you create the array.

Linear Array

Of course, you may wish to create an array along a line, and you can do this in Revit. When you create a Linear array, you enjoy the same flexibility that you have with the Radial array.

The objective of this procedure is to create an array of windows along the north and south wall on the west side of the west wing of the building. To do this, we will first need to establish two strong reference planes.

To learn how to use the Linear array command, follow along:

1. Zoom in on the west section of the west wing, as shown in Figure 4.17.

2. The next step is to add two reference planes. We will use these reference planes to establish the ends of our window array. Go to the Ref Plane command on the Work Plane panel of the Home tab.

3. On the Draw panel, keep the Line icon active, and add an offset of 1'–6" (remember you can just type **1 6**) on the Options panel.

4. Pick the corner of the radial wall where it intersects the straight wall for the first point of the reference plane, as shown in Figure 4.17.

5. Pick a second point similar to Figure 4.17 to finish the reference plane.

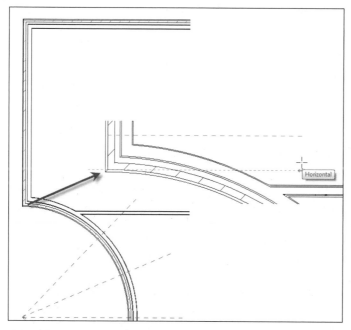

FIGURE 4.17 Creating the reference plane

6. With the Ref Plane command still running, repeat the procedure for the top of the wall. You want to pick the top, outside face of brick, avoiding the concrete ledge below, as shown in Figure 4.18.

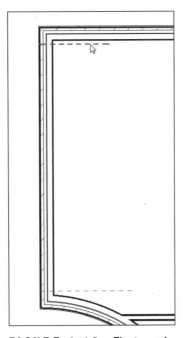

FIGURE 4.18: The two reference planes are established.

If you are drawing the reference plane, and it keeps going above the wall as opposed to below the wall, you can tap the spacebar as you are drawing the reference plane. This will flip the side of the wall it is being drawn on.

Now we need to add a window based on the bottom reference plane. This window will then be arrayed up the wall to meet the northern reference plane.

1. On the Home tab, select the Window button.

2. Change the Element Type to Fixed : 24″ × 72″.

3. Place the window approximately where it is shown in Figure 4.19. You will have to move the window in alignment with the reference plane.

4. After you place the window, press the Esc key.

5. Select the window.

6. On the Modify | Windows tab, select the Move button.

7. Move the window from the bottom, outside corner down to the reference plane, as shown in Figure 4.20.

8. Press Esc.

9. Zoom out until you can see the entire wall.

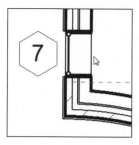

FIGURE 4.19 Adding the window to be arrayed

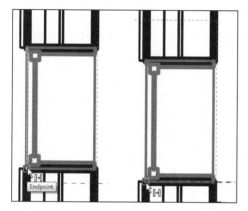

FIGURE 4.20 Moving the window into position

10. Select the window you just inserted into the wall.

11. On the Modify | Windows tab, select the Array button.

12. On the Options bar, select Linear, as shown in Figure 4.21.

13. Click Group And Associate (if it is not already selected).

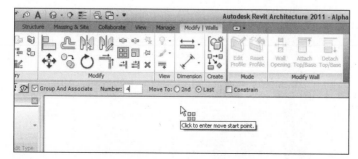

FIGURE 4.21 Choosing the Linear Array options

14. For Number, enter 4.

15. Select Move To: Last.

16. Pick the top endpoint of the bottom window.

17. Move your cursor up the wall, and pick a point perpendicular to the top reference plane, as shown in Figure 4.22.

18. After you pick the second point, you will have to wait a moment; then Revit will evenly fill the void with the two additional windows. Also, Revit will give you the option of adding additional windows. Enter a value of 5 and press Enter (see Figure 4.23).

I DON'T WANT TO MOVE ANYTHING!

The Move To: Last and Move To: Second choices are somewhat misleading. You are not actually "moving" anything. If you choose Move To: Last, for example, Revit will place an additional item in the last place you pick, keeping the first item intact. Revit will then divide the space between the two items evenly based on the number of items you specify in the options. If you specify four items, Revit still has two items left to divide.

If you choose Move To: Second, Revit will place an additional item at the second point picked (like Move To: Last), but this time Revit will add additional items beyond the second item. The distance is calculated by the distance between the first two items.

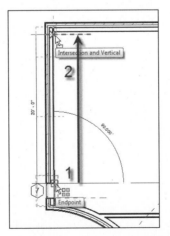

FIGURE 4.22 "Moving" the window to the top reference plane

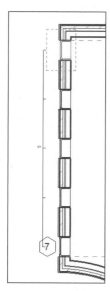

FIGURE 4.23 Changing the number of items in the array. You can always come back to the arrayed group and change this value at any time.

N O T E   After your items are grouped and arrayed, you can still move the end item. Not only can you move the end item in the direction of the array, but you can move it laterally to the array, causing a "step" in the array.

With the array completed, it is time to duplicate our efforts on the other side of the radial portion of this wall. As in CAD, at this point you have a few different choices. You can repeat the Array command, copy the items, or mirror the items.

The Mirror Command

The Mirror command works exactly as expected: it makes a copy of an object or a group of objects in the opposite orientation of the first item(s). The crucial point to remember is that you will need to specify a mirror "plane."

Although we simply could not avoid using this command in previous chapters, it's time to officially address and explore the Mirror command. The most useful aspect of the Mirror command is that if reference planes already exist in the model, you can simply pick these planes to perform the mirror, as opposed to sketching a new plane to mirror around.

The objective of the following example is to mirror the windows to the south side of the west wall:

1. Zoom in on the windows you just arrayed.

2. Select the windows starting from the upper-left corner to the lower-right corner, as shown in Figure 4.24.

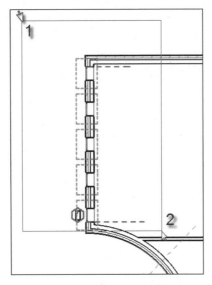

FIGURE 4.24 Selecting the items to be mirrored. Make sure you do not select the wall that the windows reside in.

 T I P   Oops! I selected the wall. That's OK. You do not need to Esc out of the selection. Simply hold down the Shift key and select the wall. It will become deselected.

3. On the Modify | Windows tab, select the Mirror - Pick Axis button, as shown in Figure 4.25.

4. Position your cursor over the center reference plane that is part of the radial array. When you pause, you will get a tooltip indicating that you are about to select the reference plane. When you see this tooltip, select the reference plane, as shown in Figure 4.26.

5. Zoom out to check out the placement of the windows. Do not assume that everything went as planned. Your Level 1 floor plan should resemble Figure 4.27.

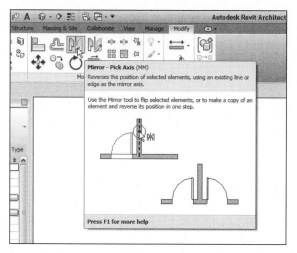

FIGURE 4.25 The Mirror buttons appear when you select an item.

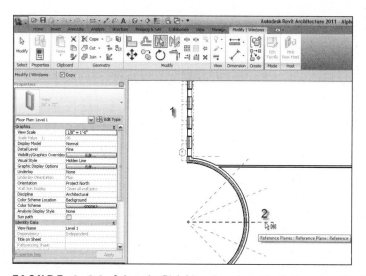

FIGURE 4.26 Select the Pick Lines icon from the Options bar. The line you are going to pick is the reference plane shown here.

NOTE If the mirror went wrong, or you are not comfortable with the results, use the Undo button and try again. Now is the time to practice!

◄

When you pick the reference plane, Revit will mirror the entire group of windows.

Now that the two straight walls have windows, it is time to array some windows within the radial portion. The problem is, however, when you insert a window along a radius, you cannot snap it to the intersection of the reference plane and the wall. This is where the Align tool becomes critical.

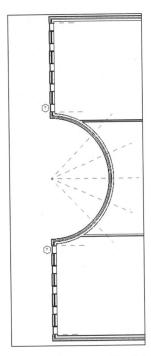

FIGURE 4.27 The finished west wall

The Align Tool

You will find yourself in situations where two items need to be aligned with one another. The Align command is a great tool for accomplishing this task. It's one of the most useful tools within Revit, and you will use it extensively. Overuse of this command is not possible! Since the Align function is a tool, you do not have to select an item first for this function to become available. You can select Align at any time.

To practice using the Align tool, follow along:

1. Zoom in on the radial portion of the west wall, as shown in Figure 4.28.

2. On the Home tab, select the Window button.

3. In the Properties dialog box, choose Fixed : 16″ × 72″.

4. Place the window in the radial wall in a similar location to Figure 4.28. Do not attempt to "eyeball" the center of the window with the reference plane. As a matter of fact, purposely misalign the window, as shown in Figure 4.28.

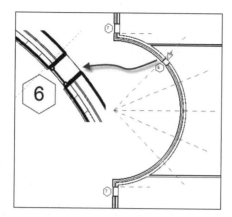

FIGURE 4.28 Place the window approximately in the area shown here.

5. On the Modify | Place Window tab, select the Align button, as shown in Figure 4.29.

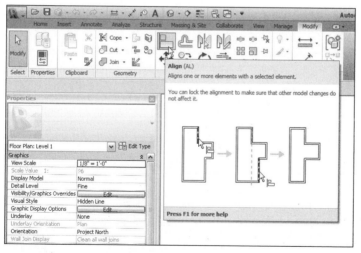

FIGURE 4.29 Select the Align button on the Modify | Place Window tab.

6. The Align tool needs you to select two items to work. First select the item you want to align *to*; pick the reference plane as shown in Figure 4.30.

7. Now you need to pick a point on the window: the centerline of the window. By looking at the window now, you will not see this line. Hover your cursor over the middle of the window and a centerline will become highlighted. When you see this centerline, pick the window.

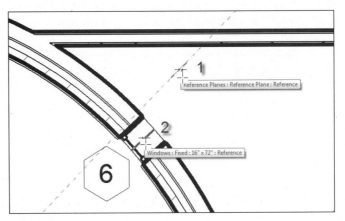

FIGURE 4.30 Choosing the items for alignment. Remember, you must choose the item you want to *align to* first.

The window will move into alignment with the reference plane, as shown in Figure 4.31.

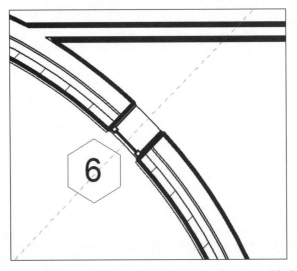

FIGURE 4.31 The window is now in alignment with the reference plane.

8. Press Esc, and then select the window.

9. Pick the Array button on the Modify | Windows tab.

10. Do a radial array of the windows with a count of five (total). You remember how, right?

N O T E   Adding reference planes, and working in a controlled environment, is very typical of Revit Architecture. You establish a reference plane, add a component, and then execute some command such as Array, Copy, or Move. Although it may seem like quite a few steps, you are now accurately, and deliberately, placing items in your model. The accuracy you apply here will propagate itself throughout the project in terms of elevations, sections, and drawing sheets.

Let's practice more with the Align tool. It is one of the most important modify tools in the Revit arsenal, and we don't want to understate its usefulness:

1. Zoom into the end of the corridor in the east wing of the building, as shown in Figure 4.32.

2. On the Home tab, select the Door button.

3. Place a Double Flush : 72″ × 84″ door in the radial corridor wall, as shown in Figure 4.32. As when you placed the window along the reference plane in the last procedure, don't try to eyeball the correct alignment; you want to purposely misalign the door.

4. Renumber the door to **100A**.

5. On the Modify panel, click the Align button.

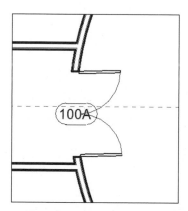

FIGURE 4.32 Adding a double door to the east wing corridor

6. Pick the horizontal reference plane.

7. Pick the centerline of the door. When the reference plane is aligned, pause for a moment without hitting Esc. You will see a little blue padlock. If you can't see it, zoom out a little. You can use this function to lock the alignment.

Another nice feature of the Align command is that, after your alignment is complete, you can physically lock the items together, allowing the two aligned items to move as one.

Locking an Alignment

After you have aligned the items, you will notice that small, blue padlock icon we just discussed. Within Revit Architecture, you can lock items together by using the Align tool. This is good and bad. It is great in the sense that, if the center reference plane moves for whatever reason, the door will also move. It is bad in the sense that, if the door moves, the center reference plane will also move.

When you align an item and you lock it, be sure this is what you want to do. It's simple: pick the padlock icon, as shown in Figure 4.33. You are now aligned and locked to the center reference plane.

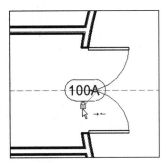

FIGURE 4.33 The door is now aligned and locked.

There will also be times when two items are already aligned, but you just want to lock the items together. To do this, you must still use the Align command to access the lock option:

1. Zoom into the west side of the east wing at the corridor intersection.

2. Start the Align command.

3. Pick the centerline of the door at that end of corridor.

4. Pick the center reference plane.

5. Pick the blue padlock to lock the doors to the center reference plane (see Figure 4.34).

Now that the Align command is out of the way, we can move on to the next item on the Modify tab: the Split command.

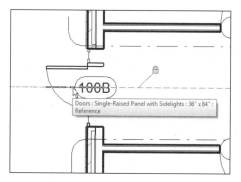

FIGURE 4.34 You can create a locked constraint by using the Align command even if the items were in alignment to begin with.

The Split Element Command

The Split Element command takes the place of the conventional Trim command because you cannot actually delete an entire area between two points in Revit using the Trim command. The Split Element command is the equivalent of the Break command in AutoCAD: you can use the Split Element command on walls and when you edit an element in Sketch Mode.

To use the Split Element command, find the model you are using to follow along. If you have not completed the previous procedures, open the file called NER-12.rvt found at the book's website, **www.sybex.com/go/revit2011ner**. Go to Chapter 4 to find the file. The objective of this procedure is to cut a notch out of a wall by using the Edit Profile function:

1. In the Project Browser, open the Sections (Building Section) called West Wing South Wall Section, as shown in Figure 4.35.

2. Select the wall beyond, as shown in Figure 4.36.

3. On the Modify | Walls tab, click the Edit Profile button, as shown in Figure 4.36.

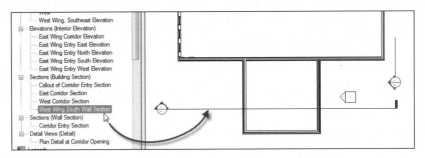

FIGURE 4.35 Open the section called West Wing South Wall Section. It will put you in the section, as shown here.

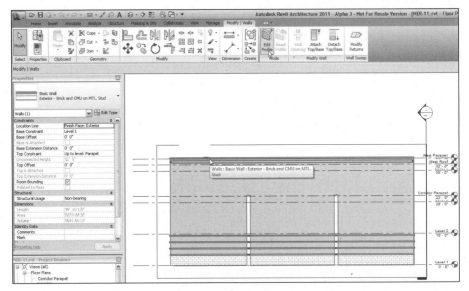

FIGURE 4.36 Select the wall beyond, and click the Edit Profile button on the Modify | Walls tab.

After you select the Edit Profile option, you will be put into Sketch Mode. You know you are in Sketch Mode because your Ribbon will end with a Finish Edit Mode and a Cancel Edit Mode that you must select to return to the full model. Also, the wall you have selected will now consist of four magenta "sketch" lines, and the rest of the model is shaded into the background.

4. On the Modify | Walls ➤ Edit Profile tab, click the Split Element button, as shown in Figure 4.37.

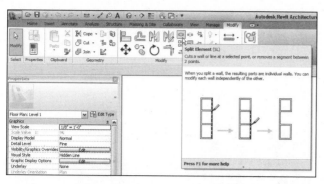

FIGURE 4.37 Select the Split Element button on the Modify | Walls ➤ Edit Profile tab.

5. After you select the Split Element button, look at your Options bar. Notice you can specify to delete the inner segment. Check the Delete Inner Segment checkbox, as shown in Figure 4.38.

6. Pick the intersection of the bottom magenta sketch line and the inside face of the left wall for the first split point, as shown in Figure 4.38.

7. Pick the intersection of the bottom magenta sketch line and the inside face of the right wall, as shown in Figure 4.38.

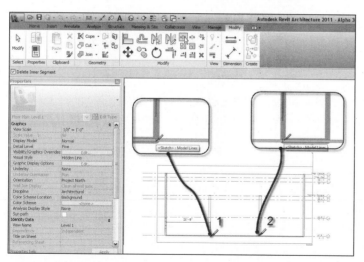

FIGURE 4.38 To remove a segment of a line, you must use the Split Element command and select Delete Inner Segment from the Options bar.

NEW TO THE 2011 SPLIT COMMAND!

There is a new split option offered in Revit Architecture 2011. This new function allows you to split an item like always, but now you can choose the size of the gap segment.

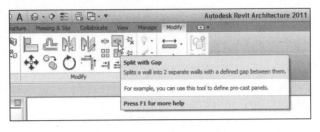

After you pick these points, the magenta sketch line will be segmented. Now you need to add more lines to the sketch. To do this, you must leave the Split Element command and follow along using the sketch tools on the Draw panel:

1. On the Draw panel of the Modify | Walls ➢ Edit Profile tab, click the Pick Lines icon, as shown in Figure 4.39.

2. Pick the inside face of the left wall (#1 in Figure 4.39).

3. Pick the Level 3 Level (#2 in Figure 4.39).

4. Pick the inside face of the right wall (#3 in Figure 4.39).

5. Press Esc.

The next step is to get the magenta lines to form a continuous loop. This means that there can be no overlapping lines. Each line starts exactly where the last line ends. There can be no gaps or overlaps:

1. Press Esc.

2. Pick (left-click) the horizontal magenta line that is traced over Level 3.

3. On each end, you will see a round, blue grip. Pick each grip and stretch the line to the intersection of the vertical magenta lines, as shown in Figure 4.40.

4. Select the left, vertical magenta line and stretch the top grip down to the intersection of the horizontal magenta line, as shown in Figure 4.40.

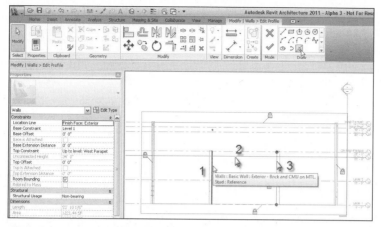

FIGURE 4.39 Tracing the walls to form a notch. This is done by selecting the Pick Lines icon and picking the walls.

5. Select the right, vertical magenta line and stretch the top down to the horizontal magenta sketch line. You should now have a continuous loop (see Figure 4.40).

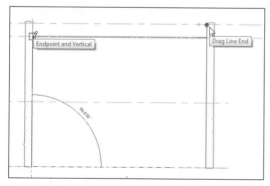

FIGURE 4.40 Modifying the sketch lines by stretching the grips to form a continuous loop

6. On the Mode panel of the Modify | Walls ➢ Edit Profile tab, select the Finish Edit Mode button, as shown in Figure 4.41.

7. Go to a 3D view at this point to check out your model, as shown in Figure 4.42. You can either click the Default 3D View button on the Quick Access toolbar, or you can pick the {3D} view from the Project Browser.

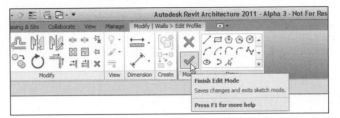

FIGURE 4.41   Click Finish Edit Mode to get back to the model.

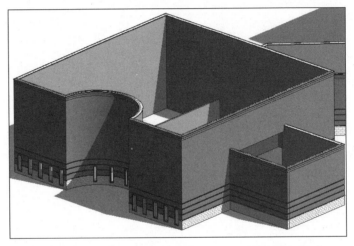

FIGURE 4.42   The building in 3D up to this point. For this image, the shadows are turned on.

REVIT WANTS IT CLEAN!

As mentioned earlier, if you click Finish Edit Mode and Revit gives you a warning, as shown in the following graphic, you *must* be sure that you have no overlapping lines or gaps in your sketch. Revit is quite unforgiving and will not allow you to proceed.

The next set of procedures will focus on basic cleanup using the Trim command. Although you can accomplish a lot with this single command, you must get used to a certain Revit method.

The Trim Command

Any time you need to "cut" an item, or extend an item, you'll use the Trim command. In any design-based application, you won't get very far without the Trim command. Similar to the Split command, the Trim command can be used on walls and within Sketch mode. As mentioned earlier, however, there are specific procedures you need to understand to be comfortable using this command.

To use the Trim command, open the model you have been working on. If you have not completed the previous chapter procedures, open the file caller NER-13.rvt found at the book's website, **www.sybex.com/go/revit2011ner**. Go to Chapter 4 to find the file.

To use the Trim command, follow this procedure:

1. With the file open, go to Level 1 under the Floor Plans category in the Project Browser.

2. Zoom in on the east wing. You will see two walls that extend beyond their destination. These walls need to be trimmed.

3. On the Modify tab, select the Trim/Extend Single Element button, as shown in Figure 4.43.

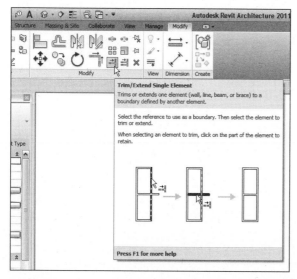

FIGURE 4.43 Click the Trim/Extend Single Element button on the Modify tab.

4. Zoom in on the area, as shown in Figure 4.44.

5. To trim the vertical wall back to the horizontal wall, you must first pick the wall you want to trim *to*. In this case, select the north face of the horizontal wall, as shown in Figure 4.45.

6. Now you must pick a point along the vertical wall. The trick here is that you must pick a point on the side of the wall that you want to *keep*. Pick a point along the vertical wall above (north of) the horizontal wall, as shown in Figure 4.45. After you do, the wall will be trimmed back.

7. Press Esc to terminate the command.

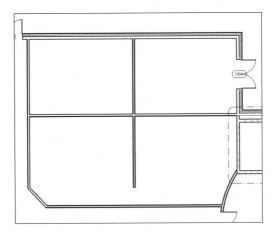

FIGURE 4.44 Zoom in to this area to start trimming the walls.

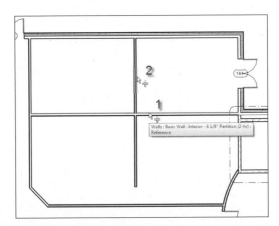

FIGURE 4.45 Pick a point along the wall to trim the wall back.

You may not always want to trim an item. There will be just as many times where you need to elongate an item to reach a destination point. In the drafting world, this procedure is better known as *extend*. The process for using the Extend feature is similar to the Trim command. First, however, you must select the wall in which you want to extend an object, and then select the object to be extended:

1. Zoom in on the south part of the east wing.

2. On the Modify tab, click the Trim/Extend Single Element button.

3. Pick the south corridor wall. This is the wall you want to extend to.

4. Pick the vertical wall that does not quite intersect. Press Esc, and your walls should now look like Figure 4.46.

5. Save the model.

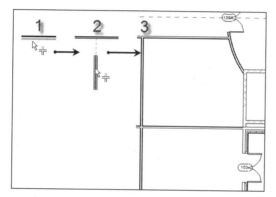

FIGURE 4.46 Stepping through the procedure to extend the wall

There is one more command to examine that is used in the day-to-day modification of a Revit model. You may have noticed that most of the commands we have used to place items in the model have had the Offset command built into the options of that specific procedure. The next section will focus on offsetting items using the stand-alone Revit Offset command.

The Offset Command

The Offset command allows you to create a copy of an item at a specified distance. As mentioned earlier, the need to offset an item crops up much less often in Revit Architecture than in a conventional drafting application. This is because, in Revit, the functionality is provided as an option in most commands. There are times, however, when you will need the good old Offset command.

To get used to using the Offset command, follow these steps:

1. Zoom in on the west part of the east wing. This is the area where the restrooms are (see Figure 4.47). The objective is to offset the vertical wall to the right of the restrooms to the middle of the open space.

2. On the Modify panel of the Modify tab, click the Offset button, as shown in Figure 4.47.

3. On the Options bar, click the Numerical button.

4. Enter 16' 2" in the Offset field.

5. Make sure Copy is checked.

6. Hover your cursor over the wall to the right of the lavatory, as shown in Figure 4.47. You will see an alignment line appear to the right of the wall.

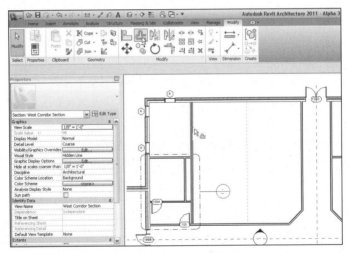

FIGURE 4.47 Choosing your options and picking the wall to be offset

7. When you see the dashed alignment line appear, pick the wall. The new wall should be in the middle of the large room.

8. Repeat the process for the walls south of the corridor, as shown in Figure 4.48.

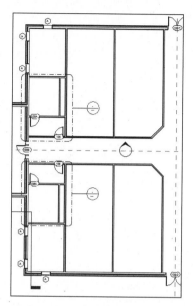

FIGURE 4.48 Completing the floor plan by using the Offset command will be a common procedure.

 WARNING   Be sure your math is correct. After you offset an item, use the Measure command. I've mentioned this before, and I will mention it repeatedly throughout this book! You will be glad you measured now rather than later.

This concludes our discussion of Offset. Because this floor plan consists of items we want to repeat on other floors, we can now explore how to do this using the Copy/Paste command right from Windows.

Copy/Paste

Yes, this is the actual Microsoft Windows Copy/Paste function. In Revit Architecture, you will use this feature quite a bit. There is no better way to complete a space or a layout on one level and then use that layout on another level by copying the geometry.

To practice using the Copy/Paste function, we will select the two lavatories on Level 1, copy them to the Windows clipboard, and paste them to the remaining floors:

1. Zoom into the east wing of the building.

2. Select the walls and doors that define both bathrooms, as shown in Figure 4.49. Also, select the corridor walls and the radial corridor wall at the east end of the building. Be sure to select the internal doors as well (see Figure 4.49).

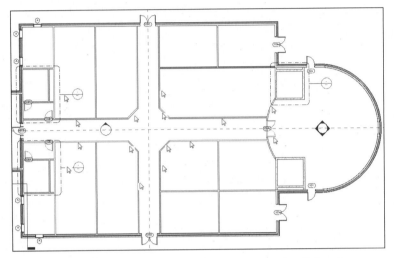

FIGURE 4.49 Selecting the items to be copied to the clipboard

3. Choose Copy To Clipboard from the Clipboard panel of the Modify | Multi-Select tab (or you can press Ctrl+V).

4. Go to a 3D view.

5. On the Clipboard panel of the Modify | Multi-Select panel, expand the Paste tool, and then click Aligned To Selected Levels, as shown in Figure 4.50.

6. In the next dialog, select Floor Plan: Levels 2 through 5, as shown in Figure 4.50.

7. Click OK.

Your model should look like Figure 4.51. If it doesn't, go back and try it again.

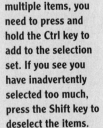

Remember, when you are selecting multiple items, you need to press and hold the Ctrl key to add to the selection set. If you see you have inadvertently selected too much, press the Shift key to deselect the items.

N O T E   Just because you copied and pasted identical items does not mean they are linked in any way. If you move, edit, or even delete any of the original walls, the new walls you pasted will not be affected.

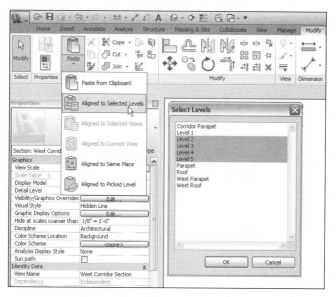

FIGURE 4.50 The Select Levels dialog allows you to choose to which levels you are pasting the information.

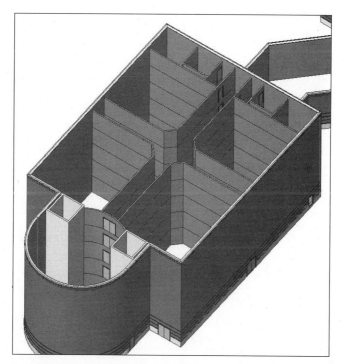

FIGURE 4.51 The east wing is starting to come together.

The last section in this chapter will focus on actual practice. We now have five floors in the east wing alone, and we must add a layout to them. We also need to add a layout to the west wing.

You Must Heed The Warning!

If you see a warning dialog while pasting elements that says you have just created a duplicate and double counting will occur, stop and undo the paste. Determine why Revit issued that warning. Did you already paste these elements to this level? Sometimes the top of the walls are above the level above. You can check this as well.

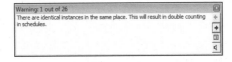

Creating the Plans

Now that you have added walls, doors, and windows, you can start to combine this experience with your knowledge of the basic Revit editing commands. In the previous section, you started to lay out the programs for your floor plans.

You can follow along with the book's examples up to floor 3. You can create your own plans for floors 4 and 5.

To get started, open the model you have been working on. If you have not completed the previous tasks, open the file called NER-14.rvt at the book's website, **www.sybex.com/go/revit2011ner**. Go to Chapter 4 to find the file.

To start building a floor plan to be copied to other levels, follow these steps:

1. In the Project Browser, go to Level 1 under Floor Plans.

2. Start adding walls, doors, openings, and windows to resemble Figure 4.52. These doors and windows can be any type you like. If your model varies slightly from the example in the book, don't be concerned.

3. In the Project Browser, go to Level 2.

4. Press Esc to clear any selection.

5. In the Properties dialog, set Underlay to None, as shown in Figure 4.53.

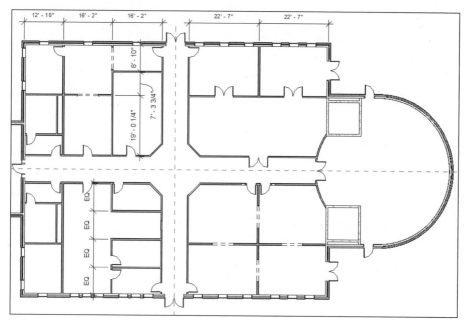

FIGURE 4.52 The first floor layout for the east wing

6. Create a floor plan layout similar to Figure 4.54. Make all of the dimensions as even and as round as possible. Use all the commands and functions you have learned up to this point.

7. For the windows, go to a 3D view, and using Copy/Paste, align them up all the way to Level 5. This way, you know your windows are aligned, and you can follow this procedure in your room layout for each floor (see Figure 4.55).

WARNING   When you use Copy/Paste, you may get the same Duplicate Value warning mentioned earlier. If you do, stop and undo. Make sure you are not pasting windows over the top of windows.

8. Go to Level 3, and create a floor plan similar to Figure 4.56. We did this by using Copy And Paste ➢ Aligned To Selected Levels from Level 1. We added one wall to the northeast suite.

9. Go to Level 4 and create your own floor plan. The book will give no example. You are on your own!

10. Create one more floor plan for Level 5. Again, design your own layout. Be as creative as you wish.

11. Save the model.

FIGURE 4.53 Switch Underlay from Level 1 to None.

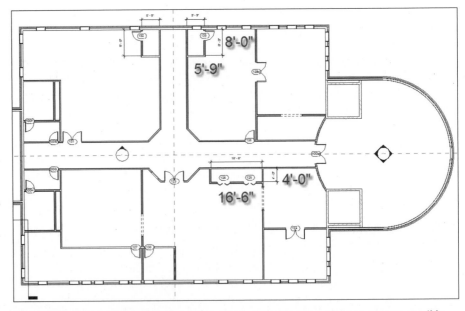

FIGURE 4.54 The layout for Level 2. Try to make the dimensions as even as possible, consistent with what is shown here.

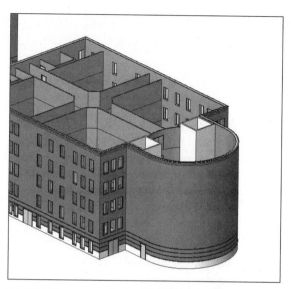

FIGURE 4.55 Using Copy/Paste, align the windows to the higher floors. This will influence your floor layout for each level.

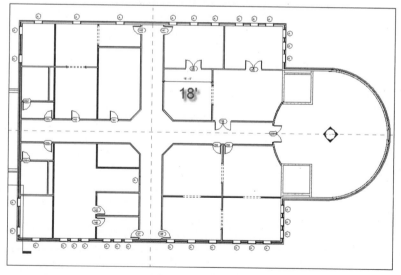

FIGURE 4.56 Level 3: This was mostly copied from Level 1 with the exception of the 18′-0″ room that was added.

If you got through that last procedure, and you are happy with the results, you are on your way to being efficient in Revit. This is because you just created a floor plan on your own. These last few steps were created to prove that Revit can be quite intuitive when approached with just a little experience.

If you are not comfortable with your results in this section, that's OK. I had an uncomfortable feeling the first time through, too. Take a deep breath, and go back through where you think you got lost. Feel free to send me an e-mail message if you have questions or concerns.

Are You Experienced?

Now you can...

- ☑ use common editing commands to alter the appearance of your model

- ☑ use reference planes to establish good, accurate methods of layout

- ☑ array items, and change the count, length, and radius if needed

- ☑ align items and keep them constrained

- ☑ use locks to constrain the alignment of one element to another

- ☑ split items to remove a segment or to turn one item into two

- ☑ use the Copy And Paste ➢ Aligned To Selected Levels commands to create multiple floors that are similar in layout

CHAPTER 5

Dimensioning and Annotating

The focus of this chapter is to give you the ability to dimension and annotate a model. After the novelty of having a really cool model in 3D wears off, you need to buckle down and produce some bid documents. This is where Revit must prove its functionality. You should ask yourself, "Can Revit produce drawings consistent with what is acceptable to national standards, and more importantly, my company's standards? And if so, how do I get to this point?" These are the questions the owners and managers will ask you. (If you are, in fact, an owner or a manager, I suppose you can still just ask yourself these questions.)

▶ **Dimensioning**

▶ **Using dimensions as a layout tool**

▶ **Placing text and annotations**

Dimensioning

The answers to these questions begin right here with dimensioning and annotations. This is where you can start to make Revit your own. Also, when it comes to dimensioning, you will find in this chapter that dimensions take on an entirely new role in the design process as well.

I think you will like dimensioning in Revit. It is almost fun. Almost. Before we get started, we should get one thing out of the way: you cannot alter a dimension to display an increment that is not true. Hooray! As you go through this chapter, you will quickly learn that when you place a dimension, it becomes not only an annotation but a layout tool as well.

The dimension command has five separate types: Aligned, Linear, Angular, Radial, and Arc Length. Each has its importance in adding dimensions to a model, and each will be covered separately.

Let's get started. To begin, open the file you have been following along with. If you did not complete the previous chapter, go to the book's website at **www.sybex .com/go/revit2011ner**. From there you can browse to Chapter 5 and find the file called NER-16.rvt.

Aligned Dimensions

The most popular of all the Revit Architecture dimensions is the Aligned dimension. This type of dimension will be used 75 percent of the time.

An aligned dimension in Revit allows you to place a dimension along an object at any angle. The resulting dimension will align with the object being dimensioned. A Linear dimension, however, will add a dimension only at 0, 90, 180, or 270 degrees regardless of the item's angle.

To add an aligned dimension, perform these steps:

1. Go to the Level 1 floor plan.

2. Zoom in on the east wing of the building.

3. On the Annotate tab, click the Aligned button, as shown in Figure 5.1.

4. On the Options bar, you will see a drop-down menu with some choices, as shown in Figure 5.2. Make sure that you have Wall Faces selected.

5. The next menu lets you pick individual references or entire walls. Select Entire Walls from the menu, as shown in Figure 5.2.

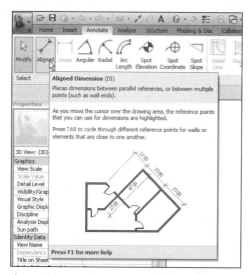

FIGURE 5.1 Starting the Dimension command from the Annotate tab

FIGURE 5.2 The Options bar for the Dimension command. Notice the Options button at the far right.

6. On the far right of the Options bar is an Options button, which leads you to options you can choose from when selecting the entire wall. Click the Options button.

7. In the Auto Dimensions Options dialog, select Intersecting Walls. Do not select any other item (see Figure 5.3), and then click OK.

8. Zoom in on the north wall, as shown in Figure 5.4.

9. Pick (left-click) the north exterior wall. Notice that the dimensions are completely filled out.

10. Pick a point (to place the dimension) approximately 8′ above the north wall (see Figure 5.4).

FIGURE 5.3 The Auto Dimension Options dialog

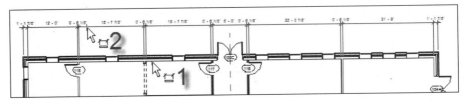

FIGURE 5.4 By choosing the Pick Entire Walls option, you can add an entire string of dimensions in one click.

11. In true Revit form, you are still in the command unless you tell Revit you do not want to be. In this case, click the Options button on the Options bar (the same one you clicked before).

12. Uncheck Intersecting Walls in the Auto Dimension Options dialog and click OK.

13. Pick (left-click) the same wall. You now have a dimension traveling the entire length of the building.

14. Move your cursor above the first dimension string you added. Notice the dimension will "click" once it gets directly above the first string.

15. When you see the dimension snap, pick that point (see Figure 5.5).

In many cases, you will need the ability to pick two points to create the dimension. What a world it would be if everything was as easy as the dimension string we just added. Unfortunately, it is not.

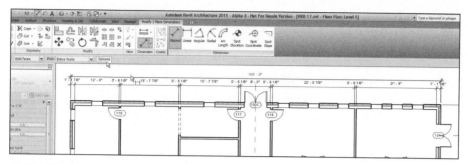

FIGURE 5.5 Adding a major dimension by turning off the Intersecting Walls choice in the Auto Dimension Options dialog

Aligned Dimensions by Picking Points

Nine times out of ten, you will be picking two points to create the dimension. Usually in Revit this is quite simple—until you get into a situation where the walls are at an angle that is not 90°. In a moment we will explore that issue, but for now, let's add some straight dimensions:

 WARNING Before you get started, note that this procedure is not easy. If it does come easily to you, great! If not, don't get discouraged. Keep trying.

1. Zoom in on the northeast portion of the east wing, as shown in Figure 5.6.

2. On the Annotate tab, click the Aligned button.

3. On the Options bar, choose Individual References from the Pick menu, as shown in Figure 5.6, and do the following:

   a. Pick the north wall.

   b. Pick the horizontal wall that ties into the radial wall, illustrated as "2" in Figure 5.6.

   c. Place the dimension about 8′ to the right of the vertical wall, as shown in Figure 5.6.

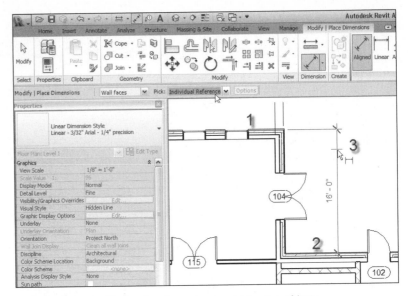

FIGURE 5.6   Placing the dimension by picking two objects

4. With the Aligned dimension command still running, pick the north wall again and do the following:

   a. Pick the outside face of the northern wall.

   b. Pick the centerline of the door, as shown in Figure 5.7, but do not press Esc, or terminate the command.

   c. Pick the horizontal wall that ties into the radial wall, illustrated as "3" in Figure 5.7.

   d. Pick a point inside (to the left of) the first dimension, as shown in Figure 5.7. This will place the dimension string and finalize the session.

 WARNING   When you add a string of dimensions, you must not stop and then resume the dimension string in the middle of the command. As you will see in a moment, when you add dimensions in a continuous line, there is a lot you can do in terms of making adjustments to the objects you are dimensioning.

You will now see that the actual dimension values are blue. Also, you will see a blue EQ icon with a dash through it. (Refer back to Figure 5.7.)

5. Click the blue EQ button, as shown in Figure 5.8. If the door was not exactly centered, this will force the door to move to an equal distance between the two walls.

6. Press Esc.

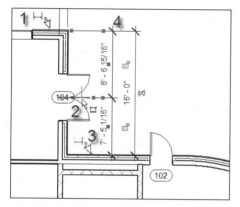

FIGURE 5.7 Adding a dimension string manually

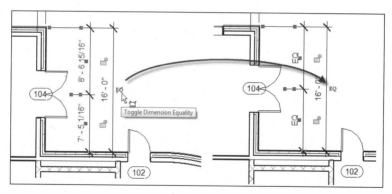

FIGURE 5.8 You can use the dimension string to move the door by clicking the EQ button.

Sometimes you may want to display the dimensions rather than the EQ that Revit shows as a default. To do so, follow along:

1. Select the dimension.

2. Right-click.

3. Choose EQ Display, as shown in Figure 5.9.

The dimensions will now show an increment.

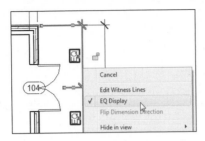

FIGURE 5.9 Toggle off the EQ Display.

Pretty cool. There is one last item involving aligned dimensions that we should address: How you dimension along an angle?

Dimensioning an Angle

No, not an "angel," an angle. Adding this type of aligned dimension is not the easiest thing to do in Revit. This is why we need to address the process as a separate item in this book.

1. Zoom in on the corridor area (the link area between the east and west wings).

2. On the Annotate tab, click the Aligned button on the Dimension panel.

3. On the Options bar, be sure Pick is set to Individual References.

4. Zoom in close to the intersection of the two walls, shown in Figure 5.10.

5. Hover your pointer over the core intersection, as shown in Figure 5.10.

6. Tap the Tab key until you see the square grip appear.

NOTE By tapping the Tab key, you tell Revit to filter through different points. When you arrive at the square grip, Revit can dimension the angled wall.

7. When the square grip appears, pick it (left-click), as shown in Figure 5.10.

8. Move to the other intersection of the angled wall.

9. Hover your cursor over this core intersection, as shown in Figure 5.11.

10. Tap the Tab key until you see the same square grip.

11. Pick the square grip.

12. Now the dimension is following your pointer. Pick a third point about 8' away from the angled wall, as shown in Figure 5.11.

13. On the left end of the Ribbon, select the Modify button. This will end the command.

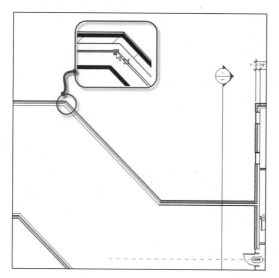

FIGURE 5.10 Press the Tab key to select the point shown.

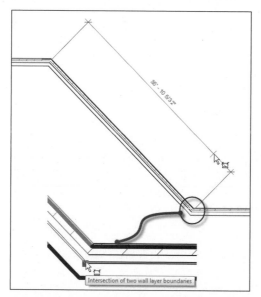

FIGURE 5.11 Picking the second point along the wall and placing the dimension

Unfortunately, we had to dimension to the core of the wall. This is the last place we would ever need to take a dimension from. At this point, the dimension needs to be "stretched" to the outside finished face of the brick, as you'll see next.

Editing the Witness Line

Every dimension in Revit Architecture has its own grip points when selected. This is similar to most CAD applications. Two of these grips control the witness line. The witness line is the line "attached" to the item being dimensioned. Because we had to take this dimension from the core of the wall, the witness lines need to be dragged to the outside face of the brick.

1. Select the angled dimension. Notice the blue grips appear.

2. On the left side of the dimension, pick and hold the grip in the middle of the dimension line, as shown in Figure 5.12.

3. Drag the blue grip to the outside face of the brick. You will know you are in the right spot because you will see a small dot appear, as shown in the magnified segment of Figure 5.12.

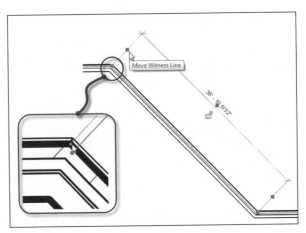

FIGURE 5.12 Dragging the witness lines grip

4. Repeat the procedure for the other side.

Trust me—this is worth practicing now, before you get into a live situation. If you have already run into this situation, you know exactly what I mean.

We need to look at one more procedure for tweaking an aligned dimension: overriding a dimension's precision.

Overriding the Precision

When you dimension a wall at an angle such as this, the dimension usually comes out at an uneven increment. In most cases, you do not want to override every dimension's precision just for this one, lone dimension to read properly. In this situation, you want to turn to the dimension's Type Properties:

1. Select the angled dimension.

2. In the Propertied dialog, click the Edit Type button as shown in Figure 5.13.

FIGURE 5.13: Clicking the Edit Type button to begin creating a new dimension style

3. Click the Duplicate button, as shown in Figure 5.14.

4. In the Name dialog box that opens, name the new dimension style **Linear - 3/32″ Arial - 1/4″ precision.** Click OK.

5. Scroll down to the Text category. There, near the bottom, you will see a row for Units Format. Next to the Units Format row is a button that displays a sample increment. Click it (see Figure 5.14).

6. Uncheck Use Project Settings.

7. Choose To the Nearest 1/4″ from the Rounding drop-down menu (see Figure 5.15).

8. Click OK twice.

9. Notice the dimension is now rounded to the nearest 1/4″. In this case, it is rounded to a whole number.

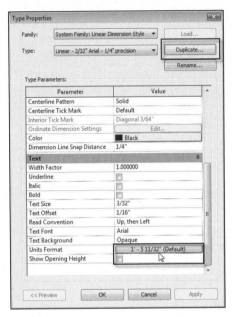

FIGURE 5.14 Select the button in the Text category to access the dimension's precision.

Although aligned dimensions will bear the brunt of your dimensioning, there are still plenty of other dimension types waiting for you to use.

FIGURE 5.15 Changing the dimension's precision. Notice some of the other available choices.

Linear Dimensions

Linear dimensions are used less frequently than most of the other dimensions. Unlike in AutoCAD, where linear dimensions are the go-to dimension, they are put on the bench for most of the game in Revit. The best use for a linear dimension is when you want to put a straight dimension across nonlinear (angled) geometry, as follows:

1. Zoom back in on the corridor area.

2. On the Annotate tab, select the Linear Dimension button. Notice that you cannot select the entire wall. That option has been taken away. Instead, Revit requires you to pick a point.

3. Move your cursor over the inside corner at the bottom intersection of the corridor, as shown in Figure 5.16. Make sure you are exactly over the exterior intersection of the brick. You will know you are there by the white dot that shows up, as shown in Figure 5.16.

4. Once you see the dot, pick the corner.

5. Pick the same spot on the other side end of the wall, as shown in Figure 5.17. When you pick the second corner, the dimension will follow your cursor in a straight direction.

6. Move your cursor to the left approximately 8′ past the first point that you picked, and pick the third point to place the dimension (see Figure 5.17).

7. Press Esc.

8. Select the new dimension.

9. In the Modify dimensions Properties dialog, select the Linear - 3/32″ Arial - 1/4″ style, as shown in Figure 5.18.

10. The dimension is now rounded to the nearest 1/4″.

Aligned and linear dimensions are the two dimension styles that pertain to straight dimensioning. The next three dimension procedures add dimensions to angled and radial geometry.

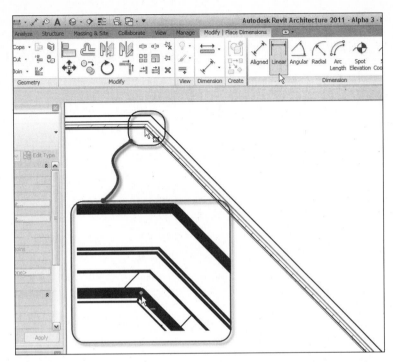

FIGURE 5.16 Selecting the finished exterior corner of the brick. You will see a small white dot appear, indicating you can pick the start of the dimension.

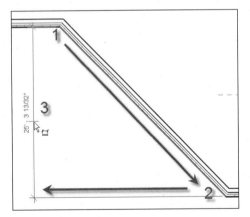

FIGURE 5.17 When you add a linear dimension to an angled wall, you will get a straight dimension.

FIGURE 5.18 Changing the dimension to reflect the new rounded dimension

Angular Dimensions

Angular dimensioning comes close to needing no introduction at all. But I will introduce it anyway.

Angular dimensions are used to calculate and record the angle between two items. These two items are usually walls. Of course, we will add an angular dimension to our lovely corridor walls:

1. Zoom back in on the corridor if you are not there already.

2. On the Annotate tab, select the Angular Dimension button, as shown in Figure 5.19.

3. For the first wall, pick the finished inside face of the upper-left corridor wall, as marked by "1" in Figure 5.19.

4. Pick the finished inside face of the angled corridor wall, as marked by "2" in Figure 5.19.

5. Move your cursor to the left about 8′, and place the dimension as marked by "3" in Figure 5.19.

6. Press Esc.

7. Repeat the steps for the bottom of the corridor.

8. Add the rest of the dimensions, as shown in Figure 5.20. This will complete the dimensioning of the corridor area.

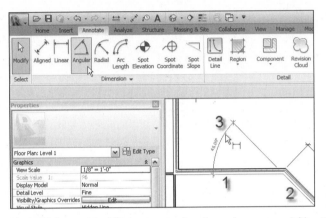

FIGURE 5.19 Placing an angular dimension means picking two walls, then a point to place the dimension.

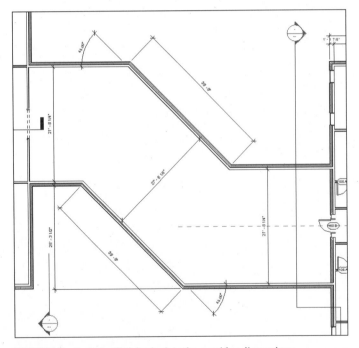

FIGURE 5.20 Finish placing the corridor dimensions.

If you would like to place the dimensions in different locations, feel free to do so.

The next set of dimensions will pertain to radial geometry. We can finally get out of this corridor!

Radial Dimensions

Radial dimensions are used to, well, measure the radius of an item. We are lucky that Revit knows that you are adding a radial dimension to a building component. This means the many different choices provided by a CAD application are taken away, leaving just the basics.

The following procedure will lead you through adding a radial dimension:

1. Zoom in on the east radial entry in the east wing.

2. On the Annotate tab, select the Radial Dimension button.

3. Pick the outside face of the radial wall, as shown in Figure 5.21.

4. Place the radial dimension somewhere that makes sense. If your model looks like Figure 5.21, you may proceed. If it does not, go back and try it again.

5. Pan all the way to the west radial end of the west wing, as shown in Figure 5.22.

Keep in mind that you can add an angular dimension to physically change the angle of the items being dimensioned. Use caution, however, and be sure the correct items are being moved when you alter the angle.

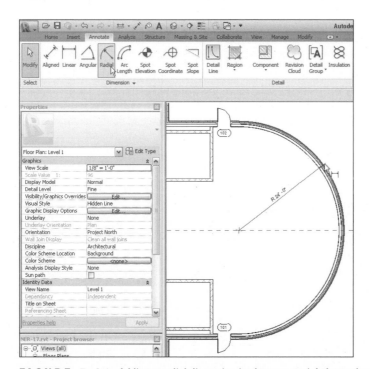

FIGURE 5.21 Adding a radial dimension is about as straightforward as it gets.

6. On the Annotate tab, select the Radial Dimension button.

7. Dimension to the finished outside face of the brick, and place your dimension in a location similar to that shown in Figure 5.22.

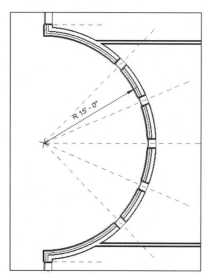

FIGURE 5.22 Adding the second radial dimension

 W A R N I N G   All too often, you can easily dimension from the wrong reference point. The reason this book is using a wall with a concrete ledge below the brick is to expose you to the fact that you need to be very deliberate in how and where you choose your references for dimensions. Don't be afraid to zoom in and out as you add your dimensions.

If you are careful in how you add a radial dimension, you will find this process quite simple. The next type of dimension, however, can be a little tricky.

Arc Length Dimensions

Measuring the length of an arc is a handy capability that was added back in the 2009 release. I have found the Arc Length dimension extremely useful in locating items such as windows along an arc. That is, in fact, what we need to do in the west wing of the building.

The following procedure will lead you through adding an Arc Length dimension:

1. Zoom in on the west radial entry of the west wing, as shown in Figure 5.23.

2. On the Annotate tab, select the Arc Length button, as shown at the top left of Figure 5.23.

3. Pick the finish face exterior face of the brick.

4. Pick the centerline of the window.

5. Pick a point along the exterior face of brick that runs along the vertical intersecting wall, illustrated as "3" in Figure 5.23.

6. Pick a point in which to place the dimension.

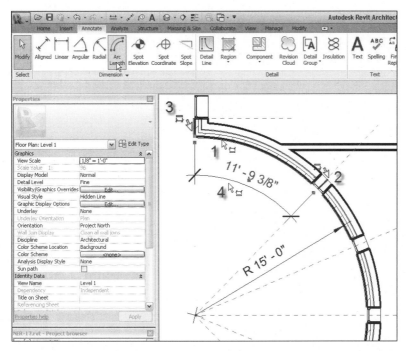

FIGURE 5.23 Placing an Arc Length dimension involves four separate picks.

Let's try it again. This time the dimension will be taken from the first window (the one we just dimensioned) to the second window. The process will be exactly the same.

1. On the Annotate tab, select the Arc Length button if you are not still in the command.

2. Pick the exterior face of brick along the radial wall.

3. Pick the first window's centerline.

4. Pick the second window's centerline.

5. Pick a point to place the dimension (see Figure 5.24.).

Now that you have experience adding dimensions to record placement of items, it is time to see how you can physically use dimensions as a layout tool.

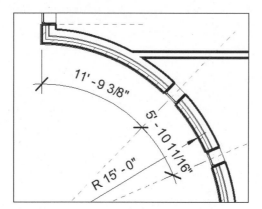

FIGURE 5.24 Adding a second Arc Length dimension

Using Dimensions as a Layout Tool

When it comes to dimensions, using them as a layout tool is my favorite topic. "Okay, fine," you may say. "I can do that in CAD." Well, not quite. You see, in Revit you cannot alter a dimension to read an increment that is not accurate. You can, however, select the item you are dimensioning, and then type a new number in the dimension. At that point, the item you are dimensioning will move. The result is an accurate dimension.

The first task we need to explore is how to equally constrain a string of dimensions. You were exposed to this task earlier in the chapter, but now, let's really dig in and gain some tangible experience using this tool.

To begin, open the file you have been following along with. If you did not complete the previous chapter, go to the book's web page at **www.sybex.com/go/revit2011ner**. From there you can browse to Chapter 5 and find the file called NER-17.rvt.

For this procedure, we will add some more walls to the west wing, and then constrain them using the EQ dimension function:

1. In the Project Browser, go the Level 1 floor plan (not a ceiling plan!).

2. Zoom in to the west wing of the building.

3. Select one of the interior corridor walls, right-click, and select Create Similar from the context menu.

4. Draw five walls, as shown in Figure 5.25. They do not have to be an equal distance from one another.

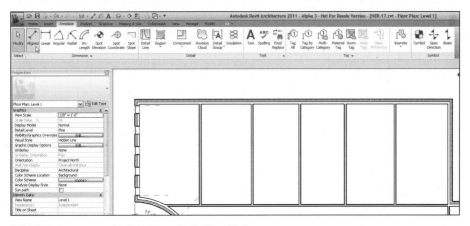

FIGURE 5.25 Adding the walls "willy-nilly"

5. On the Annotate tab, click the Aligned Dimension button.

6. Also on the Options bar, be sure the justification is set to Center Of Core (see Figure 5.26).

FIGURE 5.26 Changing the options for the dimension

7. Zoom in on the left exterior wall, as shown in Figure 5.27.

8. Hover your pointer over the wall. Notice Revit is trying to locate the center of the wall? In this instance, we do not want this (even though we just told Revit to do that).

9. We want Revit to start this dimension string using the interior face of the finished wall. To do this, hover your pointer over the inside face of the wall, as shown in Figure 5.27.

10. When your cursor is over the inside face of the wall, tap the Tab key on your keyboard three times until Revit highlights the inside face of the wall.

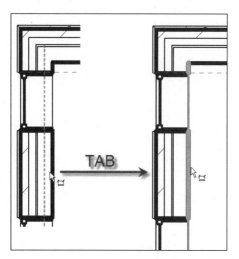

FIGURE 5.27 Press the Tab key to filter to the desired reference of the wall.

11. Pick the inside face of the wall.

12. Move your cursor to the right until you pass over the first interior wall. Notice the core centerline of the interior wall highlights. When you see this, pick the wall, as shown in Figure 5.28.

WARNING Just like when we equally constrained the door in the previous procedure, you need to keep the Dimension command running. If you press Esc, undo the last dimension and start over.

13. After you pick the first interior partition, move to the right and pick the center of the next wall.

14. Repeat the procedure until you get to the last wall (see Figure 5.28).

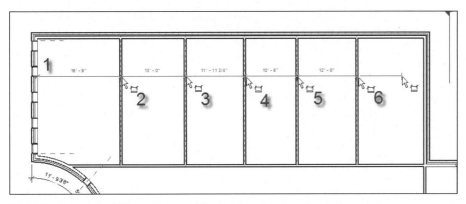

FIGURE 5.28 Adding a string of dimensions to the interior walls

When you get to the exterior wall to the right, you will encounter the same issue. You want this string of dimensions to go to the inside face, not the core of the exterior wall:

1. Hover your cursor over the inside face of the wall and tap the Tab key on your keyboard until the inside face of the wall becomes highlighted. When it does, pick the highlighted face of the wall, as shown in Figure 5.29.

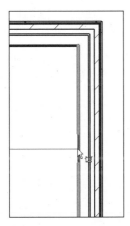

FIGURE 5.29 Press Tab to locate the inside face of the wall.

2. When you locate the inside face, pick it.

3. Move your cursor up the view. Notice the entire dimension string is following.

4. Placing a dimension in Revit is a little awkward, but you will get the hang of it. You need to pick a point away from the last dimension in the string, as shown in Figure 5.30, almost as if you are trying to pick another item that is not there. When you do this, the dimension will be in place.

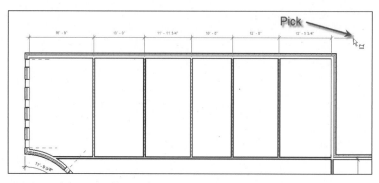

FIGURE 5.30   Picking a point away from the last dimension to place the string

Now that the dimension string is in place, it is time to move these walls to be equal distances apart from one another. Notice that, after you placed the dimension string, the familiar blue icons appeared. We can use them:

1. Find the EQ icon in the middle of the dimension string and pick it. The slash through it is now gone and the walls have moved, as shown in Figure 5.31.

2. Press Esc twice to release the selection and exit the Aligned Dimension command.

If you placed the dimension string, then escaped out of the command, that's fine. You can simply select the string of dimensions again, and you will be back in business.

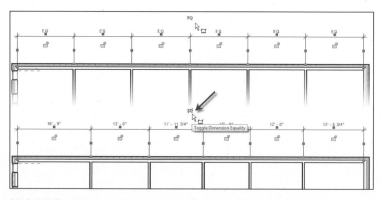

FIGURE 5.31   Before and after the EQ icon is selected

Because these walls are not constrained to always be equal, if one exterior wall is moved, these five interior partitions will always maintain an equal relationship to one another—that is, as long as this dimension string is still associated with the walls.

In Revit Architecture, you can choose to keep the walls constrained or to use the dimension only as a tool to move the walls around.

Constraining the Model

Choices you make early in the design process, such as constraining a model, can either greatly benefit or greatly undermine the project's flow. As you gain more experience using Revit Architecture, you will start hearing the term overconstrained. This is a term for a model that has been constrained in so many places that any movement of the model forces multiple warnings and, in many cases, errors that cannot be ignored.

Given that, how you choose to constrain your model is up to you. You will learn how to constrain (and of course *un*constrain) your model in this chapter, but deciding when and where to constrain your model will vary from project to project.

The string of equal dimensions we now have in place has created a constraint with these walls. To unconstrain them, follow along:

1. Select the dimension string.

2. Press the Delete key on your keyboard.

OUT OF SIGHT, OUT OF MIND

In CAD, you typed **E**, then pressed Enter to delete an item. This is no longer a good idea. If you do this to an item in Revit Architecture, it will only remove that element from the current view—not from the entire model. You are better off either selecting the item and pressing the Delete key on the keyboard, or selecting the item and clicking the delete icon, as shown in the following image:

3. Revit will now give you a warning, as shown in Figure 5.32. You must then choose whether or not to unconstrain the elements.

FIGURE 5.32 A Revit warning pertaining to the constraint of the walls

If you select Unconstrain, the EQ dimension will disappear as well as any constraint on the walls. If you move the exterior wall, the newly spaced walls will not reposition themselves.

4. Click OK. You will learn how to unconstrain these walls in a different method.

5. Select one of the interior walls that were part of the EQ dimension string.

6. On the Options bar, select the Activate Dimensions button, as shown in Figure 5.33.

N O T E   Sometimes, when you select an item that is being constrained, the dimensions will already be activated, and the Options bar won't provide the Activate Dimensions button. If you do not see the Activate Dimensions button on the Options bar for this example, your dimensions have been activated already.

7. With the temporary dimensions showing, you will now see the EQ icon. Click this icon, and it will release the constraint set for the walls. You are now free to move around the building. (Note that the EQ icon may be hiding behind a wall in the middle of the array.)

T I P   Notice in Figure 5.33 the anchor icon to the left of the dimensions. You use this icon to determine which wall will remain stationary. You can move the anchor icon to any of the items involved in the constraint. For example, if you click and drag the anchor to the middle partition, then move one of the exterior walls, the middle partition will stay in place while the other walls move an equal distance to the right and left of the anchored wall.

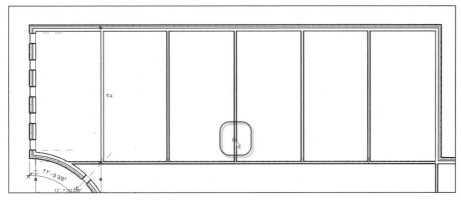

FIGURE 5.33 Activating the dimensions

Now that you have experience with dimension equality constraints, it is time to learn about a different type of constraint that involves locking items together at a distance.

Locking a Dimension

Sometimes you may want to always hold a dimension, no matter what else is going on around it. You can do this by physically adding a dimension to an item, then locking that dimension in place. For example, if you want to lock the middle space to a specific dimension, you simply add a dimension and lock it down. Sound easy? It is!

1. On the Annotate tab, click the Aligned Dimension button.

2. On the Options bar, change the alignment to Wall Faces, as shown in Figure 5.34.

3. Pick the inside faces of the two middle partitions, as shown in the upper left of Figure 5.34.

4. After you place the dimension, a blue padlock icon will appear. When it does, pick it. It should then change to an unlocked padlock icon. Once you see this, press Esc twice to terminate the command.

5. Select the left wall that has been dimensioned.

6. Move the wall to the right 2′–0″. Notice the right wall moves as well. Note that if you get a "constraints are not satisfied" message, you need to go back and "un-EQ" the five walls.

7. Click the Undo button, as shown in Figure 5.35.

8. Delete the dimension.

9. When you get the warning, click the Unconstrain button.

10. Save the model.

11. Add doors and windows to the plan, as shown in Figure 5.36. They can be any type of door or window you choose—just try to keep them similar to the ones in Figure 5.36. Also, placement does not matter. We will adjust this in the next procedure.

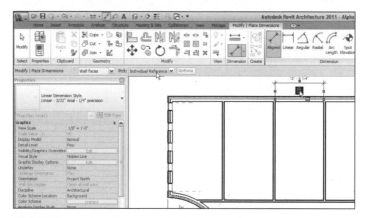

FIGURE 5.34 You can add a dimension and lock the distance between two items.

FIGURE 5.35 Click the Undo button.

In the next section, we will start using dimensions as a tool to physically move elements around. Although this one might seem like an exercise in futility, the practice is quite relevant to what you will deal with when you are on a project.

Using Dimensions to Move Objects

As I have mentioned before, you cannot type over a dimension and cause the value in that dimension to be inaccurate. Revit does provide tools to get around this. When you add a dimension and select the object being dimensioned, your

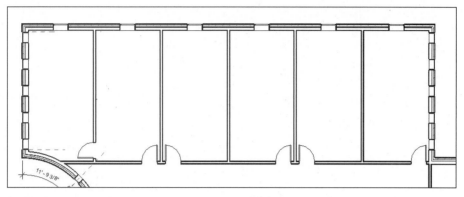

FIGURE 5.36 Adding doors and windows to the floor plan

dimension will turn blue. This is a temporary dimension, which can be edited. Consequently, the object being dimensioned will move.

The objective of this procedure is to select an item and modify the temporary dimension, in effect moving the object:

1. Zoom in on the left side of the west wing, as shown in Figure 5.37.

2. Select the door, as shown in Figure 5.37. Notice there is a blue dimension on both sides of the door. These are temporary dimensions.

3. Pick the blue text in the temporary dimension, as shown in Figure 5.37. (The text might be obscured by the wall, but if you hover over it, it will activate and then you can select it.)

4. Type 1. (This is the equivalent of 1'–0".) The door will move.

5. Press the Esc key to release the door.

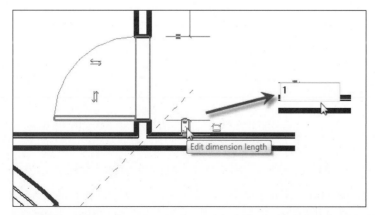

FIGURE 5.37 When you type a different value, the temporary dimension will move the object.

This procedure used a temporary dimension that appeared when you selected the item. After you edited the dimension, it went away. In the next procedure, we will add a permanent dimension and do the same thing.

1. On the Annotate tab, select the Aligned Dimension button.

2. Place a dimension between the door and the wall, as shown in Figure 5.38.

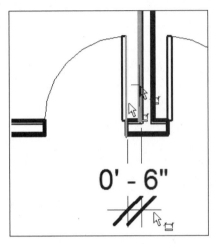

FIGURE 5.38 Placing a dimension

3. Press the Esc key twice.

4. Select the door. Notice the dimension turns small and blue. It is now ready to be modified, as shown in Figure 5.39.

5. When you see the dimension turn blue, select the text and type 1 (1′–0″). The door will adjust to the 1′–0″ increment.

6. Press the Esc key.

7. Select the dimension.

8. Notice there is a blue grip just underneath the text. Pick the grip and move the text out from between the extension lines, as shown in Figure 5.40. Notice Revit will place a leader (an arrow line extending from the model to your text) in the text.

The process of using dimensions to move objects will take some getting used to. The next procedure will delve into making further modifications to dimensions, and a nice fail-safe procedure embedded within the dimension properties.

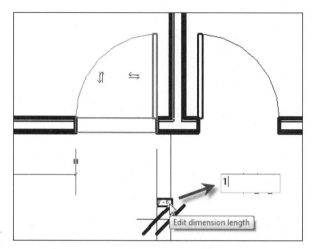

FIGURE 5.39 Making adjustments with the actual dimension

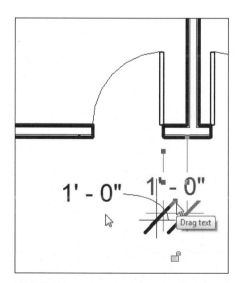

FIGURE 5.40 By grip-editing the text, you can slide it to a cleaner location. Revit will automatically place a leader for the text to the dimension line.

Dimension Text Overrides

The fact that Revit displays temporary dimensions lends itself to another common process: the double-check. All you need to do in Revit Architecture is select any item, and the temporary dimensions will appear. (If not, remember to click Activate Dimensions on the Options bar.) You can simply look at the dimension. If it reads the value you expected, great! If not, change it. It's that simple.

Although I just told you that you can't override a dimension, the following steps get around that problem. In many cases you may want text or, more commonly, a prefix or a suffix within a dimension. You can do all three can in Revit Architecture.

1. Select the 1'–0" dimension.

2. Notice the text turns blue. As you know, blue means that this item is editable in Revit. Pick the text. You should see the dialog in Figure 5.41.

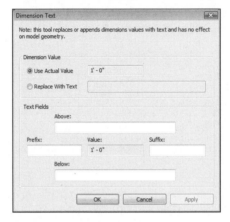

FIGURE 5.41 The Dimension Text dialog

3. Under Dimension Value, click Override Replace With Text, as shown in Figure 5.42.

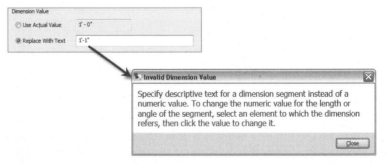

FIGURE 5.42 Any numeric value will trigger a warning in Revit. You simply cannot type a value over a dimension.

4. Type 1′–1″ and press Enter.

5. You will get an error. Revit will not allow you to do such a foolish thing. Click OK.

6. Click Use Actual Value, as shown in Figure 5.43.

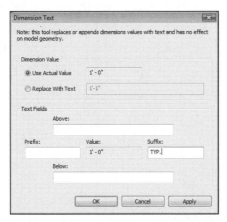

FIGURE 5.43 Under Dimension Value choose Use Actual Value, and type **TYP.** as the suffix.

7. Under Suffix, type TYP., as shown in Figure 5.43.

8. Click OK.

As a closing practice for dimensioning, move the rest of the doors along this wall to a 1′–0″ increment from the finished inside face of the wall to the door opening. Also, dimension the floor plan as shown in Figure 5.44 and Figure 5.45.

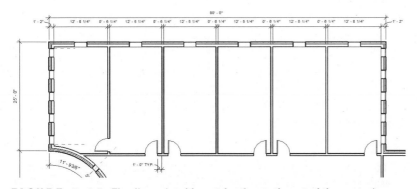

FIGURE 5.44 The dimensional layout for the north part of the west wing

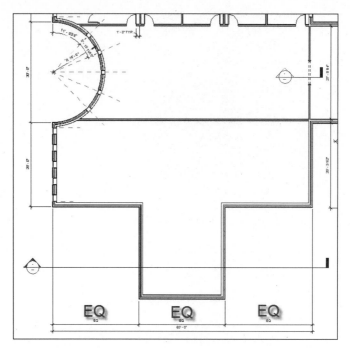

FIGURE 5.45 The dimensional layout for the south part of the west wing

Placing Text and Annotations

Text in Revit Architecture is going to be a love/hate relationship for every Revit user. You will love it, because it will automatically scale with the view's scale. You will hate it because the text editor is something of a throwback from an earlier CAD application. Either way, the procedure for adding text does not change with your feelings toward it.

To begin, open the file you have been following along with. If you did not complete the previous chapter, go to the book's web page at **www.sybex.com/go/ revit2011ner**. From there you can browse to Chapter 5 and find the file called NER-18.rvt.

The objective of this procedure is to simply add text to the model, format it, and then add and format a leader:

1. In the Project Browser, go to the Level 1 floor plan.

2. Zoom in on the east wing's radial entry area where the elevator shafts are, as shown in Figure 5.46.

3. On the Text panel of the Annotate tab, click the Text button, as shown in Figure 5.47.

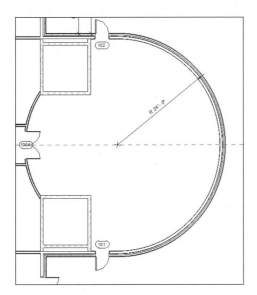

FIGURE 5.46 The radial entry

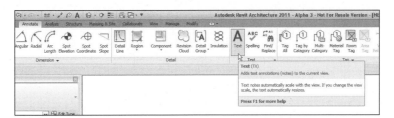

FIGURE 5.47 Click the Text button on the Text panel of the Annotate tab.

4. In the Type Properties dialog select Text : 3/32″ Arial.

5. On the Leader panel you get choices for a leader. For this example, select the None button. It is the button with the A on it, as shown in Figure 5.48.

6. To place the text, you need to pick a window. Pick the point labeled "1" in Figure 5.48.

7. Pick the point labeled "2" in Figure 5.48.

8. Type **CMU SHAFT WALL**.

9. Click a point in the view outside of the text box. You now have a note in the model.

10. Press the Esc key twice.

11. Select the text.

12. On the Options Format panel, review the choices you have to add a leader to the text.

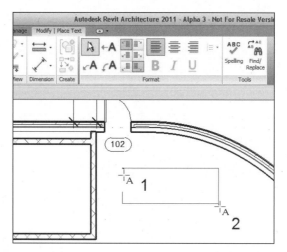

FIGURE 5.48 To place leader-less text, you must pick a window.

13. Click the Add Left Side Straight Leader button, as shown in Figure 5.49. It adds a leader to the left end of the text.

14. By clicking the grips and moving the text around, configure the text and the leader to resemble Figure 5.49.

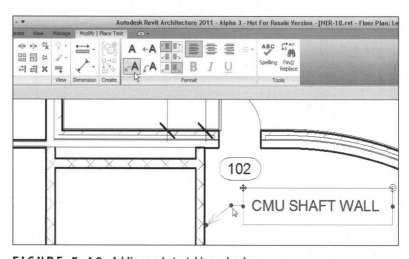

FIGURE 5.49 Adding and stretching a leader

Adding Leader Text

You can add text to a model by placing a leader first and then adding the text within the same command. Although in Revit you can add leaders to all text, you can choose to add text to a model with or without a leader.

The objective of the following steps is to place text with a leader:

1. On the Basics Text panel of the Annotate tab, select the Text button.

2. On the Options bar, click the Two Segments button, as shown in Figure 5.50.

3. Pick a point near the radial wall, as shown in Figure 5.50.

4. Pick a second point similar to "2" shown in Figure 5.50.

5. Pick a third point just to the right of the second point.

6. Type **FULL HEIGHT RADIAL WALL**.

7. Click an area outside of the text.

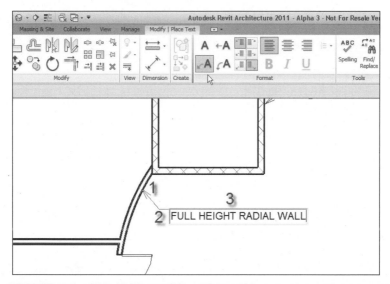

FIGURE 5.50 Adding a piece of leader text

Now that you can add text to a model, it is time to investigate how to modify the text after you add it. We can start with that arrowhead on the end of the leader.

Changing the Leader Type

It almost seems as though Revit uses the ugliest leader as a default, forcing you to change it immediately. The large arrowhead you see in Figure 5.50 is not the only arrowhead Revit provides—had that been the case, Revit would never have even gotten off the ground!

To change the arrowhead that Revit uses with a text item, follow this procedure:

1. On the Text panel of the Annotate tab, you will see a small arrow pointing down and to the right, as shown in Figure 5.51. Click it.

2. Change the Leader Arrowhead parameter to Arrow Filled 15 Degree, as shown in Figure 5.51.

3. Click OK.

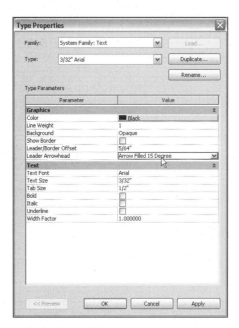

FIGURE 5.51 Changing the leader arrowhead

 TIP You will not always have to change your leader. You should set up leaders in your template before you begin. Refer to Chapter 23, "BIM Management," for management issues regarding templates.

Now that's a handsome-looking arrowhead. The next item to address is how to modify the placement of text after you add it to the model.

Modifying the Text Placement

With any text item in Revit, you can select the text in your model, and you will see grips for adjusting text: two grips on the text box, two on the leader, and a rotate icon.

Your next objective is to modify the text placement and to make the necessary adjustments.

1. Select the text you just added to the model.

2. Pick the right blue grip.

3. Stretch the text window to the left until it forces the text to wrap, as shown in Figure 5.52.

   Observe the rotate icon. You don't need to rotate the text here, but notice it is there for future reference.

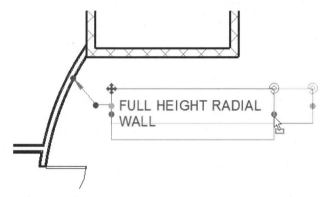

FIGURE 5.52 Wrapping the text using the right grip

Modifying the placement of text is a straightforward process. Changing the actual font and size of the text in a model is another story, and involves further investigation.

Text Properties

Of course, you can change the font for text. You can also change the height and the width. Keep in mind, however, that the text height you specify is the actual text height you want to see on the sheet. You no longer have to multiply the desired text height to a line type scale. Revit understands that text is scaled based on the view's scale. This process is eliminated for you.

To modify the text appearance, run through the following procedure:

1. Pick the Text Types arrow in the corner of the Text panel as you did when you changed the leader type.

2. Click Duplicate.

3. Call the new text **3/16″ Tahoma**.

4. Click OK.

5. Change the Text Font setting to Tahoma.

6. Change the Text Size setting to **3/16″** (see Figure 5.53).

7. Change the Width Factor setting to .8.

8. Click OK twice.

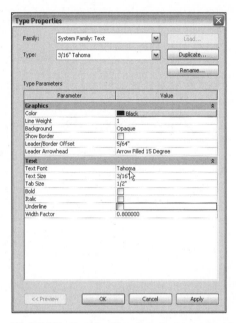

FIGURE 5.53 Changing the text values in the Type Properties dialog

You have now successfully changed the text. Of course, this large, nonuniform text is not proper in this context. You can change that easily:

1. Select the text you just changed to Tahoma.

2. In the Type Properties dialog menu on the Options bar, select 3/32″ Arial. This will change the text back to the Arial text, keeping the new text type available for another time.

I WANT TO CHANGE A BUNCH OF TEXT AT ONCE!

Now you can. New to Revit 2011, you can use the new Find/Replace feature, shown here:

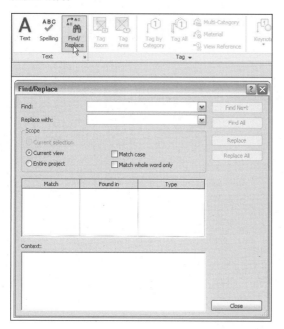

Revit does not use an SHX font. As a matter of fact, SHX cannot be used at all in Revit. It was invented by Autodesk, but only works with AutoCAD. Keep this in mind when you are setting up your company's templates. If you are using an SHX font, you will need to find an alternate font, or allow Revit to convert it to Arial. If not, this will cause issues in text formatting.

Are You Experienced?

Now you can...

☑ add a multitude of different types of dimensions to your model by simply altering the options associated with the dimension command

☑ equally constrain items in a model by adding a string of dimensions and clicking the EQ button

☑ use your dimensions as a layout tool, keeping the items constrained even after the dimension is deleted

☑ add text to a model by starting either with a leader or just a paragraph of text

☑ change the text type and arrowhead type for leader text

CHAPTER 6

Floors

It is going to be hard to convince you that floors are easy when an entire chapter is dedicated to this lone aspect of Revit Architecture. Well, floors *are* easy. The reason I'm dedicating an entire chapter to the subject is because we need to address a lot of aspects about floors.

▶ **Placing a floor slab**

▶ **Building a floor by layers**

▶ **Splitting the floor materials**

▶ **Pitching a floor to a floor drain**

▶ **Creating shaft openings**

Placing a Floor Slab

Adding a floor to a model is quite simple indeed, but in Revit Architecture, we are truly modeling this floor. That means that you can include the structure and the finish when you create your floor. When you cut a section through this floor, you get an almost perfect representation of your floor system and how it relates to adjacent geometry, such as walls.

Floors, of course, are more than large slabs of concrete; therefore, you'll also be introduced to creating materials, and you'll learn how to pitch these materials to floor drains. Further, you will examine how to create sloped slabs as well.

The first area we will explore is how to place a slab into your model. It is as simple as it sounds, but you must follow certain steps, which I'll outline next.

As you've learned up to this point, in Revit Architecture you do need to add items the way Revit wants you to add them, or you will probably generate errors or, worse, inaccuracies in your model.

To begin, open the file you have been following along with. If you did not complete the previous chapter, go to the book's web page at **www.sybex.com/go/ revit2011ner**. From there you can browse to Chapter 6 and find the file called NER-19.rvt.

The objective of the following procedure is to create a floor slab to be placed into the model:

1. In your Project Browser, go to the Level 1 floor plan.

2. In the Level 1 floor plan, zoom in to the west wing.

3. On the Home tab, select the Floor button, as shown in Figure 6.1.

4. In the Properties dialog, switch from Floor Plan: Level 1 to Floors, as shown in Figure 6.2.

5. At the top-right of the dialog, you will see an Edit Type button. Click it (see Figure 6.3).

    You are now accessing the Type Properties. This means that any change you make here will affect every slab of this type in the entire model.

 T I P   At this point, you always want to either create a new floor system or rename the current one. This will avert much confusion down the line when you have a floor called Generic - 12″ and it is actually a 6″ concrete slab on grade.

6. Click the Rename button, as shown in Figure 6.4.

7. Call it **6″ Slab on Grade**.

8. Click OK.

9. Change Function to Exterior, as shown in Figure 6.5.

10. In the Structure row, there is a long Edit button, as shown in Figure 6.5. Click it.

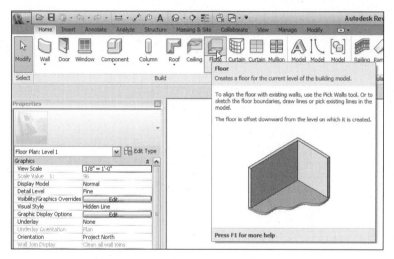

FIGURE 6.1 The Floor button on the Home tab

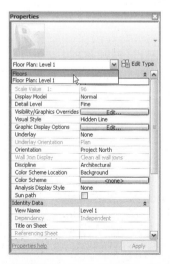

FIGURE 6.2 Changing the focus of the properties

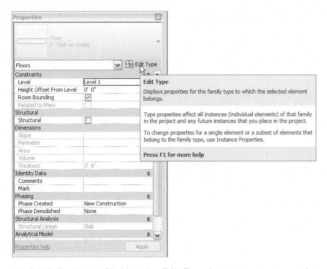

FIGURE 6.3 Clicking the Edit Type button to start creating a new floor slab

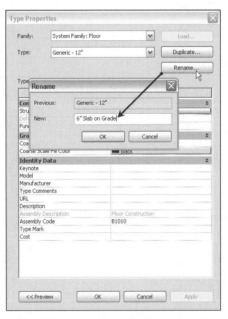

FIGURE 6.4 Renaming the current floor. You will never have a Generic 12″ floor in your model, so it is a good idea not to keep this floor around.

You are now in the Edit Assembly dialog. This is where you can specify a thickness for your slab. You can add layers of materials here as well.

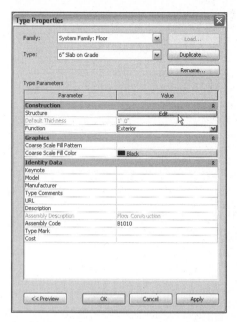

FIGURE 6.5 Clicking the Edit button to access the structure of the floor

In the middle of the Edit Assembly dialog is a large spreadsheet-type field that is divided into rows and columns. The rows are defined by a structural component, and include a boundary above and below the structure. It is the Structure row that we are interested in here:

1. You will see that the Structure row is divided into columns. Click into the Material column within the Structure row, as shown in Figure 6.6.

2. You will see a small [...] button appear when you click into the Material cell. This is an indication that you will be given a menu if selected. Click the [...] button.

The term *layer* may throw you off a bit. Revit uses layer here to describe a component of the floor. This is not to be mistaken with the AutoCAD layer.

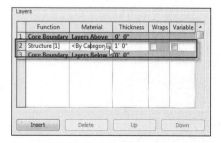

FIGURE 6.6 By clicking in the Material cell within the Structure row, you can access the Materials dialog.

3. You can now choose a material from the menu. Scroll down until you arrive at Concrete - Cast-in-Place Concrete, and select it. Notice that to the right you can see that this material will display two different hatches. There is a sand hatch that will be visible for floor plans, and a concrete hatch that is visible for sections (see Figure 6.7). These hatches allow a filling region to graphically designate specific materials.

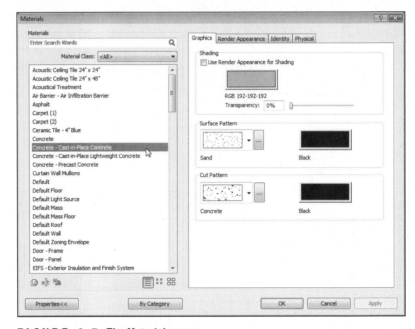

FIGURE 6.7 The Materials menu

4. Make sure Concrete - Cast-in-Place Concrete is selected, and click OK.

5. Directly to the right of the Material column is a Thickness column. Currently there is a value of 1′–0″. Click into the cell that says 1′–0″, and change it to 6″.

T I P   If you just type 6 and press Enter, you will wind up with a 6′–0″-thick slab. Be sure to add the inch (″) mark after the 6. The value needs to read 6″.

6. Click OK.

7. Click OK again to get back to the model.

Now that the slab has been created, we can place it into the model. You will notice that your Design bar has changed to Edit mode. You will now proceed to sketch the slab in place.

Sketching the Slab

You will have to adjust to the way Revit wants you to proceed with the Create Floor Boundary tab; you are basically limited to the choices provided in this menu. Not to fear, you should have plenty of choices, but you will still need to get a "feel" for how Revit works.

Here's what needs to happen: you must draw the perimeter of the slab into the model. Because this is basically a slab on grade, we will pour the concrete to the inside finished face of the wall. We won't worry about a control joint between the wall and the slab at this point.

Picking Walls

The best way to add a slab is to use the Pick Walls button as much as possible (see Figure 6.8). In doing so, you tell Revit that this edge of slab needs to move if this wall moves.

Let's start sketching the slab:

1. In the Modify | Create Floor Boundary tab, click the Pick Walls button, as shown in Figure 6.8.

F I G U R E   6 . 8 Pick Walls ensures that that edge of your slab will move if the wall moves.

2. With the Pick Walls tool running, hover your mouse over the inside face of the wall, as shown in Figure 6.9.

3. After the wall becomes highlighted and you are sure you are on the inside of the wall, pick it (see Figure 6.9).

4. With the inside face of the wall picked, you need to move on to the next wall. Pick the inside face of the north wall.

   Notice that as you pick the walls, a magenta "sketch line" appears on the inside face of the walls. This is another indicator telling you whether you are on the correct side of the wall.

WATCH WHAT YOU PICK!

As you pick the walls to place your edge of slab, be careful. If you do not pick the inside face, there is a chance Revit will try to extend the slab to the core of the wall. If you zoom into the area that you are picking, you will see an alignment line appear. Make sure this line is where you want it, as shown in the following image:

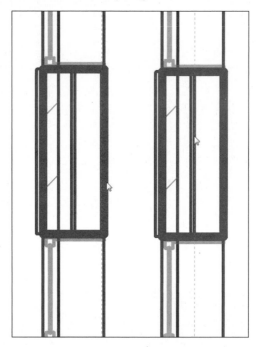

5. Keep picking the walls, as shown in Figure 6.10. You need to have a continuous loop— no gaps and no overlaps.

6. Apply some basic modify commands as well. For the right lower corner, use the Trim command to clean the corner. For the bottom line where the jog occurs, use the Split Element command (make sure the Delete Inner Segment button is checked on the Options bar).

7. After you have picked the perimeter of the west wing, click Finish Edit Mode on the Modify | Create Floor Boundary tab, as shown in Figure 6.11. It may be a good idea to check out your model in 3D just to make sure nothing went wrong. (I constantly have to do that.)

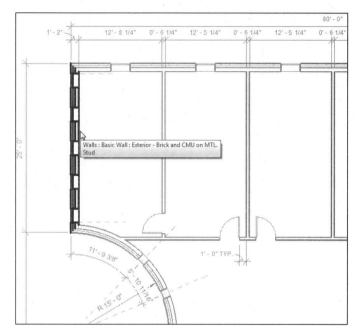

FIGURE 6.9 Picking the inside face of the first wall

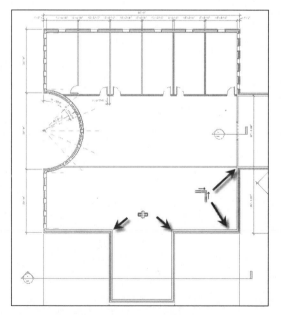

FIGURE 6.10 Selecting the walls

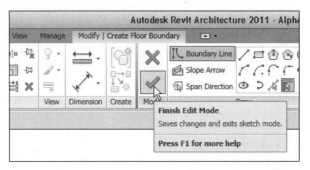

FIGURE 6.11 Clicking Finish Edit Mode to finalize the floor sketch

USING FLIP ARROWS

If you accidentally picked the wrong place in the wall, that's OK. Press Esc, then select the magenta line, and a flip arrow will appear. Pick the flip arrow, and the magenta line will flip back to the correct face of the wall, as shown in the following image. Also, if other sketch lines are on the wrong face, this one flip will take care of any connected sketch lines.

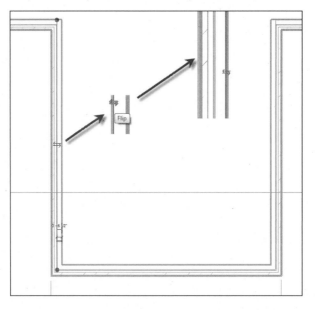

When you finish the floor, you will have plenty of opportunity to practice adding floors in this model! We need to add a floor to the corridor as well as the west wing:

1. Zoom into the corridor, as shown in Figure 6.12.

2. On the Home tab, start the Floor command.

CLEAN UP THOSE CORNERS!

Revit Architecture won't let you finish if you have a gap or an overlapping line. If you get the error shown in the following image, you need to go back into your sketch and see which corner is giving you trouble. If you do get the error dialog, you can click the Show button to have Revit show you where the issue is.

3. In the Modify | Create Floor Boundary tab, click the Pick Walls button.

4. Pick the three north walls of the corridor. Remember to keep the magenta line to the inside face (see Figure 6.12).

5. To add the east edge of the slab, Revit will not really let you pick the wall. If you do, the magenta line will go either to the core center line or to the opposite face of the wall. At this point, click the Line button on the Modify | Create Floor Boundary tab, as shown in Figure 6.13.

6. With the Line button selected, select the Pick Lines button on the Draw panel, as shown in Figure 6.14.

7. Pick the face of the east wall as shown in Figure 6.14.

8. On the Draw panel, click the Pick Walls button.

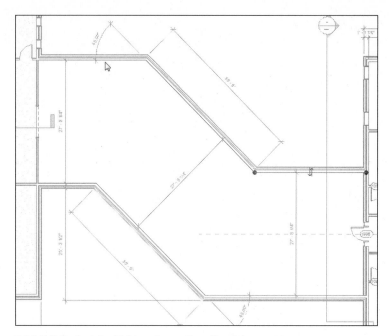

FIGURE 6.12 Picking the north walls of the corridor

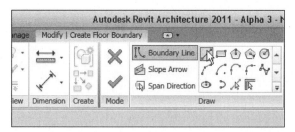

FIGURE 6.13 Sometimes you will need to click the Line button to draw the edge of the slab freehand.

9. Pick the south corridor walls. (Remember to keep the magenta line to the inside of the corridor.)

10. Pick the west wall of the corridor. This time you want to be sure that the magenta line is to the left of the wall. This will ensure that the two slabs meet. If not, you may need to use that flip arrow we were talking about earlier (see Figure 6.15).

Now that you have the process of adding sketch lines to the model, you can start to look into how to clean up the sketch so we can finish.

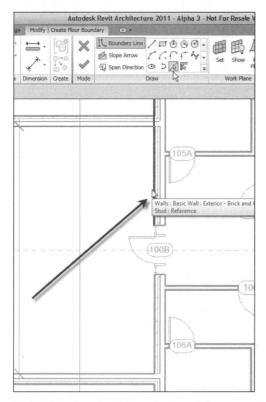

FIGURE 6.14 Picking the face of the east wall. The line will run past the corridor. That's OK. You will trim it in a moment.

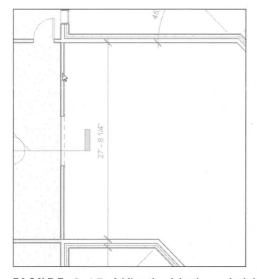

FIGURE 6.15 Adding the slab edge to the left side of the west corridor wall

Using Trim to Clean Up the Sketch

Now that the lines are placed, you need to make sure you don't have any gaps or overlaps. And you do. To fix these gaps and overlaps, you will use the basic modify commands from the previous chapter.

The east wall has a giant gap at the bottom and an overlap at the top. The command you need to use here is the Trim command:

1. Pick the Trim/Extend Single Element button from the Modify panel as shown at the top of Figure 6.16, and click the portions of the two lines you want to keep. This will remove the excess from the corner.

2. With the corners successfully trimmed, click Finish Edit Mode.

▶

When you pick the west wall of the corridor, you may find that Revit just will not let you pick the opposite face of the wall. This is OK. Pick the inside face of the wall, and then move the magenta line to the opposite face of the wall by using the flip arrows.

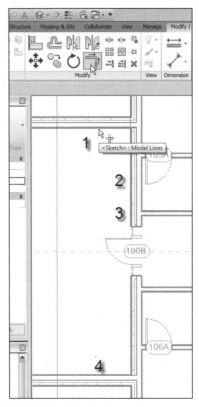

FIGURE 6.16 Picking the magenta lines in the numbered order illustrated in the figure

When Revit allows you to finish the sketch, your west wing and corridor should have a slab underneath it, as shown in Figure 6.17.

TIP Hopefully you do not get an error stating that lines are overlapping. If you do, keep going with the Trim/Extend Single Element command. Also, you may need to investigate each corner. You may also want to consider that you have accidentally placed double lines along a wall.

You can still access most of the basic editing commands such as Trim, Split Element, and Offset while you create the floor boundary.

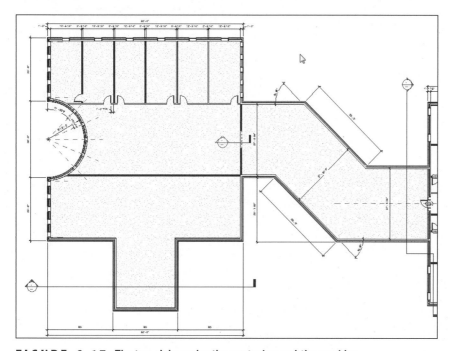

FIGURE 6.17 The two slabs under the west wing and the corridor

It is time to add a slab under the east wing. Go ahead and try it on your own. Only look at these directions if you get lost!

1. Zoom in on the east wing.

2. On the Home tab, select the Floor button.

3. In the Modify | Create Floor Boundary tab, click the Pick Walls button.

4. Pick the exterior walls of the east wing.

5. Trim any gaps or overlaps that may occur in the corners. Also, pay special attention to the radial entry. It can be tricky.

6. Click Finish Edit Mode.

Your east wing should look like Figure 6.18, which is looking at the bottom of the building from a 3D view.

Now that we have a nice slab on the first floor, we need to add some more slabs to the rest of the levels. The trick with the slabs on upper levels is that they need to extend into the core of the walls. This is where Revit can get sticky. Follow along with the next section, and let's work out this issue together.

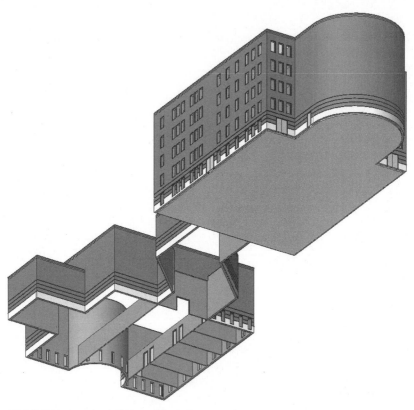

FIGURE 6.18 Adding a slab to the east wing

Building a Floor by Layers

As mentioned in the previous section, the term layer does not equate to AutoCAD's layer. It does, however, equate to layers of materials used to design a floor system. In Revit Architecture, when you create a floor system you can do it with the mind-set of how a floor is actually constructed. You can also specify which material in the floor will stop at an exterior wall and which will pass through to the core.

In this section, you will build on your experience of creating a floor. Now that the concrete slab is in place, we will start adding materials to create a floor finish.

To begin, open the file you have been following along with. If you did not complete the previous chapter, go to the book's web page at **www.sybex.com/go/ revit2011ner**. From there you can browse to Chapter 6 and find the file called NER-20.rvt.

Your objective is to create a floor system with a structure and a finish material. You will also design the floor to interrupt the exterior framing, while letting the brick façade pass from grade to parapet. Let's get started:

1. In the Project Browser, go to the Level 2 floor plan. (Remember not to go to the Level 2 ceiling plan.)

2. In the View Control bar (located at the bottom of the view window), be sure that the detail level is set to Fine.

3. On the Home tab, click the Floor button.

4. In the Properties dialog, click the Edit Type button.

5. Click the Duplicate button.

6. Call the new floor **6″ concrete with 1″ Terrazzo** (see Figure 6.19).

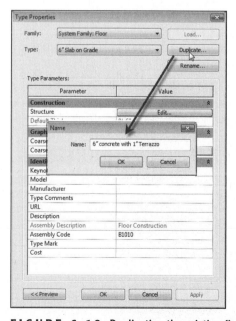

FIGURE 6.19 Duplicating the existing floor

7. Click OK.

8. In the Structure row, click the Edit button, as shown in Figure 6.20.

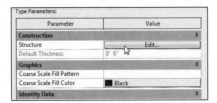

FIGURE 6.20 Clicking the Edit button in the Structure row

You are now in the Edit Assembly dialog, as you were in the previous procedure. The objective now is to add 1″ terrazzo flooring to the top of the 6″ of concrete.

Adding a Layer

Now it's time to add the additional material. To do so, you need to understand how the Edit Assembly dialog is broken down. Since we want to add a material to the top of the slab, we need to click above the concrete and insert a new layer, as follows:

1. In the Layers field, you will see three rows. Each of the three rows has a corresponding number. Click on the number 1. This is the top row that reads Core Boundary Layers Above (see Figure 6.21).

2. Underneath the Layers field, you will see an Insert button, as shown in Figure 6.21. Click it.

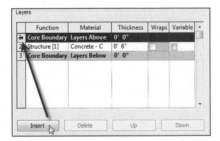

FIGURE 6.21 Inserting a new layer for the terrazzo

3. The new layer is added. You will now see that the field is divided into columns. The first column is the Function column. Currently it says that the Function is Structure. This cell is a drop box containing the

other available functions. Click the drop box arrow and select Finish 1 [4] (see Figure 6.22).

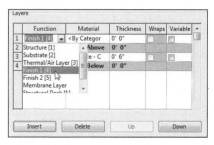

FIGURE 6.22 Choosing a layer function

4. Click into the Material cell.

5. Click the [...] button.

6. In the Materials dialog, select Terrazzo in the Materials list to the left. Click OK.

7. In the Thickness column, enter 1″. Make sure you are typing 1 inch, not 1 foot (see Figure 6.23).

8. To the far right of the rows in the Layers field are Variable checkboxes. Click Variable for the Structure row, as shown in Figure 6.23. This will enable you to slope the slab if need be. Only the layer that is set to be variable will actually slope. Any layer that is on top of this variable layer will be pitched.

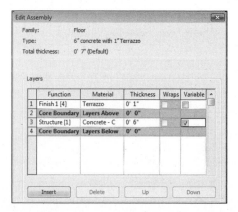

FIGURE 6.23 The completed layers for the floor system

9. At the bottom of the Edit Assembly dialog is a Preview button. Click it. After you do, you can see a graphic preview of your floor in a sectional view, as shown in Figure 6.24.

10. Click OK twice to get back to the model.

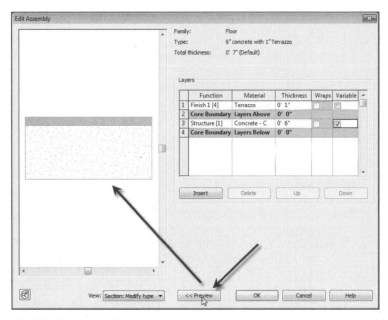

FIGURE 6.24   You can see a preview of the floor in section as it is being built.

Great job. You now have a floor with a material on it! The next step is to place it into the model.

With the new floor created, you can now place it into the model. Remember that you are in the second floor. When you place the slab, you want it to extend directly into the wall core. To do so, follow along:

1. Click the Pick Walls button on the Draw panel. You will pick every exterior wall in the east wing except for the radial wall.

2. Start picking walls, as shown in Figure 6.25. *Do not* pick the radial wall at the east entry.

3. On the Draw panel, select the Line button.

4. Draw a line from the endpoint of the magenta line at the north wall of the east entry (see "1" in Figure 6.26), to the endpoint of the magenta line in the south wall (see "2" in Figure 6.26).

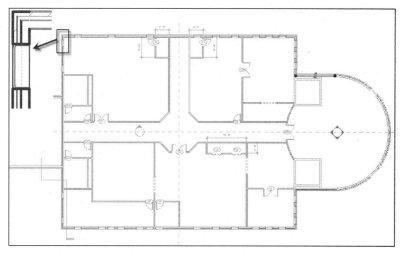

FIGURE 6.25 Picking the core centerline of the exterior walls except for the radial east wall

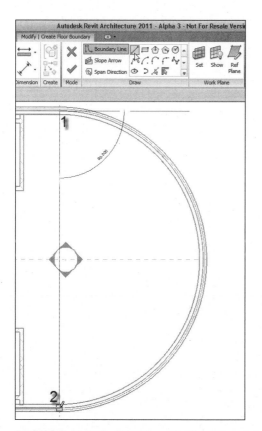

FIGURE 6.26 Sketching a line for the east portion of the entry slab

5. On the Modify | Create Floor Boundary tab, click Finish Edit Mode.

6. Revit will start asking you questions. First Revit will ask you if you want to attach the walls that go up to Level 2 to the bottom of the floor. You *do* want to do this; this will cut the walls down to meet the bottom of the floor. Any change in the floor's thickness will alter the tops of the wall. Click Yes, as shown in Figure 6.27.

7. The next message pertains to the exterior walls. Revit asks if you would like to cut the section out of the walls where the slab is intersecting. In this case you do, so click Yes in the message box, as shown in Figure 6.28.

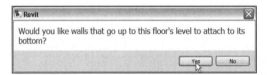

FIGURE 6.27   Click Yes to attach the walls to the floor's bottom.

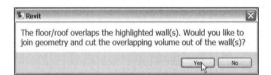

FIGURE 6.28   Click Yes if you want to cut overlapping volumes out of the exterior walls.

N O T E   As these messages come up, Revit usually does a good job of highlighting the items in the model it is addressing in these messages. Get into the habit of looking past the messages to see what items in the model are being highlighted.

With the second floor in place, you can now add it to the floors above. To do so, you can use the Copy/Paste Aligned feature you used in Chapter 3, "Creating Views." Try to do this on your own. If you don't remember how, or skipped Chapter 3, follow these steps:

1. Select the floor in Level 2. (It is easiest to select the floor at the east edge.)

2. On the Modify | Floors tab, click the Copy To Clipboard button on the Clipboard panel, as shown in Figure 6.29.

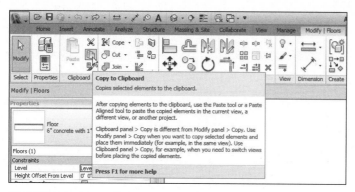

FIGURE 6.29 Clicking the Copy To Clipboard button

3. Go to the default 3D view, as shown in Figure 6.30.

4. From the Paste fly-out on the Clipboard panel, click Paste ➢ Aligned To Selected Levels as shown in Figure 6.30.

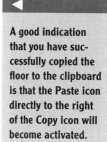

A good indication that you have successfully copied the floor to the clipboard is that the Paste icon directly to the right of the Copy icon will become activated.

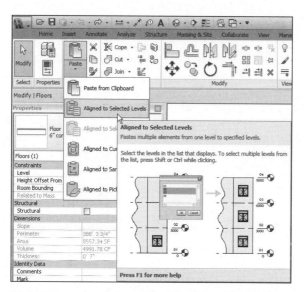

FIGURE 6.30 Using Paste Aligned To Selected Levels

5. The Select Levels dialog appears, where you will choose which levels you want to paste your floor. Choose Levels 3, 4, and 5, as shown in Figure 6.31.

6. Click OK. The floors will be pasted to the specified levels, as shown in Figure 6.32.

FIGURE 6.31 Selecting the levels where you want the slab to be copied.

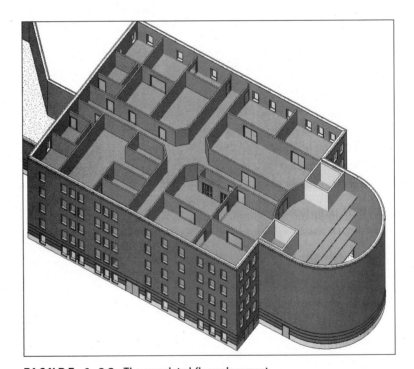

FIGURE 6.32 The completed floor placement

Notice that the fifth-level floor is not joined to any of the walls. This is because, when you pasted the floor to this level, Revit did not prompt you to cut the overlapping geometry from the exterior walls. To fix this, follow these steps:

1. After the floors have been pasted, select the fifth-level floor, as shown in Figure 6.33.

2. On the Modify | Floors tab, select the Edit Boundary button.

3. On the Mode panel of the Modify | Floors ➢ Edit Boundary button, select Finish Edit Mode.

4. Select Yes to attach the walls that go up to this floor's bottom.

5. Select Yes to cut the overlapping volume out of the walls. Figure 6.33 shows that the walls are now being cut by the slab.

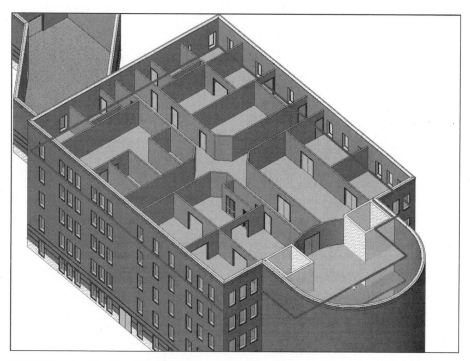

F I G U R E 6 . 3 3 The fifth floor is now cutting the walls.

6. Repeat steps 1 through 5 for floors 4 and 3.

7. Save the model.

Not too bad. You have a full building with floors placed. Now it is time to drill in to these floors (literally) and see how you can make them perform to your specifications.

The first task in the next section is to create different floor materials for a few specific areas such as the restrooms. The second task is to pitch the restroom floors to floor drains.

Splitting the Floor's Materials

If you have a floor that includes a slab, then have one single material of, say, vinyl composition tile (VCT) to the entire surface, won't that cause a problem in the restrooms? Better yet, suppose the floor is carpeted? Carpet just never seems to perform well around a toilet!

The goal of this procedure is to create a new material layer for the first floor slab, and then specify a new material for the restrooms:

1. In the Project Browser, go to the Level 1 floor plan, and zoom into an area of the east wing similar to the area shown in Figure 6.34.

2. Drag a selection window around the corner of the building, as shown in Figure 6.34.

3. On the Modify | Multi-Select tab, select the Filter button (see Figure 6.34).

4. In the Filter dialog, click the Check None button, as shown in Figure 6.35.

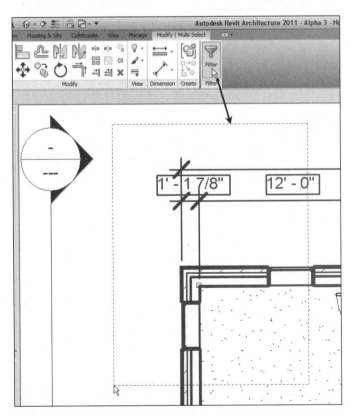

FIGURE 6.34 To select the slab, it will be easier to pick an entire area and filter the floor.

5. Check the Floors option (see Figure 6.35), and click OK.

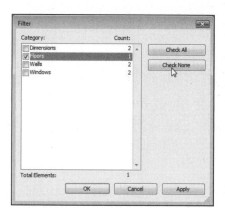

FIGURE 6.35 Uncheck all the elements, and then check Floors.

6. With the floor selected, click the Type Properties button on the Properties panel of the Modify | Floors tab.

7. Click Rename.

8. Call the floor **6″ Slab on Grade with 1″ Finish**.

9. Click OK.

10. Click the Edit button in the Structure row, as shown in Figure 6.36.

11. In the Edit Assembly dialog, select the 1 button to the left of the Core Boundary above the Structure layer, as shown in Figure 6.37.

12. Click the Insert button (see Figure 6.37).

13. Select Finish 1 [4] from the Function drop-down list.

14. Click in the Material cell.

15. Click the [...] button.

16. Find the material in the menu called Carpet (1) and click OK.

17. Give the material a thickness of 1″.

18. Click the Variable checkbox in the Structure row, as shown in Figure 6.38.

19. Click OK twice.

20. Press Esc.

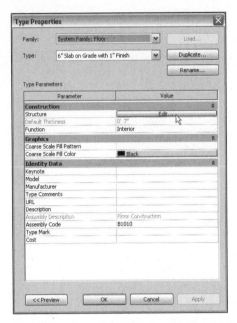

FIGURE 6.36 Editing the structure of the slab

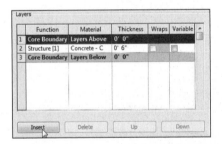

FIGURE 6.37 Adding a new layer

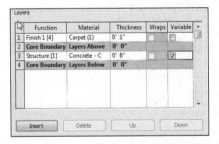

FIGURE 6.38 Adding the new material

Now that you have experience adding a new material layer to the floor (you have done it twice in this chapter), you can specify a different material for the various rooms.

Split and Paint

Adding a new material to a floor is a two-part procedure. To specify an alternate material in an area, you must first split the floor's face. Then you can add (or paint) the desired material to that area.

The objective of the next two procedures is to add an alternate material to the restrooms:

1. Zoom in on the lavatory south of the corridor.

2. On the Geometry panel of the Modify tab, select the Split Face button, as shown in Figure 6.39.

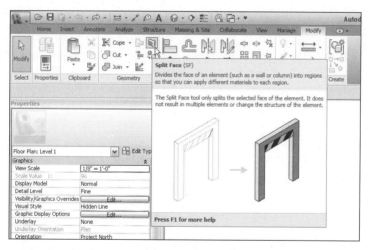

FIGURE 6.39 The Split Face button is located on the Geometry panel of the Modify tab.

3. Move your cursor into the lavatory area, as shown in Figure 6.40.

4. Notice there is a little cube at your cursor. Hover your cursor over the wall shown in Figure 6.40. You should get a tooltip telling you that you are directly over the floor. When you see this indication, pick the floor.

5. After you select the floor, you need to draw three lines around the inside face of the lavatory walls. To do so, on the Draw panel of the Modify | Split Face ➢ Create Boundary tab, make sure the Line button is checked.

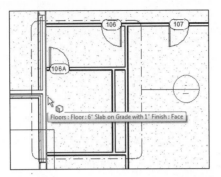

FIGURE 6.40 Finding the edge of the floor

6. Draw the three lines as shown in Figure 6.41 (you may have to trim and extend the lines).

 WARNING   Because the line you are splitting is up against the edge of the slab (as shown in the magnification in Figure 6.41), the actual floor's edge serves as one of the split lines. When you are adding the three additional lines, you *must* be snapped to the edge of the floor. There can be no overlaps or gaps.

FIGURE 6.41 Placing the three split lines around the perimeter of the lavatory

7. On the Modify | Split Face ➢ Create Boundary tab, click Finish Edit Mode.

8. The lavatory area should now be split.

Although it appears as if nothing happened, it just means you can't see it. The next step will change the material of the region. At this point it will become obvious that there is a different material.

With the floor split, it is time to add the new material to this room. This procedure is almost like adding a hatch to an area as if in AutoCAD:

1. On the Geometry panel of the Modify | Split Face tab, click the Paint icon, as shown in Figure 6.42.

2. From the Material drop-down list in the Element panel, select Ceramic Tile - 4" Blue from the menu, as shown in Figure 6.43.

FIGURE 6.42 The Paint icon on the Geometry panel

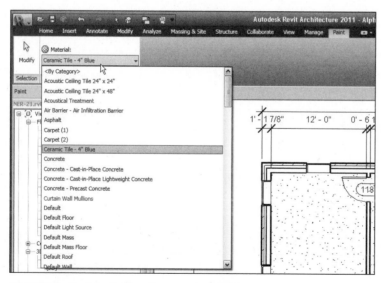

FIGURE 6.43 Finding the correct material

3. Move your cursor over the region you just created. Notice the material icon next to your cursor, as shown in Figure 6.44.

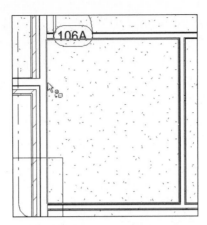

FIGURE 6.44 Filling the region with the new material

4. After you see the perimeter of the small region you created around the inside of the lavatory, pick a spot. The area will fill with the new material (see Figure 6.45).

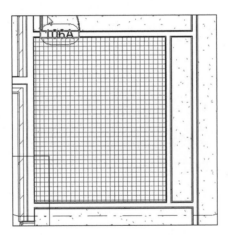

FIGURE 6.45 The completed lavatory

5. Do the same thing to the lavatory north of the corridor. If you get stuck, go back through the steps.

6. Save your model.

Now that splitting the face of the floor is out of the way, it is time to create a pitched floor situation. In some cases, this is an easy procedure. In others, it is not.

Pitching a Floor to a Floor Drain

Sure, it is the responsibility of the plumbing engineer to specify what floor drains to use, but it is generally the responsibility of the architect to specify where the floor drain needs to be, and the pitch of the floor.

That being said, let's move on to creating a pitched floor area in the restrooms. Because we have five floors to work with, let's go up to the second floor and start pitching some slabs!

The objective of the next procedure is to add points in the surface of the slab in order to pitch to a drain:

1. In the Project Browser, double-click on the Level 2 floor plan (make sure you aren't in the Level 2 ceiling plan).

2. Zoom in on the lavatory areas, as shown in Figure 6.46.

3. Select the floor.

PICKING FLOORS CAN BE PICKY

Selecting the floor can always throw people. As you'll recall, to select the floor you literally have to pick a window around multiple items, then isolate the slab in the Filter dialog. This will still be your process here. Whenever the book says to "select" an item, use all the selection methods you have gained experience with in the previous procedures and chapters.

4. Now that the floor is selected, notice on the Modify | Floors tab that you have several choices. Click the Add Split Line button (see Figure 6.46).

5. Draw lines along the finished inside face of the lavatory, as shown in Figure 6.46. As always, there can be no gaps or overlaps.

N O T E   Yes, it is true that the snapping feature is tedious at best when you're using the Split Line command. Be patient. You will need to basically get as close to the face of the wall as possible before you pick the point. This is one case where you will need to eyeball the exact pick points.

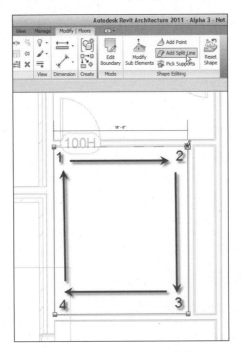

F I G U R E 6 . 4 6 Drawing a split frame around the inside of the lavatory

With the split lines drawn, you have isolated the lavatory area from the rest of the floor. Now you can pitch the floor in this area without affecting the rest of the floor. The pitch will extend only as far as the split lines.

To create a drop in the floor, follow these steps:

1. On the Home tab, select the Model Lines button, as shown in Figure 6.47.

2. Draw the line from the midpoint of the restroom's right wall, to the left 3′–0″, as shown in Figure 6.47.

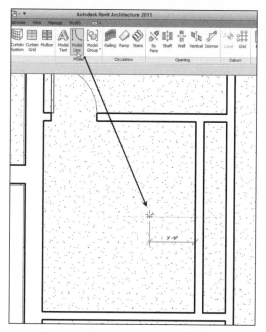

FIGURE 6.47 Drawing a line to establish the point where the floor will slope to

3. Press Esc twice.

4. Select the floor. (Remember the Filter dialog.)

5. On the Modify | Floors tab, select the Add Point button, as shown in Figure 6.48.

6. Pick the endpoint of the line you just drew, as shown in Figure 6.48.

7. Press Esc once. This will put you in the Modify Sub Elements mode. You will know you are in this mode by the icon next to your pointer, as shown in Figure 6.49.

8. Pick the point you just placed into the model. It will turn red, and a blue elevation will appear. As you know, any blue item is modifiable. Click the 0′–0″ value, and change it to –1″ (negative one inch).

9. Press Enter. Revit will drop that area of the floor and add the slope lines as if you drafted them in.

10. Press Esc twice.

11. Delete the line you drew as a guideline.

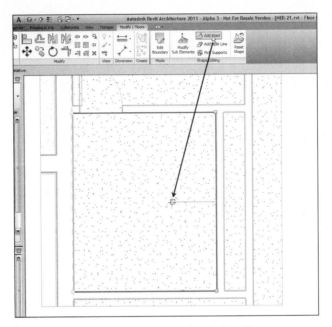

FIGURE 6.48 Picking the endpoint of the line

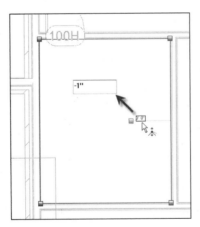

FIGURE 6.49 Dropping the elevation of the drain down 1″ from the surface of the floor

12. Save the model.

See Figure 6.50: does your floor look like this? If not, go back and see where you went wrong.

13. Repeat the steps to add a pitch to the lavatory north of the corridor.

14. Save the model (see Figure 6.51).

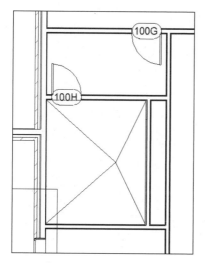

FIGURE 6.50 The final slab in the restroom

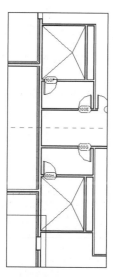

FIGURE 6.51 Both lavatories are now pitched and ready to have fixtures added.

Now that you have experience in creating and placing floors, as well as being able to pitch a floor in a specific area, it is time to look at one more item: shaft openings.

CAN I ERASE THIS AND START OVER?

Often you may just need to clear the entire slab and start again. You can do this simply by selecting the floor and clicking the Reset Shape button on the Options bar, as shown in the following image:

Creating Shaft Openings

To create a shaft opening, you just create a void through your model. This void, however, can conform to walls that are set in the model. The elevator shaft walls, for instance, will define the outside edge of our shaft opening. You may notice that the floors we added to the model are indiscriminately running uninterrupted straight through the shafts. We need to void the floor. Also, the good thing about creating a shaft opening is that if we create another floor, the shaft will be cut out automatically.

To get started, open the file you have been following along with. If you did not complete the previous procedure, go to the book's web page at **www.sybex.com/ go/revit2011ner**. From there you can browse to Chapter 6 and find the file called NER-21.rvt.

First, we need to create two more levels. We need a subterranean level (T.O. Footing) and a penthouse level to extend the elevator shaft up through:

1. In the Project Browser, go to the South elevation.

2. On the Datum panel of the Home tab, click the Level button.

3. On the Draw panel, click the Pick Lines icon, and set an offset of 10′–0″ (see Figure 6.52).

4. Hover your cursor over Level 1. Make sure the alignment line is below Level 1. When you see the alignment line, pick Level 1. You now have a new level at –10′–0″.

5. Click the Modify button on the Select panel to terminate the command.

6. Pick the level that is set to –10′–0″ and rename it to T.O. Footing (see Figure 6.52).

7. Click Yes when Revit prompts you to rename corresponding views.

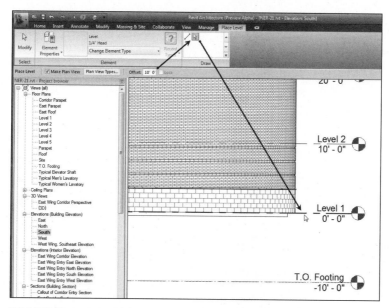

FIGURE 6.52 Adding a new Top Of Footing level

The next step is to select the CMU elevator shaft walls and modify their properties so that the bottoms are extended down to the top of the footing and the tops are extended to the penthouse level:

1. Go to a 3D view.

2. Select all of the CMU walls. Remember to press and hold the Ctrl key as you select the walls.

3. In the Properties dialog, under the Constraints category, set Base Constraint to T.O. Footing, as shown in Figure 6.53.

4. Click OK.

To select all of the CMU walls, you can simply select only one, right-click, and then click Select All Instances. Be careful, though; if there are other CMU walls of the same type in the model, they will become selected as well.

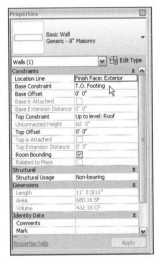

FIGURE 6.53 In the Properties dialog, change Base Constraint to T.O. Footing.

With the bottom established at the correct level, it is time to add the shaft:

1. Go to the Level 1 floor plan (note that it does not matter which floor you are actually in when you place a shaft opening).

2. On the Home tab, click the Shaft Opening button in the Opening panel. as shown in Figure 6.54.

3. On the Modify | Create Shaft Opening Sketch tab, click Pick Walls, as shown in Figure 6.55.

4. Pick the walls shown in Figure 6.55. Notice that you can have more than one shaft opening in the same command.

5. Use the Line button on the Draw panel to draw the line across the inside face of the exterior wall.

6. Use the Trim command to clean up any corners (see Figure 6.55).

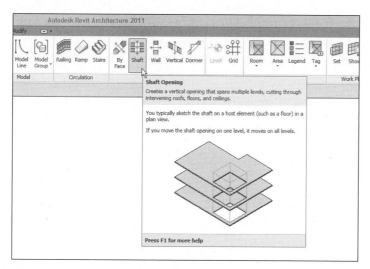

FIGURE 6.54 Selecting the Shaft Opening command from the Home tab

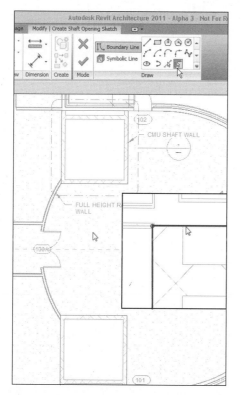

FIGURE 6.55 Adding the magenta lines to form the shaft opening to the outside of the CMU walls

Now that the perimeter has been established, it is time to establish which floors this opening will extend to. Just because we picked the CMU walls, this does not mean that a base and a top height have been established.

1. In the Properties dialog , make sure Shaft Openings is selected, as shown in Figure 6.56.

2. In the Properties dialog, set Base Constraint to T.O. Footing.

3. Set Top Constraint to Up To Level: Roof.

4. Set Top Offset to –1′–0″ (this keeps the roof from having two giant square holes in it).

5. Click Apply. Figure 6.56 shows the settings.

FIGURE 6.56 Setting the properties of the shaft opening

6. On the Modify | Create Shaft Opening Sketch tab, click the Symbolic Line button. This will allow you to sketch an opening graphic into the shaft.

7. Draw an "X" in both openings, as shown in Figure 6.57.

8. Click Finish Edit Mode.

Notice the floor is now voided from the openings. Go to a 3D view and look down the shafts. They are wide open, as shown in Figure 6.58.

 N O T E A shaft opening will only void floors and roofs. Any other geometry such as walls and structural framing will not be voided. You need to modify these elements on a piece-by-piece basis.

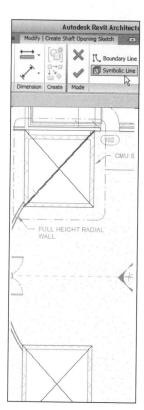

F I G U R E 6 . 5 7 You can add any "drafting" symbolic lines you deem necessary.

Now that you know how to pitch floors, you can begin using Revit for its unique capabilities. Also, you are better prepared to move into the next chapter, which focuses on creating roofs.

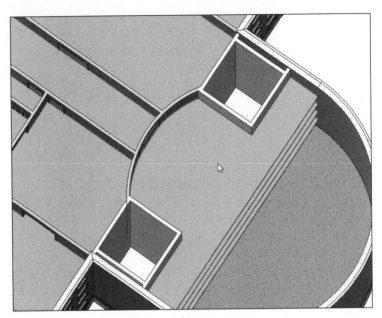

FIGURE 6.58 The completed shafts as seen in 3D

Are You Experienced?

Now you can...

- ☑ add a floor to your model by using the building's footprint as a guide by picking the walls and by drawing lines

- ☑ add additional floors to higher levels by using the Copy/Paste Aligned method of quickly repeating the geometry up through the building

- ☑ add a specific, alternate material to different parts of the floor by using the Split Face command in conjunction with the paint materials function

- ☑ split a floor into segments, and add additional points to set a negative elevation for pitching to floor drains

- ☑ create a shaft opening that will cut out any new floor slab. You also can use symbolic lines within the opening to indicate that there is an opening within the shaft.

Roofs

Roofs come in all shapes and sizes. Given the nature of roofs, there is a lot to think about when you place a roof onto your building. If it is a flat roof, pitch is definitely a consideration. Drainage to roof drains or scuppers is another consideration as well. But how about pitched roofs? Now we are in an entirely new realm of options, pitches, slopes, and everything else you can throw at a roof design. Also, there are always dormers that no pitched roof can live without! Do the dormers align with the eaves, or are they set back from the building?

▶ **Placing roofs by footprint**

▶ **Creating a sloping roof**

▶ **Roofs by extrusion**

▶ **Adding a roof dormer**

Placing Roofs by Footprint

This book can't address every situation you will encounter with a roof system, but it will expose you to the tools needed to tackle these situations yourself. The techniques we will employ in this chapter start with the concept of adding a roof to the model by using the actual floor plan footprint. As with floors, we will also build the roof's composition for use in schedules, quantities, and material takeoffs.

The command you'll probably use most often when working with roofs is the one to place a roof by footprint. Essentially, we will create a roof by using the outline of the building in plan view. There are three roof types you can place by using a footprint:

- ▶ A flat roof (OK, no roof is actually flat, but you get the point)

- ▶ A gable roof where two sides are sloped and the ends are left open

- ▶ A hip roof where all sides are sloped

You have only these options while placing a roof by footprint because you are looking at the roof in plan, which limits your ability to place a roof with nonuniform geometry. Later in the book, we will explore doing just that, but for now let's start with placing a flat roof using the footprint of the east wing.

Flat Roofs by Footprint

To begin, open the file you have been following along with. If you did not complete the previous chapter, go to the book's web page at **www.sybex.com/go/ revit2011ner**. From there you can browse to Chapter 7 and find the file called NER-22.rvt.

The objective of this procedure is to create a flat roof by outlining the building's geometry in the plan:

1. In the Project Browser, double-click on the Roof view in the Floor Plans section (be careful not to click on Roof in the Ceiling plans).

2. Zoom in to the east wing.

3. Type **VP** to access the View Properties dialog.

4. Find the Underlay row and select None from the menu, as shown in Figure 7.1.

5. Click Apply.

6. On the Home tab, click Roof ➤ Roof By Footprint, as shown in Figure 7.2.

FIGURE 7.1 Changing the view's Underlay to None

7. On the Modify | Create Roof Footprint tab, be sure the Pick Walls button on the Draw panel is checked, as shown at the top of Figure 7.3.

8. On the Options bar, uncheck Defines Slope, as shown in Figure 7.3.

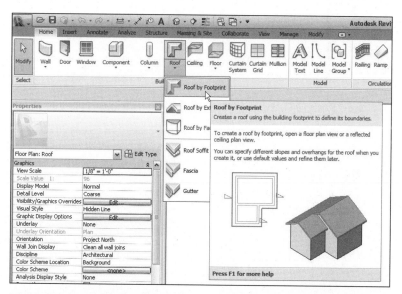

FIGURE 7.2 Clicking Roof By Footprint on the Home tab of the Design bar

9. In the Options bar, make sure the overhang is set to 0′ 0″.

10. Uncheck Extend Into Wall Core (if it is checked).

11. Hover your pointer over the leftmost vertical wall. Notice that it becomes highlighted. When you see the wall highlight, press the Tab key on your keyboard. Notice that all the perimeter walls highlight. When they do, pick (left-click) anywhere along the wall. This will place a magenta sketch line at the perimeter of the building (see Figure 7.3).

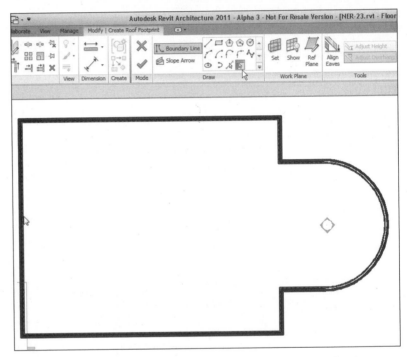

FIGURE 7.3 Adding a sketch line to the perimeter of the building by highlighting one wall and pressing Tab

12. On the Modify | Create Roof Footprint tab, click Finish Edit Mode.

13. Go to a 3D view, as shown in Figure 7.4.

With the roof added, step 1 is out of the way. Now we need to create a roof system. You will do this the same way you created your floor system in Chapter 6, "Floors."

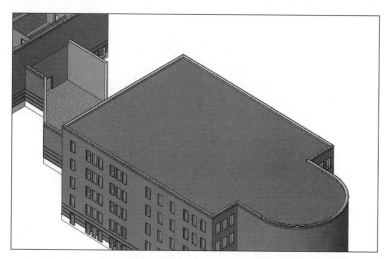

FIGURE 7.4 The roof has been added. We still have a lot of work to do, though.

Creating a Flat Roof System

Although you can use this system for a pitched roof, the steps for a flat roof system differ slightly. In Revit Architecture, there are two ways to look at a roofing system. One way is to create it using all of the typical roof materials and to create a large space for the structural framing. In this book I do not recommend that approach. Creating a roof using only the roofing components is necessary, but adding the structure will lead to conflicts when the actual structural model is linked with the architectural model. Also, it is hard for the architect to guess what the depth of the structural framing will be. In Revit, you want each component to be as literal and as true to the model as possible. The second way to look at a roofing system, as we are about to explore, is to build the roof in a literal sense—that is, to create the roof as it would sit on the structural framing by others.

The objective of this procedure is to create a roof system by adding layers of materials:

1. Select the roof. (If you are having trouble selecting the roof, remember the Filter tool.)

2. On the Modify | Roofs tab, click the Type Properties button.

3. Click Duplicate.

4. Call the new roof system 4″ Insulated Concrete Roof.

5. Click OK.

6. Click the Edit button in the Structure row.

7. Change the material of Structure 1 to Concrete - Cast-in-Place Lightweight Concrete. (You do this by clicking in the cell and by clicking the […] button. You can then select the material from the menu.) Once the material is selected, click OK.

8. Change Structure Thickness to 4″ (see Figure 7.5).

9. Insert a new layer above the core boundary. (You do this by clicking on the number on the left side of the Core Boundary row, and clicking the Insert button below the Layers section, as shown in Figure 7.5.)

10. Change the function of the new layer to Thermal/Air Layer [3].

11. Click in the Material cell.

12. Click the […] button to open the Materials dialog.

13. Select Insulation / Thermal Barriers - Rigid Insulation for the material.

14. Click OK.

15. Change Thickness to 4″.

16. Click the Variable button. When we modify the roof, this insulation layer will warp, allowing us to specify roof drain locations.

17. Insert a new layer above the Insulation.

18. Give it a Function of Finish 1 [4].

19. Select Roofing - EPDM Membrane.

20. Click OK.

21. Change Thickness to 1/4″ (see Figure 7.5).

22. Click OK.

23. Click OK again to get back to the model.

24. Press Esc.

Phew! That was a long procedure. It was worth it, though. You will be using this process a lot in Revit Architecture.

For the next procedure, we will add some roof drain locations, and then taper the insulation to drain to these locations.

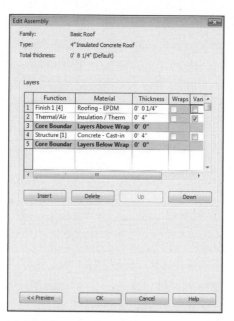

FIGURE 7.5 The complete roof system

TAKE A LOOK

It is always a good idea to keep the preview window open when you modify the roof system. If you look toward the bottom of the Edit Assembly dialog, you will see a preview button, as shown in the following illustration. Click it, and you can see the roof as it is being constructed.

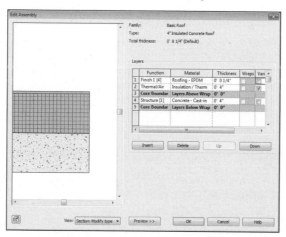

Tapering a Flat Roof and Adding Drains

If you went through the floor procedure in Chapter 6, you will see that the process for tapering a roof is similar to pitching a floor. You may have also noticed that creating a roof system is identical to creating a floor system.

To taper the roof insulation, you must first divide the roof into peaks and valleys, and then specify the drain locations based on the centering of these locations:

1. In the Project Browser, make sure you are in the Roof floor plan.

2. Select the roof. (You may have to use the Filter tool here.)

T I P   Even when you do successfully select the roof, you may not be able to tell. The roof doesn't seem to highlight. When you have the roof selected, the Options bar will show the Modify icons. Also, look in the top of the Properties dialog box—it should read Basic Roof : 4″ Insulated Concrete Roof.

3. With the roof selected, select the Create Split Lines button shown in Figure 7.6.

4. Draw a line from the points shown in Figure 7.6.

5. Press Esc.

6. Select the roof.

T I P   One really nice thing about modifying the roof is now, to select the roof, all you need to do is pick one of the ridgelines and the roof is selected.

7. To activate the points in the roof, click the Modify Sub Elements button, as shown in Figure 7.7. This will allow you to modify the points you have picked already.

8. Click the Add Point button, as shown near the top of Figure 7.8.

9. Add two points at the midpoints marked as "1" and "2" in Figure 7.8.

10. Click the Add Split Line button and draw a ridge across the entire length of the building from point 1 to point 2, as shown in Figure 7.9.

11. Press Esc twice; then, on the Home tab, click Ref Plane as shown at the top right of Figure 7.10.

12. Draw four reference planes spaced approximately the same as in Figure 7.10.

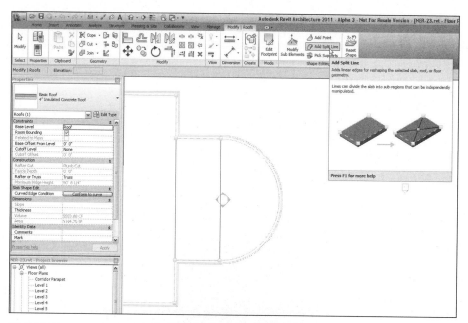

FIGURE 7.6 Start splitting the radial portion of the roof.

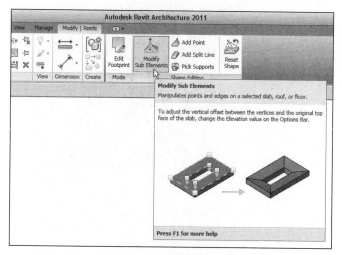

FIGURE 7.7 Click the Modify Sub Elements button to activate the points in the subassembly of the roof.

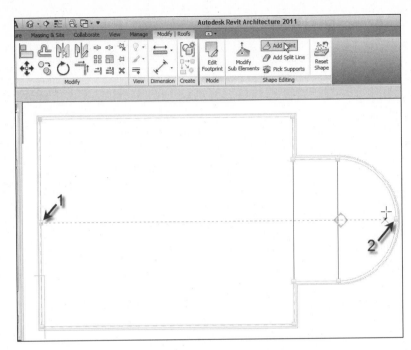

FIGURE 7.8 Adding two points

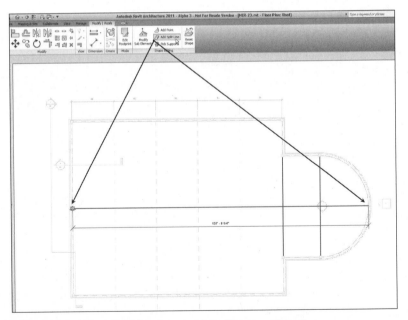

FIGURE 7.9 Drawing a new ridge from the two points shown

13. On the Annotate tab, click the Aligned Dimension button.

14. Add a dimension string starting at the exterior wall to the left and ending at the exterior wall to the right, as shown in Figure 7.10.

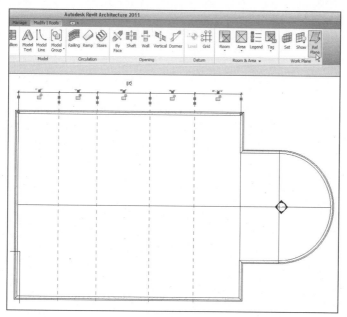

FIGURE 7.10 Add a dimension string to the reference planes shown here.

15. Click the blue EQ icon. This will equally constrain the reference planes.

16. Press Esc twice to terminate the command.

17. Select the roof.

18. Click the Add Split Line, as shown in Figure 7.11.

19. Draw four ridges at the intersections of the reference planes, as shown in Figure 7.11.

20. Press Esc.

21. On the Annotate tab, click the Detail Line button, as shown at the top of Figure 7.12.

22. Draw a diagonal line from the two points shown in Figure 7.12.

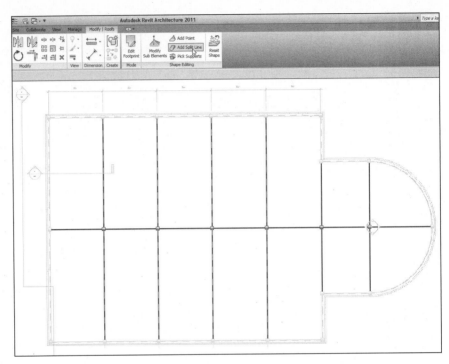

FIGURE 7.11 The ridges are in. All that is left is to create some points and start tapering the roof.

23. Press Esc, and then select the roof.

24. Click the Add Point button.

25. Pick the midpoint of the diagonal line.

26. Press Esc twice to clear the command.

27. Select the roof. Notice there is a node where you picked the point. To access the node, click the Modify Sub Elements button on the Shape Editing panel, as shown in Figure 7.13.

28. Pick the point that you just added. Notice there is a blue elevation that shows up, as shown in Figure 7.14. Click the elevation, and type –3″.

29. Press Esc twice.

This process will taper the insulation only in this bay, as shown in Figure 7.15. The objective now is to do the same thing for every bay. Because you cannot copy a point, you need to move the temporary line to the next bay and add a new point.

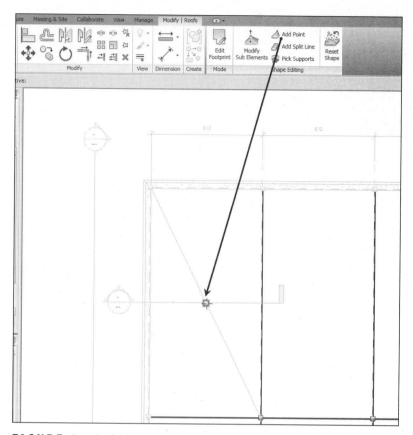

FIGURE 7.12 Add a temporary line, then pick a point to pitch the insulation to. Note there is a section marker in the illustration. We will be adding that in a moment.

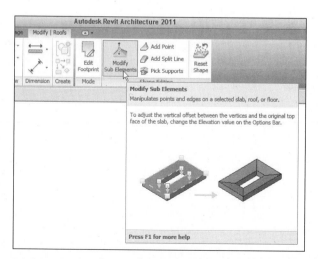

FIGURE 7.13 Click the Modify Sub Elements button to gain access to the points on the roof.

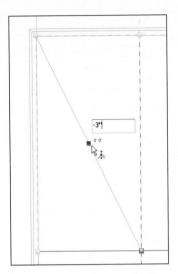

F I G U R E 7 . 1 4 Click the point to taper the roof to this point.

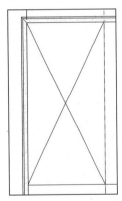

F I G U R E 7 . 1 5 The taper is in place.

Follow along to create another taper:

1. Move the diagonal line (that you drew as a reference) to the next bay to the right.

2. Select the roof.

3. Click Add Point.

4. Click the Modify Sub Elements button, and add a point to the midpoint of the line.

5. Type –3″ in the blue elevation. The roof tapers.

6. Move the line to the next bay and repeat the process.

 N O T E   Remember as you are adding additional lines in this section that I am merely recommending that you use the Move tool. At this point, you have enough experience to either draw the lines in or use any tool you have learned up to this point.

7. Complete every bay.

8. Add points to the radial area as well.

9. Your roof should look like Figure 7.16 when you have finished.

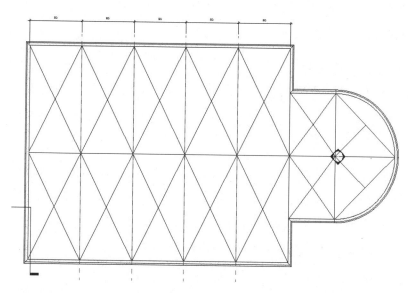

FIGURE 7.16 The completed roof

To further investigate how this roof works, and to see the benefits of this approach rather than drafting the lines in, let's cut a section through the roof and see how the detail will look:

1. On the Create panel of the View tab, click the Section button.

2. Add a section through the roof, as shown in Figure 7.17.

3. In the Properties dialog, change View Scale to 3/4″ = 1′–0″.

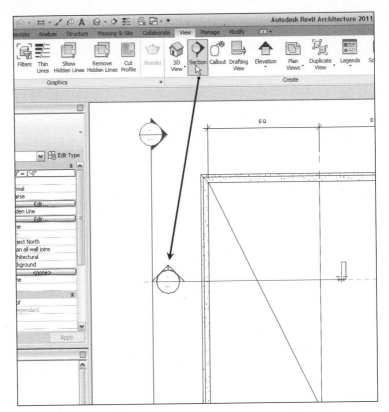

FIGURE 7.17 Adding a section through the roof at this point.

4. Change Detail Level to Fine.

5. Change the View Name option (under Identity Data) to Roof Taper Section (see Figure 7.18).

6. Click Apply.

7. Double-click on the section head (or you can find the section called Roof Taper Section in the Project Browser).

8. Adjust the crop region so you are looking only at the roof area, as shown in Figure 7.19.

This concludes modeling a flat roof. We can now move on to creating a pitched roof. Again, although these types of roofs can be easy to add in the beginning, more work will be required to get them exactly the way you want them.

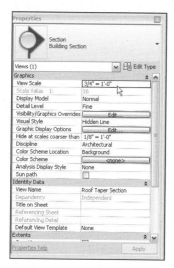

FIGURE 7.18 Changing the properties of the section

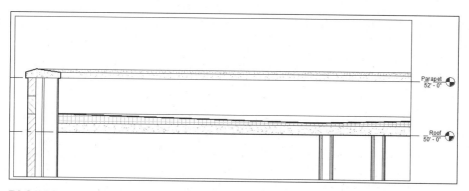

FIGURE 7.19 By adding the points to the roof, you now have an almost perfect section.

THE PROOF IS IN THE ROOF!

This is a perfect example of why the Revit approach to design documentation is the way to go. Although the sloping of the slab may have seemed tedious, in reality it didn't take much longer than if you had drafted those lines in a CAD application. But now, to produce a section, all you need to do is cut one. Also, if you change the location, or the depth of the roof pitch, your lines in plan will be accurate, as will your section.

Pitched Roofs by Footprint

We'll add a pitched roof in an identical manner in which we added the flat roof. The only real difference is that each magenta sketch line will need more attention before you finish the sketch. But, after tapering the roof's insulation, this will be a cakewalk.

We will place the pitched roof over the corridor. The problem with the corridor is that we used a wall system with a parapet cap. This is not the best wall system to receive a pitched roof. First we will change to a simpler wall system:

1. Go to a 3D view of the model.

2. Select the six corridor walls, as shown in Figure 7.20.

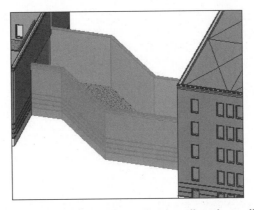

FIGURE 7.20 Select the six walls to be modified.

3. On the Modify | Walls tab, click the Type Properties button.

4. Click the Duplicate button.

5. Call the new wall system **Exterior - Brick and CMU on MTL. Stud (No Parapet)**.

6. In the Structure row, click the Edit button.

7. In the Edit Assembly dialog, make sure the Preview button has been checked, as shown at the bottom of Figure 7.21.

8. Click the Sweeps button, as shown in Figure 7.21.

9. In the Wall Sweeps dialog, you will see three sweeps. The top sweep is the parapet cap. Select sweep 1 (Parapet Cap), and click the Delete button, as shown in Figure 7.22.

10. Click OK three times.

11. Click OK one more time to get back to the model.

Your corridor walls should look exactly the same but are now void of the concrete parapet cap.

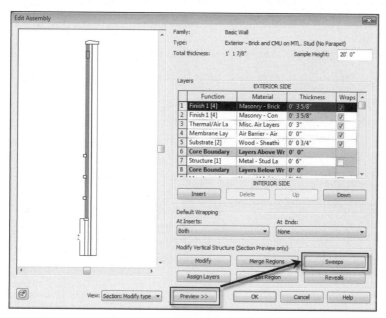

FIGURE 7.21 Without the preview checked on, you will not be able to modify the parapet sweep.

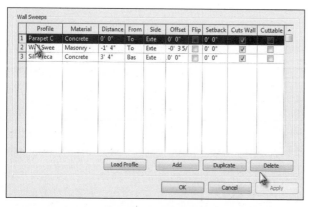

FIGURE 7.22 Deleting the Parapet Cap sweep

Remember, your preview will need to be in Section : Modify Type for all of the buttons to be active.

N O T E   Although you have pretty good experience with walls up to this point, Chapter 16, "Advanced Wall Topics," is dedicated to the advanced concepts and creation of wall systems.

It's now time to add the roof to the corridor. Because the walls our roof will bear on are now correct, the rest will be a snap!

1. Go to the Level 3 floor plan. (This is the roof level for our corridor.)

2. On the Home tab, select Roof ➤ Roof By Footprint.

3. On the Draw panel, make sure the Pick Walls button is selected.

4. On the Options bar, make sure the Defines Slope button is checked, as shown in Figure 7.23.

5. Type 1'–0" in the Overhang field.

6. Pick the six walls that comprise the corridor, as shown in Figure 7.23.

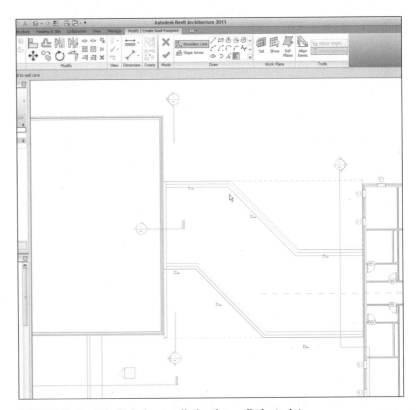

F I G U R E   7 . 2 3   Pick these walls for the roof's footprint.

With the easy walls out of the way, it is now time to create the gable ends. You should still be in the Pick Walls mode. This is OK, but there are a few things you need to change on the Options bar:

1. Click the Boundary Line button on the Draw panel, as shown in Figure 7.24.

2. On the Draw panel again, click the Pick Lines icon.

3. On the Options bar, uncheck Defines Slope.

4. For the offset, enter 0 (see Figure 7.24).

5. Pick the east wall on the west wing, and the west wall of the east wing, as shown in Figure 7.24.

As you pick the walls, notice that you now have an overhang. This overhang obviously needs to extend to the outside of the walls. Just be conscious of this as you pick the walls and watch your alignment lines as you proceed.

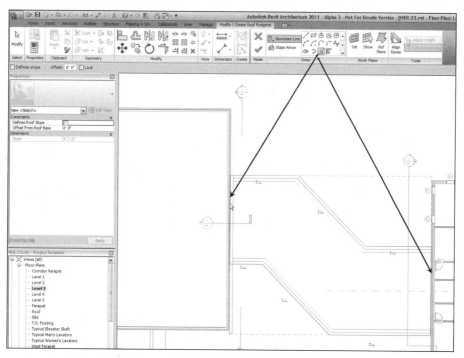

FIGURE 7.24 You must pick lines to trace the terminating walls of the roof.

It's cleanup time! Of course the magenta lines are overlapping at the long walls. This is OK—you are an expert at the Trim command by now, especially in Sketch Mode:

1. On the Modify | Create Roof Footprint tab, select the Trim/Extend Single Element command, as shown in Figure 7.25.

2. Trim the intersections that overlap. There will be four of them (see Figure 7.25).

3. On the Mode panel, click Finish Edit Mode.

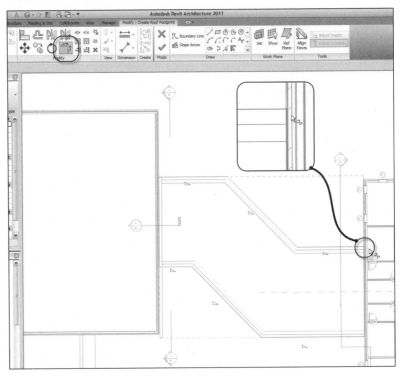

FIGURE 7.25 Using the Trim command in conjunction with the roof sketch.

One ugly roof, huh? Welcome to the world of pitched roofs in Revit. We will get the roof we want—we just need to add two roofs here. You will understand this process, but it is going to involve patience and trial and error!

To fix this roof, you simply have to make two separate roofs and join them together. This will be a common procedure for the more complicated roof systems in Revit.

1. Select the roof.

2. On the Modify | Roofs tab, click the Edit Footprint button, as shown in Figure 7.26.

3. Delete every line, other than the three shown in Figure 7.27.

4. On the Draw panel, click the Line button.

5. Draw a diagonal line from the endpoints of the two lines, as shown in Figure 7.28.

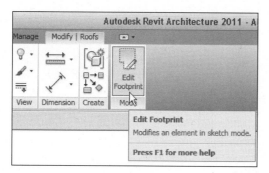

FIGURE 7.26 Selecting the roof and clicking the Edit Footprint button

FIGURE 7.27 Keep these three lines.

FIGURE 7.28 Draw a diagonal line as shown.

6. On the Modify | Roofs ➤ Edit Footprint tab, click Finish Edit Mode.

7. The roof will display. It still looks funny, but we will take care of that by altering the view range.

8. Start the Roof ➤ Roof By Footprint command again on the Home tab.

9. On your own, sketch the roof shown in Figure 7.29. Make sure the lines along the walls are defining a slope. The lines that represent the ends of the roof do not slope.

10. To add the line that matches the roof to the right, make sure you have the Boundary Line button selected on the Draw panel and that you have Pick Lines selected as well. Now, simply pick the roof to the right, and the line will appear.

11. Review Figure 7.29 to see if your sketch matches. You should have six lines total, and the right and the left ends should not have a slope.

> If you accidentally added a line with (or without) a slope, that's fine. You can change it. First, press Esc (to clear the command), and then select the line that needs to be changed. On the Options bar, you can check (or uncheck) Defines Slope.

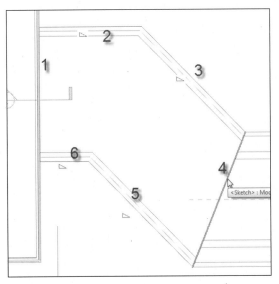

FIGURE 7.29 The new outline of the second roof

12. On the Modify | Create Roof Footprint tab, click Finish Edit Mode.

13. Go to a 3D view. Does your roof look like Figure 7.30?

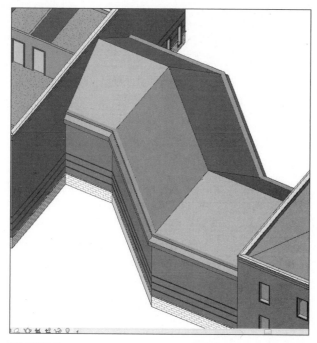

FIGURE 7.30 The corridor roof in 3D

The walls need some help! They are indiscriminately poking up through the roof. You need to do some wall cleanup. First you need to force the walls to use a mitered join at the 45° intersections. The following procedure will show you how:

1. Go to the Level 1 floor plan.

2. Zoom into the wall intersection, as shown in Figure 7.31.

3. On the Modify tab, click the Wall Joins button, as shown in Figure 7.31.

4. Move your cursor over the intersection. You will see a box form around the corner. When you see this box, pick the wall.

5. On the Options bar, click the Miter radio button, as shown near the top left in Figure 7.31. Notice the walls are now joined at a miter.

6. Perform this procedure at all four corners.

When you have suc-
cessfully mitered a
corner and are ready
to move to the next,
there is nothing indi-
cating that you can
safely pick another
corner. You do not
need it. When you
see that the walls
are at a miter, you
can pick the next
intersection. When
you have finished all
four, just press Esc.

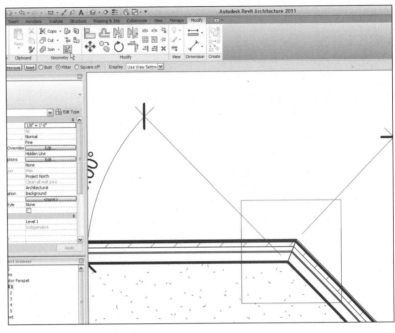

FIGURE 7.31 Modifying the wall's corners

You can now attach the tops of the walls to the bottom of the roof:

1. Go back to a 3D view and select one of the corridor walls.

2. On the Modify | Walls tab, notice there is an option to attach the top or base of the wall, as shown in Figure 7.32. Click the Attach Top/Base button.

3. Pick the roof that the wall is under. You will see that the wall no longer sticks up past the roof.

4. Perform steps 1 through 3 for each corridor wall. When you are finished, your corridor should be spanking nice, like Figure 7.33.

You don't always
have to modify the
wall's mitering. This
is a special situation
where the corners
will not attach to the
roofs properly unless
you do so. There's
really no explanation
for why and when
this will occur. Just
know you have some
tools under your belt
to get out of these
"real life" situations.

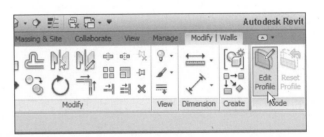

FIGURE 7.32 Attaching the top or the base

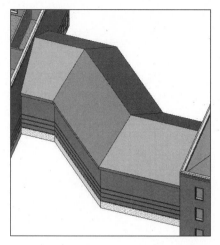

FIGURE 7.33 The completed corridor roof

BUT I GOT THIS WARNING!

Sometimes Revit does not like you hacking up its perfectly fine walls. The warning shown in the following image is common and has no effect on the model. You can just ignore it.

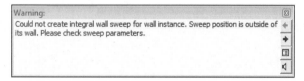

Viewing a Sloped Roof in Plan

Back in Level 3 (the level in which the corridor roof resides), we are having a view problem: the roof is only showing up to the cut plane for that level. This just cannot be. There is a procedure to correct this called a *plan region*:

1. Press Esc if the last command is still running and go to the Level 3 floor plan.

2. On the View tab, click the Plan Region button, as shown in Figure 7.34.

3. On the Draw panel, select the Rectangle button, as shown in Figure 7.35.

4. Draw a rectangle around the corridor, as shown in Figure 7.35. Be sure to snap to the exact points where the corridor walls meet the taller walls on the east and west wings.

5. In the Properties dialog, click the Edit button in the View Range row, as shown in Figure 7.36.

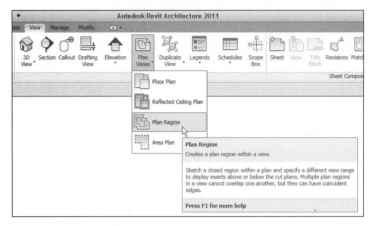

FIGURE 7.34 Using a plan region allows you to alter the view range in a specified area of a plan.

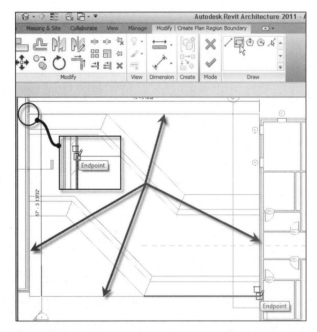

FIGURE 7.35 Creating the rectangle that forms the perimeter of the plan region

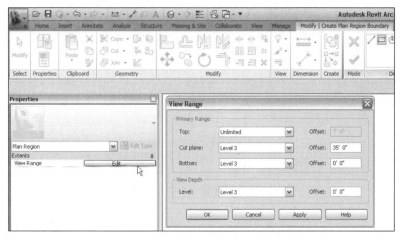

FIGURE 7.36 Setting the view range for the plan region

6. In the View Range dialog, set Top to Unlimited and Level 3 Cut Plane Offset to 35′–0″, as shown in Figure 7.36.

7. Click OK.

8. On the Modify | Create Plan Region Boundary tab, click Finish Edit Mode. You can now see the roof in its entirety, as shown in Figure 7.37.

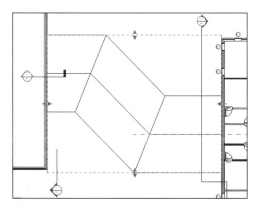

FIGURE 7.37 The finished roof plan

There is one more kind of roof to add. It will be a flat roof that has a slope in one single direction. Although you can do this by simply creating a roof with one edge specified as a pitch, there will be times where you will want a roof sloped at an odd direction that can't be handled by simply angling a roof edge.

Creating a Sloping Roof

To begin the process of creating a sloping roof, we will cap off the west wing of our building. The exterior walls used for the perimeter need to be altered. You are already a pro at this, so let's start right there:

1. Go to a 3D view.

2. Select the west wing exterior walls, as shown in Figure 7.38.

3. On the Properties panel select Exterior - Brick And CMU On MTL. Stud (No Parapet), as shown in Figure 7.38.

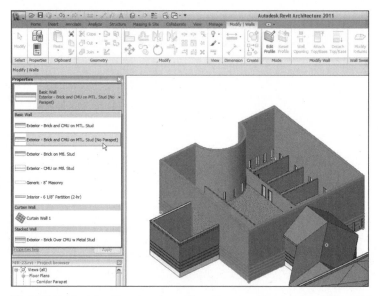

FIGURE 7.38 Changing the walls to Exterior - Brick And CMU On MTL. Stud (No Parapet)

4. In the Project Browser, go to the West Roof floor plan.

5. On the Home tab, select Roof ➤ Roof By Footprint.

6. On the Draw panel, select the Pick Walls button.

7. On the Options bar, uncheck Defines Slope.

8. Type 1'–0" for the Overhang value.

9. Move your cursor over a wall. Make sure the overhang alignment line is facing outside the walls to the exterior.

10. Press the Tab key on your keyboard. All of the walls will be selected.

11. Pick the wall. The magenta lines are completely drawn in. Your sketch should look like Figure 7.39.

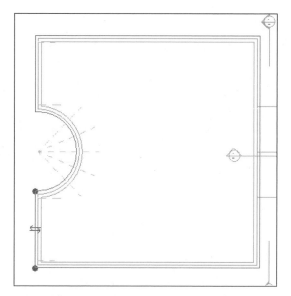

FIGURE 7.39 The perimeter of the roof is set.

Now it is time to set the slope. The objective here is to slope the roof starting at the northeast corner (as the low point) and ending at the southwest corner (the high point). This is done by adding a slope arrow:

1. On the Draw panel, select the Slope Arrow button, as shown in Figure 7.40.

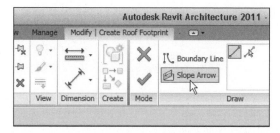

FIGURE 7.40 Clicking the Slope Arrow button on the Draw panel

2. Pick the corner at the upper right and then the corner at the lower left, as shown in Figure 7.41.

3. Press Esc.

4. Select the slope arrow you just added to the model.

5. In the Properties dialog, under Constraints change Specify to Slope.

6. Under Dimensions, change Slope to 3' / 12" (see Figure 7.42).

7. Click Finish Edit Mode on the Modify | Create Roof Footprint tab.

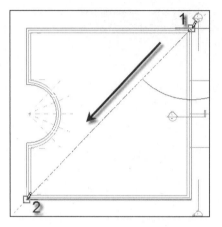

FIGURE 7.41 Adding the slope arrow

FIGURE 7.42 Changing the Slope Arrow properties

Again, we have a view range issue. You can see only the corner of the roof that sits below the cut plane. You can change that with the view range:

1. Press Esc to display the view properties in the Properties dialog.

2. Scroll down the list until you arrive at the View Range row. When you do, click the Edit button.

3. In the View Range dialog, under Primary Range set Top to Unlimited.

4. Set the Cut Plane Offset to 40'–0" (see Figure 7.43).

5. Click OK. You can now see the entire roof.

6. Go to a 3D view. You now have a cool, sloping roof, as shown in Figure 7.44.

FIGURE 7.43 Setting the view range

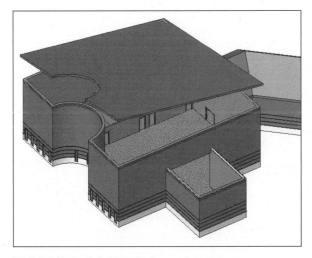

FIGURE 7.44 The sloping roof

Of course there is a wall issue. You can attach most of the walls to the roof simply by selecting them and attaching the tops. You will, however, have to modify the profile for one wall:

1. In the 3D view, select all of the exterior west wing walls, excluding the one on the east side that is west of the corridor (you can see it in Figure 7.45).

2. On the Modify | Walls tab, select Attach Top/Base.

3. Pick Top from the Options bar (it is all the way to the left).

4. Pick the sloping roof (see Figure 7.45).

5. In the Project Browser, go to the section called West Corridor Section.

6. Select the wall that does not attach to the roof.

7. On the Mode panel, click Edit Profile.

8. Trace the roof with the line tool. Be sure you delete the magenta line that established the top of the wall.

9. On the Sketch tab, click Finish Edit Mode. You now have all of the walls joined to the roof. Right now would be a good time to check out the roof in 3D just to make sure the results are pleasing to you.

10. Save the model.

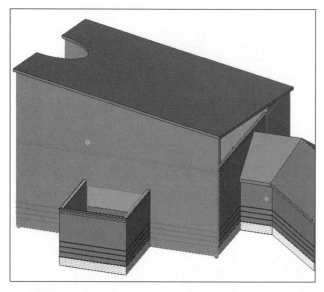

FIGURE 7.45 Attaching the tops of the walls to the sloping roof

The next item to tackle will be creating a roof by extrusion. This is where you can design a custom roof.

Roofs by Extrusion

Creating a roof by extrusion is almost always done in an elevation or a section view. The concept here is to create unique geometry that cannot be accomplished by simply using a footprint in plan. A barrel vault or an eyebrow dormer comes to mind, but there are literally thousands of combinations that will influence how our roofs will be designed.

To get started, the last roof left to be placed is the south jog in the west wing of the model. This is the perfect area for a funky roof!

The first thing to do is to change the three walls defining the jog to the Exterior - Brick And CMU On MTL. Stud (No Parapet) wall type:

1. Go to a 3D view.

2. Select the three walls that comprise the jog in the south wall, as shown in Figure 7.46.

3. From the Properties dialog, switch these walls to Exterior - Brick And CMU On MTL. Stud (No Parapet), as shown in Figure 7.46.

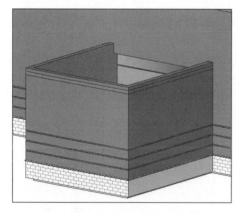

FIGURE 7.46 Changing the wall types as we have been doing all along

4. Go to the Level 1 floor plan.

5. On the View tab, select the Elevation button.

6. In the Properties dialog, be sure the elevation is a Building elevation (you are given the choice in the drop-down menu at the top of the dialog box).

7. Place the elevation as shown in Figure 7.47.

8. Pick the view extents (the blue grips at the ends of the elevation), and drag them in so you can see only the west wing.

9. Make sure you pull the view depth window back to see the wall beyond (see Figure 7.47).

10. Change View Scale to 1/2″ = 1′–0″.

11. Change Detail Level to Fine.

12. Change View Name to **South Entry Elevation**.

13. Click Apply.

14. On the Home tab, select the Ref Plane button; then, in the Draw panel, click the Pick Lines button.

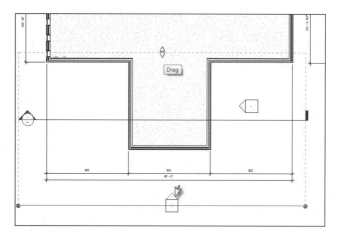

FIGURE 7.47   Adjusting the view

15. Set Offset to 1′–6″.

16. Pick the southmost wall and offset the reference plane away from the building (see Figure 7.48).

17. Press Esc twice to clear the command.

18. Select the reference plane.

19. In the Properties dialog, change the name to **South Entry Overhang**.

20. Click Apply.

21. Open the elevation called South Entry Elevation.

After you place the elevation, you will have no idea where the view is extended to. Is it to the end of the building? You just don't know. If you pick the elevation arrow (the part of the elevation marker), you can then grip-edit the elevation to see what you need.

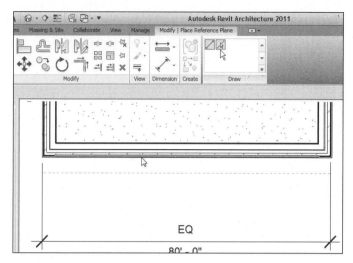

FIGURE 7.48 Adding a reference plane

The importance of that reference plane you just added becomes obvious at this point. You needed to establish a clear starting point for the roof you are about to add. Because the roof will be added in an elevation, Revit does not know where to start the extrusion. This reference plane will serve as that starting point.

1. On the Home tab, select the Roof ➢ Roof By Extrusion command, as shown in Figure 7.49.

2. When you start the command, Revit will ask you to specify a reference plane. Select Reference Plane: South Entry Overhang from the Name drop-down list, as shown in Figure 7.50.

3. Click OK.

4. In the next dialog, change the Level setting to Level 3, and click OK.

5. In the Home tab, select Reference Plane as shown in Figure 7.51, then click the Pick Lines button.

6. Offset a reference plane 3′–0″ to the left and to the right of the exterior walls, as shown by numbers 1 and 2 in Figure 7.51.

7. Offset a reference plane 4′–0″ up from the top of the wall, as shown by number 3 in Figure 7.51.

8. In the Properties dialog, click the Edit Type button.

9. Click Duplicate.

10. Call it **Canopy Roof**.

> While you are in Sketch Mode, when I tell you to click the Roof Properties button, you need to click the Roof Properties button on the right, not the one on the left. They are two different properties.

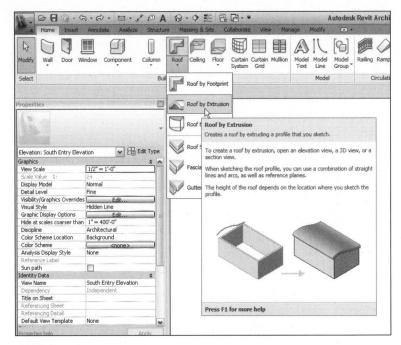

FIGURE 7.49   The Roof ➢ Roof By Extrusion command

FIGURE 7.50   Selecting the South Entry Overhang reference plane

11. Click the Edit button in the Structure row.

12. In the Edit Assembly dialog, change the structure thickness to 4″, as shown in Figure 7.52.

13. Click OK twice to get back to the model.

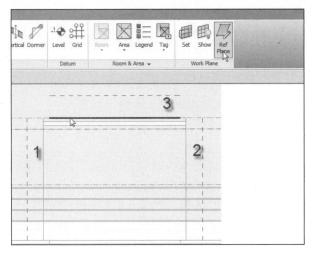

FIGURE 7.51 Adding reference planes to use as construction lines

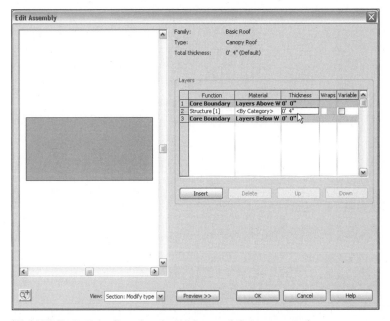

FIGURE 7.52 Changing the thickness of the canopy roof

Now it's time to put the actual roof into the model. So far we have been using great discipline in terms of setting reference planes and creating a separate roof for this canopy. Try to make this a habit!

1. On the Draw panel, click the Start-End-Radius Arc button, as shown in Figure 7.53.

2. Draw an arc from the points shown in Figure 7.53.

 T I P   When you are adding a roof by extrusion, you only need to draw one line. The 4″ thickness is defined in the actual roof you are using. After you click Finish Edit Mode, the 4″ thickness will be added to the bottom.

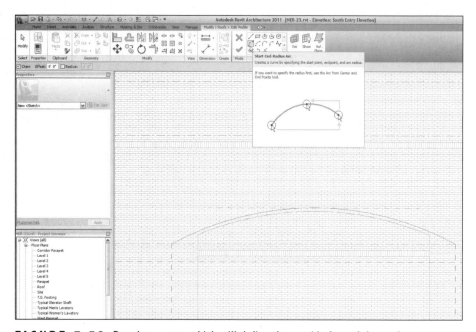

FIGURE 7.53 Drawing an arc, which will define the outside face of the roof

---

3. In the Properties dialog, set Extrusion End to –2′–0″, as shown in Figure 7.54.

4. Click Finish Edit Mode.

5. Go to a 3D view. Your roof should look like Figure 7.55.

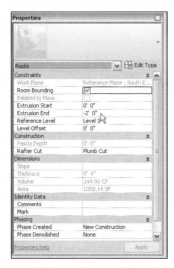

FIGURE 7.54 Setting the extrusion end

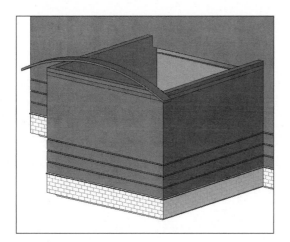

FIGURE 7.55 The almost completed canopy roof

There is just one thing left to do—and it is pretty obvious: we need to attach the roof to the wall. This can be done in one command:

1. On the Modify | Roofs tab, click the Join/Unjoin Roof button, as shown in Figure 7.56.

2. Pick the top, back arc on the canopy roof, as shown in Figure 7.56.

3. Pick the wall that the roof needs to terminate into (see Figure 7.56).

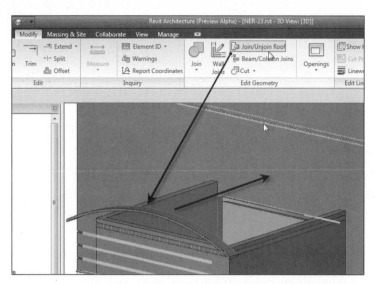

FIGURE 7.56 Picking the roof and the wall to join the two together

4. Your roof should look like Figure 7.57. Select the three walls below the roof.

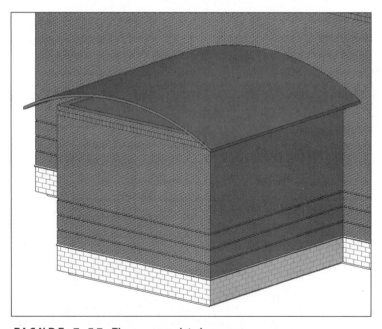

FIGURE 7.57 The now completed canopy

Picking the wall is easier said than done, mostly because it is hard to tell whether you are picking the correct wall. Simply hover your pointer over the wall until the entire face becomes highlighted. When you see this, pick the wall. The roof will then extend to the wall.

5. On the Modify | Walls tab, click the Attach Top/Base button.

6. Select the canopy roof.

The walls are now joined to the roof, as shown in Figure 7.58.

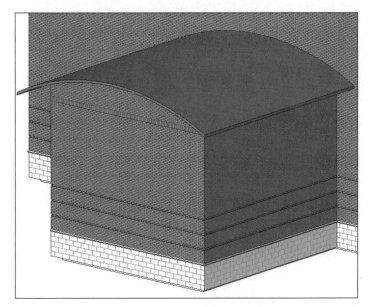

FIGURE 7.58 The walls are now attached to the roof.

All of the conventional roofing systems have been added. It is now time to move on to adding some dormers. This process will simply use a collection of the tools you have gained experience with up to this point.

Adding a Roof Dormer

The best way to add a roof dormer is to modify an existing roof. We certainly have plenty of those in this model, so there should be no shortage of roof surfaces we can use to chop up into dormers.

To begin adding a roof dormer, follow along:

1. Go to the Level 3 floor plan.

2. Zoom in on the corridor roof.

3. Select the corridor roof, as shown in Figure 7.59.

4. On the Modify | Roofs tab, click the Edit Footprint button.

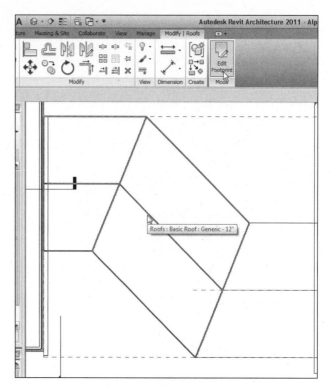

FIGURE 7.59 Selecting the roof to be modified

You are now in the Sketch Mode for this roof.

It is time to start modifying this roof. This procedure is reminiscent of climbing up on an actual roof and adding a dormer:

1. On the Modify | Roofs ➢ Edit Footprint tab, select the Split Element button, as shown in Figure 7.60.

2. On the Options bar, uncheck Delete Inner Segment.

3. Pick two points on the roof edge, as shown in Figure 7.60. The two points are an even 4′–0″ in from each edge.

4. Press Esc twice.

5. Select the middle line.

6. On the Options bar, uncheck Defines Slope.

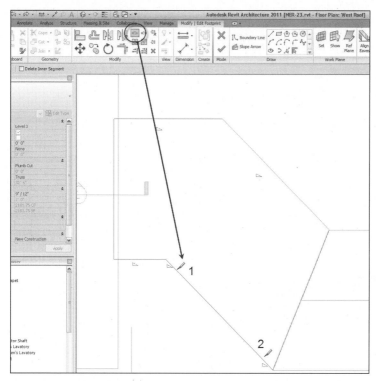

FIGURE 7.60 Splitting the line into three pieces

Now that the length of the dormer has been established, you need to indicate to Revit that you want it to be a gable end dormer. You do this by adding slope arrows:

1. On the Draw panel, click the Slope Arrow button.

2. For the first point of the slope arrow, click the endpoint of the first point you split (see number 1 in Figure 7.61).

3. For the second point of the slope arrow, pick the midpoint of the middle line (see Figure 7.61).

4. Add a second slope arrow coming from the opposite side of the ridge-line, as shown in Figure 7.62.

5. Press Esc twice.

6. Select both slope arrows.

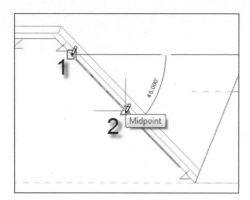

FIGURE 7.61 Adding the first slope arrow

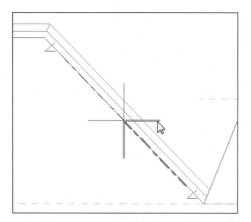

FIGURE 7.62 Adding a second slope arrow

7. In the Properties dialog, under Constraints, change Specify to Slope.

8. Under Dimensions, keep the slope at 9" / 12" (see Figure 7.63).

9. Click Finish Edit Mode.

10. Go to a 3D view to check out the dormer. It should look identical to Figure 7.64.

Adding roof dormers takes some practice to become efficient. If you do not feel confident that you can do a roof dormer on your own, feel free to either go back through the procedure or find another place in the building to add a second dormer.

FIGURE 7.63 Changing the values of the slope arrows

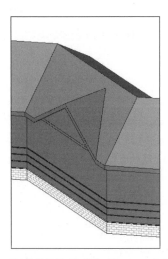

FIGURE 7.64 The completed roof dormer

 N O T E   Notice in the 3D view that the wall followed the modification in the roof. This is because you attached the wall to the roof back when you added the roof to the corridor. The walls have no choice but to comply!

Are You Experienced?

Now you can...

- ☑ place different types of roofs, including flat roofs, pitched roofs, and unconventional, sloping roofs, using the footprint of your building

- ☑ analyze tricky areas, and make multiple roofs if needed instead of relying on a single roof to flex and conform to the situation at hand

- ☑ edit wall joins to allow walls to attach to roofs after they are created

- ☑ design different roof systems based on their functionality

- ☑ create a tapered roof plan using a variable material in the roof system

- ☑ create a roof by extrusion by setting work planes and using them to lay out a custom roof

- ☑ create a roof dormer by editing an existing roof and adding slope arrows to indicate a gable end

Structural Items

Well, we can't avoid the topic of structure forever. Since we need to consider our structure from pretty much the beginning of the project, I had better add it to the first half of the book before we get too carried away!

▶ **Adding structural grids**

▶ **Adding structural columns**

▶ **Using structural framing**

▶ **Understanding foundation systems**

▶ **Adding structural footings**

▶ **Using structural views**

Structural Grids

Revit has entire books on this subject alone, so this book will address only the structural items available to people using Revit Architecture. If you are a structural engineer or structural designer, I recommend that you use Revit Structure. It is an application that is just as powerful as Revit Architecture but that is geared toward structural engineering.

That being said, the two applications share the same file extension (.rvt), which you can open and modify directly from either Revit Architecture, Revit Structure, or Revit MEP with absolutely no issues.

This chapter will delve into the structural world using available functions that have been blended in with the architectural tools.

The first item we will tackle is usually the first item in the model: structural grids. Although you add structural grids line by line, you will soon discover that these grids are just as "smart" as the rest of Revit.

The starting point for all things structural is most certainly the grid. In Revit Architecture, you will find quickly that placing a structural grid into a model is not a complicated task. Grids are essentially placed one line at a time. Those lines you place, however, have intelligence. For example, if you place a vertical grid line called "A" and then place a horizontal grid line called "1" that intersects with A, you will have a grid location. If you place a column at that intersection, the column will assume a new property called Location. That location is—you guessed it—A-1.

Let's get started. To begin, open the file you have been following along with. If you did not complete the previous chapter, go to the book's web page at **www.sybex .com/go/revit2011ner**. From there you can browse to Chapter 8 and find the file called NER-23.rvt.

Placing a Grid

Placing a grid means drawing grid lines in one by one. This task sounds tedious, but it is a welcome change from other applications that force you to create an entire, rectangular grid that you have to keep picking at until it resembles your layout. Grids are like snowflakes: no two are the same.

1. In the Project Browser, go to the Level 1 floor plan. (Make sure you aren't in the Level 1 ceiling plan.)

2. Zoom into the east wing's radial entry.

3. On the Datum panel of the Home tab, click the Grid button, as shown in Figure 8.1.

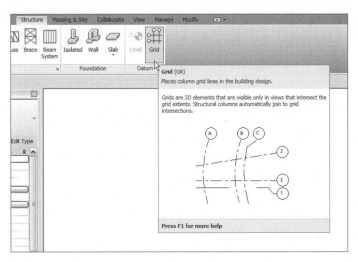

FIGURE 8.1 The Grid button on the Datum panel of the Home tab

4. On the Draw panel of the Modify | Place Grid tab, click the Pick Lines icon, as shown in Figure 8.2.

5. Pick the core centerline of the north wall, as shown in Figure 8.2.

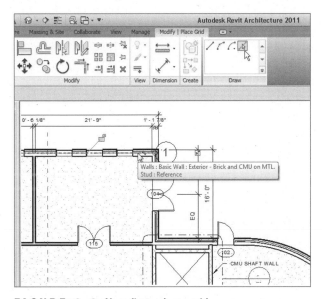

FIGURE 8.2 Your first column grid

6. The column bubble needs to be moved. Press Esc twice (to clear the command), and select the column bubble. Notice the round blue grip, similar to Figure 8.3.

7. Pick that round blue grip, and drag the column bubble to the right about 15′–0″, as shown in Figure 8.4.

8. On the Home tab, click the Grid button again.

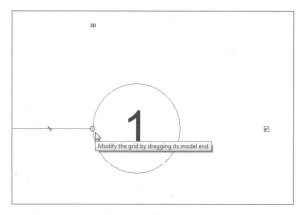

FIGURE 8.3 Examining the column grid grips

Notice these are the same levels: a column grid has similar functionality to levels, right down to the grips.

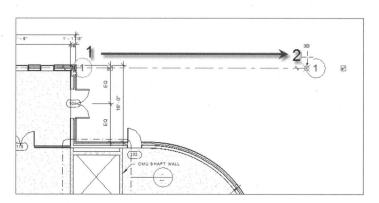

FIGURE 8.4 Dragging the column bubble to the right

9. On the Draw panel, click the Pick Lines icon.

10. Pick the core centerline of the 6 1/8″ wall that terminates at the exterior wall, as shown in Figure 8.5.

11. Drag the right end of the line to align with grid 1. After you move your line to the length of grid 1, pick the second point. An alignment line will appear.

 T I P   **Alignment lines, however useful, can be tricky to get to display. The percentage of your zoom has an effect. If you are not getting the alignment lines, simply zoom back (or in) a small amount and they will appear.**

12. On the right side of grid 2, there is a blue box. Pick it. It will turn the grid head on.

13. On the left side of grid 2, you will see a grid bubble (see Figure 8.5). You will also see the same blue checkbox. Click the checkbox to turn the grid head off at this location.

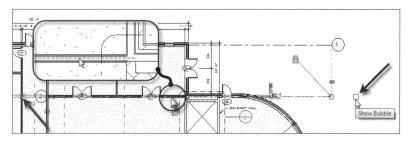

FIGURE 8.5 Adding the second grid line

14. Press Esc.

Being able to pick lines is certainly an advantage, but you are not always going to be in the situation where you have geometry in place to do so. In the following procedure, you will add grid 3 by picking two points:

1. Select the Grid button from the Home tab.

2. On the Draw panel, be sure the Line icon is selected. (It will be selected by default.)

3. Pick a point along the center reference plane, as shown in Figure 8.6.

4. Pick a second point in alignment with grid 2 (see Figure 8.6).

5. Add grids 4 and 5 to the exact opposite ends of the west wing (see Figure 8.7).

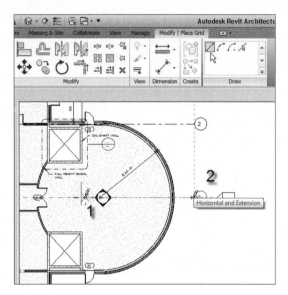

FIGURE 8.6 Adding grid 3 at the center of the building

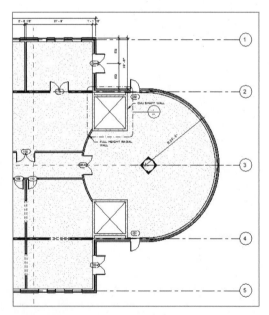

FIGURE 8.7 The completed horizontal grids

We need to add two more grids at 45° angles. This will be as easy as drawing lines. The objective here is to manipulate the grids to read the appropriate numbering.

1. On the Home tab, click the Grid button.

2. Pick the center of the radial wall.

3. Draw the line at a 45° angle until you are beyond the radial wall, as shown in Figure 8.8.

4. If you are still in the Grid command, press Esc, then rename the grid line to **2.1**.

5. Draw another grid line at a 45° angle in the opposite direction.

6. Renumber it to read **3.9** (see Figure 8.8).

 With grid lines, you can still copy, rotate, move, and mirror. Remember this when you are placing grids.

 N O T E In many instances, you will encounter elevation markers and other annotation items that get in the way. You can move these items, but be careful. After you move an item, open the referring view to make sure you did not disturb anything.

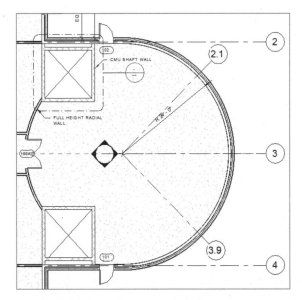

FIGURE 8.8 Adding two additional grids and renumbering them

We need two more horizontal column lines that span the length of the building. We will number these lines as **2.10** and **3.1**. The lines will run centered on the corridor walls. To do this, you will use the Pick Lines icon on the Draw panel.

1. On the Home tab, click the Grid button.

2. On the Draw panel, click the Pick Lines icon.

3. Pick the core centerline of the north corridor wall, as shown in Figure 8.9.

4. Pick the blue grip at the end of the line and stretch it to align with the already placed bubbles, as shown in Figure 8.10.

5. Click the Show Bubble button.

6. Rename the grid to **2.10** (see Figure 8.10).

7. Zoom to the other end of the grid line and uncheck the Show Bubble checkbox.

8. Repeat the process for the south corridor wall, adding an additional grid line numbered 3.1, as shown in Figure 8.11.

The grids are laying out OK, but it looks like we should make some adjustments to move the bubbles apart a little. You can do this by adding an elbow to the grid's end.

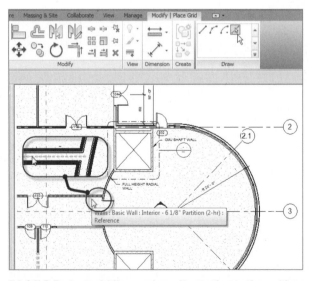

FIGURE 8.9 Adding a column line to the north corridor wall

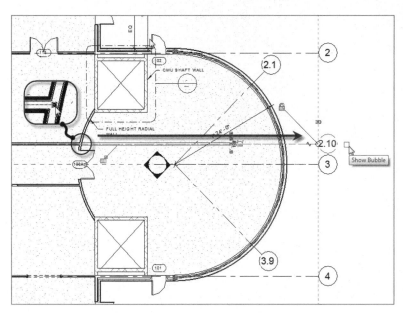

FIGURE 8.10 Dragging the line and turning on the bubble so you can rename the grid to 2.10

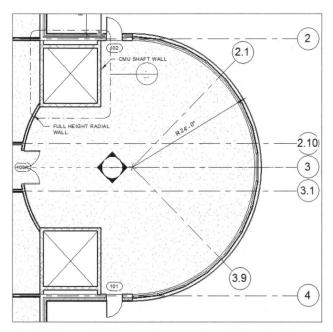

FIGURE 8.11 Adding the grids along the corridor walls

Adding Elbows

As with levels, you can add a break in the line of the grid, allowing you to make adjustments as if the grid were an arm with an elbow.

1. Select grid 2.10.

2. You will see several blue grips appear. Pick the one that appears as a break line, as shown in Figure 8.12.

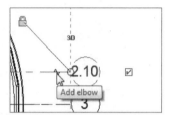

FIGURE 8.12   Clicking the Add Elbow grip after selecting the grid

3. When you pick this break line, it adds an elbow to your grid line, as shown in Figure 8.13.

 N O T E   Notice that the bubble was broken, and it was moved up and out of the way. This will not always happen. In most cases, the grid will probably move in the wrong direction. You can then select the blue grips and move the bubble in the direction you intended.

4. Repeat the procedure for grid 3.1. Your grids should now look like Figure 8.13.

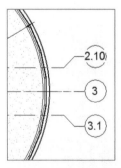

FIGURE 8.13   The cleaned-up grid bubbles

5. Save the model.

It is now time to add the vertical grids. This will be a simple process until we get to the radial entry area. At that point there will need to be some additional manipulating of the grid.

Adding Vertical Grids

The only real issue with adding vertical grids is the numbering versus lettering issue because Revit will continue the sequencing from the horizontal grids. Make sure that when you add your first grid going in the opposite direction you renumber (or rename) the first occurrence of the grid.

The objective of the next procedure is to create a grid pattern running vertically across the view:

1. Zoom out so you can see the entire east wing, as shown in Figure 8.14.

2. On the Home tab, click the Grid button.

3. On the Draw panel of the Modify | Place Grid tab, click the Pick Lines icon, as shown in Figure 8.14.

4. Pick the core centerline of the west exterior wall of the east wing, as shown in Figure 8.14.

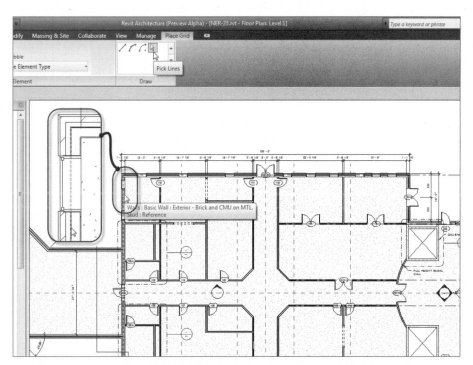

FIGURE 8.14 Adding the first vertical grid by picking the core center line of the exterior wall

5. When you pick the wall, the grid is added. It will not be the name or number you want. We will change that. But first, pick the round blue grip and drag the bubble up past the dimensions, as shown in Figure 8.15.

6. Press Esc.

7. Select the new vertical grid.

8. Click in the bubble and rename it to A, as shown in Figure 8.16.

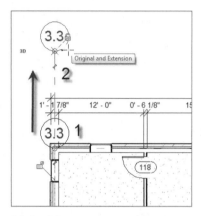

FIGURE 8.15 Dragging the new bubble out of the wall

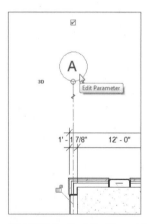

FIGURE 8.16 The grid is now named A.

It is now time to duplicate this grid. Since you have an arsenal of modify commands under your belt, the best way to duplicate this grid is to copy it, as shown in the following steps:

1. Select grid A.

2. On the Modify | Grids tab, click the Copy button, as shown at the top and center of Figure 8.17.

3. On the Options bar, make sure the Multiple checkbox is selected, as shown near the top left of Figure 8.17.

4. Pick a base point along the grid line within the wall, as shown in Figure 8.17.

5. Copy grid A to the wall centerlines, as shown in Figure 8.17. Notice that the grid lines will autosequence as you go.

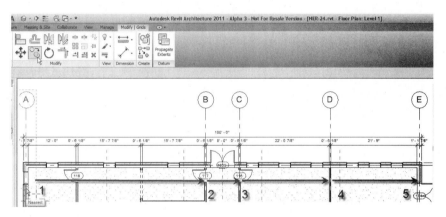

FIGURE 8.17 Copying the grid line to the other walls

6. Press Esc twice.

7. Start the Grid command again.

8. On the Draw panel, be sure the Line button is selected.

9. Pick a start point at the endpoint of the radial wall where it intersects with the straight wall, as shown near the bottom of Figure 8.18.

10. Pick the second point in line with the adjacent grid bubbles (see Figure 8.18).

11. Press Esc.

12. Pick the grip on the bottom of the line, and drag it down past the south part of the radial wall.

The next step is to add the grid to the radial entry area. This will not be as easy as simply picking a wall's centerline. The trick here will be to establish a reference point to place the grid and, subsequently, a column.

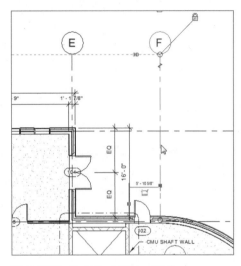

FIGURE 8.18 Adding grid F

Adding a Radial Grid Line

Sometimes, you have to think outside the box. Literally. Since we have radial geometry to contend with, we need to add a radial grid, as follows:

1. Zoom in on the radial entry of the east wing.

2. Click the Grid button on the Home tab.

3. On the Draw panel, select the Line button, as shown in Figure 8.19.

4. Type in an offset of 6″ on the Options bar.

5. Pick the finished inside face of the radial wall, as shown in Figure 8.19.

6. The actual grid bubble lands in a congested area. Fix this by adding an elbow and adjusting the bubbles, as shown by grid G near the top of Figure 8.20.

I think you get the picture on adding grids. The next procedure is to start adding columns to these grid intersections. To do so, we will explore the Structure tab on the Ribbon.

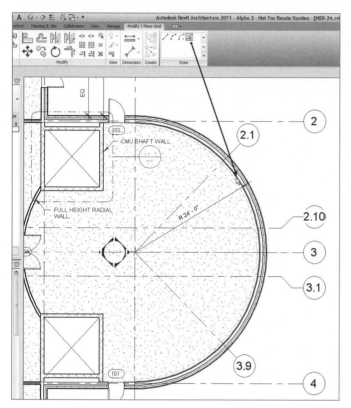

FIGURE 8.19 Adding a grid line offset from the finish inside face

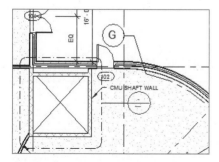

FIGURE 8.20 Adding bubbles to the radial grid line and adjusting their placements with elbows

Adding Structural Columns

The hard part is over. Determining where to put the columns is harder than physically placing them in the model. But of course there are rules to follow, and rules that need to be bent in order to accomplish the results we want to see.

This next series of procedures will include adding structural components to the model and placing framing systems in areas where a structural engineer may defer to the architect for structural integrity given their design intent.

To begin, open the file you have been following along with. If you did not complete the previous section, go to the book's web page at **www.sybex.com/go/ revit2011ner**. From there you can browse to Chapter 8 and find the file called `NER-24.rvt`.

To add columns to the model, follow this procedure:

1. In the Project Browser, go to the Level 1 floor plan.

2. Zoom into the radial entry area in the east wing.

3. On the Structure tab, click Column ➢ Structural Column, as shown in Figure 8.21.

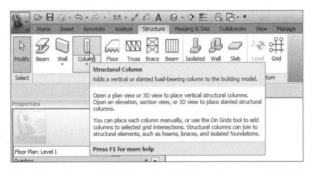

FIGURE 8.21 The Structural Column button on the Structure tab of the Ribbon

4. You will probably not have any structural columns loaded into the model. If you get the message shown in Figure 8.22, click Yes to browse for a structural column.

5. Browse to Imperial Library ➢ Structural ➢ Columns ➢ Steel.

6. In the `Steel` folder, browse to `HSS-Hollow Structural Section -Column.rfa`.

7. Double click on HSS-Hollow Structural Section-Column.rfa; you will see a dialog allowing you to select the type, as shown in Figure 8.23.

8. Select the HSS6×6×5/8 column.

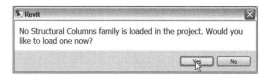

FIGURE 8.22 You'll see this message when no columns are loaded in the model. Click Yes.

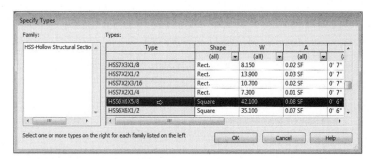

FIGURE 8.23 Select HSS-Hollow Structural Section-Column.rfa and choose the HSS6×6×5/8 type.

9. Click OK.

10. On the Options bar, make sure Height is set to Roof, as shown in Figure 8.24.

11. Place the column on the grid intersection F-1.

12. Press Esc twice.

13. Click the Column ➤ Structural Column button on the Home tab.

14. Place a column at grid intersection F-2. Before you place this column, be sure Height is set to Roof.

15. Place another column at grid intersection F-G (see Figure 8.25).

16. Select the column on the inside of the building (Column F-G). Once the column is in place, press Esc twice to release the command.

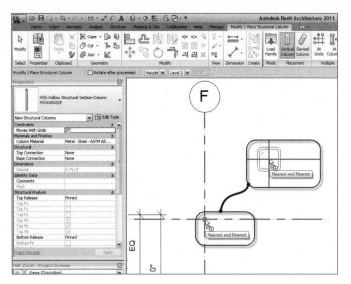

FIGURE 8.24 Placing the column on grid intersection F-1

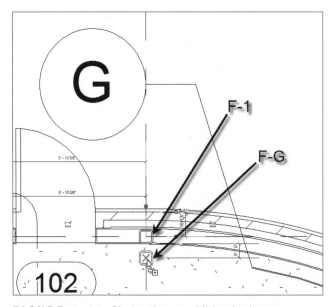

FIGURE 8.25 Placing the two additional columns

17. In the Properties dialog, make sure that the top level is set to Up To: Roof, as shown in Figure 8.26.

FIGURE 8.26 Setting the column's Top Level to extend to the roof

 N O T E Notice that Column Location is set to F-G. This is important because if the column is offset from one of these lines, Revit will still consider the column to be at that column location but with an offset dimension.

18. Mirror the three columns to the opposite side of the entry using column line 3 as the reference plane.

19. Save the model.

It's time to start adding some full-height columns at the rest of the grid locations. You will begin with the radial grid, and then place the rest of the columns in the walls of the exterior and the corridor:

1. On the Structure tab, click the Column ➢ Structural Column button.

2. On the Options bar, be sure Height is set to Roof.

3. Hover your cursor over grid intersection G-2.1. Notice that you can see the column, but it is at the wrong orientation.

4. Press the Tab key on your keyboard, and the column will rotate to align with the grid, as shown in Figure 8.27.

5. When the column is aligned, pick the intersection. The column is placed.

6. Repeat the steps for columns 3 and 3.9.

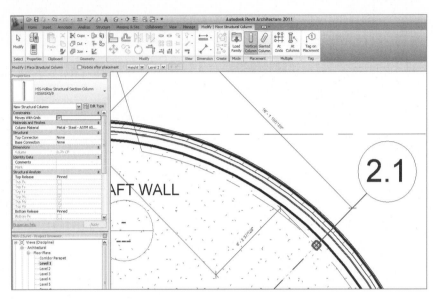

FIGURE 8.27 Placing a column at an angle

It's time now to start placing columns in the main part of the wing. Place a column at every grid location. Note that you must stretch the column lines to the left side of the wing. You should also turn the grid bubbles on at the west and south sides of the building, as shown in Figure 8.28.

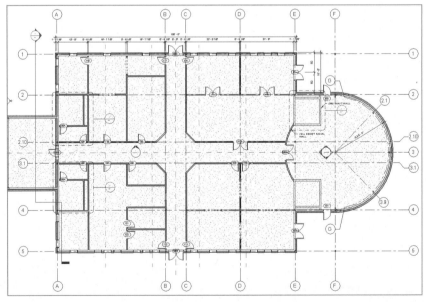

Since you rotated the first column, notice that as you follow the radius the column rotates on its own.

FIGURE 8.28 The grids should be extended and the bubbles turned on at each end.

To add columns by intersection, follow these steps:

1. Start the Structural Column command.

2. On the Modify | Place Structural Column tab, click the At Grids button on the Multiple panel, as shown in Figure 8.29.

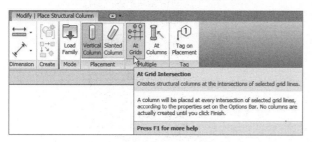

FIGURE 8.29 Using the "Place Column At Grids" function

3. Pick a window around the rectangular portion of the east wing (from right to left), as shown in Figure 8.30.

4. Notice the Modify | Place Structural Column ➤ At Grid Intersection tab now changes to allow you to either finish or cancel. Once you have the window placed, click the Finish button on the Multiple panel, as shown at the top of Figure 8.30.

5. Press Esc.

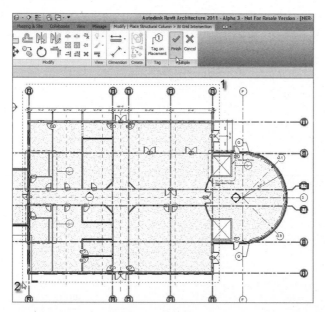

FIGURE 8.30 Picking a window where the columns will be placed

There are quite a few columns placed. You will need to move some of these columns, including the four columns in the corridor intersection area. Revit will still locate these columns at a grid intersection, except it will add the offset in the column's properties.

To move the columns and create a column offset, follow these steps:

1. Zoom into the middle of the east wing at the corridor intersection.

2. Select the two columns at the left of the corridor, as shown in Figure 8.31.

3. Move the columns 4′–0″ to the left (see Figure 8.31).

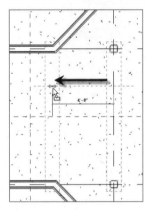

FIGURE 8.31 Moving the columns to the left 4′–0″

4. Repeat the same procedure for the other two columns (see Figure 8.32).

5. Zoom into the door shown in Figure 8.32.

6. Move the column to the left 4′–0″.

7. Save the model.

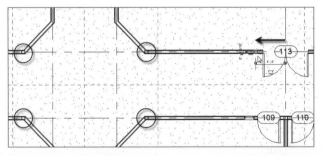

FIGURE 8.32 Making adjustments like moving a column will happen quite a bit.

That's enough columns for now. It's time to move on to adding some structural framing. The main areas where we will add framing are in the canopy areas surrounding the east entry of the east wing.

Structural Framing

Although you will not do most structural framing in Revit Architecture, there are a few areas where you will need to add some framing. Canopies with light structural framing are certainly one area that could call for the architect to wander over to the structural side of the fence.

To start adding structural framing:

1. In the Project Browser, go to the Level 2 floor plan.

2. Zoom into the radial entry area.

3. Notice you cannot see the exterior column. Adjust the view range for this view to see the item.

4. In the Properties dialog box, scroll down to the View Range row, and click the Edit button.

5. In Primary Range, set Bottom Offset to –1′–0″.

6. For View Depth, set Level Offset to –1′–0″ (see Figure 8.33).

F I G U R E 8 . 3 3 Setting the view range so you can see 1′–0″ below the level

7. Click OK. You can now see the column.

It is now time to place the structural framing. Make sure you are zoomed into the northeast corner of the east wing.

1. On the Structure panel of the Structure tab, select the Beam button, as shown in Figure 8.34.

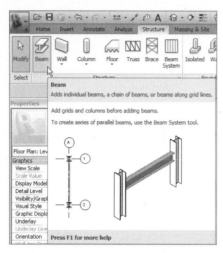

FIGURE 8.34   The Beam button on the Structure panel of the Structure tab

2. If you get the message stating that no structural framing family is loaded into the model, click Yes.

3. Browse to Structural ➤ Framing ➤ Steel.

4. Select HSS-Hollow Structural Section.rfa.

5. In the Specify Types dialog, select HSS6×6×5/8″, and click OK.

6. Pick the first point at the column to the left that is buried within the corner of the wall.

7. Pick the second point at the exterior column, as shown in Figure 8.35.

8. With the Beam command still running, pick the exterior column (F-1), then column F-2, as shown in Figure 8.36.

9. Press Esc twice.

10. Start the Beam command again.

11. Draw a beam 6″ off the finish face of the wall starting at the top beam, ending in the wall, as shown in Figure 8.37.

N O T E   Revit will not like that you are bearing a beam on a nonbearing wall. If you are asked to make this wall bearing, click Make Wall Bearing.

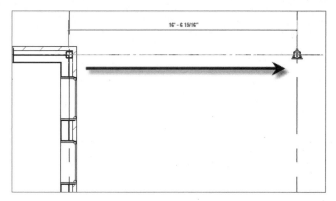

FIGURE 8.35 Adding the beam requires picking two columns.

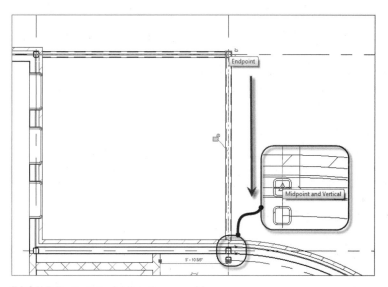

FIGURE 8.36 Adding the second beam

12. Draw another beam from the left to the right, 6″ off the finish face of the wall, as shown in Figure 8.38.

13. Save the model.

It is now time to add some filler beams. In Revit Architecture, you can add a beam system that is controlled by a specified spacing. Once the system is in place, you can control the properties for the duration of the project.

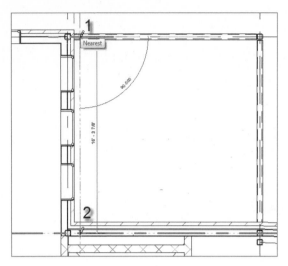

FIGURE 8.37 Adding a beam 6″ off the face of the wall to the center of the beam

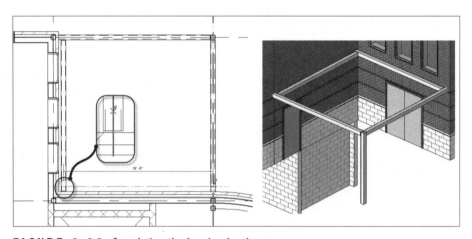

FIGURE 8.38 Completing the framing for the canopy

Adding a Beam System

Although adding beam systems is much more crucial in Revit Structure, it does have its usefulness in Revit Architecture as well. Having the ability to equally space a framing system can be quite advantageous.

To create a beam system, follow along with this procedure:

1. On the Structure panel of the Structure tab, click the Beam System button, as shown in Figure 8.39.

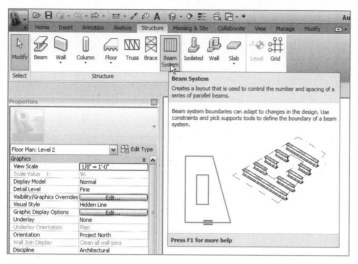

FIGURE 8.39 The Beam System button

2. On the Draw panel, click the Pick Supports button, as shown at the top of Figure 8.40.

3. Pick the four HSS members that form the canopy, as shown in Figure 8.40.

N O T E   The support you pick first determines the direction that the beams will run in. Notice the double lines in the horizontal beam? This indicates the direction of the beam system. If you want to change this direction, click the Beam Direction button on the Draw panel.

4. On the Modify panel, click the Trim/Extend Single Element button, as shown in Figure 8.41.

5. Trim the overlapping corners of the magenta sketch lines. See Figure 8.41.

6. In the Properties dialog, change the Layout Rule setting to Maximum Spacing.

7. Change the Maximum Spacing value to 4'–0", as shown in Figure 8.42.

8. Click Apply.

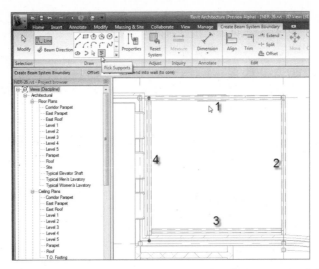

FIGURE 8.40 Picking the four beams as the supports of the beam system

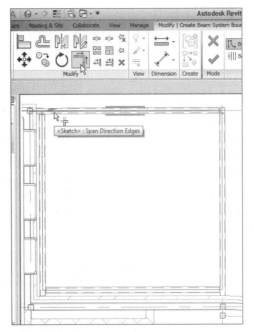

FIGURE 8.41 Cleaning up the corners of the sketch by using the Trim command

FIGURE 8.42 Changing the properties to reflect a 4′–0″ maximum spacing

9. In the Mode panel of the Modify | Create Beam System Boundary tab, click the Finish Edit Mode button. Your framing should look like Figure 8.43.

10. Mirror the canopy to the other side of the radial entry. Be careful not to accidentally mirror the columns.

11. You may receive the same message about bearing a structural member on a nonstructural wall. Click the Make Wall Bearing button.

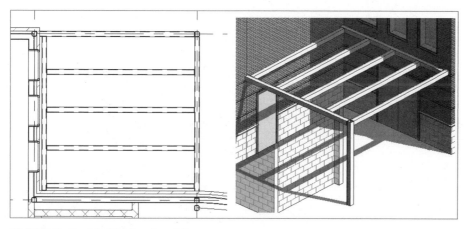

FIGURE 8.43 The framing at the canopy

By using the Beam System command, you can easily add multiple occurrences of framing members quite quickly. There will be, however, cases where you need nonuniform members on a different plane, such as lateral bracing.

Adding Bracing

It would be nice to add a rod to the top of this canopy at an angle. You can accomplish this by using the Brace command.

To use the Brace command, let's first add the rod family to our model:

1. To load the rod family, click the Load From Family ≻ Load Family button on the Insert tab.

2. Browse to Structural ≻ Framing ≻ Steel, and open the file called Round Bar.rfa.

3. Now that the file is loaded, go to the North elevation in the Project Browser.

4. In Properties panel for the North elevation, change Detail Level to Fine and Visual Style to Shaded w/Edges.

5. Zoom in on the east canopy.

6. On the Structure panel of the Structure tab, click the Brace button, as shown in Figure 8.44.

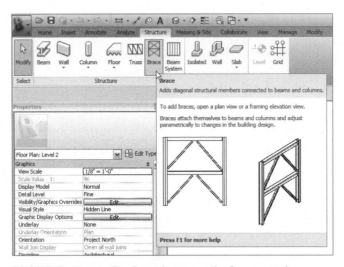

FIGURE 8.44 The Brace button on the Structure tab

7. After you select the Brace button, Revit will display a dialog asking you to specify a work plane. In the Name drop-down list, select Grid : 1, as shown in Figure 8.45, and then click OK.

8. Verify that Round Bar: 1″ is the current framing member at the top of the Properties panel.

9. Draw a diagonal bar, as shown in Figure 8.46.

10. Go to the East elevation.

11. Change Detail Level to Fine and Visual Style to Shading w/ Edges.

12. On the Structure panel of the Structure tab, click the Brace button.

FIGURE 8.45 Specifying Grid : 1 as the work plane for the bracing

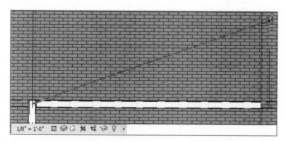

FIGURE 8.46 Adding the rod at an angle

13. Choose Grid : F as the work plane.

14. Draw a diagonal rod similar to the one in Figure 8.47.

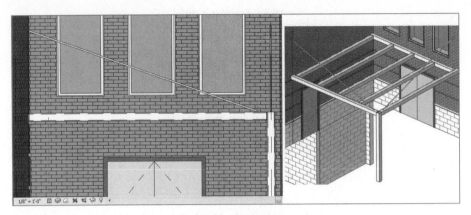

FIGURE 8.47 Adding the second rod to the canopy

> **15.** Mirror the rods to the other canopy. You can stay in the East elevation to do so.

  N O T E   If you receive a warning about a circular reference chain, simply click Unjoin Elements.

> **16.** Save the model.

That pretty much covers it for framing. The next section will bring us underground into the foundation. Although the structural engineer will usually specify the foundation system, architects must have access to foundation tools to place concrete foundation walls as well as strip and isolate footings and piers. The next section will address these topics.

Foundation Systems

The first question that arises while addressing structural foundations is, "What if the architect places a foundation in the model, and then the structural engineer places one in their model?"

What will happen is the structural engineer will use a method called Copy/Monitor whereas the engineer takes the architect's foundation and makes it their own. The engineer is then free to alter the foundation. This method will be addressed fully in Chapter 20, "Importing and Coordinating Revit Models."

The first topic in this section will focus on creating foundation walls. Although adding this type of wall is similar to adding architectural walls, there are a few things you want to look out for.

Foundation Walls

For now, let's add a foundation and deal with coordination later. The task before us here is to create a foundation wall constructed of 18″ of solid concrete. To proceed, follow these steps:

1. Go to the Level 1 floor plan.

2. Click the Wall ➤ Structural Wall button on the Structure tab, as shown in Figure 8.48.

3. In the change Element Type menu at the top of the Properties panel, select Generic 8″ Masonry.

4. Click the Edit Type button.

5. Click the Duplicate button.

6. Name the new wall **18″ Concrete**.

7. Click OK.

8. In the Function row, select Foundation from the drop-down list, as shown in Figure 8.48.

9. Just under the Function row is the Coarse Scale Fill Pattern row. Change the hatch to Concrete by clicking the […] button and selecting Concrete from the menu. Click OK.

10. Click the Edit button in the Structure row.

11. In the second row in the Layers chart, click in the Material cell.

12. Click the […] button.

13. Find Concrete - Cast-in-Place Concrete.

14. Click OK.

15. Change the Thickness to 1′–6″ (see Figure 8.49).

16. Click OK twice.

17. Press Esc.

The reason we press Esc and basically bailed out at the last second is that we are about to place a wall underneath this level. This view is currently set to not show anything below this level, forcing us to alter the view range.

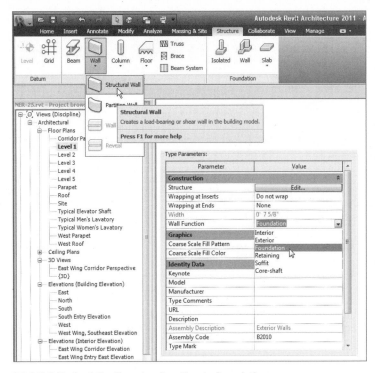

FIGURE 8.48 Changing Function to Foundation

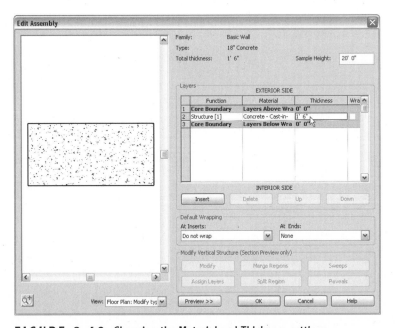

FIGURE 8.49 Changing the Material and Thickness settings

To modify the view range, follow these steps:

1. In the Properties dialog, scroll down to View Range and click the Edit button.

2. For Primary Range, set Bottom Offset to –1'–0".

3. For View Depth, set Level Offset to –1'–0".

4. Click OK.

5. Click the Wall ➢ Structural Wall button from the Home tab.

6. On the Draw panel, click the Pick Lines icon.

7. Make sure that Depth is set to T.O. Footing on the Options bar.

8. Pick the core centerline of the exterior wall, as shown in Figure 8.50.

9. Keep repeating picking the exterior walls in all three sections of the model.

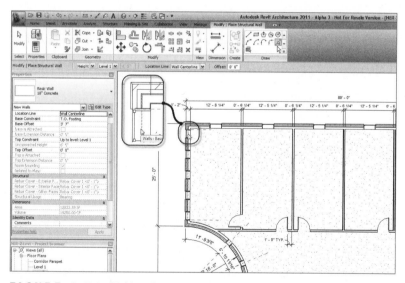

FIGURE 8.50 Picking the core centerline of every exterior wall in the entire model. This includes the corridor and both wings.

Your 3D model should look like Figure 8.51. Get into the habit of viewing the model in 3D—especially when you can't see exactly where the walls are being placed in the plan.

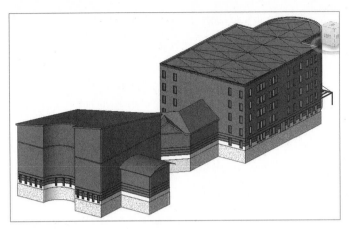

FIGURE 8.51 The foundation walls

Now we can travel into the ground and check out how our walls are joining. Some cleanup will be involved:

1. In the Project Browser, find the T.O. Footing floor plan and double-click it.

2. Zoom into the east wing area where the south elevator meets the foundation wall. There is an issue: the walls are funky, as shown in Figure 8.52.

3. Select the masonry elevator shaft wall.

4. On the blue grip, right-click and select Disallow Join, as shown in Figure 8.52.

5. Click the grip on the masonry wall (the same one you right-clicked on to disallow the join), and drag it back to the outside face of the corner, as shown in Figure 8.52.

6. The masonry wall to the right needs to be joined to the foundation wall. To do this, click the Join Geometry button on the Modify toolbar, as shown in Figure 8.53.

7. Pick the foundation wall.

8. Pick the masonry wall. The masonry wall is now notched back for the foundation.

9. Repeat the procedure for the north elevator. The condition may be slightly different than the south elevator, but the process to fix it will be the same.

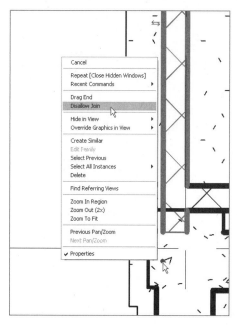

FIGURE 8.52 The walls are not behaving as we would like them to.

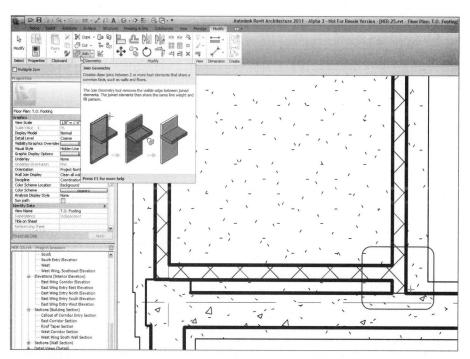

FIGURE 8.53 Disallowing the wall's join will enable the foundation walls to terminate as expected.

Moving to the west wing, there is one wall we need to fix. The command we will have to use is the Split command:

1. Zoom in on the area, as shown in Figure 8.54.

2. On the Modify tab, click the Split Element button, as shown in Figure 8.54.

3. On the Options bar, click the Delete Inner Segment checkbox (see Figure 8.54).

4. Pick the points labeled "1" and "2," shown in Figure 8.54.

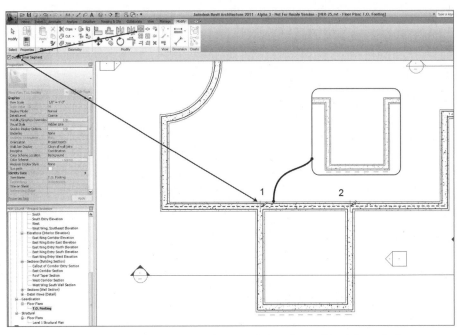

FIGURE 8.54 Splitting the foundation wall to follow the profile of the wall above

Now that the foundation walls are in place, it is time to think about what these walls are bearing on. Revit Architecture has tools to add footings to the bottom of these walls.

Adding Structural Footings

If you are going as far as placing structural foundation walls, you might as well continue on and place footings underneath them, right? Luckily this is not a difficult task.

Before we start adding the structural footings to the plan, we need to acknowledge that, by default, this view is not set up to see any objects that are physically below its level. To correct this, we must alter the view range of this specific plan.

1. Make sure you are still in the T.O. Footing plan, and click Esc twice to end any active command.

2. In the Properties dialog, go to the View Range row and click Edit.

3. Set Primary Range Bottom to Unlimited.

4. Set View Depth Level to Unlimited, as shown in Figure 8.55.

5. Click OK.

FIGURE 8.55 Again with the View Range!

6. On the Foundation panel of the Structure tab, click the Wall Foundation button, as shown in Figure 8.56.

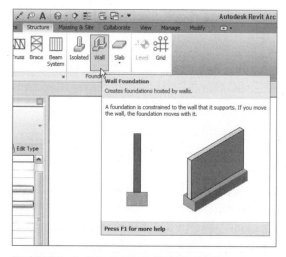

FIGURE 8.56 Adding a Wall foundation

At the top of the Properties dialog box, notice it says Bearing Footing - 36″ × 12″. This is a little big for our purposes, so let's make a new one:

Just because this specific foundation is labeled Wall does not mean it is a wall. It is labeled Wall because it is a continuous (strip) footing that has a wall bearing on it.

1. In the Properties dialog, click the Edit Type button.

2. Click Duplicate.

3. Call the new footing element **Bearing Footing - 30″ x 12″**.

4. Click OK.

5. Change the Width setting to 2′–6″, as shown in Figure 8.57.

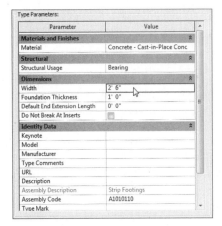

FIGURE 8.57 Changing the width to 2′–6″

6. Click OK again to get back to the model.

7. Start picking walls. This footing will be centered underneath each wall you pick.

8. When you are done picking the walls, go to a 3D view to make sure you have all of the foundations covered, as shown in Figure 8.58.

When all the footings are in place, you can see that we need to focus on the elevator shafts. Since we need an entire foundation mat underneath the elevators, we can use a structural slab.

Structural Slabs

Structural slabs are basically really thick floors. The one we are about to use is a 12″-thick solid concrete floor. Of course, Revit does not have something this thick already built in the library, so we will take this opportunity to make one:

1. Go to the T.O. Footing floor plan.

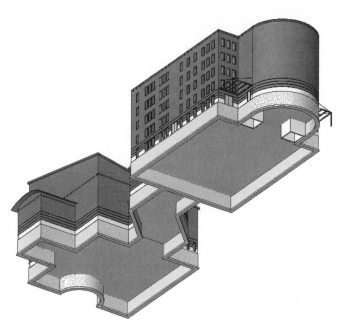

FIGURE 8.58 Doing a 3D investigation to see whether the footings are all in place

2. Zoom into the elevator area.

3. On the Foundation panel of the Structure tab, click Slab ➢ Foundation Slab, as shown in Figure 8.59.

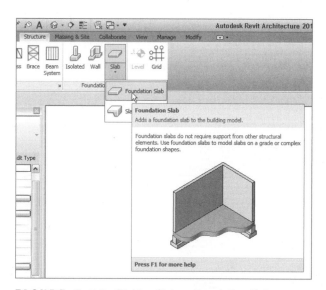

FIGURE 8.59 Clicking Slab ➢ Foundation Slab

If you hover your cursor over a wall and press the Tab key, Revit will select all connecting walls, allowing you to add the bearing footing in literally two clicks.

4. In the Properties panel, click Edit Type.

5. Click Duplicate.

6. Call the new slab **12″ Elevator Slab**.

7. Click OK.

8. Click the Edit button in the Structure row.

9. In the Layers field, change Thickness to **1′–0″**, as shown in Figure 8.60.

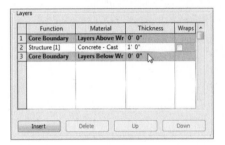

FIGURE 8.60 Changing the structure thickness

10. Click OK twice to get back to the model.

11. On the Draw panel, click the Pick Walls button.

12. On the Options bar, set Offset to 1′–0″.

13. Pick the three elevator shaft walls, as shown by the numbers in Figure 8.61.

14. Set Offset back to 0.

15. Pick the elevator shaft walls, as shown in Figure 8.61.

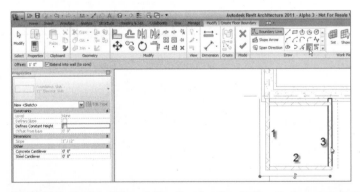

FIGURE 8.61 When picking the elevator shaft walls, be sure to include the 1′–0″ offset.

16. Set the Offset value back to 0 in the Options bar if it is not already.

17. Pick the Exterior foundation wall.

Now that the perimeter is set, it is time to start trimming the edges to make sure you have a continuous, closed loop:

1. On the Modify panel, click the Trim/Extend Single Element button.

2. Trim any overlapping corners, as shown in Figure 8.62.

3. On the Floor panel to the right of the Create Floor Boundary tab, click Finish Edit Mode.

4. Repeat the process for the south elevator.

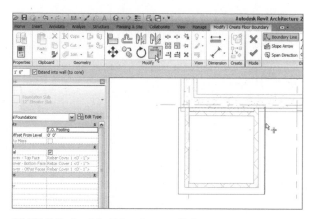

FIGURE 8.62 Trimming up all the corners

Your plan should look like Figure 8.63.

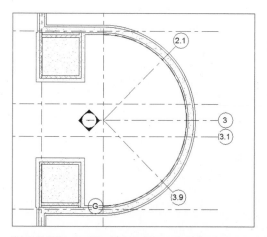

FIGURE 8.63 The finished elevator pads

Now that the footings are mostly in place, it is time to think about placing piers and spread footings in the foundation. Luckily, as you are soon to discover, you already know how to do this.

Piers and Spread Footings

Piers and pilasters, simply put, are concrete columns. This is how Revit sees these items, and this is the easiest placement method.

A nice thing about this method is the fact that the grids are in place as well as the steel columns that bear upon them. The only real trick is deciding which plan to put them in.

The objective of the next procedure is to add footings to the bottoms of the structural walls:

1. Remain in the T.O. Footing plan.

2. On the Structure panel of the Structure tab, click the Column ➢ Structural Column button.

3. On the Insert tab, click the Load Family button, as shown at the top of Figure 8.64.

4. Browse to Structural ➢ Columns ➢ Concrete.

5. Pick the file called `Concrete-Square-Column.rfa`.

6. Click Open.

7. At the top of the Properties dialog, select the 24″ × 24″ column.

8. Start placing the columns at the grid intersections, as shown in Figure 8.64.

9. Press Esc, and then go to Level 1.

10. Zoom into the corridor.

11. Move the piers under the columns.

12. Do the same for the pier under the doorway, as shown in Figure 8.65.

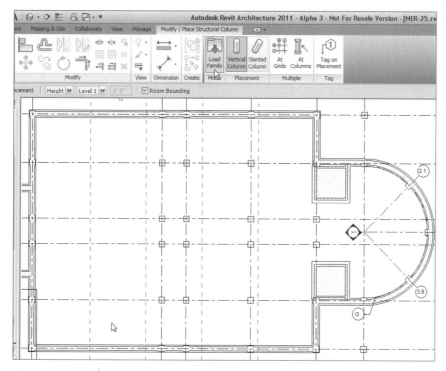

FIGURE 8.64 Start placing piers.

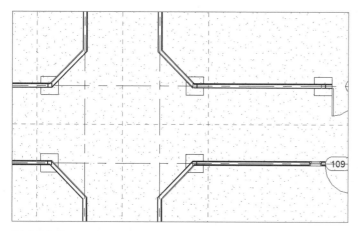

FIGURE 8.65 Making the necessary adjustments

Now it's time to add the spread footings under the piers. This process will be almost identical to the process we just went through:

1. Go back to the T.O. Footing floor plan.

2. On the Foundation panel of the Structure tab, select the Isolated Foundation button, as shown at the top of Figure 8.66.

3. No structural foundations are loaded into the project, so click Yes.

4. Browse to Structural ➤ Foundations.

5. Select the file called `Footing-Rectangular.rfa`.

6. Click Open.

7. In the Properties dialog, click the Edit Type button.

8. Click Duplicate.

9. Call the new footing 36″ x 36″ x 12″z.

10. Click OK.

11. Change Width to 36″.

12. Change Length to 36″.

13. Change Thickness to 12″.

14. Click OK.

15. Add these footings to each pier.

16. Your foundation plan should resemble Figure 8.66.

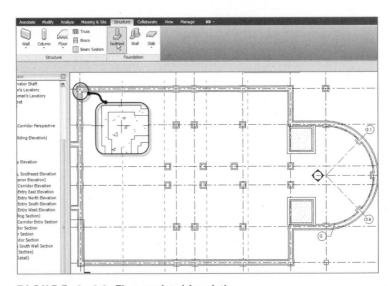

FIGURE 8.66 The completed foundation

Having a foundation in place in an architectural plan can be good and bad. It can be bad because structural items will start showing up in places you may not want to see them. The last procedure of the chapter will involve isolating the structure from the architecture.

Structural Views

By creating a structural view, you are essentially duplicating an architectural view and hiding the structural items in that view. Sound easy? That is because it is! Just follow these steps:

1. In the Project Browser, right-click on Level 1 and select Duplicate View ➤ Duplicate With Detailing, as shown in Figure 8.67.

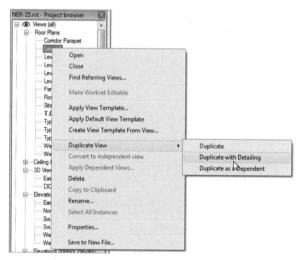

FIGURE 8.67 Selecting Duplicate View ➤ Duplicate With Detailing

2. Rename the view called Copy of Level 1 to **Level 1 Structural Plan**.

3. In the Discipline category of the Properties dialog, select Structural from the list, as shown in Figure 8.68.

4. In the Project Browser, right-click on Views (All), as shown in Figure 8.69.

5. Click Properties.

6. Change Type to Discipline, as shown in Figure 8.70, and then click OK.

FIGURE 8.68 Changing Discipline to Structural

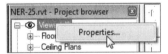

FIGURE 8.69 Right-clicking in the Project Browser

FIGURE 8.70 Changing Type to Discipline

Now the Project Browser is broken down into categories. This will be helpful for large projects with a mix of structure and architecture. Let's add the T.O. Footing plan to the Structural category:

1. In the Project Browser, right-click on the T.O. Footing floor plan.

2. Click Properties.

3. Change Discipline to Structural.

This is getting easy! The T.O. Footing plan is now categorized with its structural brethren. Let's go make the Level 1 Architectural plan truly architectural:

1. Open the Level 1 Floor plan (Architectural).

2. Scroll down to View Range.

3. Click the Edit button in the View Range row.

4. Change both –1′–0″- increments to 0.

4. Change both –1′–0″- increments to 0.

5. Click OK.

The foundation information is no longer displayed in the Level 1 floor plan.

Although the last part of this chapter was short, it is a nice look into the Project Browser and shows how you can start to get organized. If you would like more practice, go into the Project Browser on your own and start organizing it the way you think you would like.

 N O T E   If you need more structural tools than those provided within Revit Architecture, or you are, in fact, a structural engineer or designer, you may want to consider purchasing Revit Structure.

Are You Experienced?

Now you can...

☑ place a structural grid in your model using the architectural walls as a reference

☑ add additional grids at a radius or by sketch where needed

☑ add columns to the grid lines

☑ add columns at an offset, keeping the relationship to the grid intersection intact

☑ add structural beams to the model

☑ add structural beam systems, which can follow on centering rules or equal distance spacing

☑ using the Brace command, create brace framing to be used for both architectural appointments and for actual structural bracing

☑ create entire foundation systems complete with foundation walls, piers strip, and spread footings

☑ organize the Project Browser to show your model broken down into discipline

☑ change a view's discipline to Structural

Ceilings and Interiors

Now that the exterior shell is up and the rooms are basically laid out, it is time to start considering the interiors. As it stands, we have a bunch of rooms with the same wall finish, the same floor finish, and no ceilings to speak of. The restrooms don't have any fixtures, and the rooms are going to be useless without furniture.

Another issue is that we don't have any separate views such as furniture plans or finish plans. This chapter will dive into all of these items—and then some!

▶ **Creating ceilings**

▶ **Creating ceiling openings and soffits**

▶ **Interior design**

▶ **Adding alternate floor materials**

Creating Ceilings

Placing a ceiling is quite easy; the hard part is finding the view in which to do it. As you have probably noticed, the Project Browser is broken down into categories. The categories for plans are Floor Plans and Ceiling Plans. Whereas floor plans show the views standing at that level looking down, ceiling plans show the view standing at that level looking up. In Revit, you are looking at a true reflected ceiling plan.

To begin, open the file you have been following along with. If you did not complete the previous chapter, go to the book's web page at **www.sybex.com/go/ revit2011ner**. From there you can browse to Chapter 9 and find the file called NER-25.rvt.

1. Go to the Level 1 ceiling plan, as shown in Figure 9.1 (remember, this is a ceiling plan, not a floor plan).

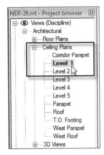

FIGURE 9.1 The Ceiling Plan category

2. On the Home tab, click the Ceiling button, as shown in Figure 9.2.

3. With the Ceiling command active, select the Change Element Type menu in the Properties dialog. You should see the same ceiling types as shown in Figure 9.3.

4. Choose 2′ × 4′ ACT System from the Type Selector.

5. Hover your mouse over the room shown in Figure 9.4. Notice the perimeter is outlined in red. This indicates that the ceiling has found at least four walls you can use as a layout.

6. When you see the red outline, pick a point in the middle of the room. Your ceiling should now look like Figure 9.5.

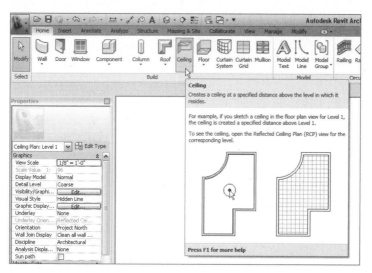

FIGURE 9.2 The Ceiling button on the Modeling tab of the Design bar

FIGURE 9.3 The available ceiling types listed in the Type Selector

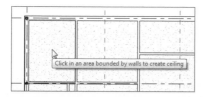

FIGURE 9.4 The ceiling finds a home.

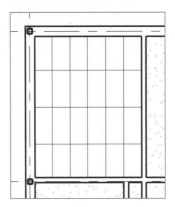

FIGURE 9.5 Placing the 2×4 tiled ceiling

7. Have at it! Add a ceiling to every room in the east wing except for the hallway, the bathrooms, East Radial Entry, and, of course, the elevator shafts, as shown in Figure 9.6.

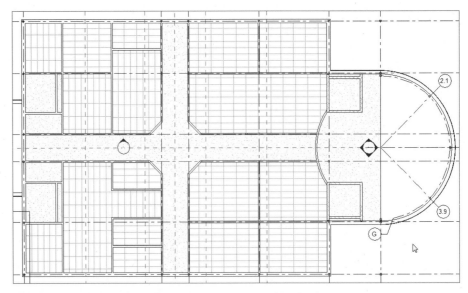

FIGURE 9.6 Adding 2×4 ACT ceilings to the specified rooms

8. With the Ceiling command still running, select Compound Ceiling : GWB On Mtl. Stud from the Type Selector.

9. Pick the bathrooms (not the chases) and the hallway.

10. Press Esc.

N O T E   If you notice that some of the grids are running in the wrong direction, don't worry. We will change that in a moment.

TRANSFERRING PROJECT STANDARDS

There will be times when you do not have the system families you need to carry out the task at hand. Ceiling types seem to be the number 1 system family that falls victim to being inadvertently deleted from a model before it gets used. If you find that you do not have the ceiling types shown in Figure 9.3, do the following:

1. On the Revit Application panel, choose New ➤ Project.

2. In the New Project dialog, click OK to start a new project using the default template.

3. On the View tab, click Switch Windows in the Windows panel, and select the Reflected Ceiling Plan from the fly-out to get back to the No Experienced Required project.

4. On the Manage tab, click Transfer Project Standards in the Settings panel.

5. In the Select Items To Copy dialog (see the following graphic), click the Check None button.

6. Click Ceiling Types.

7. Click OK.

That was just too easy! Too good to be true, right? All right, it is. You always have to make adjustments to this type of item. You probably noticed that you had no control over which direction the grids were running. Also, we have no clue how high these ceilings are. It is time to start modifying the ceilings.

Modifying Ceiling Grids

To be honest, a ceiling consists of nothing more than a basic hatch pattern applied to a material. Actually, everything in Revit is a basic hatch pattern applied to a material. That sure does make it easy to understand!

The one unique thing about hatch patterns in Revit is that you can modify them on screen. That means you can move and rotate a hatch pattern. That also means you can move and rotate a grid pattern. Let's give it a shot:

1. Press Esc to cancel the command you may be in.

2. Pick the ceiling grid line, as shown in Figure 9.7 (Make sure you're zoomed in close enough to make the Rotate command active.)

3. On the Modify | Ceilings tab, click the Rotate button, as shown in Figure 9.7.

4. Rotate the grid 45° by using the two-pick method, as shown in Figure 9.8.

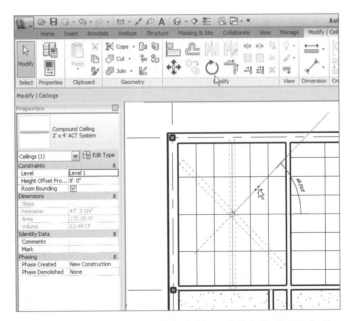

FIGURE 9.7 Select one of the grids and click the Rotate button.

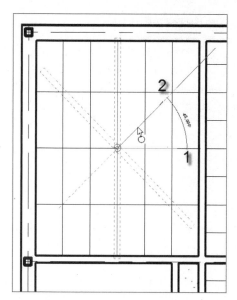

FIGURE 9.8 The Rotate process

Your ceiling should now look like Figure 9.9.

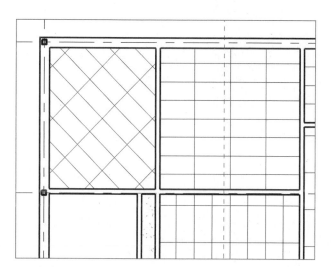

FIGURE 9.9 The ceiling at a 45° angle

Rotating a ceiling grid is a good example of the hatch functionality in Revit. You can rotate and move hatch patterns whether they are ceilings, brick, or any other pattern you need to manipulate.

Now that the ceilings are in, let's look at the ceiling's properties before we go too far. As a matter of fact, it is a good idea to investigate the ceiling's properties before you place it in the model.

Ceiling Element Properties

As I mentioned earlier, ceilings are set up in a similar fashion as floors. So, it stands to reason we will see many similar properties.

Before we get started, let's make some modifications to the west wing. The objective of this procedure is to add a hard ceiling with metal framing, gypsum, and a 3/4″ cherry substrate. To do so, however, you need to modify some of the walls:

1. Go to a 3D view of the model.

2. Select the sloped roof that covers the west wing, as shown in Figure 9.10.

3. Right-click.

4. Select Override Graphics In View ➤ By Element (see Figure 9.10).

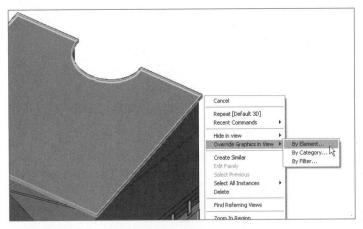

FIGURE 9.10 Selecting the roof, and right-clicking

5. In the View-Specific Element Graphics dialog, click the Transparent button in the upper-right corner, as shown in Figure 9.11.

6. Click OK. The roof is now transparent.

FIGURE 9.11 The View-Specific Element Graphics dialog

We made the roof transparent because some of the walls have to be attached to the roof. It is much easier to attach the walls in a 3D view. But to do so, we need to see the walls that we will be working on:

1. Select the wall shown in Figure 9.12.

2. On the Modify | Walls tab, select the Attach Top/Base button.

3. Pick the roof.

Your wall should look like Figure 9.12.

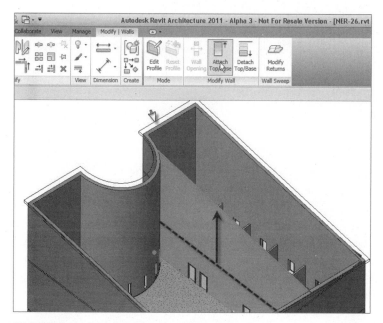

FIGURE 9.12 Attaching the wall to the roof

The next step is to constrain the partition walls in this area to Level 3. The ceilings we will add to these rooms will be much higher than the rest of the building.

1. While still in a 3D view, select the partitions shown in Figure 9.13.

2. In the Properties dialog, set the Top constraint to Up To Level: Level 3.

3. The walls are now constrained to Level 3.

4. Go to Level 1 under Ceiling Plans (if it is not open already).

The next procedure is a tad off-the-beaten-path but it fits squarely within this process. Because we have specified the walls in this area to be of a greater height than the rest of the walls in the model, we are obviously adding ceilings higher than 8'–0". This poses a problem in terms of the Level 1 ceiling plan view range.

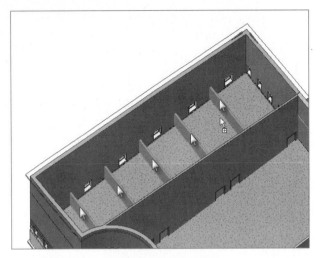

FIGURE 9.13 Selecting the partitions

Creating a Plan Region

Sometimes you will need to set your view range in a specific area that differs from the view range in the plan as a whole. In this example, we will add a ceiling at 14'–6" above the finish floor. If we do this with the current View Range settings, Revit will not display the ceiling. If you modify the View Range for the entire view, you will see the 14'–6" ceilings, but you will not see the regular 8'–0" ceilings in the rest of the building in that view.

In the following procedure we will create a region where the view range is different from the view range in the Level 1 ceiling plan:

1. In the Project Browser, make sure you are in the Level 1 Ceiling Plan.

 W A R N I N G   Double-check to be absolutely sure you are not in a floor plan. You want to be in the ceiling plan!

2. Zoom into the west wing.

3. On the View tab, select the Plan Views ➤ Plan Region button, as shown in Figure 9.14.

4. On the Draw panel, click the Rectangle button, as shown in Figure 9.15.

5. Pick a rectangle around the north portion of the west wing, as shown in Figure 9.15.

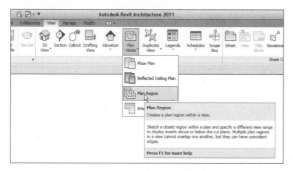

FIGURE 9.14 The Plan Region button on the Create panel of the View tab

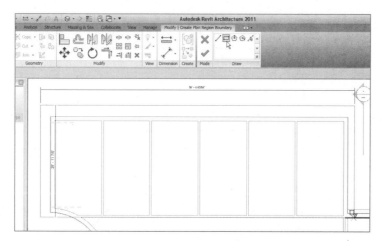

FIGURE 9.15 Defining the limits of the plan region by drawing a rectangle around a specific area

Notice that the View tab has now switched to the Modify | Create Plan Region Boundary tab. We now need to define the view range for this region:

1. In the Properties dialog, click the Edit button in the View Range row.

2. In the View Range dialog, set the Top setting to Level 3.

3. Set Cut Plane Offset to 14′–6″.

4. Set Bottom Offset to 7′–6″

5. Set View Depth Level to Level 2 with an Offset value of 16′–0″ (see Figure 9.16).

FIGURE 9.16 Configuring the View Range for the crop region

6. Click OK.

7. On the Mode panel, click Finish Edit Mode.

You now have a plan region. Although it may not seem as though you did anything in the plan, when you place a ceiling at 14′–6″, you will be able to see it.

 N O T E   The dotted line you see represents the border of the plan region. Although these borders can get annoying (especially if you start collecting several plan regions), I recommend that you keep them turned on. It is helpful to know where a plan region is in the model, and it is more important for others to know that there is a plan region in that area. Also, these borders will not plot.

With the plan region in place, we can now place a ceiling at a higher distance from the finish floor. Since we are going to the trouble of placing a high ceiling, we might as well make the ceiling something special.

Creating a Custom Ceiling

So, what do you do if your ceiling is not an acoustical tile ceiling or a gypsum system? This is Revit! You make a new one.

As mentioned earlier, creating a ceiling is similar to creating a floor or a roof. The Properties dialogs are exactly the same. This procedure will guide you through the process of creating a custom ceiling:

1. Be sure you are in the Level 1 ceiling plan, and zoom in on the northwest room.

2. On the Home tab, click the Ceiling button.

3. In the Change Element Type menu, select GWB On Mtl. Stud. To the right and below the picture of the ceiling is the Edit Type button. Click it (see Figure 9.17).

FIGURE 9.17 Clicking the Edit Type button after choosing the GWB On Mtl. Stud ceiling type

4. Click Duplicate.

5. Call the new ceiling **Wood Veneer on Metal framing**, and click OK.

6. In the Structure row, click the Edit button, as shown in Figure 9.18.

FIGURE 9.18 Clicking the Edit button in the Structure row to gain access to the ceiling's structural composition

7. In the Layers field, as shown in Figure 9.19, click on row 4. This is the Finish 2 [5] Gypsum Wall Board row.

8. Just below the Layers field is the Insert button. Click it.

9. Click the Down button to move the new row to the bottom.

10. Change the function from Structure to Finish 2 [5].

11. Click into the Material cell and click the [...] button, as shown in Figure 9.19.

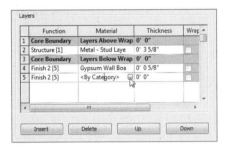

FIGURE 9.19 Clicking the [...] button in the Material cell

12. In the Materials dialog, find Wood - Cherry.

13. Give it a Surface Pattern setting of Wood 1.

14. Give it a Cut Pattern setting of Plywood, as shown in Figure 9.20.

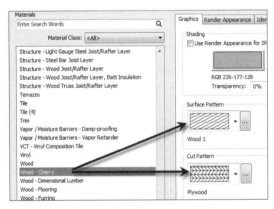

FIGURE 9.20 Selecting and configuring the material for the ceiling

15. Click OK.

16. Change the Thickness to 3/4".

17. Click OK twice.

18. In the Properties dialog, change the Height Offset from Level to 14'-6".

19. Place the ceiling in the room shown in Figure 9.21.

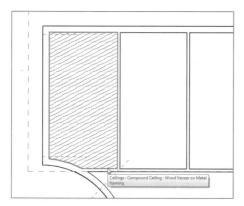

FIGURE 9.21 The cherry-veneered plywood ceiling

N O T E   Don't get discouraged if your final result is not the same as the figure. You took 19 steps to get to this wonderful cherry ceiling; any one of those steps could have gone wrong. Going back through steps and retracing your path is something you may be doing quite a bit.

For the adjacent rooms, add the same ceiling. You can keep the same height. You can follow along with these steps, but I encourage you to try to put the ceilings in from memory:

1. In the Project Browser, be sure you are in the Level 1 ceiling plan.

2. On the Home tab, click the Ceiling button.

3. In the Change Element Type menu on the Element panel, find the ceiling called Compound Ceiling : Wood Veneer on Metal framing.

4. In the Properties panel, set the height above the floor to 14'–6".

5. Pick the rooms shown in Figure 9.22. When you are done, press Esc a couple of times to clear the command.

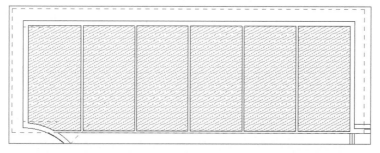

FIGURE 9.22 The north row of rooms will receive cherry ceilings!

ADDING A CEILING IN EMPTY SPACE

Note that you can add a ceiling to a model if there are no walls defining an enclosed space. To do this, start the Ceiling command in the typical manner by clicking the Ceiling button on the Home tab, as shown in the following graphic. When the Ceiling command starts, click the Sketch Ceiling button on the Ceiling tab. This will allow you to simply draft the ceiling boundaries.

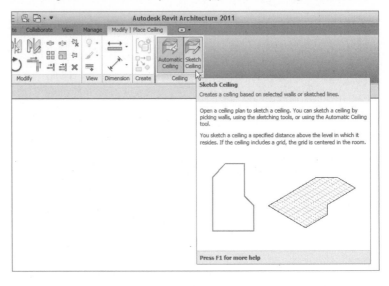

Now that you have experience placing ceilings and creating custom ceiling systems, it is time to start adding features. The first items that come to mind are lighting fixtures, but we need to go back even further and figure out how to "cut holes" in the ceilings and add soffits.

Creating Ceiling Openings and Soffits

Unless you are in a residential dwelling, or a prison, you can look up and notice that a ceiling is merely serving as a host for electrical, mechanical, and architectural appointments. Very seldom will you find a ceiling that does not require a modification in some capacity. This section of the chapter will deal with this issue, starting with creating a ceiling opening.

Creating a Ceiling Opening

To begin, open the file you have been following along with. If you did not complete the previous chapter, go to the book's web page at **www.sybex.com/go/revit2011ner**. From there you can browse to Chapter 9 and find the file called NER-26.rvt.

The objective of the next procedure is to cut an opening into a ceiling to later drop a soffit into:

1. Open the Level 1 ceiling plan.

2. Zoom into the wood ceilings in the west wing, as shown in Figure 9.23.

3. Select the ceiling in the northwest corner of the building, as shown in Figure 9.23.

 T I P Ceilings can be difficult to select. If you hover your cursor over the perimeter of the ceiling, you will see it highlight. If the wall or some other overlapping geometry highlights instead, tap the Tab key on your keyboard to filter through until you find the ceiling. When the ceiling highlights, pick it.

---

4. After the ceiling is selected, click the Edit Boundary button on the Modify | Ceilings tab, as shown in Figure 9.23. The ceiling pattern disappears and is replaced by a magenta sketch line at the perimeter of the room.

5. Switch to the Home tab, and click the Ref Plane button on the Work Plane panel as shown in Figure 9.24.

6. Draw two reference planes, as shown in Figure 9.24. Be sure to snap to the midpoints of the magenta sketch lines.

7. With the reference planes drawn, click the Pick Lines icon on the Draw panel of the Modify | Ceilings tab.

8. On the Draw panel on the Modify | Ceilings ➤ Edit Boundary tab, click the Boundary Line button. When you do, you will see an expanded list of sketch choices. Pick the Circle choice, as shown in Figure 9.25.

9. Draw a 4′-0″ radius circle at the intersection of the reference planes (see Figure 9.25).

10. On the Mode panel, click Finish Edit Mode.

11. Verify that your ceiling looks like Figure 9.26.

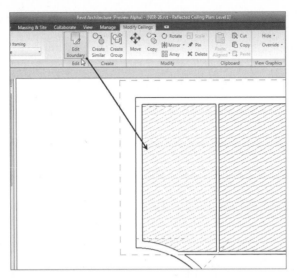

FIGURE 9.23 Clicking the Edit Boundary button on the Modify | Ceilings tab

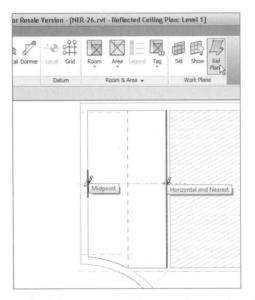

FIGURE 9.24 Drawing two reference planes to create a center intersection

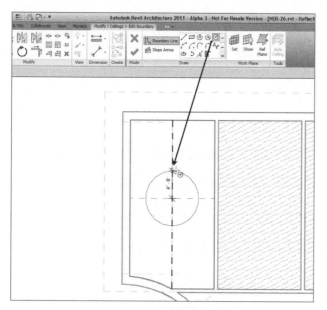

FIGURE 9.25 Sketching a 4′–0″ radius circle

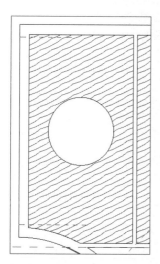

FIGURE 9.26 There's a hole in my ceiling!

With the cutout in place, we need to think about closing this feature with a soffit and, perhaps, another ceiling.

Creating a Soffit

Soffits are nothing more than walls with a base offset. This makes sense if you think about it. If your floor level moves, you certainly want the distance from the finish floor to the bottom of the soffit to remain consistent. This one is going to be easy!

1. On the Home tab, click the Wall button.

2. In the Change Element Type menu, select Basic Wall : Interior: 6 1/8" Partition (2 Hr).

3. Click the Edit Type button.

4. Click Duplicate.

5. Call the new wall 4 1/2" Soffit.

6. Click OK.

7. Click the Edit button in the Structure row.

8. Delete rows 1 and 7 (the double gypsum layer).

9. Change the gypsum thicknesses to 1/2".

10. Change the Stud layer to 3 1/2".

11. Click OK twice.

12. In the Properties dialog, set Base Offset to 14'–0", as shown in Figure 9.27.

13. Set Top Constraint to Up To Level: Level 3 (see Figure 9.28).

FIGURE 9.27 Modifying the dimensions of the 6 1/8" wall

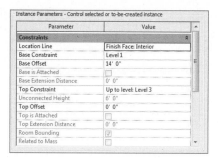

FIGURE 9.28 Setting the Top Constraint and Bottom Offset

You are now ready to place the soffit. You will add it to the radial hole in the ceiling. Normally, you would need to physically draw the wall using the Arc Sketch function. In this case, you can simply pick the radial portion of the ceiling opening.

1. With the Wall command still running, click the Pick Lines icon on the Draw panel.

2. Mouse over the radial ceiling opening. Notice a blue alignment line appears. Make sure it is to the inside of the opening, then press the Tab key twice.

3. Notice the entire circle is selected and the blue alignment line is facing the inside of the hole (see Figure 9.29). When you see this, pick a point to the inside of the hole.

4. Press Esc twice.

Your soffit is complete.

It is now time to add a secondary ceiling to the inside of the soffit. This procedure will be carried out exactly as it was when you added a ceiling to the entire room.

1. In the Project Browser, go to the Level 1 ceiling plan and zoom in on the ceiling with the soffit.

2. On the Home tab, click the Ceiling button.

3. Select Compound Ceiling : Wood Veneer On Metal Framing (if it is not the current selection already).

4. Click the Edit Type button.

5. Click Duplicate.

6. Call the new ceiling **Mahogany Veneer on Metal Framing**, and then click OK.

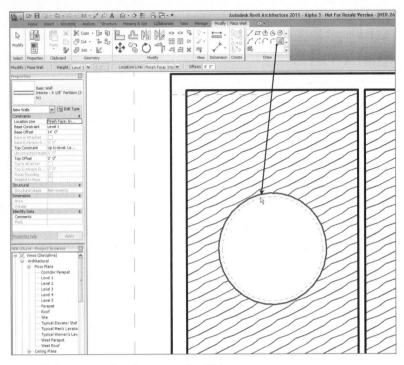

FIGURE 9.29 Creating one cool soffit!

Revit will allow you
to add the wall only
as a 180° arc. You
will need to pick
each side of the
circle to accomplish
a full 360° soffit.

7. Click the Edit button in the Structure row.

8. Click in the bottom layer, and click the [...] button to change the
   material, as shown in Figure 9.30.

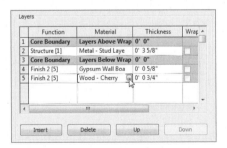

FIGURE 9.30 Click the [...] button to change the material.

9. In the Materials dialog, find Wood - Mahogany.

NEVER ASSUME ANYTHING!

They say you should never assume anything, and in this case "they" are right! Let's add a section through this entire row of rooms to gain a perspective on what is going on here.

1. On the View tab, click the Section button.

2. Cut a horizontal section through the entire side of the building, as shown here:

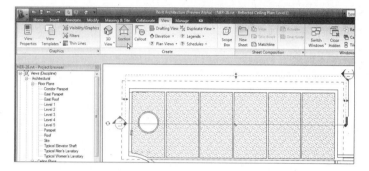

3. Select the section.

4. In the Properties dialog, change Detail Level to Fine.

5. Change the name to **Section at West Training**. (Yes, these are eventually going to be training rooms.)

6. Open the new section. You now have a clear perspective of what is going on with this area.

10. Change Surface Pattern to Wood 2.

11. Change Cut Pattern to Plywood, as shown in Figure 9.31.

12. Click OK twice.

13. Click OK one more time to get back to the model.

14. In the Properties dialog, change Height Offset From Level to 14'–1".

15. Place the ceiling inside the soffit.

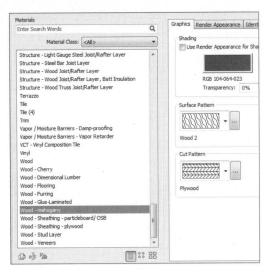

FIGURE 9.31 Altering the mahogany

You need to adjust your plan region; it has to be set so the cut plane is either below or equal to 14'–1" so you can see the lower ceiling:

> You won't be able to see the ceiling at the lower elevation, so stop picking in the middle of the circle! As a matter of fact, if you picked inside the circle more than once, undo back to the point before you started picking in the circle.

1. Pick the dotted rectangle surrounding the rooms. This is the plan region.

2. On the Modify | Plan Region tab, click the View Range button.

3. Change the Offset value for the cut plane to 14'–1", as shown in Figure 9.32.

4. Click OK.

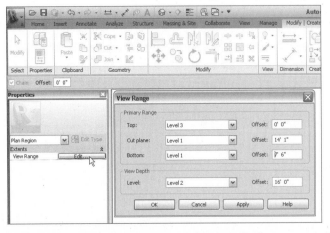

FIGURE 9.32 Changing the cut plane to 14'–1"

Your ceiling plan should look like Figure 9.33.

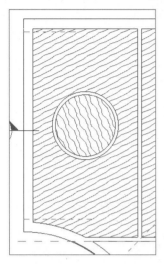

FIGURE 9.33 The completed ceiling

We are getting there with this ceiling, that's for sure! The only task left is to add some light fixtures.

Adding Light Fixtures to Ceilings

Adding lighting fixtures to a Revit Architecture model is not a difficult task, but you must follow a few guidelines to achieve success in installing lighting. For example, you must work with the Ribbon to find a face in which to insert the component:

1. Go to the Level 1 ceiling plan where you have been adding the wood ceilings.

2. On the Home tab, click Component ➢ Place Component, as shown in Figure 9.34.

3. In the Mode panel of Modify | Place Component, click Load Family, and then browse to Imperial Library ➢ Lighting Fixtures.

4. Open the file Pendant Light - Disk.rfa.

5. Place the light approximately as shown in Figure 9.35.

 N O T E   There are no snaps when you are trying to place most components. You will have to place the fixture and then move it into position. Needless to say, this is an extra step.

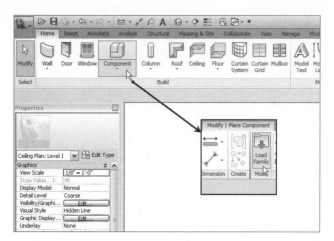

FIGURE 9.34 Click Place Component on the Home tab

6. Move the light to the center of the radial soffit. This time, you can use snaps (see Figure 9.35).

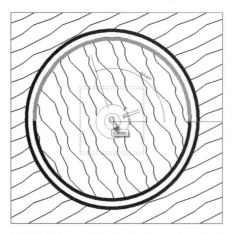

FIGURE 9.35 Moving the fixture to the correct location

7. Open the section at the West Training building section. Notice the light fixture is in the exact location you expected it to be.

N O T E   If you have directly skipped to this part of the chapter, open the file called NER-26.rfa. You will have to delete the fixtures that are in place, but you will still have the views you need.

8. Select the fixture.

9. Click the Copy button on the Modify Lighting Fixtures tab, as shown in Figure 9.36.

10. On the Options bar, be sure the Multiple button is checked.

11. Copy the fixture 3'–0" to the right and 3'–0" to the left (see Figure 9.36).

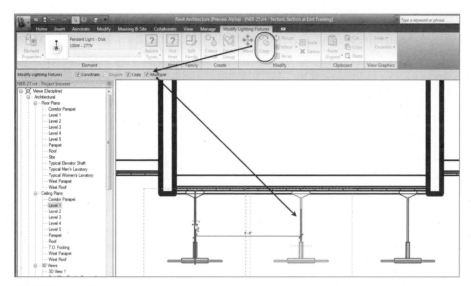

FIGURE 9.36 Copying the fixtures in the section

YIKES, THIS ISN'T TO OUR STANDARDS!

Yes, the default line thicknesses are hideous. In Chapter 23, "BIM Management," we will deal with line thickness. For now, you can click the Thin Lines icon to scale back the thickness of the lines, as shown here:

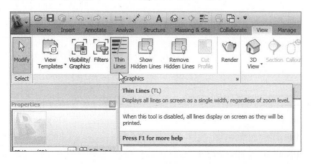

The main point of having you open a section to copy the fixtures is to illustrate that you are now in a fully modeling environment. When you switch back to plan, you will see that the fixtures have been moved. In later chapters, you will learn that this will also add line items to schedules.

Now, let's make some more fixtures:

1. In the Project Browser, go to the Level 1 ceiling plan.

2. Zoom in on the radial soffit. You will see the two new fixtures.

3. Select the right and left fixtures.

4. Click the Rotate command on the Modify | Lighting Fixtures tab.

5. On the Options bar, make sure Copy is checked.

6. Rotate the fixtures 90° to create a total of five fixtures, as shown in Figure 9.37.

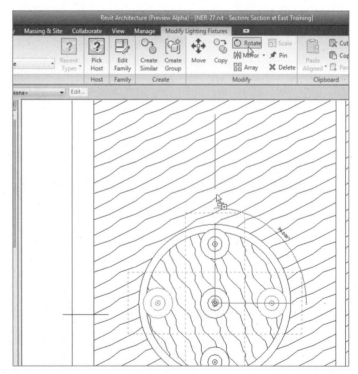

FIGURE 9.37 You are now copying and rotating as if you were in flat, 2D AutoCAD.

N O T E Notice that the fixtures overlap the gypsum soffit. This is because you are actually standing on Level 1 looking up. Revit Architecture has finally taken the confusion out of the reflected ceiling plan mystery.

Now that you have experience dealing with ceilings, it is time to start working on some interior design. Ceilings are a part of this, but what about wall treatments, trims, and architectural millwork? These items will be covered in the next section.

Interior Design

Congratulations! You have arrived at possibly the most difficult subject when it comes to 3D modeling. Why is that? Well, for starters, this is the area where nothing is easy in terms of shape and configuration. For example, suppose you want a crown molding at the ceiling where it intersects the walls. And suppose you need the same crown at the radial soffit. Of course the floors and walls are not the same material, and you need to add furniture as well.

I can go on and on listing the complications we will face here, so let's just jump in. The first part of the process will be adding plumbing fixtures and furniture.

Adding Plumbing Fixtures and Furniture

Adding a desk follows the same procedure as adding a light fixture. Notice, though, when you added the light fixture it just "knew" that it was supposed to be hosted by the ceiling. It is important to note that most furniture is not hosted by a floor; it is actually hosted by a level. This becomes very important if you have a floor system offset from a level. Your furniture will ignore the floor and stick to the level it is associated with.

To begin, we will have to knock off the less glamorous but all-too-important task of adding bathroom fixtures:

1. In the Project Browser, go to the Level 1 floor plan (floor plan, not ceiling plan).

2. Zoom in on the lavatory area, as shown in Figure 9.38.

3. As you can see, there is a callout of this area. Double-click on the callout bubble to open the view called Typical Men's Lavatory.

N O T E Now that you are more experienced with Revit, you can see the benefit of having named this view to something understandable at this stage in the game.

4. With the Typical Men's Lavatory view opened, we can start adding some fixtures. In the Insert tab, click the Load Family button.

5. In the Imperial Library directory, browse to the Plumbing Fixtures folder.

6. Select the file called Toilet-Commercial-Wall-3D.rfa and click Open.

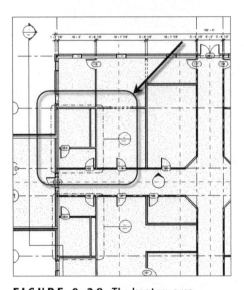

FIGURE 9.38 The lavatory area

7. In the Type Selector, make sure the 19″ Seat Height-Type toilet is selected.

8. Place it along the north wall approximately 6″ from the west wall, as shown in Figure 9.39.

Because we're not creating a military barracks from the 1960s, we need some stalls. Unfortunately Revit does not provide any stalls out of the box, but this book you bought does! To add some toilet stalls to the model, go to the book's web page at **www.sybex.com/go/revit2011ner**. From there you can browse to Chapter 9 and find these files:

▶ Toilet Stall-Accessible-Front-3D.rfa

▶ Toilet Stall-Accessible-Side-3D.rfa

▶ Toilet Stall-Braced-3D.rfa

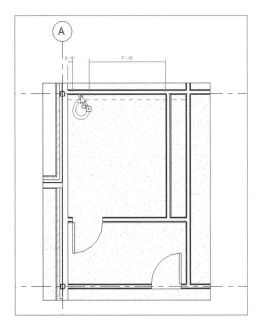

FIGURE 9.39 Placing the 19″ Seat Height toilet 6″ from the west wall, along the north wall

▶ Grab Bar.rfa

▶ Double Sink - Round.rfa

Once you locate the files, download them to the location where you keep all of your Revit families. Then follow along with the procedure:

1. On the Insert tab, click Load Family.

2. Browse to the location where the new families are kept and select the new files; then click Open. They are now loaded into your project.

3. On the Home tab, click the Place A Component button.

4. Select Toilet-Stall-Accessible-Front-3D-60″ × 60″ Clear.

5. Pick the corner of the bathroom, as shown in Figure 9.40.

T I P If you are having difficulties placing the stall directly in the corner, place it at any location along the north wall, and then move it to the corner so it looks like Figure 9.40.

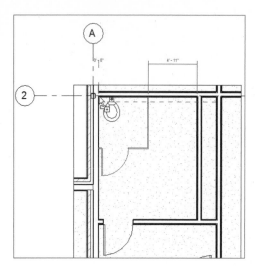

FIGURE 9.40 Placing the accessible stall

The next step is to copy the toilet and add another stall. It would be nice if the family just fit, but this is not a perfect world!

1. Copy the toilet to the right 6'-2 1/2".

2. On the Home tab, select the Place A Component button.

3. Select Toilet Stall-Braced-3D : 32" × 56" Clear from the Change Element Type menu.

4. Click the Edit Type button.

5. Click Duplicate.

6. Change the name to 59" × 60" Clear.

7. Click OK.

8. At the very bottom of the dialog, change the width to 4'-11".

9. Click OK.

10. Place the stall in the model (see Figure 9.41).

 T I P   You may have to press the spacebar as you place the stall to flip it into the correct position. Again, if you are having difficulties placing the stall directly in the corner, you can place it along the north wall at any location, and then either align or move the stall into the correct position.

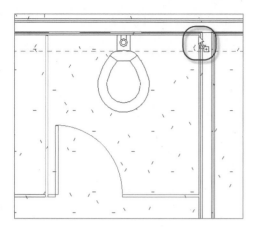

FIGURE 9.41 The two toilets in place

With the toilets and the stalls in place, you need to add a grab bar to the accessible stall. This is the same situation as before in which Revit does not provide this content. You need to either make this component yourself (this is covered in Chapter 17, "Creating Families") or use the one from the book that you downloaded with the bathroom stalls.

To add a grab bar, follow these steps:

1. Zoom in on the accessible stall, as shown in Figure 9.42.

2. Click the Place A Component button.

3. Select Grab Bar 4′–0″ Length.

4. Place along the wall, as shown in Figure 9.42.

N O T E   As you place the grab bar, it will look like it is going to be embedded into the studs of the wall. Don't worry. Once you pick the point where you want it, it will move to the finished face of the wall.

N O T E   Remember, although it kind of feels like we are just sticking "blocks" into our model, these are all 3D parametric parts. This grab bar, for all you know, is 6′–0″ above the ground or sitting on the floor. To adjust this, you do not have to cut a section or go to a 3D view. You can simply select the grab bar and, in the Properties dialog, set Elevation to 2′–0″.

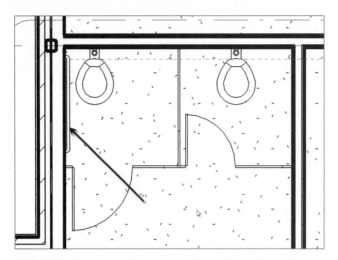

FIGURE 9.42 Adding the grab bar family to the wall

Since we are in the men's room, it is time to add some urinals. We can fit two before we start getting too close to the sink area:

1. On the Insert tab, click the Load Family button.

2. Browse to Plumbing Fixtures.

3. Select the file called Urinal-Wall-3D.rfa.

4. Click Open.

5. Place two urinals about 1′–0″ away from the front of the stall, with a 2′–0″ space between the two, as shown in Figure 9.43.

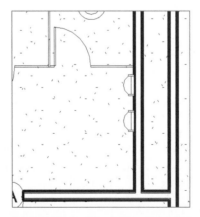

FIGURE 9.43 Adding the urinals to the men's room

What a relief to get those urinals in! The next step is to get a sink in with two stations installed into the bathroom. To do this, you can use the double sink you loaded from the book's website.

1. On the Home tab, click the Place A Component button.

2. In the Change Element Type menu, find the family called Double Sink - Round 24″ Depth.

3. Place it into the corner, as shown in Figure 9.44.

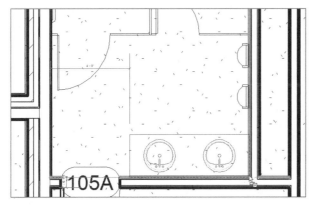

FIGURE 9.44 Placing the double sink

Because the women's room is the same size, there will be two stalls and a sink. Create the mirrored layout as shown in Figure 9.45.

Now that the first floor bathrooms are done, let's move over to some of the actual rooms and offices to furnish these rooms. The first thing we need to do is to add lighting to the ceilings.

Adding Parabolic Troffers

As you are starting to see, the procedure for adding a component does not change based on the component you are adding. This is great news. Adding a troffer, however, is slightly different. You do need to be in a ceiling plan, and you do need to specify the face of the ceiling.

At this point you may be good enough at adding these fixtures to simply look at the following figures and add the lights yourself. Or, if you desire a little help, follow along with these steps:

1. In the Project Browser, go to Level 1 ceiling plan. (Notice that we are going to a ceiling plan right now, not a floor plan.)

Of course the sink will come in at the wrong rotation. By now you know that you can tap the spacebar three times to orient the sink in the correct direction.

If you mirror the stalls, they will go "haywire." You will need to add them separately.

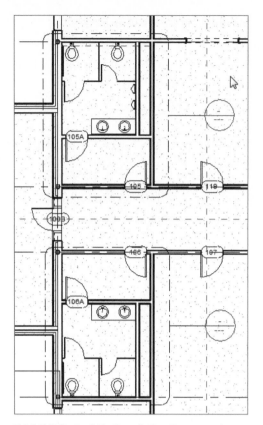

FIGURE 9.45 Completing the women's room

2. Zoom in on the northwest corner of the east wing, as shown in Figure 9.46.

3. On the Insert tab, click the Load Family button.

4. Browse to the Lighting Fixtures folder.

5. Select the file called Troffer Light – 2×4 Parabolic.rfa.

6. Click Open.

7. Click the Place A Component button; then place the fixture in your ceiling, as shown in Figure 9.46.

8. Click the Align button on the Modify tab, as shown in Figure 9.47.

9. Align the light fixture to the grid.

10. Copy the light to the location shown in Figure 9.48.

11. Add lights to the rest of the rooms in the east wing, as shown in Figure 9.48.

With the lights added to the suspended ceilings, we need to illuminate the corridors. This can be done by adding a set of wall-mounted sconces, as follows:

1. Select the Level 1 floor plan.

2. On the Insert tab, click Load Family.

3. Browse to the `Lighting Fixtures` folder.

4. Select the file called `Sconce Light - Uplight.rfa`.

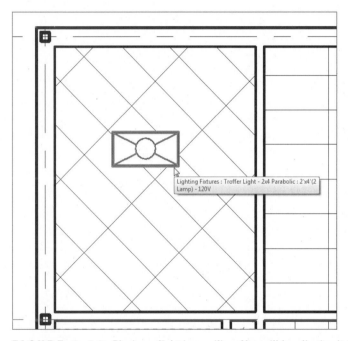

FIGURE 9.46 Placing a light in a ceiling. You will be aligning it to the grid in a moment.

5. Add the sconce to the corridor wall, as shown in Figure 9.49.

6. Add sconces to the walls of the hallways as appropriate, as shown in Figure 9.50.

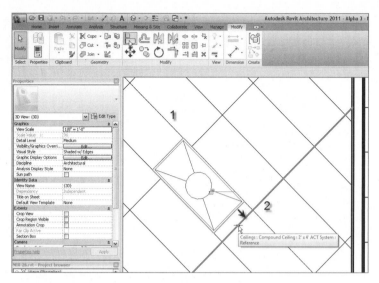

FIGURE 9.47 Aligning the fixture to the grid

FIGURE 9.48 Adding lights to the rest of the ceilings

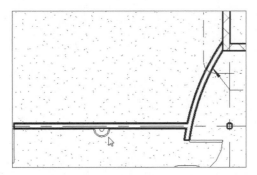

FIGURE 9.49 Adding a sconce

7. In the Project Browser, double-click on the 3D view called East Wing Corridor Perspective. This will give you a good idea of how the up-lighting influences the corridor (see Figure 9.51).

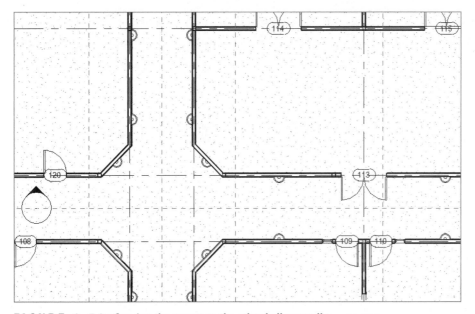

FIGURE 9.50 Copying the sconce to the other hallway walls

Well, that corridor is looking great! It's time now to start looking into the offices, and also to see if we can get a kitchen area completed.

FIGURE 9.51 Looking at the hallway in a perspective view

Adding Casework and Furniture

Adding casework and furniture is the easiest part of this chapter—that is, if you like the casework and furniture that comes right out of the Revit box. Something tells me that this is not going to be adequate. For this chapter, we will be using the out-of-the box items, but in Chapter 17, we will make some custom millwork families.

To add some office furniture, follow along:

1. Select the Level 1 floor plan.

2. Zoom into the northeast corner office, as shown in Figure 9.52.

3. On the Insert tab, click the Load Family button.

4. Browse to the Furniture folder and select the following five items:

   ▶ Cabinet-File 5 Drawer.rfa

   ▶ Chair-Executive.rfa

   ▶ Credenza.rfa

   ▶ Entertainment Center.rfa

   ▶ Shelving.rfa

5. Click Open.

6. Click the Place A Component button; then, in the Change Element Type menu, select Credenza 72″ × 24″.

7. Place the credenza desk into the room, as shown near the top of Figure 9.52.

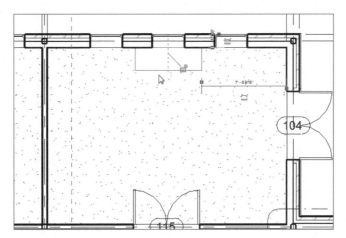

FIGURE 9.52 Placing the credenza desk into the first office

8. On the Home tab, click the Place A Component button.

9. From the Change Element Type menu, select Chair-Executive and place it in front of the credenza, as shown in Figure 9.53.

10. In the Properties dialog, select the Entertainment Center 96″ × 84″ × 30″ and place it in the corner, as shown in Figure 9.53.

11. Place four 36″ shelving units across the south wall, as shown near the bottom of Figure 9.53.

At this point, it is a good idea to take a perspective shot of this office to see if this space is developing the way you were envisioning. Although you may never put this perspective view onto a construction document, it is still a great idea to see what is going on:

1. On the View tab, select the 3D View ≻ Camera button.

2. Pick a point in the northeast corner.

3. Pick a second point beyond the southwest corner, as shown in Figure 9.54.

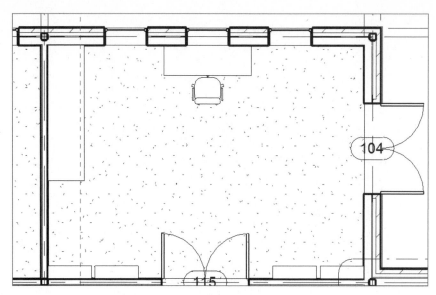

FIGURE 9.53 Adding furniture to the office

4. In the Project Browser, right-click on the new 3D view and call it **Perspective of Corner Office.**

5. You can change the Visual Style setting to Shaded w/ Edges, and even turn on shadows, if you need to do so. Remember, however, shadows are unnecessary and will slow down the view dramatically (see Figure 9.55).

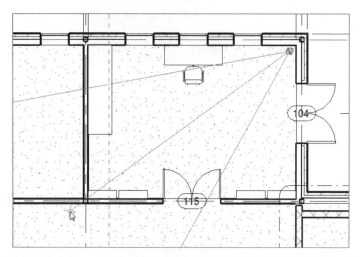

FIGURE 9.54 Adding a camera (perspective view) to the corner office

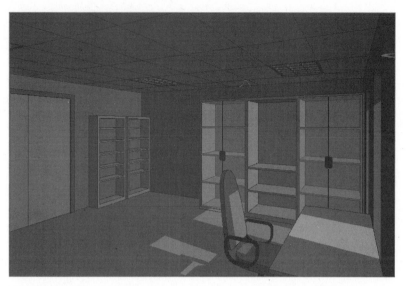

FIGURE 9.55 The perspective of the corner office. If you notice your entertainment unit is backward, you will have to go back to plan to rotate it.

It's time for a kitchen! This is such a nice office, there seems to be a need for a break area right outside. We would not want our executive to have to walk very far for a cup of coffee or a snack.

To get started, we'll load some countertops and cabinets:

1. On the Insert tab, click the Load Family button.

2. Browse to the Casework folder.

3. Open the Domestic Kitchen folder.

4. Select the following families:

   ▶ Base Cabinet-2 Bin.rfa

   ▶ Base Cabinet-Double Door & 2 Drawer.rfa

   ▶ Base Cabinet-Double Door Sink Unit.rfa

   ▶ Base Cabinet-Filler.rfa

   ▶ Base Cabinet-Single Door & Drawer.rfa

   ▶ Counter Top-L Shaped w Sink Hole 2.rfa

   ▶ Upper Cabinet-Double Door-Wall.rfa

5. Click Open.

6. Add the countertop, as shown in Figure 9.56.

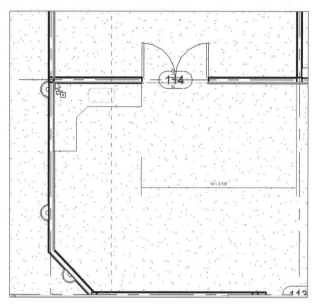

FIGURE 9.56 Adding the countertop

7. Press Esc twice.

8. Select the countertop.

9. Select the stretch arrows and stretch the leg of the counter to the end of the wall, as shown in Figure 9.57.

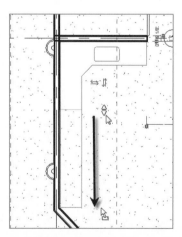

FIGURE 9.57 Lengthening the counter leg to meet the corner of the wall

10. Add the Base Cabinet-Double Door Sink Unit 30″ under the sink.

11. Align the base unit under the sink.

You now have a counter and a sink base. The problem is, you have no idea how high these items are or what they really look like. That's okay—this is Revit. You just need to create two elevations looking at these items, as follows:

1. On the Create panel on the View tab, click the Elevation button.

2. Add an interior elevation looking north, as shown in Figure 9.58.

3. Select the square marker and turn on the elevation looking west (see Figure 9.58).

4. Rename the north elevation to **Kitchen North**.

5. Rename the west elevation to **Kitchen West**.

With the elevations in, we can now flip back and forth to make sure we are putting the items in the right places, and to get a good idea of how our cabinet run is looking.

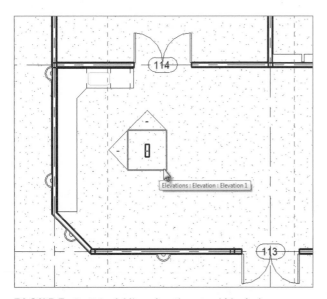

FIGURE 9.58 Adding elevations to aid in design

The remainder of the procedure will involve adding the rest of the cabinets. Let's do it!

1. On the Home tab, click the Place A Component button.

2. From the Change Element Type menu, select Base Cabinet - Single Door & Drawer 24″.

3. Place the base cabinet to the right of the sink cabinet.

4. Press Esc twice; then select the Kitchen North elevation. Does your elevation look like Figure 9.59?

5. Go back to the Level 1 floor plan.

6. Place a Base Cabinet Double Door & 2 Drawer 36″ in the position shown in Figure 9.60.

7. Press Esc twice; then select the Kitchen West elevation.

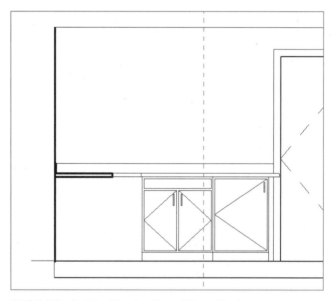

FIGURE 9.59   The elevation of the cabinet run

8. Move the base cabinet so there is a 1″ counter overhang, as shown in Figure 9.61.

9. Copy the base cabinet to the right three times (see Figure 9.62).

10. Click the Place A Component button.

11. Find Base Cabinet-Filler.

12. Click the Edit Type button.

13. Click Duplicate.

14. Change the name to **Filler - 1′–1″** and click OK.

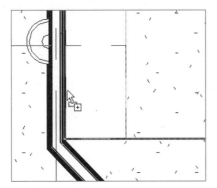

FIGURE 9.60 Placing the 36″ double door, two-drawer base cabinet

FIGURE 9.61 The base cabinets are filling the run.

15. Change the Depth 1′–1″.

16. Click OK.

17. Insert the base filler into the model, as shown in Figure 9.62.

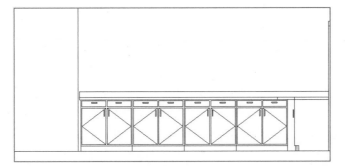

FIGURE 9.62 The base filler

18. Select the filler.

19. In the Properties dialog, change Width to 3/4".

20. Add another Base Cabinet : Filler - 1'–1" to the opposite cabinet to create the corner, as shown in Figure 9.63.

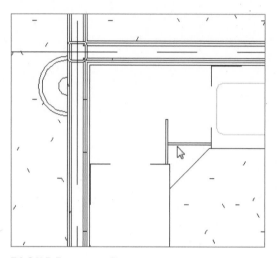

FIGURE 9.63 The completed corner

The bases are done! It is time to add some wall cabinets to the kitchen. I think at this point you will have enough experience to go on your own to populate the rest of your building as you see fit.

1. On the Home tab, click the Place A Component button.

2. In the Type Selector, select Upper Cabinet-Double-Door-Wall 36".

3. Place the wall cabinet in the model, as shown in Figure 9.64. (Don't worry too much about aligning it to the cabinet below. We will align it in elevation.)

4. Open the Kitchen West elevation.

5. Click the Align button on the Modify tab.

6. Align the wall cabinet to the base cabinet, as shown in Figure 9.65.

7. Copy the wall cabinet to the right three times.

8. Save the model.

FIGURE 9.64 Adding the wall cabinet

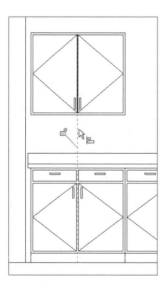

FIGURE 9.65 Aligning the wall to the base

Your cabinets should look like Figure 9.66.

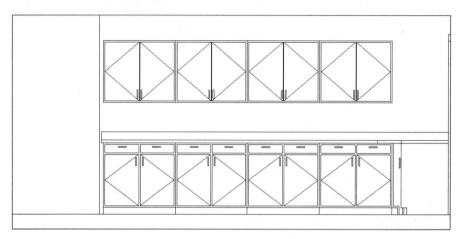

FIGURE 9.66 The finished east wall of the kitchen

Now that the kitchen is in place, it would be nice to add a tile floor only to that area. You can accomplish this without having to add extra floors to the model. You can simply split the face of the floor that is already there, and add an additional material.

Adding Alternate Floor Materials

Carpeting does not perform well in kitchens. This is information we know. What we don't know is how to add tile to a carpeted floor system without having to cut the existing floor and start piecing in sections of alternate materials. The following procedure will guide you through the steps:

1. Click the Split Face button on the Modify tab, as shown near the top right of Figure 9.67.

2. Select the entire floor. This may require finding the edge of the floor along an exterior wall (see Figure 9.67).

3. Click the Line button on the Draw panel, and draw a continuous line around the area, as shown in Figure 9.68.

4. On the Modify | Split Face ➤ Create Boundary tab, click Finish Edit Mode.

N O T E   **Remember: you cannot have any overlapping lines or gaps while adding your magenta sketch lines.**

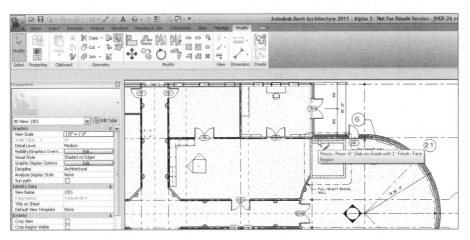

FIGURE 9.67 Clicking the Split Face button and selecting the slab edge

Although it does not seem like it, you have split the kitchen from the rest of the floor. Next you'll apply a material to the kitchen. The first step will be to create a suitable material to use.

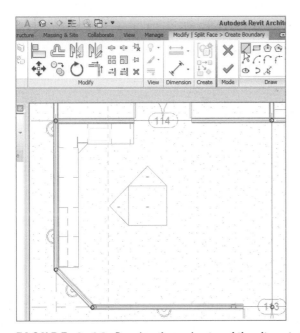

FIGURE 9.68 Drawing the perimeter of the alternate floor material

Creating a Tile Material

There is one tile material in this model, but it would be beneficial to create a new one with 12″ square tiles. This procedure will take the place of using hatching in a conventional drafting situation.

Follow along with this procedure to create a new material:

1. On the Manage tab, click the Materials button, as shown in Figure 9.69.

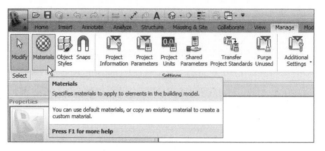

FIGURE 9.69 Choosing the Materials button on the Manage tab

2. In the Materials dialog, scroll down, and select Ceramic Tile - 4″ Blue.

3. At the bottom of the dialog, click the Duplicate button, as shown at the bottom left of Figure 9.70.

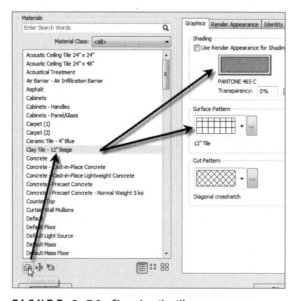

FIGURE 9.70 Changing the tile appearance

4. Call the new material **Clay Tile - 12" Beige**.

5. Change the color to Pantone 465 C.

6. Change Surface Pattern to 12″ Tile (see Figure 9.70).

7. Click the Render Appearance tab, as shown in Figure 9.71.

8. In the Render Appearance Based On field, click the Replace button.

9. From the Ceramic - Tile category of the Render Appearance Library dialog, select Mosaic Beige (see Figure 9.71).

10. Click OK.

11. Back on the Render Appearance tab, click Finish Bumps. This will make the rendering punch out (see Figure 9.72).

PANTONE WHO?

Choosing a Pantone color is the best way to get a color that can actually be made available by a manufacturer. On the Graphics tab, click the large, colored button in the Shading category. Then click the Pantone button. This will allow you to choose your color by the number.

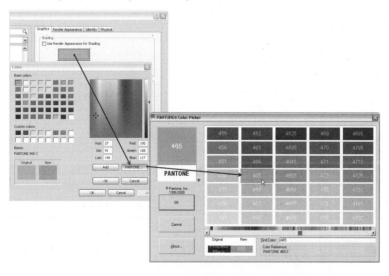

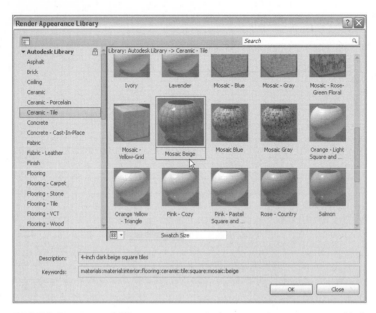

FIGURE 9.71 Adding a texture and .bmp mapping to your new kitchen floor

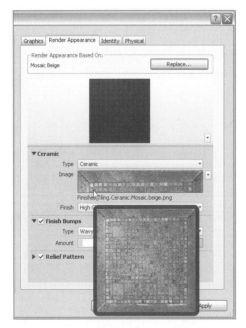

FIGURE 9.72 Configuring your render appearance for the tile floor

The new material is locked, loaded, and ready to spill onto the floor! To do this, you will paint to apply the new material to the kitchen. Follow along:

1. Click the Paint icon in the Geometry panel of the Modify tab, as shown in Figure 9.73.

2. Select Clay Tile - 12″ Beige from the Material drop-down list, as shown in Figure 9.73.

3. Put your paint icon over the edge of the kitchen floor until the region becomes highlighted.

4. When the region becomes highlighted, pick the floor. Your new tile will appear.

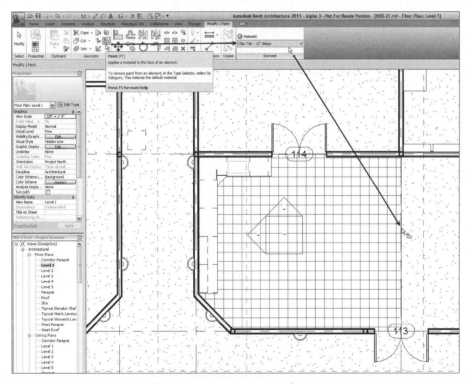

FIGURE 9.73 The new tile floor

Phew! You are gaining a good amount of experience in terms of adding components and making the interior of the building conform to your design. If you think about it, we have done nothing here that is out of the ordinary. We are simply replacing everyday drafting routines with modeling routines. What a way to go!

Since there is quite a bit of building left, go ahead and load this model up with components. If you get stuck anywhere, go back and find the procedure that pertains to your problem.

Are You Experienced?

Now you can...

- ☑ add ceilings to a room as well as create new ceilings and modify them to suit your needs

- ☑ transfer ceilings from other projects using the Transfer Project Standards function

- ☑ add soffits to your model by using a typical wall and offsetting the base

- ☑ create a plan region so you can see elements at different elevations without disturbing the rest of the view

- ☑ add components such as bathroom fixtures, office furniture, and lighting to your model

- ☑ create subregions in which to specify an alternate flooring, thus allowing you to avoid hatching

Stairs, Ramps, and Railings

A whole chapter just for stairs, ramps, and railings? You bet! If you think about it, there could be hundreds of combinations of stair and railing systems. As a matter of fact, you very seldom see two sets of stairs that are exactly the same. Kind of like snowflakes, isn't it? Okay, it's nothing like snowflakes! But you get the point. Besides, there are too many snowflake references in this book already.

▶ **Creating stairs using the Rise/Run function**

▶ **Creating a winding staircase**

▶ **Creating a custom railing system**

▶ **Creating custom stairs**

▶ **Adding ramps**

Creating Stairs Using the Rise/Run Function

To start off, this chapter will address the makings of a staircase, from commercial to a more residential feel with wood members, balusters, and spindles. During this procedure, you will see how Revit brings stairs together. After we create a common staircase, we will move on to winding stairs, custom railings, and of course, ramps.

Before we begin, I should mention that there are some features about stairs in Revit that you will love, and there are some features (or lack of features) that you will not love. As you create the stairs, keep in mind that Revit cannot always provide enough functionality to re-create every type of stair you may encounter.

N O T E   Throughout this book, you will have the opportunity to download from the book's website custom families.

In this section, we will focus on creating a staircase using the traditional Rise/Run method. Then we'll discuss modifying the actual boundary of the stairs, which allows us to create a more unusual shape than out of the box.

To begin, open the file you have been following along with. If you did not complete the previous chapter, go to the book's web page at **www.sybex.com/go/revit2011ner**. From there you can browse to Chapter 10 and find the file called NER-27.rvt.

The objective of the following procedure is to create a staircase using the Rise/Run method:

1. In the Project Browser, go to the Level 2 floor plan.

2. Zoom in on the radial entry in the east wing, as shown in Figure 10.1.

3. On the Circulation panel of the Home tab, click the Stairs button, as shown in Figure 10.1.

4. In the Modify | Create Stairs Sketch tab, click the Properties button to make sure the Properties dialog is active, as shown at the far left of Figure 10.2. If the Properties dialog is already there, you don't need to do this step.

5. In the Properties dialog, make sure that Stairs is selected from the Type menu, and then change Base Level to Level 1.

6. Change Top Level to Level 2.

7. Change Multistory Top Level to Level 5 (see Figure 10.3).

8. On the Draw panel of the Modify | Create Stairs Sketch tab, be sure that Run is selected.

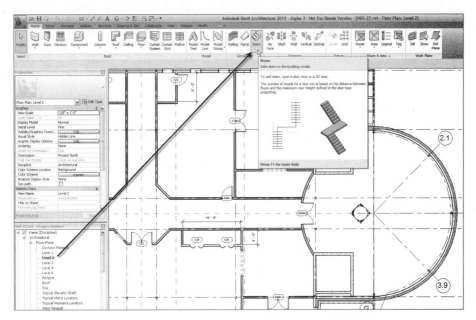

FIGURE 10.1 Click the Stairs button on the Circulation panel of the Home tab.

 N O T E By setting the base to Level 1 and the top to Level 2, you are giving Revit the dimensions it needs to calculate the rise of the stairs. When you add the multistory height, Revit will take the calculation from Levels 1 and 2, and then bring it up to the additional floors.

FIGURE 10.2 Click the Properties button on the Modify | Create Stair Sketch tab.

9. Pick the intersection of the floor edge and grid 3.1 for the first point of the stairs. This spot is labeled "1" in Figure 10.4.

10. Move your cursor to the right. You will be able to see a faint display indicating that you have a certain number of risers created and a certain number remaining.

11. Once you see that nine risers have been created, with nine risers remaining, pick the spot labeled "2" in Figure 10.4.

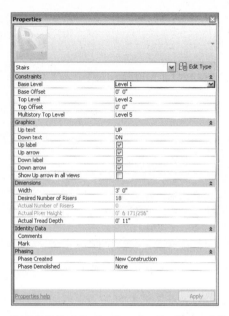

FIGURE 10.3 Changing the Element Properties of the stairs

12. Move your cursor straight up until you get to the grid intersection labeled "3" in Figure 10.4. Once you see this, pick the third point.

13. Move your cursor to the left all the way past the floor landing. Revit reports that you have 18 created, 0 remaining (see Figure 10.5).

14. Once you see the second flight completed, pick the last point. Revit will draw both flights as well as the landing (see Figure 10.6).

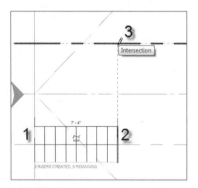

FIGURE 10.4 Adding the "L" shape to the stairs

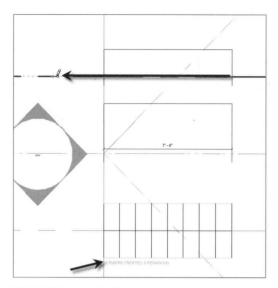

FIGURE 10.5 Make sure your cursor is way past the end of the stairs.

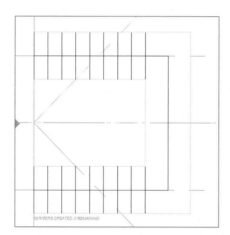

FIGURE 10.6 The stairs have been laid out.

With the basic layout completed, it is time to take a look at the perimeter of the stairs. If you are looking for any architectural design outside of the basic box that you get when you place a staircase, you want to edit the boundary.

Modifying Boundaries

With the main stairs in place and laid out, you can now start modifying the profile. Given that this is a five-tiered, multilevel staircase, the boundary will be somewhat limited, but not to the point where we can't make something pop out of our design.

To modify the boundary, follow along:

1. On the Modify | Create Stairs Sketch tab, click the Boundary button, as shown in Figure 10.7.

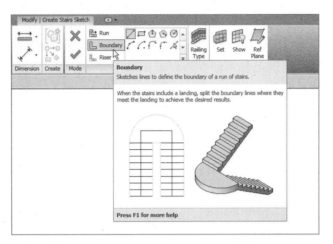

FIGURE 10.7 The Boundary button on the Draw panel

2. On the Draw panel, click the Start-End-Radius Arc button, as shown in Figure 10.8.

3. Draw an arc on the outside of the landing at an 8'–0" radius, as shown in Figure 10.8.

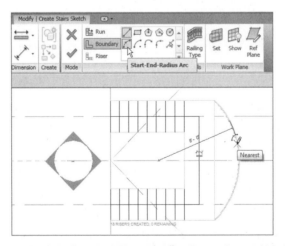

FIGURE 10.8 Add an 8'–0" radius to the outside of the landing.

With the radius drawn in, it is important to pause at this point. What we have here is an extra line. Similar to sketching a floor, if you have any overlapping line segments or gaps, Revit will not let you continue. Also, if you have any extra lines, Revit will not let you continue.

Let's clean up the stairs:

1. Press the Esc key twice and then select the straight green line at the outside of the landing.

2. Press the Delete key on your keyboard. The line is removed.

Your stairs should look exactly like Figure 10.9.

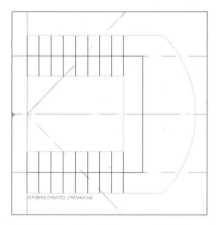

FIGURE 10.9 The completed boundary

With the boundary in place, it is time to select the railing system we are going to use. Out of the box, Revit only provides four choices. We will select one of those choices for this staircase, but we will add to the list later on in this chapter.

Adding Default Railings

Revit provides only four railing systems as a default. You can choose one of these four railings to apply to the staircase during the Sketch mode of the stairs.

Follow along with this procedure to apply a railing to the stairs:

1. On the Modify | Create Stairs Sketch tab, click the Railing Type button, as shown in Figure 10.10.

2. In the Railings Type dialog, select Handrail - Pipe, as shown in Figure 10.11.

FIGURE 10.10 Click the Railing Type button.

FIGURE 10.11 Select Handrail - Pipe in the Railings Type dialog.

3. Click OK.

With the railings in place, we are on our way to completing this staircase. As a matter of fact, round one seems to be done.

4. To complete the stairs, just click Finish Edit Mode on the Modify | Create Stairs Sketch tab. Your stairs should look like Figure 10.12.

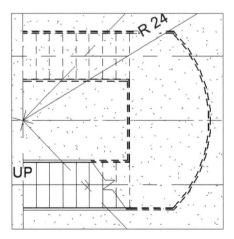

FIGURE 10.12 The stairs as displayed in plan

Normally, when you are dealing with a large, multistory staircase, you should check it out in 3D to make sure all went off as planned. This case is no exception!

1. Click the Default 3D View button on the Quick Access toolbar.

2. In the 3D view, zoom in on the radial entry.

3. Select the radial wall and right-click.

4. From the context menu, select Hide In View ➢ Elements.

You should now examine your stairs (see Figure 10.13).

FIGURE 10.13 The stairs in 3D with the radial entry "peeled back"

Here's a problem: the railing just stops dead at the stringer. This may have been acceptable practice around the time, say, when the wheel was still on the drawing boards. We need some kind of ADA compliance here at the bottom of the stairs. To accomplish this, follow along with the next procedure.

To begin, go to the book's web page at **www.sybex.com/go/revit2011ner**. From there you can browse to Chapter 10 and find the file called ADA-Pipe.rfa. You can then download it to your computer. Now perform the following steps:

1. On the Insert tab, click the Load Family button.

2. Browse to the directory where you stashed the family you just down-loaded, and load ADA-Pipe.rfa into your model.

3. Go to the Level 1 floor plan.

4. Zoom in on the bottom of the stairs.

5. On the Work Plane panel of the Home tab, click the Reference Plane button.

6. On the Place Reference Plane tab, click the Pick Lines button, as shown in Figure 10.14.

7. Offset a reference plane 9 1/2″ to the left of the bottom riser, as shown in Figure 10.14.

8. Draw another reference plane from the center line of the bottom railing to the left about 2′–0″ (see Figure 10.14).

9. On the Home tab, click the Place A Component button.

10. In the Properties dialog, select ADA - Pipe.

11. Press the spacebar once to rotate the family into place, so it is oriented as shown in Figure 10.15.

12. Place the family at the intersection of the two reference planes, as shown in Figure 10.15, then press Esc twice.

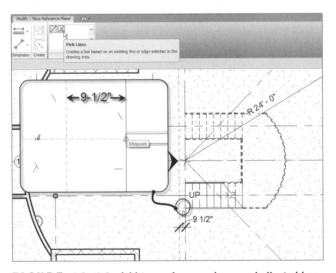

FIGURE 10.14 Add two reference planes as indicated here.

Extending the Railings

You have just added a family to finish off the stairs at the bottom. The next step is to extend the railings on the stairs to meet the new family. There is one obstacle in the way, though: the railing on the stairs already has an ending post. The trick is to remove the default ending post, and replace it with the custom ADA post you just loaded into your model.

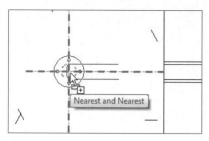

FIGURE 10.15 Inserting the ADA - Pipe family to the intersection

The objective of the next procedure is to extend the railings on the stairs to the ADA posts you just added to the model.

1. In plan, select the bottom railing, as shown in Figure 10.16. Make sure you are not selecting the stairs.

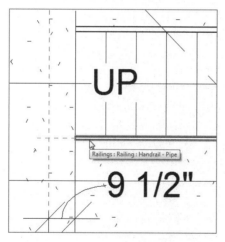

FIGURE 10.16 Selecting the railing, not the stairs

2. In the Properties dialog, click the Edit Type button.

3. Click Duplicate.

4. Call the new railing **Entry Stair Railing**.

5. Click OK.

6. In the Baluster Placement row, click the Edit button, as shown in Figure 10.17.

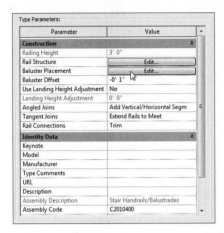

FIGURE 10.17 Click Edit next to Baluster Placement.

At the bottom of the Edit Baluster Placement dialog, you'll see a Posts category. Within the Posts category is a chance to place a post at the start, ending, or corner of the railing:

1. For the Start setting, select None from the list, as shown in Figure 10.18.

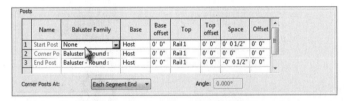

FIGURE 10.18 Setting the start of the railing to None removes the post that Revit provides only at this end of the railing.

2. Click OK twice.

3. Select the railing on the inside of the stairs.

4. In the Properties dialog, select Entry Stair Railing.

It's time to stretch the railing on the stairs to meet up with the family. This procedure is best done in plan view, where you can see exactly how far you need to stretch the railing:

1. Select the bottom (south) railing.

2. On the Modify | Railings tab, click the Edit Path button.

3. Click the Align button on the Modify | Railings ➢ Edit Path tab, as shown near the top left of Figure 10.19.

4. For the first alignment, pick the back edge of the family you loaded, as shown in Figure 10.19.

5. Now, pick the magenta railing line. (When you hover over the magenta line, you will see an endpoint icon. When you do, click it.)

   The magenta line will extend to the family (see Figure 10.19).

6. Click Finish Edit Mode.

7. Go to a 3D view to make sure the railings align (see Figure 10.20).

Notice that the line seems off center. Don't worry about this—it will line up when you finish the sketch.

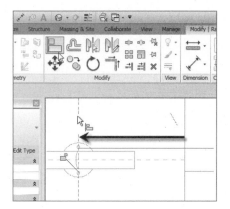

FIGURE 10.19 Aligning the end of the railing to the new family

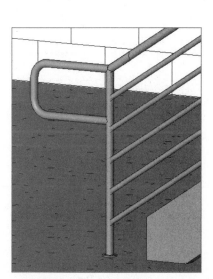

FIGURE 10.20 Check out the railing in 3D to ensure proper alignment.

It would be nice if this were the only place that this railing extension needed to go. The rest of the procedure will step you through the process of adding this extension to the inside railing and then copying it up to the other levels:

1. Copy the ADA - Pipe family up to the inside railing. Make sure you go straight up, as shown in Figure 10.21.

2. Select the inside railing.

3. On the Modify | Railings tab, click the Edit Path button.

4. Click the Align button.

5. Align the magenta line with the ADA - Pipe family, as shown in Figure 10.21.

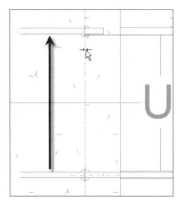

FIGURE 10.21 Copying and aligning the inner railing to the ADA family

6. Press Esc twice and then select both families.

7. On the Modify | Generic Models tab, click the Copy To Clipboard button on the Clipboard panel (it is the third panel from the left).

8. Choose Paste ➣ Aligned To Selected Levels, as shown near the top left of Figure 10.22.

9. Pick Levels 2, 3, and 4, and then click OK. Does your staircase look like Figure 10.22?

It's getting close, but it seems as though there is nothing keeping people from falling off the second, third, fourth, and fifth levels! I don't know about you, but I think this is the perfect place to put a separate railing and tie it into the stair railing.

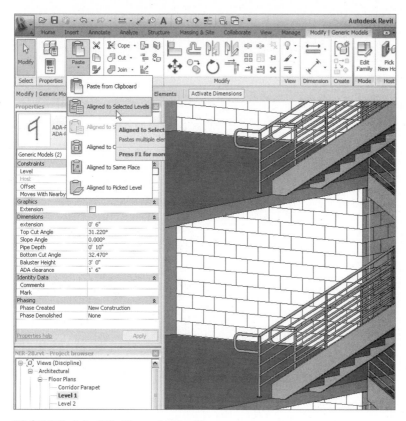

FIGURE 10.22 The copied families

Landing Railings

Railings, of course, can be drawn independently from a stair. Tying the railing into the stair, however, requires a little more patience. That being said, it starts to become obvious that Revit reflects the real world when it comes to railings. If you have a railing that is difficult to build, it is probably going to be difficult to model. Also, if you arrive at an intersection that cannot be physically accomplished in the field, then guess what? You will struggle trying to get it into Revit.

To add some railings at the landings and tie them into the stair railings, follow these steps:

1. In the Project Browser, go to the Level 2 floor plan.

2. On the Home tab, click the Railing button, as shown in Figure 10.23.

3. In the Properties dialog, make sure that Type is set to Handrail Pipe.

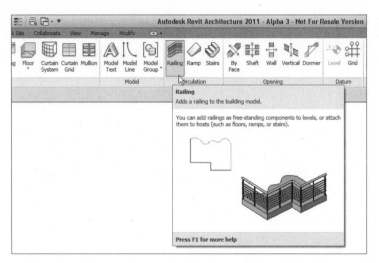

FIGURE 10.23 Click the Railing button on the Circulation panel of the Home tab.

4. On the Draw panel, make sure the Pick Lines icon is selected.

5. Change the Offset to 8 1/2" on the Options bar.

6. Pick the front edge of the floor, as shown in Figure 10.24. The sketch line should now be set back from the edge of the landing with an 8 1/2" clearance.

7. The magenta line is going to be way too long. Select it and drag the grip down to the point shown in Figure 10.24.

8. At the bottom of the railing, select the grip and drag it out of the wall as well. Once you are done, click the Finish Edit Mode button (see Figure 10.24).

NOTE   You can only have one continuous railing at a time. If there are gaps in the railing, it won't work. For example, the second floor is going to need three separate railings.

9. In the Properties dialog, click the Edit Type button.

10. Click Duplicate.

11. Call the new railing **Landing Handrail**.

12. Click OK.

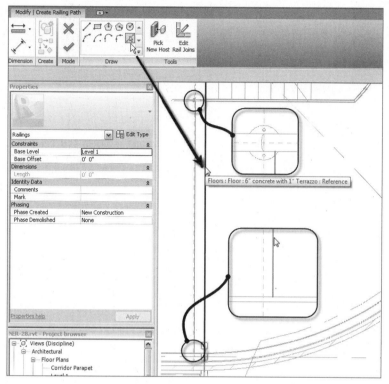

FIGURE 10.24 Adding the first railing segment

13. In the Baluster Placement row, click the Edit button.

14. In the Posts field, change the Start and End Post to None (as shown in Figure 10.25).

15. Also, just above the Posts field, change the Justify option to Center (again, see Figure 10.25).

16. Click OK twice.

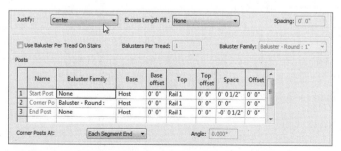

FIGURE 10.25 Configuring the railing for the landing

Your railing needs to be centered on the reference plane. It may or may not be. If it is not, select the railing. You will see a blue flip grip (double-arrow grip) in the middle of the railing. Pick it, and your railing will flip (see Figure 10.26).

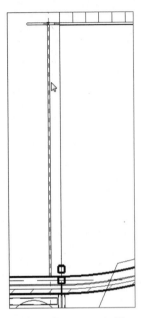

FIGURE 10.26 The railing centered on the reference plane

The next step is to create a railing between the two stair sections. This can be a tad tricky, but once you get the progression, I think you will see why it needs to be done in the following manner:

1. On the Home tab, click the Railing button.

2. In the Properties dialog, make sure Type is set to Landing Handrail, and click OK.

3. Using the same 8 1/2″ offset, draw the sketch of the railing as shown in Figure 10.27.

4. Click Finish Edit Mode.

5. If you need to flip the railing, select it, and then click the blue flip grip that appears in the middle of the railing (see Figure 10.28).

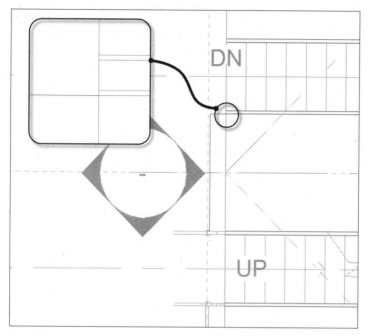

FIGURE 10.27 Adding the railing to the middle of the stair landing

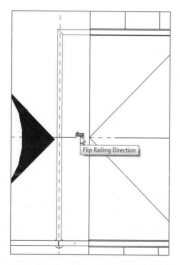

FIGURE 10.28 The finished railing

Now that the two railings are in place, you can use basic editing commands to create an occurrence of the railing on the other side of the stairs. You can either mirror the railing on your own, or if you wish, you can follow along with these steps:

It the railing is backward after you finish the sketch, you can select the flip arrow after you select the railing.

1. Select the south railing, as shown in Figure 10.29.

2. Click the Mirror - Pick Axis button on the Modify | Railings tab.

3. For the reference, pick the center reference plane.

4. Make sure the railing is abutting the north wall.

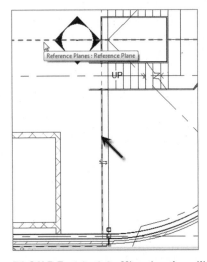

Reference Planes : Reference Plane

UP

FIGURE 10.29 Mirroring the railing to the north side of the stairs

To mirror an item, you can also select the object you wish to mirror, then type MM at the keyboard. This will start the Mirror command; however, you will have to always pick the mirror axis when doing this.

5. Select the north railing, as shown in Figure 10.30.

6. On the Modify | Railings tab, click the Edit Path button.

7. Draw a connecting piece, as shown in Figure 10.30.

8. Once the railing is sketched in, click the Finish Edit Mode button on the Mode panel to the right.

At this point, it is a good idea to check out your railing in 3D because we are about to copy it to the levels above.

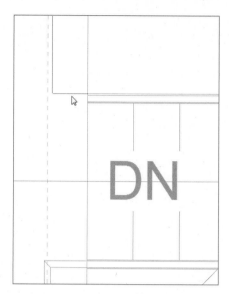

FIGURE 10.30 Adding the connecting piece to the railing

ALIGNING THE RAILING

If you are having trouble aligning the railing to the correct point of the stair railing, click the Thin Lines icon on the View tab as shown in this image:

It's copy time! The next objective is to copy these three railings up to the next three levels. You can proceed on your own and use Copy/Paste Aligned, or you can follow along with this procedure:

1. In the Project Browser, go to the Level 2 floor plan.

2. Select the three railings you added to Level 2.

3. On the Modify | Railings tab, click the Copy To Clipboard button on the Clipboard panel.

4. Click Paste ➢ Aligned To Selected Levels.

5. Select Levels 3, 4, and 5, and then click OK.

6. In the Project Browser, go to the Level 5 floor plan.

7. Delete the bottom (south) railing.

8. Select the smaller, middle railing, as shown in Figure 10.31.

9. On the Modify | Railings tab, click the Edit Path button.

10. Extend the line down to the south wall, as shown in Figure 10.31.

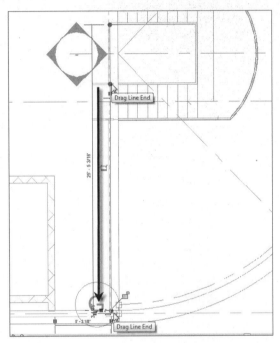

FIGURE 10.31 Extending the railing to complete Level 5

11. On the Mode panel, click Finish Edit Mode.

12. Save the model.

13. Check out the model in 3D (see Figure 10.32).

Phew! We have built a set of stairs. The good thing is that it's one sweet staircase. The bad thing is we used all the default layouts and materials. It's time to get into some more complicated shapes and styles.

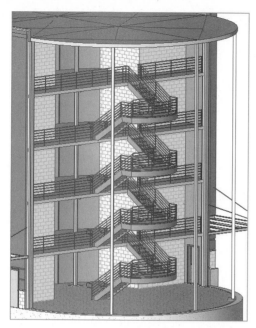

FIGURE 10.32 The entry stairs and railing

Creating a Winding Staircase

Before we get started here, you should know that this staircase will be created using the separate stair components. You can try to do a winding staircase using the Run function similar to the one we did earlier, but in many cases (especially when you run into an existing staircase in either a renovation project or an addition), you may just need to draft the stairs, then model over the top of the drafting lines. What? Drafting in Revit? Of course. How else can you expect to get anything done?

The first thing we will need to do is make modifications to the floor in a specific area to create a landing, as follows:

1. In the Project Browser, go to the Level 2 floor plan.

2. Zoom in on the area between the corridor and the east wing, as shown in Figure 10.33.

3. Select the Level 2 floor in the east wing.

4. Once the floor is selected, click the Edit Boundary button on the Mode panel of the Modify | Floors tab.

Remember, if you want to get the front radial wall out of the way, you can right-click it, and choose Hide In View ➢ Hide Element. This command will hide the wall in this view. Just remember that when you need it turned back on, you must unhide the element.

You may have to pick a window around the entire area, and then click the Filter button on the Ribbon. From there, you can select only Floors.

5. Sketch a landing that is 8'–0" long × 7'–10" wide, as shown in Figure 10.33.

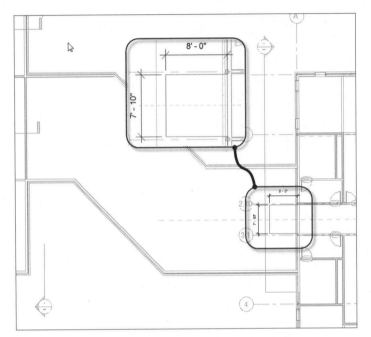

FIGURE 10.33 Creating a landing. We will add a door in a moment.

6. Once the landing is added in, click Finish Edit Mode on the Mode panel. If you are asked to attach the walls to the bottom of the floor, click Yes.

With the landing in place, we can now copy a door up to this level. To do this, we will go to the first floor and copy the door that resides there. You can do this on your own, or you can follow along with the procedure:

1. In the Project Browser, go to the Level 1 floor plan.

2. Select the door that is there (see Figure 10.34).

3. Copy the door to the clipboard (click Copy To Clipboard on the Clipboard panel).

4. Choose Paste ➢ Aligned To Selected Levels.

5. Select Level 2 and click OK.

6. In the Project Browser, go back to Level 2. The door and the landing are now in place.

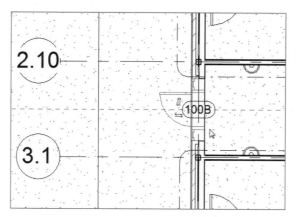

FIGURE 10.34 Copying the first floor door to the clipboard and pasting it to Level 2

With the landing and the door in place, we can now create a winding set of stairs. The first task is to simply lay out the shape in the plan, using simple drafting lines. The second step is to model over the lines we added using various stair tools, as follows:

1. Select the Annotate tab.

2. Click the Detail Line button, as shown in Figure 10.35.

3. On the Draw panel, click the Start - End - Radius Arc button, as shown near the top of Figure 10.36.

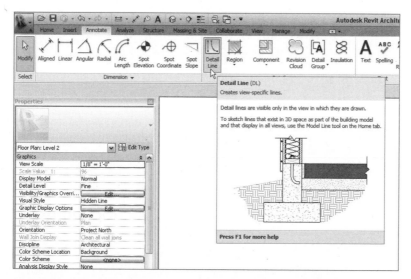

FIGURE 10.35 Click the Detail Line button on the Annotate tab.

4. For the first point of the arc, pick the midpoint of the landing, as shown in Figure 10.36.

5. Move your cursor down and at 135° from the first point picked.

6. Extend your cursor 11′–0″, as shown in Figure 10.36, and then click to set the second point.

7. To form the arc, move your cursor to the right until the radius snaps into place. When it does, pick the point, as shown in Figure 10.37.

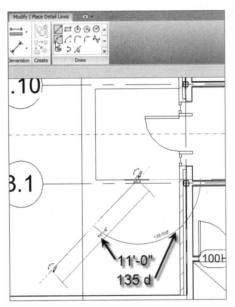

FIGURE 10.36 With the Start-End-Radius Arc, first start at the midpoint of the landing, then go southwest at an angle of 135° and a distance of 11′–0″.

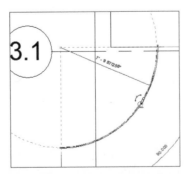

FIGURE 10.37 Picking the third point to form the arc. It will be tangent upon the first two points you picked.

8. Press Esc.

9. On the Draw panel, click the Pick Lines icon.

10. On the Options bar, add an increment of 2′–0″ to the Offset field (see Figure 10.38).

11. Offset the center arc to the right, then to the left, forming a 4′–0″ overall winder, as shown in Figure 10.38.

12. Press Esc.

13. Click the Line tool, make sure Offset is set to 0′0″, and then draw a straight line at each end of the arcs, as shown in Figure 10.39.

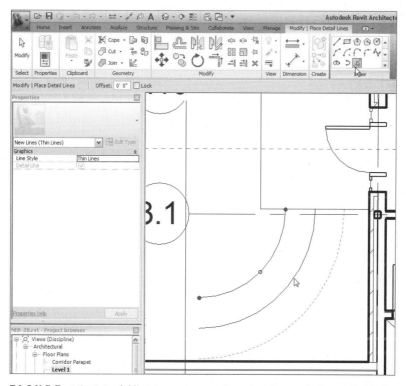

FIGURE 10.38 Adding two more arcs based on the centerline of the first

Okay, take a breather. Compare the examples in the book to what you have. Are we close? If not, go back and investigate.

 N O T E   Get used to this drafting thing; it is still very much a part of BIM, regardless of whether people say you can't draft in Revit!

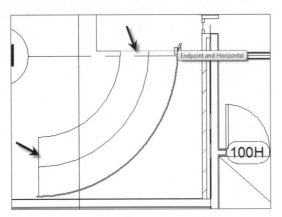

FIGURE 10.39 Adding two straight lines at each end of the arcs

The next step is to make an array of the straight lines we just added. These lines will wind up being our guidelines for our risers.

1. Press Esc, and then select the smaller arc, as shown in Figure 10.40.

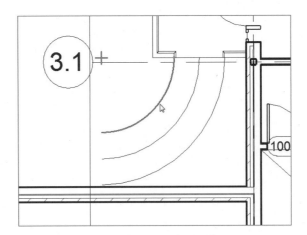

FIGURE 10.40 Selecting the smaller arc

2. Make sure the Properties dialog is active.

3. In the Properties dialog, check Center Mark Visible.

4. Select the line at the left end of the arcs, as shown in Figure 10.41.

5. Click the Array button on the Modify | Lines tab, as shown in Figure 10.41.

6. On the Options bar, be sure that Radial is selected.

7. Make sure Group And Associate is checked.

8. Type 18 for the number.

9. Click Move To: Last on the Options bar. (Remember, we aren't actually moving this line; we are simply copying to last.)

10. When these options are set, pick and drag the blue icon to the center point you turned on earlier (see Figure 10.41).

11. Pick a point along the first line (the one on the bottom left).

12. Pick the second point along the upper-right line.

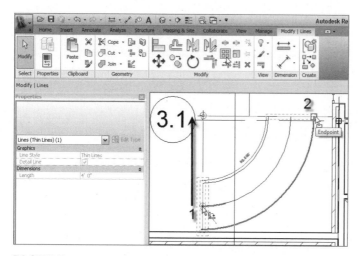

FIGURE 10.41 Arraying the line to create your own treads

Your array should now be complete. Compare your linework to Figure 10.42.

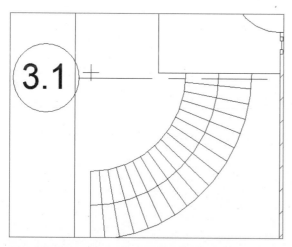

FIGURE 10.42 The stairs are taking shape.

It's time to start modeling the stairs. This procedure will be nothing more than tracing the lines you have already added to the model. To do this, we are going to utilize the tools available that we have not touched in the previous staircase, as follows:

1. On the Home tab, click the Stairs button.

2. In the Properties dialog, change Base Level to Level 1.

3. Change Top Level to Level 2.

4. Click Edit Type.

5. Click Duplicate.

6. Call the stairs **Corridor Entry Stairs**.

7. Click OK.

8. For Tread Material, click in the field where it says <By Category>.

9. You will see a […] button. Click it.

10. Choose Wood - Cherry for the Tread Material.

11. For Riser Material, do the same.

12. For Stringer Material, select Wood - Mahogany (see Figure 10.43).

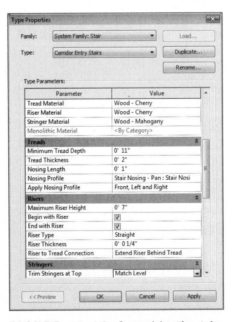

FIGURE 10.43 Customizing the stairs

13. Under the Treads category, select Front, Left And Right for Nosing Profile.

14. In the Stringers category, select Match Level for Trim Stringers At Top (see Figure 10.43).

15. Click OK to get back to the model.

It's now time to add the stairs to the model. To do this, we will first sketch the boundary:

1. On the Modify | Create Stairs Sketch tab, click the Boundary button, as shown in Figure 10.44.

2. On the Draw panel, click the Pick Lines icon.

3. Pick the two arcs defining the outside of the stairs. You will see green arcs copied directly on top of them.

FIGURE 10.44 Click the Boundary button.

4. On the Draw panel, click the Riser button, as shown in Figure 10.45.

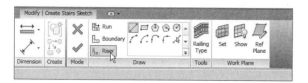

FIGURE 10.45 Click the Riser button.

5. On the Draw panel, click the Pick Lines icon.

6. Pick all of the lines you arrayed. This includes the bottom and the top lines (see Figure 10.46).

7. Click Finish Edit Mode on the Mode panel.

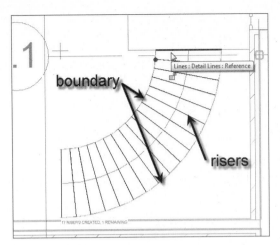

FIGURE 10.46 Picking the detail lines to lay over the stair components

With the stairs roughed in, we need to get a better look at them. If we use the default 3D view, we need to turn off way too many items to see our stairs. Let's add a perspective view just to see what's going on here!

If you are confident in adding your own perspective view, go ahead and put one in, and name it **East Entry from Corridor**. If not, follow along with the procedure:

1. In the Project Browser, go to the Level 1 floor plan.

2. On the View tab, click the 3D View ➢ Camera button.

3. Pick the first point shown in Figure 10.47.

4. Pick the second point shown in Figure 10.47.

5. In the Project Browser, find the new perspective view, and rename it to **East Entry from Corridor**.

6. In the Perspective view, turn on Shading With Edges (it is located at the View Control bar at the bottom of the view).

Now that we have a perspective on our stairs, we can see multiple issues with the railing. The first, more prominent issue is that the railings seem to be floating. This occurs when the stringers are switched from closed to open. Revit still thinks there is a stringer underneath the railings. We will need to move the railings in 2″ to fix this problem.

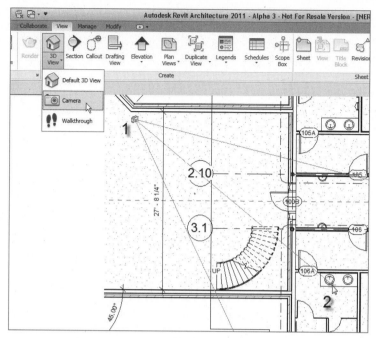

FIGURE 10.47 Adding the perspective view

Making Railing Adjustments

Yes, we have been making railing adjustments this entire chapter. Get used to constantly having to do this for each unique situation. This staircase requires us to add some posts back into the railing so it can stop and end at the stringer. But first let's move the railing back onto the actual treads:

1. Go to the Level 2 floor plan.

2. Select the top railing, as shown in Figure 10.48.

3. On the Modify | Railings tab, click Edit Path.

4. Click the Offset button on the Modify panel, as shown in Figure 10.48.

5. In the Offset field in the Options bar, type 2".

6. Deselect the Copy option.

7. Offset the railing into the stairs 2", as shown in Figure 10.48.

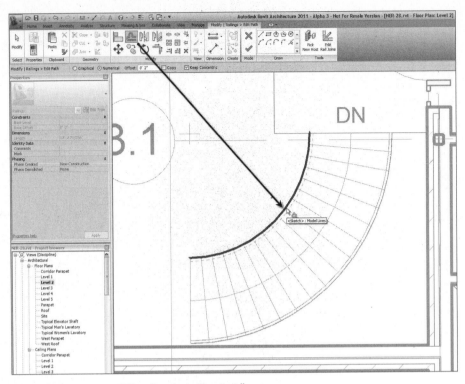

FIGURE 10.48   Offsetting the railing in 2″

    8. Click Finish Edit Mode.

    9. Select the other railing.

   10. Click the Edit Path button on the Modify | Railings tab.

   11. Offset the railing in 2″.

   12. Click Finish Sketch Mode.

Since these railings will not extend past the stringers, it is OK to add posts back to the beginning and the ends of the railings:

    1. Select both railings.

    2. In the Change Element Type menu, select Railing : Handrail - Pipe.

    3. Go to the East Entry from Corridor view. Does your stair and railing system look like Figure 10.49?

FIGURE 10.49 The almost completed stairs

The next series of steps will involve mirroring the stairs to the other side of the landing. Then, of course, we need to add a landing railing so people don't just walk out the door and off the ledge.

   1. Go to the Level 2 floor plan in the Project Browser.

   2. Select the stairs and the railings.

N O T E   To select only the stairs and the railings, you can pick a window around the entire set of lines, groups, railings, and stairs. From there, you can click the Filter button on the Ribbon, and select only Stairs And Railings.

   3. On the Modify | Multi-Select tab, click the Mirror ➤ Pick Mirror Axis button, as shown in Figure 10.50.

   4. Pick the center reference plane (I told you this thing would come in handy).

Your stairs are now mirrored to the other side of the landing, as shown in Figure 10.50.

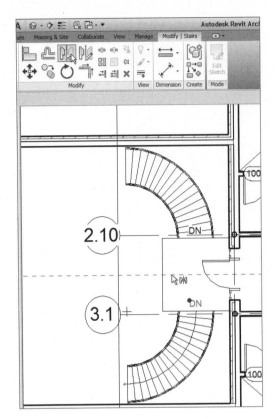

FIGURE 10.50 The mirrored stairs

It's time to tie in the railings. If you are feeling up to the challenge, try it on your own using the landing railing you used in the front entry stairs. If not, just follow along with these steps:

1. On the Home tab, click the Railing button.

2. In the Properties dialog, change the type to Landing Handrail (if it is not already), as shown in Figure 10.51.

3. On the Draw panel, click the Pick Lines icon, as shown in Figure 10.52.

4. Set Offset to 4".

5. Pick the landing lines to offset in the railing, as shown in Figure 10.52.

6. Once the offsets are complete, click the Line icon on the Draw panel, as shown in Figure 10.53.

7. Make sure the offset is set to 0.

FIGURE 10.51 Setting the Landing Handrail type

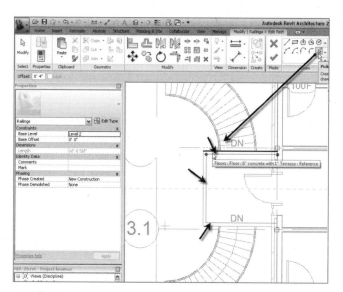

FIGURE 10.52 Adding the railings to the landing

8. Draw the lines extending from the stair railing to the landing railing, as shown in Figure 10.53.

9. Trim the corners so your railings look like Figure 10.53.

10. On the Mode panel, click Finish Edit Mode.

11. You may have to flip the railing by selecting it, then clicking the Flip arrow. Your railing should look like Figure 10.54.

12. Add two more railings between the stairs and the brick wall. Your stairs should look like Figure 10.55.

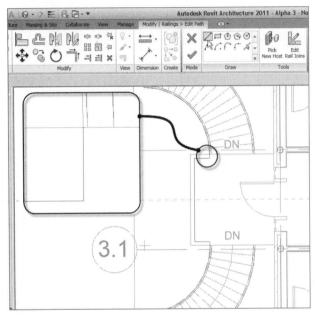

FIGURE 10.53 Connecting the landing railing to the stair railing

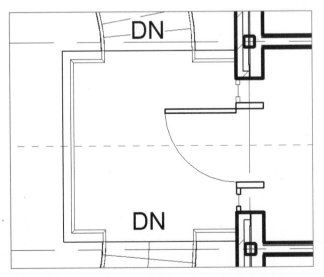

FIGURE 10.54 The railing at the front of the landing

FIGURE 10.55 The completed landing

Great! We are getting there. Now it is time to see how a staircase and the accompanying railings come together. For example, it sure would be nice to have a railing with spindles, or better yet, panels added to them. Also, a nice half-round bullnose would improve our staircase. The next section will focus on this concept.

Stair and Railing Families

Similar to the model as a whole, stairs and railings comprise separate families that come together to form the overall unit. Although stairs and railings are considered a system family (a family that resides only in the model), they still heavily rely on hosted families to create the entire element.

The next procedure will involve loading separate families into the model, and then utilizing them in a new set of stairs and railings we will create in the west wing.

1. In the Project Browser, go to the Level 3 floor plan.

2. Zoom in on the west wing.

3. On the Home tab, click the Floor button.

4. In the Properties dialog, click the Edit Type button.

5. Select the 6″ concrete with 1″ Terrazzo floor system from the Type drop-down list, as shown in Figure 10.56.

Remember, you must only do one railing at a time. If you try to do more than one continuous line, Revit will not let you proceed.

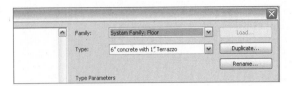

FIGURE 10.56 You must add a floor at the Level 3 floor plan for the stairs to have a landing.

6. Click OK.

7. On the Draw panel, click the Pick Walls button.

8. Pick the walls, and make sure the lines are set to the core centerline, as shown in Figure 10.57.

9. When picking the south wall, set the offset to 5'– 0" in the Options bar, as shown in Figure 10.57.

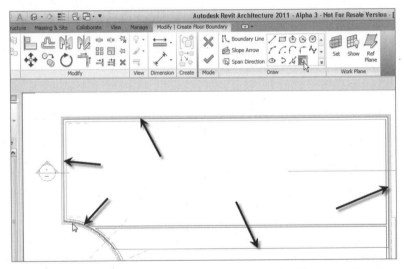

FIGURE 10.57 Adding the floor outline to the walls. Be sure to offset the line 5'-0" from the south wall. This will be the stair landing.

TIP   Again, make sure you have no gaps or overlapping lines. Use the Trim/Extend Single Element command to clean up the lines to look like the figure.

10. Once the sketch lines are in place, click Finish Edit Mode on the Mode panel.

11. Revit will ask you if you want to attach the walls that go up to this floor's bottom. Click Yes.

12. Next, Revit will ask you if you want to cut the overlapping volume out of the walls. Click Yes again.

Your floor is now in place. The next item we will tackle is creating a completely custom railing system.

Creating a Custom Railing System

It's now time to load the components that will comprise our stairs. Although Revit makes an attempt to supply you with some families, you will be downloading the families included with this book by going to the book's web page at **www.sybex.com/ go/revit2011ner**. From there you can browse to Chapter 10 and find the following files:

▶ 6210 (2-5_8).rfa

▶ landing.rfa

▶ post.rfa

▶ raised panels.rfa

▶ spindle.rfa

▶ stair nosing.rfa

To get started, we need to load the families into our model so they are available when it comes time to assemble our new railing. If you remember how to do this, go ahead and load all the families that you just downloaded from the web page. If you need some assistance, follow along with the procedure:

1. On the Insert tab, click Load Family.

2. Find the files that you downloaded from the web page.

3. Once you have found the files we listed, select all of them and click Open to load them.

4. Save the model.

The next step will be to create a new railing and add some of these items to it:

1. In the Project Browser, find the Families category and expand it, as shown in Figure 10.58.

2. Find the Railings category and expand it.

3. Find Handrail - Rectangular and double-click it (see Figure 10.58).

FIGURE 10.58 The railing family called Handrail - Rectangular

4. Click Duplicate.

5. Call the new railing **Wood Railing with Spindles**.

6. Click OK.

7. In the Rail Structure row, click the Edit button.

8. In the Rails chart, change Name to **Handrail**, as shown in Figure 10.59.

9. Change the profile to **6210 (2-5_8): 2 5/8"**.

10. Change Material to Wood - Cherry by clicking on the […] button and browsing for the material (see Figure 10.59).

11. Click OK.

12. Click the Edit button in the Baluster Placement row.

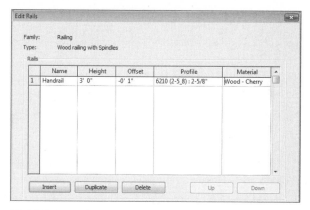

FIGURE 10.59 Changing the rail. Note that you can add as many rails as you wish. In this case, we are adding only one.

13. In the Main Pattern area, change Baluster Family to Spindle 1" (see Figure 10.60).

FIGURE 10.60 Adding the spindle to the Main Pattern

14. Just below the Main Pattern area is the Use Baluster Per Tread On Stairs option. Click it, as shown in Figure 10.61.

15. To the right, you will see a field that says Balusters Per Tread. Specify two balusters per tread (see Figure 10.61).

16. In the bottommost field is the Posts category. Change each of the three Posts to None. Our spindles are all we need (see Figure 10.61).

17. Click OK twice.

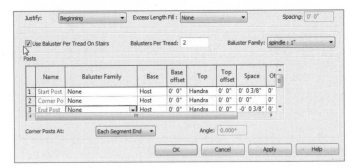

FIGURE 10.61 Specifying two balusters per tread and no actual posts

You may or may not have noticed that we did not get the opportunity to change the baluster's material as we did with the railing. This action must be done in the family itself, as follows:

1. In the Project Browser, you will see a category called Spindle just below Railing, as shown in Figure 10.62. Expand Spindle to expose the 1″ family.

2. Once you see the 1″, double-click it to open its Type Properties dialog.

FIGURE 10.62 Finding the Spindle : 1″ family to access the material

3. In the Type Properties dialog, find the Material row and click the [...] button. This will appear when you click into the field that says <By Category>.

4. Change Material to Wood - Cherry.

5. Click OK twice.

This completes the railing. Once we add it to the stairs, however, there will certainly be some required "tweaking." The next step is to customize the stairs themselves.

Creating Custom Stairs

Since this is the third staircase we have created in the same chapter, you certainly have gained some experience regarding the placement of stairs and railings into the Revit model. You are also becoming familiar with the stair and railings dialogs. This last procedure will tie all of that together.

Let's create that staircase:

1. On the Home tab, click the Stairs button.

2. In the Properties dialog box, make sure Stairs is currently in the Type Selector, and click the Edit Type button.

3. Click Duplicate.

4. Call the new staircase **Custom Bullnose Stairs**.

5. Click OK.

6. In the Type Parameters, under Construction, turn on the toggle for Monolithic Stairs, as shown in Figure 10.63.

7. Moving down the list, change Monolithic Material to Wood - Mahogany.

8. Change Nosing Profile to Stair Nosing : Stair Nosing (see Figure 10.63).

9. Under the Risers category, change Riser Thickness to 0'–3/4".

10. For Riser To Tread Connection, choose Extend Tread Under Riser (see Figure 10.63).

11. Click OK.

It is time to configure some of the layout properties. These will allow us to calculate the rise/run count as well as some basic offsets we will need.

1. In the Properties dialog, set Base Level to Level 1.

2. Set Base Offset to 6 5/8", as shown in Figure 10.64.

3. Set Top Level to Level 3. (Yes, this is going to be one long staircase!)

FIGURE 10.63 Configuring the stairs. As you can see, you have quite a few options.

FIGURE 10.64 The Base Offset value is set to 6 5/8".

The next step is to place this monster into the model. Although we did not specify a multistory staircase, we will need multiple landings to give our visitors a breather as they travel up the stairs. This layout will require a little more care in the initial planning stage.

1. On the Home tab, click the Ref Plane button.

2. Click the Pick Lines button and then offset a grid, as shown in Figure 10.65.

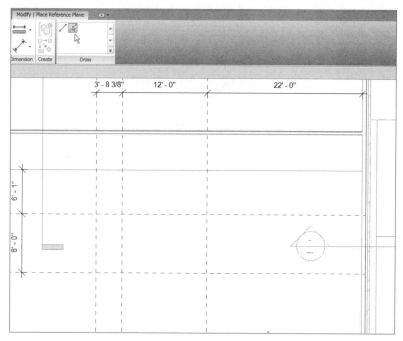

FIGURE 10.65 Using dimensions to lay out the centerlines of the stairs

3. On the Modify | Create Stairs Sketch tab, click the Run button.

4. Draw your stairs as shown in Figure 10.66. (Pick the points as the figure is sequenced.)

5. When you have picked the points, click Finish Edit Mode. Your plan should look like Figure 10.67.

The nice thing about using reference planes while in Sketch Mode is that they will disappear once you finish the sketch. If you need to go back and edit the stair, the reference planes will appear again!

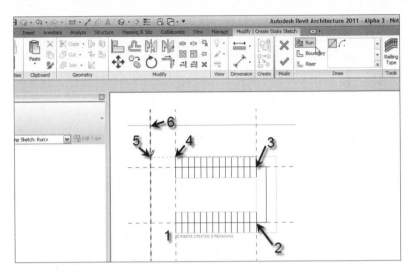

FIGURE 10.66 Picking the intersections of the reference planes to determine where the stairs will be going

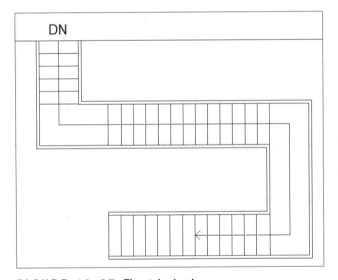

FIGURE 10.67 The stairs in place

Remember how the railings seemed to be floating when we opened the stringers in the entry staircase? We are going to have the same issue here. The next procedure is to move the railings in 2″ in plan so there is adequate bearing on the stairs:

1. In plan, select the top railing, as shown in Figure 10.68.

2. On the Modify | Railings tab, click Edit Path.

3. On the Edit panel, click the Offset button, as shown in Figure 10.68.

4. On the Options bar, enter 2" in the Offset field.

5. Uncheck Copy.

6. Hover your cursor over one of the magenta sketch lines and press the Tab key. This will select the entire railing line.

7. Make sure the dotted alignment line is facing the inside, as shown in Figure 10.68. (If it is not, press the spacebar to flip it.)

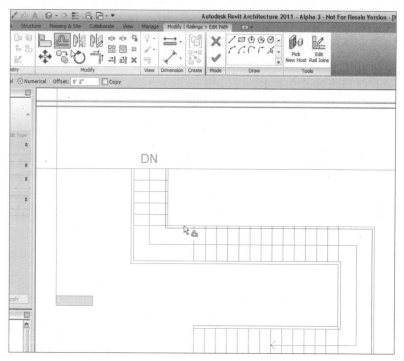

FIGURE 10.68 Offset the railing line down 2" from the original location.

8. Once the railing is offset in, click Finish Edit Mode.

9. Repeat the procedure on the other railing.

10. Go to a 3D view to check out the stairs. They should resemble Figure 10.69.

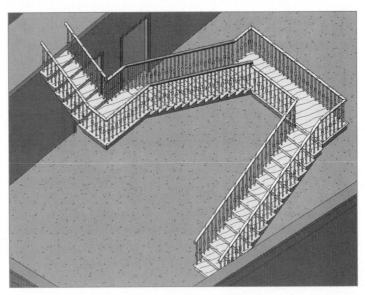

FIGURE 10.69 The stairs as shown in 3D. Notice the nice bullnose and the railings.

The next step (pun intended) is to add a landing to the bottom of the stairs. This requires creating a family. Although we will cover creating families in Chapter 17, "Creating Families," this one has been created, and you have downloaded the families needed to create this step in the stairs.

Adding a Custom Landing

The reason we left the 6 5/8″ offset for the bottom tread is because we need to introduce our own version of how that bottom tread should look. As mentioned earlier, this family has been loaded. If you have not already loaded the family, go to **www.sybex.com/go/revit2011ner**. From there you can browse to Chapter 10 and find the files called Landing.rfa and Post.rfa. After you have loaded these families, proceed with these steps:

1. In the Project Browser, go to the Level 1 floor plan.

2. On the Home tab, click the Place A Component button.

3. In the Properties dialog, find and select the family called Landing.

4. As you are inserting the family, press the Tab key to rotate the landing into the correct position.

5. Place the landing under the last tread at the point shown in Figure 10.70.

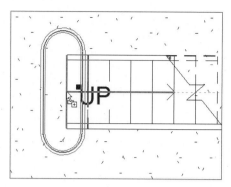

FIGURE 10.70 Placing the landing

6. Press Esc twice.

7. Select the landing.

8. In the Properties dialog, change Tread Material to Wood - Cherry.

9. Change Base Material to Wood - Mahogany and click OK (see Figure 10.71).

FIGURE 10.71 Changing the landing material to match the theme of the staircase

The next remaining task is to add a post.

Adding a Gooseneck

In this style of railing system, it would be nice to have a gooseneck that will catch the railing as it slopes downward and spiral it into the post. Of course Revit does not have families for this already built, but this book sure does! You should have downloaded the post family earlier in this chapter, but if you did not, go to the book's website at **www.sybex.com/go/revit2011ner**. From there you can browse to Chapter 10 and find the file called Post_up.rfa. After you download it and load it into the model, follow these steps:

1. In the Project Browser, go to the Level 1 floor plan and zoom in on the landing area, as shown in Figure 10.72.

2. On the Home tab, click the Place A Component button.

3. In the Properties dialog, select Post With Gooseneck.

4. As you are placing the post, press the spacebar twice to flip it into the correct orientation, as shown in Figure 10.72.

5. Place it on the landing slightly away from the stair railing, as shown in Figure 10.72.

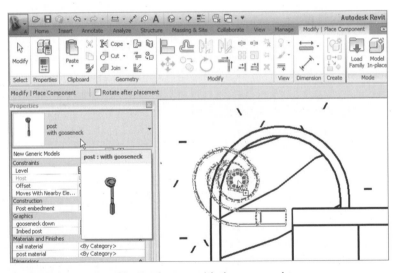

FIGURE 10.72 Placing the post with the gooseneck

6. When the post is placed, select it and change Offset to 6 5/8" in the Properties dialog.

 N O T E   If the end of the post seems to be clipped in plan, you need to adjust the view range in the Properties dialog. Right now, the 4'–0" clip plane may be a tad too low. To fix this, find the View Range row in the Properties dialog and click the Edit button. In the View Range dialog, adjust Cut Plane Offset to 4'–6".

7. Select the post again (if it is not still selected).

8. Click the Move button.

9. Move the post from the midpoint of the post's end to the midpoint of the stair railing's end, as shown in Figure 10.73.

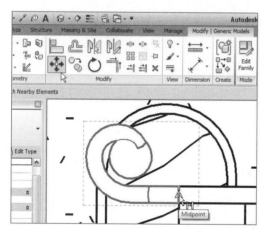

F I G U R E 1 0 . 7 3 Moving the post to align with the stair railing

10. Select the post again (if it is not selected already).

11. In the Properties dialog, go to the Materials And Finishes category and change materials for both the rail and the post to Wood - Cherry.

12. Mirror the post to the other railing.

In 3D, your landing should now look like Figure 10.74.

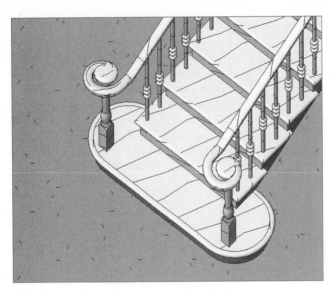

FIGURE 10.74 The completed landing

Adding a Railing to the Landing

It's now time to add the railing to the Level 3 balcony. Compared to that landing we just did, this is going to be a snap! If you feel as though you have the experience required to add your own landing railing, go ahead and take a shot. If not, just follow along with the procedure:

1. In the Project Browser, go to Level 3.

2. Zoom in on the stairs.

3. Right-click one of the railings on the stairs and click Create Similar.

4. Sketch a railing that is 4″ in from the face of the landing, as shown in Figure 10.75.

5. Make sure you have a "leg" tied into the stair railing, as shown in Figure 10.75.

6. On the Railing panel, click Finish Edit Mode.

7. Repeat the procedure on the other end (see Figure 10.76).

N O T E   To repeat the procedure on the other end, you can either mirror the railing you just put in, then edit it to reach the far end of the landing, or you can start the Railing command and do it again. I recommend mirroring the railing, selecting the new railing, and then selecting Edit Path from the Modify | Railings tab. You can then grip-edit the right end to meet the wall. This ensures you the railing will be aligned with the railing on the stair.

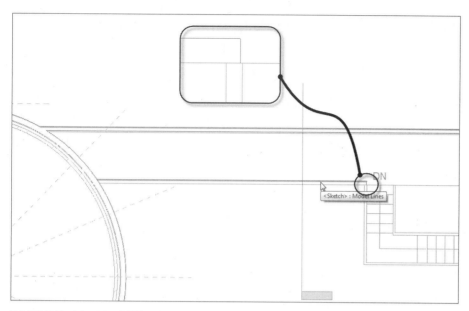

FIGURE 10.75 Adding the railing. This process is becoming old hat!

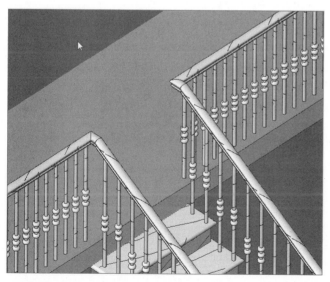

FIGURE 10.76 Both railings are in place.

The last step is to add a raised panel stile and rail system along the third floor wall.

Adding a Raised Panel Stile and Rail System

The first thing we will need to do is to add an entrance to the large Level 3 training room. The corridor will then receive a custom line-based, raised panel family.

1. In the Project Browser, go to the Level 3 floor plan.

2. On the Home tab, click the Door button.

3. In the Properties dialog, select Single-Raised Panel With Sidelights : 36″ × 84″.

4. Place it in the corridor wall aligned with the stairs, as shown in Figure 10.77.

5. Copy the door 10′-0″ to the right, as shown in Figure 10.77.

6. On the View tab, click the Elevation button.

7. In the Change Element Type menu in the Properties dialog, select Interior Elevation.

8. Pick a point, as shown in Figure 10.77; then press Esc.

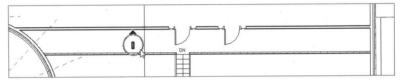

FIGURE 10.77 Pick the point as shown for the elevation.

9. In the Project Browser, right-click on the new elevation and rename it to **West Wing Balcony Elevation**.

10. Open the West Wing Balcony elevation.

11. Stretch the crop region so you can see the entire west wing.

12. On the View Control bar, change Visual Style to Wireframe.

13. On the Home tab, click the Place A Component button.

14. On the Placement panel, click Place On Face.

15. Pick the far wall, as shown in Figure 10.78.

16. In the Change Element Type menu in the Properties dialog, select the Raised Panels family.

If you do not have the raised panel family, you can download it at `www.sybex.com/go/revit2011ner`. From there you can browse to Chapter 10 and find the file called `Raised Panel.rfa`. Once it is downloaded and loaded in to the model, proceed with the next step.

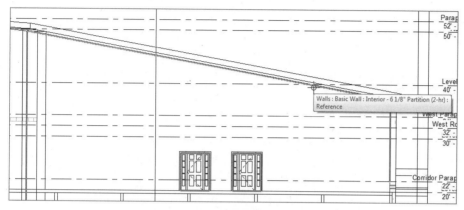

FIGURE 10.78 Picking the far wall to establish a work plane

17. Pick the base point, labeled #1 in Figure 10.79.

18. Pick the second point, labeled #2 in Figure 10.79.

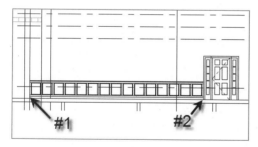

FIGURE 10.79 Adding the line-based, raised panel family

N O T E   If you just can't seem to pick the points specified in Figure 10.79, go ahead and pick two points close to the area indicated in the figure. After you place the line-based family, you can select it and grip-edit the ends to extend to the wall's edges as shown in the figure.

18. Start the Place A Component command again, and add the raised panel family between the two doors and to the right. This will complete the raised panels for this level.

19. Select all of the raised panel families on this floor (remember to hold the Ctrl key to add to the selection).

20. In the Material And Finishes category of the Properties dialog, change the panel material to Wood - Cherry.

21. Change Frame Material to Wood - Mahogany. See Figure 10.80.

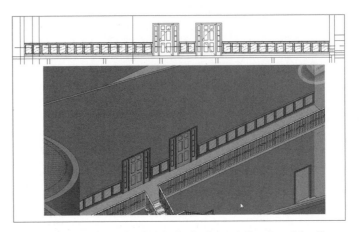

FIGURE 10.80 The finished raised panel, line-based family

Wow! That was quite a bit on stairs. If you take anything away from this chapter, take away the knowledge that stairs are not going to come easy, but you can create any staircase if you know you will need to create families.

The last section of this chapter will focus on adding ramps to the model. As far as Revit procedures go, ramps are the kid sister to stairs.

Adding Ramps

When you think of ramps in Revit, think of a one-tread, one-rise staircase at a 1/12 pitch. Ramps are placed in the model exactly in the same way as a stair. You still have the run method, and you can still sketch the ramp using a boundary.

That being said, let's start placing a ramp in your model:

1. In the Project Browser, go to the Level 1 floor plan.

2. Zoom in on the radial entry of the east wing at grid intersection F-5 (see Figure 10.81).

3. We need to create a flat landing, so on the Home tab, click the Floor button.

4. Click Edit Type in the Properties dialog.

5. Select Generic - 12″.

6. Click Duplicate.

7. Call the new floor **Exterior Concrete Slab**.

8. Click OK.

9. Click the Edit button in the Structure row.

10. Change Structure [1] Material to Concrete - Cast-in-Place Concrete.

11. Change Thickness to 6″.

12. Click OK twice to get back to the model.

13. Place the concrete at the points shown in Figure 10.81.

 W A R N I N G   **Make sure you are using the Lines mode and are picking the outside face of brick. That extra line represents the water table above this floor's level.**

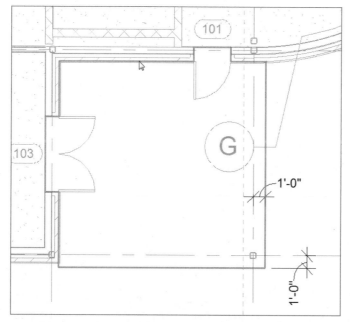

F I G U R E   1 0 . 8 1 Sketching the slab perimeter

14. When the slab is in place, click the Finish Edit Mode button.

15. Click No in the next dialog.

Now it is time for the ramp. We will set the ramp's properties for the top to Level 1, and the bottom is also going to be at Level 1 but with an offset.

1. On the Home tab, click the Ramp button, as shown in Figure 10.82.

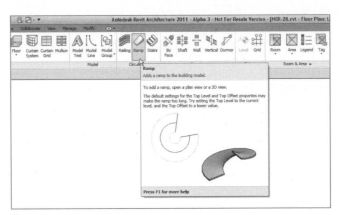

FIGURE 10.82 Click the Ramp button on the Home tab.

2. In the Properties dialog, click Edit Type.

3. Click Duplicate.

4. Call the new ramp **Exterior Concrete Ramp**.

5. Click OK.

6. Give it a 6″ thickness.

7. For Ramp Material, click the [...] button and specify Concrete - Cast-In-Place Concrete, as shown in Figure 10.83.

8. Notice the Maximum Incline Length is set to the ADA standard of 30′–0″.

9. In the Other category, notice the Ramp Max Slope is set to 1/12.

10. Click OK.

11. In the Properties dialog, set Base Level to Level 1.

12. Set Base Offset to –2′–6″, as shown in Figure 10.84.

13. Set Top Level to Level 1.

14. Set Width to 5'–0" (see Figure 10.84).

15. On the Draw panel, click the Run button.

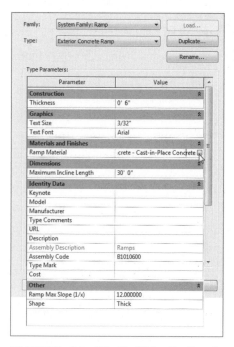

FIGURE 10.83 Modifying the Type Properties

FIGURE 10.84 Setting the properties

16. In the model, click the first point for the ramp similar to the point shown in Figure 10.85. (You will have to just place the point near the midpoint. Revit does not allow you to snap while in this Sketch Mode for some reason.)

17. Move your cursor down the view (in a southerly direction) 15′–0″ (you will see the temporary dimension), as shown in Figure 10.85.

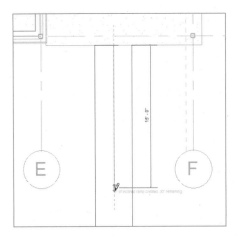

FIGURE 10.85 Pick the first point on the landing, then move your cursor down 15′–0″.

18. Pick a point about 6′–0″ below the end of the ramp in alignment with the right boundary, as shown in Figure 10.86. After you pick the second point, the view should read: "30′ of inclined ramp created, 0 remaining."

19. Move your cursor to the right until the ramp stops (see Figure 10.86).

20. On the Modify | Create Ramp Sketch tab, click the Railing Type button.

21. Select Handrail - Pipe in the Railings Type dialog that opens.

22. Click OK.

23. Click Finish Edit Mode.

24. Select the entire ramp (including the railing).

25. Move the ramp from the midpoint of the top of the ramp to the midpoint of the landing slab.

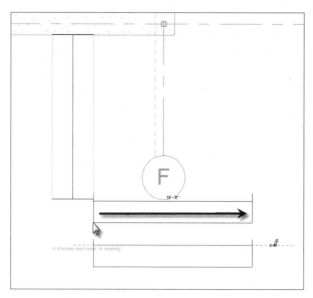

FIGURE 10.86 The second leg of the ramp

You may notice immediately that the ramp is sloping in the wrong direction. Also, we need to tie the railings into the slab. If you would like to pick around and see how to do these things on your own, go right ahead. If you would rather go through the procedure, follow along:

1. Select the ramp.

2. Notice a small blue arrow. Pick it—this will flip the direction of the ramp.

3. On the Home tab, click the Railing button.

4. In the Properties dialog, click Edit Type, change the type to Handrail - Pipe, and click OK.

5. Draw a railing in 8″ from the slab edge, as shown in Figure 10.87.

6. Mirror the slab, the ramp, and the railing to the other side of the building as shown in Figure 10.88.

7. Save the model.

Creating ramps will be a necessary evil in almost every project. Some will be easier than others, and at times they may try your patience. Keep at it and before long you will have the experience you need to feel confident.

It is best if you keep moving your cursor past the ramp, even knowing the end of the ramp has stopped. This will ensure that the entire ramp has been put in place.

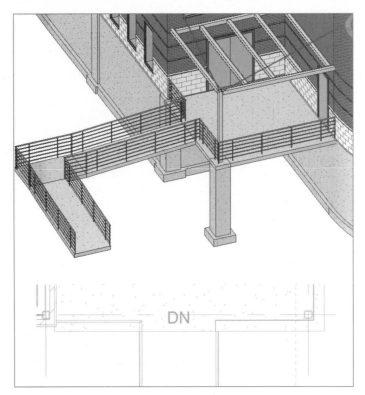

FIGURE 10.87 Adding the railing just as you have been doing this entire chapter

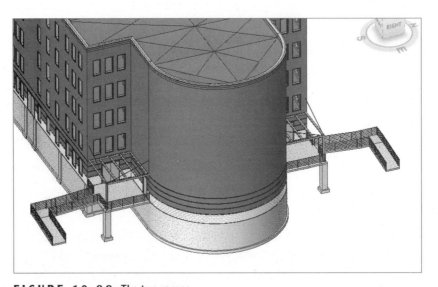

FIGURE 10.88 The two ramps

Are You Experienced?

Now you can...

- ☑ create stairs in the conventional method by using the Run command to generate the height and length you need

- ☑ create stairs by first laying out the geometry by placing linework in the model, then tracing over the lines with the stair components

- ☑ determine the difference between the boundary and the riser when you need to sketch the stair profile

- ☑ load necessary components used to customize stairs and railings such as railing types, spindles, posts, and landings

- ☑ use each separate component and access them in the Project Browser to place materials

- ☑ configure railings bases on the baluster placement and the railing placement as used in the Element Properties of the railing

- ☑ determine how to tie a railing into a stair railing by using offsets and by aligning the railing sketch with the stairs

- ☑ add a line-based raised panel family to complete millwork items

- ☑ create ramp landings and create the actual ramp

- ☑ determine the length of the ramp based on the rise and run of the slope

CHAPTER 11

Schedules and Tags

To begin, I want to clarify something specific to the people who have been using AutoCAD Architecture: you do not need to tag an item in order for it to appear in a schedule in Revit Architecture. You can't really just draft a schedule either. But this is not a bad situation to be in. Say, for example, you have a typical door schedule. Wouldn't it be nice to just add a door to the model and have that door automatically show up in the schedule?

▶ **Creating schedules**

▶ **Creating material takeoffs**

▶ **Creating key legends and importing CAD legends**

▶ **Adding tags**

▶ **Creating custom tags**

▶ **Keynoting**

Creating Schedules

Revit allows you to instantly schedule an item based on the fact that we are now using a full database. A door, for example, already has most of the information you need built into it. Didn't it seem funny that when you placed a door in the model, it was automatically tagged with a sequential door number? This is the power of BIM. We are now going beyond 3D.

Schedules do not stop just at doors and windows in Revit. You can schedule almost any item that goes into the model. Along with schedules comes the ability to quantify materials and square footages. You can even create a schedule for the sole purpose of changing items in the model. In Revit, it is always a two-way street.

The first topic we will tackle is creating the most common of the schedules in architecture: the door schedule. Once you get this procedure down, you will be off and running.

The good news is you have most of the information you need to create a multitude of schedules. The bad news is the Revit-produced schedules are not going to look like your company's schedules at all. Before we go further, it is important to note that some of you will be able to get a perfect duplication of your companies' standard schedules; some of you will not. Those of you who will not have to get as close as possible to your standards, and at that point know that sometimes the cost of doing BIM is not in the pocket but at the plotter as well.

Given that, let's get started. I think you will find creating and using schedules a wonderful experience. You are about to learn how you will save hours upon hours of work, all the while maintaining 100 percent accuracy.

Adding Fields to a Schedule

To begin, open the file you have been following along with. If you did not complete the previous chapter, go to the book's web page at **www.sybex.com/go/ revit2011ner**. From there you can browse to Chapter 11 and find the file called NER-28.rvt. The following procedure is going to focus on creating a door schedule. Grab a cup of coffee or a power drink, and follow along!

1. In the Project Browser, go to Level 1 floor plan.

2. On the Create panel of the View tab, click the Schedules ➢ Schedule/ Quantities button, as shown in Figure 11.1.

3. The next dialog box, as shown in Figure 11.2, allows you to choose which item you would like to schedule. Select Doors and click OK.

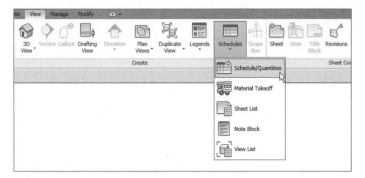

FIGURE 11.1 Click the Schedule/Quantities button on the View tab.

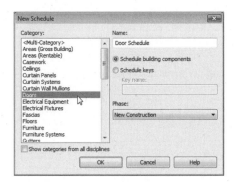

FIGURE 11.2 Select Doors and click OK.

4. The next dialog allows you to add the fields (parameters) required for your schedule. The first field you will add is Mark. To do this, find Mark in the area to the left, and click the Add button in the middle of the dialog, as shown in Figure 11.3.

5. When this field is added, add the following fields using the same method (see Figure 11.3):

- ▶ Height

- ▶ Width

- ▶ Level

- ▶ Door Finish

- ▶ Door Hardware Group

- ▶ Frame Finish

▶ Frame Jamb Type

▶ Comments

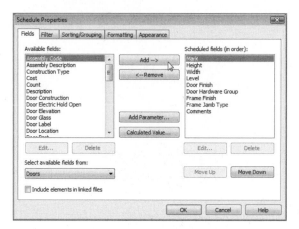

FIGURE 11.3 Adding the fields to produce a door schedule

6. Click OK. Your schedule should be similar to Figure 11.4.

Door Schedule								
Mark	Height	Width	Level	Door Finish	Door Hardware Group	Frame Finish	Frame Jamb Type	Comments
101	7' - 0"	3' - 0"	Level 1					
102	7' - 0"	3' - 0"	Level 1					
103	7' - 0"	6' - 0"	Level 1					
104	7' - 0"	6' - 0"	Level 1					
105	7' - 0"	3' - 0"	Level 1					
105A	7' - 0"	3' - 0"	Level 1					
106	7' - 0"	3' - 0"	Level 1					
106A	7' - 0"	3' - 0"	Level 1					
100B	7' - 0"	3' - 0"	Level 1					
100C	7' - 0"	6' - 0"	Level 1					
100D	7' - 0"	6' - 0"	Level 1					
100A	7' - 0"	6' - 0"	Level 1					
100E	7' - 0"	3' - 0"	Level 2					
100F	7' - 0"	3' - 0"	Level 2					
100G	7' - 0"	3' - 0"	Level 2					
100H	7' - 0"	3' - 0"	Level 2					
100I	7' - 0"	6' - 0"	Level 2					
100J	7' - 0"	3' - 0"	Level 3					
100K	7' - 0"	3' - 0"	Level 3					
100L	7' - 0"	3' - 0"	Level 3					
100M	7' - 0"	3' - 0"	Level 3					
100N	7' - 0"	6' - 0"	Level 3					
100O	7' - 0"	3' - 0"	Level 4					
100P	7' - 0"	3' - 0"	Level 4					
100Q	7' - 0"	3' - 0"	Level 4					
100R	7' - 0"	3' - 0"	Level 4					
100S	7' - 0"	6' - 0"	Level 4					
100T	7' - 0"	3' - 0"	Level 5					
100U	7' - 0"	3' - 0"	Level 5					
100V	7' - 0"	3' - 0"	Level 5					
100W	7' - 0"	3' - 0"	Level 5					
100X	7' - 0"	6' - 0"	Level 5					
107	7' - 0"	3' - 0"	Level 1					
108	7' - 0"	3' - 0"	Level 1					
109	7' - 0"	3' - 0"	Level 1					
110	7' - 0"	3' - 0"	Level 1					
111	7' - 0"	3' - 0"	Level 1					
112	7' - 0"	3' - 0"	Level 1					
113	7' - 0"	6' - 0"	Level 1					

FIGURE 11.4 The door schedule up to this point

The next step is to start organizing our data in our preferred display format. We have a long way to go, but when we are done, this schedule can be used over and over again.

 N O T E A schedule does not have to be placed on a drawing sheet. Many times you will produce a schedule to simply manipulate data without having to search for it in the model.

Sorting and Grouping

Since Revit is a database, let's think of building a schedule as simply creating a query in a database, because that's exactly what we are doing. By creating a sort, we can start to see our doors in groups and have a tangible understating of where we are. Let's get started.

1. In the Project Browser, you will see a category called Schedules/ Quantities. Open the Schedules/Quantities group and open the Door Schedule. (This procedure applies if you are not already in the schedule.)

2. New to Revit 2011, you will see that the schedule's properties are visible in the Properties dialog while you are in the schedule. However, you can still right-click and click View Properties, as shown in Figure 11.5.

FIGURE 11.5 Right-click the schedule and click View Properties.

3. In the Properties dialog, you will see a category called Other. Click the Edit button in the Sorting/Grouping row, as shown in Figure 11.6.

4. On the Sorting/Grouping tab of the Schedule Properties dialog, set Sort By to Level.

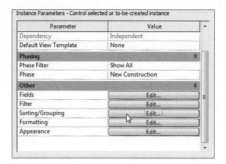

FIGURE 11.6 Click the Edit button in the Sorting/Grouping row.

5. Check the Header option.

6. Check the Footer option.

7. Select Title, Count, And Totals from the Sort By drop-down list (see Figure 11.7).

8. Click OK.

9. Save the model.

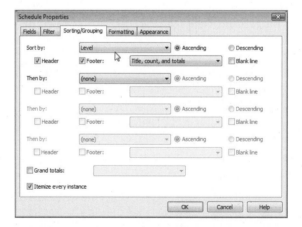

FIGURE 11.7 Sorting the schedule by level

The next step is to get the header information grouped the way we would like it. Most schedules include groups such as Door Frame and Hardware. We will create similar groupings.

Controlling Headers

Although this step is not crucial to producing an accurate, readable schedule, it is important in the attempt to get this Revit-produced schedule to look like the schedule you have been using for years in CAD. The objective of this procedure is to combine the header content into smaller groups under their own header, similar to what you can do in a spreadsheet.

To start in with controlling the schedule headers, follow these steps:

1. In the Project Browser, open the Door Schedule (if you do not already have it open).

   At the top of the schedule are the title (Door Schedule) and the headers (which include Mark, Height, Width, and Level, among others), as shown in Figure 11.8. Focus your attention here.

2. The goal is to combine Mark, Height, and Width into a group under one header called DOOR INFORMATION. To do this, click on the Width cell and drag your cursor to the left. You are selecting all three cells.

3. Once the cells are selected, click the Group button on the Headers panel.

T I P   Sometimes when you are picking the first cell to do this task, you will accidentally click into the cell. You do not want this. If this keeps happening, click into the Width cell, and then click just below the cell into the gray area. This selects the cell the way you want it. You can now pick the cell and drag your cursor to the left to highlight all the cells.

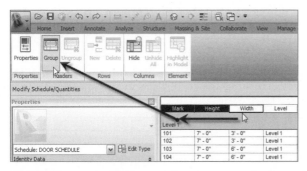

FIGURE 11.8 Clicking and dragging across the three cells. This will activate the Group button.

---

4. Click into the new cell and type **DOOR INFORMATION**.

It would be nice if the defaults in Revit were all caps, but they are not. The next procedure will rename some of the headers. This will not change any values.

1. Click in the Mark header and change it to **NUMBER**.

2. Click into Height and change it to **HEIGHT**.

3. Click into Width and change it to **WIDTH** (see Figure 11.9).

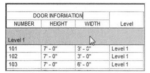

DOOR INFORMATION			
NUMBER	HEIGHT	WIDTH	Level
Level 1			
101	7' - 0"	3' - 0"	Level 1
102	7' - 0"	3' - 0"	Level 1
103	7' - 0"	6' - 0"	Level 1

FIGURE 11.9 Adding the new header and changing the descriptions

4. Change the Level header to **FLOOR**.

5. Change the rest of the headers to uppercase. This includes the Door Schedule title, as shown in Figure 11.10.

6. Select the cells DOOR HARDWARE GROUP to DOOR FINISH.

7. On the Options bar, click the Headers panel.

8. Call the new header **DOOR**.

9. Remove the word DOOR from the cell DOOR FINISH and DOOR HARDWARE GROUP (see Figure 11.10).

10. Highlight FRAME FINISH and FRAME JAMB TYPE.

11. Click the Group button on the Headers panel.

12. Call the new header **FRAME** (see Figure 11.10).

				DOOR SCHEDULE					
DOOR INFORMATION				DOOR		FRAME			
NUMBER	HEIGHT	WIDTH	FLOOR	DOOR FINISH	DOOR HARWARE GROUP	FRAME FINISH	FRAME JAMB TYPE	COMMENTS	
Level 1									
101	7' - 0"	3' - 0"	Level 1						
102	7' - 0"	3' - 0"	Level 1						
103	7' - 0"	6' - 0"	Level 1						

FIGURE 11.10 The groups are now complete.

Now it is time to start filling out some of the blank fields. This is where you can increase productivity by using schedules. Instead of going door by door in the model, you have a list of every door right in front of you!

Modifying Elements in a Schedule

In Revit, data flows in multiple directions. When you created a schedule, the data from the doors flowed into the schedule to populate it. Now, we will ask Revit to collect data that we input into the schedule to flow into the doors.

To learn how to populate the schedule, follow along with the procedure.

1. In the Project Browser, open DOOR SCHEDULE (if it is not opened already).

N O T E   **Note that Door Schedule is now DOOR SCHEDULE in the Project Browser. This is because you renamed the title in the schedule— proof that we are dealing with bidirectional information.**

2. Click into the DOOR FINISH cell for door number 101, as shown in Figure 11.11.

3. Type PT (for paint), as shown in Figure 11.11.

4. Click in the DOOR FINISH cell just below the one you just changed.

5. Notice there is a menu arrow. Click it, and notice that PT is in the list. Click PT (see Figure 11.11).

6. Save the model.

| DOOR INFORMATION | | | | |
NUMBER	HEIGHT	WIDTH	FLOOR	DOOR FINISH
Level 1				
101	7' - 0"	3' - 0"	Level 1	PT
102	7' - 0"	3' - 0"	Level 1	
103	7' - 0"	6' - 0"	Level 1	PT
104	7' - 0"	6' - 0"	Level 1	
105	7' - 0"	3' - 0"	Level 1	

F I G U R E   11.11   Once you start filling out the fields in a schedule, the items will become available in the list for future use.

Now, let's see how this affected the actual doors in the model, and perhaps find a door that needs to be tagged with a WD (wood) finish:

1. In the Project Browser, open the Level 1 floor plan.

2. Zoom in on the door between the corridor and the east wing, as shown in Figure 11.12.

3. Select the door.

4. In the Properties dialog, scroll down to the Other category and find Door Finish.

5. Click in the field and type **WD**, as shown in Figure 11.12.

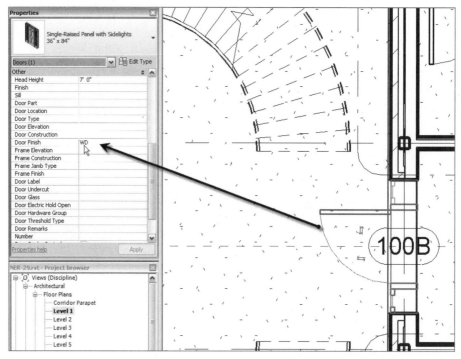

FIGURE 11.12 Changing the property of an element in the model does the same thing as changing the element in the schedule.

6. Click the Apply button at the bottom of the Properties dialog.

7. Open the door schedule. Notice that door number 100B has a WD finish.

8. Save the model.

In the interest of not getting carried away with the mundane process of filling out the entire schedule, note that this process is applicable for every field within this type of schedule. The main takeaway is the fact that you can populate a schedule by either changing the data in the schedule itself or by finding the scheduled component and changing it there.

If you click the menu drop-down arrow in the Door Finish field, you will see that PT is available. The schedules and the actual doors are "linked" together.

USING THE SCHEDULE TO FIND A COMPONENT

In some cases, while you are filling out the schedule, and you may not be sure which item you are looking at. Because schedules are "live," you can find a component from the schedule. To do this, follow these steps:

1. In the schedule, right-click on door number 114.

2. Select Show, as shown here:

Notice that Revit zooms in on the door, and even gives you choices to find other views as well:

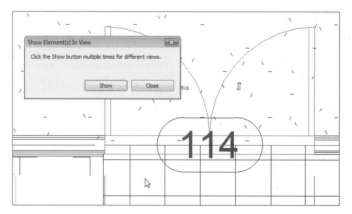

3. Click Close.

4. Close the view and go back to the schedule.

The next step is to further modify the appearance of the schedule we are working on. We can then start using this schedule to narrow in on a specific grouping of doors to change them based on a filter.

Modifying the Schedule's Appearance

As it stands, not everyone uses the same fonts, headers, and linework around the border of the schedule. Although the usefulness of this next procedure won't be evident until Chapter 14, "Creating Sheets and Printing," it is applicable at this point in the book.

The objective of this procedure is to examine what font this schedule is using as well as the line weights and spacing applied to the schedule. To learn how to adjust the appearance of a schedule, follow along:

1. In the Project Browser, open the DOOR SCHEDULE (if it is not opened already).

2. In the Properties dialog, click the Edit button for Appearance.

3. On the Appearance tab of the Schedule Properties dialog, you will see two categories: Graphics and Text. In the Graphics category, click Outline and select Medium Lines, as shown in Figure 11.13.

4. In the Text category, make sure Show Title and Show Headers are checked on (see Figure 11.13).

5. Click OK.

Your schedule will not change one bit! We have simply created a situation where the appearance of the schedule won't be apparent until you literally drag it onto a drawing sheet.

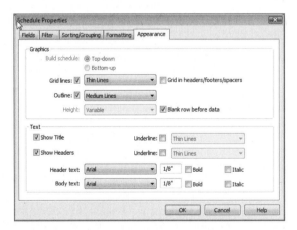

FIGURE 11.13 Configuring the schedule's appearance

HEY, THIS LOOKS FAMILIAR

You may have noticed that each time you open the properties of the schedule and click the Edit button next to a corresponding row (in this case it was the Appearance row), you are only jumping to a specific tab of the Schedule Properties dialog. Each schedule category can be accessed in one dialog, as shown in the following image:

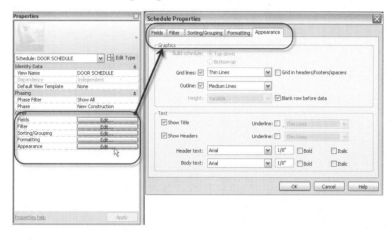

Adding a Schedule to a Sheet

Although adding a schedule to a sheet is a topic for another chapter (Chapter 14), the process is so easy, we are going to go ahead and do it right now. Not to let the cat out of the bag or anything, but you will enjoy how sheets come together in Revit. Perform the following steps:

1. In the Project Browser, find the Sheets (All) category, as shown in Figure 11.14. Coincidentally, it is located directly below DOOR SCHEDULE.

2. Right-click Sheets.

3. Select New Sheet (see Figure 11.14).

4. In the New Sheet dialog, click the Load button. This will allow you to go find a title block. Although we have not made a title block yet, Revit has a directory with some samples you can use to get started (see Figure 11.15).

FIGURE 11.14 Creating a new sheet

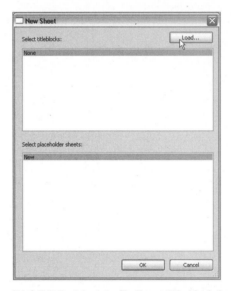

FIGURE 11.15 Finding a title block for your use

5. Browse to the Titleblocks directory. It is a folder contained within the Imperial Library directory.

6. Select the file called E1 30 x 42 Horizontal.rfa.

7. Click Open.

8. Back in the New Sheet dialog, select E1 30 x 42 Horizontal, and click OK.

You now have a new sheet, containing a blank title block, as shown in Figure 11.16.

The next objective is to click and drag the schedule onto the sheet. If the schedule fits, this is literally the easiest thing to do in Revit.

1. In the Project Browser, find DOOR SCHEDULE.

2. Click it, but do not double-click it. You want to pick it and hold down the left mouse button.

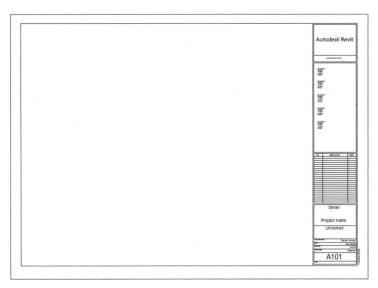

FIGURE 11.16 You now have a sheet ready to be populated.

3. With the left mouse button pressed, drag the schedule onto the sheet. You can place it anywhere you see fit (see Figure 11.17).

4. Once you have moved your cursor to the correct position, release the mouse button. If the bottom hangs over the sheet, that's okay—we will fix it in a minute.

5. Press the Esc key.

6. Select the schedule.

7. Notice the blue break grip that is located halfway up the schedule. This is the same type of grip that is used in grids, levels, and sections. Pick it, as shown in Figure 11.18.

8. With the schedule split in two, you can see that it will fit onto the sheet quite nicely. With the schedule still selected, notice there is a blue grip at the bottom of the left portion of the schedule, as shown in Figure 11.19. Pick the grip and drag. Notice you can slide the schedule so the length of each side adjusts up and down evenly.

9. Zoom in on the top of the schedule, as shown in Figure 11.20, and select the schedule.

10. Notice you have blue triangle-shaped icons at each cell in the title and the header. Pick the one on the Comments column and drag it to the right. The comments header will now be readable.

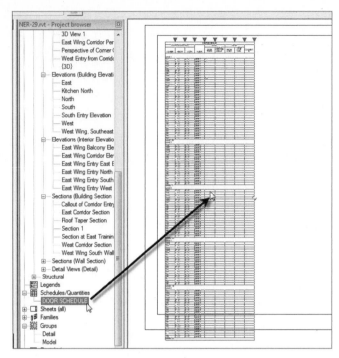

FIGURE 11.17 Clicking and dragging the schedule onto the sheet

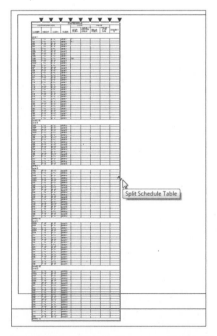

FIGURE 11.18 You can split the schedule into two (or more) sections.

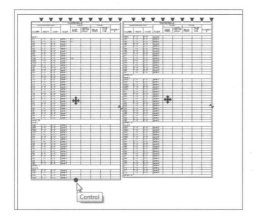

FIGURE 11.19 You can make further adjustments to the schedule by picking the round blue grip.

When you have a schedule split like this, any adjustment you make to a column will be reflected in the other half of the schedule. You do not have to make the same adjustment twice to the Comments column.

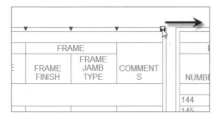

FIGURE 11.20 Pick the triangle grip to give the Comments field some more room.

We can make two more adjustments to the schedule after you place it onto a sheet. This involves rotating and joining the two columns back together again.

1. Select the schedule (if it is not already open).

   Notice that on the Modify | Schedule Graphics tab, there is a Rotation On Sheet menu on the Options bar, as shown near the upper left of Figure 11.21. You do not need to change the rotation—just note that it is there.

2. Also notice the blue move grips, as shown in Figure 11.21, located in the middle of the two schedule columns. If you pick one and drag the column back over the top of the other, they will automatically join back together (see Figure 11.21).

3. Save the model.

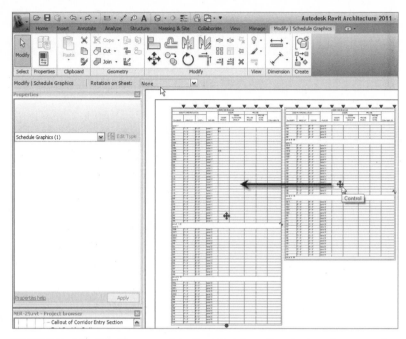

FIGURE 11.21 You can rotate the schedule on the sheet, and you can also join the columns back together if you need to.

Just to nail down the concept, let's create a window schedule now. If you like, go ahead on your own and make one. You can then compare it to the one in the book when you have finished to see if you got it right. If you would rather go step by step, that's fine too! Just follow along:

1. On the View tab, click the Schedules ➤ Schedule/Quantities button.

2. In the next dialog, select Windows and click OK.

3. In the Schedule Properties dialog, add the following fields (see Figure 11.22):

    ▶ Type Mark

    ▶ Type

    ▶ Width

    ▶ Height

    ▶ Sill Height

    ▶ Level

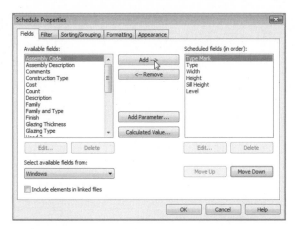

FIGURE 11.22 Adding fields to the schedule

4. Go to the Sorting/Grouping tab, as shown in Figure 11.23.

5. Sort by Type Mark.

6. Add a Footer, with Title, Count, And Totals selected.

7. Choose Level from the Then By drop-down list.

8. Check the Grand Totals option.

9. Select Title, Count, And Totals.

10. Check the Itemize Every Instance option (see Figure 11.23).

11. Click OK to get to the schedule and to see the results.

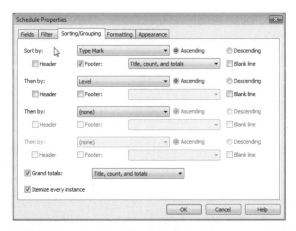

FIGURE 11.23 Specifying the settings for your window schedule

Sometimes you may want to sort items based on a field but not actually display that field. You can do this as follows:

1. Select a cell in the Level column, as shown in Figure 11.24.

2. Select the Hide button. This will hide the column.

3. Save the model.

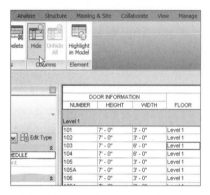

FIGURE 11.24 You can hide a column but still have Revit sort the schedule based on the hidden information.

 N O T E   It is worth noting that you can create a schedule before you add any information to the model. You can then add this schedule to a sheet and save the entire file as a template. Whenever you start a new project, these schedules will start filling themselves out and will already be on sheets!

Phew! I think you get the picture. If you like, feel free to create a bunch of schedules on your own. Practice does make perfect.

Let's venture now into creating a material takeoff. It would be a shame to have all these computations go unused!

Creating Material Takeoffs

Creating a material takeoff is similar to creating a schedule. The only difference is that we are now breaking components down and scheduling the smaller pieces. For example, we could get a schedule of all the doors in the model. That we know; we just did that. But with a material takeoff, we can now quantify the square footage of door panels or glass within the doors. To take it a step further, we can do material takeoffs of walls, floors, and any other building components we see fit to quantify.

The objective of this procedure is to create three different material takeoffs: one for the walls, one for the floors, and one for the roofs. Let's get started:

1. On the View tab, click Schedules ➤ Material Takeoff, as shown in Figure 11.25.

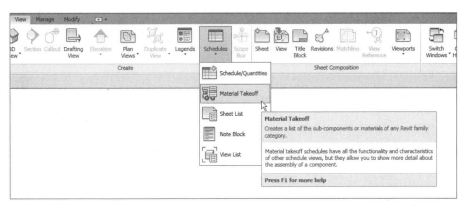

FIGURE 11.25 To add a new material takeoff, you must go to the View tab.

2. In the New Material Takeoff dialog, select Walls, as shown in Figure 11.26.

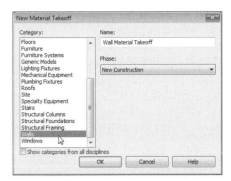

FIGURE 11.26 Select Walls in the New Material Takeoff dialog.

3. Click OK.

4. In the next dialog, add the following fields (see Figure 11.27).

   ▶ Material: Area

   ▶ Material: Name

   ▶ Count

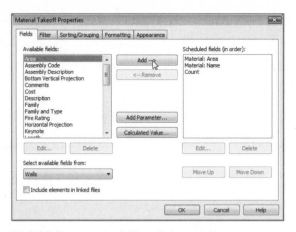

FIGURE 11.27 Adding the materials

5. Select the Sorting/Grouping tab.

6. Sort by Material: Name.

7. Add a Footer.

8. Choose Title, Count, And Totals from the menu, as shown in Figure 11.28.

9. Check the Blank Line option.

10. At the bottom of the dialog box, check Grand Totals.

11. Choose Title, Count, and Totals from the menu.

12. Select the option Itemize Every Instance (see Figure 11.28).

13. Click OK.

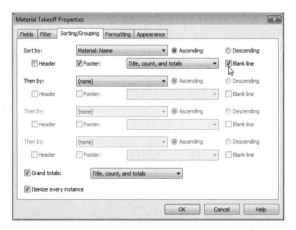

FIGURE 11.28 Configuring the parameters for the schedule

The next step is to start taking some totals on our own. The first thing we can do is have Revit automatically format a column to produce an independent total; then we can break out this takeoff and drill in to more specific line-item totals.

1. In the Properties dialog, click the Edit button next to the Formatting row to bring up the Material Takeoff Properties dialog, shown in Figure 11.29.

2. In the field to the left, select Material: Area, as shown in Figure 11.29.

3. To the bottom right, check Calculate Totals, as shown in Figure 11.29.

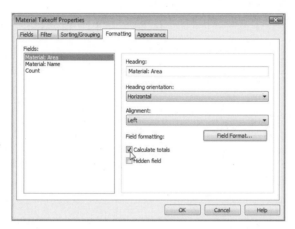

FIGURE 11.29 On the Formatting tab, you can specify Calculate Totals for the Material: Area option.

4. Click OK twice.

You now have a total square footage at the bottom of your takeoff groups, as shown in Figure 11.30.

The next step is to break down this takeoff in to smaller, more specific take-offs. Once we do this, we can provide our own calculations based on almost any formula we need.

Creating a Calculated Value Field

The objective here is to create separate schedules for Plywood and Gypsum by adding a new variable to the schedule that contains a formula we create. Yes, it is as hard as it sounds, but once you get used to this procedure, it won't be so bad! Perform the following steps:

1. In the Project Browser, right-click on the Wall Material Takeoff, and select Duplicate View ➤ Duplicate, as shown in Figure 11.31.

Wall Material Takeoff			
Material: Area	Material: Name	Count	Plywood cou
3988 SF	Air Barrier - Air Infiltration Barrier	1	83.083333
3663 SF	Air Barrier - Air Infiltration Barrier	1	76.309896
4288 SF	Air Barrier - Air Infiltration Barrier	1	89.330729
537 SF	Air Barrier - Air Infiltration Barrier	1	11.180556
831 SF	Air Barrier - Air Infiltration Barrier	1	17.314453
574 SF	Air Barrier - Air Infiltration Barrier	1	11.958333
871 SF	Air Barrier - Air Infiltration Barrier	1	18.148438
3921 SF	Air Barrier - Air Infiltration Barrier	1	81.681409
532 SF	Air Barrier - Air Infiltration Barrier	1	11.076535
771 SF	Air Barrier - Air Infiltration Barrier	1	16.062288
715 SF	Air Barrier - Air Infiltration Barrier	1	14.898688
525 SF	Air Barrier - Air Infiltration Barrier	1	10.946615
813 SF	Air Barrier - Air Infiltration Barrier	1	16.930244
3008 SF	Air Barrier - Air Infiltration Barrier	1	62.67589
1104 SF	Air Barrier - Air Infiltration Barrier	1	22.994919
2405 SF	Air Barrier - Air Infiltration Barrier	1	50.098002
1336 SF	Air Barrier - Air Infiltration Barrier	1	27.824629
3731 SF	Air Barrier - Air Infiltration Barrier	1	77.719887
1616 SF	Air Barrier - Air Infiltration Barrier	1	33.66556
295 SF	Air Barrier - Air Infiltration Barrier	1	6.156136
849 SF	Air Barrier - Air Infiltration Barrier	1	17.691708
646 SF	Air Barrier - Air Infiltration Barrier	1	13.449251
646 SF	Air Barrier - Air Infiltration Barrier	1	13.449251
605 SF	Air Barrier - Air Infiltration Barrier	1	12.59957
38268 SF			

FIGURE 11.30 The total square footage is being calculated.

2. Right-click on the new view in the Project Browser and select Rename.

3. Rename it to Plywood Takeoff.

4. Double-click on Plywood Takeoff to open the view.

5. In the Properties dialog, click the Edit button in the Filter row.

6. For Filter By, choose Material: Name.

7. In the menu to the right, select Equals from the list.

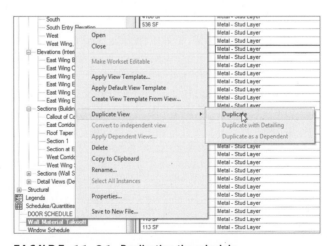

FIGURE 11.31 Duplicating the schedule

8. In the field below Material: Name, select Wood - Sheathing - Plywood (see Figure 11.32).

9. Click OK.

Your takeoff should look like Figure 11.33.

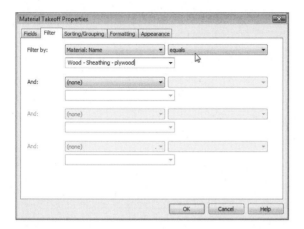

F I G U R E 1 1 . 3 2 Filter based on material

Plywood Takeoff		
Material: Area	Material: Name	Count
3878 SF	Wood - Sheathing - plywood	1
3576 SF	Wood - Sheathing - plywood	1
4178 SF	Wood - Sheathing - plywood	1
526 SF	Wood - Sheathing - plywood	1
822 SF	Wood - Sheathing - plywood	1
545 SF	Wood - Sheathing - plywood	1
842 SF	Wood - Sheathing - plywood	1
3831 SF	Wood - Sheathing - plywood	1
517 SF	Wood - Sheathing - plywood	1
761 SF	Wood - Sheathing - plywood	1
700 SF	Wood - Sheathing - plywood	1
515 SF	Wood - Sheathing - plywood	1
797 SF	Wood - Sheathing - plywood	1
2955 SF	Wood - Sheathing - plywood	1
1088 SF	Wood - Sheathing - plywood	1
2372 SF	Wood - Sheathing - plywood	1
1320 SF	Wood - Sheathing - plywood	1
3684 SF	Wood - Sheathing - plywood	1
1589 SF	Wood - Sheathing - plywood	1
286 SF	Wood - Sheathing - plywood	1
845 SF	Wood - Sheathing - plywood	1
640 SF	Wood - Sheathing - plywood	1
640 SF	Wood - Sheathing - plywood	1
587 SF	Wood - Sheathing - plywood	1
37493 SF		
37493 SF		

F I G U R E 1 1 . 3 3 The takeoff is filtered based only on plywood.

The next step is to break down the plywood into 4×8 sheets. We will need to add a formula based on the square footage given by Revit divided by 32 square feet to come up with the plywood totals.

1. Open the Plywood Takeoff schedule in the Project Browser (if it is not already).

2. In the Properties dialog, click the Edit button in the Fields row.

3. On the Fields tab in the Material Takeoff Properties dialog, click the Calculated Value button in the middle of the dialog, as shown in Figure 11.34.

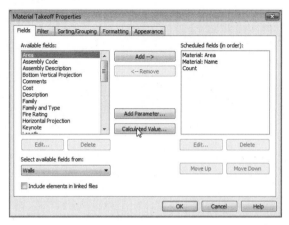

FIGURE 11.34 Click the Calculated Value button in the middle of the dialog.

4. For the name, enter **Number of Sheets**.

5. Make sure Discipline is set to Common.

6. Make sure Type is set to Number (see Figure 11.35).

7. Add the following formula: **Material: Area / 32 SF**.

8. Click OK.

9. Click the Formatting tab, as shown in Figure 11.36.

10. Select the new field called Number of Sheets.

You must type the fields being used exactly as they are displayed. For example, the Formula Material: Area must be typed exactly as specified in terms of spacing and capitalization. All formulas in Revit are case sensitive. New in Revit 2011, you can also click the [...] button to add the available fields.

FIGURE 11.35 Changing the calculated values

11. In the Field Formatting section, click Calculate Totals, as shown in Figure 11.36.

12. Click the Field Format button.

13. Uncheck Use Default Settings, as shown in Figure 11.37.

14. Change Units to Fixed.

15. Make sure Rounding is set to 0 Decimal Places.

16. Click Use Digit Grouping (see Figure 11.37).

17. Click OK.

18. Select the Sorting/Grouping tab.

19. At the bottom, deselect the Grand Totals option.

20. Click OK.

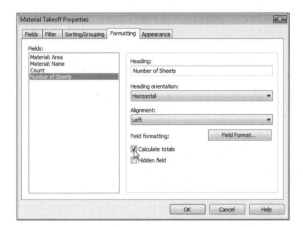

FIGURE 11.36 Clicking the Calculate Totals option

FIGURE 11.37 Overriding the units to allow this field to round

Your material takeoff should resemble Figure 11.38.

Plywood Takeoff			
Material: Area	Material: Name	Count	Number of Sheets
3878 SF	Wood - Sheathing - plywood	1	121
3576 SF	Wood - Sheathing - plywood	1	112
4178 SF	Wood - Sheathing - plywood	1	131
526 SF	Wood - Sheathing - plywood	1	16
822 SF	Wood - Sheathing - plywood	1	26
545 SF	Wood - Sheathing - plywood	1	17
842 SF	Wood - Sheathing - plywood	1	26
3831 SF	Wood - Sheathing - plywood	1	120
517 SF	Wood - Sheathing - plywood	1	16
761 SF	Wood - Sheathing - plywood	1	24
700 SF	Wood - Sheathing - plywood	1	22
515 SF	Wood - Sheathing - plywood	1	16
797 SF	Wood - Sheathing - plywood	1	25
2955 SF	Wood - Sheathing - plywood	1	92
1088 SF	Wood - Sheathing - plywood	1	34
2372 SF	Wood - Sheathing - plywood	1	74
1320 SF	Wood - Sheathing - plywood	1	41
3684 SF	Wood - Sheathing - plywood	1	115
1589 SF	Wood - Sheathing - plywood	1	50
286 SF	Wood - Sheathing - plywood	1	9
845 SF	Wood - Sheathing - plywood	1	26
640 SF	Wood - Sheathing - plywood	1	20
640 SF	Wood - Sheathing - plywood	1	20
587 SF	Wood - Sheathing - plywood	1	18
37493 SF			1,172

FIGURE 11.38 The finished Plywood material takeoff

Wow! Not too bad for only drawing a bunch of walls. As you can see, using the scheduling/material takeoff feature of Revit adds value to using this application. Well, the value does not stop there. We can use the same functionality to create legends and drawing keys as well.

Creating Key Legends and Importing CAD Legends

Here's the problem with Revit. At some point, you will need to add a component to the model that is not associated with anything. Say, for example, you have a door that you would like to put on a sheet with the door schedule. You sure don't want that door included in the schedule, and you sure don't want to have to draw a wall just to display it. This is where creating a key legend comes into play.

Adding Legend Components

The objective of the following procedure is to create a key legend adding elevations of doors that are used in the model. As it stands, a legend can mean any number of things. It could be just a list of abbreviations, it could be a comprehensive numbering system keyed off the model itself, or it could be a graphical representation of items that have already been placed into the model for further detailing and coordinating. Another special aspect of legends is that a single legend may need to be duplicated on multiple sheets within a drawing set. You don't know it yet, but this is a problem for Revit. By creating a legend, however, you can get around this.

The goal of the following procedure is to create a door type legend:

1. On the View tab, click the Legends ➤ Legend button, as shown in Figure 11.39.

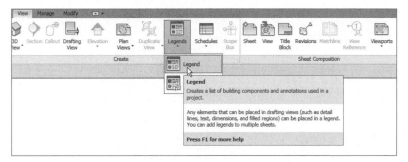

FIGURE 11.39 Click the Legends ➤ Legend button on the View tab.

2. The next dialog wants you to specify a scale. Choose 1/4″ = 1′–0″. This is fine for now (see Figure 11.40).

3. Call the view **Door Type Legend**.

4. Click OK.

FIGURE 11.40 Results of choosing 1/4″ = 1′–0″

Congratulations! You now have a blank view. This is actually a good thing, though. Think of it as a clean slate where you can draft, add components, and just throw together a legend.

OTHER FUNCTIONS HAVE BEEN ACTIVATED

Without knowing it, you have made some tools available that we have not explored yet. You will start to learn that Revit knows the type of view you happen to be in. Some commands are available in one view, but they may not be in the next. Keep this in mind as you venture through Revit and become frustrated that a command is not working. You usually just need to switch views.

The next step is to start adding some components. You will need to go to the Annotate tab for this.

1. Go to the Detail panel of the Annotate tab.

2. Click the Component ➤ Legend Component button, as shown in Figure 11.41.

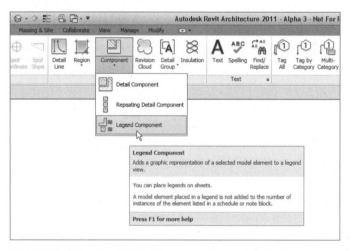

FIGURE 11.41 Clicking the Legend Component button

3. In the Options bar, choose Doors : Single - Raised Panel with Sidelights : 36″×84″, as shown in Figure 11.42.

4. Change the view to Elevation : Front.

5. Pick a point to place the elevation.

6. With the command still running, you can place another instance. This changes the view to Floor Plan. Place another instance of the door just above the elevation, as shown in Figure 11.43.

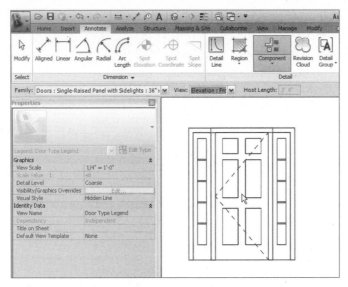

FIGURE 11.42 Changing the options for the legend

7. In the Options bar, be sure Host Length is set to 6′–0″ (see Figure 11.43).

8. With the command still running, place a Door : Double Flush : 72″ × 84″ to the right of the first door. Make sure View is set to Elevation : Front.

9. Place the corresponding plan view just above the door. Make sure Host Length is set to 6′–0″.

10. Place a bi-fold door just to the right of the second door, with a plan view to the top.

11. Set the plan view's Host Length to 6′–0″ (see Figure 11.44).

The next step is to add some text in an attempt to label the doors. These items cannot be labeled, which can be a disadvantage to breaking away from the model. This is basically a dumb sheet.

1. On the Text panel, click the Text button.

2. Make sure the text style is Text 3/32″ Arial and that the leader is set to None, as shown in Figure 11.45.

3. Place some text centered under each door elevation, and label the doors Type A, B, and C (see Figure 11.45).

4. Save the model.

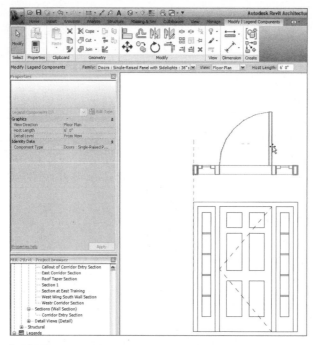

FIGURE 11.43 Placing two instances of the same door for the legend

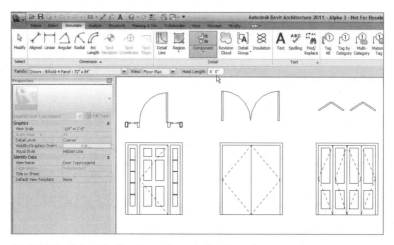

FIGURE 11.44 The three doors in the legend

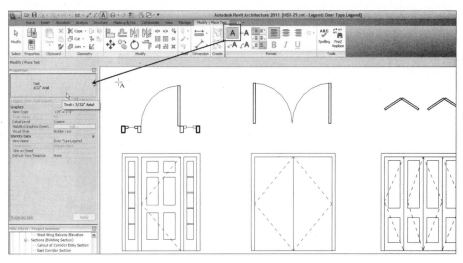

FIGURE 11.45 Placing the text underneath the doors

It is nice to have accurate "blocks" available based on what you have added to your model up to this point. By using the Revit method of building a legend like this, you are removed from the horror of stealing old legends from other jobs. I think we all know what a nightmare this turns into when they are not accurate. Plus, in Revit, you have a library of the doors you are using right at your fingertips. They do not have to be managed or updated constantly. They will always be there, and they will always be accurate.

The next step is to create a symbol legend—that is, we need to make a sheet that contains all our typical symbols. This task will be carried out in a similar manner.

Adding Symbols to a Legend

As mentioned earlier, adding symbols to a legend is similar to creating a door legend. The only difference is that you will add your typical symbols as they appear on the sheets. Every company has a sheet like this. I'm sure yours does, too.

The first objective is to create this legend from scratch using the Revit tools. The second objective is to import your legend from CAD (which I'm sure you have). After you complete the two procedures, you can decide which approach is best for your firm.

Using the Revit Symbols

To use the Revit-provided symbols, you will create a new legend view, and you will use the Annotate tab to insert the typical components. If you are feeling brave, go ahead and make a Symbol key on your own. You can follow the figures to make sure you are adding the expected components. If you would rather follow along with the procedure, let's get started:

1. On the View tab, click the Legends ➤ Legend button.

2. Set the scale to 1/4″ = 1′–0″.

3. Call the new legend **Symbol Legend**.

4. Click OK.

5. On the Symbol panel of the Annotate tab, click the Symbol button, as shown in Figure 11.46.

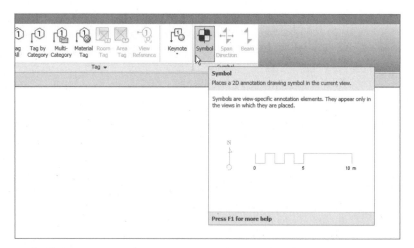

FIGURE 11.46 Clicking the Symbol button on the Annotate tab

6. In the Properties dialog, select Callout Head, as shown in Figure 11.47.

7. Place the callout head into the view, as shown in Figure 11.47.

8. With the Symbol command still running, place a door tag directly underneath the callout head, as shown in Figure 11.48.

9. Place a Room Tag With Area.

10. Place a View Title (see Figure 11.48).

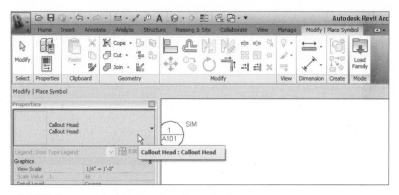

FIGURE 11.47 Placing the callout head

FIGURE 11.48 Populating the legend

The next step is to add some notes to indicate what we just added to the legend. Again, you will not be tagging the items—you are merely placing text and leaders.

1. On the Text panel of the Annotate tab, click the Text button.

2. On the Modify | Place Text tab, click the One Segment button, as shown in Figure 11.49.

3. Pick two points for the leader, and type **TYPICAL CALLOUT** (see Figure 11.49).

4. Add the following notes to the rest of the symbols (see Figure 11.50):

   TYPICAL DOOR TAG

   TYPICAL ROOM TAG

   TYPICAL VIEW TITLE

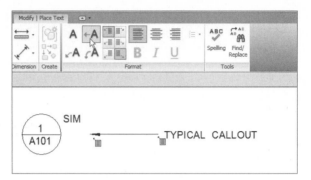

FIGURE 11.49 Adding the text to the legend

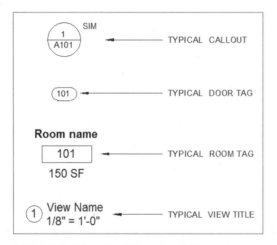

FIGURE 11.50 Adding descriptive text

The next step is to place a box around the items and then draw three equal lines to make a grid. This is done by strictly drafting lines, as the following procedure will show:

1. On the Annotate tab, click the Detail Line button, as shown in Figure 11.51.

2. In the Properties dialog, be sure Thin Lines is selected, as shown in Figure 11.52.

3. On the Draw panel, click Rectangle, as shown in Figure 11.52.

4. Draw a rectangle around the symbols and the text (see Figure 11.52).

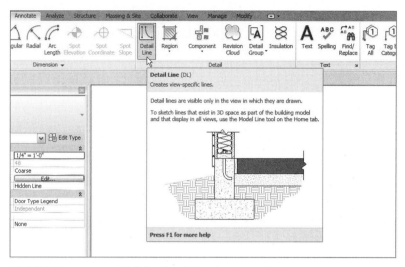

FIGURE 11.51   Click the Detail Line button on the Annotate tab.

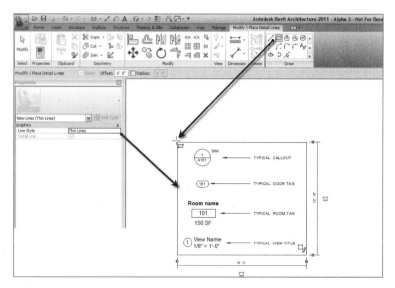

FIGURE 11.52   Adding the linework around the symbols and text

5. On the Draw panel, click the Line button.

6. Draw three horizontal lines in the box. They do not have to be equally spaced, but they should still separate the symbols.

7. Place a dimension string starting at the top of the rectangle, to the second line, to the third, to the fourth, then to the bottom of the rectangle.

8. Click the EQ button on the dimension string.

9. Move the symbols and the text to the proper positions (see Figure 11.53).

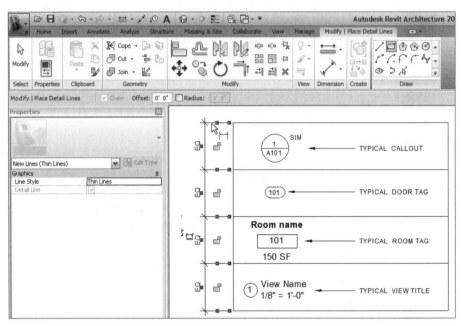

FIGURE 11.53 Draw the horizontal lines, then equally constrain them using the Dimension command.

10. Delete the dimensions.

11. Click OK in the next dialog.

12. Save the model.

Now that you have experience with creating legends using strictly Revit components and lines, it is time to investigate how we can use premade AutoCAD legends as an import.

Importing AutoCAD Legends

Just because you have switched to Revit does not mean that you must throw away over a decade of work regarding typical details and legends. Revit accepts AutoCAD and MicroStation .dwg and .dgn files just fine. Of course, there will be some "tweaking," but once you get the process down, I think you will rely heavily on this functionality.

The objective of the following procedure is to create a new legend view, and then import an existing AutoCAD legend into the view. To get started, you will need to go to the book's web page at **www.sybex.com/go/revit2011ner**. From there you can browse to Chapter 11 and find the file called Interior Partition Legend.dwg. You can then place the drawing file on your system in a place where you can retrieve it later. Now perform the following steps:

1. On the View tab, click the Legends ➢ Legend button.

2. Call the new legend **Interior Partition Legend.**

3. Make the scale 1″ – 1′–0″ (one inch equals one foot), and click OK.

4. On the Insert tab, click Import CAD, as shown in Figure 11.54.

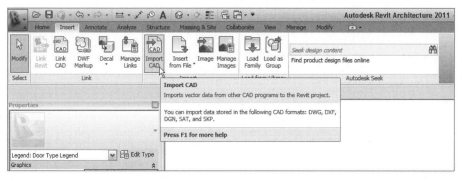

FIGURE 11.54 Importing CAD formats

5. Find the AutoCAD .dwg file called Interior Partition Legend.dwg.

 WARNING   Do not click Open until instructed to do so. There are several items we need to look at in the Import CAD Formats dialog that have a crucial effect on the imported graphics.

6. At the bottom of the Import CAD Formats dialog, notice that you have a few choices (see Figure 11.55):

   Colors   Change Colors to Black And White.

   Layers   Make sure Layers is set to All. We will be able to manipulate the AutoCAD layers after we bring the DWG file into Revit.

Import Units   Import Units should be set to Auto-Detect. In Chapter 18, "Site and Topography," we will import a site. At that point, we will have to modify this choice, but for now, leave it as Auto-Detect.

Positioning   Leave Positioning as Auto - Center to Center.

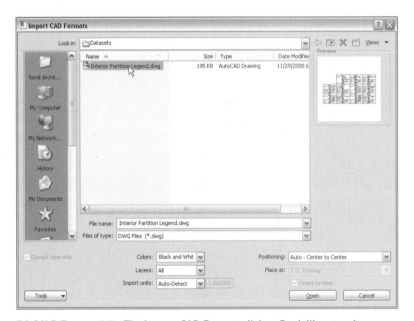

FIGURE 11.55 The Import CAD Formats dialog. Be deliberate when importing a CAD file by choosing the options at the bottom of the dialog.

     7. Click Open.

After you import the CAD file, it may be zoomed off the view so you cannot see it. Follow the procedure to zoom the CAD import into view and manipulate the data:

     1. Type **ZA** (to zoom all).

     2. You can now see the import. When the import is in view, select it.

     3. On the Import Instance panel, click the Query button, as shown in Figure 11.56.

4. Select the line shown in Figure 11.56.

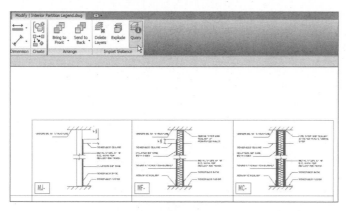

FIGURE 11.56 Clicking the Query button on the Import Instance panel

5. After you select the line, Revit will report information back to you about that line. You are also given the chance to delete the layer. Click Delete, as shown in Figure 11.57.

FIGURE 11.57 You can query items in the CAD import. You can also delete items.

6. Click OK. All of the lines on that layer are gone.

WARNING   Be careful when you delete layers. Revit is not like AutoCAD. When you delete a layer in Revit, the layer is deleted and any object that happens to be on that layer is deleted as well. You could easily delete objects inadvertently.

7. Press Esc twice.

The next step is to fix some of the text that didn't quite wrap correctly. What we will need to do is explode the import so it is broken down into Revit lines and objects.

1. Select the import again.

2. On the Modify | Interior Partition Legend.dwg tab, click Explode ➤ Full Explode, as shown in Figure 11.58.

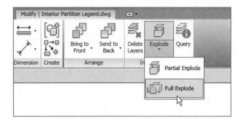

FIGURE 11.58 Click the Full Explode button on the Modify | Interior Partition Legend.dwg tab.

N O T E   The difference between Full Explode and Partial Explode is that a partial explode will break the import down to the next level of blocks. For example, if there was a block included in the drawing file, such as a column bubble, the explode would break down the import but leave the column bubble as a block. When you do a full explode, you are exploding every object in the import—blocks and all.

3. Select the text UNDERSIDE OF STRUCTURE for the MJ detail.

4. Pick the grip to the right, and drag the text box to the left until the text wraps into the correct position, as shown in Figure 11.59.

5. Do the same for the other details that have text improperly wrapped.

6. Save the model.

N O T E   You may ask, "How did Revit know what line weights to use for my import?" This is a great question. You can configure the import/export settings to translate AutoCAD colors to Revit line weights. If you are using standard AIA layering, you will have very little problem with this translation. If not, you may have some work to do. In Chapter 12, "Detailing," we will be configuring this file.

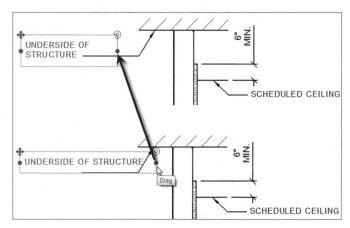

FIGURE 11.59 Fixing the improperly wrapped text

Now that you have experience with keys, it is time to move on to learn how tags work in Revit and why we address them along with schedules.

Adding Tags

Now that you are halfway through the book, you have found that some subjects, such as tags, were brushed over in earlier chapters. Tags simply cannot be avoided since they come in automatically with many items. But there is a mystery surrounding them. Where do they come from, how does Revit know what tag to associate with what element, and how the heck do you make Revit's tags look like your tags?

You can almost see a tag as a "window" looking into the item itself. A tag allows you to pull a parameter out of an item and put that parameter onto the drawing in a physical sense. Given that, tags are how we label things!

To start, let's concentrate on the simple and then move to the more complex. First you'll learn how to add a tag that did not get added automatically.

Adding Tags Individually

As you may have noticed, not everything we placed in the model received a tag—especially many of the doors and windows that we copied to different floors. The objective of the following procedures is to add tags to individual objects. The first type of tag will be By Category.

Tagging by Category

Tagging an item by category simply means that when you start the Tag command, it will look for an entire object to tag with the loaded tag that was created specifically for that object.

1. In the Project Browser, go to the Level 2 floor plan.

2. Zoom in on the area where the corridor meets the east wing, as shown in Figure 11.60.

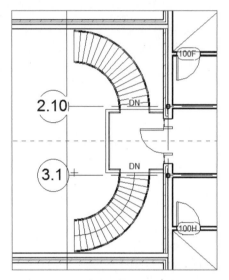

FIGURE 11.60 The area where the corridor meets the east wing

3. On the Tag panel of the Annotate tab, click the Tag By Category button, as shown in Figure 11.61.

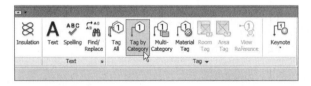

FIGURE 11.61 Click Tag By Category on the Annotate tab.

4. On the Options bar, uncheck the Leader option, as shown near the upper left in Figure 11.62.

5. Pick the door shown in Figure 11.62. Your tag is added.

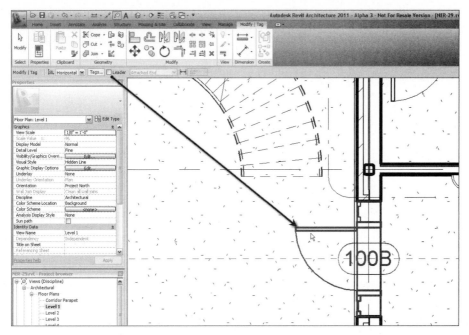

FIGURE 11.62 Tagging the door. Be sure you deselect Leader on the Options bar.

Adding tags to doors is a straightforward concept. Keep in mind, however, that doors and windows are certainly not the only "taggable" items in Revit.

Tagging Walls

Tagging walls is almost as automatic as tagging doors and windows. The only difference is that when you tag a wall, the tag will initially be blank.

To learn how to tag a wall, follow along with the procedure:

1. In the Project Browser, go to the Level 2 floor plan if you are not there already.

2. Zoom in on the east wing.

3. Click the Tag By Category button.

4. Pick the wall indicated in Figure 11.63.

5. Many times, you will not have a tag loaded for this specific type of item. When that situation occurs, you will get the message shown in Figure 11.64. Click Yes to load the tag.

6. Select Annotations ➤ Architectural ➤ Wall Tag.rfa.

7. Click Open.

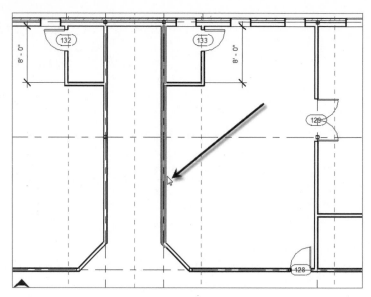

FIGURE 11.63   Picking one of the corridor partitions to tag

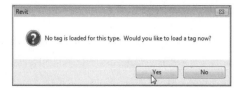

FIGURE 11.64   When you try to tag an item without a specific tag type loaded, this dialog prompts you to load the tag.

8. On the Options bar, click the Leader option so that the tag is leadered into the wall.

9. At the bottom row of the Tag panel, you will see a pull-down arrow. Click the Loaded Tags button (see Figure 11.65).

10. In the Tags dialog, scroll down to Walls, as shown in Figure 11.66.

11. In the Loaded Tags cell for Walls, pick Wall Tag : 1/2″.

12. Click OK.

13. Pick the wall again. You now have a wall tag.

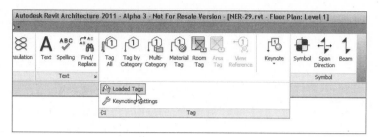

FIGURE 11.65 Click Loaded Tags.

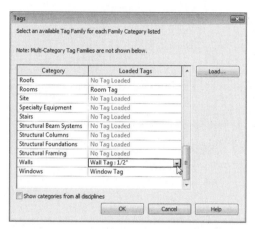

FIGURE 11.66 Changing the default tag for walls to Wall Tag: 1/2″

14. Press Esc twice.

15. Select the new wall tag (it will be blank).

16. Notice the blue items. Click the blue question mark in the tag.

17. Call it MC-1, as shown in Figure 11.67.

18. Click Yes to the warning that you are changing a type parameter.

19. Press Esc.

20. Click Tag By Category on the Annotate tab.

21. Pick any other corridor partition in the floor. Notice that this time the tag is automatically placed with the appropriate MC-1 tag filled out.

In Revit 2011, the Tag By Category button is also located on the Quick Access toolbar.

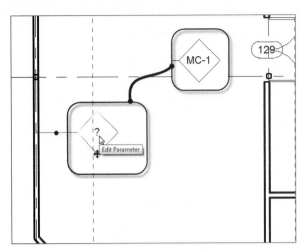

FIGURE 11.67 Adding the wall tag data

But Where Is That Information Stored?

When you modify this type of tag, it is generally the type mark that carries this data. To see where the type mark is, select any one of the interior partitions, and click Edit Type in the Properties dialog. In the Type Parameters, you can scroll down to find the Type Mark, as shown in the following image:

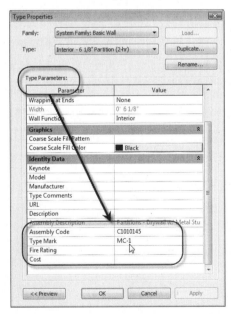

BUT WHERE IS THAT INFORMATION STORED? *(continued)*

This information is also tied into the schedule. As you are selecting fields to add to the schedule, you are selecting from the same list that Revit used to tag items in the model. This is the definition of BIM: the right information is used in the right places.

Suppose you would like to tag a number of the same items in one shot. Revit will allow you to do this by using the Tag All command.

Using the Tag All Command

The Tag All command is a favorite among Revit users. One of the most common examples of using this command is when you Copy/Paste Aligned multiple items to higher-level floors. You will almost always miss a few tags, or even all of the tags. This is where Tag All comes into play.

The objective of this next procedure is to find the Tag All feature and tag many items in one shot:

1. In the Project Browser, go to the Level 4 floor plan.

2. Notice that many doors and windows are not tagged. (If for some reason all of the doors and windows are tagged, select the tags and delete them for this procedure.)

3. On the Annotate tab, click the Tag All button, as shown in Figure 11.68.

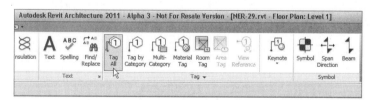

FIGURE 11.68 The Tag All button on the Annotate tab

4. In the Tag All Not Tagged dialog, click Door Tags.

5. Hold the Ctrl key and select Window Tags. This specifies that every door and window in the view is about to receive a tag.

6. Make sure the All Objects In Current View radio button is selected (see Figure 11.69).

7. Click Apply.

8. Click OK.

FIGURE 11.69 Selecting door and window tags

It almost goes without saying that Tag All is quite a valuable tool. Another valuable tool is the ability to reach into a component and tag specific material within the component itself.

Tagging by Material

Tagging By Material could be one of the most underused commands in all of Revit. The reason is most people think of a tag as, well, a tag—some kind of box with some abbreviations or letters in it. That's too bad, because we can also use tags as a means to place notes. Tagging an item's material is one way of doing just that.

The objective of the following procedure is to create a material description; then place a tag pursuant to that note:

1. In the Project Browser, go to the Level 1 floor plan.

2. Zoom in on the kitchen area in the east wing.

3. On the Tag panel of the Annotate tab, click the Material Tag button, as shown in Figure 11.70.

4. You will probably get the message stating that no material tag family is loaded into the model. If so, click the Yes button to load one.

5. Browse to Annotations ➢ Architectural ➢ Material Tag.rfa.

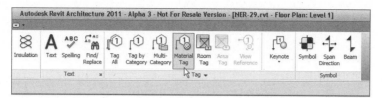

FIGURE 11.70 The Material Tag button on the Tag panel

6. Click Open.

7. Place your cursor over the tile floor as shown in Figure 11.71. Notice the tag reads Interior Finish. This is the default description that we will change in just a moment. When you see this tag, pick a point on the tile floor, and then place the note to the right, as shown in Figure 11.71.

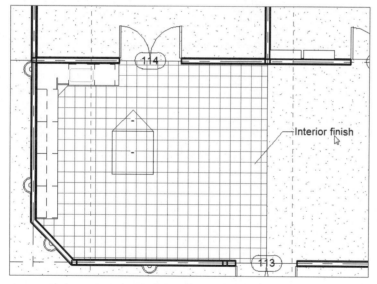

FIGURE 11.71 Placing the Interior finish note

8. Press Esc.

9. Select the tag.

10. In the Properties dialog, click Edit Type.

11. Change the leader arrowhead to Arrow Filled 15 Degree, as shown in Figure 11.72.

12. Click OK to reveal the leader. Yes, that looks much better.

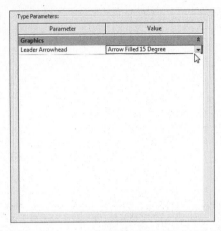

FIGURE 11.72 Changing the leader arrowhead is one of the first things you will probably have to do.

The next objective is to change what the tag says. Since we added that tag by specifying material, it is time to check out the materials to see exactly where this note came from.

1. On the Manage tab, click the Materials button, as shown in Figure 11.73.

FIGURE 11.73 Select the Materials button on the Manage tab.

2. Find the material called Clay Tile - 12″ Beige, as shown in Figure 11.74, and select it. (We made it earlier when we were doing the floors in Chapter 6, "Floors.")

3. To the right of the Materials dialog, you will see four tabs: Graphics, Render Appearance, Identity, and Physical. Click the Identity tab, as shown in Figure 11.74.

4. In the Descriptive Information section, click the Description field and type **CLAY TILE IN KITCHENS, TYP** (see Figure 11.74).

5. Click OK. See Figure 11.75 to check the changed material tag.

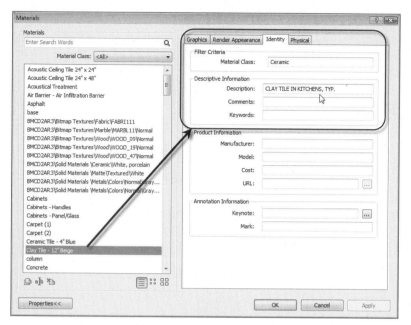

FIGURE 11.74 Changing the description of the material can result in "automatic" notation of your model.

You can see that any time you use this material, it can be annotated with the same text. This procedure also works in sections, elevations, and enlarged plans. If you decide to change the note in the materials, it will update every occurrence in the entire model.

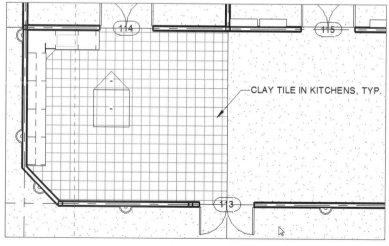

FIGURE 11.75 The material is now tagged with a leadered note.

The next topic we'll explore is where these tags come from and how we can create our own. Notation and symbols are the basis for maintaining CAD standards. If you simply use the examples given to you by Revit, you will have a set of drawings that look very generic and will immediately turn off your design team.

Creating Custom Tags

As mentioned before, templates very much drive how Revit works. Creating families is a prime example of this. To create a custom tag, you must first create a family and then load it into your drawing. The tag we will create is a casework tag. Revit does provide one, but ours needs to be smaller (based on scale), and it needs a box surrounding it.

To learn how to create a custom tag from scratch, follow along:

1. Click the Application button, and select New ➤ Family.

2. Browse to the Annotations folder.

3. Select the file called Generic Tag.rft.

4. Click Open.

Welcome to the Family Editor! The first thing you may notice is the large block of text in the middle of the view that says, "Note: Use Settings|Family Categories to set the tag's category. Insertion point is at intersection of ref planes. Delete this note before using."

This is a great note, and we need to start by taking its advice:

1. Select the note, and click the Delete button (or press the Delete key on your keyboard).

2. Click the Family Category And Parameters button, as shown in Figure 11.76.

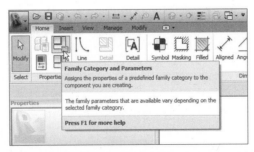

FIGURE 11.76 The Family Category And Parameters button

3. In the Family Category And Parameters dialog, select Casework Tags, as shown in Figure 11.77.

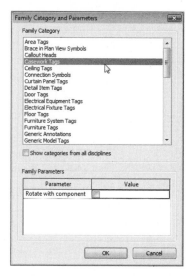

FIGURE 11.77 Selecting Casework Tags

4. Click OK.

Notice that the ribbon has changed. The only items available are designed to aid you in the creation of a family. There are many buttons that we will get to in Chapter 17, "Creating Families," but for now, we are interested in the Label button.

1. In the Text panel on the Home tab, click the Label button, as shown in Figure 11.78.

FIGURE 11.78 The Label button on the Home tab

2. Click the Type Properties button on the Properties panel, as shown in Figure 11.79.

3. Click Duplicate.

FIGURE 11.79 The Type Properties button

4. Call the new label 1/16".

5. Click OK.

6. In the Text category, change the Text Size to 1/16".

7. Change the Width Factor to 0.8.

8. Click OK.

9. In the model, place the tag directly on the intersection of the reference planes, as shown in Figure 11.80.

FIGURE 11.80 Placing the tag onto the reference plane intersection

10. In the Edit Label dialog, select Type Mark from the list to the left.

11. In the middle of the Edit Label dialog is an Add Parameter(s) To Label button. Click it. The Type Mark parameter should show up in the right field, as shown in Figure 11.81.

12. Click OK.

13. Press Esc twice.

The label has been added. It's small but it's there. The next step is to draw a rectangle around this text. The following procedure describes how:

1. On the Home tab, click the Line button, as shown in Figure 11.82.

2. On the Draw panel, click the Pick Lines icon.

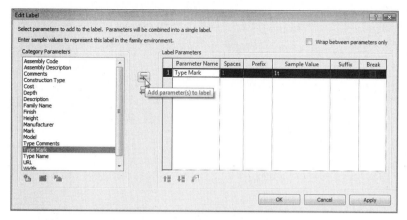

FIGURE 11.81 Adding the Type Mark parameter

3. On the Options bar, change the Offset value to **1/16"**.

4. Zoom into the label, and then offset the horizontal reference plane up 1/16" and down 1/16", as shown in Figure 11.83.

5. In the Options bar, change the Offset value to 1/8".

6. Offset the vertical reference plane to the left and to the right 1/8", as shown in Figure 11.84.

7. On the Modify tab, click the Trim/Extend Single Element button.

8. Trim the four corners so your screen resembles Figure 11.84.

9. Press Esc.

10. Save the file as **Casework Tag.rfa**. Make sure you save the file in a location where you can locate it at a later date.

11. On the Family Editor panel, click the Load Into Project button, as shown in Figure 11.85.

FIGURE 11.82 Click the Line button to start sketching the box.

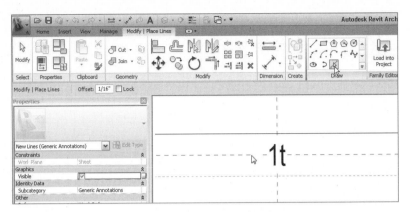

FIGURE 11.83 Offsetting the horizontal reference plane up 1/16″ and down 1/16″

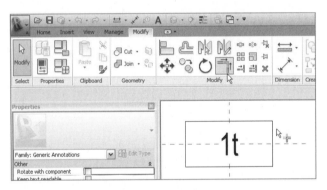

FIGURE 11.84 Creating the box

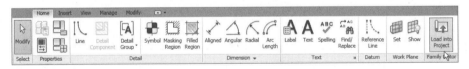

FIGURE 11.85 Loading the family into your project

With the new tag loaded into the project, we can now use it. Since it is a case-work tag, we need to find some casework to label, as follows:

1. In the Project Browser, go to the elevation called Kitchen North. You can also go to the Level 1 floor plan and zoom in on the kitchen. From there, you can double-click on the elevation marker pointing at the north leg of the kitchen.

2. Zoom in on the cabinets, as shown in Figure 11.86.

WHICH ONE DO I CHOOSE?

If you have more than one model open (other than this family), you will see a dialog asking you to select the file you wish to load the family into. If this happens, simply select NER-28.rvt (or the file you are working on) as shown here:

3. On the Tag panel on the Annotate tab, click the Tag By Category button.

4. On the Options bar, uncheck Leader.

5. Pick the base cabinet with two doors and one drawer, as shown in Figure 11.86.

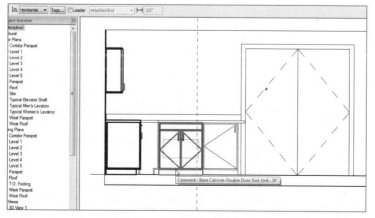

FIGURE 11.86 Picking the base cabinet with two doors and one drawer

6. After you pick the cabinet, press Esc twice, and then move the tag underneath.

7. Select the tag, if it is not still selected.

8. Select the question mark within the tag.

9. Rename it to **B2D1D**, as shown in Figure 11.87, and then click Yes.

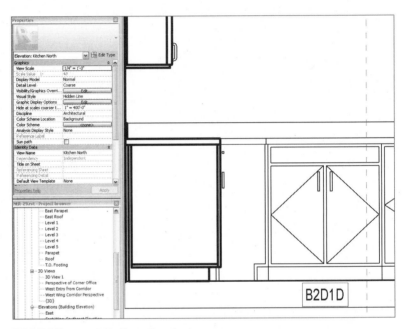

FIGURE 11.87 Renaming the tag

Because this is an annotation family, the size will change with the fluctuation of the scale. If you change the scale from 1/8″ to 1/4″, the tag will shrink by half. To do this, follow along with the procedure.

1. In the View Control toolbar, change the scale from 1/8″ = 1′–0″ to 1/4″ = 1′–0″, as shown in Figure 11.88.

2. Move the tag up so it is closer to the cabinet.

3. Add another tag to the cabinet to the right.

4. Call it **B1D** (see Figure 11.88).

As you can see, this is a huge step above inserting a block in a 2D drafting application and filling out an attribute that has nothing to do with the actual element it is labeling. In addition, the scaling feature works wonders when it comes time to create elevations and enlarged views.

The next topic to explore is creating a tag that will work in any situation we need … sort of a multipurpose tag.

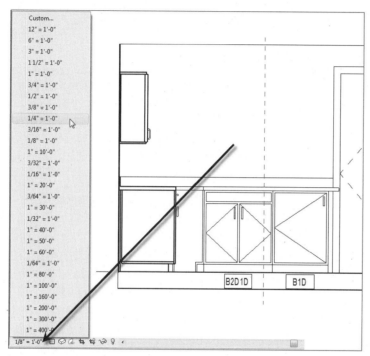

FIGURE 11.88 Changing the scale to 1/4″ = 1′–0″ and adding a second tag to the base cabinets

Using Multicategory Tags

If you think about it, we used a door tag for the doors, a window tag for the windows, and a wall tag for the walls. Jeepers! How many different tags do we need to complete a set of construction documents? Well, in Revit, you can create a multicategory tag. This will be the same tag (aesthetically) that identifies a common property in any element.

Unfortunately, Revit does not provide a sample multicategory tag, so we will just have to make one. The objective of the next set of procedures is to create a new multicategory tag, and then use it on various furniture items.

As mentioned earlier, you should create any new family by using a template. This will ensure that you are using the correct data, so the family will behave as expected. This is what we are doing right now:

1. Click the Application button, and then choose New ➢ Family.

2. In the `Annotations` folder, locate the file called `Multi-Category Tag.rft`.

3. Open the `Multi-Category Tag.rft` template.

4. Since we have started the family by using a template, the ribbon has changed. On the Home panel, click the Label button.

5. Pick the point at the intersection of the two reference planes.

6. In the Edit Label dialog, add the Family Name and Type Name parameters, as shown in Figure 11.89.

7. In the Family Name row, click the Break check box (see Figure 11.89).

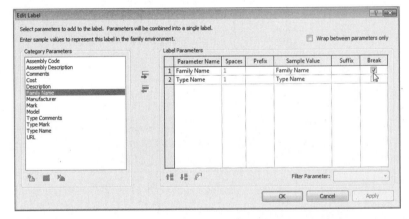

FIGURE 11.89 This time you are actually adding two parameters. By clicking the Break button, you are telling Revit to "stack" the parameters.

8. Click OK.

9. Click the Application button, and select Save As ➢ Family. Place the file somewhere you can find it later.

10. Call the new tag **Multi-Category Tag**.

11. On the Family Editor panel, click Load Into Project.

12. In the NER-28 project (or whatever project name you are currently in), go to Level 1 floor plan, and zoom in on the northeast office in the east wing.

13. On the Annotate tab, click the Multi-Category button on the Tag panel, as shown in Figure 11.90.

FIGURE 11.90 The Multi-Category button on the Tag panel

14. On the Options bar, check the Leader option, as shown in Figure 11.91.

15. Hover your mouse over the furniture items in the room shown in Figure 11.91. Notice that the tag is reporting the information for any item you hover over. Pick the entertainment unit to the left of the room.

16. Select the tag you just placed into the model.

17. In the Properties dialog, click the Edit Type button.

18. For Leader Arrowhead, select Arrow Filled 15 Degree.

19. Click OK.

20. Using the grips on the tag, move it out of the way, and adjust the leader so it looks like the one in Figure 11.91.

21. Add another tag to the credenza located on the north wall. Adjust this tag as well (see Figure 11.91).

22. Add one more tag to the shelving on the south wall of the room, and adjust the leader so it looks acceptable (again, see Figure 11.91).

Using multicategory tags is a great way to label a model. It is nice because you do not need a specific tag for the various elements. These items could have been different types of furniture and casework. As long as they have a family name and a type name, the label tag will work!

Another way to record items in a model is by adding keynoting. This procedure is done in conjunction with a schedule. The last section of this chapter will focus on this procedure.

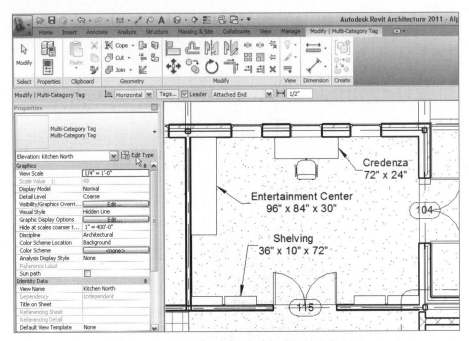

FIGURE 11.91 Adding the Multi-Category tag to the entertainment unit. Make sure you adjust the tag to show the information unobscured.

Keynoting

Keynoting has been used in construction documents dating back to the Pharaohs. Okay, maybe not that far back, but you get the point. Revit does a nice job in terms of tracking keynotes. The only issue is that nothing comes pre-keynoted in Revit. That is, a keynote value needs to be assigned to each item. If your company uses keynoting, you will have to assign a keynote to every item in Revit in your template.

That being said, let's break down keynoting and start learning how to add keynotes to your model. There are three different types of keynotes you can add to a model: keynote by element, by material, and by user. The first type of keynote is keynoting by element, which we will jump right to.

Keynoting by Element

Keynoting by element means you simply select an object and place the keynoted text. This procedure is the same as when you tagged an object, except this time the information you are reporting is actually a CSI (Construction Specifiers Institute)-formatted keynote.

To use the keynoting by element function, follow this procedure:

1. In the Project Browser, go to the Level 1 floor plan.

2. Zoom in on a hallway sconce lighting fixture.

3. On the Tag panel of the Annotate tab, select Keynote ➤ Element Keynote, as shown in Figure 11.92.

 N O T E   If no keynote tag is loaded, click Yes in the subsequent dialog and browse to Annotations ➤ Keynote Tag.rfa.

4. In the Properties dialog, click the Change Element Type menu and click Keynote Tag: Keynote Text, as shown in Figure 11.93.

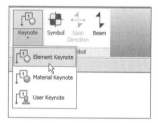

F I G U R E   1 1 . 9 2 Select Keynote ➤ Element Keynote.

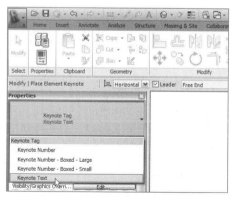

F I G U R E   1 1 . 9 3 Choosing Keynote Tag: Keynote Text

 N O T E   At this point, it is up to you to determine which style of keynoting your firm uses. Do you keynote the plans with the CSI number, with the Keynote description, or with a combination of the number and the description? Either way, we will be making a keynote schedule with these items in a list.

5. Pick the wall sconce shown in Figure 11.94.

6. Pick a second point for the leader line.

7. Pick a third point to place the keynote text (see Figure 11.94).

8. Select the tag.

9. In the Properties dialog, click Edit Type13. Change Leader Arrowhead to Arrow Filled 15 Degree.

10. Click OK.

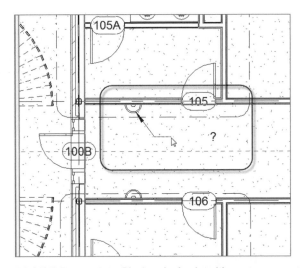

FIGURE 11.94 Placing the leadered keynote

Since there has been no keynote assigned to this family, it is time to specify one now. Revit lets you specify keynoting information by either assigning the information through the Properties dialog or by simply placing a keynote tag, after which Revit will prompt you to specify the missing information.

After you pick the third point, Revit will provide you with the Keynotes menu shown in Figure 11.95. Follow these steps to place the keynote value into the sconce family:

1. Scroll to Division 26 Electrical.

2. Go to the group 26 51 00 Interior Lighting.

3. Go to group 26 51 00.B2 Wall Mounted Incandescent Fixture, as shown in Figure 11.95.

4. Click OK.

FIGURE 11.95 Selecting the proper keynote value for the sconce

5. Drag the text to the right to see the arrow and the note clearly.

6. On the Tag panel of the Annotate tab, select Keynote ➤ Element Keynote again.

7. Pick another wall sconce and place the keynote. Notice this tag is consistent throughout.

Now that you have experience keynoting by element, it is time to reach into the materials and see how we can apply a keynote value in this capacity.

Keynoting by Material

Similar to keynoting by element, you can tag material with a keynote as well. It is good practice to use the Material dialog to assign keynotes.

To assign keynotes to a material, follow these steps:

1. On the Manage tab, click the Materials button.

2. In the Materials dialog box, find Wood - Cherry, as shown in Figure 11.96.

3. To the right of the dialog box, click the Identity tab, as shown in Figure 11.96.

So, Where Is This Information Coming From?

Now that you have added the information to the tag, you can see where it is stored in the Element Properties dialog:

1. Select a sconce.

2. In the Properties dialog, click Edit Type.

3. Scroll down to the Keynote field. Notice it now contains information, as shown in the following image:

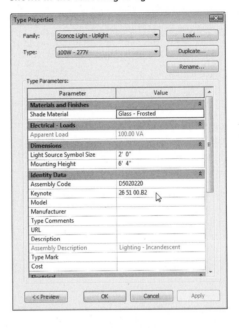

4. At the bottom of the dialog in the Annotation information group, click the [...] button next to the Keynote field (see Figure 11.96).

5. Go to Division 06 Wood, Plastics, and Composites.

6. Go to 06 40 00 Architectural Woodwork.

7. Select 06 40 00.A2 Wood Laminate (see Figure 11.97).

8. Click OK.

9. Click OK again.

10. Go to the Level 1 floor plan.

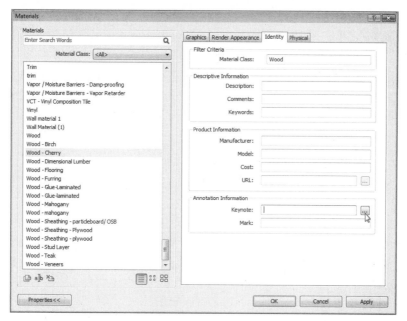

FIGURE 11.96 Browsing for a new keynote

11. Zoom into the stairs in the west wing.

12. On the Tag panel of the Annotate tab, click Keynote ➢ Material Keynote.

FIGURE 11.97 Finding 06 40 00.A2 Wood Laminate

13. Pick the stair landing's surface.

14. Place the keynote as shown in Figure 11.98.

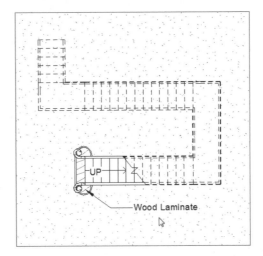

FIGURE 11.98 Placing the material keynote

Now that you have experience adding a keynote value to material, it is time to buckle down and assign keynotes to all of your materials. It is also important to note that, as your firm develops more materials, you need to be diligent in adding keynotes to the new materials as they are created.

The next style of keynoting allows you to specify an alternate keynote to an element. To begin, we will physically open the keynote text file and add some custom notes.

Keynoting by User

There will be times when you need a completely custom keynote. Although you should try to stick to the CSI formatting, there will always be reasons to add your own. To do so, the first thing we need to look at is how to customize the Keynote list.

1. Save your model, and close out of Revit Architecture completely.

2. Using a text editor, open the file C:\Documents and Settings\All Users\Application Data\Autodesk\RAC 2011\Imperial Library\ RevitKeynotes_Imperial_2004.txt.

WARNING   Before you start typing anything, you need to know that, when you need a separator between texts, you must press the Tab key. If not, the code won't work. Also, before you do this, be sure to make a copy of the original file.

3. Scroll down the list until you find the note: 06 43 00.B1→3/4" Plywood Treads And Risers→06 43 00.

4. Click in the end of the note, press Enter to start a new line, and add the row 06 43 00.B2→Custom Hardwood Stairs→06 43 00 (see Figure 11.99).

```
06 22 00.A5     1x5 wood Trim    06 22 00
06 22 00.A6     1x6 wood Trim    06 22 00
06 22 00.A7     1x8 wood Trim    06 22 00
06 22 00.A8     1x10 wood Trim   06 22 00
06 22 00.A9     1x12 wood Trim   06 22 00
06 40 00        Architectural Woodwork  Division 06
06 40 00.A1     Plastic Laminate       06 40 00
06 40 00.A2     wood Laminate    06 40 00
06 40 00.A3     Metal Laminate   06 40 00
06 43 00        Wood Stairs and Railings      Division 06
06 43 00.A1     2x_ Stringer     06 43 00
06 43 00.A2     2x12 Stringer    06 43 00
06 43 00.B1     3/4" Plywood Treads And Risers  06 43 00
06 43 00.B2     Custom Hardwood Stairs        06 43 00
06 43 00.C1     1 3/8" x 2 1/2" Rail Cap       06 43 00
06 43 00.C2     1 1/2" Round Rail       06 43 00
06 43 00.C3     1 9/16" x 3 3/8" Rail Cap      06 43 00
06 43 00.C4     1 3/4" x 3 3/8" Rail Cap       06 43 00
06 43 00.D1     5/16" x 3 1/4" Stair Nosing    06 43 00
06 43 00.D2     3/4" x 3 1/4" Stair Nosing     06 43 00
06 46 00        Wood Trim        Division 06
06 46 00.A1     3/4" x 5 7/8" Crown Molding    06 46 00
```

FIGURE 11.99 Adding the row 06 43 00.B2→Custom Hardwood Stairs→06 43 00

5. Save the file.

6. Open Revit Architecture.

7. Open your project file.

8. In the Project Browser, go to Level 1 floor plan.

9. On the Tag panel of the Annotate tab, click Keynote ➢ User Keynote.

10. Pick the stairs, as shown in Figure 11.100.

11. In the Keynotes dialog box, your new keynote will be at the top of the list, as shown in Figure 11.101.

12. Pick the new keynote.

13. Click OK.

The stairs now have a custom keynote.

Now that we have every kind of tag imaginable placed in our model, we need to create one more legend to close the chapter: a keynote legend.

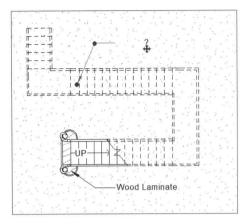

FIGURE 11.100 Picking the stairs to place the keynote

FIGURE 11.101 The new keynote

Creating Keynote Legends

Creating keynote legends is similar to creating schedules. Sometimes there is a fine line between what a schedule is and what a legend is. Keynotes seem to almost fall between these two concepts. Either way, follow this procedure to create a keynote legend:

1. On the View tab, click Legends ➤ Keynote Legend.

2. The name Keynote Legend is fine, so click OK at the dialog that appears.

3. In the Keynote Legend Properties dialog, only two fields are available, and they are both added to the legend. All you need to do is click OK, and the legend has been created (see Figure 11.102).

Keynote Legend	
Key Value	Keynote Text
06 40 00.	Wood Laminate
06 43 00.	Custom Hardwood Stairs
26 51 00.	Wall Mounted Incandescent Fixture

FIGURE 11.102 The new keynote legend

Well, that was easy! As mentioned before, if the data is there, it is not hard to create a query such as this to display the information.

One more item to address is where Revit looks for information regarding keynotes: in the Settings listings.

Keynote Settings

To find the keynote settings, follow this procedure:

On the Tag panel of the Annotate tab, click the drop-down arrow on the bottom of the panel. This will allow you to click the Keynoting Settings button, as shown in Figure 11.103.

Although we are not going to change anything, it is noteworthy that the default path is by library location. This is desired, because when you upgrade Revit and you have a custom keynote file, you can move it to the same directory, and Revit will read it into the model.

By specifying by project, you will have only one keynote legend. If you specify by sheet, you can then drag the legend onto multiple sheets and only the keynotes that are visible on that specific sheet will be included in the legend. We will cover this process in further detail in Chapter 14.

As you can now see, there are many items that can be tagged, keynoted, and scheduled. If you feel as though you could use more practice, go ahead and create some more schedules, tags, and keynotes!

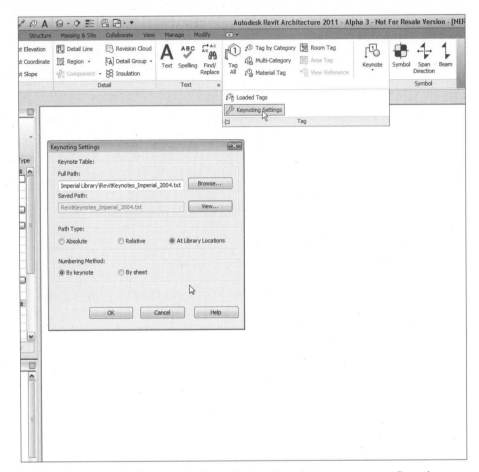

FIGURE 11.103 Keynoting Settings displays where the keynotes are configured.

Are You Experienced?

Now you can...

- ☑ create several different types of schedules

- ☑ add custom fields to the schedules that calculate values

- ☑ create material takeoffs that give you up-to-the-second information as you add items to the model

☑ create legends by using a blank view and basically drafting items into the model

☑ import AutoCAD-generated data to create a legend that looks exactly like your CAD

☑ create drawing sheets, add a schedule, and manipulate a schedule to fit on the sheet

☑ add tags to the model in addition to the tags that were automatically added when you placed the components

☑ place tags that "reach into" a component and display different materials

☑ create custom tags to display any information

Detailing

Simply put, if detailing does not work, then you will use Revit only as a schematic design application. It is imperative that you can detail in Revit efficiently. When firms fail in the attempt to use Revit, it is because of detailing. In fact, many of you who have bought this book may jump straight to this chapter. And why is that? It is because many people (this author included) buy into the concept of really cool 3D perspectives and one-button modeling.

▶ **Working with line weights**

▶ **Drafting on top of the detail**

▶ **Adding notes**

▶ **Creating blank drafting views**

Working with Line Weights

Once we understand Revit, we find out immediately that the real hurdle in getting it to work lies in the detailing. Sure, you can cut sections and create callouts, but how do you add that fine level of detailing needed to produce a set of documents that you are willing to stamp and sign? This chapter addresses the issues surrounding detailing.

The first thing that comes to mind when dealing with CAD standards is line weights, right? In AutoCAD it's layers, in MicroStation it's levels, but on paper it is line weights that control 75 percent of our company's standards. As you will learn in this chapter, Revit can be a good 2D drafting application as well. As we learn how to control our line weights in the 3D elements, we can also control line weights, well, line by line.

To begin, open the file you have been following along with. If you did not complete the previous chapter, go to the book's web page at **www.sybex.com/go/ revit2011ner**. From there you can browse to Chapter 12 and find the file called **NER-29.rvt**.

The objective of this procedure is to format the line weights and to see where, and how, they are read by Revit.

1. In the Project Browser, open the section called Roof Taper Section.

2. Notice the perimeter of the walls and the roof are extremely heavy in contrast to the finer lines that divide the submaterials. This is what we will change. On the Settings panel of the Manage tab, click the Object Styles button to the left of the Ribbon, as shown in Figure 12.1.

FIGURE 12.1 Object Styles is located to the left of the Manage tab.

3. In the Object Styles dialog, you will see a list of every object category available in Revit. The first items we want to change are the roofs. In the category column, scroll down until you see Roofs, as shown in Figure 12.2.

Glancing up at the headers that describe the columns, you will see the Line Weight column. This column is divided into two sections: Projection and Cut. The Projection column controls the line weights of objects as they are viewed in plan or elevation. The Cut column controls the line weights as they are shown in section. So, to reiterate, *projection* means plan and elevation, and *cut* means section. Our objective is to modify the line weight for both the cut and the projection of the floor.

4. In the Roofs row, change the Cut value to 3, as shown in Figure 12.2.

5. Click the plus sign next to Roofs to expand the category.

6. Notice all of the subelements are shown, and you can control the line weights accordingly. Change the Cut value of Fascias to 3.

7. Change the Cut value for Gutters to 3.

8. Change the Cut value for Roof Soffits to 3 (again, see Figure 12.2).

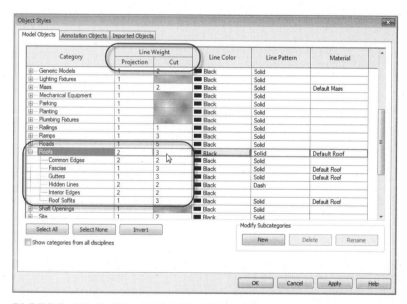

FIGURE 12.2 Changing the object line weights

9. Find Floors, and change Cut Line Weight to 3.

10. Find Walls, and change Cut Line Weight to 3.

11. Click OK and you will see the change to your outline (see Figure 12.3).

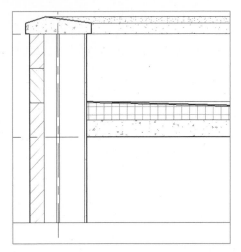

FIGURE 12.3 Your section's outline should start looking a lot better.

It's Template Time!

Many of the procedures we cover here in the first section of this chapter lend themselves well to the topic of standards and templates. You need to change the line weights of objects in a Revit template. BIM management and templates are discussed in full in Chapter 23, "BIM Management."

Now we can start adding our own items to the section. The next group of procedures focuses on inserting and creating detail components to use in the sections.

Drafting on Top of the Detail

As mentioned before, Revit provides a good number of 2D details that we can insert at any time. When Revit does not have the component we need, we can always create one. It is not that hard to do.

In this section, we will physically create a detail. The procedures we will apply consist of adding detail components, linework, filled regions, and some good old-fashioned drafting!

Using Predefined Detail Components

The first procedure focuses on inserting predefined detail components. The great thing about this is that you do nothing that you have not done repeatedly throughout this book—it's just a matter of finding the right button to get it all started.

1. Make sure you are still in the detail called Roof Taper Section.

2. On the Detail panel of the Annotate tab, click Component ➤ Detail Component, then click the Load Family button as shown in Figure 12.4.

FIGURE 12.4 The Load Family button on the Mode panel of the Modify | Place Detail Component tab

3. Browse to the Detail Components directory. (It is located in the Imperial Library directory.)

4. Open the Div 01-General folder.

5. Click the file called Break Line.rfa.

6. Click Open.

7. In the Type Selector of the Properties dialog, be sure that Break Line is selected, as shown in Figure 12.5.

8. Press your spacebar twice. (This will flip the break line into the correct orientation.)

9. Pick a point similar to the one shown in Figure 12.5.

The next step is to simply start drafting. As mentioned earlier, you are only going to get so far with 3D modeling before you have to take matters into your own hands and simply draft. The way we can approach this in Revit is to take the parts of the detail we want to keep and hide the rest. After we hide portions of the detail, it is time to start adding our own ingredients such as detail components and good old-fashioned lines.

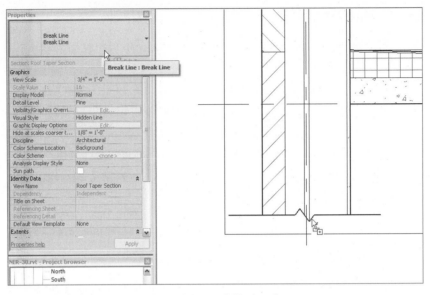

FIGURE 12.5 Placing the break line and flipping the component

THIS FLIPPIN' BREAK LINE IS BACKWARD!

If you forgot to flip the break line as you were inserting it and it is now masking the wrong region, that's OK. Simply press Esc, and then select the break line. Now you can press the spacebar twice to flip the break line, as shown in the following image:

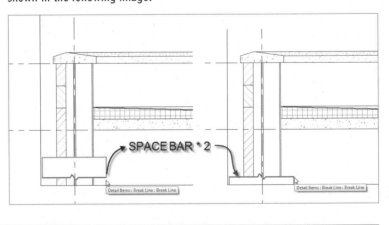

Masking Regions

To let you hide portions of the detail, Revit has added a nice feature called a masking region. Instead of wrestling around with items you ultimately have little or no control over, you can hide these items to make way for your detailing.

To learn how to apply a masking region, follow these steps:

1. Make sure you are still in the detail called Roof Taper Section.

2. On the Detail panel of the Annotate tab, click Region ➤ Masking Region, as shown in Figure 12.6.

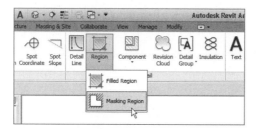

FIGURE 12.6 Region ➤ Masking Region on the Annotate tab

3. In the Properties dialog you'll see some choices in the Subcategory. Choose Invisible Lines, as shown in Figure 12.7.

N O T E By selecting Invisible Lines, you ensure that the perimeter of the masking region will not be visible once you exit Sketch Mode.

4. Again on the Draw panel, click the Rectangle button.

5. Draw a rectangle at the approximate points shown in Figure 12.7.

6. After you place the rectangle, click the Finish Edit Mode button on the Mode panel.

The area is now masked. The problem is, though, some areas such as the break line are a little *too* masked. The next procedure will step through changing the display order of a detail's objects:

1. Select the break line, as shown in Figure 12.8.

2. On the Modify | Detail Items tab, click the Bring To Front button, as shown in Figure 12.8.

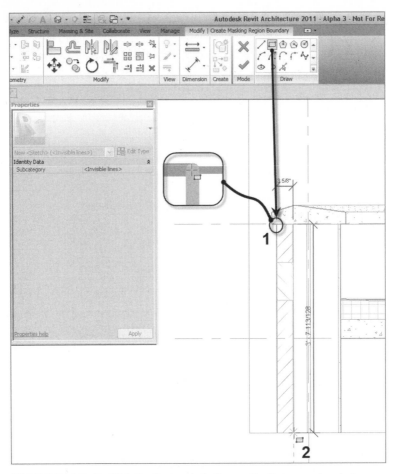

FIGURE 12.7 Click the Rectangle button on the Draw panel and place a masking region as shown.

Your detail should now look like Figure 12.9.

The next step is to add a brick face. Yes, Revit did show the brick before we masked it, but we need to show coursing, as well as how the façade is tied back to the wall. To do this, we will use a function called a repeating detail.

Repeating Details

Revit has a procedure that allows you to add a detail component as a group. You do this by basically drawing a line, and Revit adds the detail in an array based on the points you pick.

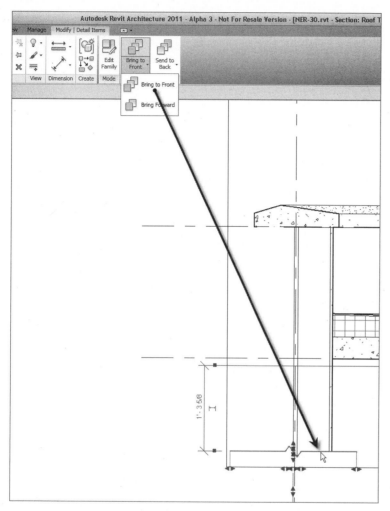

FIGURE 12.8 Click the Bring To Front button on the Modify | Detail Items tab after selecting the break line.

To learn how to add a repeating detail, follow this procedure:

1. On the Detail panel of the Annotate tab, select Component ➤ Repeating Detail Component, as shown in Figure 12.10.

2. In the Properties dialog, choose Repeating Detail : Brick from the Type Selector, as shown in Figure 12.11.

3. Pick the point labeled "1" in Figure 12.11.

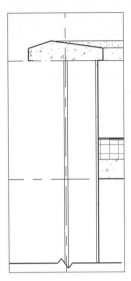

FIGURE 12.9 The detail with the completed masking region

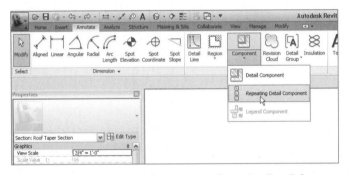

FIGURE 12.10 Select Component ➤Repeating Detail Component.

T I P   Picking that point is going to be a little harder now that it's not there! The objective is to draw an actual façade based on the existing points where the Revit-generated brick once resided. When you hover your mouse over where the brick was, you will see the masked detail appear, as shown in Figure 12.11. Once it appears, you will see the point you need to pick.

4. After you pick the first point, move your cursor down the view.

5. Notice the brick is facing the wrong side. Press the spacebar to flip the brick into the wall, as shown in Figure 12.11.

6. Pick the point labeled "2" in Figure 12.11.

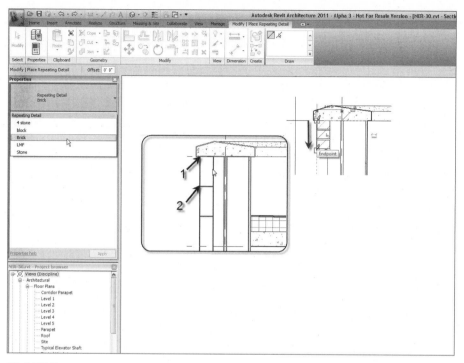

FIGURE 12.11 Adding the repeating detail based on the points shown

Your detail should look like Figure 12.12.

The next step is to keep going with the repeating detail. The problem we are faced with here is that we need to deal with the soldier course that is in the exterior wall. We can add that in a moment. Right now we need to complete the brick down past the break line.

If you feel like you are getting the hang of adding this repeating brick detail, go ahead and add the second repeating detail. If you would like some instruction, follow along:

1. Click the Component ➤ Repeating Detail Component button on the Detail panel on the Annotate tab.

2. Pick point 1, as shown in Figure 12.13.

3. Press the spacebar.

4. Pick point 2, as shown in Figure 12.13. Make sure you pick the second point well past the break line, or the brick will stop short.

5. Press Esc twice. Look at Figure 12.14. Does your detail look the same?

> Remember, you can add a second repeating brick detail by right-clicking on the first one you added and selecting Create Similar.

6. Select the break line.

7. On the Arrange panel, click the Bring To Front button. The repeating detail is now behind the break line.

The next step is to add the soldier course. This will be done in the same way as adding the break line. In this respect, Revit offers a good library broken down into the CSI format.

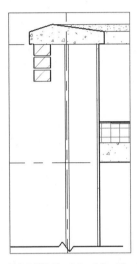

FIGURE 12.12 The first repeating detail

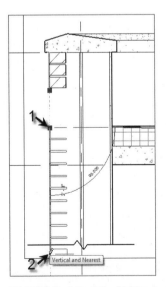

FIGURE 12.13 Picking two points

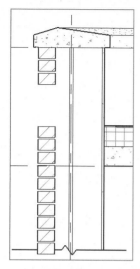

FIGURE 12.14 The bricks are being placed.

To add the soldier course, follow along with the procedure:

1. On the Detail panel on the Annotate tab, click the Component ➤ Detail Component button, then click the Load Family button.

2. Browse to the Detail Components folder.

T I P   If you have not noticed, when you click the Component ➤ Repeating Detail Component button, you *always* go to the Detail Components **folder. This may go without saying, but it took a few months for this author to understand this simple concept.**

3. Go to the Div 04-Masonry folder.

4. Go to the 041200-Clay Unit Masonry folder.

5. Select the Bricks-Top.rfa file.

6. Click Open.

7. When the file is loaded, select Bricks-Top : Standard - 3/8″ Joint from the Type Selector, as shown in Figure 12.15.

8. Press the spacebar once to flip the detail to a vertical plane.

9. Place the detail as shown in Figure 12.15. As you are placing the detail, you will notice that Revit will snap it into the proper position.

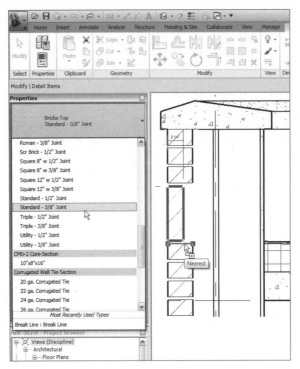

FIGURE 12.15 Placing the Bricks-Top : Standard - 3/8″ joint detail component

Well, the soldier course is in place, but that fat line weight is horrendous! It would be nice if everything that came out of the Revit box looked nice and met our specifications, but alas, that is not the case. It is time to modify this component to make it look presentable.

Modifying a Detail Component

Right about now is when every CAD/BIM manager around the globe raises an eyebrow—for good reason. Revit allows you to modify a component by actually opening the file! But don't worry; you have to issue a Save As to save the detail. If even this is a concern, we will address proven BIM management methods in the last chapter (Chapter 23) of this book. For now, just follow along, and we will talk about management later.

The objective of the following procedure is to create a texture on the brick detail and to use a line weight that the user can control in the model.

1. If you still have a command running, click the Modify button to the left of the Ribbon, or press the Esc key.

2. Select the Bricks-Top family that you just placed.

3. On the Modify | Detail Items tab, click the Edit Family button, as shown near the top of Figure 12.16.

4. The next dialog may ask you if you want to open this file to edit it. Click Yes if you get the message.

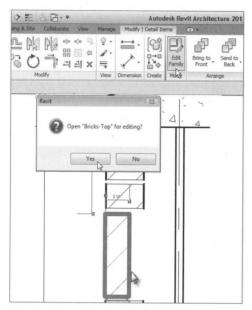

FIGURE 12.16 Click Yes to open Bricks-Top for editing after selecting the Bricks-Top family.

The detail component family is now open. It is time to operate, Doctor. The next set of procedures will focus on modifying the linework of the brick and adding what is called a filled region.

Modifying Filled Regions

A filled region is similar in nature to a masking region in that you proceed in applying both in the same manner. A filled region, however, contains a hatch pattern that is visible when the region is completed. This is how we hatch in Revit. It takes the place of the conventional hatch command found in AutoCAD and MicroStation.

The objective of the next procedure is to modify the filled region that comprises the brick. We will also use the region's outline to define the perimeter and the texture of the brick itself.

1. Select one of the heavy lines that comprise the outline of the brick, as shown in Figure 12.17. Revit will indicate that this is a filled region,

as revealed in the tooltip that appears when you hover your pointer over one of the boundaries.

2. On the Mode panel of the Modify | Detail Items tab, click the Edit Boundary button, as shown in Figure 12.17.

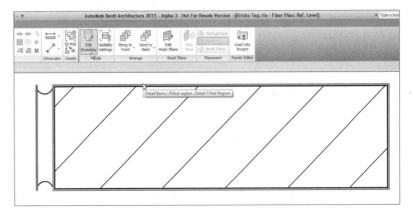

FIGURE 12.17 Click the Edit Boundary button on the Mode panel after selecting the filled region.

3. Select all four lines that make up the brick (the long horizontal lines) and delete them, as shown in Figure 12.18.

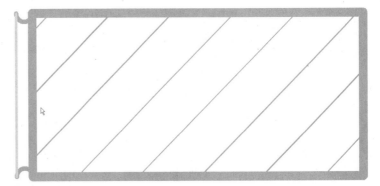

FIGURE 12.18 Deleting the four lines

N O T E   As you may notice, manipulating lines is almost identical to AutoCAD in terms of the process in changing a line's *layer*. You select the line, then change that line's line type in the Type Selector.

4. On the Draw panel, select the Line button, as shown near the top of Figure 12.19.

5. In the Properties dialog, select Detail Items from the Type Selector.

6. Draw a series of jagged lines, as shown in Figure 12.19.

7. Do the same for the bottom.

8. Draw the right and the left straight lines back in.

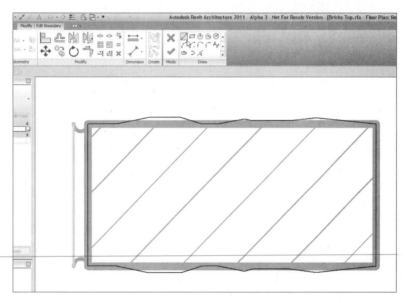

FIGURE 12.19 Adding a texture to the brick family

9. After you finish sketching the texture in, click the Edit Type button in the Properties dialog.

10. Change the background from Opaque to Transparent, as shown in Figure 12.20.

11. Click OK.

12. Click Finish Edit Mode.

13. Select the mortar joint to the left of the brick, as shown in Figure 12.21.

14. On the Mode panel, click the Edit Boundary button.

15. Select the arced lines.

16. Place them on Detail Items, as shown in Figure 12.21.

17. On the Mode panel, click Finish Edit Mode, and your brick should look like Figure 12.22.

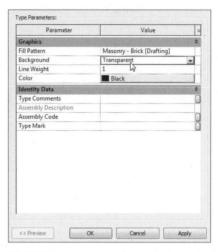

FIGURE 12.20 Changing the background to Transparent

 NOTE By putting all of the lines on the Detail Items line type, you are telling Revit that you do not want to specify a line weight here, but rather let the user specify the line weight by changing the Detail Items in the Object Properties dialog after you load the detail back into the model.

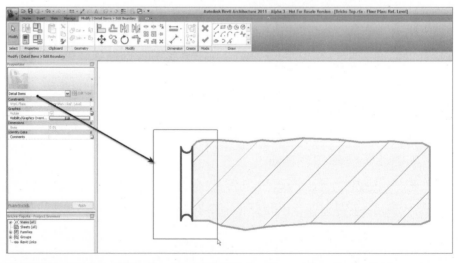

FIGURE 12.21 Editing the mortar joint filled region and then placing the lines on Detail Items

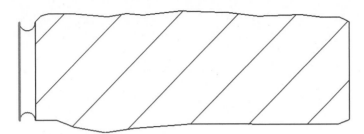

FIGURE 12.22 The brick is looking the way you want it to.

The next step is to add shading underneath the brick pattern. To do this, we will create an entirely new filled region and add it to the brick by tracing over the existing filled region.

1. On the Detail panel of the Home tab, click the Filled Region button, as shown in Figure 12.23.

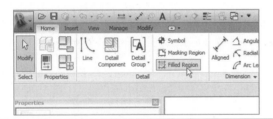

FIGURE 12.23 Click the Filled Region button on the Detail panel.

2. In the Properties dialog, click the Edit Type button and change the Type to Solid Fill - Black, as shown in Figure 12.24.

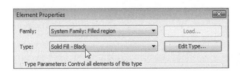

FIGURE 12.24 Changing the region to Solid Fill - Black

3. Click Duplicate.

4. Call the new region **Light Shade**.

5. Click OK.

6. In the Fill Pattern row, click into the Solid Fill [Drafting] field. You will see a [...] button in the right corner. Click it.

7. Notice that you can select any hatch pattern you wish. Make sure Solid Fill is selected, as shown in Figure 12.25, and click OK.

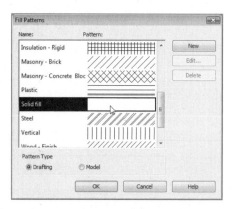

FIGURE 12.25 Select the Solid Fill pattern and click OK.

8. In the Color row, you will see a button that is labeled Black. It also has a little black box icon included. Pick the black box.

9. In the Color dialog, click the Gray tile, as shown in Figure 12.26. (The color is actually RGB 192-192-192.)

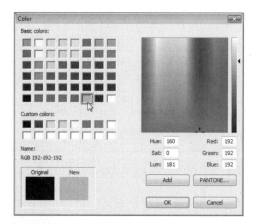

FIGURE 12.26 Selecting the gray color (RGB 192-192-192)

10. Click OK twice.

11. On the Draw panel, click the Pick Lines button, as shown in Figure 12.27.

12. Hover your cursor over one of the jagged lines of the brick face, and press the Tab key.

13. When you press Tab, all of the lines you are trying to trace are highlighted. After the lines are all highlighted, pick any one of the lines, as shown in Figure 12.27. Revit will draw the region based on these points.

14. On the Mode panel, click Finish Edit Mode, and then press Esc. Your brick should look like Figure 12.28.

15. When the Filled Region is in place, select it by clicking on the boundary.

16. On the Arrange panel, click the Send To Back button, as shown near the top of Figure 12.29.

You may find that nothing happens when you press Tab. If this is the case, click into the view in any location. Revit just needs to focus on the view. You can also hold down the wheel button on your mouse to pan a little. This will also switch the focus from the Options bar to the view window.

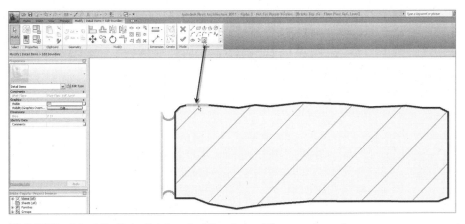

FIGURE 12.27 Press Tab to select the chain of lines, as shown here.

FIGURE 12.28 The solid pattern will cover the previous pattern. We will fix this in a moment.

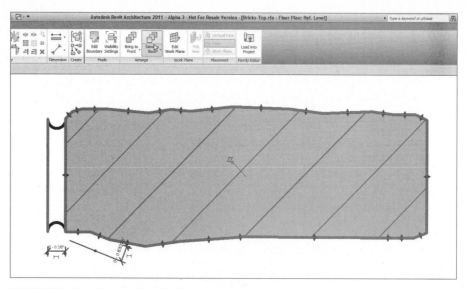

FIGURE 12.29 Sending the light shade to the back

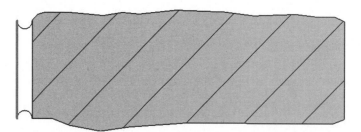

FIGURE 12.30 The finished brick

17. Press Esc. Your brick should now look like Figure 12.30.

18. Click the Save icon.

19. Save the file to a separate location other than the root folder. The file is also available at the book's web page: **www.sybex.com/go/ revit2011ner**. From there you can browse to Chapter 12 and find the file called Bricks-Top.rfa.

20. On the Family Editor panel on the Create tab, click the Load Into Project button, as shown in Figure 12.31.

21. Click to overwrite the family, but do not check Overwrite Parameter Values Of Existing Types.

WHERE DO I WANT TO SAVE THIS?

Notice that when you clicked the Save icon, Revit did not just save over the original file. You are forced to do a Save As. You have one of three choices here:

▶ If the file is not write-protected and you have administrative access to the original folder, you can simply save over the original file. (Do I need to mention that you had better make sure this is what you want to do?)

▶ Save the file as a different file altogether in either the same directory or somewhere else.

▶ Do not save the file at all and load it into your project. Revit will still update the project with the changes even if you did not save the family file.

You can even close out of the family file and not save any changes. Your model will still hold the changes. If you choose to edit the file at a later date, you can select the family in the model and click Edit Family. Revit will open a copy of the modified family.

22. Go back to your model to verify that your detail looks like Figure 12.32.

23. Save the model.

FIGURE 12.31 The Load Into Project button

The next group of procedures focuses on editing the bricks used in the repeating detail. We certainly want the same face texture, and it would be nice if there was a mortar joint between them.

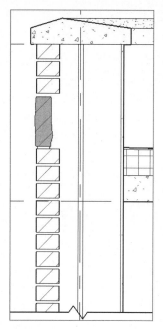

FIGURE 12.32 The new soldier brick in the model

Before we modify the bricks, let's explore how a repeating detail is created. The objective of the next procedure is to discover how a repeating detail works and how we can create a new one.

1. Make sure you are in the detail called Roof Taper Section.

2. Select one of the repeating details, as shown in Figure 12.33.

3. In the Properties dialog, click the Edit Type button, as shown in Figure 12.33.

4. Click into the Parameter list. Notice that every detail component listed in your model is available. The detail component being used here is Brick Standard : Running Section.

   Notice also that you can change the spacing and the patterns of how the repeating detail will perform.

5. Click Cancel.

The next objective is to modify the specific detail component that the repeating detail is using. To do so, we must add an instance of the detail component (in this case it is Brick Standard : Running Section) and then edit the family. Once we load it back into the model, the repeating detail will be up-to-date.

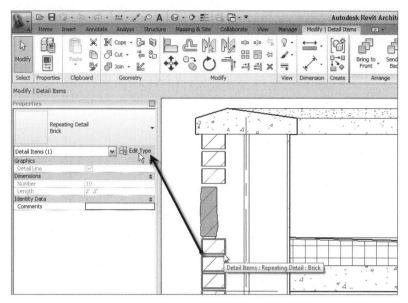

FIGURE 12.33 Click the Edit Type button after selecting one of the brick repeating details.

If you would like to give it a shot and do it on your own, go ahead. If you would rather have some guidance, follow along:

1. On the Detail panel of the Annotate tab, click the Component ➤ Detail Component button.

2. In the Type Selector on the Properties dialog, pick the Brick Standard : Running Section detail component. (Remember, this was the component that we discovered the repeating detail was using.)

3. Place the detail component off to the side of the wall, as shown in Figure 12.34.

4. Press Esc twice.

5. Select the Brick Standard : Running Section you just inserted.

6. On the Mode panel, click the Edit Family button.

7. Select the filled region.

8. On the Mode panel, click Edit Boundary.

9. Delete the right and left thick lines.

10. On the Draw panel, click the Line button.

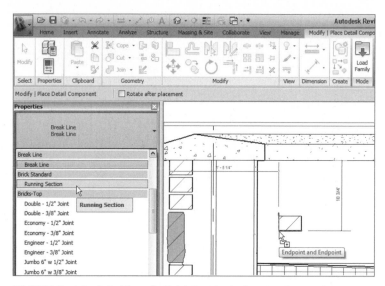

FIGURE 12.34 Place the Brick Standard : Running Section detail component off to the side. You will later delete this occurrence of the component.

11. In the Type Selector menu in the Properties dialog, click Detail Items.

12. Draw the jagged lines in both sides, as shown in Figure 12.35.

13. Click Finish Edit Mode on the Mode panel.

14. On the Home tab, click the Line button.

15. On the Draw panel, click the arc passing through three points button.

16. In the Properties dialog, be sure Detail Items is chosen from the Type Selector list.

17. Draw an arc on both sides of the brick, as shown in Figure 12.35.

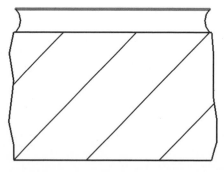

FIGURE 12.35 Draw the textured face while you are in the Edit mode for the filled region. Draw the arcs for the mortar joint using lines.

18. When you are finished, save the new brick. You can also find this brick at the book's web page in Chapter 12; it's called Brick Standard.rfa.

19. On the Family Editor panel, click Load Into Project.

20. In the project, click to overwrite the family.

21. Delete the stray detail component you placed. We were only using it for access to the family.

Compare your detail to the detail in Figure 12.36.

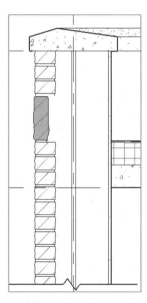

FIGURE 12.36 The brick actually looks like brick!

The next step is to anchor this façade back to the wall. Two things need to be added. We will first add a structural relief angle above the soldier course, then a brick tieback to a lower course.

1. On the Annotate tab, click the Component ➤ Detail Component button.

2. On the Mode panel, click the Load Family button.

3. Open the Detail Components folder.

4. Go to Div 05-Metals.

5. Go to 051200-Structural Steel Framing.

6. Double-click on the file AISC Angle Shapes-Section.rfa.

7. In the Type list, select L6X4X5/16.

8. Click OK. You will have to use the spacebar to flip the instance.

9. Place it into the model as shown in Figure 12.37.

10. Press Esc twice.

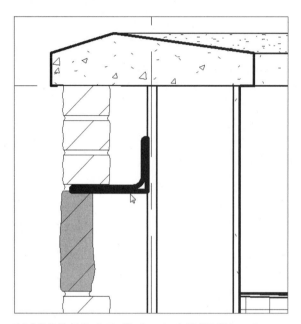

FIGURE 12.37 Placing the L6X4X5/16 angle

Of course the line weight is basically a blob, so we must modify the family in order for it to look accurate. The next procedure is almost a review of what we had to do to the bricks.

1. Select the angle.

2. On the Mode panel, click Edit Family.

3. In the Family Editor, select the filled region (it is the entire angle), and click Edit Boundary on the Mode panel.

4. Select all the lines that comprise the perimeter of the angle.

5. In the Type Selector menu in the Properties dialog, select Detail Items. (We are switching from heavy lines to Detail Items.)

6. On the Mode panel, click Finish Edit Mode.

7. On the Family Editor panel, click Load Into Project.

8. Click Overwrite The Existing Version.

9. Adjust the angle so it looks like Figure 12.38.

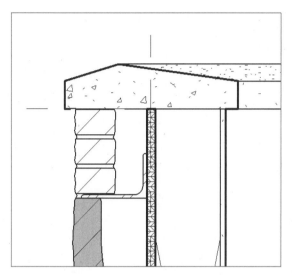

FIGURE 12.38 The angle in place and looking like an angle

The next step is to find a fastener to anchor the angle back to the wall's substrate. There is a problem, however. The type of bolt we need is a lag bolt that is power-driven from the exterior into the wall. Revit does not provide one out of the box. Luckily the book you bought does! To find the lag bolt provided with the book, go to the book's web page, browse to Chapter 12, and find the file called A307 Lag_Bolt-Side.rfa.

1. To load the lag bolt into your model, go to the Insert tab and click the Load Family button. Browse to the directory where you put the A307 Lag_Bolt-Side.rfa file.

2. With the lag bolt loaded, click the Component ➢ Detail Component button on the Annotate tab.

3. Select A307 Lag_Bolt-Side : 3/4" from the Type Selector.

4. Insert the lag bolt into the angle as shown in Figure 12.39.

5. Press Esc twice.

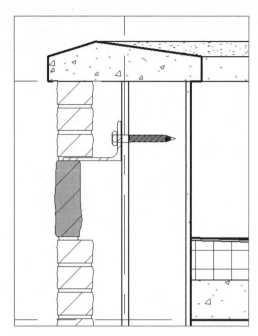

FIGURE 12.39 Inserting the lag bolt

The next step is to add a corrugated wall tie to the brick below the soldier course. Since the brick is a pretty good distance away from the wall, we will also need to add some wood blocking to the model.

1. On the Insert tab, click the Load Family button.

2. Go to the Detail Components folder.

3. Go to Div 06-Wood And Plastic.

4. Go to 061100-Wood Framing.

5. Click the file called Nominal Cut Lumber-Section.rfa.

6. Select the 2×6 type, and click OK.

7. Go to the Annotate tab, click the Component ➢ Detail Component button, and place the 2×6 into the wall, as shown in Figure 12.40.

8. Press Esc twice.

9. Select the blocking you just added and right-click it.

10. Select Override Graphics in View ➢ By Element.

11. In the Projection Lines category, change the weight to 2.

12. Click OK. Your blocking should look like Figure 12.40.

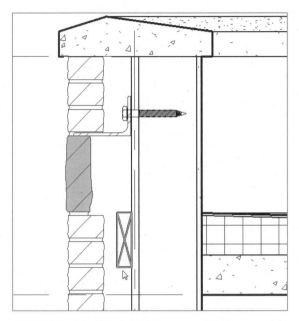

FIGURE 12.40 Adding the wood blocking

The next step is to add the corrugated wall tie. This will be done in the same manner, except that it is located in a different directory.

1. On the Insert tab, click the Load Family button.

2. Go to the Detail Components folder.

3. Go to Div 04-Masonry.

4. Go to 040500-Common Work Results For Masonry.

5. Go to 040519-Masonry Anchorage And Reinforcing.

6. Select the file called Corrugated Wall Tie-Section.rfa.

7. Use the Detail Component button to place the wall tie into your model, as shown in Figure 12.41.

8. Press Esc twice.

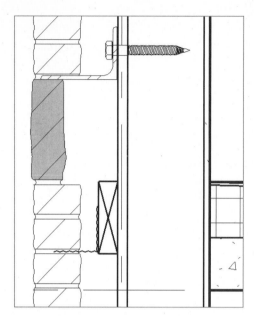

FIGURE 12.41 Placing the corrugated wall tie

The next step is to add some blocking along the concrete parapet cap. Also, we need additional blocking along the lag bolts. If you would like, go ahead and copy the 2×6 blocking around the model to mimic the figure at the end of this series of steps. Or you can follow along:

1. Select the 2×6 blocking.

2. On the Modify | Detail Items tab, click the Copy command.

3. Pick the base point of the upper-right corner, as shown in Figure 12.42.

4. Copy the blocking to the point shown in Figure 12.42.

5. Select the new blocking and rotate it into position, as shown in Figure 12.42. (You will also have to nudge the blocking, using the arrow keys to center it into the wall.)

6. Copy the blocking down to double it, as shown in Figure 12.43.

7. Copy and rotate blocking to the positions shown in Figure 12.43 to allow for support of the lag bolt.

8. Select all the blocking that has the heavy line weight, right-click, and choose Override Graphics in View ➢ By Element. Change the projection line weight to 2.

9. Compare your detail to Figure 12.43.

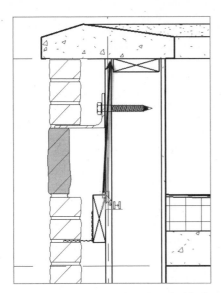

FIGURE 12.42 Rotating the blocking after copying it

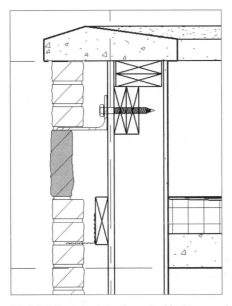

FIGURE 12.43 Copy the blocking as shown.

The next type of detail component we will add is a line-based component. The 3/4″ void in the middle of the wall is plywood sheathing. You can add the plywood "hatch" in one of two ways: add a filled region that has the plywood hatch built into it, or add a detail component.

Your bolt may become obscured by the blocking. This is OK. Simply select the bolt and use the Draw Order tool to bring the bolt to the front.

Let's do the latter. To add a line-based detail component, follow along:

1. On the Insert tab, click the Load Family button.

2. Browse to the Detail Components directory.

3. Select Div 06-Wood And Plastic.

4. Select 061600-Sheathing.

5. Double-click the file called Plywood-Section.rfa.

6. Click the Detail Component button on the Annotate tab; then, in the Properties dialog, make sure Plywood Section : 3/4″ is current in the Type Selector.

7. Click point 1 and point 2, as shown in Figure 12.44.

8. After you draw in the plywood, make sure the bottom is down past the break line. When it is, select the plywood, click the Draw Order button on the Modify Detail Items tab, and choose Send To Back.

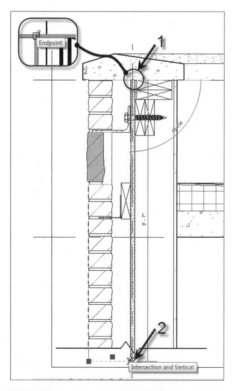

FIGURE 12.44 Drawing the plywood into the core

Now that you have a good grasp of adding detail components, we need to figure out how to control the line weight so the outlines of the bricks look a little bolder.

If you remember, some of the detail components were modified based on the line weight of the filled region perimeter. This thickness was taken from Heavy Lines to Detail Items. We need to set the Detail Items to a thickness we can live with.

1. On the Manage tab, click the Object Styles button.

2. Scroll down the list until you see Detail Items.

3. Change the Projection line weight to 2, as shown in Figure 12.45.

Object Styles			
Model Objects	Annotation Objects	Imported Objects	

Category	Line Weight		Line Color
	Projection	Cut	
⊞ Casework	1	3	■ Black
⊞ Ceilings	2	2	■ Black
⊞ Columns	1	4	■ Black
⊞ Curtain Panels	1	2	■ Black
⊞ Curtain Systems	2	2	■ RGB 000-127-000
⊞ Curtain Wall Mullions	1	3	■ Black
⊞ Detail Items	2		■ Black
⊞ Doors	2	2	■ Black

FIGURE 12.45 Changing the Detail Items Projection line weight to 2

4. Click OK. Your detail now has a bolder perimeter.

 N O T E   It is a great idea to plot this detail right now! Although Revit does a nice job of letting you see the contrasting line weights on the screen, it may be a different story at the plotter. Do yourself a favor and make sure this is the line weight you want.

Another item left to explore in terms of adding detail to a view is the simple concept of drawing lines.

Drawing Detail Lines

As mentioned before, in Revit you can simply draw lines. You can only get so far with detail components, and then you need to pick up the pencil and add your lines.

The next set of procedures will focus on adding lines to your model; then we will look deeper into how these lines are created and modified.

1. In the Project Browser, make sure you are in Sections (Building Sections : Roof Taper Section).

2. On the Detail panel of the Annotate tab, click the Detail Line button, as shown in Figure 12.46.

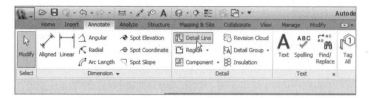

FIGURE 12.46 Click the Detail Line button on the Annotate tab.

3. In the Type Selector in the Properties dialog, click Medium Lines, as shown in Figure 12.47.

4. On the Options bar, uncheck the Chain option.

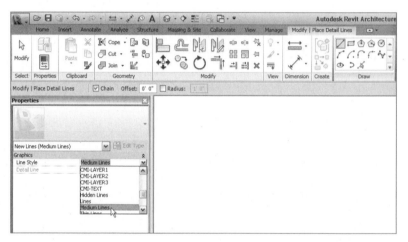

FIGURE 12.47 Select the Medium Lines option from the Line Style parameter in the Properties dialog.

N O T E Does this seem familiar? If you are used to the AutoCAD method of drafting, this is the same as starting the Line command and choosing the correct layer.

5. Draw a line, as shown in Figure 12.48. Be sure to use your endpoint and perpendicular snaps.

6. With the Line command still running, click the Pick Lines icon on the Draw panel.

7. Change the Offset to 1 1/2", as shown in Figure 12.49.

8. Offset the line you just drew down 1 1/2", as shown in Figure 12.49.

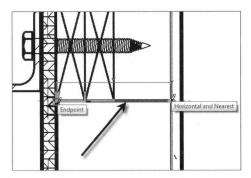

FIGURE 12.48 Drawing a medium line

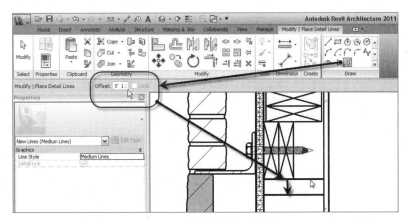

FIGURE 12.49 Offsetting the line down 1 1/2" to create a second line

9. With the Line command still running, change to Thin Lines in the Properties dialog.

10. In the Draw panel, click the Line button.

11. Change the offset to 0.

12. Draw the "X" for the blocking, as shown in Figure 12.50.

13. Copy the blocking down to form a double plate, as shown in Figure 12.50.

14. Draw another "X" below the plates to indicate a stud, as shown in Figure 12.50.

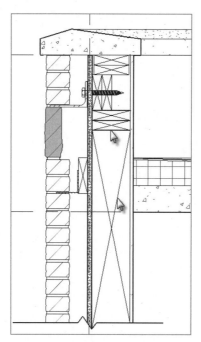

FIGURE 12.50 Adding the detail to indicate studs and plates by using detail lines

So, what makes a Medium Line medium and a Thin Line thin? This is a part of Revit that we need to have full control over. After all, your biggest challenge will be getting your plotted sheets to match your old CAD plotted sheets. Specifying line weights is crucial.

Specifying Drafting Line Weights

Just like in CAD, you would not dare to draw even a single line if you did not know the proper "layer" it was being drafted on, right? So why should Revit be any different?

The objective of the next procedure is to investigate where the line weights are stored and how they relate to the lines you are drawing:

1. On the Manage tab, choose Additional Settings ➤ Line Styles.

2. In the Line Styles dialog, expand the Lines category by clicking the plus sign next to Lines.

Notice there are some line styles that appear to have been generated in AutoCAD—they were. These line styles were imported when you brought in the legend back in Chapter 11, "Schedules and Tags."

3. Click into the Wide Lines category and change the value from 5 to 4, as shown in Figure 12.51.

4. Click OK.

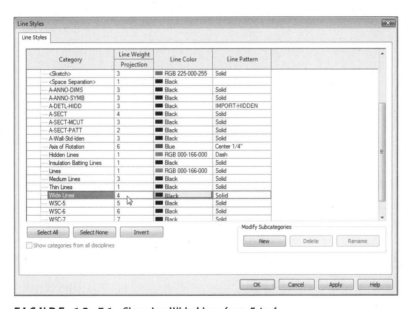

FIGURE 12.51 Changing Wide Lines from 5 to 4

To learn more about setting up line weights and how to establish a good useful template, hop over to Chapter 23. This chapter is dedicated solely to BIM management.

The next item to tackle is the fact that this detail looks naked without any text or dimensions added to it! Although we have applied both of these items in past chapters, we need to use them as they are relevant to detailing.

But What Do "5" and "4" Represent?

In Revit, line weights are sorted from thinnest to heaviest. You can add additional line weights, but I recommend that you stick to the 16 available. To see where these settings are stored, choose Additional Settings ➢ Line Weights. In the Line Weights dialog, notice that numbers 1 through 16 are listed. These numbers represent what you see in the Line Styles dialog. Also notice that the thicker line weights degrade in thickness as the scale is reduced (see the following graphic).

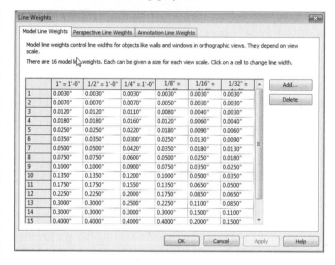

Adding Notes

In Revit, adding notes to a section can take on a whole different meaning than in CAD. You may remember back in Chapter 11 when we were able to specify materials and then tag them in a plan. Well, you can do the same thing right here in Revit.

Or, if you wish, adding notes to a detail can be exactly like it was back in CAD. Sometimes sticking to the tried-and-true isn't such a bad thing either!

The objective of the next set of procedures is to add notes by tagging materials, and to add notes by simply leadering in some text.

Adding Notes by Material

Because we have some experience adding information to materials, it would be nice to leverage that experience here. The next procedure will involve going to the material settings and adding a description to the brick that reads BRICK FACADE. Then we will add that tag in the section.

If you are confident, you can go and do this on your own. Your finished detail should look like Figure 12.54 at the end of this series of steps. If you would like some instruction, follow along:

1. On the Manage tab, click the Materials button on the Settings panel.

2. Select Masonry - Brick in the list to the left, as shown in Figure 12.52.

3. On the right side of the dialog, go to the Identity tab, as shown in Figure 12.52.

4. In the Description, type **BRICK FACADE**.

5. Click OK.

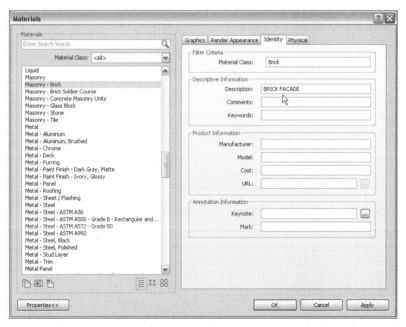

FIGURE 12.52 Changing the Description to BRICK FACADE in the Identity tab

6. In the Project Browser, make sure you are in the section Roof Taper Section.

7. On the Annotate tab, click the Material Tag button on the Tag panel, as shown in Figure 12.53.

8. Once you place your cursor over the brick, you will see the tag fill in. Place the tag as shown in Figure 12.54.

FIGURE 12.53 On the Annotate tab, click the Material tag button on the Tag panel.

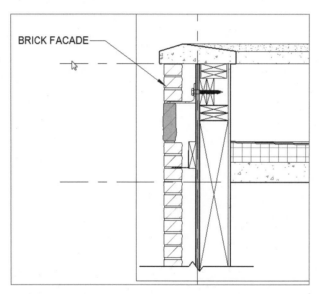

FIGURE 12.54 Placing the material tag

Another method of applying a description to a material is to tag the item first and then fill out the tag. If you do so, the material will automatically be identified, and the tag will be filled out the next time you tag the same material.

1. On the Annotate tab, click the Material Tag button on the Tag panel.

2. Place a tag, as shown in Figure 12.55, on the tapered roof insulation. Notice there is nothing but a question mark. This means Revit does not yet have a description for the material.

3. Press Esc twice; then click the question mark. It turns blue.

4. Click the question mark again and type **TAPERED RIGID INSULATION** (see Figure 12.56).

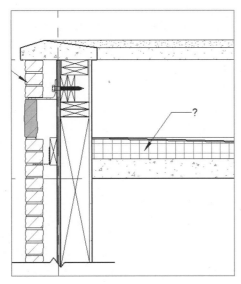

FIGURE 12.55 Adding a material tag to the insulation

 N O T E   When you add a material tag in this manner, you will usually have to move the text to the right or the left to make it readable. In this case, select the text and move it to the right using the drag grip.

Now it's time to just add some freeform notes. The great thing is, we have already done this, and we have gone as far as setting up our own leaders for that text.

Adding Textual Notation

We are duplicating efforts with text to drive home the fact that Revit lets you add text indiscriminately of the view, and also indiscriminately of the scale. Text in a plan is the same as text in a detail. And we are going to prove it in the next procedure:

1. On the Annotate tab, click the Text button.

2. On the Modify | Place Text tab, click the Align Right button on the Format panel, as shown at the top of Figure 12.57.

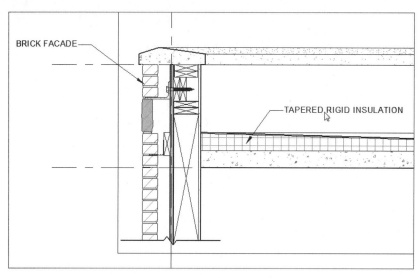

BRICK FACADE

TAPERED RIGID INSULATION

FIGURE 12.56 Add the note TAPERED RIGID INSULATION.

3. Again, on the Modify | Place Text tab, click the Two Segments leader (the uppercase A in the lower-left corner of the Format panel) (see Figure 12.57).

4. Also on the Format panel, click the Leader At Top Right button (this is a new feature in Revit Architecture 2011).

5. In the section, pick the first point of the leader (labeled "1" in Figure 12.57).

6. Pick the second point above and to the left of the first point (labeled "2" in Figure 12.57).

7. Pick the third point for the second segment, as shown in Figure 12.57.

8. Type the note **CORRUGATED BRICK TIE ON 2X6 BLOCKING.**

9. Click off the text into another part of the model, and your text will justify to the leader.

10. Press Esc twice.

11. Select the text.

12. Pick the grip to the left, and drag the box to resemble Figure 12.58. Your text will wrap.

13. Save the model.

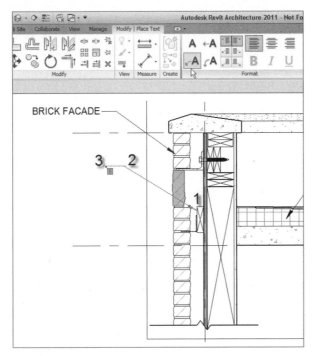

FIGURE 12.57 Adding the leadered text

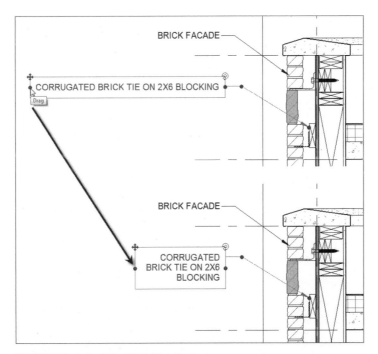

FIGURE 12.58 Wrapping the text

These steps are the most common procedure for adding detail to a model. In other words, take what you can from the model, then add linework and detail components to the view. You will, however, find yourself in the situation where you would rather just draft your detail from scratch. This can be done as well, as you'll see in the next section.

Creating Blank Drafting Views

Over the years, Revit has been labeled as a "poor drafting application." This is unfortunate, because it can be a very good drafting application when given the chance. The only challenge is to figure out where to start!

The objective of the next procedure is to create a blank view, and then learn how to simply draw lines:

1. On the View tab, click the Drafting View button, as shown in Figure 12.59.

2. In the New Drafting View dialog, name the new view **TYPICAL WALL TERMINATION**.

3. Change the scale to 3/4" = 1'–0" (see Figure 12.60).

4. Click OK.

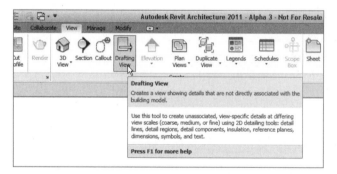

FIGURE 12.59 Click the Drafting View button on the View tab.

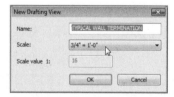

FIGURE 12.60 Changing the view name and scale

You are now in a completely blank canvas. Anything you draw here is truly drafting and is not tied back to the model whatsoever.

The objective of the next procedure is to start adding lines and more detail components. The item we will draft is a detail showing a flexible top track of a metal stud partition.

1. On the Annotate tab, click the Detail Line button.

2. In the Properties dialog, click Medium Lines.

3. Draw a horizontal line about 4′–7″ long, as shown in Figure 12.61.

4. With the Detail Lines command still running, change the Offset setting in the Options bar to 8″.

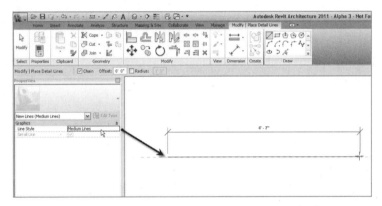

FIGURE 12.61 Drawing a detail line approximately 4′–7″

5. Using the two endpoints of the first line, draw another line below.

GET DOWN THERE!

Remember, if your line is above the first line you drew, press the spacebar, and it will flip the line down below the first, as shown in this image:

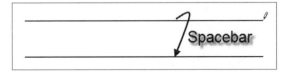

6. Press Esc twice.

7. Start the Detail Line command again.

8. On the Draw panel, click the Pick Lines icon.

9. Again on the Options bar, change the offset to 1 1/2", as shown in Figure 12.62.

10. Offset the bottom line down 1 1/2". Your detail should look like Figure 12.62.

11. With the Detail Line command still running, click the Line button and set the Offset value to 3", as shown in Figure 12.63.

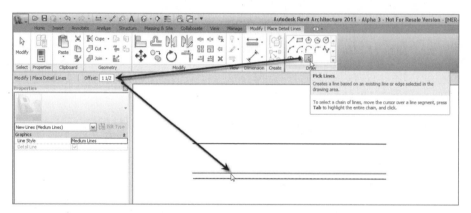

FIGURE 12.62 Using Pick Lines and adding an offset of 1 1/2"

12. On the Options bar, make sure the Chain option is checked on.

13. For the first point of the line, pick the midpoint of the bottom line, as shown in Figure 12.63.

14. For the second point of the line, pick a point about 1'–9", straight down as shown in Figure 12.63. (This draws a line offset 3" to the right from the center of the line above.)

15. To draw the other line, pick a point aligned with point 2 (shown as point 3 in Figure 12.63) and the midpoint of the bottom line.

16. Pick a point perpendicular to the bottom line (see Figure 12.63).

17. Press Esc twice.

18. Compare your lines with the lines in Figure 12.64.

19. Click the Trim/Extend Single Element button on the Modify tab, as shown in Figure 12.65.

20. Trim the edges of the top of the wall, as shown in Figure 12.65.

The next step is to add the track to the bottom of the floor. You will do this by creating three wide lines. The trick here is to do a good amount of offsetting. If you want to explore and try the procedure on your own, go ahead and try to match the figure at the end of this series of steps dimensionally. Remember, we are using wide lines for the track.

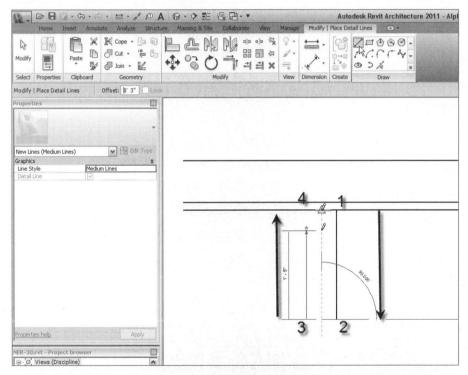

FIGURE 12.63 By setting an offset of 3″, you can draw two lines using a common centerline.

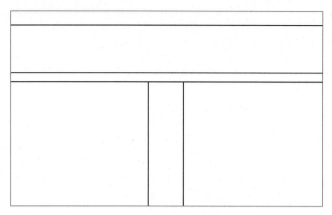

FIGURE 12.64 The detail up to this point

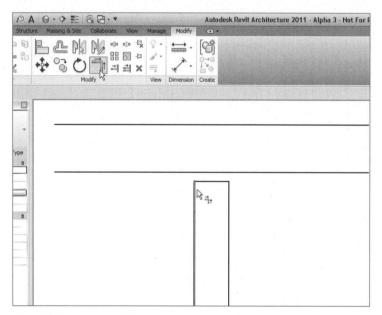

FIGURE 12.65 Trimming the corners

If you would rather have guidelines, follow these steps:

1. On the Annotate tab, click the Detail Line button.

2. In the Properties dialog, click Wide Lines.

3. On the Draw panel, click the Pick Lines button.

4. On the Options bar, set the offset to 1/8".

5. Offset the bottom of the floor down 1/8″. (It will look like the bottom line simply got thicker, but once we trim it up, it will look right.)

6. With the Detail Line command still running, set the offset to 3/8″.

7. Offset the left and the right lines, as shown in Figure 12.66.

8. Offset the bottom of the "floor" down 3″.

9. Extend the tops of the left and right thick vertical lines to the thick horizontal line.

10. Trim the bottoms of the thick, vertical lines to the 3″ horizontal line, as shown in Figure 12.67.

11. Trim the top horizontal line to the new vertical lines.

12. Delete the 3" horizontal line. Your detail should now look like Figure 12.68.

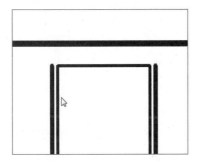

FIGURE 12.66 Offsetting the heavy lines 3/8″ to the right and to the left

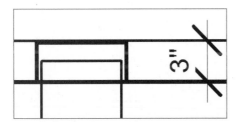

FIGURE 12.67 Offsetting the thick lines

Now it is time to add the gypsum to both sides of the wall. By using the same method as before, we will simply use thin lines to denote two layers of 5/8″ gypsum on both sides of the stud. If you are ready to complete this task on your own, go ahead. (Remember, we are adding two layers of 5/8″ gypsum to both sides of the wall, and we are using thin lines to denote this.)

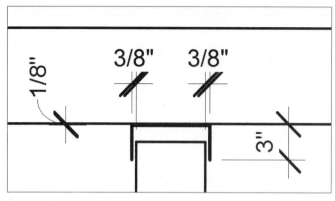

FIGURE 12.68 The top track is now in place.

If you would rather have some guidelines to practice with, let's step through the procedure:

1. On the Annotate tab, click the Detail Line button.

2. Select Thin Lines in the Properties dialog.

3. On the Draw panel, click the Pick Lines icon, as shown in Figure 12.69.

4. Type 5/8" in the Offset field.

5. Offset two lines in from the right and the left, as shown in Figure 12.69.

Look at this! The steps are getting shorter. As you can see, we used only the Detail Line command but yet have successfully offset every line we needed without leaving the command we were running at the time. Who says you can't draft in Revit?!

The next procedure will involve adding a filled region to the "floor." Although we don't want to be too specific about what we are calling out here, we do still need some contrasting hatch.

If you would like to venture out on your own, try to duplicate the figure at the end of this series of steps. You will need to add a filled region using diagonal lines. If you would rather follow the procedure, let's get started.

1. On the Annotate tab, click the Region ➤ Filled Region button.

2. In the Line Style panel, click Invisible Lines, as shown in Figure 12.70.

3. Draw a boundary, as shown in Figure 12.70, and press Esc.

4. On the Properties dialog, click the Edit Type button, as shown in Figure 12.70.

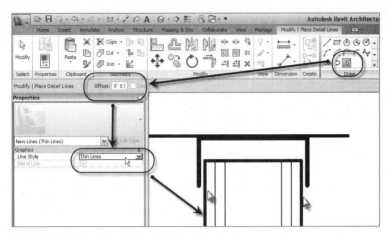

FIGURE 12.69 Adding the lines for the gypsum

5. Click Duplicate.

6. Call the new region ROOF.

7. Change Fill Pattern to Diagonal Up-Small [Drafting].

 N O T E   Remember to change the Fill pattern by clicking the [...] button after you click in the Material cell. You can then browse to find the pattern you are looking for in the menu.

8. Click OK.

9. Click Finish Edit Mode on the Mode panel. Your pattern should look like Figure 12.71.

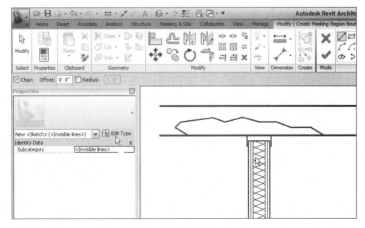

FIGURE 12.70 Click the Edit Type button.

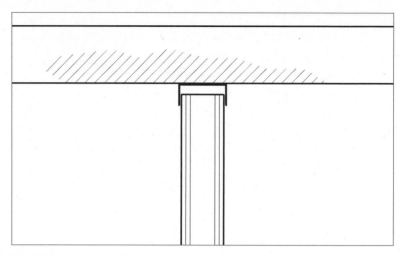

FIGURE 12.71 The detail with the hatching included

This detail is looking good—so good that it would be nice to never have to draw it again. Let's proceed with creating a special group that we can just drag onto another view.

Creating a Detail Group

Groups can be extremely advantageous to the drafting process. Although I mentioned at the start of this section that details and drafting views are not linked to the model, we can still provide some global control within the details themselves by creating a group. This will give us further control over every instance of this specific detail within the entire model.

The objective of the following procedure is to create a new group and add it to another view:

1. Select everything in the view by picking a window.

2. On the Create tab, click the Create Group button, as shown in Figure 12.72.

3. In the Create Detail Group dialog, call the new group **Typical Slip Track**. Click OK.

4. The group has been created. You will see an icon similar to the UCS icon in AutoCAD. This is your origin. Pick the middle grip and drag it to the left corner of the track (where it meets the floor), as shown in Figure 12.73.

5. Save the model.

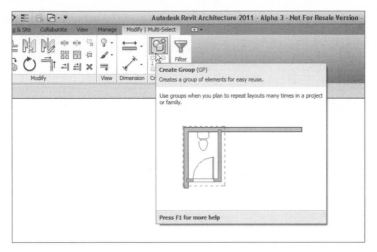

FIGURE 12.72 The Create Group button on the Create tab

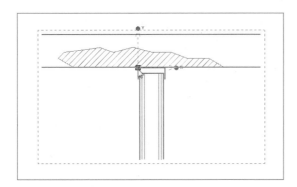

FIGURE 12.73 Move the origin to the location shown here.

With the group created, it is time to add it to another view. Since not every view shows exactly the same thing, we can alter the group's instance to conform to the detail it is being placed into.

The objective of this next procedure is to physically add the new detail group to the Roof Taper Section:

1. In the Project Browser, find the Sections (Building Section) called Roof Taper Section.

2. On the Annotate tab, click Detail Group ➤ Place Detail Group, as shown in Figure 12.74.

3. Move your cursor over the underside of the roof. Notice you get a snap. This is the origin point of the detail.

4. Pick a point along the bottom of the roof similar to what is shown in Figure 12.75.

5. Once the group is placed, press Esc.

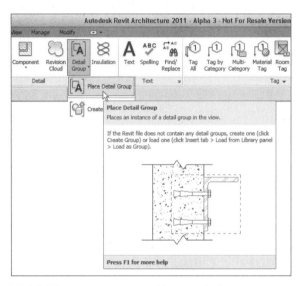

FIGURE 12.74 Choose Place Detail Group.

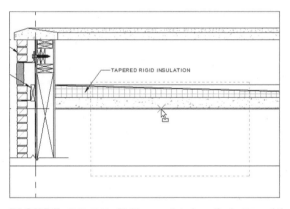

FIGURE 12.75 Picking a point along the bottom of the roof to place the group

The next step is to remove some of the extraneous hatch and lines. You can do this within a group, but you must be careful not to edit the group in a way that affects all other instances.

The objective of the next procedure is to remove the extra lines and hatch from the group:

1. Hover your cursor over the thick line representing the bottom of the floor in the group, as shown in Figure 12.76.

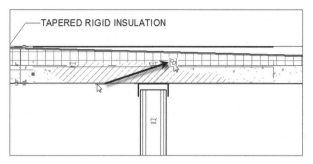

FIGURE 12.76 Excluding an element from the group

2. Press the Tab key. This allows you to get to the second level of the group and highlight the single line.

3. Pick the line, as shown in Figure 12.76.

4. You will see a small, blue group icon appear. When you hover your mouse over it, it says that you can exclude this member from the group. This is what we want to do, so click the button.

5. Repeat the process for the top line.

6. Repeat the process for the hatch.

7. Save the model. Your detail should now look like Figure 12.77.

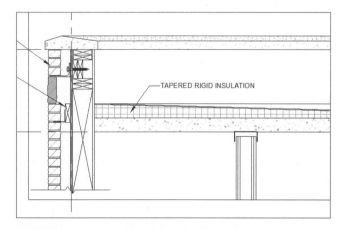

FIGURE 12.77 The slip track without the extra lines

The next step is to make modifications to the original group to see how each insertion of a group is influenced. This is where the advantage of using groups in a model comes into play.

The objective of the next procedure is to open the original group and modify it. Once the modifications are completed, the other groups will be updated.

1. In the Project Browser, find the TYPICAL WALL TERMINATION view under Drafting Views (Detail) and open it.

2. Select the group.

3. On the Modify | Detail Groups tab, click Edit Group. You will now see the Edit Group panel toward the right of the ribbon.

4. On the Detail panel of the Annotate tab, click the Insulation button, as shown in Figure 12.78.

5. Place the insulation starting at the midpoint of the top of the stud and terminate the insulation at the bottom of the stud, as shown in Figure 12.79.

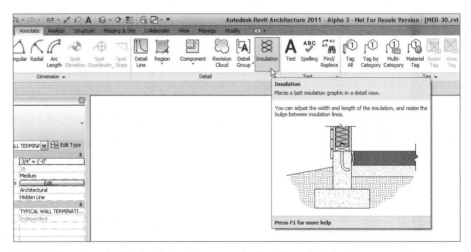

FIGURE 12.78 The Insulation button on the Detail panel of the Annotate tab

6. Click the Finish button on the Edit Group toolbar, as shown in Figure 12.80.

7. Open the Roof Taper Section and observe that the insulation has been added.

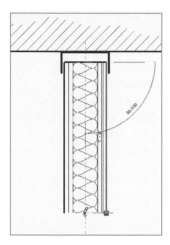

FIGURE 12.79 Drawing the insulation

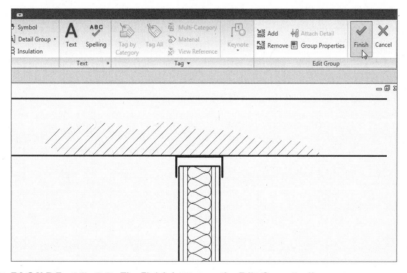

FIGURE 12.80 The Finish button on the Edit Group toolbar

So, we are starting to get detailing covered pretty well. There are two issues left to discuss. First, it would be nice to reference these details from the plan even knowing that they are not physically tied into the model. Second, we want to know how to import CAD into a detail.

ALWAYS BE AWARE OF THE PROJECT BROWSER

You can add a group from the Project Browser as well. If you scroll down in the Project Browser, you will see a category called Groups. Expand the Groups category, and you will see the Detail category. Expand this, and you will see the Typical Slip Track group, as shown in the following graphic. All you need to do is click this group and drag it into the model.

Adding a Section to Another View

You already know how to add a section marker in plan. What you may not know is how to tell Revit that you would rather specify the reference.

The objective of the next procedure is to go to the Level 1 ceiling plan and add a section pointing to our drafting view:

1. In the Project Browser, open the Level 1 ceiling plan.

2. Zoom in on the area of the east wing, as shown in Figure 12.81.

3. On the View tab, click the Section button.

4. Before you place the section, look up at the Options bar. There you will see a button labeled Reference Other View. Click it.

5. In the menu to the right of the Reference Other View label, expand the drop-down and select Drafting View: TYPICAL WALL TERMINATION.

6. Place the section into the model, as shown in Figure 12.81.

7. Press Esc.

8. Double-click on the section marker that you placed in the model. It will open your drafting view.

9. Save the model.

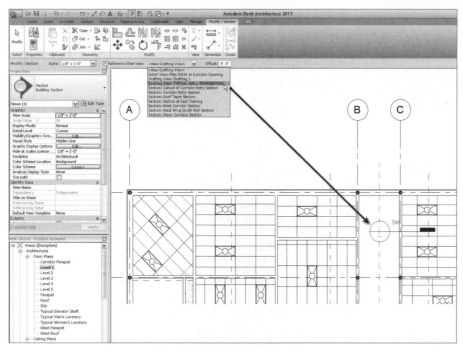

FIGURE 12.81 Choosing the correct options while placing the section

 WARNING Be careful here! In AutoCAD and MicroStation, we got used to doing this type of referencing daily. In Revit, your coworkers may not be accustomed to this inaccurate style. Be deliberate when you add sections referring to other views, and try not to do this too often.

With creating a drafting view behind us, it is time to look at our old friend CAD. (Some may say the new acronym is Ctrl Alt Delete.) Regardless of the existing sentiment toward CAD, it did get us this far. And we still need it—more so in the drafting capacity. Yes, you can import CAD into a detail.

Importing AutoCAD into a Drafting View

I will go out on a limb and venture to guess that you have a handful of CAD details that you use on a daily basis. The question always is, "What do I do with this pile of details I spent years, and thousands of dollars, to create?" Well, you can still use them.

The objective of the next procedure is to create a new drafting view and import an AutoCAD detail. If you would like, you can attempt to import your own detail, or you can use the file provided. Just go to the book's web page at **www.sybex.com/ go/revit2011ner**. From there you can browse to Chapter 12 and find the file called base cabinet.dwg. You can then place it on your system for later retrieval.

The objective of this procedure is to import a CAD detail into a drafting view:

1. In the View tab, click the Drafting View button.

2. In the next dialog, name the new view **TYPICAL BASE CABINET**.

3. Set Scale to 1 1/2" = 1'–0", then click OK.

4. On the Insert tab, click the Import CAD button.

5. Browse to the location where you placed your CAD file.

6. Select the file, but do not click Open yet.

7. At the bottom of the Import dialog, set Colors to Black And White.

8. Set Layers to All.

9. Set Import Units to Auto-Detect.

10. Set Positioning to Auto - Center To Center.

11. Click Open.

12. Type ZA. The detail should now be in full view.

13. Select the detail.

14. On the Modify | Base cabinet.dwg tab, click Explode ➤ Full Explode.

15. Select one of the filled regions.

16. In the Properties dialog, click Edit Type.

17. Change the Fill Pattern to Sand - Dense and select the Drafting radio button.

18. Click OK.

19. Click OK one more time to get back to the model.

20. Make sure your cabinet is hatched properly.

21. Save the model.

Use the Builder Button!

To change the pattern to Sand, make sure you click the [...] button next to the area where it says Solid Fill, as shown in the following graphic. From there, you can choose the hatch pattern.

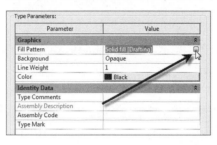

As you may notice, the line weights are all one weight. If you would like to address this matter now, jump to Chapter 23 and go to the section on Import/Export settings.

Up to this point, we have been using detail lines for our drafting. The one issue here is that detail lines are visible only in the specific view you are working in. Suppose you wanted linework to show up both in plan/elevation as well as a 3D view. In this situation you want to use the actual Lines tool.

Adding 2D and 3D Lines to the Model

Just because we are drafting, that does not mean we can't do it in a 3D function. Revit has a tool that is simply called Lines, and you use it to project lines into multiple views. You apply the Lines tool just like a detail line, only it behaves the same as a Revit 3D family in that you can see it in every view (unless you turn it off).

The objective of the next procedure is to add detail lines to the west sloping roof. They are nothing fancy, but you will quickly get the picture on how to use this feature.

1. In the Project Browser, find the West Roof floor plan and open it.

2. On the Home tab, find the Work Plane panel to the right of the Ribbon and click the Set button, as shown in Figure 12.82.

3. In the Work Plane dialog, click the Pick A Plane radio button, as shown in Figure 12.83.

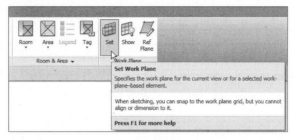

FIGURE 12.82 The Set Work Plane button on the Work Plane panel of the Home tab

FIGURE 12.83 Click the Set button.

4. Click OK.

5. Pick the roof, as shown in Figure 12.84.

6. On the Model panel of the Home tab, click the Model Line button.

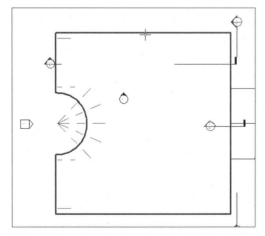

FIGURE 12.84 Picking the roof. Your work plane is now set to slope with the roof. Anything you draw will be on this sloping plane.

7. In the Properties dialog under Line Style, click the Medium Lines line type, as shown in Figure 12.85.

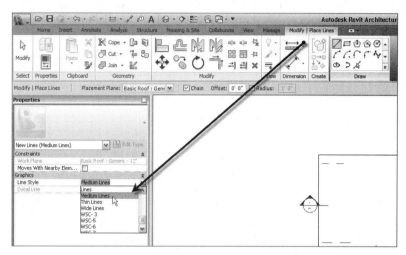

FIGURE 12.85 Click the Medium Lines button under Line Style in the Properties dialog.

8. On the Draw panel, click the Start-End-Radius Arc button, as shown in Figure 12.86.

9. Draw an arc from the two endpoints shown in Figure 12.86. Make the radius 80′–0″.

10. Go to a 3D view. You can still see the arc.

11. Save the model.

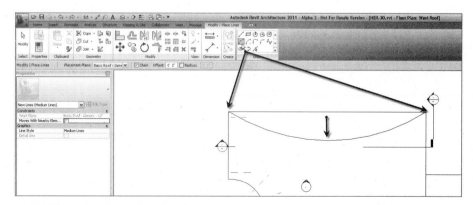

FIGURE 12.86 Drawing an 80′–0″ radius arc

It is a good idea to keep this feature in mind. This drafting tool will become quite useful when it comes to sketching in 3D. There are going to be many situations when you use this little nugget!

Are You Experienced?

Now you can...

- ☑ modify and add line weights to be used in both the 3D and 2D environment

- ☑ add linework in a drafting view as well as a 2D and 3D view

- ☑ create both masking regions and filled regions to provide hatching to a model

- ☑ mask an area so you can draft over it

- ☑ add detail components to the model and create repeating details

- ☑ modify detail families to suit your needs

- ☑ create a group to be used in multiple drafting views and change the group and update each copy in each view

- ☑ create a new Drafting view to draft from scratch and import a CAD file into a drafting view

Creating Specific Views and Match Lines

As you can see, Revit is all about the views. In fact, by using Revit, not only are you replacing the application you use for drafting, but you are also replacing your existing file storage system as well. This is largely because we are now using one model, and we are simply using views of that model for our project navigation.

▶ **Duplicating views**

▶ **Creating dependent views**

▶ **Adding match lines**

▶ **Using view templates**

Duplicating Views

That being said, I wanted to dedicate an entire chapter to project navigation. Although you have steadily gained experience in this area, we can expand on much more to round out your Revit expertise.

The first item we will tackle in this chapter is the process of duplicating a view to create another. Although it is a straightforward procedure, a lot is riding on the hope that you proceed with this function correctly. As you are about to find out, this command is not a simple copy-and-paste operation.

Revit will change how you organize a project. You will no longer open a file and save it as another file so you can make changes without affecting the original. As you know, Revit is all-inclusive in terms of files. Well, there is only one. From that one file, there are views that reside within the Project Browser.

Of course I am not telling you anything you have not learned. If you have gone through the book from page 1, you have already gained experience in creating views (especially in Chapter 3, "Creating Views"). If you are just jumping to this chapter, you most certainly have had some exposure to view creation. The reason this topic is broken into two chapters is to help you gain a more in-depth understanding of how you can manipulate and organize views.

Now let's duplicate some views! To begin, open the file you have been following along with. If you did not complete the previous chapter, go to the book's web page at **www.sybex.com/go/revit2011ner**. From there you can browse to Chapter 13 and find the file called NER-30.rvt.

The objective of the following procedure is to create a furniture plan of Level 1, then turn off the furniture on the original Level 1.

1. In the Project Browser, find the Level 1 floor plan and right-click.

2. Select Duplicate View ➢ Duplicate With Detailing, as shown in Figure 13.1.

3. You now have a view called Copy of Level 1. Right-click on it in the Project Browser.

4. Rename it to **Level 1 Furniture Plan**.

5. Make sure you are still in Level 1. In the Level 1 view window, type **VG**. This will bring up the Visibility/Graphics Overrides window.

6. In the Visibility column, deselect Casework, Furniture, and Furniture Systems.

7. Click OK.

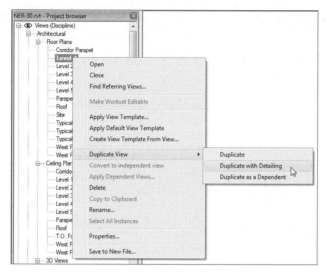

FIGURE 13.1 Right-clicking on the Level 1 Floor Plan in the Project Browser

Now any time you add furniture or casework, it will only show up in the furniture plan. You do not need to deal with a layer or display configuration.

The ability to create a copy of a view and then modify its visibility graphics to display certain items is a critical function within Revit. Another similar task is also available: creating coordinated match line divisions in a model by creating dependent views.

Creating Dependent Views

You create a dependent view in much the same way you duplicate a view. In fact, you are duplicating a view. The function of a dependent view is to "nest" a duplicate of a view within the host view (or the view you are making the duplicate of). This nested view is dependent on the host view in terms of visibility graphics and View Properties. You can have multiple dependent views categorized under the host view. The reason we create dependent views is to add match lines. Yes, you could simply duplicate a view and move its crop region, but when you have dependent views—as you will see in Chapter 14, "Creating Sheets and Printing" —you can tag those views in a specific way for Revit to keep track of the sheets they are on. Dependent views also give the advantage of making your Project Browser much less cluttered, without unnecessary floor plans.

The difference between choosing Duplicate With Detailing and Duplicate is that Duplicate With Detailing will also copy all the tags and annotations you have in the original view. Duplicate will only copy the geometry.

The objective of the next procedure is to make a dependent view of the Level 1 Floor Plan.

1. In the Project Browser, right-click on the Level 1 floor plan.

2. Select Duplicate View ➤ Duplicate As A Dependent. You now have a view that is nested under Level 1. As you can see, Level 1 is now expanded to show its dependencies.

3. Right-click on Level 1 again.

4. Select Duplicate View ➤ Duplicate As A Dependent. You now have two views nested under Level 1 (see Figure 13.2).

5. Right-click on the Dependent (2) on Level 1 dependent view.

6. Rename it to **Level 1 East**.

7. Rename the other dependent view to **Level 1 West** (see Figure 13.2).

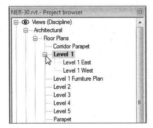

FIGURE 13.2 Creating the two views dependent on Level 1

Now that the views are duplicated and nested within the host view, it is time to divide the Level 1 floor plan. We will do this by adjusting the crop region.

Adjusting the Crop Regions

Every view in Revit has a crop region. Crop regions play an important role when your plan is too large to fit on a sheet. All we need to do at this point is to slide the east and the west crop regions to display the correct views.

The objective of the next procedure is to adjust the crop regions to display the appropriate parts of the plan based on the name of the views.

1. Open the Level 1 West dependent view.

2. Select the crop region, as shown in Figure 13.3.

3. Drag the right side of the crop region to the position shown in Figure 13.3.

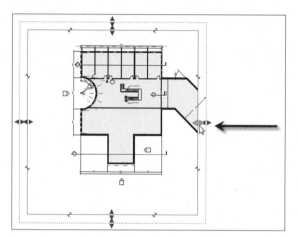

FIGURE 13.3 Dragging the crop region in the Level 1 West view

4. Open the Level 1 East view.

5. Select the crop region.

6. Drag the left side of the region to the right, as shown in Figure 13.4.

STRETCH THAT VIEW

You will notice that there are two stretch grips. One is for the actual crop region, and the other is for the annotation crop region. We will cover what the annotation crop region means in a moment. For now, pick the stretch grip to the inside as shown in this image:

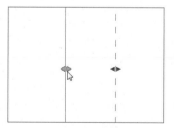

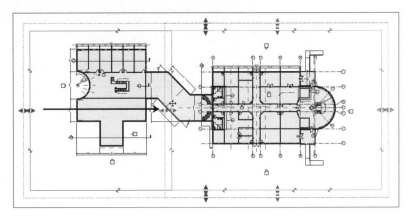

FIGURE 13.4 Dragging the crop region to the right

7. Select the crop region again if it is not selected already and right-click.

8. Choose Go To Primary View to open the Level 1 floor plan.

9. When you are in the Level 1 floor plan, turn on the crop region by clicking the Display Crop Region button on the View Control toolbar, as shown in Figure 13.5.

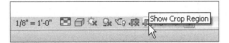

FIGURE 13.5 Turning on the crop region from the View Control toolbar

Now you can see the area where you need to draw the match line. The crop region should overlap in the corridor. If not, drag the crop regions so that they match Figure 13.6.

 N O T E   If you would like to turn a dependent view back to an independent view, you can simply right-click on the dependent view and select **Convert To Independent View**. This will break the link to the host view.

Unfortunately, if you have a match line situation in your project, you must follow this procedure with each floor plan separately. For multifloor projects, this can become time-consuming. Or you can right-click on a view that has dependencies, and select Apply Dependent Views. From there you can select which views the dependent views will be added to.

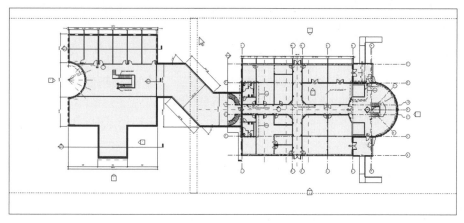

FIGURE 13.6 Adjusting the crop regions to overlap in the corridor

As you can see, adjusting the crop region is how you specify which part of the plan is going to show up on your sheet. This poses one issue. If you have text that you would like to lie outside of the crop region—that is, if you have a leadered note pointing to an item within the cropped boundary—you may not see the note. This is where we can adjust the annotation crop region.

Adjusting the Annotation Crop Region

Since the crop region cuts off the model at a specified perimeter, what is to become of our text that needs to lie outside of this boundary? This is where the annotation crop region comes in handy. You will always have the situation where leadered text must be outside of the geometry it is labeling. We can make adjustments to ensure this can happen.

The objective of the next procedure is to adjust an annotation crop region to clean up a plan.

1. In the Project Browser, find the Level 1 West dependent view and open it.

2. Select the crop region, as shown in Figure 13.7. Notice the two perimeters: one is a solid line type and the other is a dashed line type.

3. In the corridor, there is a dimension that seems to be floating. This is because the crop region allows this dimension to show. With the crop region still selected, pick the outside stretch grip (as shown in Figure 13.8) and stretch the annotation crop region in until the dimension disappears.

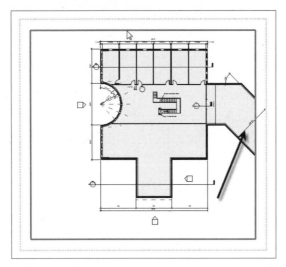

FIGURE 13.7 Selecting the plan's crop region. Notice the additional region on a dashed line type—this is the annotation crop region.

THE SECOND LINE

If you do not see the second line, follow these steps:

1. Type **VP** in the view window.

2. In the Properties dialog, scroll down until you get to the Extents area.

3. Make sure the Annotation Crop option is checked, as shown here:

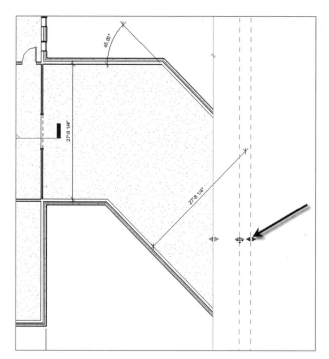

FIGURE 13.8 Stretching the annotation crop region to the left

N O T E   The annotation crop feature is available in any view. This example used a plan, but you can do the same procedure in a section or an elevation as well.

Now that you understand how to add crop regions and display them appropriately, it is time to add the match line.

Adding Match Lines

In CAD, adding a match line is nothing more than the simple practice of drawing a line. In Revit, adding a match line is nothing more than the simple practice of drawing a line—only in Revit, you draw that line in Sketch Mode, and you can propagate that line to other views. Also in Revit, after you place that line it does in fact register as having two sides of a model. In Chapter 14, when we drag our views onto sheets, Revit will know where each side of the model is in terms of being placed on a sheet.

The objective of the next procedure is to place a match line into the model.

   1. Open the Level 1 floor plan.

2. On the Sheet Composition panel of the View tab, click the Match Line button, as shown in Figure 13.9.

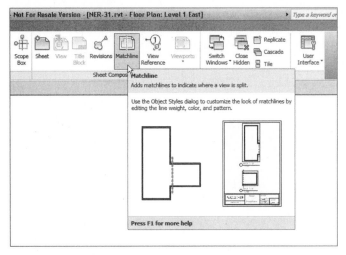

FIGURE 13.9 The Match Line button on the View tab

3. In the Properties dialog, make sure the Top and Bottom Constraints are set to Unlimited.

4. On the Draw panel, click the Line button.

5. Draw the match line as shown in Figure 13.10.

6. Click Finish Edit Mode on the Mode panel.

Your match line will now appear as a bold dashed line. Since the physical appearance of a match line never seems to be the same from firm to firm, we can adjust the appearance of the line.

Match Line Appearance

A match line is not an actual line by definition; it is an object. Therefore, we can control its appearance by using the Object Styles dialog.

The next procedure will focus on changing the appearance of the match line:

1. On the Manage tab, select the Object Styles button toward the left of the Ribbon.

2. Click the Annotation Objects tab, as shown in Figure 13.11.

3. Scroll down until you see Matchline.

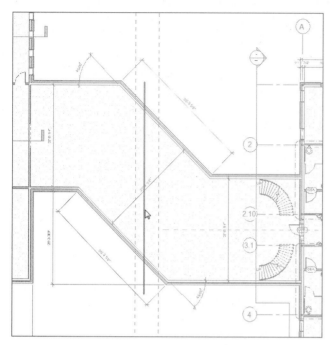

FIGURE 13.10 Placing the match line

4. Click into Line Pattern (the Dash cell).

5. After you click into the cell, you will see a menu arrow. Click it and select Dash Dot 3/8″ (see Figure 13.11).

6. Click OK. Your match line is now a different line type.

Category	Line Weight Projection	Line Color	Line Pattern
Furniture Tags	1	Black	Solid
Generic Annotations	1	Black	Solid
Generic Model Tags	1	Black	Solid
Grid Heads	1	Black	Solid
Keynote Tags	1	Black	Solid
Level Heads	1	Black	Solid
Lighting Fixture Tags	1	Black	Solid
Mass Floor Tags	1	Black	
Mass Tags	1	Black	Solid
Matchline	8	Black	Dash Dot 3/8″
Material Tags	1	Black	Solid
Mechanical Equipment Tags	1	Black	Solid
Multi-Category Tags	1	Black	Solid
Parking Tags	1	Black	Solid
Plan Region	1	RGB 000-127-000	Dash
Planting Tags	1	Black	Solid
Plumbing Fixture Tags	1	Black	Solid
Property Line Segment Tags	1	Black	Solid
Property Tags	1	Black	Solid

FIGURE 13.11 Changing the Matchline line pattern to Dash Dot 3/8″

Now that the match line is in place and the plan is split into two halves, it is time to add an annotation to label the match line.

For the match line annotation, we will simply place a piece of text that says MATCHLINE. But when we are referencing each side of the plan, we will need to add view references.

Adding View References to a Match Line

After the plan is split and the match line is in place, we can tag each side of the match line. When we drag the view onto a drawing sheet, the tag will be filled out with the correct page name. It is important to note, however, that although this process is automatic, it is not fully automatic. You do need to specify the correct view name as you are placing the tag.

The objective of the next procedure is to place a piece of text that says MATCHLINE along the match line, and to add a view reference to each side of the match line.

1. In the Project Browser, open the Level 1 floor plan view.

2. On the Annotate tab, click the Text button, as shown at the top right of Figure 13.12.

N O T E   Unfortunately when you are placing text, you cannot rotate the text until after you have added it. In this procedure, simply place the note, rotate it, and then move it into position.

3. On the Place Text tab, you have leader options. Click the No Leader button (the A), as shown in Figure 13.12.

4. Pick a window near the match line for the text.

5. Type the word **MATCHLINE** and click off the text, as shown in Figure 13.12.

6. Select the text (if it is not selected already).

7. Click the rotate grip and rotate the text 90 degrees.

8. Click the move grip, and drag the text over to the match line so it is positioned as shown in Figure 13.13.

9. On the Sheet Composition panel of the View tab, click the View Reference button.

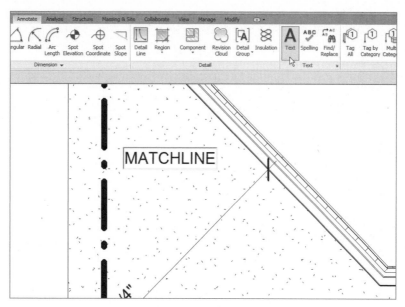

FIGURE 13.12 Typing the text MATCHLINE

10. On the Options bar, you will see a Target View menu. Make sure Floor Plan: Level 1 West is current, as shown in Figure 13.13.

11. Pick a point to the left of the match line (see Figure 13.13).

12. With the view Reference command still running, change the Target View to Floor Plan: Level 1 East.

13. Place a view reference to the right of the match line.

14. Press Esc. You have two view references, and you are now ready to add these views to a drawing sheet for the next chapter.

One last item to discuss before we close this chapter is how to create and use settings from a single view after we determine that we want to repeat the view settings.

Using View Templates

When we created the furniture plan in the beginning of the chapter, we manipulated the data in the Visibility/Graphics Overrides options to hide furniture in a specific plan. It would be nice to build settings like these into a template so we could simply apply that template to a view the next time the situation arose.

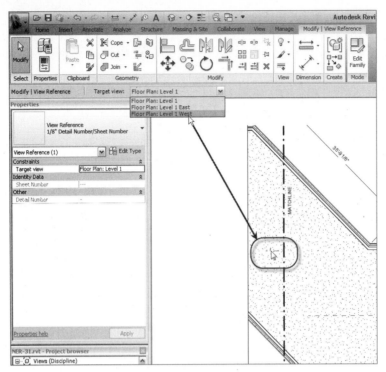

FIGURE 13.13 Adding a view reference includes choosing the correct target view from the Options bar.

The objective of the next procedure is to create a view template and apply it to another view.

1. In the Project Browser, right-click on Level 1 floor plan.

2. Select Create View Template from View.

3. In the Name dialog, call the template **Without Furniture or Casework** then click OK.

4. In the View Templates dialog, Revit allows you to further control the view properties and visibility graphics. Since we don't need to make any further adjustments, click OK.

5. Right-click on Level 2 floor plan.

6. Select Apply View Template.

7. In the View Template dialog, select the Without Furniture Or Casework template, as shown in Figure 13.14.

8. Click OK.

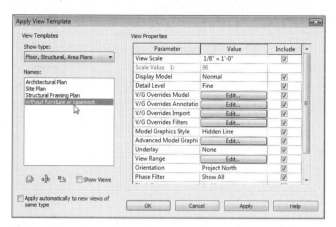

FIGURE 13.14 Selecting the Without Furniture Or Casework template

As you can see, using view templates will help you immensely with maintaining company-wide standards. Use templates as often as possible. For more information on setting up standards, flip to Chapter 23, "BIM Management."

Are You Experienced?

Now you can...

☑ **create duplicates of views, and tell the difference between duplicating with detailing and simply duplicating a view**

☑ **create dependent views, allowing separate views to be nested under one host view**

☑ **add match lines and view reference tags**

☑ **create and use view templates**

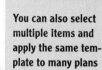

You can also select multiple items and apply the same template to many plans if so desired.

Creating Sheets and Printing

Our deliverable product is a set of construction documents and specifications. So it stands to reason that the application we use to produce these construction documents is at its strongest in this arena. Unfortunately, when you see marketing campaigns related to Revit, all they show are huge skyscrapers and realistic renderings. And of course you see the slide of the architect handing a model to the contractor, and then the contractor handing it to the owner. Don't get me wrong—all that stuff is good, but the most powerful feature of Revit Architecture is its ability to create sheets. You would not think this is the standout feature, but when it is 4:30 in the afternoon and the job is going out the door at 5:00, you will never go back to a drafting application after you have used Revit at the 11th hour.

▶ **Creating and populating sheets**

▶ **Modifying a viewport**

▶ **Adding revisions to a sheet**

▶ **Addressing project parameters**

▶ **Generating a cover sheet**

▶ **Printing from Revit Architecture**

Creating and Populating Sheets

The first part of the chapter will focus on the creation of a sheet, and how to populate it with views. Although you have completed this task back in Chapter 11, "Schedules and Tags," it is time to drill into the ins and outs of sheet creation.

Luckily, when we create and populate sheets, Revit holds true to form—that is, we still don't have to start setting up different drawings or models to simply reference them together. We will create sheets much as we created most other views, because that is all a sheet is: a view. But a sheet goes one step further. Look at a sheet as a view that collects other views for the purpose of printing.

The objective of the following procedure is to create a new sheet. To get started, open the model you have been working on. If you missed the previous chapter, go to the book's web page at **www.sybex.com/go/revit2011ner**. From there you can browse to Chapter 14 and find the file called NER-31.rvt.

1. In the Project Browser, scroll down until you see a category called Sheets, as shown in Figure 14.1.

2. Right-click on Sheets and select New Sheet (see Figure 14.1).

3. In the Select Titleblocks area of the New Sheet dialog box, select the E1 30 × 42 : Horizontal title block. (It is probably the only one available.)

4. Click OK.

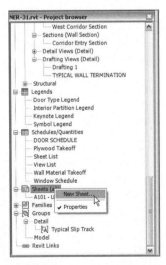

FIGURE 14.1 Selecting a new sheet

N O T E   The title block we are using is a standard Autodesk-supplied title block. Later in the chapter, we will look at how to make custom title blocks. Also, your new sheet may be numbered differently from the example in the book. This is OK; we are going to change the numbering in a moment.

Congratulations! You now have a blank sheet. The next procedure will involve adding views to the sheet by the click-and-drag method.

1. On the View tab, click Guide Grid, as shown in Figure 14.2.

2. In the Guide Grid Name dialog, call the guide **Grid 30x42**, and click OK.

3. Select the guide grid, and drag it into place by using the blue grips, as shown in Figure 14.2.

4. With the guide grid still selected, change Guide Spacing to 3" in the Properties dialog, as shown in Figure 14.2.

 N O T E   Note that you do not have to add a guide grid. The guide grid keeps your plans in the same spot from sheet to sheet, and can be a good idea.

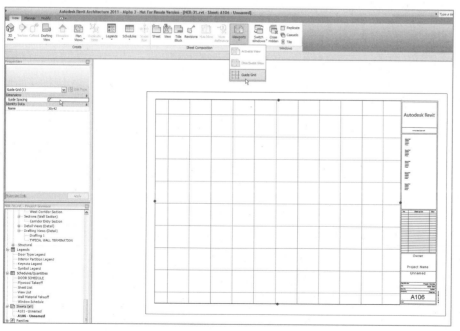

F I G U R E 1 4 . 2 New to Revit 2011, you can add a guide grid to a sheet.

5. In the Project Browser, find the dependent view called Level 1 West, as shown in Figure 14.3.

6. Pick the view, and hold down the pick button.

7. Drag the view onto the sheet, as shown in Figure 14.3.

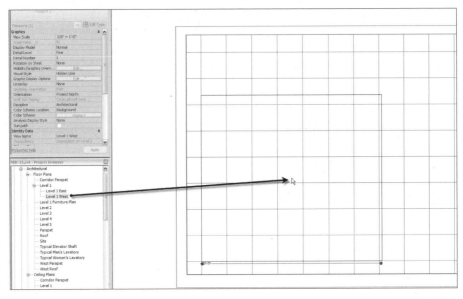

FIGURE 14.3 Dragging the view onto the sheet

8. When the view is centered in the sheet, let go of the pick button. You will now see the view following your cursor. Try to align the lower-left corner of the viewport with a guide grid, and then click. This will place the view onto the sheet.

This is how you populate a sheet using Revit—quite the departure from CAD. One nice detail is that the title is filled out, and the scale will never be incorrect. The next step is to start renumbering sheets so we can create a logical order.

Sheet Organization

If you have been following along with the book, you will already have a sheet numbered A101. It would be nice if we could give this sheet a new number and start our sequence over again. Revit lets you do just that.

The objective of the next procedure is to change the sheet numbering and to add more sheets, allowing Revit to sequentially number the sheets as they are created.

1. In the Project Browser, find the sheet A101 - Unnamed and right-click.

2. Select Rename, as shown in Figure 14.4.

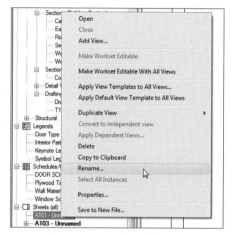

FIGURE 14.4 Renaming the sheet

3. Change the sheet number to **A601**.

4. Change the name to **SCHEDULES AND GENERAL NOTES**.

5. Click OK.

6. Right-click on sheet A103 (if it is not named A103, it is the only other sheet other than A601, the sheet you just created).

7. Select Rename.

8. Change the number to **A101**.

9. Change the name to **WEST WING FIRST FLOOR PLAN**.

10. Click OK.

Your Project Browser should now resemble Figure 14.5.

With the sheets organized, we can now proceed to create more. As we do, we will see that not only do the sheets number themselves, but all of the sections, elevations, and callouts will start reading the appropriate sheet designations.

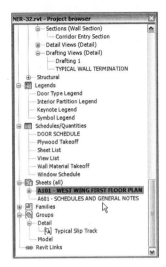

FIGURE 14.5   The reorganized Project Browser

The objective of the next procedure is to create more sheets and to add views to them.

You may also notice a plus sign (+) next to A101. If you expand the tree by clicking on the +, you can see the views that are included on this view. This can prove to be immensely useful because you cannot add a view to another sheet (or the same sheet for that matter) if it is already included in a sheet.

1. Right-click on Sheets (All) in the Project Browser.

2. Select New Sheet.

3. Click OK to add the title block.

4. At the bottom of the Properties dialog, select 30x42 as the guide grid, as shown in Figure 14.6.

5. In the Project Browser, find the dependent view called Level 1 East and drag it onto the new sheet.

6. Pick a point on the sheet to place the view aligned with the guide grid, as shown in Figure 14.6.

7. In the Project Browser, double-click on the A101 sheet, opening the view. Notice that the view reference next to the match line is filled out with the appropriate designation.

8. Double-click on A102 to open the view again.

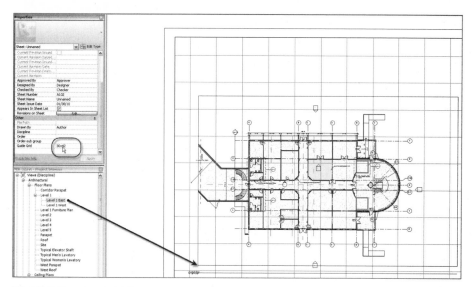

FIGURE 14.6 Adding another sheet

You may notice in the Project Browser that sheet A102 is still unnamed. The next procedure will describe a different way to rename and renumber a sheet.

1. With Sheet A102 opened, zoom into the right side of the view, as shown in Figure 14.7.

2. Select the title block. Notice that a few items turn blue. If you remember, any item that turns blue can be modified.

3. Click into the text that says Project Name and type **NO EXPERIENCE REQUIRED.**

4. Click into the text that says Unnamed and type **EAST WING FIRST FLOOR PLAN** (see Figure 14.7).

5. Create another sheet using the 30x42 Horizontal title block.

6. Number it A201.

7. Name it **ENLARGED PLANS.**

8. Add the 30x42 grid guide.

9. Drag the following views onto the sheet:

▶ Typical Elevator Shaft

▶ Typical Men's Lavatory

▶ Typical Women's Lavatory

10. Arrange them so they are in a row, as shown in Figure 14.8.

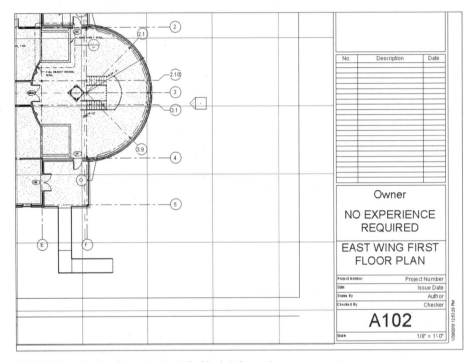

FIGURE 14.7 Changing the title block information

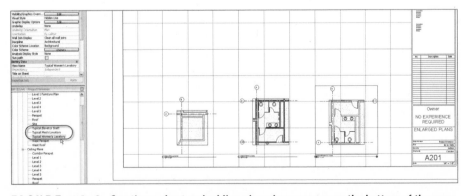

FIGURE 14.8 Creating a sheet and adding views in a row across the bottom of the page

N O T E   Also notice that the title block is filled out. The page number and the sheet name are filled out because we edited these names when we made the sheet, but the project name will appear on every new sheet that we create.

Now that the first floor plans and typical enlarged plans are placed on a sheet, it is time to move on to adding the details that we created.

If you feel as though you have enough experience creating a sheet and adding views, go ahead and proceed on your own. Your new sheet will be numbered A301 and called Building Sections, and you will add the views East Corridor Section, West Corridor Section, Section at West Training, and West Wing South Wall Section. Your sheet should look like the figure at the end of the procedure.

If you would like some assistance in putting the section sheet together, follow along with this procedure:

1. In the Project Browser, right-click on the Sheets category.

2. Select New Sheet.

3. Select the E1 30×42 Horizontal title block, and click OK.

4. In the Project Browser, right-click on the new sheet and select Rename.

5. Give the new sheet a number of **A301** and a name of **BUILDING SECTIONS**.

6. In the Properties dialog, add the 30x42 grid guide.

7. In the Project Browser, find the Sections (Building Sections) category.

8. Drag the section called East Corridor Section onto the lower-left corner of the sheet.

9. Drag the section called Section at East Training onto the sheet to the right of the East Corridor Section.

10. Drag the section called West Corridor Section onto the sheet and place it into the upper-left corner. Be sure you align it directly above the East Corridor Section.

11. Drag the section called East Wing South Wall Section to the right of the West Corridor Section and directly above the Section of West Training. Notice the alignment lines will allow you to accurately place the section. After you have these four sections in place, your sheet A301 should look like Figure 14.9.

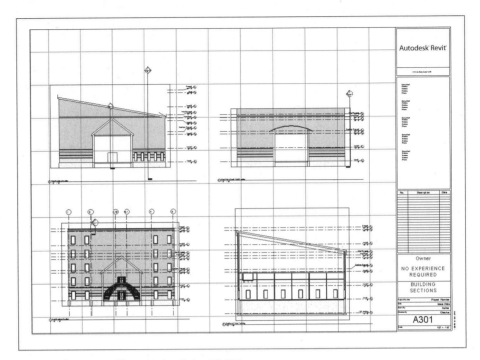

FIGURE 14.9 The completed sheet A301

Now that we have created a few sheets, you may want to make some adjustments to the view without leaving the sheet. The next section of this chapter will focus on the properties of a viewport and how to make it *live* on the sheet so we can make modifications.

Modifying a Viewport

Wait a second. Isn't a viewport AutoCAD vernacular? Yes, it is. But a viewport in AutoCAD and a viewport in Revit are two different things altogether.

In Revit, when you drag a view onto a sheet, a linked copy of that view becomes a viewport. This is what you see on the sheet. Any modification you make to the original view will immediately be reflected in the viewport, and vice versa. See Figure 14.10 for a graphical representation.

The objective of the next procedure is to activate a viewport to make modifications on the sheet, and also to explore the Element Properties of the viewport.

1. Open the sheet A301 (if it is not open already).

2. Zoom in on the viewport West Wing South Wall Section, as shown in Figure 14.11.

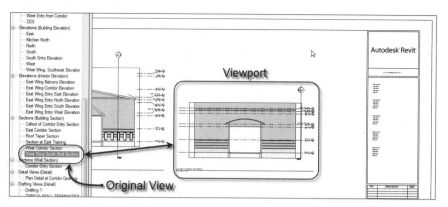

FIGURE 14.10 The relationship between the original view and the viewport

3. Select the view.

4. Right-click and select Activate View, as shown in Figure 14.11.

5. With the view activated, you can work on it just as if you had opened it from the Project Browser. Select the crop region, as shown in Figure 14.12.

6. Stretch the top of the crop region up so you can see the entire view.

7. Stretch the bottom of the crop region down to expose the bottom of the section.

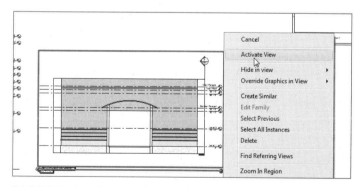

FIGURE 14.11 Activating a view

 NOTE   By activating the view in this manner, you are essentially opening that view. The only difference between physically opening the view in the Project Browser and activating the view on the sheet is that by activating the view, you can now see the title block, which will help in terms of layout.

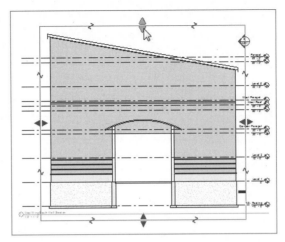

FIGURE 14.12 Stretching the crop region so you can see the entire view

8. In the View Control toolbar, select Hide Crop Region.

UNSIGHTLY CROP REGIONS BE GONE!

By selecting Hide Crop Region, as shown in this image, you are simply cleaning up the view. As we will explore in this chapter, you can keep the crop region on and tell Revit not to print it.

9. Right-click and select Deactivate View.

10. Right-click on the view to the left of the West Wing South Wall Section (it is the view called West Corridor Section), and select Activate View.

11. Stretch the crop region down so you can see the entire foundation.

12. Hide the crop region.

13. Right-click and deactivate the view.

With the view widened, it is coming close to the actual title. You can move the viewport or the title independently of one another. The objective of the following procedure will involve moving the viewport up, then moving the view title down to provide some more room.

1. Select the West Wing South Wall Section viewport.

2. Hold down the pick button, and move the entire viewport up. As you move the viewport up, an alignment line will appear. This means that the views are physically aligned. When you see the alignment line, release the pick button.

3. Press Esc.

4. Select the view title, as shown in Figure 14.13.

5. Move it down. As you move the view title, it will snap in alignment to the view title to the left, as shown if Figure 14.13.

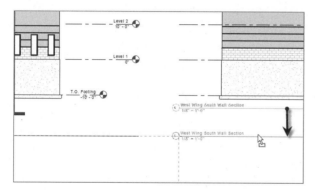

FIGURE 14.13 You can select the view title independently of the actual viewport.

 N O T E   You can also customize the view titles. This procedure, however, falls under the category of BIM management. Chapter 23, "BIM Management," has a section dedicated to creating a view title.

Now that we have some experience creating sheets and making adjustments to the views and viewports, we can easily create one more sheet that contains sections.

The following procedure will focus on creating a detail sheet. If you feel as though you can create this sheet on your own, go ahead. The sheet will be sheet number A401, it will be named DETAILS, and the views to be added are

Corridor Entry Section, Callout of Corridor Entry Section, Roof Taper Section, and TYPICAL WALL TERMINATION. Your finished sheet should look like the figure at the end of the procedure.

If you would rather have some assistance, follow along with this procedure:

1. In the Sheets category in the Project Browser, right-click on the Sheets title.

2. Select New Sheet.

3. Number it A401 and name it **DETAILS**.

4. In the Project Browser, drag the Sections (Wall Section) called Corridor Entry Section and place it in the sheet all the way to the right.

5. In the Project Browser, drag the Sections (Building Section) called Callout of Corridor Entry Section onto the sheet to the top left of the previous section (see Figure 14.14).

6. Drag the section called Roof Taper Section to the bottom left of the first view you added.

7. Drag the view called TYPICAL WALL TERMINATION to the sheet directly to the left of Callout of Corridor Entry Section (see Figure 14.14).

8. Zoom in on the view title for the Corridor Entry Section, as shown in Figure 14.15.

9. Select the Corridor Entry Section viewport. Notice there are blue grips on the view title.

10. Extend the line by stretching the grip on the right to the right, as shown in Figure 14.15.

11. Save the model.

Pan and zoom around to investigate all of the reference markers. They are starting to fill themselves out based on the sheets where you placed the referring views.

N O T E   You can place only one instance of a view on a sheet. You also cannot place a view on multiple sheets. This is Revit's way of keeping track of what view is on a page and which page that view is on. The only type of view that you can place on more than one sheet is a Legend view. If you would like to place a view on a sheet more than once, you will need to duplicate the view in the Project Browser.

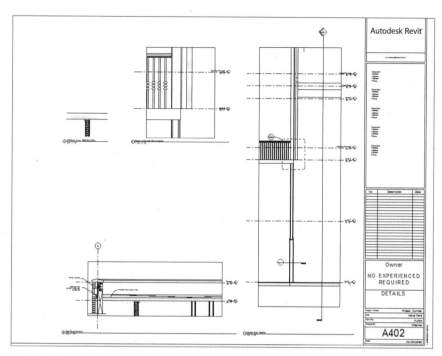

FIGURE 14.14 Building the A401 DETAILS sheet

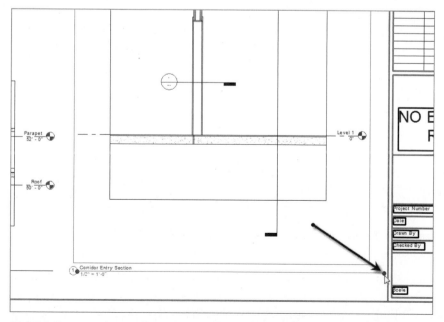

FIGURE 14.15 Stretching the view title line to the right via the blue grip

Now that we know how to manipulate a viewport, it is time to take a look at the viewport's properties. I think you will be glad to see how familiar these properties are.

Viewport Properties

Just like anything else in Revit, viewports have associated properties. You just select the viewport and click the Properties button on the Ribbon if the Properties dialog isn't already open.

The objective of the following procedure is to look through the viewport's properties and to make some minor modifications.

1. Open the view A401 - DETAILS (if it is not already).

2. Select the Corridor Entry Section view (the tall section to the right of the sheet).

 N O T E   Notice that the properties for the viewport are exactly the same as those for a typical view. When you change the properties of a viewport, you are actually changing the properties of the corresponding view.

3. In the Properties dialog, scroll down the list until you arrive at the Title On Sheet, as shown in Figure 14.16.

4. Change the Title On Sheet to **SECTION AT ENTRY CORRIDOR**.

5. Click Edit Type.

6. In the Type Parameters, you can choose which view title you will be using, or if you want any view title at all. We will address creating custom view titles in Chapter 23, so for now just click OK.

7. Zoom in on the detail and notice that the name has changed.

Now that we have pretty much exhausted creating and manipulating sheets, it is time to explore another sheet function: adding revisions.

Adding Revisions to a Sheet

An unfortunate reality in producing construction documents is that you must eventually make revisions. In CAD, you normally create a duplicate of the file, save that file into your project directory, and then create the revisions. The only way to keep track of them is to add a revision cloud and change the attribute

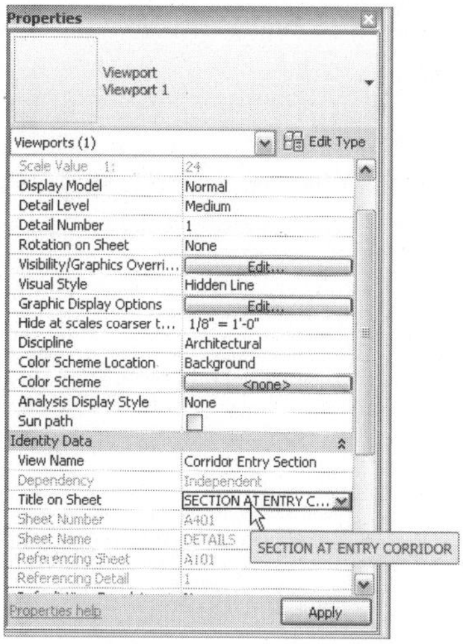

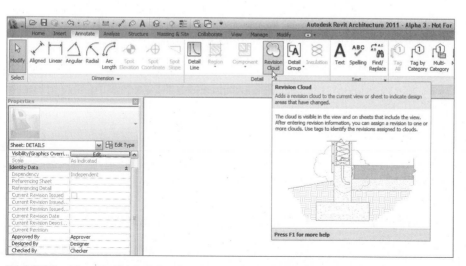

FIGURE 14.16 You can make the title on the sheet different from the view name.

Notice that when you select the viewport, the name and detail number turn blue. This means that you can change the values right on the sheet.

information in the title block. In Revit, however, you are given a revision schedule and the means to keep track of your revisions.

The objective of the next procedure is to add a revision cloud and to populate a schedule that is already built into the sheet.

1. In the Project Browser, open Sheet A101.

2. On the Annotate tab, click the Revision Cloud button, as shown in Figure 14.17. Notice you are now in Sketch Mode.

FIGURE 14.17 The Revision Cloud button on the Annotate tab

3. Place a revision cloud around the plan, as shown in Figure 14.18.

 T I P   **To get the revision cloud drawn accurately, you must work in a clockwise manner. Unfortunately, if you err in getting the cloud on the sheet, you should probably undo and start over.**

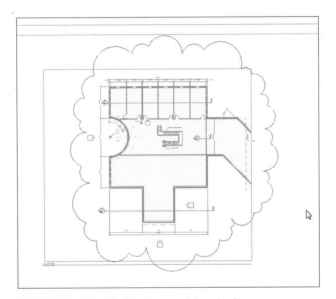

FIGURE 14.18 Placing a revision cloud

4. On the Modify | Create Revision Cloud Sketch tab, click Finish Edit Mode.

5. On the Annotate tab, click Tag By Category, as shown in Figure 14.19.

6. Pick the revision cloud.

7. You will probably get a dialog stating that you do not have a tag loaded for this category. If you see this dialog, click Yes to load one.

8. Select Annotations ➢ Revision Tag.rfa.

9. Pick the revision cloud. You now have a tagged revision cloud, as shown in Figure 14.19.

Zoom closer to the title block. You will also notice that the revision schedule has the first revision added to it. Revit is now keeping track of your revisions.

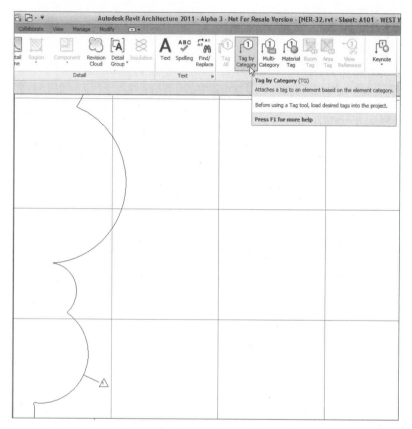

FIGURE 14.19 The revision tag has been added to the cloud. Also, notice the title block has Revision 1 added to it.

The next procedure will focus on making modifications to the revision scheme so we can better keep track of the revision schedule.

1. On the View tab, click the Revisions button on the Sheet Composition panel, as shown in Figure 14.20.

2. In the Sheet Issues/Revisions dialog, change the date to today's date.

3. For the description, type **First Floor Revisions**.

4. Click the Add button, as shown in Figure 14.20.

5. Give the new revision a date in the future.

6. For the description, enter **Revised Sections** (see Figure 14.20).

7. For the Numbering, click the Per Project radio button.

8. Click OK.

9. In the Project Browser, open the sheet A301 - BUILDING SECTIONS.

10. On the Annotate tab, click the Revision Cloud button.

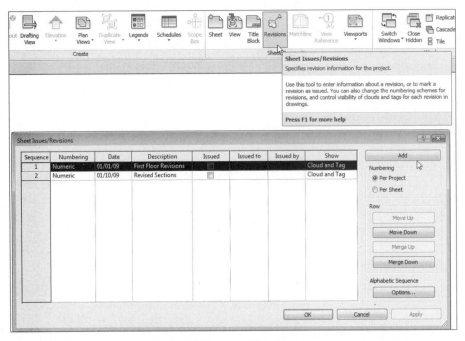

FIGURE 14.20 The Sheet Issues/Revisions dialog

11. Place a cloud around the upper-right detail.

12. On the Mode panel, click Finish Edit Mode.

13. Select the cloud you just added.

14. On the Options bar, make sure you have Seq. 2 - Revised Sections selected, as shown in Figure 14.21.

15. On the Annotate tab, select Tag By Category.

16. Place the revision tag on the cloud. You may also notice that the schedule in the title block is filled with only the appropriate revision relevant to this sheet.

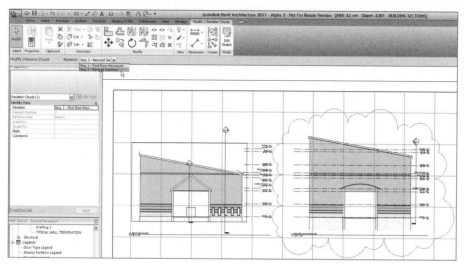

FIGURE 14.21 By selecting the revision cloud, you can specify the sequence from the Options bar.

Now that we have experience with the concept of how sheets and revisions come together, we need to explore one more avenue with populating sheet information. You may have noticed that the title blocks are not yet complete. The empty fields relate to project information that needs to be included on each sheet. This is where project parameters come in.

Addressing Project Parameters

Since Revit is built upon a database, it makes sense that items like Project Name and Project Number will be added to the design in a different manner than that in CAD. In CAD, you fill out attributes sheet by sheet, or you simply externally reference a title block with the sheet information. In Revit, you fill out the project information in one place. The information you add to the database propagates down to the sheets. When, or if, this information changes, it is done quickly and accurately.

The objective of the next procedure is to locate the project parameters and populate the model with the job information.

1. On the Manage tab, click Project Information, as shown in Figure 14.22.

2. Click the Edit button next to Energy Settings, as shown to the right in Figure 14.22. The resulting dialog allows you to add the project's geographical information as well as energy data. This will allow you to export the information to GBXML as well as provide information so your architectural model can be imported into Revit MEP.

SAVE THAT MODEL!

You may have noticed that a save reminder keeps popping up (see the following graphic). Revit likes to ask you if you want to save the model *before* you execute a command. This process has greatly reduced the amount of crashes as compared to AutoCAD.

3. Click OK.

4. You can fill out the rest of the information as follows (see Figure 14.22):

   ▶ Project Issue Date: 1/30/10

   ▶ Project Status: 100%

   ▶ Project Name: NO EXPERIENCE REQUIRED

   ▶ Project Number: 20090342

N O T E   Notice the NO EXPERIENCE REQUIRED text has already been entered. This is because you added it to the appropriate field in the title block. Remember, when you are dealing with Revit, and databases in general, it is a two-way flow of information.

5. Click OK.

6. Open any sheet and examine the title block. All of the information should be filled out.

Now that we can populate the information in a sheet, there is one more item to cover quickly before we jump into printing: adding a drawing list.

FIGURE 14.22 Filling out the project data

Generating a Cover Sheet

It goes without saying that this ingenious method of creating and managing sheets would not be quite perfect unless you could generate a sheet list and put it on a cover sheet. Well, this is Revit. Of course you can! The best part is you already have the experience necessary to carry out this procedure.

The objective of the next procedure is to create a sheet list and add it to a cover sheet.

1. On the View tab, click Schedules ➢ Sheet List, as shown in Figure 14.23.

2. In the Sheet List Properties dialog, add Sheet Number and Sheet Name, as shown in Figure 14.24.

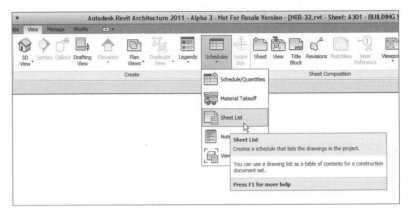

FIGURE 14.23 The Sheet List button on the View tab

3. Click the Sorting/Grouping tab.

4. Sort by Sheet Number.

5. Select Ascending.

6. Click OK.

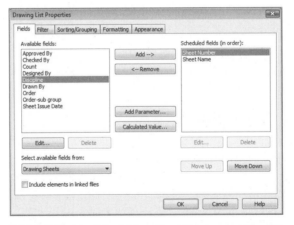

FIGURE 14.24 Adding Sheet Number and Sheet Name (in that order)

Wow! Creating a schedule is so easy, you will probably be doing this on your lunch break instead of playing Internet games! While you are still in the schedule, you can add a new row. This row will constitute a filler sheet that we can add to the Project Browser at a later date. To add a filler sheet, follow along.

1. Make sure you are in the Sheet List schedule.

2. On the Rows panel, click the New button, as shown in Figure 14.25.

3. Call the new row **COVER SHEET A001**, as shown in Figure 14.25.

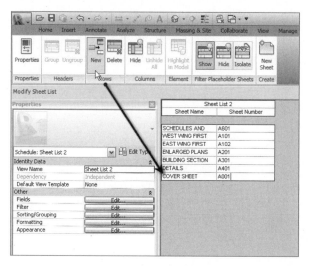

FIGURE 14.25 New to Revit 2011, you can add a placeholder row.

For now, let's keep this schedule in the Project Browser and create a cover sheet that we can drag it onto. The objective of the next procedure is to create a new title block family, add it to the project, and then drag the drawing list onto the cover.

1. Click the Application button and choose New ➤ Title Block, as shown in Figure 14.26.

2. Select E1 - 42 x 30.rft.

3. Click Open.

4. On the Text panel of the Home tab, click Label, as shown in Figure 14.27.

5. In the Properties dialog, click Edit Type.

6. Click Duplicate.

7. Call the new tag **TITLE** and click OK.

8. Make sure the Text Font is Arial.

9. Change Text Size to 1".

10. Click Bold.

11. Click OK.

12. On the Format panel, click the Center Middle button.

13. Pick a point in the upper center of the sheet.

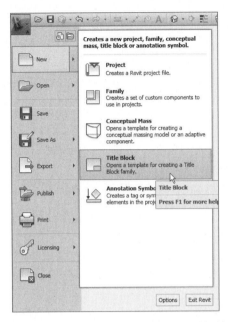

FIGURE 14.26 Creating a new title block

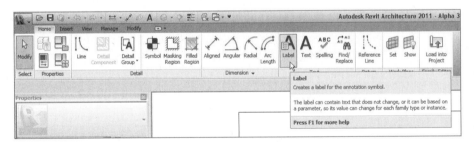

FIGURE 14.27 Selecting Label from the Create tab

After you place the tag, you will immediately see the Edit Label dialog. This dialog will allow you to add the label you wish. When you load this cover sheet into the project and add it to a new sheet, the project information will become populated automatically.

The objective of the next procedure is to add the correct tags to the sheet.

1. Select Project Name, and click the Add Parameter(s) to Label button, as shown in Figure 14.28.

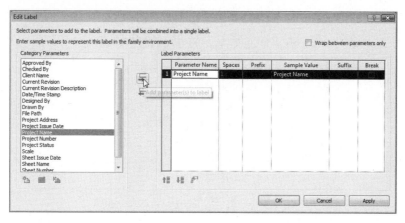

FIGURE 14.28 Adding the project name to the label

2. Click OK.

3. Click the label and widen the grips. You may have to adjust the label so it is centered in the sheet, as shown in Figure 14.29.

4. Click the Application button and then click Save As ➢ Family.

5. Save the file somewhere that makes sense to you. Call it **Title Sheet**.

6. Click Load Into Project.

If you have more than one project opened, you will see a dialog allowing you to choose which project to load the sheet into. If this is the case, choose the No Experience Required project you are working on.

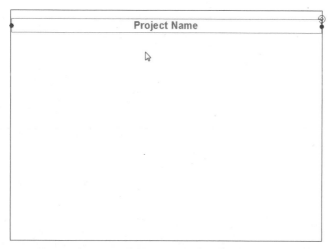

FIGURE 14.29 Adjusting the label so it is centered in the sheet

7. In the Project Browser, right-click on Sheets and select New Sheet.

8. In the New Sheet dialog, select Title Sheet.

9. Also in the New Sheet dialog, you will see that placeholder sheet you added to the schedule. Select it, as shown in Figure 14.30.

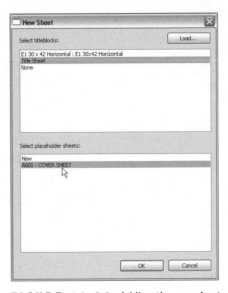

FIGURE 14.30 Adding the new sheet

10. Click OK. You will see your tag is now populated with the project information.

11. In the Project Browser, find the Sheet List (it is in the Schedules/Quantities category) and drag it onto the sheet.

12. Select the schedule and adjust it so the text is readable. Your title sheet, although not very glorious, should look like Figure 14.31.

FIGURE 14.31 The completed title sheet

In most cases, we don't want the actual cover sheet to be an item in the schedule. We can fix this. While still in the cover sheet, uncheck Appears In Sheet List in the Properties dialog, as shown in Figure 14.32.

FIGURE 14.32 Deselect the Appears In Sheet List option.

Perfect! We have a handful of sheets. The beauty is that you do not have to leave the model to see how these sheets are shaping up. In Revit, they are always just a click away!

Since we have these sheets, it is time to explore how we send them to the plotter. After all, it is paper construction documents that we are producing.

Printing from Revit Architecture

Luckily, printing is one of the easiest things you will be confronted with in Revit. There are, however, some dangerous defaults that you must consider when printing. I can go out on a limb and say that printing from Revit is too easy in some cases.

The objective of the next procedure is to print a set of drawings. Pay special attention to the warnings, though—they will steer you clear of danger.

1. Click the Application button and select Print.

2. For the printer name, select the printer you wish to print to.

3. If printing to a file, you can choose to combine all files into one or create separate files. Choose to combine into one file. If you are not printing to a file, ignore this choice.

4. For Print Range, you can print the current window or the visible portion of the current window, or you can choose Selected Views/Sheets. Choose Selected Views/Sheets.

 T I P When you choose to print the current window, you are printing the current view. When you choose to print the visible portion of the current window, you are printing the area that you are currently zoomed into. In Revit, you do not pick a window like you do in CAD.

5. Click the Select button, as shown at the bottom left in Figure 14.33.

6. At the bottom of the View/Sheet Set dialog, uncheck Views.

7. Now only the sheets are listed. Click on all of the sheets.

8. Click OK.

9. Revit will ask you if you want to save the settings for a future print. Click No.

10. In the lower-right corner, you will see a Settings area. Click the Setup button, as shown in Figure 14.34.

FIGURE 14.33 Choosing the options to print the drawings

T I P   Printing from Revit is similar to an AutoCAD paper space model space environment where you can simply print a specific view or print an entire sheet. The only difference is you are not bothered by scale. The sheets and views are printed at the scale specified in Revit.

F I G U R E   1 4 . 3 4   Clicking the Setup button

W A R N I N G   Make a habit of selecting the Setup button before you print. There are some crucial settings in the resulting dialog that need to be verified.

11. For Paper, choose the correct paper size you wish to print to.

12. For Paper Placement, choose Center.

13. For Zoom, select Zoom: 100% Of Size.

W A R N I N G   The Fit To Page radio button should never be selected unless you know that you are not plotting to scale. If you would like a reduced set of drawings, you can specify Zoom and then move to a smaller percentage (50% is a half size set).

14. For the options, check Hide Ref/Work Planes.

15. Check Hide Unreferenced View Tags.

16. Hide Scope Boxes.

17. Hide Crop Boundaries.

18. Click OK.

19. Click OK again, and your plot is off.

20. Save the file.

Well, there you have it. The book does not create a sheet for every single view. If you feel like your experience is still lacking regarding creating sheets and printing, go ahead and create more sheets, and keep printing away until you feel confident to move on to Chapter 15, "Creating Rooms and Area Plans."

Are You Experienced?

Now you can...

☑ **create sheets by simply dragging views and creating viewports**

☑ **configure project parameters to populate the sheets**

☑ **create a drawing list for a cover sheet**

Creating Rooms and Area Plans

This chapter brings us to a great point in Revit. We are in a position now where we can start to build on what we have added to our model up to this point. By creating rooms and areas, we are starting to merge the model with the database. In Chapter 11, "Schedules and Tags," we did the same thing, but by adding rooms and areas we are physically building our construction documents, while at the same time adding crucial information to the model's database.

▶ **Creating rooms**

▶ **Adding a room schedule**

▶ **Adding a color fill plan**

▶ **Adding room separators**

▶ **Creating an area plan**

Creating Rooms

The first topic we will tackle is the task of creating a room and adding it to the model. The procedures that follow will focus on finding where to launch the room and areas, and the parameters Revit looks for while placing a room into the floor plan.

Because Revit draws from a database to gather information, the process of creating a room boils down to you adding some notes to an already built form. When you place the room in the model, Revit will automatically tag it. Unlike other drafting applications, however, Revit does not rely on the tag for its information. Once a room is in the model, it can either contain or not contain a tag. This is a great way to organize the flow of room information.

To get started, open the model you have been working on. If you missed the previous chapter, go to the book's web page at **www.sybex.com/go/revit2011ner**. From there you can browse to Chapter 15 and find the file called NER-32.rvt.

The objective of the following procedure is to find the Room & Area panel on the Home tab, and to configure and add some rooms to the model.

1. In the Project Browser, find the dependent view called Level 1 East, and open it.

2. In the Room & Area panel on the Home tab, click the Room button, as shown in Figure 15.1.

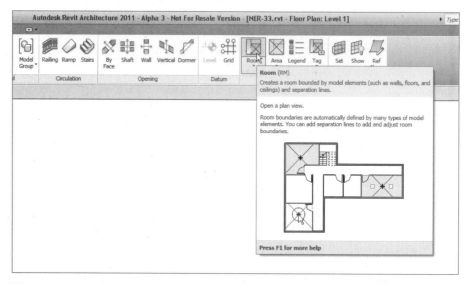

FIGURE 15.1 Clicking the Room button on the Room & Area panel of the Home tab

3. Hover your cursor over the southeast room, as shown in Figure 15.2. Notice that there is an X and the outline of a room tag.

4. When you see the X show up, pick a spot in the middle of the four walls.

5. Press Esc.

If you do not have the Room & Area tab shown, right-click on any tab in the Ribbon. You will see a list of tabs that are not currently displayed. Find Room & Area, and select it. You will now have the proper tab displayed on the Ribbon.

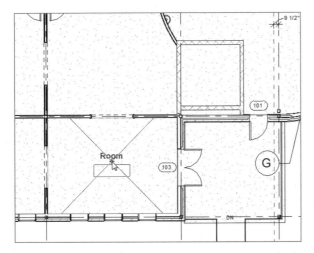

FIGURE 15.2 When you hover your mouse over the intended area of the room, you will see an indication that Revit has found the bounding edges.

You now have a room added to the model. Of course, it is a nondescript room name with a nondescript room number. The following procedure will correct that. The objective here is to change the room name and number on the screen.

1. Select the room tag that you just added to the model.

N O T E   You may be sick of hearing this by now, but I'll say it again: when you select a component in Revit, the items that turn blue are always editable.

2. Click the Room text.

3. Change the name to **SOUTHEAST CORNER OFFICE**.

4. Click on room number 1.

5. Change the number to **101** (see Figure 15.3).

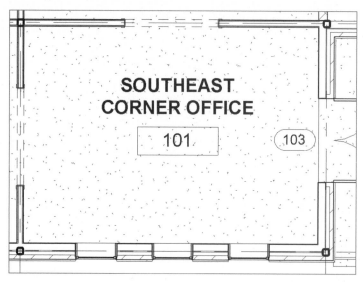

FIGURE 15.3 Changing the room name and number to SOUTHEAST CORNER OFFICE, 101

Now that we have a room in place and it is named properly, we can start cooking in terms of adding additional rooms. This is because Revit will begin to sequentially number the rooms as they are placed into the model.

The objective of the next procedure is to populate the rest of the east wing with rooms.

> When you modify the fields within a tag in Revit, the best method to finalize the data is to simply click on an area away from the tag itself. This will ensure that you do not inadvertently create an additional line in the tag's value.

1. On the Room & Area panel of the Home tab, click the Room button.

T I P   If you get the save reminder, be sure to save the model. In no situation is this ever going to be a bad idea!

2. Place a room in the adjacent area, as shown at the bottom center of Figure 15.4.

3. Call the room **SOUTHEAST CONFERENCE** (see Figure 15.4).

N O T E   Did you notice that the room tag was trying to align itself with the adjacent tag? This is a fantastic feature in Revit Architecture!

4. On the Room & Area panel of the Home tab, click the Room button again.

5. Place a room in the radial entry area.

6. Rename the room to **EAST ENTRY**.

7. Renumber the room to **001**.

8. Place a room in the south elevator shaft.

9. Rename and renumber it to **SOUTHEAST ELEVATOR** and **010**.

10. Place a room in the north elevator shaft.

11. Rename and renumber it to **NORTHEAST ELEVATOR** and **011**.

12. Place a room in the corridor.

13. Call it **EAST WING CORRIDOR** and number it **100**.

14. Just north of the SOUTHEAST CONFERENCE and SOUTHEAST CORNER OFFICE, place two rooms, each called **GATHERING**. Number them **103** and **104** (see Figure 15.4).

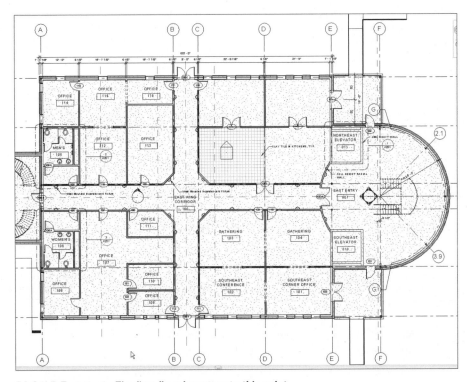

FIGURE 15.4 The first floor layout up to this point

15. Zoom over to the west portion of the east wing where the lavatories are.

16. In the north lavatory, add a room named **MEN'S 105** as shown in Figure 15.5.

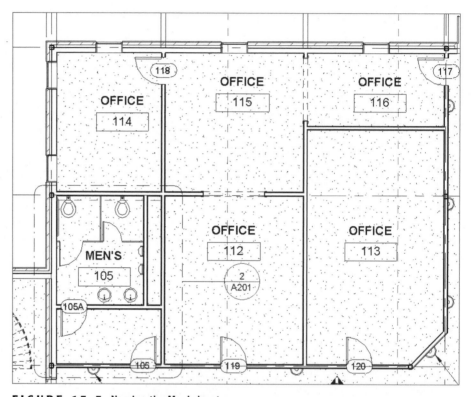

FIGURE 15.5 Naming the Men's lavatory

17. In the south lavatory, add a room named **WOMEN'S 106** as shown in Figure 15.6.

I think you are getting the concept of adding rooms! Although we have a good amount of rooms added to the east wing, we need to start adding some plain old offices. The next procedure will involve adding offices to the rest of the spaces in the east wing of Level 1. From there we can look at a room's properties and figure out how to alter the room information.

1. Make sure you are in the east wing area of the model, on Level 1.

2. On the Room & Area panel of the Home tab, click the Room button.

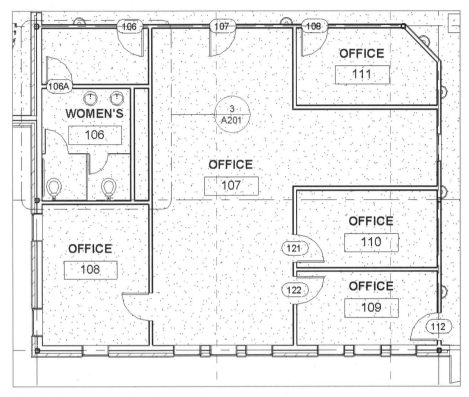

FIGURE 15.6 Naming the Women's lavatory

3. Pick the large area to the right of the women's lavatory, as shown in Figure 15.7.

4. Rename the room to **OFFICE**. Change the number to **107**, as shown in Figure 15.6.

N O T E   **If the numbering starts to become inconsistent with the examples in the book, that is okay. This will happen from time to time in Revit. You can either accept the differences between the book and your model, or you can simply renumber the rooms to match. Either way, this will not affect the outcome of the procedures.**

5. On the Room & Area panel of the Home tab, click the Room button.

6. Add rooms to the rest of the vacant areas. (Skip the Kitchen area and the room to the right of it, as shown in Figure 15.8).

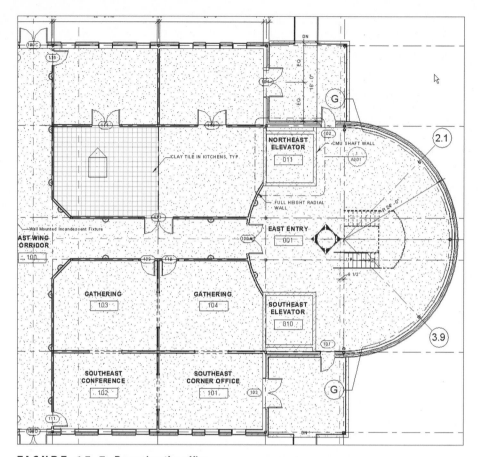

FIGURE 15.7 Renaming the office

Now that all of the rooms are in (at least in this section of the building), we can start examining the specific properties to see how we can add functionality and further populate the database information pertaining to each room.

Configuring Properties

Each room will have specific properties associated with it. There will be floor finishes and wall finishes as well as ceiling types and finishes. It would be nice if Revit picked up this information by "reading" the ceilings, walls, and floors, but it does not. And for good reason. Imagine having to create a different wall type for each paint color, and then splitting each partition as it passes through each room. In Revit, you will specify these individual room finishes in the properties of the room itself.

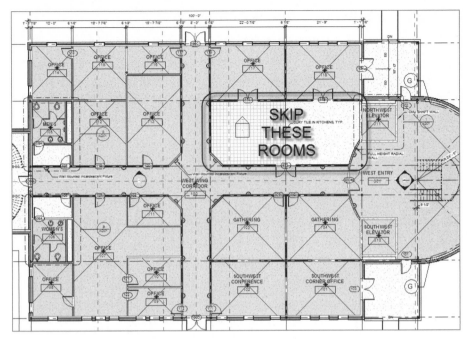

FIGURE 15.8 Adding rooms to the remainder of the spaces

The objective of the next procedure is to generate additional room information in the properties of the room.

1. Zoom in on the SOUTHEAST CORNER OFFICE 101 room.

2. Hover your cursor over the room until you see the X show up, as you can see in Figure 15.9.

 TIP Any time you wish to view the properties of a room, you need to click on the actual room, not the room tag. Sometimes selecting the room can be difficult because the room itself is invisible until you hover over it. With some practice, this process will soon become second nature.

3. When you see the X, pick the room.

4. In the Properties dialog, scroll down to the Identity Data group, as shown in Figure 15.10.

5. Add WD-1 to Base Finish.

6. Add ACT to Ceiling Finish.

7. Add PT to Wall Finish.

8. Add VCT to Floor Finish (see Figure 15.10).

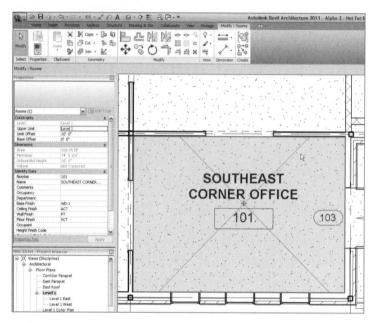

FIGURE 15.9 Hover the cursor over the room until the X appears.

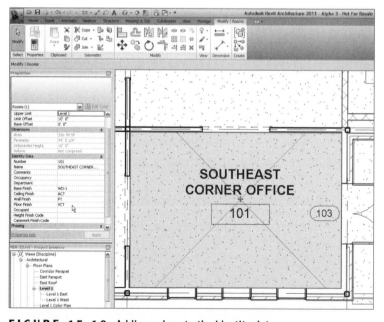

FIGURE 15.10 Adding values to the identity data

9. Select the SOUTHEAST CONFERENCE room.

10. In the Properties dialog, click into the Base Finish field. Notice there is a pull-down menu. Click the arrow and select WD-1, as shown in Figure 15.11.

11. Change the rest of the fields using the previous entries.

12. Save the model.

FIGURE 15.11 Once a field has been added to the database, it is available for the rest of the rooms.

Changing a room's properties is a simple task. There is, however, one more item to discuss. This pertains to a room that spans multiple floors such as the east entry.

The objective of the next procedure is to change the height of the east entry room's properties.

1. Zoom in on the east entry area and select the room, as shown in Figure 15.12.

2. In the Properties dialog, change Upper Limit to Roof.

3. Change Limit Offset to 0. This will set the east entry room to extend from Level 1 to the roof.

Now that we have experience changing the properties of the rooms, it is time to take a look at the properties of the actual walls that divide the rooms. Certainly you noticed that when you placed the rooms in the lavatories, the

If you are having trouble selecting the room, remember, you can pick an entire window around the area and use the Filter button on the Filter panel.

room did not fill the small entry areas. We can correct this by changing the wall's room bounding properties.

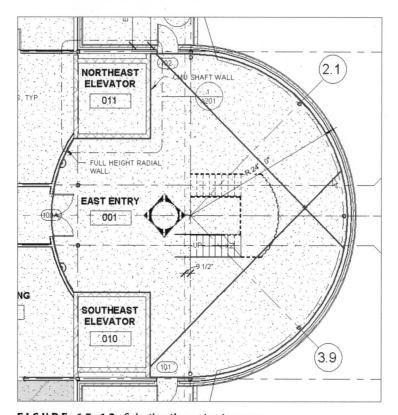

FIGURE 15.12 Selecting the east entry room

Room Bounding Properties

By default, each wall you add to the Revit model will automatically define a room boundary, and this is what we want to see 95 percent of the time. There are some situations, however, where we do not want a wall to separate the room itself. In such cases, we can modify the instance parameters of the wall to disallow the division of the room.

The objective of the following procedure is to "turn off" the room bounding in certain walls.

1. In the East Wing floor plan, zoom in on the lavatory area.

2. Select the wall that divides the Men's toilet area from the Men's lavatory entry area, as shown in Figure 15.13.

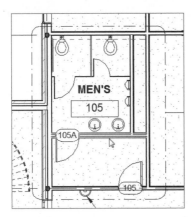

FIGURE 15.13 Selecting the partition within the Men's lavatory

3. In the Properties dialog, scroll down to the Room Bounding row.

4. Uncheck Room Bounding, as shown in Figure 15.14.

FIGURE 15.14 Unchecking Room Bounding

5. Repeat the procedure in the Women's lavatory.

6. Save the model.

Having the ability to add rooms and manipulate the information in the Revit database easily gives you a tremendous advantage as you move forward with the rest of the model. Also, that information is relayed into the room's tag, which is automatically added as you place the room into the model.

This concept brings us to our next topic: how to change the actual tag to display the information on the drawings that we desire.

Placing and Manipulating Room Tags

As mentioned earlier, the room tag is merely a vehicle to relay the room's data to the construction documents. As a default, a room tag is added automatically as you place the room into the model. A default room tag is included, but we are not stuck with this room tag.

The objective of the next procedure is to add an alternate room tag to the room, and to open the tag's family editor to investigate the composition of the tag.

1. Zoom into the SOUTHEAST CORNER OFFICE.

2. Select the room tag.

3. In the Properties dialog, select Room Tag With Area, as shown in Figure 15.15.

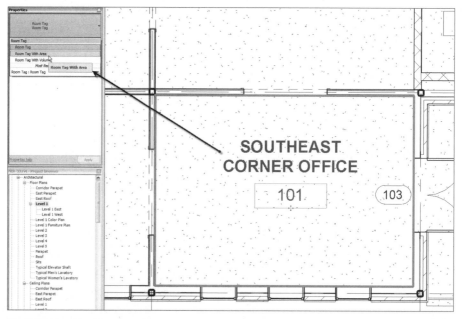

FIGURE 15.15 Change the type to Room Tag With Area

Now that was just way too easy! Let's take a closer look at what we just did. A room tag is nothing more than the cover sheet we created back in Chapter 14, "Creating Sheets and Printing." All we need to do is simply open the file, and place a tag into the family.

To open the tag's Family Editor, follow this procedure:

1. Select the room tag for the SOUTHWEST CORNER OFFICE.

2. On the Modify | Room Tags tab, click the Edit Family button.

3. With the family file open, click on the Room Name piece of text that is visible. (These pieces of text are actually tags.)

4. On the Modify | Label tab, click the Edit Label button.

5. In the Edit Label dialog, the list to the left displays all the parameters that you can easily add to the room tag (see Figure 15.16). Do not change anything and click OK.

FIGURE 15.16 A list of available parameters you can add to the room tag

WARNING   If you are modifying the room tag, do yourself and the rest of your design team a huge favor and inform everyone that you are in there modifying your company's standards! If you are the BIM manager, set the permissions to this network directory accordingly.

6. Close out of this file without saving any changes.

Now that you know what tag Revit uses while placing a room, and how to manipulate that tag, it is time to tie the tag into something more robust. Since a tag is just a reflection of the room data, we can add another Revit object that does the same thing: a room schedule.

Adding a Room Schedule

Up to this point in our careers we have been adding room information twice, sometimes three times. And why is that? It's because we had to fill the tag out in the plan, then fill the same information out in the room schedule. If you were in the unfortunate situation where you had an enlarged plan, then you added the information yet again for a third time. Now when you have to change that information you need to do it in multiple places. Now, I'm not saying that Revit will end all your problems, but it sure will make life easier!

The objective of the next procedure is to create a room schedule. We will then finish filling out the room information from the actual schedule, thus saving time and increasing accuracy.

1. On the View tab, click Schedules and then click the Schedule/Quantities button, as shown in Figure 15.17.

2. In the New Schedule dialog, select Rooms from the list to the left.

3. Click OK.

4. In the Fields tab of the Schedule Properties dialog that opens, add the following fields in the specified order (see Figure 15.17):

   Number

   Name

   Base Finish

   Floor Finish

   Wall Finish

   Ceiling Finish

   Comments

   Level

5. Click the Sorting/Grouping tab.

6. Sort by Number.

7. Click OK. Your schedule will look similar to Figure 15.18, with the probable exception of the Room 0.

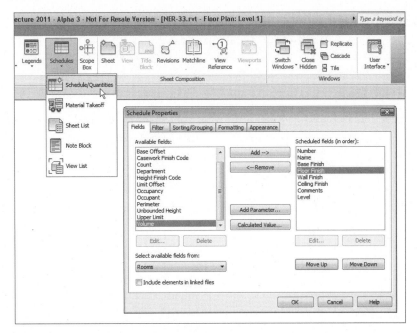

FIGURE 15.17 Adding the fields to the schedule

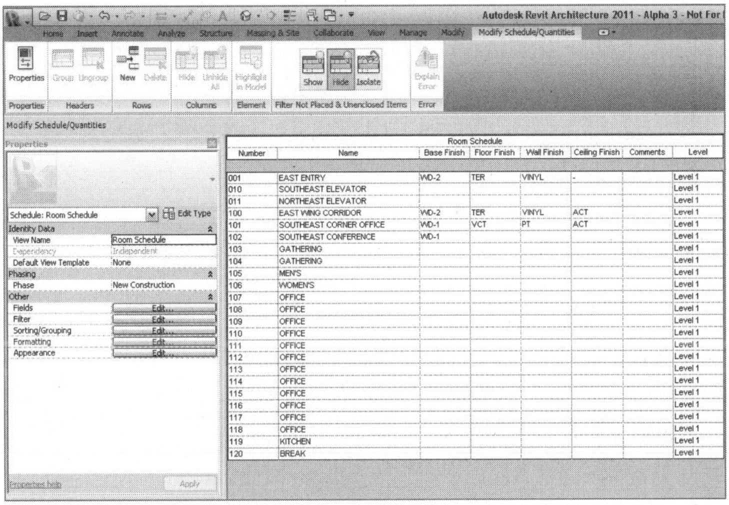

FIGURE 15.18 The room schedule

8. With the schedule still open, click into the EAST ENTRY Base Finish cell, and type **WD-2**.

TURNING OFF UNWANTED ROOMS

The schedule in the book has an errant room that does not belong in the schedule. Because going step by step through a book does not give you a true feel for a real-world scenario, I can tell you that you will wind up with some misplaced rooms. This is OK, because you can turn them off in the schedule. If you click the Not Placed/Not Enclosed menu, you will see that you can show, hide, or isolate unwanted data. For this example, I will choose Hide to remove the row (see the following graphic).

9. Click into the Floor Finish cell and type **TER** (for Terrazzo).

10. Click into the Wall Finish cell and type **VINYL**.

11. Click into the Ceiling Finish cell and type a hyphen (-).

12. Click into the EAST WING CORRIDOR Base Finish cell. Notice there is a menu arrow, as shown in Figure 15.19. Click it. You now have a choice between two base finishes. Choose WD-2.

13. Change the other values to TER, VINYL, and ACT (see Figure 15.19).

| | | Room Schedule | |
Number	Name	Base Finish	Floor Finish
001	EAST ENTRY	WD-2	TER
010	SOUTHEAST ELEVATOR		
011	NORTHEAST ELEVATOR		
100	EAST WING CORRIDOR	WD-2	TER
101	SOUTHEAST CORNER OFFICE	WD-1	VCT
102	SOUTHEAST CONFERENCE	WD-2	
103	GATHERING		
104	GATHERING		
105	MEN'S		

FIGURE 15.19 Filling out the room schedule

Now that we have the rooms in place and a schedule filled out, it is time to move to a more colorful aspect of adding rooms to the model: adding a color fill plan.

Adding a Color Fill Plan

Another benefit of using the Room feature in Revit is that you can add a color plan at any time, and you can virtually create any type of color scheme or pattern scheme you desire. And here's the best part: adding one is so easy it is almost fun!

The objective of the next procedure is to make a duplicate of the East Wing floor plan and to create a color scheme based on room name.

1. Right-click on the Level 1 floor plan view and select Duplicate View ➤ Duplicate, as shown in Figure 15.20.

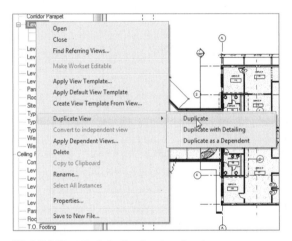

FIGURE 15.20 Duplicating the view

2. Right-click on the new view and select Rename.

3. Rename the view to **Level 1 Color Plan**.

4. Click OK.

5. Open the new plan if it is not open already.

6. In the Room & Area panel of the Home tab, click the Legend button, as shown in Figure 15.21.

7. After you click the Legend button, you can place the legend into the model. Place it into the upper-right corner of the view (inside the crop region), as shown in Figure 15.21.

8. In the Choose Space Type And Color Scheme dialog, change Space Type to Rooms and Color Scheme to Name (see Figure 15.22).

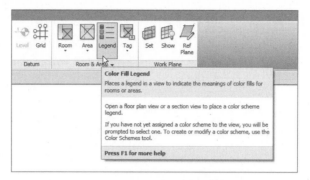

FIGURE 15.21 Clicking the Legend button

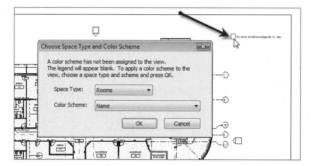

FIGURE 15.22 Placing the legend and specifying the color scheme

9. Click OK. You now have a nice color plan.

10. Select the actual Color Scheme legend.

11. Click the Edit Scheme button on the Modify | Color Fill Legends tab, as shown in Figure 15.23.

12. Notice, in the Edit Color Scheme dialog that opens, you can alter the color and the fill pattern for each room. After you investigate this area, click OK.

Pretty cool concept! You may notice that the two rooms we skipped are still white. It is time to take a look at the situation we have here. The problem is, there are no walls dividing the two rooms, but it would be nice to have two separate rooms anyway! To do this, we can add a room separator.

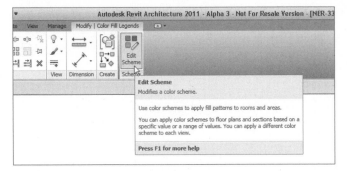

FIGURE 15.23 Proceeding to edit the scheme

Adding Room Separators

Although it seems like a small issue, the topic of adding room separators has been known to confuse some people. Within Revit, you can physically draw a room without any walls at all. Or you can simply draw a "line in the sand" between two rooms that are not separated by an actual wall. This is known as adding a room separator.

The objective of the next procedure is to separate the kitchen from the break room by adding a room separator.

1. In the Level 1 floor plan, zoom in on the area shown in Figure 15.24.

2. On the Room & Area panel of the Home tab, click the Room button.

3. Place a room over the top of the tile flooring, as shown in Figure 15.24.

4. On the Room & Area tab of the Home tab, click the Room Separation Line button, as shown in Figure 15.25.

5. On the Draw tab, click the Pick Lines icon.

6. Pick the edge of the flooring, as shown in Figure 15.26.

7. Press Esc twice.

8. Click the Room button.

9. Place a room to the right of the kitchen area.

10. Change the room to the left to **KITCHEN**.

11. Change the room to the right to **BREAK**.

12. On the Annotate tab, click the Tag All button.

13. Select Room Tags and click OK.

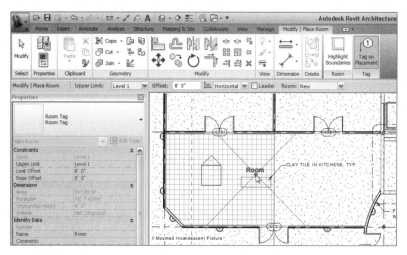

FIGURE 15.24 Place a room over the tiles (it will spill into the adjacent room).

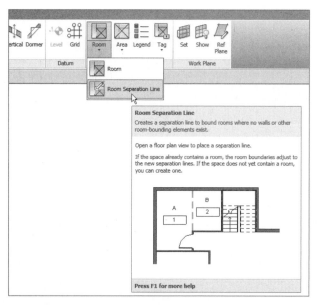

FIGURE 15.25 Click the Room Separation button on the Room & Area panel of the Home tab.

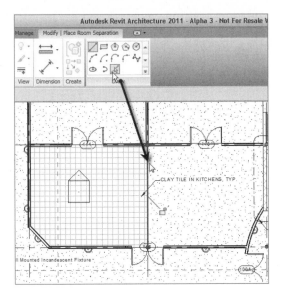

FIGURE 15.26 Adding the room separation line

We are really moving along here! We now have a fully coordinated room schedule tied into a room color fill plan that can be modified by simply changing a room tag. How did we ever live without Revit?

The next item to discuss is how to create a gross area plan. The process is similar but slightly more involved than creating a room color plan.

Creating an Area Plan

Almost any job of considerable size will require an area plan at some point in the early development of the project. This normally occurs in the programming phase, but the need for this type of plan can persist well into the later stages of a project.

The objective of the next procedure is to create a separate floor plan, then to divide it up into areas.

1. On the Room & Area panel of the Home tab, select Area and click the Area Plan button, as shown in Figure 15.27.

2. In the New Area Plan dialog, choose Gross Building from the Type list, and choose Level 1 for the Area Plan Views.

3. Click OK.

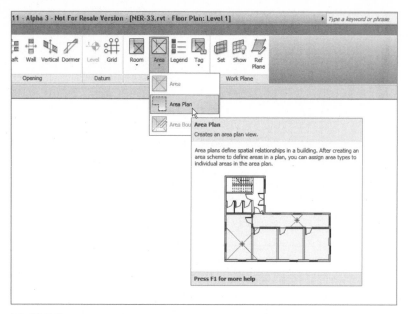

FIGURE 15.27 Clicking the Area Plan button

4. Click Yes to automatically create area boundaries. You now have a new floor plan with a blue boundary around the perimeter of the entire building.

5. On the Room & Area panel, click the Area Boundary Line button, as shown in Figure 15.28.

6. Draw a line, as shown in Figure 15.28, separating the corridor from the east wing.

7. Draw another similar separator between the west wing and the corridor.

N O T E   If your lines are not exactly snapping to the endpoints, this is not that big a deal. Unlike Sketch Mode, Revit is much more forgiving when it comes to creating area separations.

8. On the Room & Area tab, click the Area button, as shown in Figure 15.29.

9. If Revit says a tag isn't loaded, click Yes to load the family. Browse to Annotation ➢ Area Tag.rfa.

10. Place an area in the west wing, then in the corridor, and then in the east wing, as shown in Figure 15.30.

11. Select the tag in the west wing.

12. Rename it to **WEST WING**.

13. Click the Corridor tag.

14. Rename it to **LINK**.

15. Click the East Wing tag.

16. Rename it to **EAST WING**.

17. On the Room & Area panel, click the Legend button.

18. Place the legend in the upper-right corner of the view, as shown in Figure 15.30.

19. In the Choose Space Type And Color Scheme dialog, choose Areas (Gross Building) for Space Type and Gross Building Area for Color Scheme.

20. Click OK.

21. Select the Color Scheme Legend.

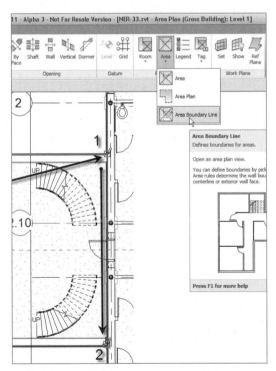

FIGURE 15.28 Drawing the area separator

22. Click the Edit Scheme button on the Modify | Color Fill Legends tab.

23. For Color, change Area Type to Name.

24. Click OK at the warning.

25. Click OK to return to the model (see Figure 15.30).

26. Save the model.

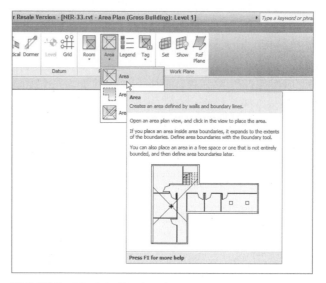

FIGURE 15.29 The Area button

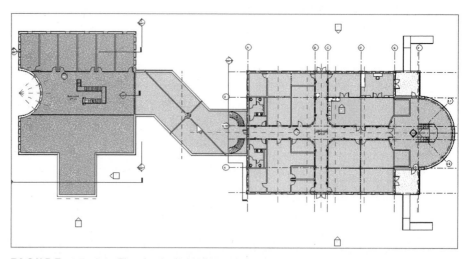

FIGURE 15.30 The plan is divided into three areas.

Great job! You now have experience with creating area plans. If you feel as though you could use some more practice before you start on a real project, you have five more floors in this model you can work on. You can either work on your own or step back through this chapter's procedures.

Are You Experienced?

Now you can...

- ☑ **add rooms to the model**

- ☑ **add room separators to the model**

- ☑ **create color scheme plans**

- ☑ **create area plans**

- ☑ **create room schedules**

- ☑ **update the rooms in the model directly from a room schedule**

Advanced Wall Topics

More on walls? Really? It seems as though all we do is walls. Well, that's because our buildings are composed mainly of walls. As you may have noticed, the exterior walls are compound wall structures with reveals and parapet caps. In the west wing, we have a staircase that is completely unsupported. It would be nice to add a wall to make those stairs less spongy. Given the fact that the west wing is a high-end architectural woodwork area, that wall could use some trims that can be added right to the wall's profile. Also, we have not touched on a curtain wall of any kind whatsoever.

▶ **Creating compound walls**

▶ **Adding wall sweeps**

▶ **Creating stacked walls**

▶ **Creating curtain walls**

▶ **Adding a wall to a massing object**

Creating Compound Walls

The first item to tackle is how to develop a wall with different materials. The exterior walls we have been using in this model are a prime example of a compound wall. The bottom 3′ of the wall consists of concrete block and the rest of the wall is brick. When you cut a section through the wall, you can see that the wall has an airspace as well as a metal stud wall backup.

Usually these chapters start with a claim that "the following procedure is so easy a caveman could do it" (or something of that nature). The development of compound walls is not the easiest thing you will tackle in Revit. This procedure is somewhat touchy, and doing it well takes practice. In this section, we will create an interior wall with a wood finish on the bottom along with different wood material on the top. We will also extrude a chair rail along the wall.

To get started, open the model you have been working on. If you missed the previous chapter, go to the book's web page at **www.sybex.com/go/revit2011ner**. From there you can browse to Chapter 16 and find the file called NER-33.rvt.

The objective of the next procedure is to create a compound wall from a basic wall and then add a sweep profile.

1. Open the Level 1 West dependent view.

2. On the Home tab, click the Wall button.

3. In the Type Selector in the Properties dialog, choose Basic Wall : Generic - 6″.

4. In the Properties dialog, click the Edit Type button.

5. Click Duplicate.

6. Call the new wall **Stairwell 3 support wall** and click OK.

7. Click the Edit button in the Structure row.

8. Click into the Material cell for the Structure row, as shown in Figure 16.1.

9. Click the […] button.

10. In the Materials dialog, select Wood - Stud Layer, and click OK.

11. Change the thickness to **5 1/2″**, as shown in Figure 16.1.

12. At the bottom of the Edit Assembly dialog is a Preview button. Click it (see Figure 16.2).

13. With the preview open, change View to Section: Modify Type Attributes.

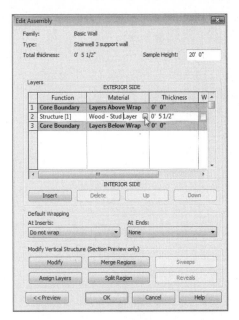

FIGURE 16.1 Changing the structure to a 5 1/2″ wood stud

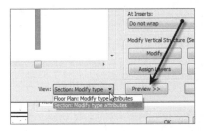

FIGURE 16.2 Changing the view to a section

It doesn't seem like we have done much, but we have set the stage to start building our wall. It is time now to focus back on the Layers field.

Adding Layers to the Compound Wall

If you are an AutoCAD veteran, the term layer now takes on a different meaning. In Revit the term layer, as it pertains to a wall assembly, represents a material layer that will be assigned an actual thickness as well as its own material.

As you can see in Figure 16.3, the Layers area is broken down into two categories: Exterior and Interior. For the following procedure, we will add materials to both the exterior and interior portion of the wall.

To create a new compound wall, follow these steps:

◀

Adding a preview to the Edit Assembly dialog is not only a nice feature, it is also absolutely necessary to continue with the editing of the wall. As you will soon see, you will not have access to certain buttons without the preview being displayed in a sectional view.

1. In the Layers area, click on the number 1, as shown in Figure 16.3 (it is the field just above the Layers Above Wrap row).

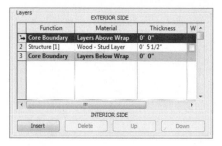

FIGURE 16.3 Clicking on row 1 to highlight the entire row

 T I P   Note that when you are trying to highlight an entire row in the Layers area, you must click right on the actual number. A small black arrow will appear, indicating that you can click that spot to highlight the entire row.

2. Click the Insert button.

3. Change Function to Finish 1 [4].

4. Click into the Material cell, and click the […] button.

5. Select Finishes - Interior - Gypsum Wall Board (5/8″).

6. Click OK in the Materials dialog.

7. Change Thickness to 5/8″.

8. Click on row 4 (Layers Below Wrap).

9. Click the Insert button.

10. Click the Down button, as shown at the bottom right of Figure 16.4. It is located below the Layers area.

11. Change Function to Finish 1 [4].

12. Click into the Material cell, and click the […] button.

13. Find Finishes - Interior - Gypsum Wall Board (5/8″).

14. Click OK in the Materials dialog.

15. Change Thickness to 5/8″. Your Layers field should resemble Figure 16.4.

> Notice that the preview is instantly adding the changes to the wall. This interaction will be of great benefit down the road.

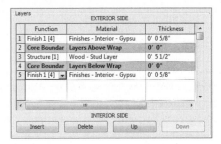

FIGURE 16.4 Adding a 5/8" gypsum layer to the interior side of the wall

Now that the wall is wrapped with one layer of 5/8" gypsum on each side, it is time to start placing the veneered plywood layers to the exterior of the wall.

The objective of the next procedure is to add a 3/4" plywood layer to the exterior of the wall.

1. Click on 1 Finish 1 [4] (the top layer).

2. Click Insert.

3. Change Function to Finish 2 [5].

4. Change Material to Wood - Mahogany (it is the mahogany material that has Plywood for the cut pattern). Click OK.

5. Change the Thickness to 3/4". Your wall's layers should resemble Figure 16.5.

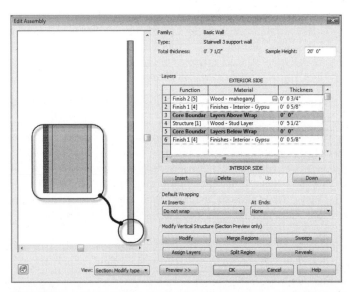

FIGURE 16.5 Adding the 3/4" mahogany veneered plywood material

6. At the bottom of the dialog, click the OK button.

7. Click Apply.

In the preview, you can hold down the wheel button on your mouse and pan around. You can also wheel in and out to zoom in and out of the preview.

WARNING   By clicking OK, then Apply, you are basically saving your work. In the Edit Assembly dialog, there is no Save or Apply button as you create the wall. Also never press Esc. This will cancel every change you have made and will almost certainly result in costly repairs to your computer as you rain blows upon it.

Now it's time to go back in and split the wall materials in two. It would be nice if we could have cherry at the top and mahogany at the bottom. Revit gives you the ability to do this.

Adding New Materials by Splitting a Region

If you want more than one material along the face of a wall, you will use the Split Region command that you'll find in the Edit Assembly dialog. The objective of the following procedure is to add a new material, then apply it to the top half of the plywood face.

1. Click the Edit button in the Structure row.

2. Click on Layer 1 (the top layer).

3. Click Insert.

4. Change Function to Finish 2 [5].

5. For Material, select Wood - Cherry, and click OK. (Do not give it a thickness.)

6. Click the Split Region button, as shown in Figure 16.6.

7. Move your cursor up the plywood face. Notice that your cursor turns into a knife. You will also see a short, horizontal line within the plywood. This indicates where the region will be cut.

NOTE   You are going to find that splitting the correct region can be extremely difficult even if you have done this procedure many times. Make sure you zoom into the area, take a deep breath, and try it again if you are getting frustrated.

8. Once you see 3′–0″ in the temporary dimension, pick the point as shown in Figure 16.6. *Do not press Esc when you are finished!*

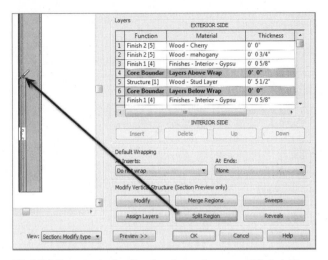

FIGURE 16.6 Cutting the plywood at a specific height

You have now split the plywood. The only thing left to do is to apply a new material to the upper region. You can accomplish this by using the Assign Layers button.

Assigning Material to Different Layers

The Assign Layers command will allow you to choose where you would like to assign a layer. This is quite useful within the context of this dialog because now you are not "stuck" without the ability to just move the layers around the wall as you need. Of course, when you split the wall as we just did, you will notice that the thicknesses of the two wood layers are set to 0 and Variable. Revit needs us to assign an alternate layer at this point.

The objective of the following procedure is to assign the cherry layer to the upper portion of the plywood.

1. Pick the Layer 1 row (Wood - Cherry), as shown in Figure 16.7.

2. Click the Assign Layers button, as shown in Figure 16.7.

3. Move your cursor over the upper region of the plywood layer and pick. Cherry is now assigned to the upper portion of the wall, and the thicknesses are now set to 3/4" (see Figure 16.7).

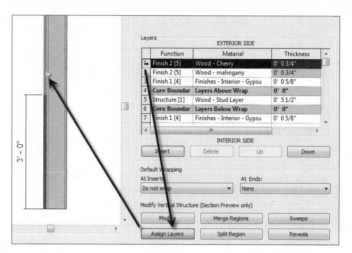

FIGURE 16.7 Assigning the cherry layer to the upper portion of the wall

4. At the bottom of the dialog, click OK.

5. Click Apply.

6. Click the Edit button in the Structure row to get back to the Edit Assembly dialog.

7. Pan to the top of the wall in the display, as shown in Figure 16.8.

8. Click the Modify button, as shown in Figure 16.8.

9. Hover your cursor over the top of the 3/4″ plywood, as shown in Figure 16.8.

10. Once the top of the plywood becomes highlighted, pick the line.

11. Unlock the blue padlock (see Figure 16.8).

12. Click OK.

13. Click OK one more time to get to the model.

14. Click the Modify button on the Home panel.

15. Save the model.

By unlocking the layer, you can now move that layer up or down depending on what you need. Another good example of the usefulness of this functionality is when you need to slide a brick ledge down past a foundation.

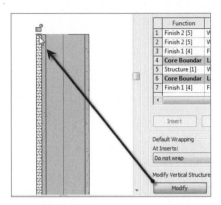

FIGURE 16.8 Unlocking the plywood to enable independent movement once the wall is placed into the model

Some people find splitting the regions in the Edit Assembly easy while others find it to be more difficult. I found the procedure difficult at first. If you are like me, this technique will require more practice until you have done a few more walls. Don't worry—it only gets easier as time passes.

Adding an automatic sweep along this wall would be nice. Come to think of it, a nice wood base and a chair rail would finish off this wall perfectly.

Adding Wall Sweeps

The concept of adding a wall sweep is as close to actual construction as you can come without actually setting up a chop saw. That is because, when we want to add a specific profile to sweep along a wall, we need to go outside the model, find (or create) the profile, and then bring it into the model. This process is similar to ordering trim and installing it.

The objective of the following procedure is to load a base and a chair rail trim into the model. We will then include these items in the wall we have been working on.

1. On the Insert tab, click the Load Family button.

2. Go to the Profiles directory.

3. Load the files Base 1.rfa and Casing Profile-2.rfa. (Use Ctrl to select both files.)

4. On the Home tab, click the Wall button.

5. Make sure the current wall is Stairwell 3 Support Wall.

6. In the Properties dialog, click the Edit Type button.

7. Click the Edit button in the Structure row.

8. Click the Sweeps button, as shown in Figure 16.9.

FIGURE 16.9 Adding a sweep to the wall

9. In the Wall Sweeps dialog, click the Add button, as shown near the bottom of Figure 16.10.

10. For Profile use Base 1 : 5 1/2″ × 5/8″.

11. For Material, use Wood - Mahogany (the one with the cut pattern that is set to the Wood Small hatch). Click OK.

12. Click the Add button again.

13. The new profile will be Casing Profile-2 : 5 1/2″ × 13/16″.

14. Set Material to Wood - Mahogany.

15. Set Distance 2′–6 1/2″ from the base, as shown in Figure 16.10.

16. Click OK and zoom in on the wall where the sweeps are so you can confirm they are placed as expected.

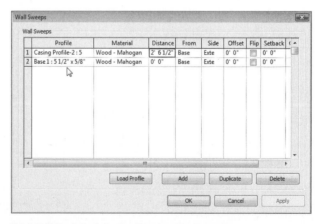

FIGURE 16.10 Configuring the two sweeps

17. Click OK again.

18. Click OK one more time to get back to the model.

19. In the Properties panel, make sure Base Offset is set to 0′–0″.

20. In the Options bar, set Height to Unconnected with a height of 10′–0″.

21. Set Location Line to Finish Face: Exterior.

22. Set Offset to –1″ (see Figure 16.11).

23. Draw the wall by snapping to the inside of the stringers, as shown in Figure 16.11. You want to go in a clockwise direction, so start with the northern part of the staircase, as illustrated by the 1 in Figure 16.11.

24. On the Geometry panel on the Modify | Place Wall tab, click the Wall Joins button.

25. Using the Wall Joins tool, go to each wall corner and make the join Mitered.

 T I P   **If you receive a warning stating that a sweep cannot be added, ignore it. This warning is sometimes generated when there is a sweep on the face of a wall.**

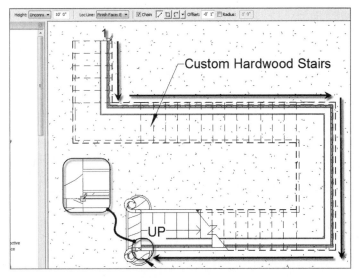

FIGURE 16.11 Placing the wall clockwise in the model

The wall has been added to the model. Since we are placing it underneath a staircase, there will be issues with the actual profile of the wall. This brings us to the next section of this chapter, which guides you through modifying a wall's shape after it has been placed into the model.

Modifying a Wall's Profile In-Place

Although we have touched on modifying a wall profile back in Chapter 2, "Creating a Model," we are going to take this procedure to the next level. You can make a wall conform to any odd geometric shape you wish if you follow a few simple rules and procedures.

The objective of the following procedure is to edit the profile of the new walls to conform to the profile of the stairs.

1. On the View tab, click the Elevation button.

2. Place an interior elevation as shown in Figure 16.12.

3. Open the elevation.

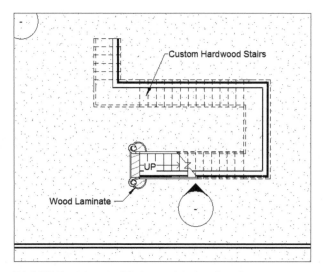

FIGURE 16.12 Placing an interior elevation

4. Select the wall, as shown in Figure 16.13.

5. On the Mode tab, click Edit Profile, as shown in Figure 16.13.

6. On the Draw panel, click the Pick Lines icon.

7. Pick the underside of the stairs. Follow the profile exactly.

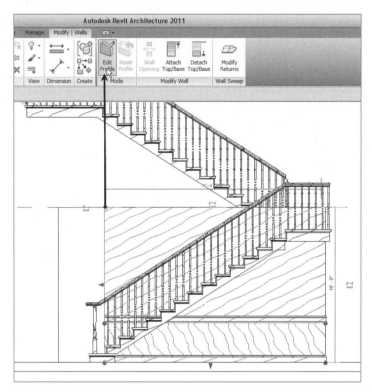

FIGURE 16.13 Selecting the wall to be modified and clicking the Edit Profile button

8. Delete the existing top magenta line and the existing left magenta line by selecting them and pressing the Delete key. All you should have left is the profile shown in Figure 16.14.

9. Use the Trim/Extend Single Element command to clean up all the corners. Revit will not allow you to continue if you don't (see Figure 16.14).

10. Click Finish Edit Mode. Your wall is now trimmed to the underside of the stairs.

 N O T E   If your wall does not look right, select it again and click Edit Profile. Keep working on the wall until you are satisfied.

11. Repeat the procedure for each wall under the stairs. Remember to add elevations for each. Your finished walls should look like Figure 16.15.

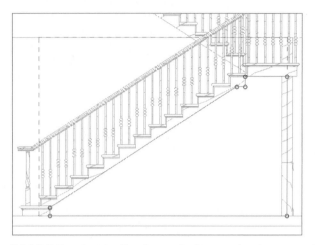

FIGURE 16.14 Cleaning up the lines so they form a continuous loop

Now that we can create a compound wall and modify it to fit in an odd place, it is time to learn how to manually add some sweeps.

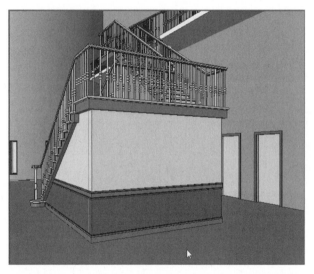

FIGURE 16.15 The finished walls should follow the profile of the stairs.

Manually Adding Host Sweeps

The problem with the wall scenario that we created in the previous procedure is that we have only horizontal wall sweeps. Suppose we need some vertical wall sweeps? This is where host sweeps come into play.

A host sweep is exactly like the sweeps we just added to the wall's properties, only by adding a host sweep, we can add sweeps manually.

The objective of the next procedure is to configure and add a host sweep to the model.

1. Go to the elevation shown in Figure 16.16.

2. On the Home tab, click the down arrow on the Wall button and select Wall Sweep, as shown in Figure 16.16.

3. In the Properties dialog, click the Edit Type button.

4. Click Duplicate.

5. Call the new sweep **Chair Rail Sweep**. Click OK.

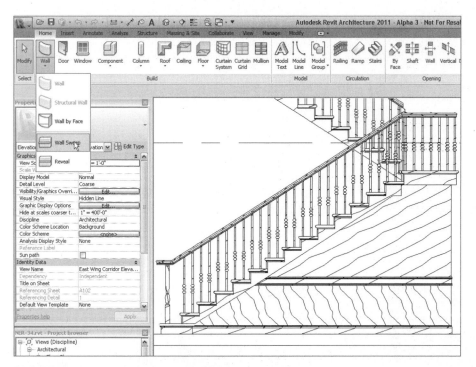

FIGURE 16.16 Choosing the Wall Sweep command

6. For the profile, choose Casing Profile-2 : 5 1/2" x 13/16" from the list, as shown in Figure 16.17.

7. For the Material, choose Wood - Mahogany (see Figure 16.17).

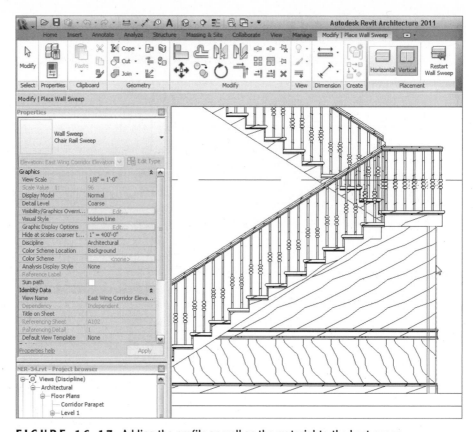

FIGURE 16.17 Adding the profile as well as the material to the host sweep

8. Click OK.

9. On the Modify | Place Wall Sweep tab, click Vertical on the Placement panel, as shown in Figure 16.17.

10. Make sure your Chair Rail Sweep is current in the Type Selector menu.

11. Place a vertical rail about 1'–0" in from the right corner, as shown in Figure 16.18.

N O T E   If you are having trouble placing the sweep on the corner, you still need to go to the plan and select Edit Wall Joins from the Tools toolbar. Pick the corner of the walls, and select Mitered from the Options bar. If you need further assistance with this procedure, go back to Chapter 2 and read up on creating mitered wall joins.

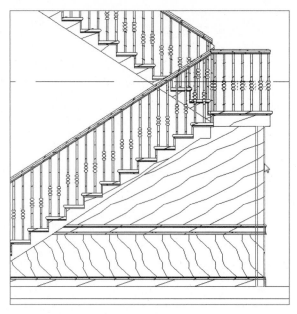

FIGURE 16.18 Placing the sweep on the corner

12. After the trim is placed, press Esc.

13. Select the vertical trim. Notice there are grips on the top and the bottom. Pick the bottom grip and drag it up to meet the top chair rail, as shown in Figure 16.19.

14. Add another sweep about 3′–0″ to the left of the first sweep.

15. Once the sweep is in, select it. You will see a temporary dimension appear. Change the dimension to 3′–0″.

16. Drag the bottom up.

17. Repeat the procedure so your elevation looks like Figure 16.20.

18. Add vertical rails at a 3′–0″ +/– to the other walls as well. Your walls should look like Figure 16.21.

So, we can now make modifications to a simple wall in any direction. We have experience adding sweeps to the wall's composition, and we can add sweeps free-hand when we need to.

One other type of wall that we should cover before we get to curtain walls is a stacked wall. When you need a compound wall, the outside face must always be in alignment. When you run into this situation, you have to construct an entirely new wall.

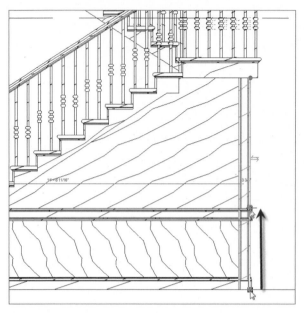

FIGURE 16.19 Dragging the sweep up to the chair rail

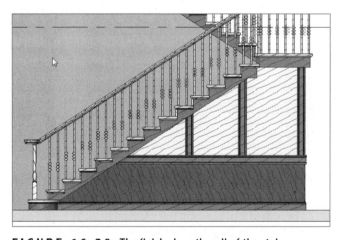

FIGURE 16.20 The finished south wall of the stairs

Creating Stacked Walls

A stacked wall, simply put, is a wall created by stacking two premade walls together. You can't have a stacked wall without at least two basic walls that you can join together. The good thing about stacked walls is that you can stack as

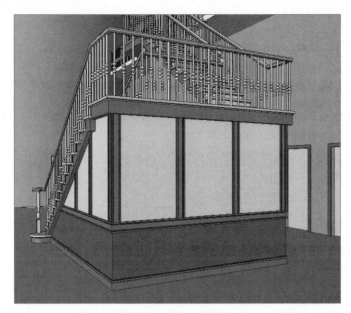

FIGURE 16.21 The final walls with the sweeps added

OPEN THIS DOOR ONLY IN CASE OF EMERGENCY!

Although it is true that a stacked wall is basically the only good way to create a wall system with an offset face, stacked walls are notoriously bad in terms of hosting items and joining to other walls. Also one of the biggest drawbacks to stacked walls is they won't show up in a schedule.

many as you like. I recommend that you use some restraint, though—these walls can start to use up memory if you get too carried away.

The objective of the following procedure is to join three basic walls together to create one stacked wall. The outcome will create an alcove for architectural casework.

1. On the Home tab, click the Wall button.

2. In the Type Selector menu in the Properties dialog, select Basic Wall : Interior 6 1/8" Partition (2Hr).

3. Click the Edit Type button in the Properties dialog.

4. Click Duplicate.

5. Call it **18" Soffit Wall**, and click OK.

6. Change Wrapping At Inserts and Wrapping At Ends to Interior.

7. Click the Edit button in the Structure row.

8. In the Layers area, click on 3 Core Boundary (Layers Above Wrap), and click Insert.

9. Set Function to Structure [1].

10. Set Material to Air Barrier - Air Infiltration Barrier.

11. Set Thickness to 8 1/4".

12. Click Insert (to insert another layer above).

13. Set Function to Substrate [2].

14. Set Material to Metal - Stud Layer.

15. Set Thickness to 3 5/8" (see Figure 16.22).

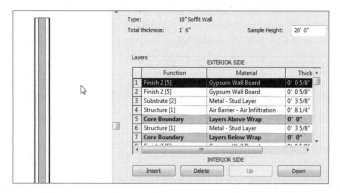

FIGURE 16.22 The walls layers

16. Click OK twice.

17. To the left of the Ribbon, click the Modify button (this clears the Wall command).

Now it's time to start building the stacked wall. Since we have two walls to work with, we can specify them in the Edit Assembly dialog for the stacked wall.

The objective of the next procedure is to join the 18″ soffit wall with the 6 1/8″ partition wall.

1. On the Home tab, click the Wall button.

2. Scroll down the Type Selector until you arrive at Stacked Wall: Exterior - Brick Over CMU w Metal Stud, and select it.

> A good way to establish the overall thickness is to look at the top of the Edit Assembly dialog. There you can see the total thickness.

3. Click Edit Type.

4. Click Duplicate.

5. Call the new wall **Recessed Wall**, and click OK.

6. Click Edit in the Structure row.

7. For Offset, select Finish Face: Interior.

8. In the Types area, change Wall 1 to 18″ Soffit Wall.

9. Change Wall 2 to Interior - 6 1/8″ Partition (2-Hr).

10. Change Height to 5'–6".

11. Insert a wall below the Interior - 6 1/8″ Partition (2-Hr) wall.

12. Change the third wall to 18″ Soffit Wall.

13. Change the height to 3'–0".

14. At the top of the dialog, change Sample Height to 10'–0" (see Figure 16.23).

15. Click OK twice.

16. Draw the wall in the west wing, as shown in Figure 16.24. (If you wish, you can create an elevation, or cut a section through the wall.)

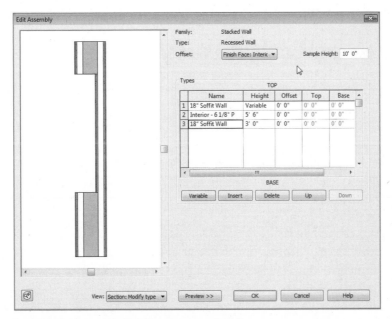

FIGURE 16.23 Creating the stacked wall

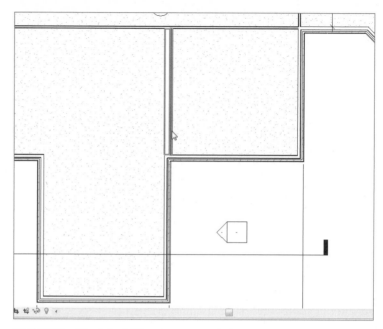

FIGURE 16.24　Adding the new stacked wall to the model

With the concept of stacked walls behind us, we can now move into the crazy world of curtain walls. Although curtain walls are complex in nature, Revit handles them quite well.

Creating Curtain Walls

The topic of curtain walls brings us away from the conventional mind-set of walls. Curtain walls are placed into the model the same way as conventional walls, but curtain walls have many more restrictions and Element Properties that should be examined before you go throwing one into your model.

Given that, curtain walls also provide the most dramatic effect on your building. As this section will explain in detail, a curtain wall is composed not only of glass and aluminum extrusions. A curtain wall can be constructed from building materials such as brick, CMU, and wood. You can also predefine the materials and the spacing, or you can create them grid by grid, depending on your situation.

The first part of this section will focus on adding a predefined curtain system to the model.

Adding a Predefined Curtain Wall

The quickest way to model a curtain wall is to use one that has already been created for you. The out-of-the-box curtain walls that are provided with Revit have enough instance and type parameters available to make the curtain wall conform to your needs for each situation.

The objective of the next procedure is to add a predefined curtain wall system to the radial east entry wall.

1. In the Project Browser, open the Level 1 East dependent view.

2. Zoom in on the east entry.

3. On the Home tab, click the Wall button.

4. In the Properties dialog, select Curtain Wall: Storefront.

5. Click Edit Type.

6. Click Duplicate.

7. Call the new curtain wall **East Entry** and click OK.

8. Notice that you can configure many parameters. For Vertical Grid Pattern, change Spacing to 4'–0".

9. Check Adjust For Mullion Size.

10. For Horizontal Grid Pattern, change Layout to Maximum Spacing. Also check Adjust For Mullion Size.

11. Click OK.

12. In the Instance Properties dialog, change Base Offset to 3'–7".

13. Set Top Constraint to Up To Level: Roof.

14. Set Top Offset to –1'–0" (that's minus 1'–0").

15. On the Draw panel, click the Pick Lines icon.

16. Pick the radial entry wall, as shown in Figure 16.25. Make sure you are picking the wall centerline.

17. Go to a 3D view. Your curtain wall should resemble Figure 16.26.

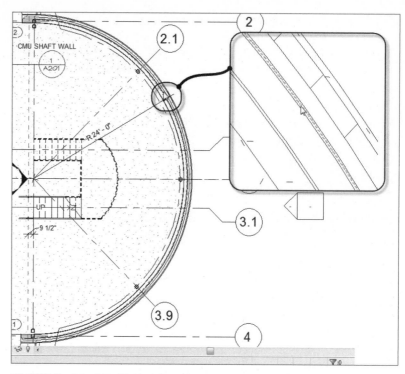

FIGURE 16.25 Picking the radial entry wall to add the curtain wall

REVIT CAN BE TOUCHY

You may receive a warning that says "Could not create integral reveal for wall instance. Sweep position is outside of its wall. Please check sweep parameters" (see the following graphic). If you do, just click the red X in the upper-right corner of the warning to dismiss it.

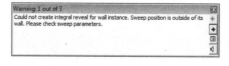

The ability to create an automatic curtain wall such as the radial one in the west entry way is quite an advantage when it comes to quickly modeling

a curtain system. However, you will not always be presented with a perfectly square vertical shape. This is where creating a blank curtain wall comes in handy. You can then add grids and mullions at spaces that are at odd intervals.

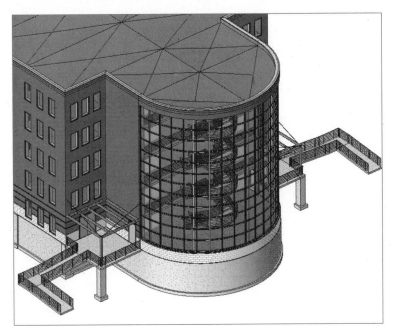

FIGURE 16.26 The curtain wall in 3D

Adding a Blank Curtain Wall

A blank curtain wall is nothing but a giant chunk of glass. By adding a blank curtain wall, you are telling Revit, "Don't bother spacing the panels, I'll do it myself."

The objective of the next procedure is to create a blank curtain wall and add it to the model. We will then go to an elevation and edit the profile of the panel.

1. In the Project Browser, open the Level 1 West dependent view.

2. On the Work Plane panel of the Home tab, click Ref Plane, and then click Pick Lines on the Draw panel.

3. Offset a reference plane 2′–0″ from the face of brick, as shown in Figure 16.27.

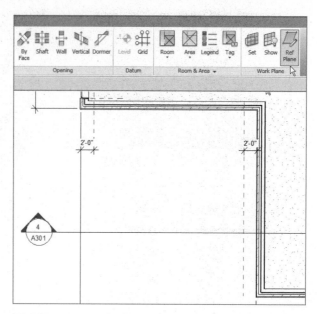

FIGURE 16.27 Offsetting two reference planes 2'–0" from the face of brick

4. On the Home tab, click the Wall button.

5. In the Properties dialog, pick Curtain Wall: Curtain Wall 1 from the list.

6. Click Edit Type.

7. Click Duplicate.

8. Call the new curtain system **South West Entry** and click OK.

9. Check the Automatically Embed check box.

10. Click OK.

11. For the Base Offset, change the value to 0'–0".

12. For Top Constraint, set the value to Up To Level: Level 5.

13. For Top Offset, change the value to 0'–0".

14. Draw the wall at the centerline of the wall between each reference plane, as shown in Figure 16.28.

15. In the Project Browser, open South Entry Elevation.

16. In the South Entry Elevation, change Visual Style to Shaded With Edges (this is so we can see the glass wall better).

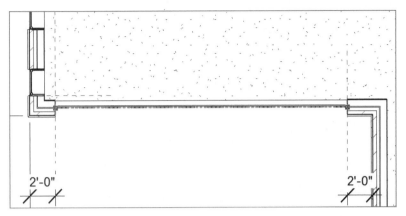

FIGURE 16.28 Drawing the curtain wall at the centerline of the wall between the two reference planes

Now that we have the wall drawn and are looking at the elevation, we can begin to alter the profile and add some curtain grids of our own. The objective of the next procedure is to edit the curtain profile.

1. Select the curtain wall.

2. On the Modify | Walls tab, click Edit Profile.

3. On the Draw panel, click Pick Lines.

4. Using the Options bar, offset the roof down 2′–0″, and trim the edges of the curtain wall to the offset line.

5. Delete the horizontal magenta line that is now floating.

6. Click Finish Edit Mode. Your curtain wall's profile should resemble Figure 16.29.

> To select the curtain wall, you will have to hover your pointer over an edge. When the curtain wall's perimeter becomes highlighted, select it.

With the shape of the curtain wall finished, it is time to create some divisions along the vertical and horizontal plane of the wall. In Revit, these are called curtain grids.

Creating Curtain Grids

Because all we have is a single pane of glass, we will need to "dice" this glass up. In this situation, we can start dividing the glass panel by using the Curtain Grid command. When we have finished, we can add mullions, doors, and even materials to the panels.

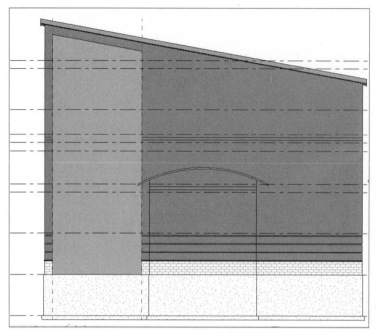

FIGURE 16.29 The complete curtain wall profile

The objective of the next procedure is to add curtain grids to the glass panel.

1. On the Build panel of the Home tab, click the Curtain Grid button, as shown in Figure 16.30.

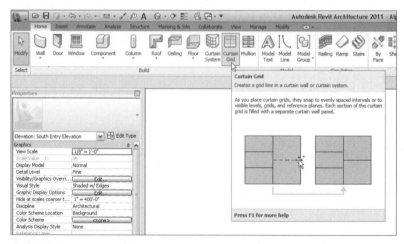

FIGURE 16.30 Click the Curtain Grid button on the Build panel of the Home tab.

2. On the Modify | Place Curtain Grid tab, click the All Segments button, as shown in Figure 16.31.

3. Move your cursor up the left side of the curtain wall and pick a horizontal point that is 8′–0″ up from the base of the wall, as shown in Figure 16.31.

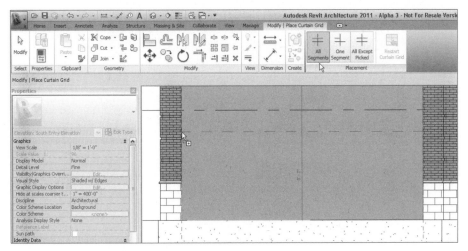

FIGURE 16.31 Picking a point 8′–0″ up from the base of the wall

4. Press Esc twice.

5. Select the horizontal grid.

6. Click the Copy button on the Modify panel.

7. Copy the grid up 4′–0″.

8. Copy the 4′ grid up 2′–0″.

9. Repeat this pattern until you have reached the top of the wall (see Figure 16.32).

10. Click the Curtain Grid button.

11. Slide your cursor along the base of the panel (notice the grid is extended in a vertical direction).

12. On the Placement panel, click the button for One Segment.

13. Pick the midpoint of the panel. (You should only have segmented the bottom panel.)

14. Press Esc twice.

15. Select the vertical grid.

16. On the Modify toolbar, click the Move icon.

17. Move the grid to the left 3′–0″.

18. Copy the grid to the right 6′–0″. Your wall should now look like Figure 16.33.

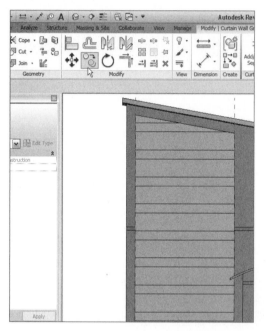

FIGURE 16.32 Copying the grids to form the custom curtain wall

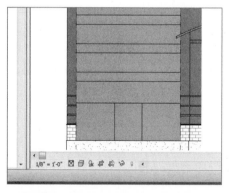

FIGURE 16.33 Chopping up the panel. (Note that the levels have been removed for clarity.)

Now that the panel is broken up, it is time to start adding some materials. One material you may not think of is an actual door! Yes, in Revit curtain walls, you add a door to a curtain panel as a material.

Adding Materials

Aside from doors, we can add any material that is present in the model. We can even add separate wall systems as well.

The objective of the next procedure is to add a door to the curtain system; then we will add brick belts that fill the 2′–0″ sections.

1. On the Insert tab, click the Load Family button.

2. Browse to Doors, then open the file called Curtain Wall-Store Front-Dbl.rfa.

3. Zoom in to the 6′×8′ panel.

4. Hover your cursor to the top of the panel.

5. Press the Tab key twice. The panel will now be highlighted. When the panel is highlighted, pick it (see Figure 16.34).

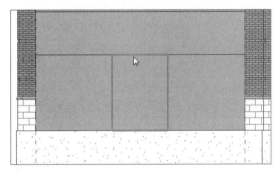

FIGURE 16.34 Selecting the 6′×8′ panel

6. In the Properties dialog, pick Curtain Wall-Store Front-Dbl: Store Front Double Door from the Type Selector. A door now appears in the panel.

7. Select the 2′–0″ panel above the door.

8. In the Properties dialog, pick Basic Wall: Generic - 12″ Masonry.

9. Press Esc.

10. Fill the rest of the 2′–0″ bands with the same Generic 12″ Masonry.

HEY, THIS IS GRAY!

If the wall is showing up backward (if the wall appears gray), then you need to physically flip the entire curtain wall. To do so, go to the Level 1 West plan and select the curtain wall. After you select the wall, you can click the little double arrow in the middle of the wall as shown in the following graphic. This will flip the direction of the entire curtain wall.

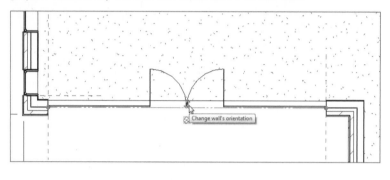

With the panels in place, it is time to start filling in the mullions—which brings us to our next step: adding mullions to the grid.

Adding Mullions to the Grid

The next logical step is to create the mullions that will be attached to the grid we just added. Since we have a few areas where there should not be any mullions, the job becomes more tedious.

The next example could go one of two ways. One procedure will involve adding mullions *piece by piece*, whereas the other procedure will allow you to add mullions all at once and then delete the mullions you do not need. This procedure will take the latter approach; we'll add the mullions all at once and then remove the superfluous mullions.

1. On the Build panel of the Home tab, click the Mullion button, as shown in Figure 16.35.

2. In the Properties dialog, choose Rectangular Mullion: 2.5″ × 5″ Rectangular.

3. Pick the grid above the door, as shown in Figure 16.36.

4. Press Esc.

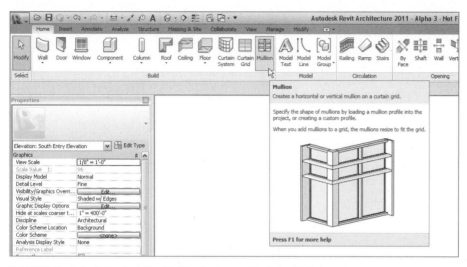

FIGURE 16.35 Click the Mullion button on the Home tab.

5. Click the Mullion button again.

6. On the Placement panel, click All Grid Lines.

7. Pick anywhere on the grid. The mullions have been added to the entire system.

8. Press Esc.

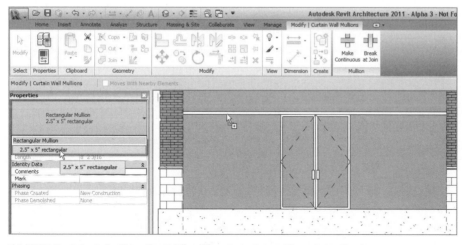

FIGURE 16.36 Place the 2.5″ × 5″ rectangular mullion above the door.

With the mullions added, we have actually gone too far! There is now an aluminum extrusion that separates the CMU from the adjacent brick. The objective of the next procedure is to remove these pieces of mullion.

1. Zoom into an area where the CMU meets the brick, as shown in Figure 16.37.

2. Select the small mullion piece that lies between the brick and the CMU. (You will have to press the Tab key several times to accomplish this.)

3. With the mullion selected, notice you can either modify the join (as shown in Figure 16.37) or you can press the Delete key and remove the mullion. In this case, delete the mullion. Repeat the procedure for other similar areas.

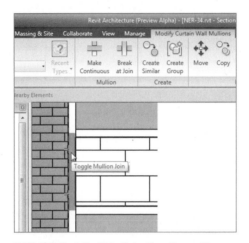

FIGURE 16.37 Selecting the mullion

So, what have we accomplished here? Well, we have embedded a predefined curtain wall to a radial profile, and we have added a curtain system to a giant glass panel by hand. The only thing left to do is to apply a curtain wall to a sloping surface.

Adding a Wall to a Massing Object

Sometimes in architecture, artistic expression is required on a project, such as curved and laterally sloping walls that cannot be accomplished using straight, linear components. Most of the time some form of expression will be added to a project. We need to be able to deal with that in Revit, and we can!

The process involved in adding a sloped wall is to first create a massing object, and then apply the wall to the face of that object. The objective of the next procedure is to create a mass along the south entrance of the building.

1. In the Project Browser, open the West Corridor Section.

2. In the West Corridor Section view, turn on the crop region, as shown in Figure 16.38.

3. Select the crop region as shown in Figure 16.39.

4. In the Properties dialog, scroll down to the Far Clipping row.

5. Click the Clip Without Line button, as shown in Figure 16.40.

6. In the Far Clipping dialog, click the No Clip button (see Figure 16.40).

7. Click OK.

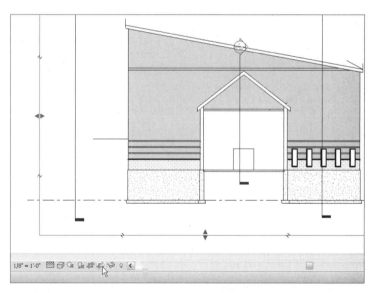

FIGURE 16.38 Turning on the crop region and adjusting the line

Now that the view is set up, we can take full advantage. The objective of the next exercise is to place a mass. After we place the mass, we can add a wall and a roof to it.

1. On the Massing & Site tab, click the In-Place Mass button, as shown in Figure 16.41.

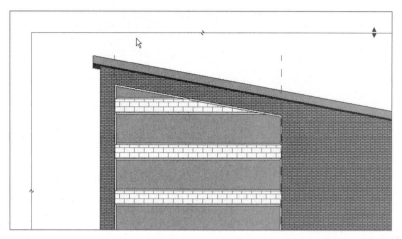

FIGURE 16.39 The crop region is selected. You can tell by the grips and the break icons.

FIGURE 16.40 Adjusting the view's clipping

2. If you get the Show Mass Enabled dialog, just click Close.

3. Name the mass **South West Entry** and click OK.

4. On the Draw panel, click the Start-End-Radius Arc button, as shown near the top left in Figure 16.42.

5. You will be prompted to pick a work plane. Pick the far wall, as shown in Figure 16.42.

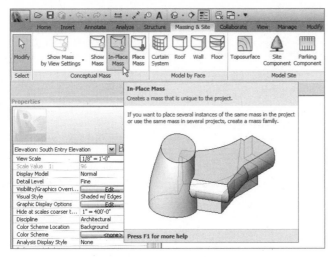

FIGURE 16.41 Click the In-Place Mass button.

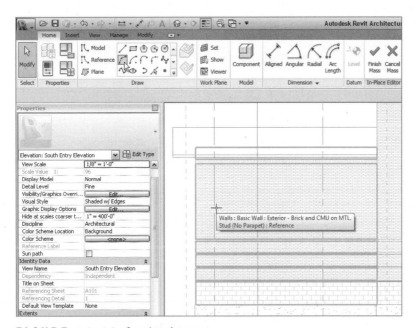

FIGURE 16.42 Starting the mass

6. Draw an arc, as shown in Figure 16.43.

7. On the Draw panel, click the Line button, and draw three lines forming a box, as shown in Figure 16.43.

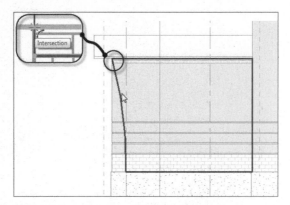

FIGURE 16.43 Adding the 3D mass

8. On the Quick Access bar, click the Default 3D View button.

9. Zoom in on the perimeter you have sketched and select it, as shown in Figure 16.44.

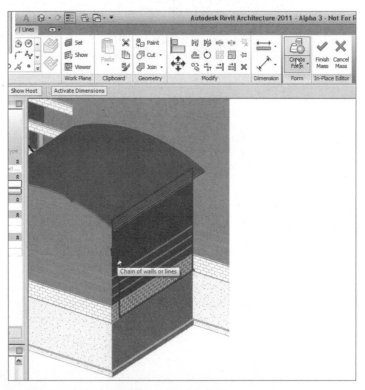

FIGURE 16.44 The Create Form button

10. On the Form panel of the Modify | Lines tab, click the Create Form button, as shown in Figure 16.44.

11. Pick (left-click) and drag the right-facing arrow so that the mass is in alignment with the corner of the building, as shown in Figure 16.45.

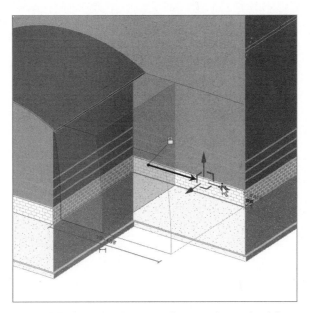

FIGURE 16.45 Dragging the extrusion to the right

12. Pick the top, front edge of the mass.

13. Click the arrow facing up and drag the edge down, causing a slope. You can eyeball the distance, then type 18' 4" in the temporary dimension, as shown in Figure 16.46.

14. Click Finish Mass.

15. On the Model By Face panel, click the Roof button, as shown in Figure 16.47.

16. Pick the top of the mass, as shown in Figure 16.48.

17. After you pick the top of the mass, click the Create Roof button, as shown in Figure 16.48.

18. Press Esc.

19. On the Massing & Site tab, click the Curtain System button.

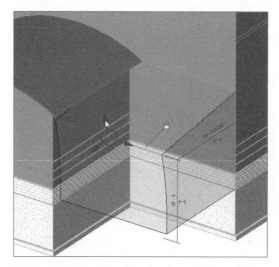

FIGURE 16.46 Creating the roof slope

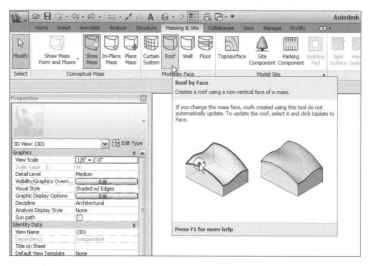

FIGURE 16.47 The Roof button on the Model By Face panel

20. In the Properties dialog, click the Edit Type button.

21. Click Duplicate.

22. Name the new curtain system **Southwest Entry**.

23. Click OK.

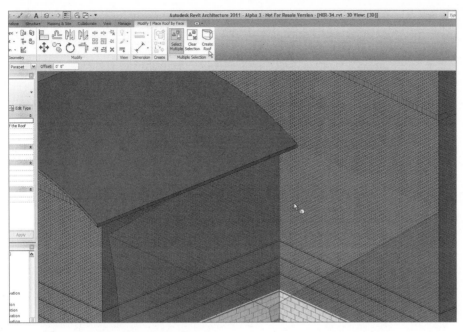

FIGURE 16.48 Creating the roof

24. Change Curtain Panel to System Panel : Glazed.

25. Set Join Condition to Border and Grid 1 Continuous. For the Grid 1 Pattern, set Layout to Maximum Spacing.

26. Set Spacing to 3′ 0″.

27. Repeat the layout and the grid spacing for the Grid 2 Pattern.

28. Change all of the mullions to use Rectangular Mullion : 2.5″ × 5″ rectangular (see Figure 16.49).

29. Click OK to get back to the model.

The next step is to apply the curtain system to the face(s) of the mass. The objective of the next series of steps is to apply the new curtain system to the front and the left side of the mass.

1. Pick the front face of the mass.

2. Pick the left face of the mass.

3. Click Create System. Your walls should resemble Figure 16.50.

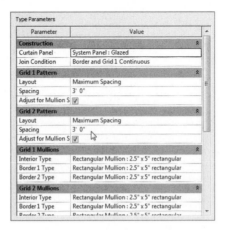

FIGURE 16.49   Changing the grid

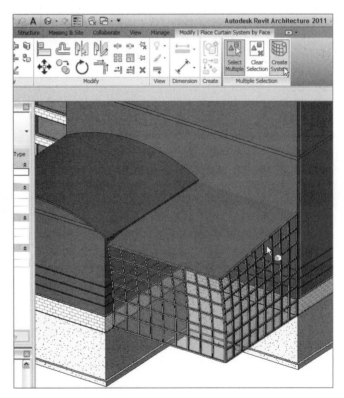

FIGURE 16.50   The new curtain wall

As you can see, we are just at the doorway of massing. Literally. There is no way to get into this little portico we just created. In the next chapter, we will discuss creating families and we will delve much deeper into the massing that comprises Revit Architecture 2010.

Are You Experienced?

Now you can...

- ☑ create custom compound walls by using the Edit Assembly dialog

- ☑ create stacked walls by joining compound walls together

- ☑ create sweeps in both the walls profile as well as free-form sweeps

- ☑ create curtain walls by using a predefined wall system and from a blank panel

- ☑ create vertically angled walls by applying a curtain system to a massing object

Creating Families

As you are probably becoming acutely aware, having the right content will make or break a Revit project. I am sure you are also acutely aware that, other than the content that Autodesk has provided and the content you downloaded from this book's web page, you don't have anywhere near the amount of content you need to start a project! That being said, it is time to buckle down and dig into how Revit works, and see how having adjustable, parametric families will turn you into a Revit fan for life.

▶ **Creating a basic family**

▶ **Using a complex family to create an arched door**

▶ **Creating an in-place family**

Creating a Basic Family

The first item we will tackle is how to create a basic family. We will start with the creation of a wall sweep, and then move into creating an arched doorway. As you become fluent with these two basic family types, it's going to be like a ball rolling down a hill!

Well, you have to start somewhere. To be honest, no good family is "basic," but some are simply easier to create than others. The concept is the same, however.

Essentially a family has three basic components:

Reference Planes   Yes, reference planes drive the family. Look at these as the skeleton of the family.

Constraints   Constraints are simply dimensions with a parameter associated with them to give the skeleton its flexibility.

3D Massing   3D massing is locked to the skeleton. We'll call this the skin. Corny, I know, but it gets the point across.

To get started, we need to figure out where to get started. Any family that you want to insert into a Revit model needs to start with a template. Choosing the correct template, as you will soon discover, will make your life much simpler.

The objective of the next procedure is to start a new family by choosing a template within Revit.

1. Open Revit Architecture.

2. In the Recent Files screen, click the New link in the Families row in the middle of the dialog (or you can click the Application button and select New ➤ Family).

3. In the Imperial Templates folder (this is where the family templates are stored), select Profile-Hosted.rft, and then click Open.

As mentioned earlier, first you will notice the reference planes. A good family starts and ends with these. Next you will notice some text. Revit adds some "advice" in each of its family templates. After you read the advice, you can delete it. We will do that in a moment, but first let's add some reference planes to the family.

Adding Reference Planes to a Family

The one bad thing about creating a family is that you can get away with making a family without using reference planes at all. This is bad because a family made with no (or not enough) reference planes will be faulty at best. This author has learned that lesson the hard way. Although it may seem redundant to add reference planes, I strongly advise you to use them and use them often.

The objective of the following procedure will be to offset some reference planes to create the wall sweep.

1. On the Datum panel of the Home tab, select the Reference Plane button, as shown in Figure 17.1.

2. In the Draw panel, click the Pick Lines button.

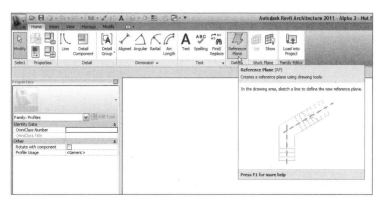

FIGURE 17.1 The Reference Plane button on the Home tab

3. On the Options bar, set Offset to 1'–0".

4. Hover your cursor over the center, vertical reference plane. When you see the blue reference line appear to the right of the vertical plane (as shown in Figure 17.2), pick the center reference plane. You will now have two vertical reference planes spaced 1'–0" apart.

5. With the Reference Plane command still running, pick the horizontal reference plane and offset it down using the same offset increment of 1'–0". Your family should now resemble Figure 17.3.

These two reference planes represent the actual body of the sweep. We will now add two secondary reference planes for more control over the family.

The objective of the following procedure is to add two more reference planes to the family.

1. Set Offset to 2".

2. Offset the top horizontal reference plane down.

3. Offset the left vertical reference plane to the right (see Figure 17.4).

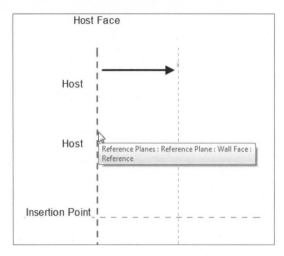

FIGURE 17.2 Adding a second vertical reference plane

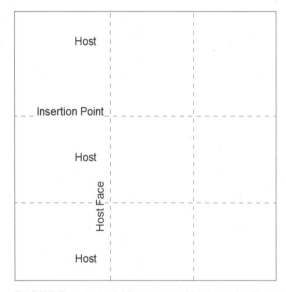

FIGURE 17.3 Adding a second horizontal reference plane downward

With the reference planes in place, we can now move on to adding some dimensions to the reference planes. After we add the dimensions, we can then add actual parameters to those dimensions to make our family flexible when we add it to the model.

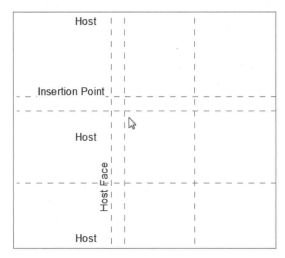

FIGURE 17.4 Offsetting two more reference planes

Adding Dimensions and Parameters to a Family

We are now looking at one of the most outstanding features of Revit. Because you can create a parametric component easily, and then allow the end user to change the dimensions, you can put your company into overdrive in terms of pushing BIM through and having success with Revit in general.

The first procedure involves adding dimensions to the reference planes we have already put into place. The second procedure will be to add parameters to the dimensions we have added.

1. On the Measure panel of the Modify | Place Reference Plane tab, click the Aligned Dimension button.

2. Add a horizontal dimension from the left reference plane to the right reference plane. The dimension should be 1′–0″.

3. Add a second dimension from the top reference plane to the bottom reference plane. The dimension should be 1′–0″.

4. Add a dimension from the left reference plane to the 2″ reference plane to the right.

5. Add a dimension from the top reference plane to the reference plane 2″ down (see Figure 17.5).

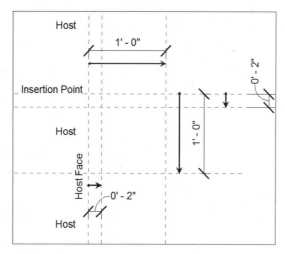

FIGURE 17.5 Adding the dimensions to the reference planes

The next step is to make this family come alive! Since we are in the Family Editor, when we select a dimension we can choose to add a label to the dimension. This label is tied to a parameter that can be modified.

To add a label to a dimension, follow these steps:

1. Press Esc twice; then select the top, horizontal 1′–0″ dimension.

2. On the Options bar, click the Label field and choose Add Parameter (see Figure 17.6).

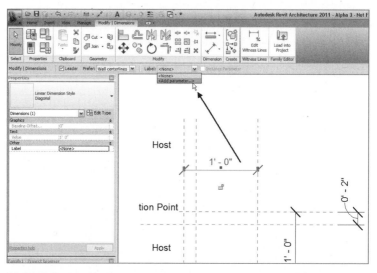

FIGURE 17.6 Choosing Add Parameter on the Options bar

3. In the Parameter Properties dialog under Parameter Data (as shown in Figure 17.7), type **Width** for the Name.

 N O T E   When you add a name to the parameter, you are actually adding part of a formula. There is a chance that this name will be part of a mathematical expression. When naming parameters, be deliberate, and give it some thought. Also, the mathematical expressions built into the parameters are case sensitive. If you capitalize the first letter of each word, be consistent.

---

4. In the Group Parameter Under field, select Dimensions.

5. Click the Type toggle (see Figure 17.7).

6. Click OK. The parameter is now added to the dimension.

7. Select the 1′–0″ vertical dimension.

8. On the Options bar, click the Label field.

F I G U R E 1 7 . 7 Configuring the parameter

---

9. Select Add Parameter from the menu.

10. For the Name, type **Height**.

11. Group the parameter under Dimensions.

12. Make it a Type parameter.

13. Click OK.

14. Select the two 2″ dimensions.

CHOOSING INSTANCE OR TYPE

The decision to use instance or type could be the most important decision you will make when creating family parameters. As you have noticed when you are modifying a family in the model (such as a wall, door, or window), you can either make a change to the one instance of the component you have selected, or you can click Type and change the component globally within the model. This is because, when the parameter was created, either the Instance or the Type toggle had been checked. So, when you are creating a parameter, you need to ask yourself, "Do I want the user to modify only one instance of this family by changing this parameter, or do I want the user to change every instance of this family by changing this parameter?"

Also, to complicate matters, if you plan to use this parameter in a mathematical expression, every parameter in that expression must be of the same type. For example, you cannot add an instance parameter to a type parameter. Revit will not allow it.

▶

Remember, if you hold the Ctrl key, you can select multiple items. The objective of selecting both of the 2″ dimensions is that we are going to create one parameter to put both of the items on it.

15. On the Options bar, click the Label menu.

16. Select Add Parameter.

17. For the name, type **Reveal**.

18. Group it under Dimensions.

19. Make it a Type parameter.

20. Click OK.

21. Click Esc to clear the selection.

Now that the reference planes are in place and the dimensions are set with the parameters, it is time to go behind the scenes and see how these families operate by examining the family types and adding formulas to the parameters.

The Type Properties Dialog

Within the Family Editor lies a powerful dialog that allows you to organize the parameters associated with the family you are creating. The Type Properties dialog also allows you to perform calculations, and to add increments in an attempt to test the flex of the family before it is passed into the model.

The objective of the following procedure is to open the Family Types dialog and configure some parameters.

1. On the Properties panel, click the Family Types button, as shown to the left in Figure 17.8.

FIGURE 17.8 The Family Types button on the Properties panel

2. In the Family Types dialog, click into the Formula cell in the Height row.

3. Type **Width**, and press the Tab key on your keyboard (see Figure 17.9).

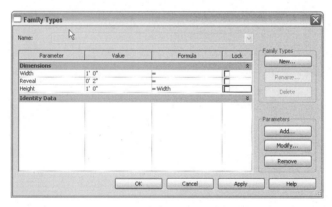

FIGURE 17.9 The Height parameter is now constrained to the Width parameter.

4. Click into the Width value (the area in the Width row that has the 1′–0″ increment).

5. Change Width from 1′–0″ to 6″. Notice the Height value changes too.

6. Click OK. The 1′–0″ dimensions are reduced to 6″.

7. Click the Family Types button.

8. Change the Width back to 1′–0″.

9. Click Apply.

10. Click the New button in the Family Types area, as shown in Figure 17.10.

11. Call the new type **12"x12"** and click OK (see Figure 17.10).

12. Click the New button again.

13. Call the new type **6"x6"**, and click OK.

14. Change Width to 6".

15. Change Reveal to 1".

16. Click Apply.

17. Change the Type back to **12"x12"**.

18. Click OK.

19. Click Save and save the family somewhere you will be able to retrieve it later. Name the file **Cove sweep.rfa**.

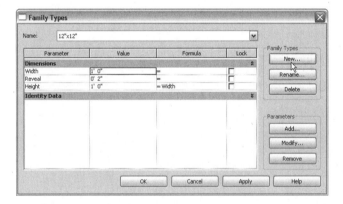

FIGURE 17.10 Creating a new family type

Now that we have the reference planes and parameters in place, we can flex the family to make sure that it will work properly when we load it into the project.

The next step is to add the physical lines that comprise the perimeter of the sweep. Given that this was created using the wall sweep template, the actual family is merely going to be a 2D profile. The family won't become a 3D object until we pass it into the model and use it as a wall sweep.

The objective of the next procedure is to draw the perimeter of the cove sweep.

1. On the Detail panel of the Home tab, click the Line button.

2. Draw a line from the intersection labeled "1" in Figure 17.11 to the intersection labeled "2" in Figure 17.11.

3. Draw a line from point 2 to point 3.

4. Press Esc.

5. Draw a line from point 1 to point 4.

6. Draw a line from point 4 to point 5.

7. On the Draw panel, click the Start-End-Radius Arc button and draw an arc from point 5 to point 3. Once the two points are snapped in place, move your cursor to the left until the radius snaps into place. Your family should look like Figure 17.11.

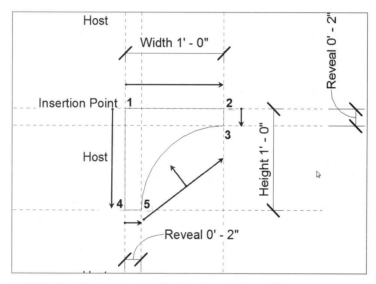

FIGURE 17.11 Drawing the boundary of the profile

IT'S TIME TO FLEX YOUR FAMILY!

Now that the family is complete, you need to go back to the Type Properties dialog and change the parameters to see where this family will break. This testing is called *flexing* in the Revit world and should be done as often as possible.

With the family completed, it is time to load it into the model and use it as a wall sweep. This is where you get to enjoy the fruits of your labor. To get started, open the building model you have been working on. If you missed the previous chapter, go to the book's web page at www.sybex.com/go/revit2011ner. From there you can browse to Chapter 17, and find the file called NER-34.rvt.

1. Open the Cove Sweep file (if you have closed it).

2. On the Family Editor panel, click the Load Into Project button.

3. In the NER-34 project, select one of the exterior walls in the east wing.

4. In the Properties dialog, click Edit Type.

5. Click the Edit button in the Structure row.

6. Make sure the preview is on and that it is showing a section.

7. Click the Sweeps button.

8. In the Wall Sweeps dialog, click the Add button.

9. For the Profile, select Cove Sweep : 12″×12″ from the list (notice the 6″× 6″ is available too).

10. For the Material, apply Concrete - Precast Concrete.

11. Set Distance to –1′ 4″.

12. In the From column to the right, make sure it says Top.

13. In the Side column, make sure the choice is Exterior.

14. Click OK twice.

15. Click OK yet again.

16. Zoom in on the walls—there should be a sweep, as shown in Figure 17.12.

You are getting a taste for what you can do with this powerful tool. And as you can see, we are only scratching the surface of the fun we can have. Now you are ready to try a real family!

The next section of this chapter will be spent creating an opening with a radial header. Think about the lessons learned in the cove sweep, and let's start really digging in.

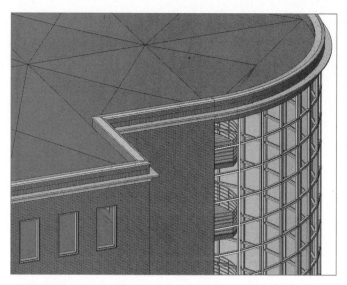

FIGURE 17.12 The new precast concrete wall sweep

Using a Complex Family to Create an Arched Door

Now that the "easy" family is out of the way, it's time to start blending the procedures of creating a parametric frame with actual 3D extrusions and sweeps. These 3D extrusions and sweeps will behave exactly like the cove family we just made. Once you learn how to create one type of family, the lessons you learned will transfer to the next.

This section of the chapter will start with a blank door template and proceed with modifying a wall cut, then move to adding casing, a jamb, and then a door.

The objective of the next procedure is to start a new family and create a door opening with an arched top.

1. Click the Application button and select New ➢ Family.

2. Find the template called Door.rft and click Open.

3. The first thing you will notice is that quite a bit of work has been done for you. This is great, but you don't need all the items in the template. Select the doorjambs, as shown in Figure 17.13, and delete them from either side of the door.

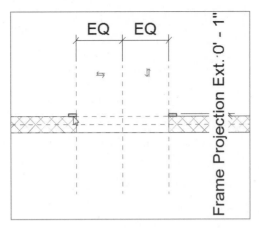

FIGURE 17.13 Deleting the jambs from either side of the door

4. In the Project Browser, find the Exterior elevation, under the Elevations (Elevation 1) category, and open it.

5. In this view you will see a wall and an opening. Select the bottom of the opening, as shown in Figure 17.14.

N O T E   The wall that you see is provided by Revit in order for you to design your opening to be flexible with any sized wall in the model after you load this family. Once the door family is in the project, this wall is removed. It is provided merely as a purpose for layout.

6. On the Options bar, click Transparent In: Elevation.

7. Next, click the Edit Sketch button on the Opening panel (see Figure 17.14).

8. By clicking Edit Sketch, you are now in Sketch Mode. On the Draw panel, click the Start-End-Radius Arc button, as shown in Figure 17.15.

9. Draw an arc, as shown in Figure 17.15.

10. Delete the leftover top line. Your door opening should be a continuous perimeter.

11. Click Finish Edit Mode.

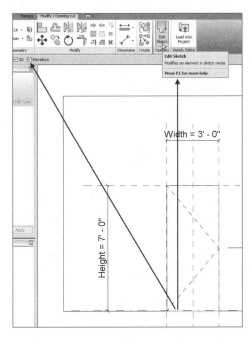

FIGURE 17.14 Editing the door opening

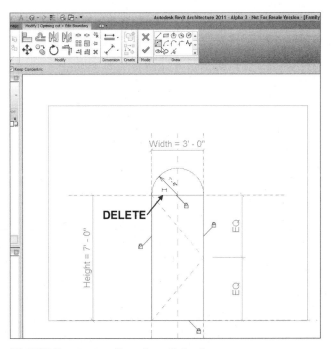

FIGURE 17.15 Rounding off the door top

With the opening in place, it is time to start testing! Yes, we need to test the width to see if the actual radial top will behave as expected. Taking the time to do this now is an extremely small concession to the pain of deleting half the family, later trying to find what "broke" the family.

The objective of the next, short procedure is to test the width of the opening.

1. Click the Family Types button on the Properties panel.

2. Change the value for Width to 4'–0".

3. Click OK.

4. Verify that the arc behaved as expected. If it did not, you need to reedit the opening and make sure you are snapped to the correct points.

I told you that would be quick. That is all the time it takes to make sure your family is good to go up to this point.

Now it's time to start adding some components to the family. The first item we will tackle is the doorjamb. This will be done by creating a solid form and then a solid extrusion.

Creating a 3D Extrusion within a Family

Other than the curtain wall we applied to a face of a mass in the previous chapter, we have been working in this massive 3D program without actually doing one single 3D operation. Well, that has come to an end. At some point, you will need to deal with 3D and massing. When it comes to learning families, you cannot avoid it.

3D within a family, however, is slightly different than any 3D item you may have created in the past. The wonderful thing about creating 3D items within a family is that these items are fully adjustable after they are created.

The objective of the next procedure is to create a doorjamb using solid extrusion. We will then lock the faces of the extrusion to the walls so the family will adapt to any wall thickness when passed into the model.

1. Make sure you are in the exterior elevation.

2. On the Forms panel of the Home tab, click the Extrusion button.

3. In the Work Plane panel, click the Set button, as shown in Figure 17.16.

4. In the Work Plane dialog, click Pick A Plane and click OK.

5. Pick the face of the wall, as shown in Figure 17.17.

6. Now that the work plane has been set, click the Pick Lines icon on the Draw panel.

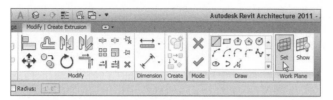

FIGURE 17.16 The Set button in the Work Plane panel

 WARNING   Step 3 has you setting the work plane to the face of the wall. *This step is of utmost importance.* If you skip this step, your door will not respond to the change in the wall's thickness when you load it into the model.

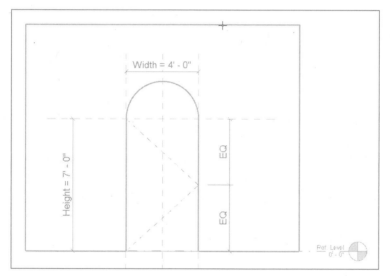

FIGURE 17.17 Setting the face of the wall as the work plane

7. On the Options bar, check the Lock toggle, as shown in Figure 17.18.

8. Pick the inside face of the opening, as shown in Figure 17.18.

9. After you pick the inside face, change the offset on the Options bar to 1″.

10. Pick the same lines offsetting the inside face of the jamb into the opening 1″.

11. Zoom into the bottom of the jambs.

LINE IS TOO SHORT?

You may get an error at some point as you pick these lines, as shown in the following image. This is more of a nuisance than anything else. All you need to do is click OK, delete the line(s) that were set into the wrong spot, and redo the same command. You will have more success the second time through.

12. Set the offset on the Options bar to 0″.

13. Draw a line connecting the bottom of each jamb, as shown in Figure 17.18.

14. In the Properties dialog, make sure the type is set to Extrusion, as shown in Figure 17.19.

15. Set Extrusion End to –3″, as shown in Figure 17.19.

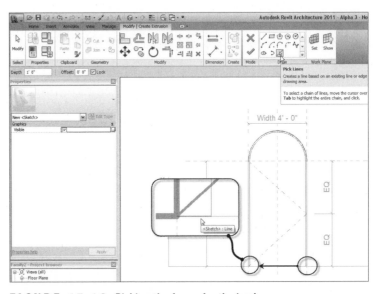

FIGURE 17.18 Picking the frame for the jamb

16. Click the small button to the right of the Material row, as shown in Figure 17.19.

FIGURE 17.19 Clicking the button to add a material parameter

17. Click Add Parameter at the bottom-left corner of the dialog.

18. Name it **Jamb Material**.

19. Group it under Materials And Finishes.

20. Keep it a Type parameter.

21. Click OK.

22. Notice the Material field is no longer active. Click OK again.

What did we just do? By not selecting the actual material in the properties of the extrusion, we created a parameter so users could specify whatever material they deemed necessary. This is a valuable step in family creation. It's called flexibility.

Speaking of flexibility, this jamb is held at a steady 3″. This is an incorrect value and will remain static unless we do something about it. We will do so right now. The objective of the next procedure is to align the inside face of the jamb with the inside face of the wall and to lock that alignment in place.

1. Go to a 3D view, and make sure you are "spun around" so you can see the inside face of the wall where the jamb does not align.

2. Click the Align button, as shown in Figure 17.20.

3. On the Options bar, select Wall Faces for Preference.

4. Pick the inside face of the wall.

5. Pick the inside face of the jamb.

6. Click the open padlock icon that appears (see Figure 17.20).

7. Press Esc.

8. Click the Save icon.

9. Save the door into a directory where you will be able to find it.

10. Call it **Arched Door.rfa**.

11. Make sure your project is open.

12. In the Arched Door.rfa file, click Load Into Projects.

13. In the model, open the Level 1 West dependent view.

14. On the Home tab, click the Door button.

15. Insert it in the wall, as shown in Figure 17.21. (Do not worry too much about placement.)

16. Select the door.

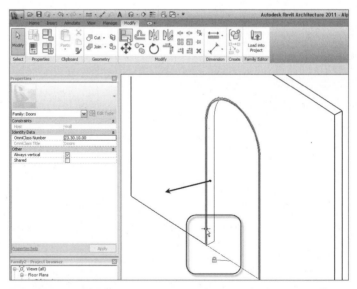

FIGURE 17.20 Aligning and locking the inside face of the jamb to the wall

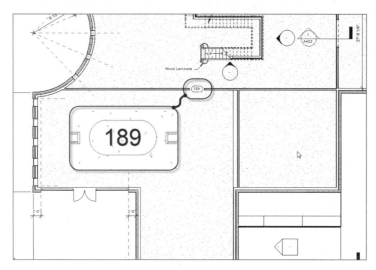

FIGURE 17.21 Adding the family to the project

17. In the Properties dialog, click Edit Type and observe the parameters. Look familiar? You created them!

18. Click OK.

19. Go back to the door family.

Wow! So this thing actually works. Good deal. The next trick is to add some casing to the outside of the frame. To do so, we will have to use a solid sweep.

Creating a 3D Sweep within a Family

Going along the same lines (literally) as the extrusion, we can create a situation where we actually sketch a path and extrude a profile along that path. The trick is to make sure that this sweep can flex along with the door.

The objective of the next procedure is to create the door casing by using a 3D sweep.

1. Go to a 3D view (if you are not there already) and position the view so it looks like Figure 17.22.

2. On the Home tab, click the Sweep button.

3. On the Sweep panel, click the Pick Path button.

4. Pick the inside corner of the jamb starting with the left side, as shown in Figure 17.22.

5. Click Finish Edit Mode on the Mode panel.

6. On the Sweep panel, click the Load Profile button.

7. Go to the Profiles folder and select Casing Profile-2.rfa.

8. Click Open.

9. In the menu on the Sweep panel, click the Profile drop-down and select Casing Profile 2:5 1/2″ × 3/16″ (notice the red dot is now replaced with the actual profile).

10. On the Options bar, type –0′–5 3/4″ for the Y offset. Notice the profile is pushed back onto the wall with a 1/4″ reveal.

11. Click Finish Edit Mode.

12. In the Properties dialog, click the small button to the right of the Material category.

13. Click Add Parameter.

14. Call the parameter **Casing Material**.

15. Group it under Materials and Finishes.

16. Click OK twice.

17. Repeat steps 1 through 20 on the other side of the door. (Do not try to mirror it. It will not work.)

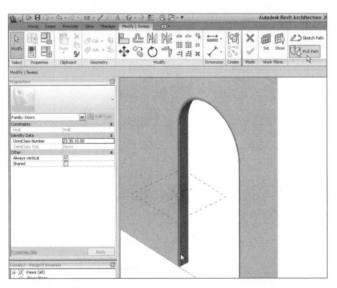

FIGURE 17.22 Picking the path for the sweep

18. Save the family.

19. Load it into the project.

20. In your model, select the door.

21. In the Properties dialog, click Edit Type.

22. Change the Width value to 3′–0″.

23. Click OK.

Your door is still working properly and is looking better as shown in Figure 17.23.

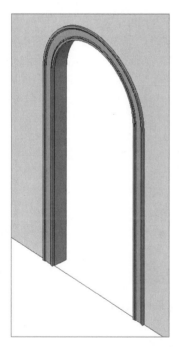

FIGURE 17.23 The finished sweep

Let's move forward and start working on adding a door to the family. The biggest challenge here will be the plan swing representation, but with a few new items to learn, this will be no problem.

The objective of the next procedure is to add a door, a stop, and some plan symbolic linework.

1. Open the door family.

2. Go to the exterior elevation.

3. On the Home tab, click the Extrusion button.

4. On the Draw panel, click the Pick Lines icon.

5. Set the offset to 1/8″.

6. Offset the two sides and the radial top to the inside 1/8″.

7. Set the offset to 1/2″.

8. Offset the bottom up (see Figure 17.24).

9. Trim the bottom corners so the door is one panel.

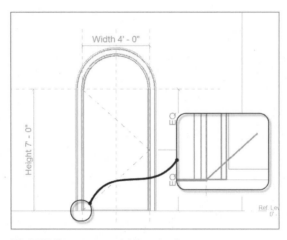

FIGURE 17.24 Adding the door

10. In the Properties dialog, make sure Extrusion is current in the Type menu.

11. For the Extrusion end, type -1 3/8″.

12. For the material, click the button to the right of the Material field, and add a new parameter called **Door Material**.

13. Categorize it under Materials And Finishes.

14. Click OK.

15. Click Finish Edit Mode.

16. In the Project Browser, go to the Ref. Level floor plan view.

17. Click the Thin Lines button on the View tab, as shown in Figure 17.25. You door should look like this figure.

18. Load the door into your project. (Click Yes to overwrite the door that is there.) Verify that the door looks correct.

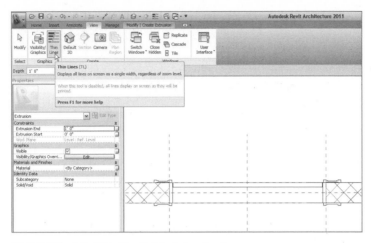

FIGURE 17.25 The finished door in plan

Now that you have created the door, it is time to fix up the plan view. What we need to do is add a door swing. Also, we don't want to see the door panel in plan, so we can create a view state to turn it off in the plan view.

The objective of the next procedure is to create a door swing and to make the door panel invisible in plan.

1. On the Annotate tab, click the Symbolic Line button, as shown in Figure 17.26.

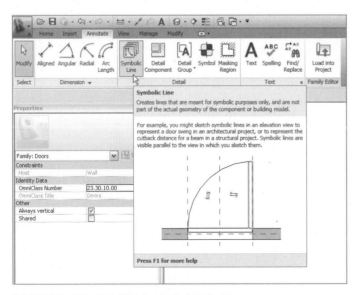

FIGURE 17.26 The Symbolic Line button

2. Draw a line straight up from the right corner of the jamb (on the exterior side of the wall) 4'–0", as shown in Figure 17.27.

3. Draw another line to the right 1 3/8".

4. Draw another line straight down 4'–0".

5. Draw another line to the right 1 3/8" (see Figure 17.27).

6. Click the Symbolic Line button again.

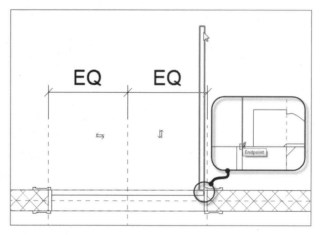

FIGURE 17.27 Drawing the symbolic door swing

7. Draw an arc from the left side of the jamb to the top of the symbolic swing, as shown in Figure 17.28.

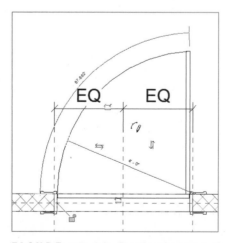

FIGURE 17.28 Drawing the plan swing arc

With the plan swing in place, we can now turn off the actual door panel. This process is quick and painless!

1. Select the door panel.

2. On the Modify | Extrusion tab, click the Visibility Settings button on the Mode panel.

3. Uncheck Plan/RCP.

4. Uncheck When Cut In Plan/RCP (If Category Permits).

5. Click OK.

6. Save the family.

7. Load it into the project. If it didn't explode, your door is complete!

As you can see, it is not all that difficult to create a family. This topic could be a book within a book. Start experimenting with your own families. If you run into a snag, send me an email at ewing@cscos.com, and we can work on it.

The next type of family we will study is one that literally can't be avoided. Eventually you will need the surrounding geometry of the model to create the family. This is called an *in-place family*.

Creating an In-Place Family

An in-place family gives you the best of both worlds. When you start the In-Place Family command, your model turns into the Family Editor. You can make a family exactly the same way you just did, except that it is native to the model. Many times you will need this flexibility when you have a family you will never use again in any other building. This also gives you the flexibility to create custom content that cannot be created using the conventional Revit commands.

To create an in-place family, follow along with this procedure:

1. Open the model you have been working on.

2. Open the section view called West Wing South Wall Section.

3. On the Home tab, click Component ➢ Model In-Place, as shown in Figure 17.29.

4. Set Family Category to Doors; then click OK.

5. Call the new door **West Opening**.

6. Click OK.

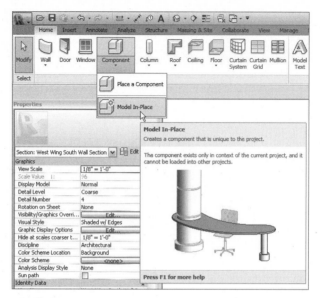

FIGURE 17.29 Starting an In-Place family

7. On the Model panel of the Home tab, click the Opening button.

8. Pick the brick wall facing you.

9. Sketch an opening, as shown in Figure 17.30.

10. Click Finish Edit Mode.

11. Go to a 3D view.

12. On the Forms panel of the Home tab, click the Sweep button.

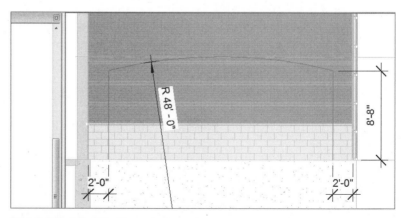

FIGURE 17.30 The arched opening

13. On the Sweep panel, click the Pick Path button.

14. Pick the exterior corners of the opening forming the arc and the two straight lines to either side of the opening (see Figure 17.31).

15. Click Finish Edit Mode on the Mode tab.

16. In the Project Browser, go to the Level 1 West floor plan.

17. Click the Select Profile button on the Sweep panel.

18. On the Sweep panel, click the Edit Profile button (see Figure 17.32).

19. Sketch the profile, as shown in Figure 17.32.

When you are picking the lines for the path, you will find that you cannot pick the entire line on either the two sides or the arc. All you need to do is pick any line on the three corners, and then trim them to meet at the corners.

FIGURE 17.31 Picking the exterior edge for the sweep's path

20. Click Finish Profile.

21. In the Properties dialog, make sure Sweep is current, and then click the little gray button to the left of the Materials row.

22. Add a parameter called **Casing Material**.

23. At the bottom of the dialog in the Other category, click the Trajectory Segmentation.

24. Set Maximum Segment Angle to 1.

25. Click OK.

26. Click Finish Sweep.

27. Click Finish Model.

28. Go to a 3D view; your opening should look like Figure 17.33.

The moral of this story is this: when you have a custom situation within the model that cannot be created using the conventional Revit tools, create an in-place family. You should also make it as flexible as possible, and give the user some choices, such as materials, so anyone can manipulate the family as if Autodesk itself provided it.

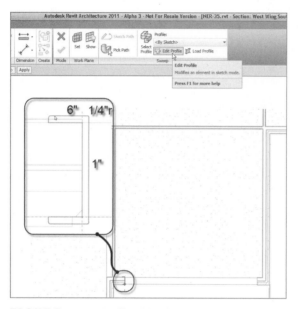

FIGURE 17.32 Sketching the profile

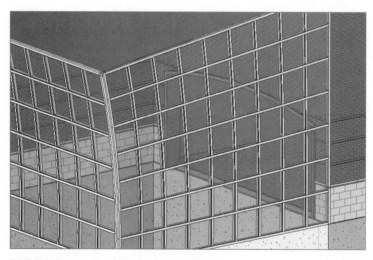

FIGURE 17.33 The finished family

Are You Experienced?

Now you can...

- ☑ create a cove sweep family
- ☑ identify the family template you need to use to start a family
- ☑ create a door family
- ☑ add symbolic lines to a family
- ☑ create an in-place family
- ☑ create sweeps and extrusions
- ☑ create parameters

CHAPTER 18

Site and Topography

You might be asking yourself if there is a fourth Revit. No. It would be nice if there was a "Revit Civil," but there isn't such a thing. So, we are left to our own devices when it comes to adding a site to our model. This is fine, because in many cases Revit is well equipped to take on the challenge. Unfortunately, also in many cases Revit is dependent on AutoCAD or MicroStation to provide a real-case scenario for a site that can be imported (similar to importing a plan or a detail). Fortunately, Revit provides tools to add a topographic surface to an imported CAD site.

▶ **Adding a site within Revit**

▶ **Splitting the surface**

▶ **Creating subregions**

▶ **Adding site components**

▶ **Adding building pads to displace earth**

▶ **Adding a property line**

▶ **Creating a toposurface by instance**

▶ **Creating a graded region**

▶ **Orienting a site**

Adding a Site within Revit

To get started, let's do something easy, and then migrate into the more difficult areas such as importing a CAD file. The first item we will tackle will be to start a site using datum points that you will manually pick using the Toposurface function on the Ribbon's Massing & Site tab.

The first major function within Revit Architecture for adding a site is the topographic surface. Revit has a separate tab on the Ribbon called the Massing & Site tab that lets you access this feature.

So, let's get cracking. To get started, open the model you have been working on. If you missed the previous chapter, go to the book's web page at **www.sybex.com/ go/revit2011ner**. From there you can browse to Chapter 18 and find the file called NER-35.rvt.

The objective of the next procedure is to add a topographical surface by choosing datum points and elevations.

1. In the Project Browser, find the floor plan called Site and open it.

2. On the Massing & Site tab, click the Toposurface button, as shown in Figure 18.1.

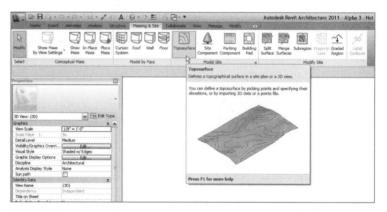

FIGURE 18.1 Click the Toposurface button on the Site tab of the Design bar.

3. On the Options bar, set the elevation to –6″ (that's negative 6″).

4. Pick points in a circle around the footprint of the building, as shown in Figure 18.2.

N O T E   Notice that after you clicked the Toposurface button, Revit launched the Sketch Mode. The button that is selected by default within the Toposurface Sketch Mode is the Points button.

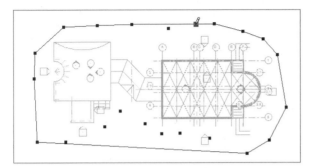

F I G U R E   18.2 Adding the first contours

5. With the Points command still running, set Elevation on the Options bar to –1′–0″.

6. Pick a circle surrounding the inside contour lines, as shown in Figure 18.3.

7. With the Points command still running, set Elevation on the Options bar to –3′–0″.

8. Add a third contour line surrounding the second, as shown in Figure 18.4.

9. Click Finish Surface (the green checkmark).

10. Select the topographical surface; then, in the Properties dialog, click into the Material field, and click the […] button.

11. Choose Site - Grass from the Materials list and click OK.

12. Go to a 3D view and check out your site, as shown in Figure 18.5.

Next let's see how we can modify a site after we create it. We will have to deal with the fact that the ramps at the west entry are buried in our site now.

Modifying a Toposurface

Since you must always make modifications to a toposurface, you will need to learn how to do so. The method is basic. Select the site, click Edit, and away you go!

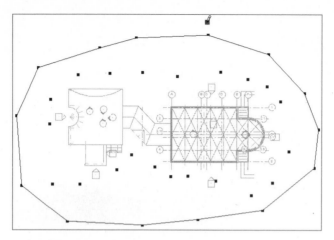

FIGURE 18.3 Adding the second contour to the site

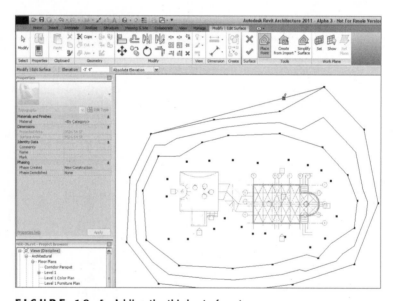

FIGURE 18.4 Adding the third set of contours

The objective of the next procedure is to modify the toposurface to allow for the ramps to land on earth.

1. Go back to the Site plan.

2. Zoom in on the east entry area where the ramps are located, as shown in Figure 18.6.

3. Select the site (you may have to find an edge).

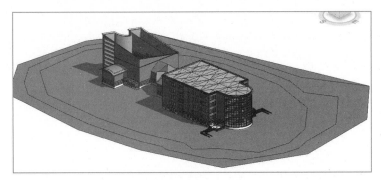

FIGURE 18.5 The toposurface

4. On the Modify | Topography tab, click Edit Surface.

5. On the Tools panel, click the Place Point button.

6. On the Options bar, set Elevation to –2′–6″ (negative 2′–6″).

7. Pick a series of points, as shown in Figure 18.6.

8. Click Finish Surface on the Surface panel.

9. Go to a 3D view to make sure the ramps are terminating at grade.

10. Save the model.

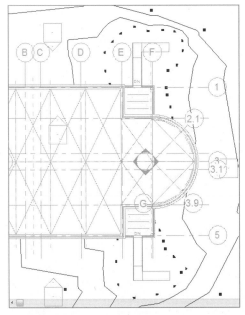

FIGURE 18.6 Adding the –2′–6″ points

Excellent! You are getting the hang of this. Next, we need to create some raised areas (small hills) where we can eventually add some plantings and different materials. The problem is, to create a small hill, we need the site to sharply rise to the new elevation. To achieve this, we have to physically split the surface.

Splitting the Surface

When you need a drastic change in the surface's elevation without influencing the rest of the site, you must split the surface. Just to warn you up front, be deliberate about when and where you do this because you are physically cutting a hole in the surface and adding a secondary toposurface to the void. Although you can merge these surfaces back together, in some situations it can be difficult to merge cleanly.

The objective of the next procedure is to split the toposurface and create smaller toposurfaces.

1. In the Project Browser, go back to the Site plan.

2. On the Massing & Site tab, click the Split Surface button, as shown in Figure 18.7.

3. Select the toposurface.

4. Zoom in on the corridor area that links the east and the west wings, as shown in Figure 18.8.

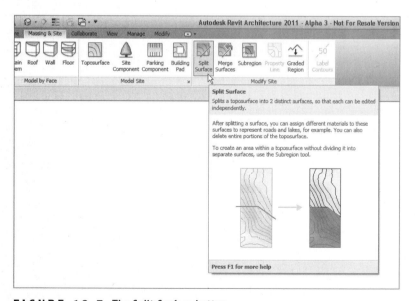

FIGURE 18.7 The Split Surface button

5. On the Draw panel, click the Line button.

6. Sketch a perimeter similar to the one in Figure 18.8.

7. Click Finish Edit Mode. You now have a new toposurface.

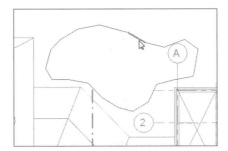

FIGURE 18.8 The split surface sketch

Now we can manipulate this surface without influencing the main topography. This is the ideal situation for creating bumps and berms.

The objective of the next procedure is to raise this toposurface to an elevation of 4′–0″. We do this by using a point and placing the datum in the middle of the berm.

1. Select the newly formed toposurface as shown in Figure 18.9.

2. Click the Edit Surface button on the Modify | Topography tab.

3. On the Tools panel, click the Place Point button.

4. On the Options bar, enter a value of 4′–0″ in the Elevation field.

5. Pick three points near the center of the hill, as shown in Figure 18.9.

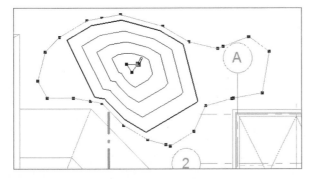

FIGURE 18.9 Adding a new datum elevation

6. Click Finish Surface.

7. Go to a 3D view, and orbit around so the hill is visible.

8. Select the hill.

9. In the Properties dialog, in the Material field, click the [...] button.

10. In the Materials dialog, select Site - Earth.

11. Click OK.

12. Deselect the topography. Your site should resemble Figure 18.10.

After you place the points in the model, you can still pick the points and drag them left and right, as well as up and down. Also, if you look at the site in section or elevation, you can pick the points and drag them up and down, too.

NOTE Yes, you can copy these little hills around just like anything else in Revit—I am very glad you asked! After you copy the hills, you can edit them just like any other toposurface.

Well, I think you can see where this is all going. When you work with sites, it is just good to have some kind of procedure. This takes us to our next perplexing situation. Suppose we just want to keep the contours and the dips and hills intact, and we only want to specify a new material in a subregion of the main topography? Well, we can!

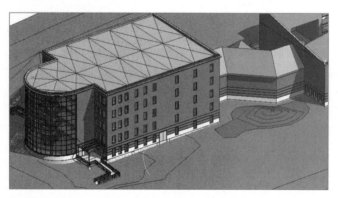

FIGURE 18.10 The raised area of the site

Creating Subregions

The purpose of a subregion is to match two surfaces together so any change in elevation or lateral movement will be reflected within both regions. We need this ability for walks and most roadways. When you split the toposurface into subregions, you give yourself the freedom to manipulate two different materials within the same datum. Another benefit to subregions is that the file size will remain as if there was still one toposurface. If you were to split the surface every time you needed a path or a roadway, your file size would bloat.

The objective of the following procedure is to create a walkway path using the subregion command.

1. Go to the Site plan.

2. Zoom in on the east entry.

3. On the Massing & Site tab, click the Subregion button, as shown in Figure 18.11.

4. On the Draw panel, click the Start-End-Radius-Arc button.

5. Draw a path similar to the one shown in Figure 18.12. (It does not have to be exact.)

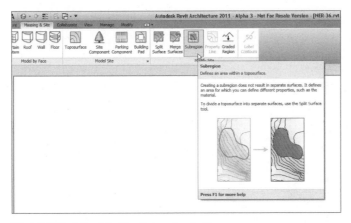

FIGURE 18.11 The Subregion button

6. Click Finish Edit Mode.

7. Select the subregion.

8. In the Properties dialog, change Material to Site - Earth.

9. Create another subregion extending to the bottom ramp. Use your imagination.

10. Go to a 3D view and compare yours with Figure 18.13.

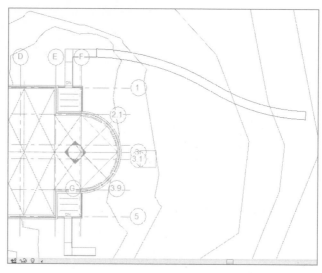

FIGURE 18.12 Sketching the subregion

 NOTE You cannot cross over and exceed the extents of the original boundary. If you do, Revit will not allow you to finish the sketch. Also, this subregion must form a continuous loop with no gaps or overlapping lines. You will need a straight line at each end of the path.

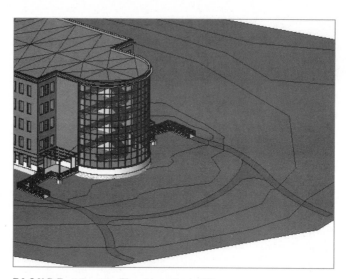

FIGURE 18.13 The sidewalks in 3D

How did you do? If you don't like the line in the sidewalk, you can simply redo the two separate sidewalks and create just one.

Not too shabby! There definitely is something missing from this site, though. It sure would be nice to start adding some trees and plantings. The great thing about adding plantings after you have your topography in place is that any site component added to the model will be hosted by the topography. This means you do not have to determine the elevation.

Adding Site Components

Adding a site component to Revit is no different than adding a desk or a door. A component is a component as far as Revit is concerned. As you have learned, a component is hosted by a system component. For example, when you are inserting a window, there needs to be a wall, or Revit will not allow such a foolish transaction to occur. The same goes for a site component. You need dirt to plant a tree!

The objective of this next procedure is to add various trees and plantings to the Revit model. First, however, we need to load some bushes.

1. On the Insert tab, click the Load Family button.

2. Scroll to the Planting directory.

3. Load every file in the directory.

4. In the Project Browser, go to the Site plan.

5. On the Massing & Site tab, click the Site Component button, as shown in Figure 18.14.

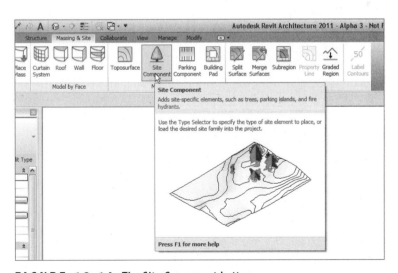

FIGURE 18.14 The Site Component button

6. In the Change Element Type menu In the Properties dialog, click the RCP Shrub Boxwood 2′–9″ and line your walkway, as shown in Figure 18.15.

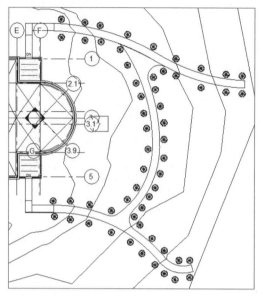

FIGURE 18.15 Adding the shrubs to the walkway

7. Click the Site Component button again.

8. From the Change Element Type menu, select any tree you wish, and plant it on our little hill.

9. Put some shrubs around it.

10. Go to a 3D view and compare it to that shown in Figure 18.16.

Now that we have all the contours and plantings in place, we need to knock out a small maintenance issue. There is a function that will allow you to automatically add contour labels to the site. This is a great feature in Revit Architecture.

Adding Contour Properties and Labels

Since nothing in Revit Architecture is "dumb," we can take advantage of a topographic surface having some "smarts" as well. Even the contour lines of a site are smart.

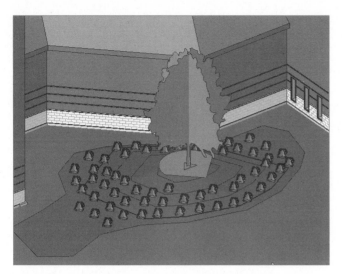

FIGURE 18.16 The trees and shrubs on the hill

 N O T E   Now that looks simply horrible! Don't worry. When we move to the next chapter, we will focus on rendering. This is where the trees literally come to life.

The objective of this next procedure is to examine some site settings and throw some labels into the contours. It is a quick set of steps, but important nonetheless. To examine the Site Settings, run through the following procedure:

1. Click the arrow in the lower-right corner of the Model Site panel, as shown in Figure 18.17.

2. In the Site Settings dialog, you will see a field that contains additional contours. In the Increment panel, change the value of 1′ 0″ to 6″, as shown in Figure 18.17.

3. Click OK. Notice the contours are tighter.

With the contours in place, it is time to label them. Luckily there is a function in Revit that allows you to do it all in one shot. All you need to do is draw a *line* specifying the alignment of the contours, and let Revit add the labels automatically.

FIGURE 18.17 Changing the additional contour increment

Follow these steps to add contour labels to the site:

1. On the Massing & Site tab, click the Label Contours button, as shown in Figure 18.18.

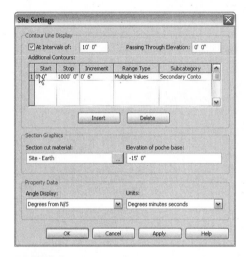

FIGURE 18.18 The Label Contours button

2. Pick a point to the outside of the toposurface, labeled "1" in Figure 18.19.

3. Pick a second point near the building, labeled "2" in Figure 18.19. After you pick the second point, the contours are labeled.

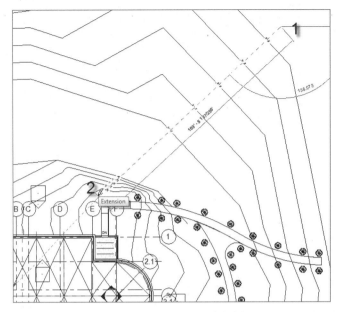

FIGURE 18.19 Adding the contour labels

With the site in place, it is time to address a situation that has arisen unbeknownst to you. You see, we never defined any areas where we may not want earth to "spill into," such as the basement. This will affect every section that we have. We can place a *pad* to displace the earth in the basement.

Adding Building Pads to Displace Earth

When you need to displace a volume of earth, you use a tool exclusive to the Massing & Site tab to do so. By placing a building pad into your model, you tell Revit that you want to cut the earth away from this area while still leaving the earth beneath a certain elevation. For example, if you wanted to remove the earth from the basement (which we will be doing) but you still needed the earth to exist beneath the basement, you must place a building pad.

To place a building pad into the model, follow this procedure:

1. In the Project Browser, go to the T.O. Footing plan. It is located in the Structural category.

2. On the Massing & Site tab, click the Building Pad button, as shown in Figure 18.20.

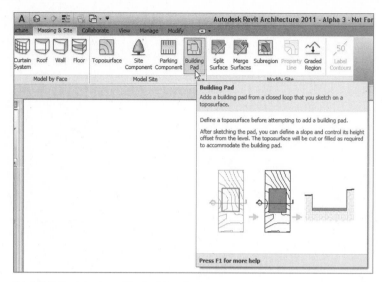

FIGURE 18.20 The Building Pad button

3. In the Properties dialog, make sure Pads is current, and click Edit Type.

4. Click Duplicate.

5. Call the pad **Footprint**, and click OK.

6. For the Structure, click the Edit button.

7. Change the Thickness to 6″.

8. Click OK twice.

9. Change Height Offset From Level to 6″.

10. Place the pad against the outside of the foundation wall underneath the entire model, as shown in Figure 18.21.

11. Click Finish Edit Mode.

12. In the Project Browser, open the East Corridor Section.

13. You can see the pad sitting on top of the footing extending past the wall, as shown in Figure 18.22. Select it.

14. When the pad is selected, right-click and select Hide In View ➢ Elements, as shown in Figure 18.22.

15. Go to the Model Site panel and click the Site Settings arrow.

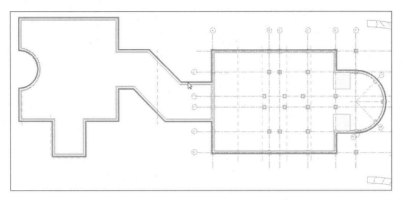

FIGURE 18.21 Place the pad to the outside of the wall.

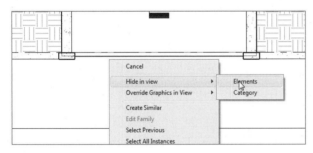

FIGURE 18.22 Hiding the pad in the view

16. In the Section Graphics area, change the Elevation Of Poche Base value to –15′ 0″.

17. Click OK. The earth hatch is now beneath the slab area.

With the pad in place, we can now rest assured that our sections are showing the earth where it is supposed to be.

The next item we will cover is creating a property line. In most conventional drafting applications, this involves nothing more than adding a polyline around the site. In Revit that approach is the same, but the property line can tell you much more about the boundary it is incasing.

Adding a Property Line

If you want to add a property line, Revit provides you with the tool you need. Of course this is Revit here, so we are not just adding a "dumb line" to the model. When you start the Property Line command, Revit will ask you if you want to create the property line either by using bearing distances or by Sketch (which can be converted to a bearing table after it has been placed).

To add a property line, follow this procedure:

1. In the Project Browser, go to the Site floor plan.

2. In the Massing & Site tab, click the Property Line button, as shown in Figure 18.23.

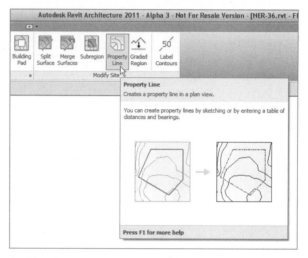

FIGURE 18.23 The Property Line button

3. In the Create Property Line dialog that appears, click the Create By Sketching choice.

4. Draw a series of lines around the perimeter, as shown in Figure 18.24.

5. Click Finish Edit Mode.

6. Select the property line.

7. On the Modify | Property Lines panel, click the Edit Table button.

8. Click Yes if you get a "do you want to continue" dialog.

9. Close the Property Lines dialog, and save the model.

You now have a table of deed data that can be modified as you see fit.

The next item on the agenda is a powerful tool when it comes to creating a site in Revit. As much as it would be nice to never depend on CAD, most of our topographical information will be coming from the CAD world. Revit has a "By Instance" function that can facilitate this procedure.

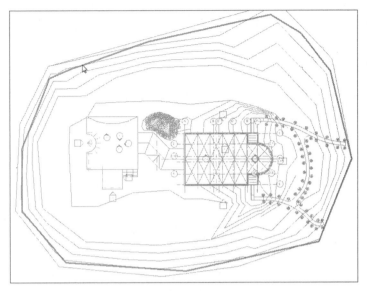

FIGURE 18.24 Sketching the property line

Creating a Toposurface by Instance

Creating a toposurface by instance requires that you import a CAD file. After you import the CAD file, you can go to the Toposurface command. Within the Toposurface command is the choice to use an imported instance to drape a surface from Revit.

To get started, you can either choose a site that was created in CAD that you may want to experiment with, or you can go to the book's web page at **www.sybex.com/go/revit2011ner**. From there you can browse to Chapter 18 and find the file called contours.dwg.

To use an imported instance to create a toposurface, follow these steps:

1. In Revit, create a brand-new project.

2. Save it as Imported Site.rvt.

3. In the Project Browser, go to the Site plan.

4. On the Insert tab, click the Import CAD button.

5. Browse to the contours.dwg file you downloaded. (If you have your own site .dwg, that's fine too.)

6. Before you click Open, change Colors to Black And White, Layers to All, and Import Units to Feet. Also, change Positioning to Auto - Origin To Origin.

7. Click Open.

8. Type **ZA** to see the entire site.

9. On the Massing & Site tab, click the Toposurface button.

10. On the Tools panel, click Create From Import ➤ Select Import Instance, as shown in Figure 18.25.

FIGURE 18.25 Select Import Instance command

11. Select the imported CAD file.

12. Uncheck Layer 0 and Defpoints in the Add Points From Selected Layers dialog.

13. Click OK.

14. In the Properties dialog, change Material to Site - Grass.

15. Click OK to get back to the model.

16. Click Finish Surface.

17. Go to a 3D view. Your topography should look like Figure 18.26.

Now that would be a hard toposurface to create entirely within Revit! The next item we need to explore is how to grade a surface, giving us areas of cuts and fills. The process itself is straightforward, but as you are about to learn, we need to first deal with *project phasing*.

Creating a Graded Region

This section of the chapter will focus on creating cuts and fills within a site. We do this by lowering and raising points that already exist within the topography. The problem is, after we alter the site, we do not know which part of the site is original, or existing, and which part is new. This means that we have two issues at hand.

FIGURE 18.26 The new toposurface in Revit

The objective of the following procedure is to move the site to an existing phase to prepare it for the grading procedure.

1. Type VG.

2. In the Visibility/Graphic Overrides dialog, click the Imported Categories tab.

3. Uncheck contours.dwg.

4. Click OK.

5. Select the toposurface.

6. In the Properties dialog, change Phase Created to Existing.

7. On the Massing & Site tab, click the Graded Region button, as shown in Figure 18.27.

8. In the next dialog, click Create A New Toposurface Exactly Like The Existing One.

9. Select the toposurface.

10. You will get a warning stating that you may not be able to see all the points. Click the X to close the warning.

11. In the Properties dialog, change the type to Floor Plan: Site.

12. Scroll down to the View Range field, and click the Edit button.

13. Choose Unlimited for both Primary Range: Bottom and View Depth Level.

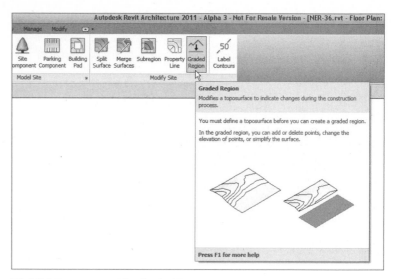

FIGURE 18.27 The Graded Region button

14. Click OK.

15. Select a window around the center of the site (this will select a bunch of points), as shown in Figure 18.28.

16. In the Properties dialog, enter a value of 0 for the elevation.

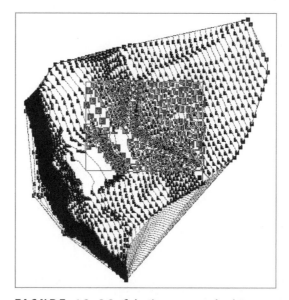

FIGURE 18.28 Selecting a range of points

17. Click Finish Surface.

18. Verify that your site appears similar to Figure 18.29.

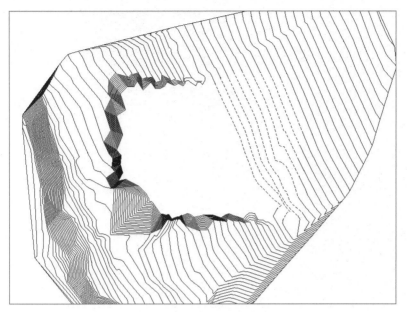

F I G U R E   1 8 . 2 9 The site with cuts and fills

19. Save the model and close it.

Now that we know how to create graded regions in a site, it is time to delve into physically rotating a site to true north.

Orienting a Site

How do we rotate a site to true north while keeping the rest of the model positioned in the 0 degree orientation? Well, there is a specific procedure, which you will learn by following along:

1. Open the NER-35.rvt file you have been working on (or any file with a site that you may be using).

2. Go to the Site plan (if it does not open there) and find the Orientation category in the Properties dialog; change it from Project North to True North.

3. On the Project Location panel of the Manage tab, click Position ➤ Rotate True North.

4. In the Options bar, type **130** for the CCW Rotation Angle value, as shown in Figure 18.30.

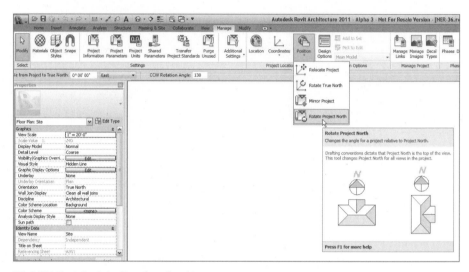

FIGURE 18.30 Rotating the site

5. Go to the Level 1 floor plan; the site will still be oriented to Project North while the site plan is of a different orientation. Of course, now this mindset makes the North Wing and the East Wing nomenclature irrelevant to the actual orientation of the site (see Figures 18.31 and 18.32).

T I P   **You must physically reposition the property line based on the northing easting coordinates that were preset. In the future, add the property lines after you rotate the site to true north.**

Now that we have accomplished rotating the site, what happens if we need to move the entire model to a datum point recorded from sea level? As it stands, we just started modeling from an elevation of 0. This situation needs to be addressed.

The objective of the following procedure is to relocate the datum elevation to 100′–0″:

1. In the Project Browser, open the South elevation.

2. Select one level marker.

3. In the Properties dialog, click Edit Type.

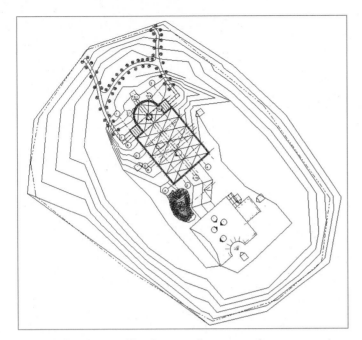

FIGURE 18.31 The site rotated to true north

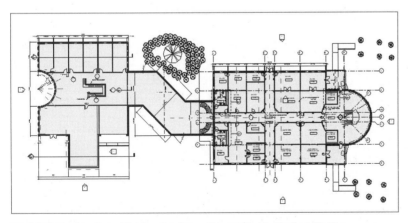

FIGURE 18.32 The Level 1 floor plan rotated to Project North

4. For Elevation Base, select Shared.

5. Click OK.

6. On the Manage tab, click Position ➤ Relocate Project (see Figure 18.33).

7. Pick the point labeled "1" in Figure 18.33.

8. Move your pointer directly up from the first point.

9. Type 100 (see Figure 18.33).

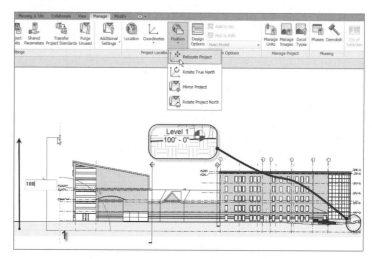

FIGURE 18.33 Relocating the project

Now that you know how to position your entire model laterally and vertically, you can adapt to whatever condition you need to design to.

Are You Experienced?

Now you can...

- ☑ **add a topographical surface to your site by using points**

- ☑ **create a topographical surface in your site by using an imported CAD file**

- ☑ **add site components**

- ☑ **split and divide a site's topography**

- ☑ **rotate a project to true north**

- ☑ **relocate a project's datum elevation**

Rendering and Presentation

Well, here we are! The chapter you have probably been chomping at the bit to get into—and for good reason! It's the output that we create from this chapter that will make our bosses, and better yet, our clients get behind our presentations. Like I always say, none of this software is any good if you can't capture the work to begin with. That being said, in this chapter we will focus on creating renderings and adding animations and provide solar studies based on the project's geographical location.

▶ **Creating an exterior rendering**

▶ **Interior rendering**

▶ **Creating walkthroughs**

▶ **Creating a solar study**

Creating an Exterior Rendering

The first item we need to tackle is how to go about creating an exterior rendering. Just trying to address the subject of rendering as a whole would convolute the matter. The thing is, when we create a rendering, lighting obviously plays a major role. Day lighting and artificial lighting are two completely different bears; one will influence the effect of the other. For example, if you are rendering an exterior scene, there are bound to be windows. If this rendering appears at night, or at dusk, the interior lights will be turned on.

The objective of the first section of this chapter is to create a rendering from the exterior of the building using day lighting scenes, sky, and shadowing to create the rendering we need.

In the previous chapter, we completed one of the hardest tasks when it comes to creating a proper exterior rendering: how a building is rotated in terms of true north. It stands to reason that your rendering will not be accurate if you have a glass curtain wall that is facing north but still have sunlight pouring through it. The correct building orientation is crucial, and we have accomplished that part. If you didn't read Chapter 18, "Site and Topography," you can still proceed with this chapter, but I strongly recommend that you review the last section of Chapter 18 as soon as you get the chance.

To get started, open the model you have been working on. If you missed the previous chapter, go to the book's web page at **www.sybex.com/go/revit2011ner**. From there you can browse to Chapter 19 and find the file called NER-36.rvt.

The objective of the first procedure is to create a camera view that we can use for our first rendering. We will then adjust the view controls and look at the sunlight effects.

1. In the Project Browser, open the Level 1 floor plan.

2. Zoom in on the corridor area in the middle of the building.

3. Add some curtain walls to the corridors, as shown in Figure 19.1. (Come on, I know you can do it.) These are Level 1 to Level 3 with a –6" offset from Level 3. You can use the Curtain Wall Storefront.

4. On the View tab, select 3D View ➢ Camera.

5. Create a camera view of the area shown in Figure 19.1.

6. Find the view in the Project Browser. It will probably be 3D View 3 under 3D Views.

7. When you find the view, rename it to **Rendering View Corridor**.

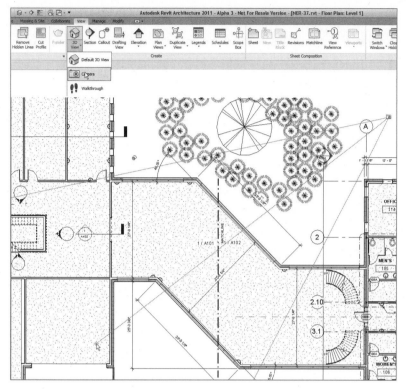

FIGURE 19.1 Creating the camera view

8. Open the Rendering View Corridor view.

9. In the View Control bar, set Detail Level to Fine.

10. Change Visual Style to Realistic.

11. For the Shadows, select Graphic Display Options, as shown in Figure 19.2.

FIGURE 19.2 Selecting Graphic Display Options

12. In the Graphic Display Options dialog, click Cast Shadows and Ambient Lighting.

You can also access
the Graphic Display
Options dialog by
clicking the small
black arrow in the
right corner of the
Graphics panel.

13. Turn on the Gradient background (at the bottom of the dialog).

14. Click the […] button to the right of the Sun Setting field (at the top of the dialog in the Lighting area). This will bring up the Sun Settings dialog.

15. Choose your geographic location for the settings Date, Time, and Location. (I am choosing Syracuse, NY, and my birthday [05/10 is the default].) You can change these settings if you would like (see Figure 19.3).

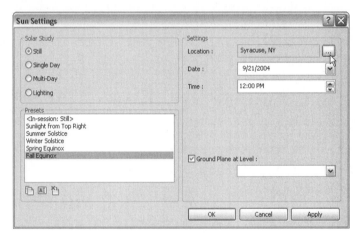

FIGURE 19.3 The Sun Settings dialog

16. Click OK.

17. Click OK again to get back to the model.

18. Click the Show Render Dialog button on the View Control bar, as shown in Figure 19.4.

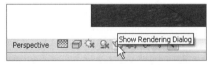

FIGURE 19.4 The Show Render Dialog button

In the Rendering dialog, you will see quite a few choices. Each choice will vary depending on the scene you are trying to capture. The following procedure will move through the Rendering dialog from top to bottom.

At the top of the Rendering dialog, you will see a button that says Render. This is actually the last button you will click. This starts the rendering process in motion. For the rest, follow these steps:

N O T E   The Region toggle (the toggle to the right of the Render button) allows you to pick a window to be rendered. Since the scene in this example is somewhat small, we won't need to click this button. If you were rendering a much larger scene, you would render a region. That way, it won't take hours upon hours to complete the rendering, and the resulting rendered scene would be a smaller size.

1. For Output Settings, set Resolution to Printer and to 300 dpi.

2. For the Lighting category, set Scheme to Sun And Artificial.

3. Set Sun to Sunlight From Top Right by clicking the [...] button in the Sun Settings row.

4. For the Background category, set Style to Sky: Few Clouds (see Figure 19.5).

5. Click the Rendering button. After the scene is rendered, it should appear similar to Figure 19.6.

T I P   Before you click the Render button, find something else to do for about two to three hours because at this resolution, Revit needs about that much time to render this scene. I recommend that you have Revit installed on another machine at your place of business. You do not want to watch the rendering process as it is similar to gazing into a campfire. Plus, if your model is being rendered on another machine, you can get some work done.

So you waited half your day for this rendering to complete. If you are like me, you then carefully move your mouse around wondering how long it will be before something happens and you lose your rendering.

FIGURE 19.5 The Rendering dialog

FIGURE 19.6 The 300 dpi rendering

The next procedure will look at how to save the rendering to the model, and also how to export the rendering to an image:

1. In the Rendering dialog, click the Save To Project button, as shown in Figure 19.7.

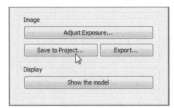

FIGURE 19.7 Saving the rendering to the project

2. Call the new rendering view **Exterior Rendering at Corridor**; then click OK.

3. Click the Export button.

4. Save the file somewhere where you can retrieve it. You can choose whatever file format you prefer.

5. At the bottom of the Rendering dialog in the Display section, click Show The Model. The rendering now reverts back to the original graphics style.

6. Click the Show The Rendering button. The rendering shows back up.

WARNING The ability to jump back and forth from the model to the rendering is a nice feature, but it is short-lived. After you close this view, the rendering is no longer available. Do not close this view until you have finished saving the view to the model and exporting it (if you wish to do so).

With our first rendering under our belts, it is time to create another exterior rendering. This time, however, we need to start adding some lighting and produce this rendering at night. There is nothing like a good before-and-after rendering to sell a project.

The objective of the next procedure is to add some exterior and interior lighting to create a nighttime rendering scene.

1. In the Project Browser, go to the Level 1 ceiling plan (that's *ceiling plan* in case you missed it).

2. In the Home tab on the Ribbon, click the Component button.

Rendering may or may not come easy to you. It may take some trial and error. I know you are not made of money, but setting up a separate machine just for rendering is not a bad idea.

3. On the Mode panel, click the Load Family button.

4. Go to the `Lighting Fixtures` folder.

5. Within the `Lighting Fixtures` directory, go to the `Exterior` folder.

6. Select the family called `Wall Pack Light - Exterior.rfa` and click Open.

7. Place the lights at the locations shown in Figure 19.8.

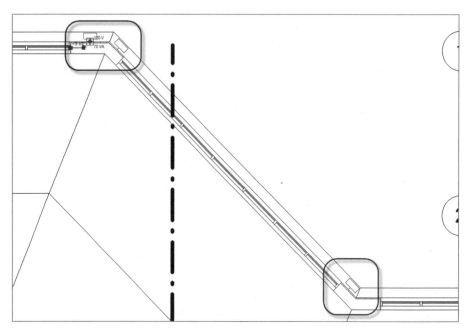

FIGURE 19.8 Placing the exterior lights

8. In the Project Browser, open the Level 1 floor plan.

9. On the Home tab, click the Component button.

10. In the Properties dialog, choose the Sconce Light - Uplight 60W - 120V family, as shown in Figure 19.9.

11. Place seven lights on the walls of the northeast corner classroom, as shown in Figure 19.9.

Now that some lights are in place, it is time to look at how we can efficiently group the various types of lighting fixtures to create a nice lighting scene.

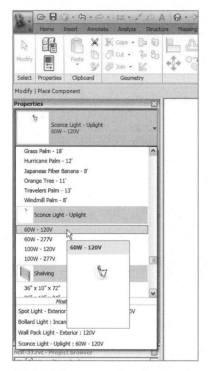

FIGURE 19.9 Choosing the sconce

Creating Lighting Groups

All too often, we render scenes with no real consideration for the actual lighting that has been added to the model. Because we lean heavily on Revit to produce accurate scenarios to present to our clients, we should spend some time thinking through our lighting before we create a rendering.

The objective of the next procedure is to create two lighting groups and to render the same view using a nighttime setting.

1. Select one of the sconces you just added to the model, as shown in Figure 19.10.

2. On the Options bar, click the Light Group menu, and select Edit/New from the list, as shown in Figure 19.10.

3. In the Artificial Lights - Level 1 dialog, click the New button in the Group Options area, as shown in Figure 19.11.

4. Call the new group **Interior Lighting Northwest**.

Remember, some components are more fickle than others. Lighting fixtures sometimes take some finesse. Make sure you are zoomed back enough to see a large portion of the wall, or Revit may not place the fixture where you expected.

5. Scroll down to the bottom of the list and locate the lights Sconce Light - Uplight : 60W - 120V. Select all of them, as shown in Figure 19.12.

6. Click the Move To Group button under Fixture Options.

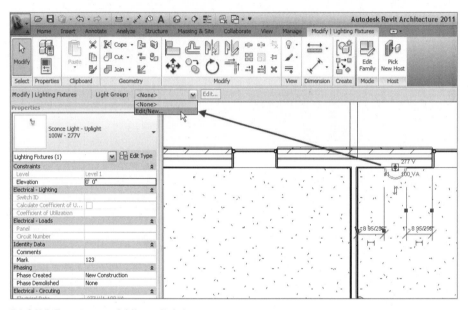

FIGURE 19.10 Adding a lighting group

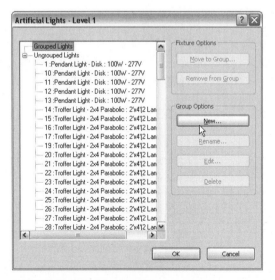

FIGURE 19.11 Creating a new group

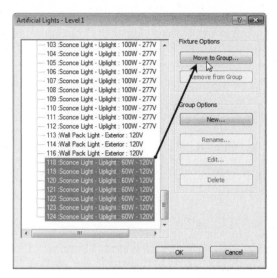

FIGURE 19.12 Moving the selected lights to the new group

7. Choose the Interior Lighting Northwest group in the Light Groups dialog and click OK.

8. Click OK to close the dialog.

9. In the Project Browser, go to the Level 1 ceiling plan.

10. Select one of the exterior lights.

11. On the Options bar, click the Light Groups menu, and select Edit/New.

12. Create a new group called **Exterior Corridor**.

13. Locate the exterior wall pack lights and add them to the group.

14. Click OK.

15. Go back to the Level 1 floor plan.

16. Add the same sconce lights to the interior of the corridor at each corner, and at the ends of the walls.

17. Create a new lighting group called **Corridor Interior**, and add the corridor lights to the group. You now have three lighting groups.

18. In the Project Browser, go to the Rendering View Corridor view.

19. On the View Control bar, click the Sun Path button (it is the picture of the sun with the small red x), and click Sun Settings.

20. Click the Duplicate button, as shown at the bottom left in Figure 19.13.

21. Call the new scene **Syracuse at dusk** (you can replace "Syracuse" with your location), then click OK.

22. Set the time for 7:30 PM (see Figure 19.13).

23. Click OK; your scene should look like Figure 19.14.

24. Click the Show Rendering Dialog button on the View Control bar.

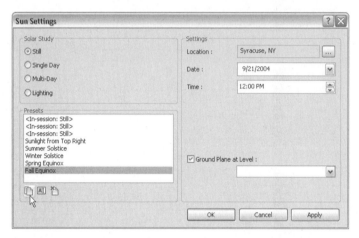

FIGURE 19.13 Changing the scene to dusk

FIGURE 19.14 The rendering at night

25. Set the Setting value to High.

26. Set Lighting Scheme to Exterior: Sun And Artificial.

27. Click the Artificial Lights button to make sure all your groups are present, and then click OK.

28. Click the Render button. Your scene should look like Figure 19.15.

FIGURE 19.15 The rendering in daylight

If you are actually in Syracuse during the winter, it would probably be a good idea to get inside! While we are in there, we can bring the experience that we just gained inside with us to create an interior rendering scene.

Interior Rendering

We create an interior rendering in almost exactly the same as an exterior rendering. Of course, we will definitely use artificial lighting. We will also use sunlight, just to make sure we account for any natural light that comes into the building.

The objective of this procedure is to create an interior lighting scene using a premade 3D perspective of a hallway:

1. In the Project Browser, find the 3D view called East Wing Corridor Perspective.

2. On the View Control bar, click the Show Rendering Dialog button.

3. Set the Quality setting to High.

4. Set Resolution to Printer and to 300 dpi.

5. Set Lighting Scheme to Interior: Sun And Artificial.

6. Set Sun to Sunlight From Top Right.

7. Make sure Background Style is set to Color.

8. Click the Render button. Your hallway should resemble Figure 19.16.

FIGURE 19.16 The interior corridor

This is getting almost too easy! I suppose we could keep rendering all week, but in the interest of saving some trees, I encourage you to render just a little more. If you run into any trouble during your foray into additional rendering, give me a shout at ewing@cscos.com and ask your question. The winding stairs heading up to the balcony in the west wing would make a nice scene to hang on your cubicle or office wall!

If you feel as though you have enough experience with rendering, let's jump to the next section and tackle creating a nice walkthrough for a presentation.

Creating Walkthroughs

For some reason, you can show a client a beautiful rendering of a space or building you plan to design for them and still meet with a blasé, half-hearted reaction. Now, if you show them the same space, but as though you are walking through it ... well then! The client perks right up.

Although this part of the chapter is not crucial to your expertise in Revit, it is certainly worth a glance. Sometimes it is the special tools that you can pull out of your belt that can win a job or impress your friends on a Saturday night. A walkthrough is a series of points you pick in a sequence in a plan view. It's sort of like connecting the dots, but these dots will advance a frame as if you were walking to the points you picked.

The objective of this procedure is to create a walkthrough of the building and to export the walkthrough to an AVI file:

1. Go to the Level 1 floor plan.

2. On the View tab of the Ribbon, choose 3D ➤ Walkthrough, as shown in Figure 19.17.

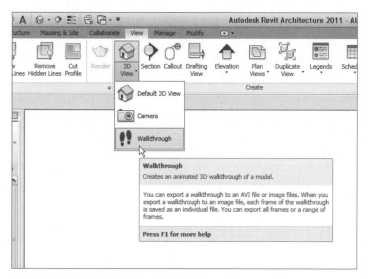

FIGURE 19.17 Finding the Walkthrough command

3. Zoom in on the east entry.

4. Start picking points, as shown by the numbers in Figure 19.18.

5. Keep picking points down the hallway, into the corridor, and into the west wing, as shown in Figure 19.19.

6. On the Modify | Walkthrough tab of the Ribbon, click Finish Walkthrough.

7. On the Modify | Cameras tab of the Ribbon, click the Edit Walkthrough button.

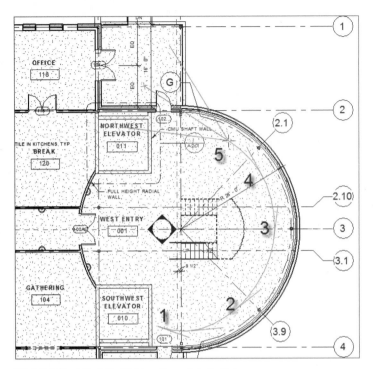

FIGURE 19.18 Picking the points in the sequence

Note that you can adjust the camera height on the Options bar. This is especially useful for walking up and down stairs.

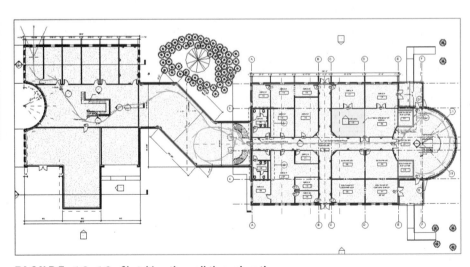

FIGURE 19.19 Sketching the walkthrough path

8. In the Project Browser, find the Walkthroughs category and open the Walkthrough 1 view.

9. On the Options bar, change the first frame to 1, as shown in Figure 19.20.

10. In the View Control bar, click Realistic.

11. Select the crop region.

12. On the Modify | Cameras tab, select the Edit Walkthrough button (again).

13. On the Modify | Cameras tab, click the Play button, as shown in Figure 19.20.

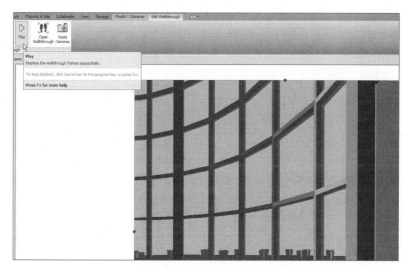

FIGURE 19.20 Clicking the Play button to start the walkthrough

14. When the walkthrough is done, you can click the button that contains the value of 300 (this is the number of frames) on the Options bar, as shown in Figure 19.21.

15. In the Walkthrough Frames dialog, change the Frames Per Second value to 20.

16. Run the Walkthrough again. This time it is sped up.

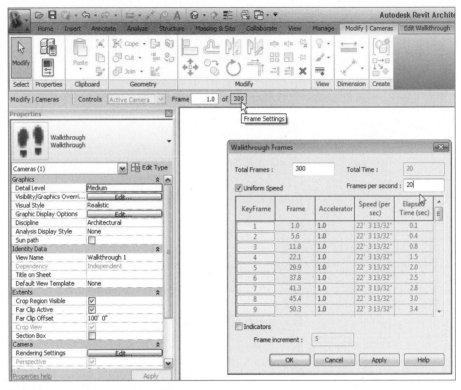

FIGURE 19.21 Changing the frames

The walkthrough is complete. One thing you certainly will be asked is if you can "give" the walkthrough to someone for a presentation. Luckily the answer is yes, and the person presenting does not have to be Revit literate, or even own the application.

Exporting an Animation

Exporting an animation is a great, but slightly hidden, feature. The Export function is not located on the Ribbon—you will find it in the Application menu, as shown in Figure 19.22. By exporting a walkthrough, you are creating an animated vector image (AVI) that will translate the native Revit walkthrough. It is quick and almost completely painless!

To create an AVI of the walkthrough, follow these steps:

1. Click the Application button.

2. Choose Export ➢ Images And Animations ➢ Walkthrough, as shown in Figure 19.22.

3. Select the defaults in the next dialog, then click OK.

4. Find a location for the file and click Save.

5. Click OK in the Video Compression dialog. (You will have to sit and wait for Revit to go through the walkthrough as it creates the AVI.)

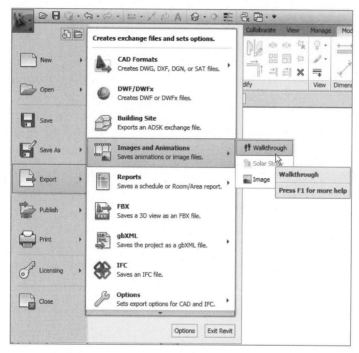

FIGURE 19.22 Choosing to export the walkthrough

6. Find the AVI and run it to make sure it works.

 NOTE Just in case you are wondering, yes, the size of this AVI is over a gig. If necessary, you can attempt to compress the file as you export it, but the quality will probably degrade. Besides, memory is cheap these days.

With the walkthrough complete, there is one more animation that we need to look at. It's not as cool as the walkthrough, but it is just as interesting. This animation is called a solar study.

Creating a Solar Study

A solar study, put simply, is a shaded 3D view that provides a time-elapsed visual image of how the building will cast shadows over the course of either a day or multiple days.

The objective of this procedure is to create a single-day solar study by specifying the geographical location of your building:

1. Go to the view {3D} in the Project Browser.

2. Right-click and choose Duplicate View ➤ Duplicate With Detailing.

3. Rename the new 3D view to **One Day Solar Study**.

4. On the View Control toolbar, click the Sun Path button, and choose Sun Settings.

5. In the Sun Settings dialog, click the Single Day radio button, as shown in Figure 19.23.

6. Click the Duplicate button.

7. Call the new configuration **Single day Syracuse, NY**.

8. Make sure Place is set to Syracuse, NY (or wherever you find yourself these days).

9. Change Date to **05/10/2009**.

10. Set Time Interval to One Hour (see Figure 19.23).

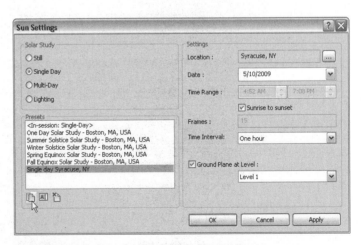

FIGURE 19.23 Setting up the solar study

11. Click OK.

12. On the View Control bar, click the Shadows button, then select Preview Solar Study, as shown in Figure 19.24.

13. On the Options bar, click the Play button, as shown in Figure 19.25.

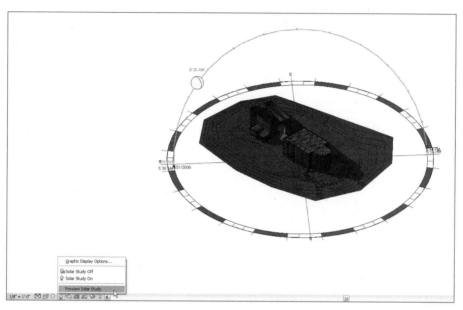

FIGURE 19.24 Previewing the solar study

FIGURE 19.25 Clicking Play to start the solar study

 NOTE Unfortunately, you need to have a high-performance machine to perform this study. If you do not, this one-day solar study could take one full day to complete. It will be in real time.

Creating animations such as solar studies and walkthroughs are a couple of the unique features of Revit that aid you in capturing work. Keep these features in mind next time you are working up a proposal and a presentation.

Are You Experienced?

Now you can...

☑ **create an exterior rendering by specifying a day lighting scene based on your geographic location**

☑ **create an exterior rendering scene at dusk using lighting**

☑ **create an interior rendering using a mixture of day lighting and artificial lighting**

☑ **create a walkthrough and export it to an AVI**

☑ **create a solar study that allows you to visualize the shadowing effect**

Importing and Coordinating Revit Models

It is amazing that we are up to Chapter 20, and I'm sure many readers are still unclear about how BIM fits in here. Yes, most of the previous chapters showed you how you benefit from BIM when you change an item in one place, and it changes in another, yada, yada, yada. But you were probably sold on the whole "coordinating with your consultants" thing back when you were considering purchasing Revit. Well, here we are. It's time to tackle that mystical ideology that has put our industry in a loose headlock.

▶ **Linking a Revit Structure model**

▶ **Activating Copy Monitor**

▶ **Running interference detection**

▶ **Importing and exporting AutoCAD**

Linking a Revit Structure Model

The first section of this chapter will focus on the actual event of importing a Revit Structure model. As you start the process, you will see that this procedure is not unfamiliar if you have any CAD background whatsoever. If you do not have a CAD background, I think you will find these procedures to be intuitive enough to get through importing Revit models with no experience.

As you proceed into design development, you must get your structural engineer on board. This consultant may be an external or an in-house resource. Either way, this individual will have a different model that you need to coordinate with.

This section will focus on the procedures involved with importing a Revit Structure model. We will also cover the concept of creating a live monitoring system with the structure as well as interference detection.

To get started, open the model you have been working on. If you missed the previous chapter, go to the book's web page at **www.sybex.com/go/revit2011ner**. From there you can browse to Chapter 20 and find the file called NER-37.rvt. You will also need to locate the model called NER-37_STRUCTURAL.rvt. Save this file in a location where you can retrieve it.

The objective of the following procedure is to import and link a Revit Structure model.

1. In the Project Browser, go to the Level 1 floor plan.

2. Delete every structural grid and column. (Keep the canopy framing intact. Do not delete the beams and columns in these two areas.)

 N O T E   Why are you deleting these structural members you worked so hard to add? Because the structural consultant laid out their grid based on yours. You are going to copy their grid back in, and monitor any movement that may occur throughout the life of the project. As far as the columns, we are simply going to use the structural engineer's columns for our elevations, plans, and sections from this point on.

---

3. On the Link panel of the Insert tab, click the Link Revit button, as shown in Figure 20.1.

4. Browse to the NER-37_STRUCTURAL.rvt file, but do not click Open just yet.

5. Select the file.

6. At the bottom of the dialog, you will get a choice of positioning. Select Auto - Origin To Origin, as shown in Figure 20.2.

7. Click Open. Your structural model is now linked.

8. Open the 3D view East Entry From Corridor.

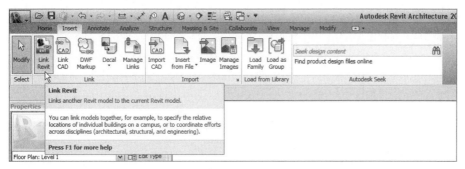

FIGURE 20.1 The Link Revit button on the Link panel of the Insert tab

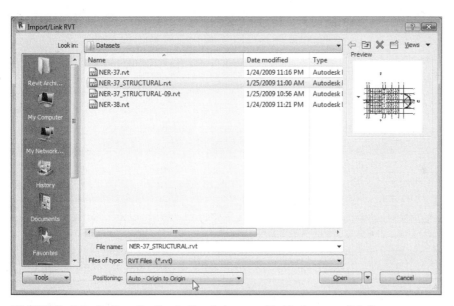

FIGURE 20.2 Pay attention to the choices provided before you click Open.

You can now see the wood framing the structural engineer added to support the cantilevered slab, as shown in Figure 20.3.

Already we are seeing the benefits of a collaborative model, and we have done nothing more than insert one model into another. This is not new technology, and we are certainly not doing anything profound here. The real benefit comes from how we can now keep track of what the structural model is doing underneath our model. We can actually copy items from the structural model, and then monitor any changes made from the linked model. This is the definition of BIM.

FIGURE 20.3 The supporting framing under the cantilevered slab at the east link

Activating Copy Monitor

You can almost sum BIM up in one command: Copy Monitor. I hate to break down the most import acronym in our industry since CAD into such simple terms, but *building information modeling* is the process of monitoring and tracking change, and that process starts right here!

The objective of the following procedure is to copy the structural grids and apply a monitoring system that will alert you when the grids have moved. Although this book will focus solely on copying and monitoring the grids, your takeaway will be the experience required to recognize the procedure and the importance of this function.

To create a copying and monitoring system, follow this procedure:

1. Go to the Level 1 floor plan.

2. On the Coordinate panel of the Collaborate tab, click the Copy/Monitor button. On the fly-out, click Select Link, as shown in Figure 20.4.

3. Hover your pointer over one of the grids. You will see an outline of the Revit Structure model that you have linked in. When you see the outline, pick the grid (see Figure 20.5).

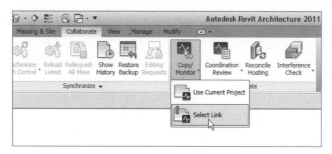

FIGURE 20.4 The Copy/Monitor button on the Coordinate panel of the Collaborate tab

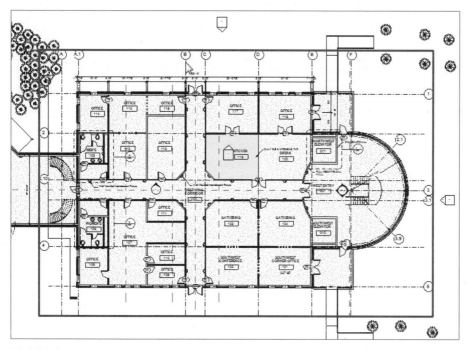

FIGURE 20.5 Selecting the link to Copy/Monitor

4. On the Copy/Monitor tab, click the Copy button, as shown in Figure 20.6.

5. On the Options bar, check the Multiple option.

6. While pressing the Ctrl key, select all of the grids in the linked model.

7. When you are finished, click Finish on the Options bar, as shown in Figure 20.7.

FIGURE 20.6 Clicking the Copy button

8. You will get a warning saying that "The following types already exist but are different." Just click OK. Your grids should look like Figure 20.8.

9. Close out of any warnings stating that new items have been renamed. This is inconsequential information.

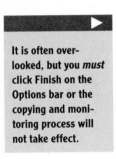

It is often overlooked, but you *must* click Finish on the Options bar or the copying and monitoring process will not take effect.

FIGURE 20.7 The Finish button on the Options bar

Now that the grids are being monitored, it is time to take a look at what we can copy and monitor from our consultant's models by configuring the Copy/Monitor settings.

Adjusting the Copy/Monitor Options

By copying the grids into the architectural model, we are actually proceeding with the most common, and by far the safest, function of this command. If you do choose to copy and monitor items such as foundations and columns, you can automatically replace the items being copied with an alternate component. For example, you could use Copy/Monitor on a foundation wall that is 12" thick but automatically replace it with a foundation wall that is 10" thick. I am using this example to emphasize something you would not want to do. Be careful while replacing components you are getting from the structural model.

The objective of the next procedure is to look at the Copy/Monitor settings.

1. On the Copy/Monitor tab, click the Options button on the Tools panel, as shown in Figure 20.9.

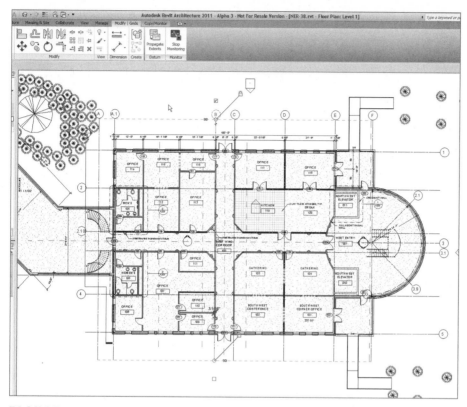

FIGURE 20.8 The copied grids!

2. Notice that Revit will replace any column indiscriminately with a 24″-square concrete column. Click into the first column category and replace the entry with **Copy Original Type** (see Figure 20.10).

3. Change the rest of the columns to **Copy Original Type** and click OK.

4. On the Copy/Monitor panel of the Copy/Monitor tab, click Finish, as shown in Figure 20.11.

5. Save the model.

FIGURE 20.9 The Options button on the Tools panel of the Copy/Monitor tab

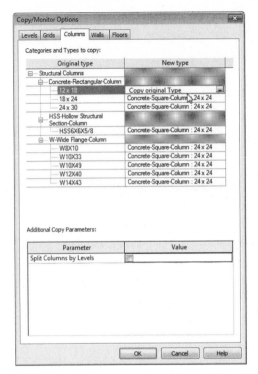

FIGURE 20.10 Changing to Copy Original Type

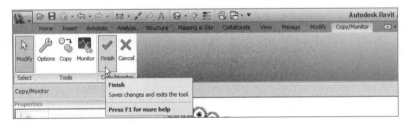

FIGURE 20.11 Clicking Finish

Now that we have a relationship with the structural model, it is time to put this relationship to the test and generate a coordination alert. I suppose you could say that the honeymoon is over!

Coordination Alert

Suddenly we have been thrust into a completely different way of working. We have a structural model inserted into our architectural model that will bark at us every time something changes. There's nothing wrong with that. Sure, occasionally there will be some annoyances, but these occasional annoyances are a small concession for being truly tied in with the structure.

When something changes in the structural model that is involved with an active monitor, you will be alerted. This alert will occur when you either open your model, or when you reload the linked Revit file.

To review the coordination alert, follow this procedure:

1. Save and close your model.

2. Open the NER-37_STRUCTURAL.rvt model.

3. In the NER-37_STRUCTURAL.rvt model, open the Level 2 structural view; then move grid A to the left so it is in alignment with the beam located between grids 2.10 and 3.1, as shown in Figure 20.12.

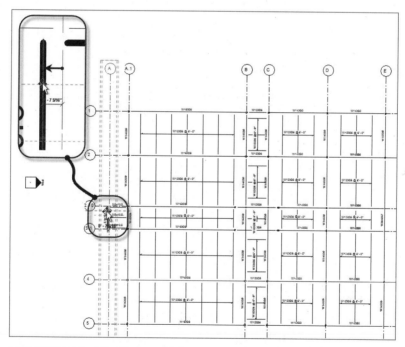

FIGURE 20.12 Moving grid A

4. Save the model and close.

5. Open the architectural model. When it opens, you may get the warning shown in Figure 20.13.

6. Click OK to continue opening the model.

7. Go to Level 1.

8. Select the link (you may have to hover your mouse over one of the grids and press the Tab key).

FIGURE 20.13 The Coordination alert

9. On the Monitor panel of the Modify | RVT Links tab, click the Coordination Review button, as shown in Figure 20.14.

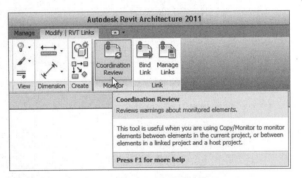

FIGURE 20.14 The Coordination Review button on the Monitor panel of the Modify | RVT Links tab

10. In the Coordination Review dialog, expand the category for the Grids (under the New/Unresolved category), as shown in Figure 20.15.

11. Expand the Grid Moved category.

 T I P   The category that says Grid Moved is the actual alteration that occurred in the structural model. Finally! Somebody is telling us what they changed without fear of us getting mad at them.

12. To the right of the Grid Moved category, you will see an Action column. Click into the cell that says Postpone and look at the list. You will see four categories:

> **Reject** Reject will postpone the change. Each time you run a coordination review, this instance will be listed as rejected. You will still have a chance to modify the instance at a later date.

> **Accept Difference** Accept Difference basically skips the error. You will still be able to change it at a later date.

> **Rename** Rename will take action. If the difference is the name (which it is in this case), Revit will rename the grid. If the grid moves, Revit will move the grid for you. (Basically any modification that needs to be made can be automatically made right here.)

13. Select Modify Grid 'A'.

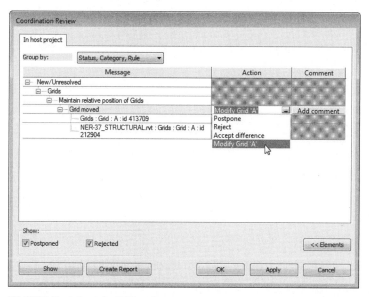

FIGURE 20.15 Telling Revit to automatically move the grid

 N O T E You can also add a comment pertaining to the change. Typically it is a note to yourself, but in some situations, you will need it when you are involved in friendly discussions about who started the chain of events.

14. Click the Create Report button at the bottom of the dialog.

15. Save the HTML file to a location where you can find it.

16. Click OK in the Coordination Review dialog. (Notice that grid A moved.)

17. Open Windows Explorer, find the HTML report, and open it. This gives you an uneditable report on the coordination effort that just occurred.

18. Close the report.

19. Save the model.

20. To check and see if there are any more issues, click the Coordination Review ➤ Select Link button on the Coordinate panel of the Collaborate tab, as shown in Figure 20.16.

21. Select the linked structural model. The report should be empty.

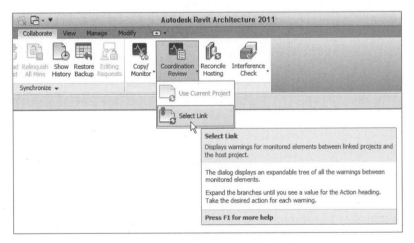

FIGURE 20.16 The Coordination Review button on the Coordinate panel of the Collaborate tab

A coordination report is an excellent way to track changes, but we are alerted of these changes only if we have the elements copied and monitored. So, how are we supposed to know if other elements are colliding with one another? This question is answered by using the Interference Detection function built into Revit.

Running Interference Detection

What came first? The chicken or the egg? That's a tough call. Another tough call is if the beam comes before the duct or wall. Ask a structural engineer, and he will answer that the beam does in fact come before the wall, door, and any other architectural appointment. On the opposite hand, the architect will request to move or eliminate a structural component altogether. But, the fact is, if the architect and the structural engineer are having this argument, that means they know there is an interference, and their disagreement about the chicken and the egg is actually a good thing.

You use the interference detection within Revit to keep the contractor from asking the question. If the contractor is asking questions, then we have a problem, don't we? This means a collision occurred that nobody caught. Don't worry—you can still have the chicken argument, only it is now called litigation.

To use interference detection, you do not have to do anything more than open a single dialog. In this dialog, you can select specific elements that you are worried about colliding. Of course, in true Revit form, you can create a report and even zoom in on the issue.

The objective of the following activity is to find some clashes between the architectural model and the structural model:

1. On the Coordinate panel of the Collaborate tab, click the Interference Check ➢ Run Interference Check button, as shown in Figure 20.17.

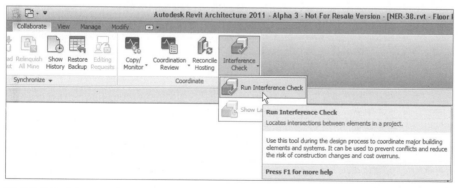

FIGURE 20.17 The Run Interference Check button on the Coordinate panel of the Collaborate tab

2. In the panel to the left of the Interference Check dialog that opens, select Current Project as the Categories From setting.

3. Select Doors and Stairs from the list, as shown in Figure 20.18.

4. In the Categories From menu to the right, select the NER-37_ STRUCTURAL.rvt file.

5. Select Structural Framing and Structural Columns (see Figure 20.18).

6. Click OK.

7. The Interference Report dialog will show where we have a collision (it looks like all of our stairs are safe). Click on Doors : Double-Flush 72″ × 84″.

8. At the bottom of the dialog, click the Show button (see Figure 20.19).

9. Revit will zoom right in on the issue. Click the Export button.

10. Click the Export button and save the report in the same directory as the coordination report.

11. Click Close.

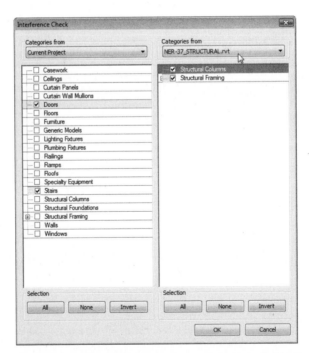

FIGURE 20.18 Selecting the components to find in the interference report

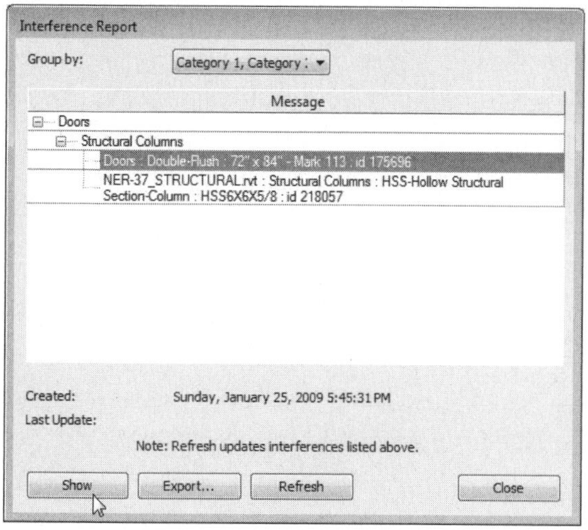

FIGURE 20.19 The offending items are discovered!

What Do You Mean, Close? We Didn't Fix Anything!

Yes, that's right—we only identified the issue. Revit does not breach into another model to fix your consultant's work. It does, however, give you a specific, detailed report for your meeting. Remember, Revit doesn't negate the need for open discussion during a project.

Boy! That is some good stuff. Lucky for you, your consultants are all up and running on Revit! Oh, they aren't? Now what kind of world are we living in here?

It's true. Your consultants aren't all going to be on Revit. If you're lucky, one in ten uses Revit in the capacity where they are ready to share a model with you. This is okay—don't panic. We are still in a great position. We can easily import AutoCAD (or MicroStation), and we can export our model just as easily.

Importing and Exporting CAD Formats

The first process we will delve into is the process of importing an AutoCAD structural floor plan. Although we have imported CAD in this book numerous times, we have yet to do so in the context of a coordinated floor plan. The mind-set is a little different. And why is that? It is because we now care about where this AutoCAD drawing lands in relationship to our model, and we care also about maintaining that relationship.

For the CAD file used in the following procedure, go to the book's web page at **www.sybex.com/go/revit2011ner**. From there you can browse to Chapter 20 and find the file called NER-37.rvt. You will also need to locate the model called NER-37_STRUCTURAL.dwg. Save this file in a location where you can retrieve it.

The objective of the following procedure is to import an AutoCAD 2D floor plan, and pin down its coordinates.

1. Go to the Level 1 floor plan.

2. Right click on the Level 1 view in the Project Browser, and click Duplicate ➤ Duplicate With Detailing, as shown in Figure 20.20.

3. Rename the new view **Level 1 CAD Coordination**.

4. Open the new view.

5. Type **VG** (for Visibility Graphics).

6. Click the Revit Links tab.

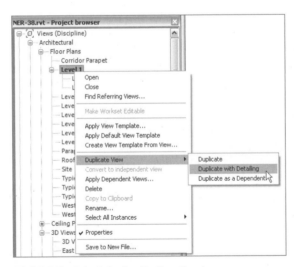

FIGURE 20.20 Duplicating the view

7. Uncheck the NER-37_STRUCTURAL.rvt model.

8. Click OK.

9. On the Link panel of the Insert tab, click the Link CAD button, as shown in Figure 20.21.

Sometimes, Revit will produce a warning that you are pasting a view that references itself. This is an erroneous warning. Click Delete Element(s) and Revit will let you proceed.

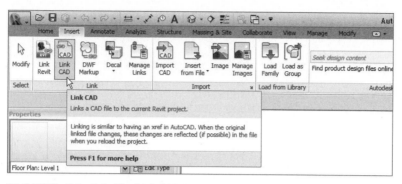

FIGURE 20.21 The Link CAD button on the Link panel of the Insert tab

10. At the bottom of the Link CAD Formats dialog, click the Current View Only check box.

11. Set Colors to Black And White.

12. Set Layers to All.

13. Set Import Units to Auto-Detect.

14. Set Positioning to Auto - Origin To Origin.

15. Click Open.

16. On the View Control bar, click the Wireframe button so you can see the AutoCAD structure, as shown in Figure 20.22.

FIGURE 20.22 Clicking the Wireframe button on the View Control bar

The next step is to make sure that the coordinates in our Revit model stay true in the DWG file. With one simple procedure, we can publish the coordinates of the Revit model to the DWG file to ensure accuracy while importing.

1. On the Project Location panel of the Manage tab, click Coordinates ➢ Publish Coordinates, as shown in Figure 20.23.

2. Select the AutoCAD link by left-clicking on it in the view.

FIGURE 20.23 Publishing the coordinates

3. In the Site tab of the Location Weather and Site dialog, click the Duplicate button.

4. Call the new location **Revit Position**, then click OK.

5. Click Make Current.

6. Click OK.

7. Press Esc, then select the AutoCAD link.

8. In the Properties dialog, verify that the Shared Site is now Revit Position.

9. Save the Revit model.

10. Once you save the Revit model, you will be prompted to save the new coordinates in the DWG. Click the Save button, as shown in Figure 20.24.

So, that's importing. Suppose we need to send our model to our clients and consultants who don't have Revit? This can be taken care of quickly and deliberately.

Exporting a Model to CAD

For some of you, this may be a nice-to-know subject. For most of you, this is a need-to-know subject. Taking the plunge into Revit means that you may be taking that plunge alone. Just because you are using Revit, that does not mean you don't need the ability to give someone CAD drawings based on your models.

This section will focus on the process of exporting your Revit model to both 2D and 3D CAD.

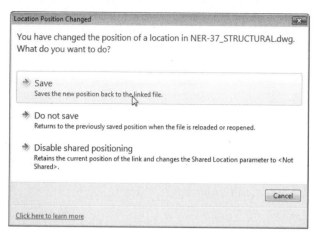

FIGURE 20.24 Saving the coordinates to the AutoCAD file

Exporting a 2D Model

Most of the time, your deliverable to your clients will be a 2D model. Also, if your consultants aren't on Revit, that also usually means that they are not using 3D CAD either. This format is the lowest common denominator. Not that a 2D model is bad—it just means we need to export our model in a way that the client can just pick it up and run with it.

The objective of the next procedure is to export our model to a 2D AutoCAD drawing file.

1. In the Project Browser, open the Level 1 floor plan.

2. Click the Application button, and select Export ≻ CAD Formats ≻ DWG Files, as shown in Figure 20.25.

3. On the View/Sheet Set panel, select In Session View/Sheet Set from the Export drop-down list.

4. For the Show In List option, select All Views And Sheets In The Model.

5. Scroll down to the bottom of the list and make sure your Level 1 floor plan is checked on (see Figure 20.26). You may check on any others as you please.

6. Click the DWG Properties tab.

7. At the bottom, click Export Rooms And Areas As Polylines.

8. Click the Next button.

9. Browse to the directory of your choosing then click OK.

FIGURE 20.25 Exporting the model to CAD

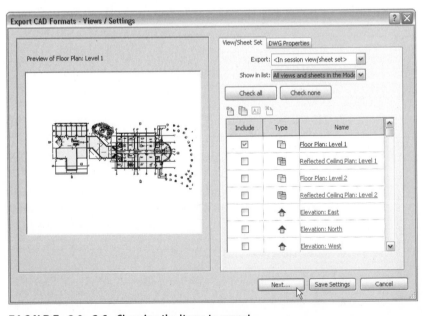

FIGURE 20.26 Choosing the items to export

Now that we can export to a flat 2D file, it is time to take our model and export it as a full 3D entity. The process is similar to exporting as 2D.

Exporting the Model to 3D CAD

It is such a shame to "dumb down" our 3D model to flat 2D CAD. It feels as though we are taking a step backward each time we do it. When you find yourself in the situation where your consultants are using CAD but are using the 3D modeling, you can give them the gift of 3D.

The objective of the next procedure is to export a model to 3D CAD.

1. Go to the Default 3D view.

2. Select Export ➢ CAD Formats ➢ DWG Files.

3. Set the Export option to Current View/Sheet Only.

4. Click the Next button.

5. Find a place to save the 3D model, then click OK.

6. Save the model.

The most important step in exporting to a 3D CAD format is to be in a 3D view.

As you can see, it's not a difficult process. In Chapter 23, "BIM Management," we will explore setting up the export in such a way that the layers are correct if your client is not standardized on the AIA format.

Are You Experienced?

Now you can...

☑ **import a Revit Structure model**

☑ **copy and monitor the Revit model**

☑ **run interference checking on a linked Revit model**

☑ **export a Revit model to CAD formats (2D and 3D)**

Phasing and Design Options

Of all the projects I have been involved with over the years, I can only remember a handful that didn't involve some kind of existing condition. It would be nice if we could find a giant, flat field to construct our buildings, but those projects are few and far between.

▶ **Managing project phasing**

▶ **Creating an existing phasing plan**

▶ **Demolishing components**

▶ **Examining phase filters**

▶ **Creating design options**

Managing Project Phasing

The term phasing in Revit is often taken quite literally, and can often become misunderstood as construction sequencing. When we talk about phasing in the context of how Revit views it, we are talking about adding new construction to an existing building, and the demolition of the existing structure. Although you can use Revit to track all aspects of construction, the base use and the purpose of phasing is for existing conditions.

The first section of this chapter will focus on the setup of your actual phasing scheme. By default, Revit Architecture provides two phases: Existing and New Construction. As it stands, everything we have placed into our model for the last 20 chapters has been exclusively on the New Construction phase. We will now alter that.

I have seen this scenario played out more times than I would like. People get Revit, build a model, and then start clicking the Demolish button found on the Phasing panel on the Modify tab, as shown in Figure 21.1. Yes, it forces hidden lines, now you are demolishing walls that were constructed in the same phase as they are being removed. You can't just do that!

With some practice, and by following the procedures in this chapter, you will be able to swing that hammer around all you want. But for now, to get started go to the book's web page at **www.sybex.com/go/revit2011ner**. From there you can browse to Chapter 21 and find the file called NER-Phasing.rvt. (If you prefer, you can follow along with your own model as well.)

The objective of the following procedure is to create a *demo* phase and insert that phase between the Existing phase and the New Construction phase.

1. Open the file called NER-Phasing.rvt you downloaded.

2. On the Manage tab, click the Phases button on the Phasing panel, as shown in Figure 21.1.

3. In the Phasing dialog, click on the number 1. This is the control for the Existing phase row.

4. To the right of the dialog is the Insert section. Click the After button.

FIGURE 21.1 Clicking the Phases button

5. Rename the phase that is now in the middle to **Demolition**, as shown in Figure 21.2.

6. Click OK.

7. Make sure you are in Level 1; then on the View tab, click Duplicate View ➤ Duplicate View, as shown in Figure 21.3.

8. Right-click the new view and rename it to **Level 1 Existing**.

9. Open the Level 1 Existing plan.

For now, that is all we need to do to start setting up the plans. We will create a demo plan as well, but not until we start getting some items moved over to the Existing phase.

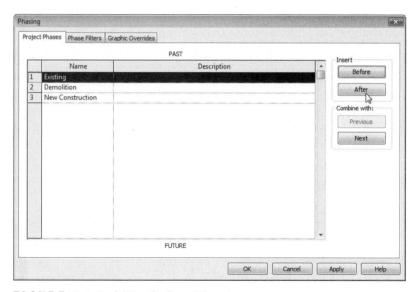

FIGURE 21.2 Adding the Demolition phase

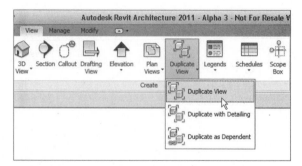

FIGURE 21.3 Duplicating the view

Creating an Existing Phasing Plan

Just because you just called it "existing" does not, by any means, qualify this plan as an existing plan. We have a good amount of work left to do before we can consider this existing.

First we need to physically select each item and move what we want over to the Existing phase. After we finish that task, we need to assign the Existing phase to this plan.

The objective of the following procedure is to physically move components to the Existing phase:

1. Pick a window around the entire west wing as well as the corridor link, as shown in Figure 21.4.

2. On the Modify | Multi-Select tab, click the Filter button, as shown in Figure 12.4.

3. In the Filter dialog, click the Check None button, and then check Walls.

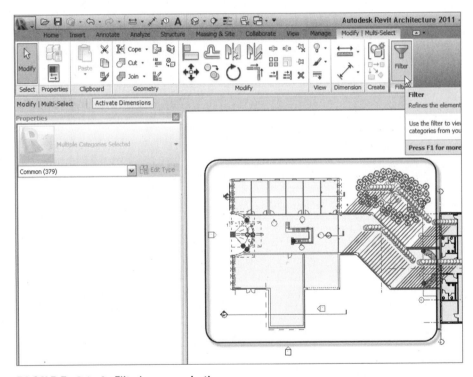

FIGURE 21.4 Filtering your selection

4. Click OK.

5. In the Properties dialog, scroll down to the bottom where you see Phasing. For Phase Created, select Existing (see Figure 21.5).

6. Pick the same window around the entire east wing.

7. Click the Filter button.

8. Select only Windows and click OK.

9. In the Properties dialog, change Phase Created to Existing.

Zoom in on the plan. Notice the items that have been moved to Existing are gray and have lost their detail level, as shown in Figure 21.6. Also notice that some of the items are still on a heavy line weight. These items need to be selected and then moved to the Existing phase.

FIGURE 21.5 Setting Phase Created to Existing

Keep selecting items and moving them to the Existing phase. Continue until you have every item in the east wing and the corridor link. This includes the floors and foundations, too. The only thing you want to keep is the winding stairs that connect the link to the east wing. You can select items in the 3D view as well.

Okay, it's time to create the existing plan. The only thing that separates an existing plan from a new construction plan is a single property.

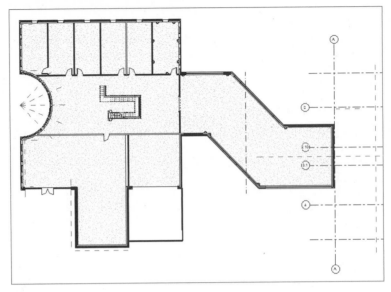

FIGURE 21.6 The existing walls

The objective of the next exercise is to change the plan to an existing plan:

1. Press the Esc key to clear any running command.

2. Scroll down the list to the Phasing category.

3. Change Phase to Existing (see Figure 21.7).

Some of the items you are trying to select are still part of an array group. Since you can't move an array group to a phase, you can hover your cursor over one of the arrayed items, and then press your Tab key until the individual item is selected. Once it is selected, right-click and choose Select All Instances.

FIGURE 21.7 Changing Phase to Existing

N O T E   If you are not catching what is going on here, here's the deal. We just added the building components to the Existing phase. Now, to see the existing items only, we are changing the actual view's phase to Existing.

4. In the east end of the link, zoom in on the end. You will see a wall missing. Select one of the exterior walls, and select Create Similar from the Modify Walls tab, as shown in Figure 21.8.

5. Draw a wall across the front of the opening, as shown in Figure 21.8.

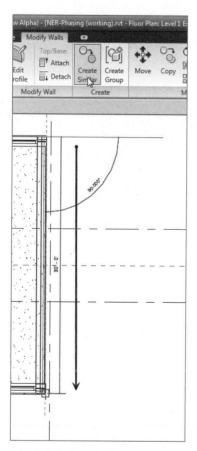

FIGURE 21.8 Drawing a new wall in the existing plan. This wall will later be demolished.

6. In the Project Browser, right-click on the {3D} view, and select Duplicate View ➢ Duplicate.

7. Rename the new 3D view to **Existing**.

8. Select the wall you just added and attach the top to the roof.

9. With the wall still selected, make sure Phase Created is set to Existing in the Properties dialog.

10. Change Phase Demolished to Demolition.

11. Go to the existing 3D view. It should look like Figure 21.9.

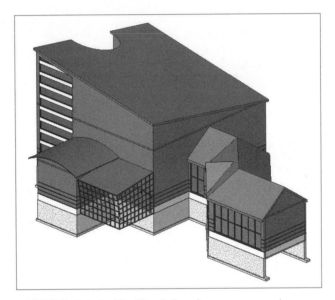

FIGURE 21.9 The 3D existing view

Now we're getting it. The next step is to add a small addition to the north side of the east wing. We will then demo a portion of the wall.

1. In the Project Browser, go to the Level 1 floor plan.

2. Turn on the Crop region and drag the north region up about 20 or 30 feet. Do the same for the dependent crop region. It should look similar to Figure 21.10.

3. On the Home tab, click the Wall button.

4. Select Exterior - Brick And CMU On MTL. Stud.

5. On the Options bar, change the height to East Roof, and set Location Line to Wall Centerline.

6. Pick the start point, as shown in Figure 21.10.

7. Draw the wall 40′ to the north.

8. Draw another horizontal wall centered on the partition to the right, as shown in Figure 21.10.

9. Draw one more wall across the front connecting to the west wing exterior wall.

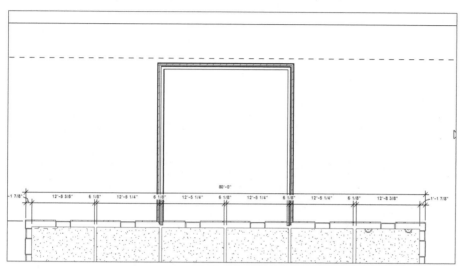

FIGURE 21.10 Drawing a small box addition

Great! The addition is added. We could put a roof on and add some floors, but let's jump right to the good stuff. We need to start knocking out some major demolition areas. The first items we will look at are those windows, and then the area that leads into the main building.

Demolishing Components

Now that our phasing is properly set, we can do some renovations. Since we need to cut a huge gaping hole in the north face of the building, it seems we need to demo some interior partitions back as well. Also, there are some windows that need to be demolished and in-filled. Let's start there.

The objective of the next exercise is to demolish the north exterior windows and create an automatic in-fill.

1. Go to the North elevation.

2. Zoom in on the west wing.

3. On the Manage tab, click the Demolish button (with the hammer icon) on the Phasing panel, as shown in Figure 21.11.

4. Pick the two windows to the right and the left of the addition (four demolished windows total).

5. Press Esc twice and then select the four windows.

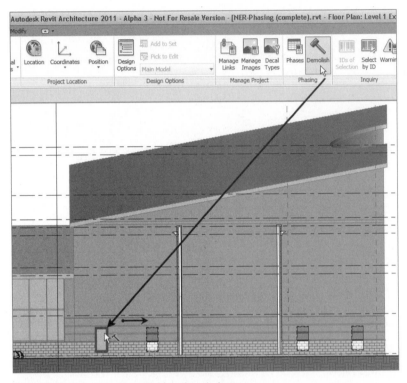

FIGURE 21.11 Demolishing the windows

 WARNING   Hang on there, Thor! Do you know what phase you are in? You were about to demolish those windows in the New Construction phase! We need to change that.

6. In the Properties dialog, change Phase Created to Existing, and Phase Demolished to Demolition.

 NOTE   For all you LEED professionals, remember that you can schedule anything in Revit. You can also schedule only windows that are being demolished. With an accurate monitor of material being demolished, you can suddenly have a running tally of reusable building materials.

Because the Phase Created of the north elevation is set to New Construction, when you demolish an item in a previous phase (the demolition phase occurs before the new construction phase), that item should not appear in the current phase. Instead of leaving a gaping hole, Revit added in-fill to the window opening.

The next demolition item will not be as easy. The next exercise will involve cutting a large hole out of the north wall at the perimeter of the addition. The height will be constrained to Level 4.

1. Make sure you are in the North elevation.

2. Select the north wall of the west wing.

3. On the Modify | Walls tab, click the Edit Profile button.

4. On the Draw panel, click the Pick Lines button.

5. Pick the inside faces of the two new walls, as shown in Figure 21.12.

6. Pick the Level 4 level (again, refer to Figure 21.12).

7. Split the bottom line between the two walls. This forms the continuous loop.

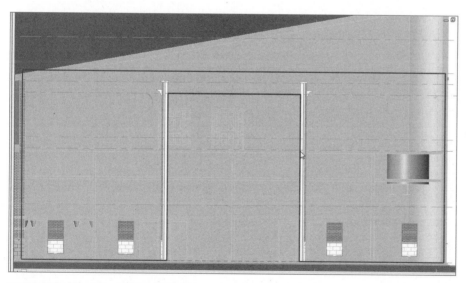

FIGURE 21.12 Cutting the hole

8. On the Modify | Walls tab, click Finish Edit Mode.

9. Go to the Level 1 floor plan. Notice that the wall joins are inaccurate.

10. Select the horizontal wall. You will see arrow grips, as shown in Figure 21.13. You will also see a small T-shaped grip. This is an important grip.

11. Pick the T-shaped grip first. This will physically disallow the walls to be joined.

12. Pick the arrow grip, and drag the wall until it is aligned with the new addition wall, as shown in Figure 21.13.

13. Do the same for the other side.

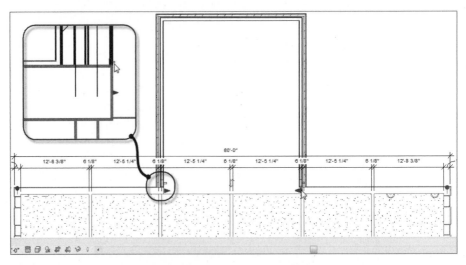

FIGURE 21.13 Cleaning the join between new and existing

N O T E   Wall cleanups such as the cleanup illustrated in the current procedure will be common during the phasing sequence. Don't think that Revit will automatically clean it how you would like it to. I can assure you, it will not.

14. Go to the Level 1 Existing plan.

15. Zoom in on the same intersections we just adjusted.

16. Select the middle wall, and grip-edit the walls back to the abutment, as shown in Figure 21.14.

17. Type ZA.

18. Select one of the structural grids, right-click, and select Hide In View ➢ Category.

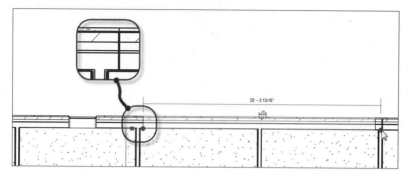

FIGURE 21.14 Cleaning the join in the existing plan

19. Repeat the procedure for the reference planes.

20. Save the model.

Now that we have an existing plan and a new construction plan, it is time to create a demo plan. Since all of the elements have been placed in the correct phases, and the phases are in place, this is the fun part!

Creating a Demo Plan

The fact that you can track a project from existing to demolition to completion without a single overlapping line is astounding. This is the type of coordination that is keeping Revit around. Granted, this sometimes does not come as easily as you may like, and you can find yourself picking around at wall joins to get them to display correctly. But overall, this is a marked advantage over 2D or even 3D CAD drafting.

Creating a demo plan is no more difficult than creating an existing plan. The process involves making a duplicate of Level 1, and then changing the phase to Demolition.

1. Open the Level 1 floor plan.

2. On the View tab, click Duplicate View ➢ Duplicate View, as shown in Figure 21.15.

3. Rename the new view to **Level 1 Demolition**.

4. Open the Level 1 Demolition plan.

5. In the Properties dialog, set the phase to Demolition (see Figure 21.16).

6. Hide the structural grids and the reference planes.

> As you are building your model with view upon view, always be diligent in naming these views you are introducing to the model. It is just good practice.
>
>

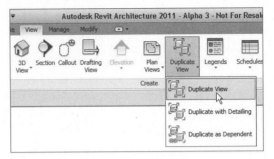

FIGURE 21.15 Duplicating the Level 1 floor plan

 TIP Now that you have a demo plan in place, I recommend that you do all your demolishing here. You can just hammer away at the walls you wish to demolish without being bothered by the new construction, and you can see your work clearly and free of obstruction.

7. On the Manage tab, click the Demolish button, as shown in Figure 21.17.

8. Demolish the wall and the door shown in Figure 21.17. (Again, since we are in the demo plan, this process has never been easier.)

FIGURE 21.16 Changing Phase to Demolition

With the three plans assembled, it is time to make one more plan view. Although we have essentially run out of phases, we can create a new plan that will simply show the model in its completed form by using a *phase filter*.

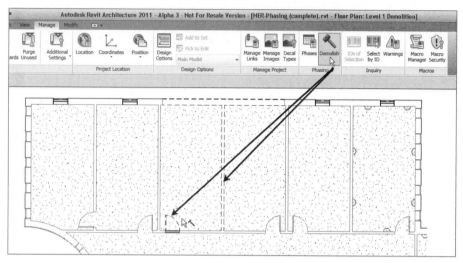

FIGURE 21.17 Demolishing the wall and door

Examining Phase Filters

Phase filters allow the user to specify what phases they want to see in a view. For example, if your view's phase is set to New Construction, you will see the existing as well as the new information, but you won't see the demolition. In Revit, you can set up a filter to show the demolition in a new construction plan if so desired. Also, by using phase filters, you can even change how items are displayed in a specific state.

The objective of the following procedure is to create a new plan showing the model in its completed state.

1. Duplicate the Level 1 plan (without detailing).

2. Rename the new view to **Level 1 completed**.

3. Go to the view's Properties.

4. Change Phase Filter to Show Complete, as shown in Figure 21.18.

5. Investigate the plan. It looks as if we never moved anything to Existing.

6. On the Manage tab, click the Phases button.

7. In the Phasing dialog, click the Phase Filters tab. Notice this tab contains the filtering you are using in this project. You can add or modify these filters at any time (see Figure 21.19).

8. In the Phasing dialog, click the Graphic Overrides tab. Here you can see that you can change the line types and the shading for each phase status (see Figure 21.20). Click OK.

FIGURE 21.18 The Show Complete phase filter

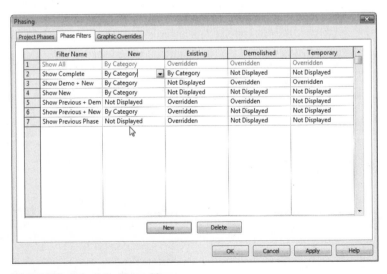

FIGURE 21.19 Phase filters

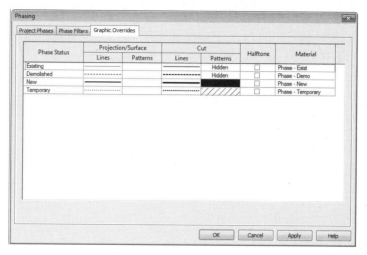

FIGURE 21.20 Graphic Overrides tab

Typically in a set of drawings, you are not going to have a *show complete* view, but it can be extremely helpful with internal coordination throughout the life of the project. You can quickly see where major deficiencies happen when you view a model as completed.

One problem with all this phasing is that, on some projects, your Project Browser will become confusing and crowded quickly. Let's look at dividing the browser up into phases.

1. In the Project Browser, right-click on the Views (Discipline) heading, as shown in Figure 21.21, and click Properties.

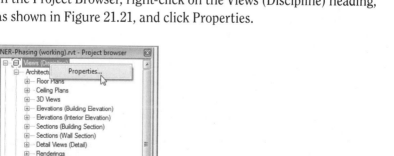

FIGURE 21.21 Opening the browser's properties

2. Click the Edit button in the Folders row.

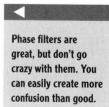

Phase filters are great, but don't go crazy with them. You can easily create more confusion than good.

3. You will see that the browser is already organized by Discipline. Focus on the Then By section, and change the Then By category to Phase (as shown in Figure 21.22).

4. Click OK twice to get back to the model.

Well, I think you can see that browser organization can help you organize a project. Be careful, though. Adding random, multiple categorizations could get out of hand and wind up more confusing than if you had just left the Project Browser alone.

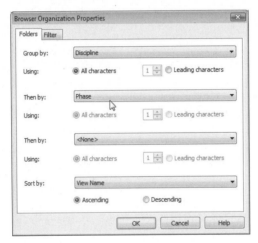

FIGURE 21.22 Changing Then By to Phase

WHAT THE "???" IN THE PROJECT BROWSER MEANS

What the heck is that? As you can see in the following graphic, there are three question marks in our Project Browser. This will happen when you start organizing the browser by a specific property that some views do not contain. The views categorized in the ??? heading are drafting views, and they do not have a phase property.

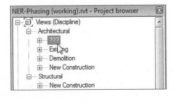

Another functionality of Revit that we need to venture into is similar to phasing, but has an entirely different meaning when it comes to tracking aspects of a project. This functionality is called design options.

Creating Design Options

Revit is equipped with the functionality to allow you to model different options in one model, better known in the design world as bid alternates. The great thing about how Revit handles this functionality is that any alternate design will never be (or at least will seldom be) a completely new structure. There will be items that are in more than one option. Revit allows you to keep like items intact while creating new or different items that belong to different options. This creates a situation where you only need to model the common items once, so you can focus on the alternates.

That being said, there is a lot to be added to this functionality. Many of the examples in this section of the chapter will deal more with flaws in Revit than with actual design option procedures.

To get started, go to the book's website at **www.sybex.com/go/revit2011ner**. From there you can browse to Chapter 21 and find the file called NER-38.rvt. Follow along with the procedure.

1. On the Manage tab, click the Design Options button, as shown in Figure 21.23.

2. In the Design Options dialog, click the New button under Option Set.

 N O T E   **You can have as many option sets as you choose. There will be cases where you have other, unrelated options in other places in your model.**

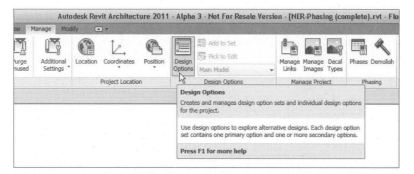

FIGURE 21.23 Clicking the Design Options button

3. Select Option Set 1.

4. In the Option Set category, click the Rename button.

5. Call the option set **West Entry**.

6. Select Option 1 (Primary).

7. In the Option category, click Rename.

8. Rename it to **With Entrance**.

9. In the Option category, click the New button.

10. Rename the new option **Without Entry** (see Figure 21.24).

FIGURE 21.24 Adding options

11. Click Close.

12. In the Project Browser, go to the Level 1 floor plan.

13. Select the curtain wall to the left of the entry, as shown in Figure 21.25.

14. Click the Cut to Clipboard button, as shown in Figure 21.25.

15. Delete the door family in the middle of the wall.

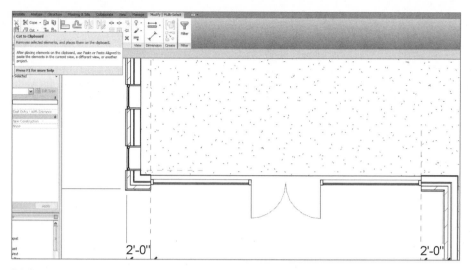

FIGURE 21.25 Cutting the curtain wall out of the host wall

TIP If you have a lot of in-place families, you are going to have an extremely difficult time with design options. When you know you might have design options, create all your families outside the model.

16. Select the walls as shown in Figure 21.26, and click the Add To Set button in the Design Options panel on the Manage tab. (You will have to click the Manage tab.)

17. In the Add To Design Option Set, only check With Entrance (Primary), and click OK.

18. Select the floor.

19. Click the Add To Set button.

20. Add the floor to both options. (Keep both items checked.) Click OK.

21. Go to a 3D view.

22. Select the curtain walls and the roof. (Use your filter and only check Curtain Systems and Roof.)

23. Click Add To Set.

24. Add the curtain walls and the roof to the With Entrance (Primary) option only, and click OK.

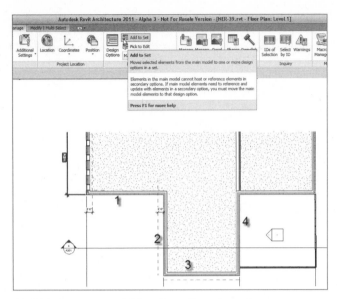

FIGURE 21.26 Adding the walls to the option set

Phew! Let's take a breather! The next thing we need to do is put that curtain wall back into the model. To do this, we need to make the option we want this wall to be in current. It is almost like making a layer current in AutoCAD.

To start placing objects in a specific option, follow along with these steps:

1. On the Design Options panel of the Manage tab, click the Active Design Option menu, and select With Entrance (Primary), as shown in Figure 21.27. (This that you are making this option current.)

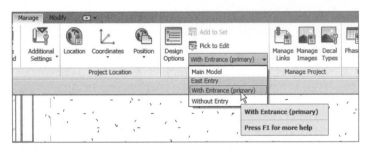

FIGURE 21.27 Making the design option current

2. On the Modify tab, click Paste Aligned ➢ Same Place. Your curtain wall is back in action.

3. Go to the Level 1 floor plan.

4. On the Design Options panel, select the Without Entry option.

5. Select the floor, and click the Edit Boundary icon on the Modify | Floors tab.

6. Eliminate the jog in the floor, leaving only a straight line.

7. Click Finish Edit Mode, and click No for the next two questions.

8. On the Home tab, click the Wall button.

9. In the Change Element Type dialog, select the Exterior - Brick And CMU On MTL. Stud (No Parapet) wall type.

10. Draw a wall across the front of the building, as shown in Figure 21.28.

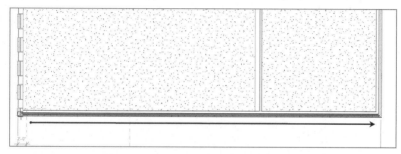

FIGURE 21.28 Drawing a new wall across the front of the building

IS THAT WALL NOT WORKING OUT?

At the ends of the walls, you may run into a join situation. If this is the case, be sure to set wall joins to Mitered.

11. Go to a 3D view. Attach the wall to the roof. Notice that the foundation and the pad are causing trouble. You can add these items to the current option as well. To do so, return to the previous exercise.

12. Click the Active Only button off at the bottom of the screen, as shown in Figure 21.29.

13. Select the entire site, including plantings and walkways, and click Hide In View ➢ Category.

14. Select the five foundation walls under the entry and the long wall, and add them to the set.

15. Go to the T.O. Footing Structural Plan.

16. Change Option to Without Entry.

17. Draw a new foundation wall and add a footing to it.

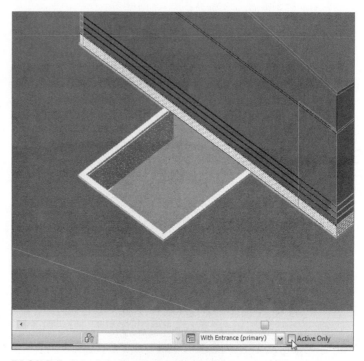

FIGURE 21.29 The Active Only button

18. Go to a 3D view.

19. Change Current Option to None.

Now that the options are set, we can toggle the views to reflect the option we desire. To do so, we will create a duplicate view and have two different option sets for a 3D view.

1. In the Project Browser, right-click on the {3D} view, and duplicate it.

2. Call the new view **West Entry - With Entry.**

3. Duplicate the view again, and rename the second view to **West Entry - Without Entry**.

4. Open the West Entry - Without Entry view.

5. Type VG.

6. On the Design Options tab, select Without Entry from the Design Option menu, as shown in Figure 21.30.

7. Open the West Entry - With Entry view, and change the option to With Entry.

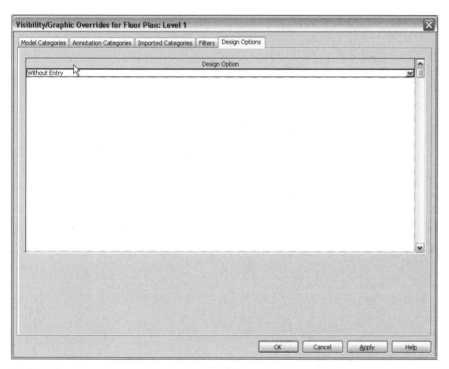

FIGURE 21.30 Choosing the correct option

Your options are set. Do not expect to have a graceful experience with this the first time you venture into design options. However, once you get the technique down, you will start to see the advantages of using this feature.

ACCEPTING THE PRIMARY OPTION

You will notice that when you are working in design options, you can only edit items belonging to the current option. If your options set is set to None, then you are actually in the Main Model option. When you are finished with the options and an alternative has been accepted, you can make the accepted option the primary option and click Accept Primary. This deletes all other options, leaving just the one option. (Make *sure* you have a backup before you do this.)

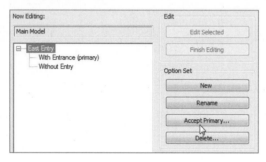

Are You Experienced?

Now you can...

- ☑ configure project phasing settings by adding new phases

- ☑ change and add phase filters, and create phasing graphical overrides

- ☑ create existing and demo plans

- ☑ organize the Project Browser to reflect your phasing

- ☑ create design options

Project Collaboration

It is quite ironic that the second-to-last chapter of this book contains information that many of you will need to get your first Revit project off the ground. That is, how do we work on a project when multiple people need to be in the model? Revit is only one model, right?

▶ **Enabling and utilizing worksharing**

▶ **Working in the Revit shared environment**

Enabling and Utilizing Worksharing

You may be surprised, but the answer, and the procedure, is not as difficult as some make it out to be. I have seen many explanations on the subject of project collaboration that are far-reaching and convoluted, thus causing an air of uneasiness. Collaboration is not as horrible as it sounds, and this chapter will explain project collaboration in the simplest terms possible.

First we'll establish exactly what we are trying to accomplish and how to go about doing it. The backbone of project collaboration is within the functionality of *worksharing*.

The concept of worksharing in Revit, broken down into its simplest form, is this:

1. Open the model.

2. Issue a Save As command.

Now you have two models. The model you just saved is linked to the original model. Any change made in your model is saved back to the original model. Subsequently, any changes from other users will be brought into your local model.

Your coworker can now open the original model and choose Save As. Now there are three models. Any change you make is saved to the original model and to your coworker's model. Any change your coworker makes is saved to the original model and to your model.

The *original* model is to be considered the *central* model. The file you save is called a *local* copy. So to reiterate: you open the central model, and then choose Save As. The file you now have is the local copy (see Figure 22.1). Another good way to view this setup is as a basic computer network. You have a file server, along with several desktop computers that are networked to it.

OK, so that's the concept of worksharing. It's now time to drill down and see how to activate this network of linked files. As mentioned before, Revit has a function called worksets. The worksets are the backbone of this entire concept.

Enabling Worksets

The worksets function in Revit influences your model and the way you go about working more than anything you can do. Worksets is a mode you literally have to enter into. After you enable worksets, there is no going back. Worksets are to the Undo button as Kryptonite is to Superman.

Essentially, worksets are a way to divide your model. You can almost look at this like phasing. Every element in your model, once you activate worksharing, will have a workset associated with it. As you will see in a moment, levels and grids will be on their own workset while everything else in the model will automatically be assigned Workset 1. This *assignment* is in the form of a parameter that you can see in the Properties dialog, and you can change that parameter.

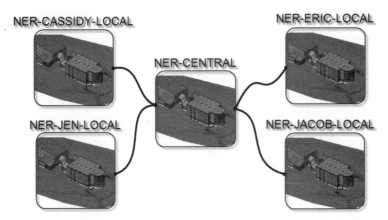

FIGURE 22.1 The basic file-sharing configuration

Why would you want to change it? Good question. Here's an example: say you are modifying an interior partition and your coworker (who is working on her local model) tries to edit that same wall. Your coworker will be denied access to the wall. But there is nothing stopping her from working on another wall in the same area, one that you intended on making the same modifications to. This could get messy fast. To avoid this situation, you can add all your interior partitions to a workset called Interior Partitions and actually *lock* everybody else out of any item that has been placed on this workset.

Now that's the way to work!

Obviously this process is not without its rules, quirks, and parts that need further explanation, so to get started, go to the book's web page at **www.sybex.com/go/revit2011ner**. From there you can browse to Chapter 22 and find the file called NER-38.rvt.

To enable worksets and start the worksharing process, follow these steps:

1. Open the NER-38.rvt file.

2. On the Collaborate tab, click the Worksets button on the Worksets panel, as shown in Figure 22.2.

3. You will get a Worksharing dialog that welcomes you to the point of no return. Accept the defaults for Shared Levels And Grids and for Workset 1, as shown in Figure 22.3, and click OK.

FIGURE 22.2 Once you pass this point, there is no turning back.

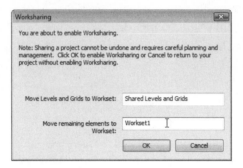

FIGURE 22.3 The Worksharing dialog

 N O T E   Turning on your worksets is a onetime activation process. You do not have to do this every time you want to work on the project.

4. The next dialog you arrive at is named Worksets, as shown in Figure 22.4. As you can see, your two worksets are present in a spreadsheet format. It says they are both Editable and that you own them. Congratulations. There is plenty to explain here:

  ▶ Active Workset indicates the workset where any new item will be either drawn on or inserted on (sort of like the current *layer* in AutoCAD). There is also a Gray Inactive Workset Graphics option. When checked, this will shade the items not on the current workset.

  ▶ The Show area at the bottom of the Worksets dialog will allow you to add specific families, project standards, and views to the workset list (see Figure 22.4).

5. Click OK to get back to the model.

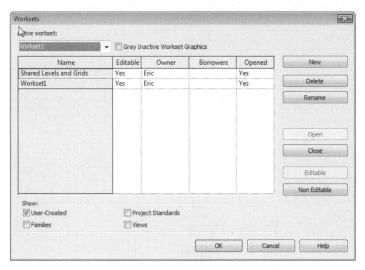

FIGURE 22.4 The Worksets dialog

NOTE   You can turn on additional items in the Show category. Unless there is a compelling reason to do so, don't—especially if this is the first project your team is taking on in Revit. Try to keep your worksets as simple and painless as possible. Just because you *can* assume ultimate control over your users does not mean you *have* to.

Now that you have activated the worksets and saved the model, it is time to create the central model. This will always be the next step in the process.

Creating a Central Model

Creating the central model generally will be a onetime deal. You create it immediately after you enable your worksets. Also, the individual who creates the central model needs to be your best Revit user.

Okay, best Revit user, follow this procedure to learn how to create the central model:

1. Click the Application button and choose Save As ➤ Project, as shown in Figure 22.5.

2. In the Save As dialog, click the Options button in the lower-right corner.

FIGURE 22.5 Saving the project using Save As

3. In the File Save Options dialog, change the Maximum Backups to 1 (see Figure 22.6).

 N O T E   Notice that the Worksharing area is not active. This is because you are saving the file for the first time after activating worksharing. You have no choice but to make this the central model.

4. Click OK.

5. Call the file NER-CENTRAL.rvt.

6. Click Save.

7. On the Collaborate tab, click Synchronize With Central ➢ Synchronize Now, as shown in Figure 22.7. This saves any changes made.

8. On the Worksets panel in the Collaborate tab, click the Worksets button.

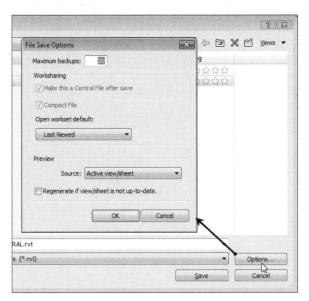

FIGURE 22.6 Modifying the settings before you save the central file

FIGURE 22.7 Clicking the Synchronize Now button

Notice that on the Quick Access toolbar the Synchronize button is now available. Since this is the central model, the actual Save icon is inactive.

9. Change both worksets by choosing No for the Editable column (see Figure 22.8).

10. Click OK. (Don't worry—I will explain what all this means in a moment.)

11. Click the Synchronize Now button.

The reason we made these worksets not editable is because when you are working in the central file, you always want to leave it with no editable worksets. That way, users do not have access to these worksets in their local models.

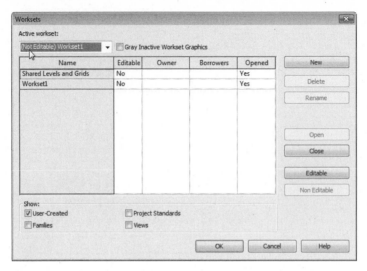

FIGURE 22.8 Releasing the worksets by clicking No for Editable

The next task we need to tackle is how to make a new workset and move some components onto the new workset.

The objective of the following procedure is to create a Site workset and to move the topography and the site components to this workset:

1. Click the Worksets button on the Collaborate tab.

2. In the Worksets dialog, click the New button, as shown in Figure 22.9.

3. In the New Workset dialog, call this workset Site, and then click OK.

4. Set Editable for Workset1 to Yes.

5. Click OK.

6. Go to the default 3D view.

7. Select the toposurface.

8. In the Properties dialog, find the Identity Data category, find the Workset row, and change the workset to Site.

9. Select the rest of the site components, including the split surfaces, the tree, and the shrubs.

10. Put these items on the Site workset.

11. On the Collaborate tab, click the Synchronize Now button.

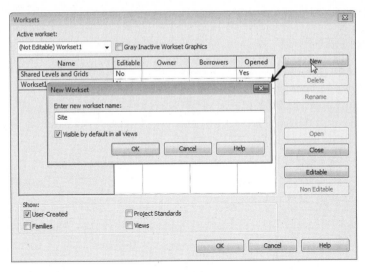

FIGURE 22.9 Creating a new workset

12. On the Collaborate tab, click the Worksets button.

13. Make all worksets not editable, as shown in Figure 22.10, and then click OK.

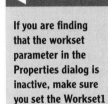

If you are finding that the workset parameter in the Properties dialog is inactive, make sure you set the Workset1 workset to Active.

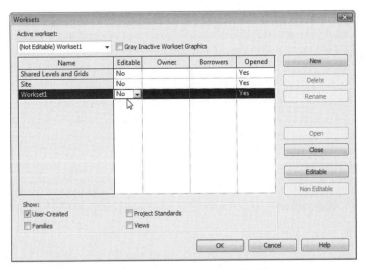

FIGURE 22.10 Making all worksets not editable

14. Click the Synchronize Now button.

N O T E   The reason we are making sure all the worksets are not editable is that, in the central model, everything needs to be turned off. Look at the central model as merely a *hub* that serves as a conduit for passing data as your team collaborates on the project.

It is now time to create your local model. Luckily, you have done all the difficult work. Setting up the central file is the hardest part of the worksharing process, and is usually done by the BIM manager or at least the BIM lead person on the project. The act of creating a local file is as simple as issuing a Save As.

Creating a Local File

With the central file in place, you are ready for the rest of your team to have at it. Although I keep mentioning how easy most of this stuff is, there are some dangers to look out for. The first danger is to never open the central file and stay in it. When you are in the process of creating a local file, you open the central file, do a Save As, and work in your new file.

N O T E   Some firms also like to have their users physically copy the central file in Windows Explorer and rename it. I err on the side of caution, and have my users open the central file and choose Save As. You may be saying to yourself, "Self, why wouldn't I just take the advice of the book's author?" All I can say is, it only takes one time to have a user open the central model and start working. This generates errors and will cause the other users to be unable to make any edits.

This section of the chapter will guide you through the process of creating a local file by opening the central model and saving the local copy as your own:

1. Make sure you are still in the central model.

2. Click the Application button, and choose Save As ➤ Project.

3. Find the folder where your central model is, and create a new folder.

4. Call the new folder **Local User** and open that folder.

5. In the Save As dialog, click the Options button.

6. In the File Save Options dialog, change the number of backups to 1, and click OK.

7. Save the model in this folder, naming it **NER-LOCAL-ERIC.rvt** (obviously you enter your name here).

Congratulations! You are the proud owner of a new Revit file that knows your name and everything! Yes, it knows your name.

You see, when you create the local file, it is yours to keep. As a matter of fact, if someone else opens your file from their computer, they will not be able to make any modifications. Not only does your local file keep a live link back to the central file, it actually knows who it belongs to. Revit does this for a good reason. This file now represents you within the team.

Working in the Revit Shared Environment

With the local model saved, you are free to work away. As you'll recall, the central model was created with three worksets: Shared Levels And Grids, Workset1, and Site. You, as a local user, can just start working away! As you start making edits to the model, however, Revit is making a note that you are actually borrowing a workset. Revit is also making a note that you physically own the item you are editing.

Borrowing? OK, let's stop right there, and take a look at what this all means. In Revit worksharing, you can either be a borrower of a workset or an owner of a workset. If you are a borrower, the rest of the design team can make modifications to elements in the workset but not to the specific element you are working on.

The objective of the next exercise is to make a modification to the site and to investigate what happens in the Worksets dialog:

1. Go to the default 3D view.

2. Delete one of the shrubs. (Remember, we put the shrubs on the Site workset.)

3. On the Collaborate tab, click the Worksets button.

4. In the Worksets dialog, notice that you are now borrowing the Site workset, as shown in Figure 22.11. Click OK.

Since there is no good way to have you go through an exercise, you can take your hand off the mouse and read for a few paragraphs. If you are at work and have another willing participant, have them create their own local file, and ask them to start making edits to the model.

Notice that the Site workset still says No for Editable. This means that if Cassidy comes along and starts working on the shrubs right next to the one you just deleted, she still can. You don't own the workset—you are just borrowing it. Now, if you simply changed the shrub to a tree (or made any modifications whatsoever to the shrub), Cassidy cannot make any edits to the new tree. When she tries to edit the tree, she will get the error shown in Figure 22.12.

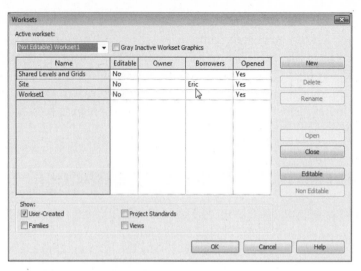

FIGURE 22.11 Borrowing a workset

GET IN SYNC

Now that you have created the local model, you can see what others are doing, as well as publish what you are doing for the other users. Just click the Synchronize Now button on the Quick Access toolbar, and you and your users are in sync.

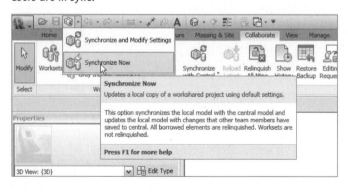

You may notice in Figure 22.12 that there is a button that allows Cassidy to place a request. When she clicks this button, a request to relinquish is sent to you (see Figure 22.13). Also, she can check to see if any team members have placed a request to her.

FIGURE 22.12 Eric is modifying the element.

ERIC A.K.A. CASSIDY

If Eric decides to not relinquish an item to Cassidy, then decides to close his model and leave to go on vacation (ignoring repeated warnings), then we have a situation, don't we? His office door is locked, and we don't know his password. What you can do in these trying times is click the Options button at the bottom of the Application menu. Select the General tab, and change the username to the offender's name. You can now open Eric's local file and relinquish the worksets. (See the following graphic.)

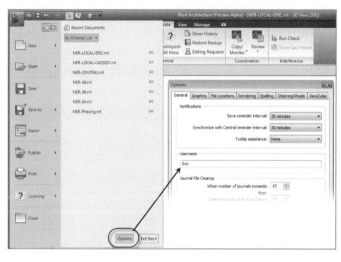

On the other side of the fence, there is no notification to you that anyone is asking you to cough up some site! You can check, though, by clicking Editing Requests on the Collaborate tab. From there, you will be able to expand a list of requests, as shown in Figure 22.14.

FIGURE 22.13   Requesting a relinquish

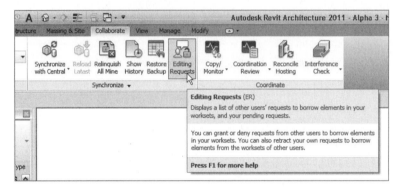

FIGURE 22.14   Checking to see who is begging

Now, once you see that Cassidy is begging you to release an item, you get to do the right thing and grant her the request. You do this by simply clicking the Relinquish All Mine button on the Collaborate tab, as shown in Figure 22.15.

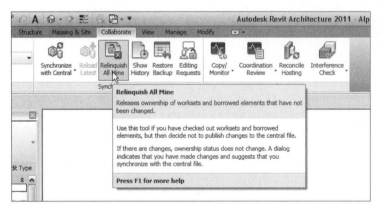

FIGURE 22.15   The Relinquish All Mine button

See? We *can* all get along! Until you pull the next move. Suppose you didn't want anybody else on the team to modify anything in the entire Site workset. There are times when this will occur. To figure out how to do this, follow along:

1. On the Collaborate tab, click the Worksets button.

2. In the Site workset, select Yes in the Editable field, as shown in Figure 22.16. Although Cassidy is a borrower, you can still take over the workset.

3. Click OK.

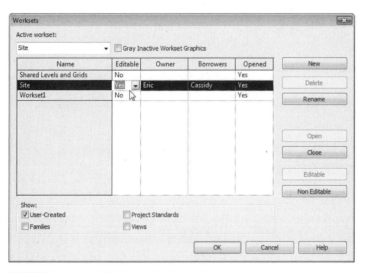

FIGURE 22.16 Occupying the entire workset

 N O T E   If Cassidy was in the middle of an active edit on any items in the workset, you would not have been able to take over. You would then have to place an editing request to her. See? You should have given her the shrub when she asked for it earlier!

And so the workday goes in an environment of sharing and getting along. Speaking of environment, suppose you could not care less about the site? There is a good chance you don't even want to see it. Well, you are in luck. Because you have worksets enabled, you can make it so Revit doesn't even load the site into your local model.

Loading or Not Loading a Workset

I'm making a big deal out of a simple task only because this simple task can speed up your performance, and nothing can bog down a Revit model more than a huge site, complete with landscaping and maybe an image.

Simply switching the Opened status to No in a workset will force Revit to not load it into your model. If you make an edit that has an influence on the site, don't worry. Revit will take care of that in the central model.

To turn off the site, follow this procedure:

1. Click the Worksets button on the Collaborate tab.

2. In the Site workset, change the Opened status to No, as shown in Figure 22.17.

3. Click OK. Notice something missing?

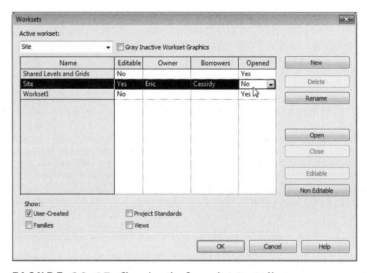

FIGURE 22.17 Changing the Opened status to No

Having the ability to turn off large portions of a model can be a tremendous advantage as you move forward in Revit. You do need to exercise caution, however. You could easily deceive yourself into thinking that some portions of the model have not been created yet.

Are You Experienced?

Now you can...

- ☑ activate worksharing in a Revit project
- ☑ create a central file
- ☑ create a local file
- ☑ manipulate worksets

BIM Management

Well, here we are: the last chapter. The ironic thing here is that the last chapter contains much of the information you will need to proceed with any of this BIM stuff. All too many times I have seen firms do poorly with Revit Architecture due to one fact: they weren't prepared. "We did not find that Revit worked for us," someone tells me. I ask them what they used for a template to get started with their first project. "The default one" is always the answer.

▶ **Setting up the template**

▶ **Managing settings**

▶ **Creating and understanding shared parameters**

Setting Up the Template

If you think you are going to start a real project with deadlines and budget with no prior setup, you are going to fail. So don't. If you take nothing away from this chapter other than this small bit of advice, it has been successful. Granted, you don't have to get it all, but you need as smooth of a transition as possible. Also, once you start down the Revit path, don't look back, and don't say, "We can always just push it out to AutoCAD." I have found that if you think you have something to fall back on, well, you will fall.

You don't have to spend weeks upon weeks preparing for the Coming of Revit. You can knock this stuff out if you do it in an orderly fashion, and the first order of business is creating your company's templates.

If you do nothing more than simply save the default template and give it your company name, you are off to a good start. People who are jumping to a new way of working will be looking for any comfort they can find. No, this is not like giving someone a sugar pill for a migraine, because we will populate the template with custom content.

The objective of the following procedure is to save a default template and to "map" Revit to this template.

1. Open Revit.

2. In the Projects menu, click New, as shown in Figure 23.1.

3. Click the Application button, and select Save As ➤ Template, as shown in Figure 23.2.

4. Save this file to your network. The file in our examples will be called NER-TEMPLATE.rte. You can call yours whatever you see fit.

NOTE   When I say save this file to your network, give this simple instruction some thought. We will be mapping our network deployment to this directory. Also, don't get into the habit of having errant templates scattered around your network that you are "practicing" on. You will get confused. (This author still needs to practice what he preaches regarding this matter.)

The file is now saved as NER-TEMPLATE.rte. The .rte extension indicates that you have indeed created a template and that you are now working in it.

The next order of business is to tell Revit that every time you wish to start a new project, Revit should choose this template.

1. Click the Application button. At the very bottom of the menu, you will see an Options button, as shown in Figure 23.3. Click it.

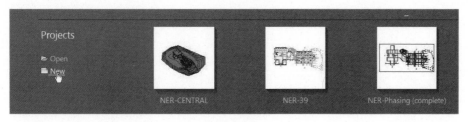

FIGURE 23.1 Clicking New on the Projects menu

FIGURE 23.2 Saving as a Revit template

2. In the Options dialog, click the File Locations tab, as shown in Figure 23.4.

3. For the default template file, click the Browse button, and locate your newly saved template.

4. Once you have browsed to the .rte template, click Open.

So, it's official. You have a separate template for your company to get started with. Now the fun begins!

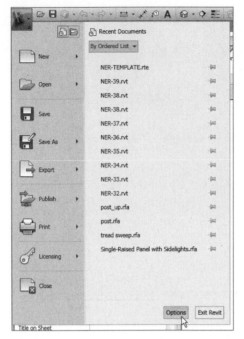

FIGURE 23.3 Finding the Options button

In your options, if you go to the File Locations tab, you can map your Revit to always use this template as your default.

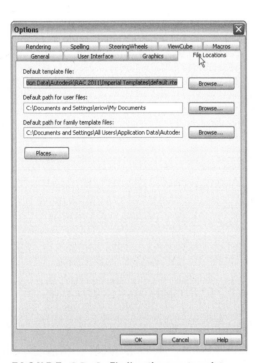

FIGURE 23.4 Finding the new template

The first item we will address for setting up this template to your company's standards is the nagging line-weight issue that has persisted throughout this book. You take care of this issue by managing your Revit settings.

Managing Settings

Given that Revit is such a robust, deep application, you would think that there would be an endless stream of convoluted settings (like AutoCAD Architecture). Although Revit has quite a few settings, you will find that they are straightforward. In fact, the mapping of the default template is almost the only mapping that you will need as you set up and work in Revit.

The objective of this section is to locate the settings for your line weights and then apply them to your object styles.

1. In Revit, select the Manage tab on the Ribbon.

2. Click the Object Styles button as shown in Figure 23.5.

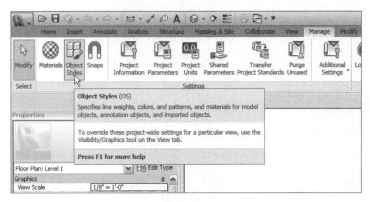

FIGURE 23.5 Selecting Object Styles

3. With the Object Styles dialog open, notice that there are categories. Click on the + next to the Casework category, and you'll see the subcategories.

To the right of the category field is the Line Weight column. There is a Projection and a Cut. *Projection* refers to whether you view the item in plan, elevation, or a 3D view. *Cut* refers to whether you view the item in section. (Boy, this beats layers, huh?) Notice that you can change the line color, the pattern, and the rendering material each item will use (see Figure 23.6).

Well, that was easy. I wish I could tell you specifically what number to assign each item, but that is up to you!

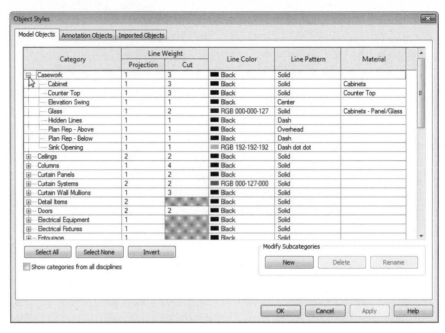

FIGURE 23.6 The Object Styles dialog

What do all those 1s and 2s mean? You're used to seeing something like "0.35mm" for a line weight, but now we are looking at plain numbers!

Don't worry—Revit has it figured out. You see, these numbers refer to a chart where you will see these familiar line weights. Also, these are line weights that comply with NCS 4.0 standards.

To find the line weights associated with the object styles, follow these steps:

1. On the Settings panel of the Manage tab, click Additional Settings ➤ Line Weights, as shown in Figure 23.7.

   In the Line Weights dialog (see Figure 23.8), notice that not only are numbers 1 through 16 assigned a pen thickness, but the thickness will actually degrade as the line weights get scaled down!

NOTE   You may be inclined to start tampering with these line weights, but hold off doing that. You are probably seeing the industry finally shifting to some form of unified line weight system. This is the NCS (National CAD Standards). These line weights are set to these standards. Change the object styles all you want, but I recommend that you keep these pen assignments just the way they are.

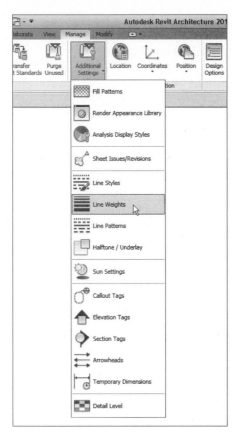

FIGURE 23.7 Clicking Additional Settings ➢ Line Weights

2. Click the Perspective Line Weights tab on the Line Weights dialog. Notice that you can alter your line weights for an object in a perspective view, independent of a standard plan, elevation, or isometric view.

3. Click the Annotation Line Weights tab. Again, notice that you can set your line weights for your annotation. This tab will come in handy as you start to set up your templates. Remember it is available.

4. Click Cancel to leave this dialog.

I wish I could tell you that you don't have tons of work ahead of you in terms of trying to match your AutoCAD line weights, but many of you will be inundated with the effort of adjusting line weights for quite a while. You will have to make at least some tweaks before you can submit a set of drawings with your name on them.

That being said, suppose your submittal includes sending CAD files. Hang on here, we use Revit! You can do that?

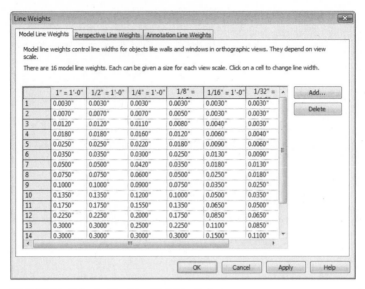

FIGURE 23.8 The Line Weights dialog

Import/Export Settings

Of course, you can import and export CAD files! The beauty of it is, you can import and export to a predefined set of layers. This works wonders for firms that find themselves surrounded by "CAD people."

The objective of this section is to learn how to deal with the issue of importing a CAD model into Revit, so follow along with this procedure:

1. Open the last model you have been working on. At this stage of the game, it does not matter which one.

2. On the Insert tab, click on the down arrow in the lower-right corner of the Import panel, as shown in Figure 23.9.

3. In the Import Line Weights dialog, notice that all the line weights are set to 1. This does not make for a very spectacular drawing. At the upper-right corner of the dialog is a Load button, as shown in Figure 23.10. Click it.

4. You will automatically be taken to the directory where you mapped Revit to find your line weights files. They are simple text (.txt) files. Find the file called importlineweights-dwg-AIA.txt and click Open. Your line weights have been adjusted, as shown in Figure 23.11.

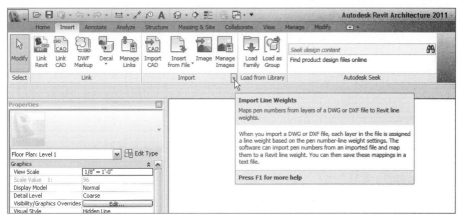

FIGURE 23.9 Clicking the down arrow on the Import tab

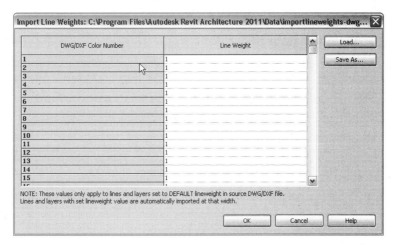

FIGURE 23.10 Importing some line weights

5. Notice that you have a Save As button. Change a few line weights around and click the Save As button.

6. Save the file in the same directory as NER Line Weights.txt.

As mentioned before, you will probably have a good amount of work to do configuring these line weights. If you have been sticking to the AIA or NCS layering conventions, you will not have an issue. If not, then you have some translating to do!

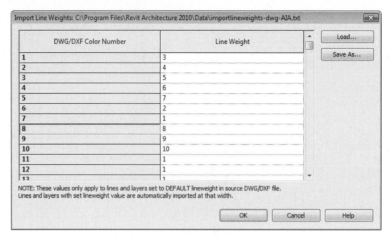

FIGURE 23.11 The adjusted line weights

Great! We have importing down. Suppose we want to export a Revit model to CAD. It's a little different, but the concept is the same. You need to physically *map* the Revit objects to AutoCAD or MicroStation layers or levels.

The objective of the next exercise is to examine export settings when sending a model to CAD:

1. On the Application Menu button, select Export ➤ Options ➤ Export Layers DWG/DXF.

   In the Export Layers dialog notice that all of your Revit objects are represented and are given a unique layer name. That layer name is also assigned an AutoCAD pen number. This assigns the layer a color. You can change both of these items in this dialog (see Figure 23.12).

WAIT! I DON'T HAVE THAT CHOICE

When you click the Application button and look for an item, you will notice an arrow in a wide blue strip at the bottom of the menu. If you hover your pointer over this blue strip, you will see the menu scroll up so you can see more choices, as shown here:

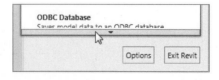

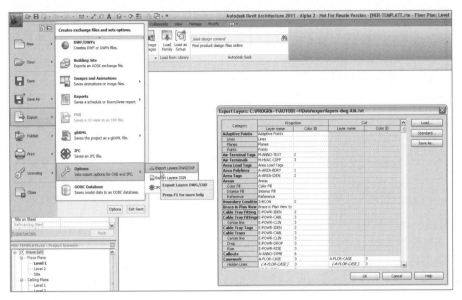

FIGURE 23.12 The Export Layers dialog

2. In the Export Layers dialog, click the Standard button.

3. The Undefined Layering Standard dialog opens, as shown in Figure 23.13. Here you get a choice of four standards. By default, the American Institute of Architects Standard (AIA) will be current, but you can change to one of the other three. Choose a standard or click Cancel.

FIGURE 23.13 The four choices for standards

4. If you want to change your layering scheme, go right ahead. Because the AIA standard is saved to an external .txt file, you will not have to worry about "messing up" that file. If you do make your changes, however, click the Save As button and save your .txt file somewhere that makes sense to you.

5. Click OK to get back to the model.

Now we are cooking here! We now know how to adjust our line weights, and how to make sure those adjustments are valid when we export the model and when we import CAD. It's time to move on to other graphical features that need to be controlled within the Revit template. These are the annotation features.

Controlling Annotations

To begin with, Revit does not accept .shx fonts. The only font that Revit accepts is a TrueType font (.ttf). If a font is not in your Windows fonts directory, forget it. Given that, don't worry if your AutoCAD fonts are set to an SHX. Revit will convert them to Arial when you import them. If Arial is unacceptable, you will have to figure out an acceptable font. I recommend Arial, but most of the SHX fonts, such as architxt.shx, are available in a .ttf format. You can either find them online or email me at the address in the front of the book.

The annotation we will address first is the everyday text that you will use in your models and the accompanying leaders.

Formatting Annotations and Leaders

Just like any drafting application, Revit needs to have the text set up. Yes, you can just use it out of the box, but I assume you have standards that look better than the boxed sample styles that are provided.

The objective of the next procedure is to set up our default text and leaders:

1. To get started, make sure you are in the NER-TEMPLATE.rte file or the template you created.

2. On the Text panel of the Annotate tab, click the down arrow in the lower-right corner of the panel, as shown in Figure 23.14.

3. In the Type Properties dialog, switch the Type: to 3/32" Arial.

4. Click the Rename button.

5. Call the new text NER-3/32" (of course you can call it whatever you want) and then click OK.

6. In the Type Parameters, change the leader arrowhead to Arrow Filled 15 Degree.

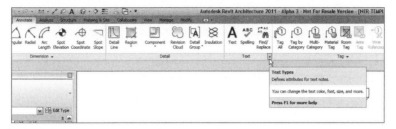

FIGURE 23.14 Clicking the down arrow in the Text panel

7. Change Width Factor to .800000 (see Figure 23.15).

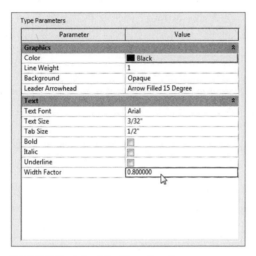

FIGURE 23.15 Changing the text

8. Click OK.

9. On the Annotate tab, click the Text button.

10. In the Properties dialog, make sure the NER-3/32″ text is current.

11. Add one leadered piece of text into your model. (It's always a good idea just to check it to make sure the text came out as expected.)

With the text and leaders out of the way, it is time to venture into text's close cousin: the dimension.

CLEANLINESS STARTS HERE!

We now have an extra text style kicking around. We should purge our model immediately to avoid a messy template.

1. On the Manage tab, click the Purge Unused button, as shown here:

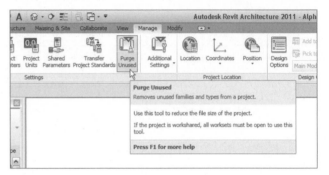

2. In the Purge Unused dialog, you must first click the Check None button. If you just click OK, you will have purged your entire model with no warning.

3. Scroll down near the bottom of the list, find the Text category, and expand it.

4. Check the 1/4" - Arial text style.

5. Click OK. The text style is now deleted.

Formatting Dimensions

We can format dimensions in the same manner. You will, however, find this process unwieldy because each type of dimension needs to be formatted. You cannot do just one dimension and expect it to propagate to the other styles.

The objective of the next procedure is to format your dimension styles.

1. On the Annotate tab, click the bottom of the Dimension panel (click where it says Dimension). This will expose your Dimension settings, as shown in Figure 23.16.

2. Click the Linear Dimension Types button.

3. In the Type Properties dialog, click Rename.

4. Rename the value to **NER-3/32"**, and click OK.

5. Scroll down to the Text group, and change the Width Factor value to .8.

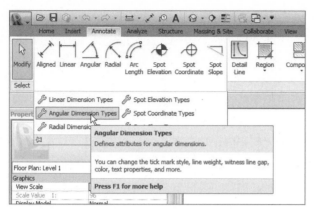

FIGURE 23.16 Accessing the Dimension settings

6. Click the button to the right of the Units Format category.

7. Uncheck Use Project Settings.

8. Change the Rounding to the nearest 1/8".

9. Check Suppress 0 Feet (see Figure 23.17).

10. Click OK twice.

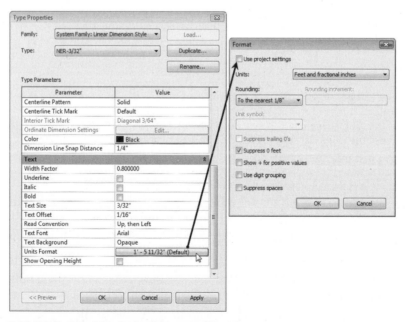

FIGURE 23.17 Customizing your dimensions

Unfortunately you need to repeat this setup with the rest of the dimension types. I recommend you do so.

Okay, moving along with annotations, we need to control our levels and our structural grid bubbles. Since we made slight adjustments to our text and dimensions, we have to alter our datum items as well. Doing so, however, is not as straightforward.

Formatting Grids, Elevations Markers, and View Titles

If you have had any experience with Revit, I'm sure you quickly realize that there is no button to change the appearance of grids and elevations. It's not impossible to make specific alterations to these items, but you must do it by editing the annotation family that is loaded into your project.

The objective of the following procedure is to alter a structural grid bubble and to modify a level indicator:

1. In Revit, click the Open button on the Quick Access toolbar.

2. Go to your Imperial Library folder.

3. Open the Annotations folder.

4. Select the file Grid Head - Circle.rfa and click Open.

5. Select the large 0. This is a tag.

6. Click the Edit Type button in the Properties dialog.

7. Check Bold.

8. Change the Width value to .8.

9. Click OK.

10. Save the file. Notice that Revit wants you to save a separate file. If you are the BIM manager, and nobody is going to yell at you, save it right over the existing file. If not, save it somewhere else.

11. Click the Load Into Project button.

12. You will get a warning that this family already exists, as shown in Figure 23.18. Click Overwrite the existing version.

Sweet! You just replaced the grid bubble. See the trick? Some elements can be edited within the model, while some you have to go ferret the family out of its hiding place. Let's keep rolling and do a level head!

1. On the Quick Access toolbar, click the Open button.

> If you don't feel like navigating through buried folders in Windows Explorer, you can click the Imperial Library button in the menu to the left of the Open dialog. This will take you directly to your default library.

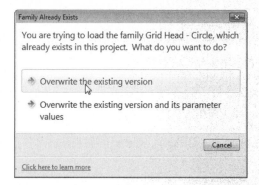

FIGURE 23.18 Overwriting the existing version

2. Browse to the Imperial Library and then the Annotations folder.

3. Select the file Level Head - Circle and click Open.

4. Select the text Name.

5. In the Properties dialog, click the Edit Type button.

6. Click Bold.

7. Change the Width Factor value to .800000.

8. Click OK.

9. Save the file.

10. Click Load into Project, as shown in Figure 23.19.

FIGURE 23.19 Clicking Load into Project

11. Select Overwrite the existing version.

12. Go to an elevation view just to make sure the change worked.

YEAH, BUT WHERE DID THIS FAMILY GO?

You loaded the file into your project and it just magically worked, right? No. There is no magic here. In the elevation view, if you select the level, click the Properties button, and then click Edit Type, you will see that the symbol this specific family is using is the one we just modified, as shown in the following image. Also, this means that you can load any level head into the model and apply that to the family.

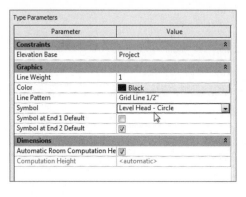

Okay, now this is just getting to be downright fun. Let's go ahead and modify a view title, shall we?

1. On the Quick Access toolbar, click the Open button.

2. Browse back to the Annotations folder.

3. Select the file View Title.rfa and click Open.

4. Select the View Name tag.

5. In the Properties dialog, click the Edit Type button.

6. Check the Bold option, and change Width Factor to .8000000.

7. Click OK.

8. Select the 1/8″ = 1′–0″ tag.

9. In the Properties dialog, click Edit Type.

10. Click Duplicate.

11. Call the new tag 3/32″ and then click OK.

12. Change the text size to 3/32″.

13. Click OK.

14. Save the view title family.

15. Load it into your project.

16. Overwrite the existing version.

17. Stand up and clap loudly because you are actually creating a nice template! (Optional.)

This is looking great. Now for the harder stuff. When it comes to additional information that Revit does not provide, you will need an outside influence. Or, at least you will need to physically create a text file loaded with some of your "oddball" parameters that you can share between projects, families, and possibly other disciplines.

Creating and Understanding Shared Parameters

Shared parameters is a convoluted subject, so I am going to try to explain it in terms that I can understand—because this concept had to be explained to me over and over until I finally got it.

Suppose you are doing a project for a school. All of your drawings need to have an SED (State Education Department) number. (I'm in New York, so if it is called something different in your state, province, or country, please forgive me.) This SED number belongs in with your project parameters so when you are filling out the job information, this SED number can be included. The issue is we need to add this parameter to the project you are working on *and* this same exact parameter needs to be added to the title block family. When you insert the title block into the project, this SED number will populate the title block.

Still foggy? Okay, let's just do it and see what shakes out! The objective of the following exercise is to create a shared parameter .txt file and add it to a title block and your project.

1. In the Manage tab, click the Project Parameters button, as shown in Figure 23.20.

2. In the Project Parameters dialog, click the Add button.

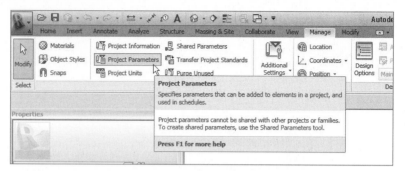

FIGURE 23.20 Clicking the Project Parameters button

3. In the Parameter Properties dialog, click the Shared Parameter radio button.

4. In the Categories field, check Project Information.

5. In the middle of the dialog, click the Select button.

6. You will get a dialog stating that you have not specified a shared parameter. Click Yes to choose one.

7. In the next dialog, there is still an issue because you don't actually have a shared parameter file. Click the Create button.

8. Save the file as **NER-Shared Parameters**. (Of course you can name it anything you choose.)

9. In the Groups field, click the New button as shown in Figure 23.21.

10. Call the new parameter group **Project Information** and click OK.

11. In the Parameters field, click New.

12. Name it **SED Number**.

13. Click OK.

14. Keep clicking OK until you are back to the model.

15. On the Manage tab, click the Project Information button. Notice that SED number has been added to the list. See Figure 23.22.

If you type your long SED number, where does this number wind up? This is where the shared part comes into play. Suppose we need this SED number displayed in our title block. It's just a matter of adding this same parameter to the title block family.

FIGURE 23.21 Filling out the information for the shared parameter

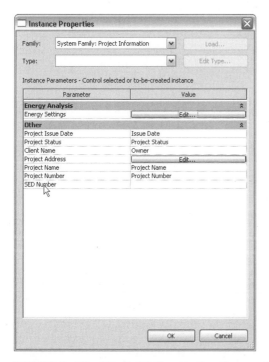

FIGURE 23.22 Voilà! The new shared parameter!

Still don't believe me? Okay, let's add the same exact shared parameter to a title block, and then load it into the model:

1. On the View tab, click the Sheet button, as shown in Figure 23.23.

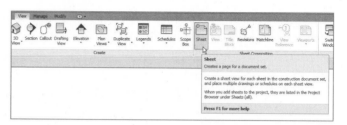

FIGURE 23.23   Creating a new sheet

2. Click OK in the next dialog.

3. Select the title block, and click the Edit Family button in the Modify | Title Blocks tab, as shown in Figure 23.24.

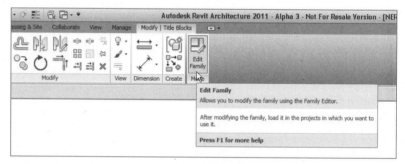

FIGURE 23.24   Editing the title block family

4. Zoom into the lower-right corner, and select the Date label, as shown in Figure 23.25.

5. Click the Create Similar button on the Create panel, as shown in Figure 23.25.

6. Pick a point, as shown in Figure 23.25.

7. Once you pick the point, you will see an Edit Label dialog. Click the Add Parameter button, as shown at the lower left in Figure 23.26.

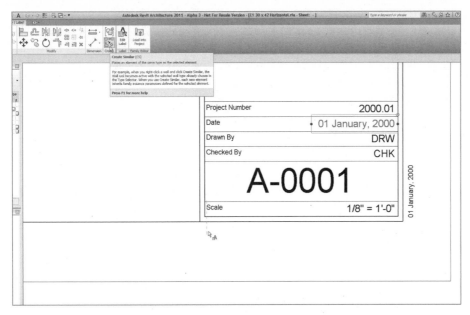

FIGURE 23.25 Adding the tag

8. In the Parameter Properties dialog, click Select. (I think you know where we are going here.)

9. Select the SED number (it is the only one), and click OK.

10. Click OK again.

11. Click the Add Parameter(s) To Label button located between the two large fields.

12. Click OK.

13. Load the title block into the project.

14. Click Overwrite The Existing Version.

15. Nothing changed? Well, let's see about that! Click the Project Information button on the Manage tab.

16. Give it an SED number such as 123.456.789.

17. Click OK. The title block now contains this information.

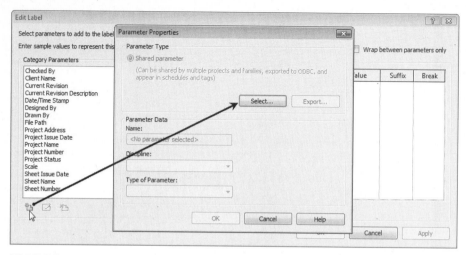

FIGURE 23.26 Adding the parameter to the label

Now, that's how you create and utilize shared parameters. Although this trick is useful for project parameters, it is useful for object parameters as well. This is just another way we can control the flow of information.

The funny thing is, this book ended with the chapter that will come first when you start using Revit. If you do not establish templates and the flow of information, that first project will be unnecessarily cumbersome.

If you establish these templates, you and your users will have a much better chance of seeing the full capabilities of BIM, and how Revit Architecture is the front-running software in its class.

Are You Experienced?

Now you can...

☑ **begin to set up a companywide template**

☑ **set up text styles and dimension styles**

☑ **edit the families of various symbols used in your models**

☑ **create and utilize shared parameters**

INDEX